Rule One

The middle term of a valid syllogism must be distributed in at least one premise. A violation of this rule is known as the **fallacy of the undistributed middle.**

Rule Two

A term that is distributed in the conclusion of a valid syllogism must also be distributed in the premise in which the term occurs. A violation of this rule is known as the **fallacy of the illicit major** or **the fallacy of the illicit minor,** depending on which term is not distributed in its premise.

Rule Three

A valid syllogism cannot have a negative premise unless it has a negative conclusion, in which case it must have exactly one negative premise. Violating this rule involves committing one of three different fallacies—the **fallacy of two negative premises, the fallacy of affirmative conclusion from a negative premise,** or the **fallacy of a negative conclusion from affirmative premises.**

[Rule Four—applies only to Boolean Interpretations]

*In a syllogism **on the Boolean interpretation** a particular conclusion cannot be validly deduced from two universal premises.*

Probability

General Conjunction Rule

If x and y are any outcomes whatever (either dependent or independent), then
$$P(x \text{ and } y) = P(x) \times P(y \text{ given } x).$$

General Disjunction Rule

For any outcomes x and y,
$$P(x \text{ or } y) = P(x) + P(y) - P(x \text{ and } y)$$
[*where P(x and y) can be determined using the general conjunction rule*].

Fourth Edition

Robert Baum

University of Florida

Harcourt Brace College Publishers

Fort Worth   Philadelphia   San Diego   New York   Orlando   Austin   San Antonio
Toronto   Montreal   London   Sydney   Tokyo

Vice President, Publisher	Ted Buchholz
Editor in Chief	Christopher P. Klein
Senior Acquisitions Editor	David Tatom
Developmental Editor	J. Claire Brantley
Senior Project Editor	Charles J. Dierker
Production Manager	Debra Jenkin
Text design	John Ritland
Cover Design	Melinda Welch

Photo credits

The portraits on the following pages are used courtesy of The Granger Collection, New York: 4, 20, 41, 46, 113, 196, 208, 230, 242, 246, 356, 364, 380, 384, 475, 555, 560, 596, 603. The photo on page 361 is used by permission. Copyright © 1987 by Mark Murphy. The photo on page 464 is courtesy AP/Wide World Photos.

ISBN: 0-15-501617-2

Library of Congress Catalog Card Number: 95-77198

Preface

The success of the previous editions of *Logic* has demonstrated that introductory logic textbooks do not have to be modeled on graduate mathematics or linguistics books, particularly with regard to style and format. Previous editions of *Logic* have also demonstrated that "real" logic *can* be presented in a clear and interesting way, and that a logic textbook *can* have an aesthetic dimension that goes beyond the inclusion of "elegant" abstract proofs. It is gratifying to observe that an increasing number of such textbooks resemble in style and appearance the last two editions of this book, as well as recent textbooks in physics and psychology.

At the other extreme from formal logic, there has been a proliferation over the past ten years of books and courses dealing with "informal" logic, although for the most part even those textbooks are austere in style and content. The trend toward informal books and courses may, however, mean throwing out the baby with the bath water. Most students in such courses get little or no significant exposure to the concepts of formal logic. They can get credit for a logic course without being able to test an argument for validity or even being able to define 'valid,' which is as bad as getting credit for an English course without being able to write a grammatically correct sentence or to distinguish a participle from an infinitive. I firmly believe that there is much of value in traditional formal logic, that formal logic can be related to "real" arguments in interesting and useful ways, and that all of this can be done in an aesthetically satisfying way.

In previous editions of *Logic*, the rigorous presentation of the various concepts and methods of formal logic was retained, while a substantial amount of new material was added on the ways in which formal logic relates to the analysis of everyday arguments. All of this was presented in a package that had an aesthetic dimension never before attempted in a logic textbook. That this fourth edition is now appearing is convincing evidence that the innovations in the second and third editions have had real pedagogical value. The changes to this edition represent a "fine tuning" of the text to make it an even more effective tool for stimulating students' interest in logic and for teaching them the basic concepts and skills.

Although earlier editions of *Logic* were distinguished by their flexibility, this edition is even more flexible. Most of the chapters can be included or excluded from a particular course depending on the goals of the course and the time available. The only constraints on flexibility are that Chapter 4 (on the syllogism) must be preceded by at least the first four sections of Chapter 3 (that is, through section 3.4). And the material in Chapters 5 through 8 (propositional and quantificational logic) must be taken in the sequence in which it is presented, although it can be cut off at any point (such as after the treatment of truth tables in Chapter 6) without affecting the coverage of any other chapters. The chapters on Mill's methods and scientific method have been combined into a single chapter (10), but either part can be used independently of the other. The chapters on informal fallacies, definitions, and probability may each be scheduled at any point in a course after Chapter 2. Also, more difficult or specialized topics at the ends of chapters (such as the discussion of the Boolean interpretation at the ends of Chapters 3 and 4) can be omitted at the instructor's discretion.

Most of the changes in structure and organization in this edition were made on pedagogical grounds. For example, the discussion of the rules for deductive proofs in Chapter 6 has been broken up into a number of subsections, and whole sets of new exercises have been inserted to allow students to focus on and develop their skills with regard to only two or three rules at a time. Furthermore, hundreds of new exercises have been added throughout the book. The ancillary package now includes a Study Guide for students that provides a number of other pedagogical aids. Instructors may request an Instructor's Manual, a set of Transparency Masters, and Computerized Test Banks, all newly developed to accompany *Logic*, Fourth Edition.

It is impossible to acknowledge by name in this limited space all of those who have contributed to this book. Perhaps my greatest debt is to my students, who have provided me with as much of a learning experience as I have been able to provide for them. It is, of course, impossible to identify the precise sources of the many ideas, concepts, and methods contained in an introductory textbook such as this one. But certainly, whatever their historical origins, they have been transmitted to me, consciously or otherwise, by my own teachers, colleagues, and the authors of the numerous books I have used and studied over the years.

Numerous individuals, some good friends and others not known personally by me at all, provided helpful comments on the first three editions and/or drafts of this new edition. I want to single out and thank again David Wieck, who helped me in a variety of ways on the first two editions. With apologies to those persons whose names have fallen through the cracks of my record-keeping system and memory, I also want to mention explicitly the following for their constructive criticisms and suggestions over the years that have contributed to making this edition better than any one person could ever have made it: Professors Ronald Beanblossom, Donald A. Cress, Manuel Davenport, Robert Ellis, James A. Gould, Robert Gurland, Allen Harder, Bruce Hauptli, James Heffernan, George Isham, William F. Lawhead, John Lincourt, Robert Long, Russell McIntire, Jr., Richard Oliver, Philip Pecorino, Joel L. Peterson, Paul

Peterson, Nelson Pole, William Prior, Janine S. Randal, John Schumacher, John Sertic, and Otto Tetzlaff. My thanks go to the following professors who served on the review panel for this edition: Ronald R. Cox, San Antonio College; Harold Greenstein, State University of New York-Brockport; Kelly J. Marino, Texas A&M University; George I. Mavrodes, University of Michigan; John E. Sallstrom, Georgia College; and Nancy A. Stanlick, University of South Florida. I look forward to additional feedback from these persons and other users of this new edition that will permit the continuation of the fine-tuning process.

The editors of the first three editions made many substantive contributions that still add value to the present edition, so I must express appreciation again to Nicholas Falletta, Sarah Parker, David Boynton, Jeanette Johnson, Karen Dubno and Pamela Forcey. I also want to thank David Tatom, Claire Brantley, and Charles Dierker, who did a highly professional job of shepherding this edition through a lengthy gestation and production process. Others who have contributed in various ways to the writing of this book include Eric Baker, Kym Bergendahl, William Briel, Michael Buchholtz, Michael Francis, Joseph Jackson, Myron Jefka, Kent Johnson, Jo Kaufman, Donald Kieffer, Deborah Kransberg, Richard Loringer, Terri Nally, John Peoples, Thong Pham, John Rotondo, Daniel Salvano, John Shook, Rose Slomowitz, Marlin Thomas, Rory Weiner and Wayne Wright. As always, responsibility for errors and matters of judgment rests entirely with me.

Table of Contents

Preface   iii

Introduction   1

    I.1 The Value and Uses of Logic   2
    Exercises   5

    I.2 What Can Be Learned about Logic and How Can It Be Learned?   9
    Exercises   11

    I.3 Logic versus Psychology   16

    I.4 The Organization of This Book   19
    Exercises   20

CHAPTER 1
Informal Analysis of Statements   30

    1.1 Sentences   31
    Exercises   31

    1.2 Cognitive and Noncognitive Uses of Sentences   32
    Exercises   33

    1.3 Statements   34

    1.4 Recognizing Sentences Used to Express Statements   35
    Exercises   37

    1.5 Self-Evident and Supported Statements   38
    Exercises   40

    1.6 Logical Relationships between Two (or More) Propositions   44

    1.7 Consistency   45
    Exercises   48

    1.8 Real versus Apparent Disagreements   49
    Exercises   52

    1.9 Verbal Disagreements   52
    Exercises   53

    1.10 Implication   54

    1.11 Logical Equivalence   55

    1.12 Independence   56
    Exercises   57

Summary   60

CHAPTER 2
Informal Analysis of Arguments   62

    2.1 Inferences and Arguments   65
    Exercises   67

    2.2 The Logical Sense of 'Argument'   70
    Exercises   71

    2.3 Premises and Conclusions   72
    Exercises   74

    2.4 Problems in Recognizing Intended Arguments   75
    Exercises   77

    2.5 Supplying Missing Statements   78

    2.6 Deductive and Inductive Arguments   80
    Exercises   83

    2.7 Criteria for Good Arguments   92
    Exercises   93

    2.8 Dealing with Enthymemes   94
    Exercises   96

    2.9 Complex Argument Structures   96

    2.10 Analyzing Sample Arguments   100

    2.11 Some Basic Elements of Argument Analysis   107
    Exercises   108

Summary   110

CHAPTER 3

Aristotelian Logic: Statements   113

3.1 Categorical Statements   113
Exercises   118

3.2 Abbreviations   120

3.3 Schemas   121
Exercises   128

3.4 Venn Diagrams and Categorical
Statements   129
Exercises   132

3.5 Logical Relations between Categorical
Propositions   133
Exercises   136

3.6 Immediate Inferences   136
Exercises   140

3.7 The Traditional Square of
Opposition   140
Exercises   141

3.8 The Boolean Interpretation   142
Exercises   144

Summary   152

CHAPTER 4

Aristotelian Logic: Arguments   155

4.1 The Categorical Syllogism   156
Exercises   157

4.2 Standard-Form Syllogisms   158
Exercises   161

4.3 Mood and Figure   164
Exercises   166

4.4 Testing the Validity of
Syllogisms   166

4.5 Testing by Counterexamples   167
Exercises   169

4.6 Testing with Venn
Diagrams   170
Exercises   171

4.7 Testing by Rules   182
Exercises   190

4.8 The Boolean Interpretation   191

4.9 Syllogistic Arguments in Ordinary
Language   192
Exercises   192

Summary   199

CHAPTER 5

Propositional Logic: Statements   202

5.1 Compound Propositions and Logical
Operators   202

5.2 Truth-Functional Operators   203
Exercises   205

5.3 Propositional Abbreviations and
Schemas   205
Exercises   208

5.4 Conjunction   209
Exercises   213

5.5 Truth Tables   214

5.6 Negation   215
Exercises   216

5.7 Disjunction   217
Exercises   219

5.8 Material Implication   219
Exercises   225

5.9 Material Equivalence   225
Exercises   226

5.10 Propositions with More Than One
Logical Operator   228
Exercises   231

5.11 Truth Table Construction   233
Exercises   237

5.12 Logically Equivalent
Statements   238

5.13 Logical Equivalence and Material
Equivalence   239
Exercises   242

5.14 Tautologies   242

5.15 Contradictions   244

5.16 Contingent Statements   245
Exercises   246

Summary   247

CHAPTER 6

Propositional Logic: Arguments   251

6.1 Truth-Functional Validity   252

6.2 Contradictory Premises and
     Tautological Conclusions   253

6.3 Abbreviating Truth-Functional
     Arguments   254

6.4 Schematizing Truth-Functional
     Arguments   255
     Exercises   257

6.5 Testing Validity by Truth
     Tables   260
     Exercises   269

6.6 The Short Truth Table Method   270
     Exercises   272

6.7 Truth-Functional Arguments and
     Corresponding Conditionals   273
     Exercises   276

6.8 The Propositional Calculus   276

6.9 Constructing a Formal
     Proof   277

6.10 Inference Rules   281
      Exercises   284

6.11 Rules of Thumb for Proof
      Construction   294

6.12 The Rule of Rigor   296
      Exercises   297

6.13 The Replacement Rule   300
      Exercises   304

6.14 Conditional Proof   321
      Exercises   325

6.15 Indirect Proof   325

6.16 Deductive Completeness   327
      Exercises   328

Summary   329

CHAPTER 7

Quantificational Logic: Statements   333

7.1 Predicates and Individuals   333

7.2 Variables and Constants   335
     Exercises   337

7.3 Compound Propositions   337
     Exercises   339

7.4 Existential Quantifiers   339
     Exercises   342

7.5 Universal Quantifiers   346
     Exercises   347

7.6 Negation and Quantifier
     Exchange   352
     Exercises   354

7.7 Multiple Quantifiers   357
     Exercises   361

Summary   366

CHAPTER 8

Quantificational Logic: Arguments   368

8.1 Universal Instantiation   369
     Exercises   371

8.2 Existential Generalization   372
     Exercises   374

8.3 Existential Instantiation   375
     Exercises   378

8.4 Universal Generalization   378
     Exercises   381

Summary   387

CHAPTER 9

Inductive Arguments   389

9.1 Enumerative Inductions   391
     Exercises   397

9.2 Relative Strength of Enumerative
     Inductions   402
     Exercises   405

9.3 The Possible Elimination of Inductions
     by Analogy   425
     Exercises   427

9.4 Statistical Inductions   428
     Exercises   434

Summary   438

CHAPTER 10
Scientific Method   441

10.1 The Hypothetico-Deductive
     Method   441
     Exercises   443

10.2 Hypothetico-Deductive Method and
     Inductive Generalization   447
     Exercises   449

10.3 Crucial Experiments   452

10.4 Scientific Method   459
     Exercises   460

10.5 Causal Explanations   462

10.6 Kinds of Cause   463
     Exercises   467

10.7 Mill's Method   474
     Exercises   482

10.8 Replicability and Controls   489
     Exercises   491

10.9 The Role of Logic in
     Science   501
     Exercises   503

Summary   505

CHAPTER 11
Probability   509

11.1 Some Basic Terminology   510
     Exercises   512

11.2 Two General Principles of
     Probability   513
     Exercises   513

11.3 Three Theories of Probability   514
     Exercises   516

11.4 Independent and Mutually Exclusive
     Outcomes   522

11.5 The Probability Calculus   524
     Exercises   526

Summary   534

CHAPTER 12
Informal Fallacies   537

12.1 Disguised Nonarguments   538
     Exercises   545

12.2 Valid but Fallacious
     Arguments   546
     Exercises   553

12.3 Other Informal Fallacies   564
     Exercises   564

Summary   568

CHAPTER 13
Definitions   571

13.1 Kinds of Definitions   572
     Exercises   573

13.2 Uses of Definitions   581
     Exercises   584

13.3 Criteria for Good Definitions   594
     Exercises   597

Summary   598

CHAPTER 14
Applied Logic   601

14.1 Burden of Proof   602

14.2 The Principle of Induction   604
     Exercises   606

14.3 Choosing the Appropriate
     System   607
     Exercises   623

Summary   623

**Answers to Odd-Numbered
Exercises   625**

Index   687

Introduction

The point of the cartoon is blatantly obvious. But is it TRUE?

The answer is a definite YES! But it is of course reasonable for you to want *proof* of such a claim. And the very fact that you instinctively want proof is evidence that you already recognize the value and utility of logic, for logic is (in part) the study of proofs—how to construct proofs and how to evaluate their quality. But logic is concerned with much more than proofs. Another example of the nature and use of the concepts of logic is provided by the following statement:

1

> **You will pass this course if and only if you get a grade of 60 or better on each of the four midterm exams while attaining a minimum average of 70 points, unless you get a grade of 90 or better on the optional final exam, in which case you will pass the course even if you had less than 60 points on one or more exams; all the above notwithstanding, in the event that you do not fail to take all of the exams (including the final exam) you will pass the course even if you fail to receive a grade of 60 or higher on one or more of said exams.**

This statement may be a bit difficult to understand, but compared to the kinds of statements included in some apartment leases, consumer loan agreements, employment contracts, insurance policies, and IRS tax return instructions, it's relatively simple and straightforward. Logic provides tools and sharpens skills that can improve your ability not only to understand such complex statements, but also to discover potentially significant things about their logical structure. (Was it *obvious* to you that the statement about the course asserts that if you take all four midterm exams and the final you will pass the course, no matter what grades you get on the exams?)

I.1 The Value and Uses of Logic

Although the study of logic has been a central element of education in the Western world for more than two thousand years, it is not as easy to describe or explain the value or uses of logic as it is for subjects such as accounting, medicine, or engineering. Part of its value is, in fact, its use in these more directly applied fields—logical analysis is an integral part of the practice of accounting, medicine, engineering, and most other fields that involve problem solving or decision making. Logic is perhaps most directly applicable in fields such as computer programming and law, but knowledge of the concepts and methods of logic presented in this book can also be of considerable use and value in dealing with a wide range of situations that we all encounter in everyday life.

One piece of evidence that logical skills are relevant to most if not all professional fields is that they are tested for on most exams for admission to law schools (the LSAT), medical schools (MCAT), business schools (GMAT), and graduate schools in general (GRE). Although no guarantees can be given that mastery of the tools presented in this book will result in higher entrance exam scores, over the years many students have reported that they have taken the LSAT, GMAT, or other exams both before and after their logic course, and their grades have almost always been higher after the course. A number of the exercises in this book have been designed to resemble the kinds of questions included on graduate and professional school entrance exams.

One other area in which the study of logic can be of relatively direct value is the area of relations between individual persons and between groups (defined in terms of ethnic, religious or other characteristics) of individuals. Two

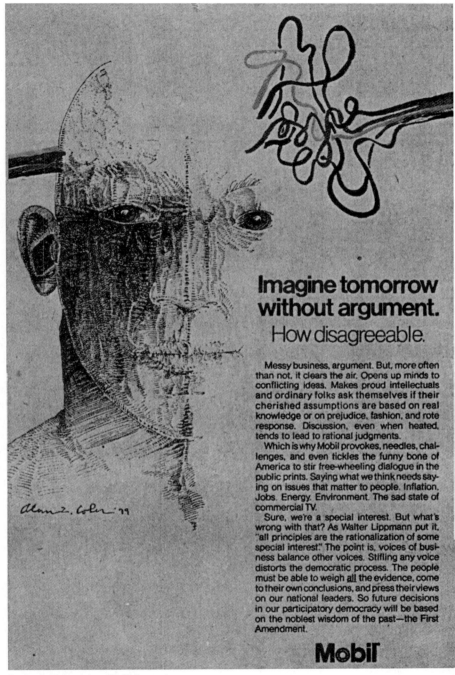

Imagine tomorrow without argument.
How disagreeable.

Messy business, argument. But, more often than not, it clears the air. Opens up minds to conflicting ideas. Makes proud intellectuals and ordinary folks ask themselves if their cherished assumptions are based on real knowledge or on prejudice, fashion, and rote response. Discussion, even when heated, tends to lead to rational judgments.

Which is why Mobil provokes, needles, challenges, and even tickles the funny bone of America to stir free-wheeling dialogue in the public prints. Saying what we think needs saying on issues that matter to people. Inflation. Jobs. Energy. Environment. The sad state of commercial TV.

Sure, we're a special interest. But what's wrong with that? As Walter Lippmann put it, "all principles are the rationalization of some special interest." The point is, voices of business balance other voices. Stifling any voice distorts the democratic process. The people must be able to weigh all the evidence, come to their own conclusions, and press their views on our national leaders. So future decisions in our participatory democracy will be based on the noblest wisdom of the past—the First Amendment.

Mobil

The above advertisement provides an argument in support of arguments. Do you think this is a good argument? Why or why not? Return to this argument after you have studied various parts of this book and reevaluate it.

Calvin and Hobbes

by Bill Watterson

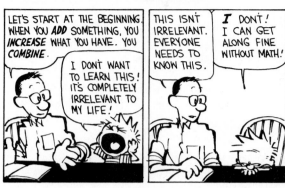

The rule about combining that Calvin's dad is trying to teach is actually a fundamental principle of logic. All of the concepts and principles of the elemenary mathematics that we use in everyday life can be derived from the basic concepts and principles of logic. Thus, it is even more true of logic than of mathematics that it is required by *every* job.

inescapable facts of human existence as we all must live it today are (1) the reality of conflicts—much too often hostile and even violent—between individuals and groups of individuals and (2) the necessity to make difficult judgments and decisions that affect our own lives and well-being as well as the lives and well-being of others. When confronted by conflicts, we often try to understand the positions of the parties involved as a first step in the process of working to resolve the conflict. When faced with a difficult decision having potentially significant effects, we usually want to make every effort to consider the pros and cons of the various alternatives from which ultimately we must choose.

The study of logic can help us in various ways to deal with conflicts and decisions in a more reasonable and satisfactory way than would be possible without the understanding and skills provided by such study. Unfortunately, it is impossible to explain or demonstrate briefly here how this can be; indeed, the primary objective of this entire book is only to begin to give some idea of the ways in which the study of logic can be relevant to and useful in dealing with conflicts and decisions.

Since argument is not recognized as a means of arriving at truth, adherents of rival dogmas have no method except war by means of which to reach a decision. And war, in our scientific age, means, sooner or later, universal death.

BERTRAND RUSSELL

If Russell's judgment is correct, the acceptance of logical analysis of arguments could be of far-reaching significance.

EXERCISE I–1

The following questions are similar to those on various admissions tests for post-graduate programs such as law, business and medicine. Many people are able to work out the correct answers using their general reasoning skills, although it may take quite a bit of time for a single question. See how many of these you can answer correctly now. In addition to writing down your answer, also record the amount of time (in seconds) that it takes you to answer each question. After you have finished your study of logic, come back to these questions and compare the number that you get correct and the amount of time taken at that time with your performance on this initial working of the problems.

1. (I) Any good candy is made with real sugar.
    (II) Choo-choo Chews are made with real sugar.
    (III) Choo-choo Chews are good candy.

    Which of the following statements is/are true?

    a. The truth of (I) alone entails the truth of (III).
    b. The truth of (II) alone entails the truth of (III).
    c. The truth of (I) and (II) together entails the truth of (III).
    d. The truth of (I) and (III) together entails the truth of (II).
    e. None of the above is true.

2. (I) The jar holds x liters.
    (II) The number of beans that fits in a liter is y.
    (III) Some beans are heavier than others.

    Which of these statements is/are sufficient to entail that the jar holds y times x beans?

    a. (I) alone   b. (II) alone   c. (I) and (II) together
    d. (II) and (III) together   e. None of the above

3. (I) Only Margot, Jess, or Flowers could have spiked the punch.
    (II) Margot didn't spike the punch.
    (III) Jess didn't spike the punch.

    Which of these statements is/are sufficient to entail that Flowers spiked the punch?

    a. (I) alone   b. (II) alone   c. (III) alone
    d. (I) and (II)   e. (I), (II), and (III)

4. (I) There are ten students in Jones' class.
    (II) Smith is in Jones' class.
    (III) The top ten students in Jones' class get As.

    Which of these statements imply that Smith gets an A in Jones' class?

    a. (I) alone   b. (II) alone   c. (III) alone
    d. (I) and (II)   e (I), (II), and (III)

5. No one without hairspray can be on the debate team. If Ed is not on the debate team, Pat won't marry him.

Which of the following statements must be true, given these conditions?

a. If Ed gets hairspray, he will be on the debate team.
b. If Ed gets hairspray, Pat will marry him.
c. If Ed makes the debate team, Pat will marry him.
d. If Pat married Ed, Ed had hairspray.
e. If Ed has hairspray, he'll marry Pat.

6. Anthropologists report that some form of family structure has been present in all known human societies. Indeed, the family structure is still strong in the modern world. In light of the high divorce rate in the U.S., it might be thought that families in the U.S. are dying out. But this is false, since the U.S. has the world's highest rate of remarriage.

Which of the following is a reasonable inference from the above statements?

a. Everywhere there is a high divorce rate, there is a high rate of remarriage.
b. The basic family structure remains the same as it was in early societies.
c. The family is not dying out in the U.S., but changing.
d. The high U.S. divorce rate is the sign of a healthy family structure.
e. People in other countries share the U.S. outlook on families.

7. I act like you. Therefore I am an actor. All the world admires an actor. Therefore you admire me.

Which of the following has a logical structure most similar to this argument?

a. Gymnastics toughen the body. You do gymnastics. So, you have a tough body. People with tough bodies are cruel. Therefore, you are cruel.
b. An infinite universe had to be created by an omnipotent God. The universe is infinite. Therefore God is omnipotent. An omnipotent God would not allow suffering. So, you won't ever suffer.
c. I love talking to Jo. So, I'm a good listener. Everyone trusts a good listener. So, Jo trusts me.
d. Van bathed this morning and every morning for the past three weeks. So, Van is clean. Clean people are pleasant. So, Van is pleasant.
e. Eve is a woman. Women are humans. So, Eve is a human. Humans are finicky. So, Eve is finicky.

8. If the school doesn't raise tuition, it must reduce the stipends of teaching assistants. Reducing stipends will anger the union. If the union gets angry, the faculty may strike. If the faculty strikes, there will be no classes. But if the school raises tuition, the students will protest.

Which of the following statements must be true if all of the above are true?

a. Either the students will protest or the union will be angry.
b. Raising tuition will cause greater stipends.
c. A faculty strike will cause higher tuition.

    d. It is impossible for the school to maintain its present number of classes at the present level of tuition.

    e. If the school doesn't raise tuition, then classes will be canceled.

9. The best answer to an ethical question is most reliably found through dialogue. Though an individual might make a moral inquiry and reach an answer, that answer must both overcome objections and surpass other possible answers in correctness, if it is to be confidently accepted. Recognizing this necessity, Plato wrote several inquiries into the nature of good in the form of dialogues between Socrates and his peers.

    According to this passage, if Jan has an answer to an ethical question, but has not heard objections or alternatives to it, then she could believe that it is the right answer for any of the following reasons EXCEPT:

    a. Jan thinks it is the best answer.

    b. Most people think that it's the right answer.

    c. It fits Jan's intuitions about right and wrong.

    d. Jan knows that it is the best of all possible answers.

    e. It appears to explain certain facts about human nature.

10. The existing minimum wage laws have been justified by the argument that they are necessary to assure everyone a decent standard of living, since otherwise employers would take advantage of workers. But since many workers are not worth minimum wage, they are shut out of the job market by such laws. So, there is no justification for minimum wage laws.

    Which of the following is an assumption on which the above argument rests?

    a. Government can't really enforce minimum wage laws.

    b. It is not the job of the government to guarantee financial assistance to anyone who needs it.

    c. Employers will not pay minimum wage for workers who are not worth minimum wage.

    d. Government should interfere with business as little as possible.

    e. Without restrictive laws, employers would never treat their workers fairly.

Refer to the following facts when answering questions 11–14.

Alma, Buck, Cal, Denise, and Eloise, shy spectators at a rodeo, would "hee-haw" if the announcer asked them to, but none of them would hee-haw without the announcer's request.

If Alma were asked to hee-haw, she would do it.

If Buck were asked to hee-haw, he would hee-haw only if Eloise also did.

If Cal were asked to hee-haw, he would only if Denise hee-hawed as well.

If Denise were asked, she would hee-haw only if Alma did not.

If Eloise were asked to hee-haw, she would hee-haw only if Cal did not.

11. If all five were asked to hee-haw, how many would hee-haw?

    a. 1   b. 2   c. 3   d. 4   e. 5

12. If all but Alma were asked to hee-haw, how many would hee-haw?

    a. 0   b. 1   c. 2   d. 3   e. 4

13. If only Alma, Buck, and Cal are asked to hee-haw, which of them will?

    a. Alma only   b. Buck only   c. Cal only
    d. Alma and Buck only   e. Alma and Cal only

14. Which of the following pairs of people could not hee-haw together?

    a. Alma and Buck   b. Alma and Cal   c. Alma and Eloise
    d. Buck and Eloise   e. Cal and Denise

15. Since every part of the universe is finite, the universe must be finite.

    The primary mistake in the above argument is that it

    a. argues from a general principle to a specific instance.
    b. draws a general inference from particular examples.
    c. involves a contradiction.
    d. suggests that when two things share some properties, they must share all their properties.
    e. suggests that a whole must have some property if all of its parts have that property.

16. It should be legal to have opaque windows on one's car. Car windows are just like windows anywhere else, so if the law requires free visibility through windows into all cars, it should require free visibility through windows into all homes. But we have a tradition in the U.S. of protecting the privacy of the individual, and a legal requirement of free visibility to the interior of any private property violates that tradition.

    Which of the following statements, if true, is most damaging to this argument?

    a. Automobiles are meant for motion, while homes stand still.
    b. Tradition in the U.S. protects privacy rights only in residential areas.
    c. Cars with opaque windows are often used for illegal acts.
    d. Opaque windows have never been legal.
    e. Most lawyers hold that opaque car windows should be banned.

17. It has even been maintained by Smith that since it is obvious that many people desire anarchy, we cannot avoid the conclusion that anarchy is desirable, unless we are willing to give up the conviction that things that many people see are visible. Of course, this position overlooks the important difference in modality between the words 'visible' and 'desirable'; the former we define as 'that which one can see,' while the latter means 'that which one should desire.'

    The objection stated in the second half of this passage points out that

    a. nobody really desires anarchy.
    b. Smith is an anarchist herself.

    c. Smith has not proved that people desire anarchy.

    d. we must give up the conviction that everything that we see is visible.

    e. Smith has not proven that anarchy is desirable.

18. Some ethical theorists have held that an act's moral value derives not from any consequences of the act, but from the principle from which the act follows.

    The ethical theorists mentioned in this statement would deny that which of the following acts could have moral value?

    a. An act committed without regard to its consequences.

    b. An act chosen because it accords with a questionable principle.

    c. An act committed to follow the Golden Rule.

    d. An act that had good consequences, even though it was motivated only by selfish desires.

    e. An act committed by someone who didn't consider whether it was in his or her best interest to commit that act.

19. An anthropologist has suggested that there is a correlation between shoe size and personal charm. Her evidence for the claim is that nearly 60 percent of the people that her survey determined to be most charming wear size-nine shoes.

    To assess the validity of the anthropologist's claim it is most important that we answer which of the following questions?

    a. What percentage of persons not considered most charming wear size-nine shoes?

    b. What percentage of the total population wears shoes?

    c. What is the meaning of 'charming' as the anthropologist uses it?

    d. How many people are considered most charming?

    e. What percentage of the total population is not charming?

I.2 What Can Be Learned about Logic and How Can It Be Learned?

You probably were able to correctly answer many if not all of the questions in the preceding set. But this does not mean that nothing can be gained from the study of the material in this book. Because many admissions exams are given under severe time constraints, *speed with accuracy* is essential. And being able to correctly answer all of the questions in the preceding set definitely does NOT mean that you will be able to get an A in a logic course without hard work!

No one can be taught to be logical. This does not mean that the study of logic is a waste of time. Rather, saying this is comparable to telling native speakers of English that none of them can be taught English; they can't be taught it because *they already know it* and because English is the language that would have to be used to teach it! What can be taught to native speakers of English is not how to speak English, but how to speak it ***better***.

ASK MARILYN®

BY MARILYN VOS SAVANT

In your responses to questions, the logic of your explanations makes it appear so effortless. Do you think that problem-solving and critical-thinking skills can be learned and developed? If so, how?

—Stephanie Zinger, Howard Beach, N.Y.

I'm confident that they can be learned, and the key is having the right attitude. Think of mental exercise like physical exercise. If you do only as much physical exercise as you need to accomplish your day-to-day tasks, you'll soon find yourself incapable of doing anything more. And any little bit of exertion that you save—like driving around the department store's parking lot to find the parking space that's closest to one of the doors—narrows your physical world just that much more. If you operate only within your comfort zone, you not only do not expand it, but your comfort zone also quietly shrinks.

I was at a concert hall last week and watched at least 100 people line up at the escalator to ride up the equivalent of two sets of stairs. A broad marble staircase was right next to the escalator. There were fewer than half a dozen people on it. It's the same way with mental exercise. Every day, you must press yourself to do a little more than you can do easily. Play games that make you *think*—not games of chance. Read a book that's a bit difficult for you. Take a course in any academic subject. Will this make you feel dumb at first? Yes. It's just like the feeling you get when you go to the gym for the first time. You feel out of breath and out of shape. And you are! But, with time, all the old abilities will come back, and you'll feel just great. Try it!

Reprinted with permission from Parade, *copyright © 1993.*

We have all learned our basic logical skills the same way that we learned our basic English-speaking skills—through informal practical use starting at birth (or perhaps even before birth). The fact that you were able to identify the correct answers on at least some of the questions in Exercise I–1 provides concrete evidence that you have some fairly sophisticated logical skills. But we all can progress further in our ability to use the English language and our ability to reason well by formally studying to learn new skills and concepts that are not normally learned in the course of everyday use of our language and reasoning abilities.

I.2.1 Logical Form and Structure

The most basic concept in the study of logic is that of **logical *form***. To get a rough idea of what this concept involves, consider the following sentences.

> Pat likes logic.
> Lee likes logic.
> Jan likes logic.

These statements have quite different meanings insofar as they are about three different persons, but they also resemble one another in a basic way. One way of describing this similarity among the three statements is to say that they have the same logical structure or form. The statement 'Pat likes calculus' also shares this form, even though it differs from the second and third sentences in two ways. The similarity of form among these statements can be most clearly shown by using blanks as follows:

_____ **likes** ....

Any sentence we might construct by putting appropriate nouns in the blanks would have the same logical form as our original three statements. Thus, 'Rover likes dog food' and 'Pat likes Jan' also share the same logical form. The best way to understand this concept is to work through exercises such as the following.

EXERCISE I–2

Put words in the blanks to create five different sentences with the same logical form.

1. _____ is larger than ....
2. All _____ are ....
3. _____ believe(s) that ....
4. Not every _____ is a(n) ....
5. Either _____ or ....
6. Whenever _____ also ....
7. I sometimes _____, but I never ....
8. If I thought that _____, I would ....
9. No _____ are ....
10. If _____ then ....

EXERCISE I–3

Look for words that are contained in both components of the following pairs of sentences. Display the *common* form by replacing with blanks the words which do NOT appear in the same positions in both sentences.

1. Dan is happy. / George is happy.
2. This car is red. / This car is blue.
3. Joe joined the army. / Joe joined the chess club.
4. Joe joined the chess club. / Karen joined the chess club.
5. Ben swam to France and Dave swam to England. / Ben swam to Albania and Dave swam to Turkey.
6. Pam very likely swam the channel. / Morris very likely scrubbed the hide.
7. If Mt. Julio is taller than Everest, then if I climbed Mt. Julio, I'm famous. / If Mt. Julio is taller than Everest, then if I climbed Mt. Julio, I'm foolhardy.

8. If Alex says that he is irritable, you'd better believe it. / If Alex says that he is crazy, you'd better stay out of his way.

9. Either roses are red or violets are blue. / Either roses are violet or violets are vermillion.

10. If all roses are red, then probably some violets aren't blue. / If some people are nasty, then probably Ross is one of them.

11. Either I ate the cake or I ate the pudding. / Either I ate the bagel or I ate the oatmeal.

12. Either I ate the cake or Dave ate the pudding. / Either Seth swam the river or Jane tugged the rope.

13. If Jon passed the ball then the Blankets won the game. / If Douglas passed the ball then the Blankets lost the game.

14. Terry will marry you if and only if you are caring. / Terry will scorn you if and only if you are selfish.

15. Terry will marry you if and only if you are caring. / Ken will trip you if and only if you are tall.

16. If Dave plays the tambourine, Ben sings, and Mike plays guitar, then the band is in business. / If Dave holds his breath, Ben hops on one foot, and Mike walks on hot coals, then the circus is in business.

I.2.2 Formal and Informal Logic

We have already indicated that logic is concerned with the structure of individual statements and the relations that exist between two or more statements. One way of approaching this task is by focusing on the basic logical structure or form of statements and arguments, with no consideration of their nonlogical content. Exercises I–2 and I–3 involve the logical forms of relatively simple statements. The following example involves the slightly more complex logical structure of a set of interconnected statements that constitute an argument.

> **If Pat works to improve her logical skills, she also will probably be a better lawyer.**
> **Pat is working to improve her logical skills.**
> **Thus, Pat will probably be a better lawyer.**

The basic logical structure of this set of statements can be exhibited in a variety of ways using different systems of logic. One possible way is the following:

> **If _____, then ....**
> **_____.**
> **Thus, ...**

If we are concerned only with the form or structure of these statements, it is not at all important (or even relevant) what terms might be plugged into the various blanks. When the meanings of the nonlogical terms are not being considered and only the logical form is of interest, we are working in the domain known as **formal logic.**

Some logicians study only formal logic; that is, they work only with abstract models that have purely logical substance and content. Although such an activity can be as intellectually challenging and interesting as the game of chess, it has additional value in that it can be applied to the analysis and evaluation of statements and arguments that are part of our everyday lives. It is for this reason that logic courses are part of most college curricula while chess is not.

Relating the abstract systems of formal logic to "real" statements and arguments is not part of formal logic itself; it requires the consideration of many issues and factors beyond the basic logical forms of the statements and arguments. The study of the factors other than logical form relevant to the analysis and evaluation of statements and arguments of the kind that occur in everyday situations is known as **informal logic.** This study includes consideration of such things as: identification and clarification of vague or ambiguous statements; identification of unstated assumptions, presuppositions, or biases and making them explicit; recognition of frequently used but highly questionable premises; and assessment of the strength of analogies between more or less similar cases.

EXERCISE I–4

Match each of the following arguments to its closest relative in form. To do this, you will probably be disregarding (either consciously or unconsciously) the non-logical content of the statements comprising each argument.

1. Alex is a lot like Al.
   Al is a menace to the Goodfellows.
   So, Alex is a menace to the Goodfellows.
   a. Chet is a lot like Wynn.
      Wynn eschews undergarments.
      So, Chet does also.
   b. Baggs knits only if Simms does.
      Simms knits only if Mel does.
      So, Baggs is a lot like Mel.
   c. Bud is a lot like Snell.
      So, if Snell is a lot like Prynne, then Bud is a lot like Prynne.

2. All mammals are like humans.
   So, if we shouldn't harm humans for the purposes of science, we shouldn't harm any mammals for the purposes of science.
   a. All books are like magazines.
      So, if we shouldn't read books then we shouldn't read magazines.
   b. Paper is like plastic.
      So, even if we can't use them both for all the same things, we should recycle both.
   c. Love is like a full moon.
      So, many children believe that love is made of green cheese.

3. Since humans have a profound capacity to feel dread and pain, certain things should never be done to them.
But chimpanzees, orangutans, and apes all have a profound capacity to feel dread and pain.
So, certain things should never be done to chimpanzees, orangutans, or apes.

   a. Since water is a liquid, it can make you wet.
     Maple syrup is a liquid.
     So, maple syrup contains water.
   b. Wherever we find goodness, we find hope.
     But hope is identical to faith.
     So, wherever we find goodness, we find faith.
   c. Since Janus has a cold, she could make you sick.
     But Cinch has a cold, too.
     So, Cinch could make you sick.

4. All gongs are drums.
Some gongs are loud.
Therefore, some drums are loud.

   a. All fibs are lies.
     Some fibs are songs.
     So, all fibs are fibs.
   b. All chicks are babies.
     Some chicks are yellow.
     Therefore, some babies are yellow.
   c. All spies are liars.
     All liars are sneaks.
     Therefore, all liars are spies.

5. Jody and Bobbie are usually at the well when they're not at the stables.
They're not at the stables.
So, they're probably at the well.

   a. Craig and Kelly are usually licking their fingers when they're not poking the cake.
     They're not poking the cake.
     So, they're probably licking their fingers.
   b. Seth and Dijon are either unhealthy or malicious.
     They're malicious.
     So, they're not unhealthy.
   c. Skip and Ralph are both excellent and radical.
     They're excellent.
     So, they're radical.

6. Avery and Arden can't both be president.
Skip is chief justice only if Avery is president.

Biff is chief justice only if Arden is president.
Avery is president.
So, Biff is not chief justice.

a. Bambi and Barbi can't both love fishing.
   Welch loves casting only if Bambi loves fishing.
   Pops hates casting only if Barbi loves fishing.
   Barbi doesn't love fishing.
   So, Welch loves casting.
b. Rupe can be president and Sal can be chief justice.
   Chad can be chief justice if Rupe is president.
   Dell can be chief justice if Sal is president.
   Rupe is president.
   So, Dell is not chief justice.
c. Mill and Waters couldn't both be liars.
   Grendel was misled only if Mill is a liar.
   Salvo was misled only if Waters is a liar.
   Mill is a liar.
   So, Salvo was not misled.

7. A state always has a larger population than any state with a smaller area.
   California is smaller in area than Alaska.
   Therefore, Alaska has a larger population than California.

a. Chancellors have more power than provosts.
   Tina and Max are both chancellors.
   Therefore, Tina and Max have more power than provosts.
b. People are generally younger than their uncles.
   Bim is Simcha's uncle.
   So, Simcha is probably younger than Bim.
c. No two numbers are identical.
   Twelve and three are two numbers.
   So, twelve is less than three.

8. Most clowns are very sad.
   Kim is always happy.
   So, Kim is probably not a clown.

a. Most mercenaries are religious.
   Jeb is not religious.
   So, it's unlikely that Jeb is a mercenary.
b. Most criminals are deeply ironic.
   Crab is a criminal.
   So, Crab is probably deeply ironic.
c. Bo is a southpaw.
   All southpaws are lefties.
   So, Bo is a lefty.

I.3 Logic versus Psychology

As a discipline, logic dates to the Greek philosopher Aristotle, who wrote the first text on the system of syllogistic logic that will be studied in Chapters 3 and 4 of this book. For more than two thousand years, Aristotelian logic was regarded as the only possible kind; it was not until the nineteenth and twentieth centuries that alternative systems were developed. Yet, in all this time, no simple, precise, universally accepted definition of logic has ever been formulated. Of the various definitions that have been offered, a good many have been more confusing than helpful. Nevertheless, it is worthwhile to examine some of them to gain some insight into the nature of the discipline.

One common definition is that logic is the study of the laws of thought. The problem with such a definition is that it is too inclusive. Many mental activities—for example, imagining a unicorn, or daydreaming about being a millionaire—would qualify as thought in this sense of the term. However, few of these activities would be of interest to the logician. Logic is concerned primarily with the type of thinking called **reasoning,** the process by which an inference or conclusion is drawn from a statement or series of statements. Can logic then be properly defined as the study of the laws of reasoning? This is certainly more specific, but it is still too broad. The discipline of psychology is also concerned with what can properly be called laws of reasoning; and yet logic is not a branch of psychology but of philosophy.

If this is confusing, it is probably because we commonly use the term 'law' in two quite different senses. A law may be a **descriptive** statement about the way something in fact happens; or it may be a **prescriptive** statement about how something should be done.

When we speak of the laws of nature or scientific law, we are using the term 'law' in its descriptive sense. The law of gravitation, the laws of motion, and the laws of heat exchange, to give just a few examples, were not created by a human legislature, and they cannot be repealed. They describe what experts consider to be the closest approximations to the ways the components of the universe behave under given conditions. Nothing and no one can choose to obey or not to obey these laws. If I drop a brick from the top of the Empire State Building, my knowledge of several descriptive laws would enable me to predict rather accurately the ensuing course of events. And if, instead of dropping a brick, I myself step off the top of the Empire State Building, I will also behave according to those same descriptive laws; I obviously cannot choose to do otherwise.

Another way of characterizing descriptive laws is in terms of how we normally deal with exceptions to them. Descriptive laws are generally considered to have no exceptions. Thus, if we encounter an apparent exception, either we must find some explanation as to why it is not really an exception, or else we must change our descriptive law so that it includes this exceptional behavior. For example, if a physicist is told that a brick that was dropped off of the

Empire State Building did not accelerate during its fall to the ground (as is required by the descriptive laws of physics), the physicist would have to do one of three things:

1. reject the observation as being defective;

2. find evidence that special circumstances can explain the exceptional behavior (for example, the brick was attached to a parachute); *or*

3. make a revision to the laws of physics.

It would not be logically correct for the physicist to accept the claim about the brick as true and as involving no special factors (such as the parachute) *and* to keep the basic laws of physics unchanged. (For well-established and long-held descriptive laws, we almost always wind up rejecting the observation of an exception on the grounds that the observation is in some way defective.)

Laws of behavior may also be descriptive; that is, they may purport to describe the ways in which individuals or groups of people tend to react to given conditions, on the basis of biological structure or social conditioning. If we assert that hungry people are more likely than well-fed people to riot against a corrupt government, we are stating what we believe to be a descriptive law. We are describing a way in which people do frequently tend to act.

Prescriptive laws, on the other hand, are concerned with the way people *ought* to act. Moral laws are prescriptive; the laws of a political entity such as a nation or a city are prescriptive; the constitution and bylaws of an organization are prescriptive. Such laws are usually established by deliberate choice, as a means of attaining a desired goal; they can be broken. If a motorist sees a street sign setting forth the prescriptive law, "Speed Limit 20 mph," it is possible for her to ignore it and push the speedometer up to 50. The consequences might be unfortunate, or they might not: The driver might arrive at her destination in one piece, having skidded off no cliff, struck no pedestrian, and picked up no speeding ticket. But nothing requires that the law be changed because of this violation, and as a matter of fact, we almost never change prescriptive laws as the result of a relatively small number of violations. (One reason given for the repeal of the constitutional amendment prohibiting the production and sale of alcoholic beverages was that there were so many violations of it that it was proven to be unenforceable. But there were other reasons for its repeal, and other prescriptive laws with quite large numbers of violations have not been repealed.)

To return now to our comparison of logic and psychology: *Psychology* is concerned with the laws of reasoning insofar as it is concerned with *describing* the ways in which people actually *do* tend to reason. For instance, psychologists may seek to discover the ways in which people form generalizations. To do so, they observe, interview, and test a number of subjects. One subject might be a college student who, after struggling with three difficult mathematics courses, has concluded that all mathematics courses are difficult. Another might be a person who has purchased meat twice from a particular store, found it tough on both occasions, and concluded that all meat sold by that store is of poor quality. Still others report similar experiences, so, on the basis of this information, the psychologists might propose a descriptive hypothesis that all people form generalizations on the basis of fewer than ten specific instances. The psychologists' conclusion says nothing about whether this is a good or a bad way to reason; it merely purports to describe a way in which people do reason.

In contrast, the laws of reason with which *logic* is concerned are more of the *prescriptive* type. Logic seeks to set standards for the ways in which people ought to reason if they wish to reason well. The prescriptive laws of reason are based on logicians' collective judgment that certain ways of reasoning are, by their very nature, better than other ways of reasoning. Therefore, like speed limits, the prescriptive laws of logic can be ignored, but persons who ignore them are likely to find themselves saddled with the results of mistaken conclusions. For example, a politician running for reelection in a district where abortion is a major issue might poll a sample of nine residents and conclude from their responses that an anti-abortion stand will ensure her victory. But if the nine people she talked to are not typical of the majority of voters in her district, she is probably in for a rude shock when she sees the election returns. In arriving at her conclusion, she indeed reasoned according to the process described by the psychologist in the previous paragraph. However, from a logical point of view, her reasoning was poor—not because she was relying on other people's opinions, but because the opinions were drawn from a very small and unrepresentative sample of voters.

Logic can also be characterized as the study of reasoning in a descriptive sense. On this account, logic provides descriptions of basic logical structures of statements and of the relations that hold among them. For example, logic tells us that the statement 'The sun is shining or it is not shining' is true because of its logical structure. Logic also tells us that the statement 'The sun is shining' implies the statement 'It is not the case that the sun is not shining.' These exemplars of some basic laws of logic are at least as true (descriptively) as the laws of physics and are more widely accepted than most if not all of the descriptive laws of psychology.

Thus, in this respect, logic is similar to psychology, but it differs in that it is descriptive of the logical structures of—and the logical relations among—statements, not of human minds or reasoning processes. In brief, psychology is concerned with describing the way people reason while logic is concerned with evaluating this reasoning (possibly by using rules that describe the essential nature of logical structures). In this text, we shall focus on methods for distinguishing good reasoning from bad reasoning, and we will present formal criteria for evaluating inferences and arguments as well as techniques and procedures for applying these criteria to concrete cases. These criteria, techniques, and procedures are of value not only to logicians but also to psychologists, students, business people, politicians, detectives, farmers, athletes, and anyone else who uses a variety of reasoning processes to make inferences and reach conclusions. In truth, we all require standards for determining which of these processes are good and which are poor, which is the same as to say that our reasoning and arguments are subject to logical evaluation.

I.4 The Organization of This Book

Although the study of logic is similar to the study of English in many ways, it is different in at least one important way: One common core constitutes English grammar, but many different systems of logic have been developed, each of which is useful for dealing with certain kinds of statements and arguments in certain ways. Only a few of the more frequently used systems of logic are discussed in this book. However, a careful study of even two or three of the different systems presented in this book will be sufficient to give you a good idea of the nature of logic in general and of its uses and limitations.

Many systems have been developed during the past two thousand years for analyzing the structure of and relations between statements. We shall be studying at an elementary level only a few of the more widely known and widely used systems. In Chapters 3 through 8, we will examine three different *formal* systems for analyzing statements and arguments composed of sets of statements. In dealing with each of these systems, we will deal first with their respective concepts and methods for analyzing the logical structures of individual statements and the relatively simple logical relations between pairs of statements, particularly the relations of consistency and implication (Chapters 3, 5, and 7). After the techniques and procedures for dealing with individual statements have been mastered, we will study the more complex logical relations that hold among sets of statements, particularly the relation known as 'validity' (Chapters 4, 6, and 8).

Although the discussion of *informal* factors and methods will be incorporated as appropriate and necessary into the chapters on formal deductive logic, informal logic will also be discussed in more general and detailed ways in several separate chapters. Chapter 1 focuses on methods and concepts for the informal analysis of the logical structure of individual statements, with particular focus on the different kinds of statements that do not require arguments in their support. Chapter 2 presents the general principles of informal analysis of arguments, particularly as relevant to the application of formal techniques dealt with in Chapters 3 through 8. Chapter 12 presents a method of informal analysis for identifying certain kinds of common fallacious or defective arguments. Chapter 14 ties together material presented throughout the book by providing sample analyses of relatively complex sets of statements of the kind that are regularly encountered in everyday contexts.

In summary, you should be prepared to find some things in your study of this book that will be of relatively immediate use and value, both to your other areas of study and to various everyday situations you might encounter. But much of what you will learn from the study of logic will be only indirectly

In the space of one hundred and seventy-six years the Lower Mississippi has shortened itself two hundred and forty-two miles. That is an average of a trifle over one mile and a third per year. Therefore, any calm person, who is not blind or idiotic, can see that in the old Oolitic Silurian Period, just a million years ago next November, the Lower Mississippi River was upward of one million three hundred thousand miles long, and stuck out over the Gulf of Mexico like a fishing-rod. And by the same token any person can see that seven hundred and forty-two years from now the Lower Mississippi will be only a mile and three-quarters long, and Cairo and New Orleans will have joined their streets together, and be plodding comfortably along under a single mayor and a mutual board of aldermen. There is something fascinating about science. One gets such wholesale returns of conjecture out of such trifling investment of fact.

MARK TWAIN, *Life on the Mississippi* (1875)

Although your intuitions are probably (correctly) strong that Mark Twain's argument is mistaken somewhere, it may be fairly difficult for you to specify precisely what is wrong with it. The study of logic should help you deal with such problems—and also with more practical ones—if you work at it conscientiously.

useful—sometimes only in the long run. Thus, you should approach the subject with patience and the understanding that its lack of apparent "relevance" to your current interests and concerns does not mean that it is not worth studying as part of your overall educational program. Every effort has been made in this book to make explicit the ways in which logic relates to many aspects of life and human activity, and it can be stated with confidence that if you pursue the study of logic conscientiously you will discover many other interesting and useful ways in which the methods and concepts to be discussed here relate to other areas of your life.

EXERCISE I–5

Each of the following articles, cartoons, and advertisements contains at least one argument. Try to identify the arguments and make an "educated guess" as to whether each is "good" or "bad." Save your written guesses. We will return to these arguments several times later so that you can assess the improvement in your skills of argument analysis.

1.

THE WIZARD OF ID   by Parker and Hart

By permission of Johnny Hart and Creators Syndicate, Inc.

2.

George F. Will

Commentary

Anyone with a small child feels as Cardinal Wolsey felt about Henry VIII: "Be well advised and assured what you put in his head, for ye shall never pull it out again." The aim of advertising directed at children, especially on Saturday morning, is not just to set visions of sweets dancing in small heads. The aim also is to make children even less like angels than it is their natural inclination to be. The aim, a candid assessment has said, is to turn them into "very successful naggers."

Conclusive evidence that advertising achieves this aim is the hundreds of millions of dollars spent each year on such advertising. Advertisers are not fools; they would not spend so much if they did not have hard evidence that it pays to bombard little people, even though little people have no money. Little people successfully belabor big people.

3.

**"Fair enough--let's give them a cut
out of what we take tonight"**

Copyright 1975 by Herblock in The Washington Post.

4.

Homeless families are real, need help

This is a magical time of year. But there are children — tens of thousands of them — who never heard the jingle of sleigh bells or the clatter of reindeer on the roof.

It's not that Santa Claus forgot or that he doesn't care. He simply couldn't find them. Their address is the street.

People who run emergency shelters say they're seeing more and more kids. Not just in the big cities on the East and West coasts, but even in the heartland.

Some say the problem's exaggerated. The National Coalition for the Homeless disagrees. It estimates there are as many as 500,000 children without permanent shelter.

Hard numbers are difficult to come by: The children who weren't home for Santa weren't there for the census takers, either.

The U.S. Conference of Mayors — no bleeding hearts — says the need for emergency lodging increased 21% on average this year in the 26 cities it surveyed. Last year, it was up 20%.

Children and their parents now make up a third of the homeless population, the mayors say. That's a 32% increase over 1986. Two out of every three people seeking emergency rations are moms, dads or their kids — up 18%.

One-year-old Elizabeth Jowders is too young to realize that living in a windowless warehouse sets her apart. The warehouse, a stone's throw from the Dallas Convention Center, is used by churches for people who have no other choice. It's a palace compared to the squalor available in some cities. But it's no place for a baby to be growing up.

Elizabeth's dad has a strong back. He wants to work. But his skills don't match the marketplace.

Even if Bill Jowders finds a job, there's no guarantee he'll be able to make ends meet. One out of five homeless people works but can't pay the bills, the mayors say.

Housing shortages and inadequate or outmoded job skills are among the major causes of homelessness. Violence often sends women and their children packing. For people living at the margin, a medical crisis, a temporary job loss or a big rent hike can be a one-way ticket to the street.

Whatever the reasons, we can't have kids consigned to converted warehouses and sleazy hotels. Too many of them are missing out on the immunizations they need. They're not eating right. Their teeth receive no care. If they attend school at all, they become the butt of bad jokes. They fall behind. They get in trouble. A piece of a generation is lost.

That is a sad waste. It is cruel. And it is wrong.

Long-term remedies will require a joint effort by communities and the federal government.

Uncle Sam can more effectively encourage local initiatives. Some of the churches, charities, foundations, cities and states have shown a knack for creative thinking. Their successful innovations should be strongly supported and widely publicized.

The stakes are high. Before another Christmas rolls around, we've got to find the ways and means to get more kids' addresses to the North Pole.

5.

PETER B. GEMMA, JR.
An opposing view

Homeless families are a bleeding-heart myth

ARLINGTON, Va. — Professional bleeding hearts pick up and cast off causes like seasonal clothing.

Remember the spate of TV docudramas selling tragic stories of battered wives like soap? And how about that business of holding hands across the country, thinking happy thoughts, while trying to feed the hungry?

Country and Western festivals for FarmAid, rock concerts for Amnesty International, and perennial hunger strikes against all the injustices ever perpetrated have turned the politics of guilt and pity into a growth industry. Enter here today's urgent but chic issue: homeless families.

I'm not Scrooge or the Grinch who stole Christmas, but it is obvious that the homeless problem is being oversold and overplayed.

Of course, there are indigent people who desperately need our help. Apparently, the myriad of local, state and national private and public welfare programs missed some needy people — or perhaps the poor missed these programs.

In any case, over the din of movie moguls promoting their schmaltzy productions of Hollywood's idea of homelessness and the street protesters shouting, "Somebody *do* something," let's look at some facts.

On one hand, professional activists for the homeless claim 2 million or more of the nation's poor have no place to sleep. But unless there is a conspiracy of federal employees dedicated to denying assis-

Peter B. Gemma Jr. is a contributing editor of Conservative Digest.

tance to the needy, recent studies produced by both the Housing and Urban Development and the Agriculture departments actually estimate the number of homeless to be in the range of 250,000 to 350,000.

And this figure can be reduced by carefully studying why people are indeed homeless: by choice or by chance.

During the four "compassionate" years of the Carter administration, 41,198 federally constructed homes were completed at a cost of $21.5 billion. During the first four "lean and mean" years of the Reagan era, $37.4 billion of our money was spent by Washington to build 111,195 housing units for the poor — yet guess who is portrayed as the bogyman of the homeless.

New York City spent $300 million — in addition to federal infusions of tax monies — trying to assist its approximately 36,000 homeless people last year. Add to this equation 300,000 abandoned apartments due to the city's strangling regulations and anti-free market rent controls, and you get "bureaucratic help" at its efficient best.

You don't have to be stingy, cynical, or unsympathetic to keep the plight of the homeless in perspective. Homeless families don't really need Big Monies or Big Brother Government programs. All they really need is you and I and some common sense.

6.

THE DOORS OF INJUSTICE

SENECA FALLS, New York—In 1976, an ex-policeman disappeared while fishing on Seneca Lake in Upstate New York. Two men were arrested and accused of his murder, even though the body was never found.

Carol Ritter, court reporter for Gannett Rochester Newspapers, went to cover the pretrial hearing for the accused.

When she arrived at the courtroom, Ritter and other reporters were barred from the hearing on the pretext that the accused would not be able to get a fair trial if the pretrial hearing was covered by the press.

The Gannett Rochester Newspapers strongly disagreed and challenged the judge's right to close the doors of justice to the people, including the press. They took that challenge to the Supreme Court of the United States.

Gannett believes no judge should have the right to shut the people and their free press out of such pretrial hearings, where an overwhelming majority of criminal prosecutions are resolved.

Can you imagine up to 90 percent of all court cases being settled in secret? Gannett could not. But on July 2, 1979, the Supreme Court ruled it could happen.

Gannett protests vigorously this abridgment of the First Amendment. Not only has the Court limited journalists' access to gathering and reporting the news for the public, but it has also trampled on the people's freedom to know, the cornerstone of our rights as a free people in a free society.

The freedoms of the First Amendment must be cherished, not shackled.

At Gannett, we have a commitment to freedom in every business we're in, whether it's newspaper, TV, radio, outdoor advertising or public opinion research.

And so from Burlington to Boise, from Fort Myers to Fort Wayne, every Gannett newspaper, every TV and radio station is free to express its own opinions, free to serve the best interests of its own community in its own way.

Gannett
A world of different voices where freedom speaks.

7.

Which Side Do You Believe?

There are two sides to the issue of nuclear power. Both sides feel strongly that their position is correct—which makes it difficult for Americans to form a responsible position on whether our country needs this source of energy.

Americans are bombarded with conflicting views and statements from numerous self-proclaimed energy experts. Some have even said that nuclear power—which currently provides 12% of the nation's electricity—should be halted altogether.

But consider the *sources* of the loudest anti-nuclear noise. Among those leading the attack on nuclear power are a host of actors and actresses, rock stars, aspiring politicians and others who think America has grown enough.

The Issue Isn't Just Nuclear

Nuclear power is not the only thing they oppose. These are often the same people who have been against development of geothermal energy in California . . . stopped new hydro-electric plants in Maine and Tennessee . . . blocked a new oil refinery for southern California . . . opposed new pipelines to deliver natural gas to the East . . . fought the building of more coal-fired plants. And they're the same people opposed to President Carter's plan for developing a synthetic fuels.program. One wonders what they are *for*, and how they propose meeting America's energy needs?

For many of these people, stopping nuclear power is but one part of a political objective to slow growth across the board in America. This no-growth philosophy of the anti-nuclear leadership was clearly expressed by Amory Lovins, one of the world's leading nuclear critics, when he admitted, "If nuclear power were clean, safe, economic . . . and socially benign per se, it would still be unattractive *because of the political implications* . . ."

Support For Nuclear Widespread

On the other hand, consider the many organizations that have *endorsed* nuclear power for America's future. They include: the AFL-CIO . . . the NAACP . . . the National Governor's Conference . . . Consumer Alert . . . and many more. These groups recognize that America's need for electric power is growing at a rate of 4% each year.

Consider also that the health and safety record of nuclear power has been endorsed by a vast majority of the *scientific* community—including such organizations as the National Academy of Sciences, the World Health Organization, the American Medical Association, and the Health Physics Society.

We're not saying that nuclear power is risk free. The truth is that risks are involved in *all* energy technologies. However, the overwhelming scientific evidence is clear: nuclear power is at least as clean and safe as any other means available to generate electricity—more so than most.

Where will Americans get the electricity that is needed if not, in part, from nuclear power? That's the real question in the nuclear debate. It's the one for which the anti-nuclear leaders have no answer.

Nuclear Power. Because America Needs Energy.

America's Electric Energy Companies, Department E. Post Office Box 420. Pelham Manor. New York 10803

Courtesy Committee for Energy Awareness

8.

Pick a Color

Several months ago, I was required to complete a typical prying federal form, one which, among other things, inquired of my "minority status." Now that the courts have decided to implement "racial balance," the bureaucrats are right there demanding racially "mixed" neighborhoods, even apartment buildings, and "hire by quota" is the thing in the building trades.

After all, if you're going to bus kids or hire apprentices, you must know which is the "right" race, and in what correct proportion, to use, lest you fail to create that great magical amalgam "race harmony."

But what *is* race? What are those things which comprise "racial characteristics?" Was I (check one): a) white (nonminority); b) Negro/black; c) American Indian; d) Spanish-American; e) Oriental; f) Other minorities not under above.

Well, what the hell. I *felt* like being a "Negro/black" that day, and checked the box.

The forms attendant noticed the discrepancy as my white hands moved the pen on to another section of the form, and called my attention to my "error."

"It's no error," I replied. "I *am* Negro."

Still doubtful, the HUD bureaucrat said, "Bullshit!"

Being newly Negro/black, and not about to take any crap from a government employee, I returned his remark with, "You don't know my mother." That stopped him dead in his pencil pushing, the specter of my Negro/black mother haunting him.

Somewhere, some federal form now lists me as Negro/black. Next time, maybe, I'll choose "Oriental," or perhaps "Other" and insist I'm a Basque.

All of which makes me ask: how does anyone, anywhere, *know* who is black, or who is white, or who is whatever?

The answer is that the labels are applied on the basis of how the labeler *thinks* a black, a white, an Oriental, or an "Other" looks, whether appropriate or inappropriate. I have been assured by the more conscientious pickers and choosers of race among local school personnel that they assess "cultural differences" in determining category. Fine. When asked to define that, I get no coherent reply.

Underneath it all is the ultimate racist thought: *we* are talking about and labeling *them*, and everybody knows who *they* are. Indeed, *they* know who they are.

At what point on the chromatic scale, or whatever is used, does a person cease being "Negro/black" and become "white (nonminority)"? Or cease being "white" and become "Oriental"? Is there, deep in the recesses of HEW's Washington headquarters, a model of "whiteness" and "blackness"?

No, there are no models, because there are no legal definitions of what it takes to be "Negro/black," "Spanish-American," or "Other." There are no guidelines either. There are only prejudices and assumptions.

Actually, anyone may legally claim to be whatever nice color he wants to be. He may, under present laws, even choose to be of the opposite sex, if he/she so desires.

There are no United States equivalents to the Nazi Nuremberg Laws of Racial Purity.

Which means that if a community faced with some HEW massive busing plan should just claim that 50 per cent of its group is already black, or white, what official would oppose it? Or *could* oppose it?

Some citizen might go to court over the matter, but short of exhuming long-dead ancestors to check for coloration, no court could solve the question, unless a color code were formulated. That would be an American dilemma.   —LARRY MAY

Reprinted with permission of National Review, *150 East 35th St., New York, N.Y. 10016.*

9.

In Henry Aaron's Footsteps: The Man Who Isn't There Yet

(c) 1974 New York Times News Service

NEW YORK — Okay: Hank Aaron has overtaken Babe Ruth. who's next?

Anyone? Ever? In the foreseeable future?

It is safe enough to say that no one currently recognized as a major league homerun hitter has much chance of reaching 700, let alone whatever figure beyond that Aaron finally establishes. And anyone starting now would need, as Aaron and Ruth did, 20 years of averaging 35 homers a year to get three — which would be 1994.

The two players who come closest to having even a million-to-one chance of catching Aaron are Johnny Bench and Reggie Jackson. But. assuming each plays to the age of 40, Bench would have to average 83 homers a year for the next 14 years and Jackson would need 40 a year for the next 13 years to pass 700.

So even if Jackson did it, that would be in 1987 and it can be flatly asserted that Halley's Comet, due back in 1986, will return before anyone challenges Aaron's mark.

And it is extremely unlikely that anyone will threaten it during the rest of the 20th century.

Such projections are simple enough to make, because while no one can predict any man's actual career homerun total, it is quite possible to calculate a "maximum probable" total that a player will not exceed.

For example: Of all active players, Harmon Killebrew has hit homeruns with greatest frequency: 546 in 7,502 at-bats, or one homer every 13.74 times at bat. (These and all other figures are as of the start of this season.) It is reasonable to assume that he will not play past the age of 40, and that he will not average more than 500 at-bats a season in the remaining three years.

(Actually, Killebrew has averaged 394 at-bats the last three years, and Aaron 445, so 500 is a safe "outside limit" for players that age.)

Well, if Killebrew hit homers at his career pace for an-

other 1,500 at-bats, he would add 109 to his total and finish with 655.

The same kind of estimate can be made for all players, young and old, and the results underline the magnitude of Aaron's achievement.

There are three categories for comparison: those players, still active, who already have high totals (like Killebrew); those who have established their slugging credentials but are much younger (like Bench and Jackson); and those who have acknowledged potential but are so young — under 25 — that they haven't yet produced a reliable form chart.

The first category is startling: there are only five players with even half the number of homers Aaron has: Frank Robinson 552, Killebrew 546, Willie McCovey 413, Al Kaline 386, and Billy Williams 376. All are 35 or over, so they simply don't have time to catch up.

In the second group, the tasks confronting Bench and Jackson have already been mentioned. Assuming age 40 as a cutoff, Earl Williams would have to average 41 homers for 15 years, Bobby Bonds 45 for 12 years, Darrell Evans 45 for 14 years, Nate Colbert 46. for 12 years and Dick Allen would have to average 52 for eight years. They won't make it.

John Milner of the Mets and John Mayberry of Kansas City are 24-year-olds with proven power. To reach 700, Mayberry would have to average 40 homers and Milner 42 for the next 16 years.

Cesar Cedeno of Houston, Greg Luzinski of Philadelphia and Jeff Burroughs of Texas are 23-year-olds with just as much power. For the next 17 years, Cedeno would have to average 38 homers a year and the other two 39 to reach 700.

Ruth's mark lasted 39 years. If Aaron's should last as long, that would bring us to the year 2013. Don't bet against it.

10.

Listen Smokers:
You don't have to wait 20 years for cigarettes to affect you.
It only takes 3 seconds.

In just 3 seconds a cigarette makes your heart beat faster,
shoots your blood pressure up, replaces oxygen in your blood with
carbon monoxide, and leaves cancer-causing chemicals
to spread through your body.
All this happens with every cigarette you smoke.
As the cigarettes add up, the damage adds up.
Because it's the cumulative effects of smoking—adding this
cigarette to all the cigarettes you ever smoked—
that causes the trouble.

And tell that to your dog, too.

U.S. DEPARTMENT OF HEALTH, EDUCATION, AND WELFARE • This Space Contributed as a Public Service

11.

Everyone thinks Unisys is just a computer company.

Everyone's wrong.

Chapter 1

Informal Analysis of Statements

Logic should be a required course for all students.
Logic is similar to mathematics.
Logic is an art, not a science.
Logic is my favorite course.

Sentences, such as those above, can be used to express a variety of thoughts, some of which are true and others of which are false. They sometimes stand alone, but they also frequently are used in connection with other sentences that express related thoughts. The thoughts expressed are known in logic as **statements.** Sometimes one statement supports the truth of another statement. Sometimes a statement contradicts other statements. And some statements are such that they do not require any support from any other statements, and they cannot be undermined by any other statements.

In this chapter we focus on the logical structures of individual statements and on some basic logical relationships between pairs of statements. In the next chapter we proceed to the more complex sets of statements that comprise arguments.

The truth or falsity of some statements can be established without any proof, while the truth or falsity of other statements requires proof; for both kinds of statement, we must have special conceptual and methodological tools for analyzing both their meaning and logical structure. Some of the basic informal concepts and methods for working with the meaning and structure of statements are presented in this chapter.

1.1 Sentences

Statements are generally expressed or communicated by sentences. Strictly speaking, a **sentence** is *both a physical **and** linguistic entity that can be used to communicate information and to perform a variety of other tasks.* A sentence is a physical entity insofar as it consists of a collection of ink marks on a page or sound waves traveling through the air. It is a linguistic entity insofar as it is a collection of letters or words, organized according to grammatical rules of a particular language (such as English or Swahili). Certain highway signs, such as the one in the margin, are physical entities used to transmit information (e.g., the road ahead curves to the right) but they are not sentences because they are not linguistic entities.

Sentences of any kind, when taken as mere physical and linguistic entities, are of little value or interest to most people. However, like hammers and forks and pens, sentences can be of significant value when they are used in appropriate ways in certain contexts. Some of the many uses of sentences include—but certainly are not limited to—praying, cursing, greeting friends, deceiving, asking questions, thanking, giving orders, presenting facts, expressing anger, making jokes, and reporting on events.

EXERCISE 1–1

Compile a list of at least twenty additional uses of sentences.

EXERCISE 1–2

Identify at least one (don't hesitate to look for more than one!!!) use for each of the following sentences in specific contexts.

1. With this ring, I thee wed.
2. Where's the parachute?
3. I question her motives.
4. I pledge allegiance to the crown.
5. Go away.
6. Amen.
7. If they've bought off the government, who's going to stop them?
8. Take out paper, class.
9. What's in a name?
10. Disgusting!
11. I dub thee 'Macintyre.'
12. I promise we'll just stay for five minutes.

Create your own examples of sentences and identify their uses in specific contexts.

1.2 Cognitive and Noncognitive Uses of Sentences

The almost limitless number of uses of sentences might be overwhelming to anyone trying to study them in any systematic way. Fortunately, to help sort out the uses of language relevant to the logician, philosophers have developed a method of classification that distinguishes between just two fundamental uses of sentences—cognitive and noncognitive. A sentence is said to be **cognitive** when *it is being used to express or assert something about which it makes sense to say that it is true or false.* The following sentences, as commonly used in everyday contexts, provide examples of sentences being used cognitively:

> **Logic is easy for Heather.**
> **Bill forgot to study for today's exam.**
> **The sun will rise at 7:02 A.M. tomorrow.**
> **Elephants are reptiles.**
> **Whales are mammals.**
> **I believe that the moon is made of green cheese.**

When uttered in ordinary contexts by native English speakers, sentences such as these can be used to do a variety of things, such as to declare, report, classify, assert, inform, deny, predict, explain, argue, and admit. However, these sentences all have one use in common: each is normally used to express a statement of which it is appropriate to say that it is true or false. It does not matter whether the statement being expressed is, in fact, true or false. 'Elephants are reptiles' and 'Whales are mammals' can both be used cognitively, even though the first normally would be used to express a false statement and the second normally would be used to express a true statement.

A sentence is said to be **noncognitive** when *it is being used to do something other than express a true or false statement.* Noncognitive uses of language include issuing commands or giving orders, making requests, asking questions, and arousing emotions. In everyday situations, each of the following sentences or phrases is normally used noncognitively:

> **Shut the door.**
> **Did you study for the exam?**
> **Please pass the salt.**
> **Wow!**
> **Go for it!**
> **Echhhh!**

It is never proper to ask of any question, command, or expression of feelings, "Is it true or false?" For instance, if the sentence 'Shut the door' is being used to express a command, we may ask, "Is the command appropriate or inappropriate?" or "Should the command be obeyed or not obeyed?" But we cannot appropriately ask of the command itself, "Is it true or false?" Similarly, it is normally inappropriate to ask whether the question 'Did you study for the exam?' is true or false. Once again, we may challenge the appropriateness of the question, ask whether or not one ought to respond to it, and debate the answer given to it. But we cannot properly ask, "Is it true or false?" of the question itself. It is equally improper, assuming ordinary context, to ask, "Is it true or false?" of such expressive utterances as 'Wow!' 'Go for it!' and 'Echhhh!'

The subtlety and complexity of natural languages make it difficult to determine whether certain sentences are being used in a cognitive or noncognitive ways in specific contexts. One whole category of sentences has been the subject of debate among philosophers for many years, and no agreement has yet been reached as to whether such sentences are normally used cognitively or noncognitively. This category is the set of sentences used to make value judgments such as:

> **Everyone ought to study logic.**
> **Valid arguments are better than invalid arguments.**
> **Cheating on a logic exam is wrong.**
> **You have a responsibility to yourself to do your best.**

Some philosophers have argued that such sentences are used only to express positive or negative feelings about the subjects being referred to. Others claim that these sentences are used mainly to make commands or give orders. On both of these views, such sentences are being used noncognitively. Other philosophers have asserted that such sentences are normally used cognitively, although they do not all agree as to exactly what kind of true or false statement is being expressed. In this book we assume that sentences being used to express value judgments are being used cognitively, but we do not impose any specific cognitive interpretation on them.

EXERCISE 1–4

The following sentences could be used cognitively or noncognitively depending on the context. For each sentence provide: (a) a context in which the speaker would be using language cognitively; (b) a context in which the speaker would be using the language noncognitively.

1. Close the window, you polar bear!
2. George, wasn't that Barbara I saw you with last night?
3. Do you really believe in Santa Claus?
4. Drive with care.
5. Kill the umpire!
6. Don't try to tell me that Lincoln wasn't a great president.

7. Get out of here!
8. You're not going to wear that again?
9. Why should tax credits be allowed for those who send their children to private schools?
10. Professor Adams, have a heart!

1.3 Statements

It is awkward and inconvenient to use repeatedly the lengthy phrase "sentences being used cognitively." There is also disagreement among logicians and philosophers as to what exactly it is that we apply the terms 'true' and 'false' to. Some assert that it is the sentence itself that is true or false. But many other logicians and philosophers argue that it is not the sentence that is true or false; rather, it is the meaning or thought conveyed or statement expressed by the sentence that is true or false.

We cannot elaborate on this problem here—and we certainly can't resolve the problem to everyone's satisfaction—so we will simply stipulate the following rule: We shall use the term **statement** to refer to *the (true or false) thought that is being conveyed by a sentence that is being used cognitively.* We shall use the term **proposition** as being *synonymous, and therefore interchangeable, with the term 'statement.'* We shall restrict the term **sentence** to refer to the physical and linguistic entities—e.g., the marks on the paper—used to convey the meanings. We will not talk about sentences as being true or false. It might be helpful to think of a statement as standing in essentially the same relationship to a sentence as a meaning stands to a word.

To determine whether a sentence expresses a statement[1] in a particular context, we simply need to ask if that which is being expressed can be said to be true or false. Don't forget! Falsity, not just truth, indicates that a sentence is expressing a statement. Thus, both of the following sentences are normally used to express statements:

Sentences can be used to express statements.
Sentences are animals that can fly.

The first happens to be true, whereas the second is patently false; nevertheless, both sentences express statements.

---

[1]Technically, sentences do not convey or express anything in and of themselves: they must be used by someone to communicate information (or express feelings or anything else). For the sake of brevity, we shall take the liberty in the remainder of this book of talking about 'the sentence that expresses the proposition such-and-such' in place of the technically correct but more lengthy formulation, 'the sentence that is being used by so-and-so to express the proposition such-and-such.' Similarly, the introduction to any statement ought to be phrased 'the proposition (or statement) expressed by the sentence "such and such".' For simplicity, however, we will often use 'the proposition (or statement) "such and such" ' as an abbreviation for the proper wording.

Logicians have also investigated the nature of, and relations among, sentences used in various noncognitive ways and have developed new fields such as the logic of questions and the logic of commands. However, in this book we focus on the systems of logic that deal with sentences being used cognitively to express statements.

1.4 Recognizing Sentences Used to Express Statements

Although the basic distinction between cognitive and noncognitive uses of sentences can be formulated quite concisely and straightforwardly, it is not always easy to determine how a particular sentence is being used in ordinary discourse. While grammatical structure can provide valuable clues as to whether a sentence is being used cognitively or noncognitively, the structure is all too often misleading.

Declarative sentences, with a subject term followed by a verb and ending with a period, commonly are used cognitively. Interrogatives (ending with question marks) and imperatives (with the verb preceding the subject) usually are used noncognitively to ask questions and issue commands, respectively. However, the context in which the sentence is being used plays a significant role in determining how the sentence is being used. Thus, depending on the context, the same sentence can be used to express two or more different statements, or it can be used to perform some noncognitive function, or it can do several different things at once. Also, different sentences can be used in appropriate contexts to express the same statement. These facts about sentences explain why it is not always easy to determine how a particular sentence is being used in a specific context.

As an example of the fact that nondeclarative sentences may express statements, consider the following sentence.

Didn't I see Linda with you today?

The sentence is interrogative in form, but in some contexts the same meaning could just as well be expressed by

I saw you with Linda today.

Thus, an interrogative sentence can be used to make an assertion; in fact, negative interrogatives very often are used to do this.

The context of a sentence may have much to do with whether it expresses a statement. 'Duuhhh!' does not by itself appear to convey a true-or-false assertion. But if it is uttered in response to the question 'Did you understand the lecture on atomic physics?' it might reasonably be understood as expressing the same meaning as 'I did not even remotely begin to understand the lecture.' This sentence clearly asserts something that is either true or false.

Again, the sentence 'I'm beat' is declarative in form; but does it express a statement? If it is uttered to a group of people who want you to go skiing, it conveys information, and does indeed express a statement. If it is uttered to an empty room as you come in and collapse on the bed, it is possibly purely exclamatory, in which case questions of truth or falsity are quite irrelevant, and it does not express a statement.

Context, then, is at least as important as grammatical form in determining whether a sentence expresses a statement. All propositions *can* be expressed by declarative sentences, but not all of them *are* so expressed; declarative sentences do not invariably express statements.

Even the context is not always sufficient for determining the intended use of a particular expression, as Linus reveals to Charlie Brown in the comic strip.

A single statement also might be expressed by different sentences either in the same or different languages. For example:

The house is very lovely.
La maison est tres belle.
La casa es muy bella.

These are clearly three different physical and linguistic entities—they are composed of different sets of letters and words; they occupy different spaces on the page—yet if uttered in the same context, the sentences express essentially the same statement. Of course, the richness and flexibility of many languages makes it possible to express the same statement through different sentences in a single language:

Jane put the jelly donuts on that windowsill.
The jelly donuts on that windowsill were put there by Jane.
On that windowsill are jelly donuts which Jane put there.

Though it may seem to be splitting hairs, consider these:

The sky is cloudy.
The sky is cloudy.

Reprinted by permission of UFS, Inc.

Even here, two different sentences are expressing the same statement. One of them can be cut out of the page and thrown away, but the other would remain. Logicians have introduced additional terminology to describe such cases; but it is sufficient to note for the purposes of this text that these are two distinct sentences, both of which can be used to express the same statement.

It is also important to understand that different propositions can be expressed by the same sentence, insofar as a change in context changes the statement expressed by a given sentence. Consider the following sentence:

> **The official candidate of the Democratic party in the most recent presidential election was a governor at that time.**

If asserted in 1993, this would have been expressing a true statement about Bill Clinton. But in 1985 it would have expressed a false statement about Walter Mondale, since Mondale did not hold any elected office during the 1984 campaign.

Contextual factors other than time can also affect what is being expressed by a given sentence. For example, the sentence 'This lake is quite large' might express a statement about Lake Superior, Lake Pontchartrain, or the Great Salt Lake, depending on the location of the speaker.

Remember!

1. A sentence is a physical and linguistic entity that can be used to perform a variety of tasks, such as asking questions, issuing commands, and making assertions.

2. A statement or proposition is that which is expressed by certain sentences in certain contexts, and of which it is proper to say that it is true or false.

3. Different statements can be expressed by the same sentence being used in different contexts.

4. Different sentences can express the same statement.

EXERCISE 1–5

In an everyday context, would each of the following sentences express statements—that is, do they primarily involve cognitive or noncognitive use of language? Explain each of your answers.

1. The Second World War ended in 1945.

2. Thank God, Hitler was defeated in the Second World War.

3. Take your umbrella with you today.

4. More than half a million human beings speak Mandarin Chinese.
5. The original *Webster's Dictionary* was written by Noah Webster, not Daniel Webster.
6. What time is it?
7. Aha!
8. Be sure to sign your tax return before mailing it.
9. The melting point of lead is 327.5°C.
10. Do you know if she did it?
11. The causes of smog are highly complex and not fully understood.
12. Why is it difficult for you to accept that smoking causes cancer?
13. Workers of the world, unite; you have nothing to lose but your chains!
14. The best-laid plans of mice and men will often go astray.
15. If you touch my little brother again, I'm going to report you.
16. The weatherman says it's going to rain.

1.5 Self-Evident and Supported Statements

We have already made one major distinction—between sentences being used cognitively (that is, to express statements) and sentences being used noncognitively. It is now necessary to examine a basic distinction between two different kinds of statements: statements whose truth or falsity is in some way self-evident or self-contained and statements which are such that their truth or falsity is grounded to some extent in something outside the statements themselves. *Statements that require evidence in their support* are **supported statements.** *Statements that can stand on their own and that require no further evidence or support* are **self-evident statements.** (Technically, some statements are actually self-refuting, but they can be subsumed under the general category of self-evident statements, using concepts to be developed later, so we won't discuss them as a separate category of statement.)

In general, we can characterize self-evident statements as statements that most people will accept as being true unless someone can provide a compelling proof to the contrary. Statements of this kind are designated as axioms in both formal and informal systems—that is, statements that can be used to prove other statements but that don't require proof themselves. Many theories have been formulated in the attempt to clearly specify what exactly qualifies a statement for this category and what exempts it from the need to be itself proved or supported. The consideration of this question and the study of these theories belongs for the most part not to logic but instead to the subfield of philosophy known as epistemology or the theory of knowledge. We shall, therefore, examine briefly only two of the most common types of self-supporting statements that relate most directly to the study of logic.

In their choice of wording for the declaration of their independence from the king of England, Thomas Jefferson and his colleagues presented their case as a set of self-evident statements. The absence of alternative procedures for agreeing on whom the burden of proof rested resulted in the Revolutionary War. The possibility of mutual nuclear destruction today puts even more importance on the need for finding more reasonable means of resolving conflicts and for increasing our tolerance of positions different from our own even if we don't accept them.

The most important kind of self-evident statement in logic is known as an **analytic statement.** Actually, there are two types of analytic statement: (1) those that are true or false by virtue of their logical structure or form, and (2) those that are true or false because of the meanings of key words in them. For example, the truth of statements such as 'It is raining or it is not raining' and 'If some dogs are beagles, then some beagles are dogs' results from their logical form—that is, it is impossible for any statement having the same forms to be false. Likewise, the falsity of the statement 'If all beagles are dogs, then no beagles are dogs' results from its logical form. *Statements that are true or false by virtue of their logical form* are called **syntactically analytic propositions** (or syntactically analytic statements).

Some syntactically analytic statements can be readily identified as such because they have a relatively simple logical structure. For example, any proposition with one of the following forms is always syntactically analytically true.

1. **Either X or not X.**
2. **If X, then X or Y.**
3. **All A are A.**
4. **Some A are A.**
5. **If all A are B, then some A are B.**
6. **If some A are B, then some B are A.**

It is assumed that in each example the X and Y are replaced by the same *sentence* (in 1 and 2) and that A and B are replaced by the same *word* (in 3 through 6) in both places in the sentence. Similarly, any proposition with one of the following forms is always syntactically analytically false.

    7. **Both X and not X.**

    8. **X if and only if not X.**

    9. **No A are A.**

   10. **Some A are not A.**

   11. **If no A are B, then some A are B.**

We introduce tools in later chapters that make clear *why* sentences with the above forms are analytically true or false and that will help us identify even the most complex examples of syntactically analytic propositions. Until we have such tools, you will have to simply memorize the 11 basic patterns above so that you will be able to recognize instances of them. You should not consider a statement to be syntactically analytically true or false unless the form of the sentence expressing it is *exactly* the same as one of the patterns above, with the one exception that the negation can be located in a more natural position than would be required to exactly fit one of the patterns. For example, pattern 8 would allow only sentences such as 'Tom is happy if and only if not Tom is happy,' which is far from a natural form of expression; our exception to the requirement that sentences must have *precisely* one of the above forms will allow 'Tom is happy if and only if Tom is not happy' to count as being syntactically analytically false.

EXERCISE 1–6

For each of the following syntactically analytic statements, identify which of the 11 basic forms it has and whether it is therefore true or false.

  1. Either the taxi's coming or the taxi's not coming.

  2. It's raining and it's not raining.

  3. If you're married, then you're married or all dogs are fish.

  4. All lemons are lemons.

  5. Some shoes are not shoes.

  6. If some singers are poets, then some poets are singers.

  7. If no chickens are carrots, then some chickens are carrots.

  8. Some cupcakes are cupcakes.

  9. No earwigs are earwigs.

10. Julia rides horses if and only if Julia doesn't ride horses.

11. If all pigs are dirty, then some pigs are dirty.

12. If you drank the wrong potion, then you drank the wrong potion or you're a frog.

13. You are the magical wizard if and only if you are not the magical wizard.

14. Some operas are not operas.

15. John's crazy and John's not crazy.

16. If some dancers are brilliant folks, then some brilliant folks are dancers.

The second type of analytic statement can be produced by replacing one of the components of a syntactically analytic statement by part or all of its definition. For example, if we replace either occurrence of the term 'bachelor' in sentence I below with its definition ('unmarried adult male'), the statement expressed by the resulting sentence (II or III) is still one whose truth would be considered to be self-evident by most native speakers of English.

I. All bachelors are bachelors.
II. All bachelors are unmarried adult males.
III. All unmarried adult males are bachelors.

We cannot see that II and III are true simply by looking at their logical form, for on the surface they are indistinguishable from statements expressed by sentences such as

IV. All students in this class are women.

But II and III are different from IV in that if we know the meanings of the words in II and III, we know that they are true, whereas even if we know exactly what the words in IV mean, we must go to a meeting of the class and make observations about the students in it before we know whether it is true or false. Statements such as II and III are called **semantically analytic statements.** They are sometimes described as being true or false by definition, although it is a bit more precise to say that *their truth or falsity is dependent solely on the meanings of the words in the sentences expressing them.*

Semantically analytic statements also sometimes result when we replace a word with part of its definition, but in such cases great care is necessary. For example, we can replace one occurrence of the word 'bachelors' with 'males' in sentence I in two different ways shown as V and VI below.

V. All bachelors are males.
VI. All males are bachelors.

When more and more people are thrown out of work, unemployment results.

CALVIN COOLIDGE

This "immortal remark," attributed to President Coolidge, is a good example of a statement whose truth results directly from the meanings of the words comprising it—that is, it is semantically analytic.

Statement V is semantically analytically true, whereas VI is not. Although you might be tempted to call VI semantically analytically false, a closer look should convince you that nothing in the definition of the word 'male' specifies anything about marital status, and thus its falsity cannot be considered self-evident. We need to look around in the world until we find at least one male who is married in order to know that VI is indeed false.

As with syntactically analytic statements, semantically analytic statements can also be false. Statement VII is an example of a semantically analytically false proposition.

VII. All bachelors are women.

EXERCISE 1–7

Determine which of the following are semantically analytic and which are syntactically analytic.

1. No whales are birds.
2. If John's in the dungeon, then John's in the dungeon.
3. Pat is not Pat.
4. If Dale is a Carnegie, then Dale is not a Carnegie.
5. All singers are vocalists.
6. No cubes are spheres.
7. If Pat likes to read in the nude on the roof, then Pat likes to read naked on the roof.
8. If Paul was one of the Beatles, then Paul was a rock musician.
9. No mud wrestlers are mud wrestlers.
10. If Bo is happy, then Bo is not sad.

A statement that is *neither syntactically nor semantically analytic* is called a **synthetic** or **contingent proposition** or statement. In other words, a synthetic or contingent proposition is one whose truth or falsity is *not* determinable either by virtue of its logical form or by the definitions of the words expressing it: its truth or falsity must be ascertained by other means. To determine the truth or falsity of the synthetic statement 'The lights are on in this room,' we must open our eyes and look.

Given that a statement is analytically true, there is no way that its truth can be challenged. It is *necessarily* true. Likewise, if it is analytically false it is *necessarily* false. It is not always possible, however, to prove that a particular sentence in a specific context is being used to express an analytic statement, especially a semantically analytic statement. For example, the sentence 'All spiders are creatures with eight legs' might be interpreted as being true by definition. On this interpretation, it is impossible to prove the statement false by any observations of spiders. If we produced one or even a million creatures

Copyright © Selby Kelly, Ex.

Is Churchy's "discovery" that Friday the thirteenth falls on Friday this month the discovery of a analytic truth? How could it be interpreted as nonanalytic?

with six legs, this would prove nothing. The person for whom 'having eight legs' is part of the definition of 'spider' would simply reply that any creature with fewer than eight legs is not a spider, by definition. The only way to attack this kind of an assertion is to challenge the definition.

EXERCISE 1–8

For each of the following, determine whether the sentence expresses a syntactically analytic, semantically analytic, or synthetic (contingent) proposition.

1. The moon is smaller than the earth.
2. It is snowing or it is not snowing.
3. All actresses are women.
4. All blind persons are humans.
5. Some humans are blind.
6. If all cheese is made from milk, then some cheese is made from milk.
7. Some liars never tell the truth.
8. No circles are squares.
9. If all persons are mortal, then some persons are mortal.
10. Either John is lazy or John is not lazy.
11. George Washington had false teeth made of wood.
12. If some students are poets, then some poets are students.
13. If no squares are circles, then no squares are round.

14. If some trees are things that are taller than twenty feet, then some things that are taller than twenty feet are trees.

15. If no valorous, fearless heroes who sweep the plains in grand gestures of selfless protection are sociopaths, then some valorous, fearless heroes who sweep the plains in grand gestures of selfless protection are sociopaths.

16. Either Sam is a jaded and overworked private detective who is beginning to realize that at a young age she made unfortunate decisions that would largely determine the shape of her life, or Sam is not a jaded and overworked private detective who is beginning to realize that at a young age she made unfortunate decisions that would largely determine the shape of her life.

1.6 Logical Relationships between Two (or More) Propositions

In addition to having internal logical structures, propositions also have logical relationships to one another. We can get an intuitive understanding of the kinds of logical relationships that exist between propositions by comparing them with human relationships.

As persons, we have a variety of different relationships with other persons. We feel attracted to some people; some—but usually not all—of these people also feel attracted to us. We don't feel any particular attraction to most people in the world, but we don't have any negative feelings about them either. We even feel repulsed by some people, and in some cases the feeling might be mutual. If we use the word 'like' to express in a simplistic way a person's relatively strong feeling of attraction for another and 'dislike' to express a relatively strong degree of repulsion, the possible combinations include the following:

Ab likes Bo and Bo likes Ab.
Ab likes Bo but Bo neither likes nor dislikes Ab.
Ab likes Bo but Bo dislikes Ab.
Ab neither likes nor dislikes Bo but Bo likes Ab.
Ab neither likes nor dislikes Bo and Bo neither likes nor dislikes Ab.
Ab neither likes nor dislikes Bo but Bo dislikes Ab.
Ab dislikes Bo and Bo likes Ab.
Ab dislikes Bo but Bo neither likes nor dislikes Ab.
Ab dislikes Bo and Bo dislikes Ab.

Human relationships obviously are more subtle and complex, but this list is sufficient to give a rough idea of some of the possibilities. The list, of course, does not even begin to consider interpersonal relationships involving more than two people. (Most movies, novels and popular songs deal with at least three-person romantic "triangles.")

Another useful analogy can be drawn with magnets and nonmagnets. Two magnets are attracted to one another if they are arranged so that the north pole of one is aligned with the south pole of the other. However, if the north pole of one is aligned with the north pole of the other, they repel each other. If we have only one magnet and a second object of some other material, different relationships hold. For example, with some materials such as iron there is also an attraction, although it is only one way—the magnet exerts an attractive force on the iron, but the iron does not exert any force on the magnet. And other materials (such as glass and paper) are not affected by, nor do they affect, the magnet.

Relationships exist also between propositions; they are analogous to many of the relationships involving people and also magnets. For example, one proposition can logically imply a second proposition while the second does not imply the first. Or two propositions can each logically imply each other. Or two propositions can be logically incompatible.

As with the internal logical structures of propositions, we cannot usually identify—nor can we fully understand—the specific logical relationship between two propositions without using special logical tools and techniques such as those presented later in this book. At this stage, we can only introduce at an intuitive level—using the analogies with personal relationships and magnetic attractions—several of the most common and important logical relationships that can hold between two (or more) propositions.

1.7 Consistency

The most central and important logical relationship between statements is the one known as 'consistency.' Two statements are **consistent** when *it is possible for both to be true*. Two statements are thus **inconsistent** if *it is impossible for them both to be true*. Saying that it is possible for two statements to be true is similar to saying that it is possible for two people to stay in the same room with each other. To say that it is *possible* for them to stay in the same room does not require that they actually be in the room; it means only that they are sufficiently compatible that *if* they were in the same room at some time neither would feel compelled to leave. Similarly, to say that it is possible for two statements to both be true does not require that both of them be true; it only means that they are (logically) compatible to the extent that *if* one of them is true, the other would not necessarily have to be false.

Consider the following example. Assuming that the following sentences are being used in their normal way in the same context, they express inconsistent propositions.

Pat got an A on the first logic exam.
Pat did not get an A on the first logic exam.

If one of these statements is true, then the other must be false. In contrast, the following two statements are consistent because the truth of one does not rule out the possibility of the other being true—that is, it is possible for both to be true.

> **Pat got an A on the first logic exam.**
> **Jan did not get an A on the first logic exam.**

We don't need to know whether either is actually true in order to know that it is logically *possible* for both to be true.

To use our analogy with magnets, consistent propositions can be like pieces of paper or glass (which have no attractive force between them) or like a piece of iron and a magnet (where only one exerts an attractive force on the other) or like two magnets with their opposite poles aligned (where there is a mutual attraction). The only relationship that is ruled out is that of mutual repulsion.

The term 'possible' is emphasized in the definition of consistency to make clear that one—or even all—of any set of consistent statements might be false. All three of the following statements are consistent with each other, even though two of them are false.

1. **China is in Asia.**
2. **Bill Clinton was the first president of the U.S.**
3. **Winston Churchill is the current king of England.**

These statements are consistent because the fact that 1 is true does not logically prevent the others from also being true. Statements 2 and 3 are false because of the way the world is, not because 1 is true; it is *logically* possible for them to be true.

People are often tempted to add the qualifier 'at the same time' to the definition of 'consistency'—that is, they want to say that it must be possible for two consistent statements to be 'true at the same time.' This extra qualification is unnecessary and in fact makes no sense given our definition of 'statement.' If we adhere to our distinction between sentences and statements, we must recognize that statements are timeless.

If we use the *sentence* 'Pat got an A in logic' at two different times, we might very well be using it to express two different propositions—one of which is true and the other false. For example, the word 'Pat' might be referring to two different people in the two contexts, one of whom did get an A in logic

I am persuaded that the world has been tricked into adopting some false and most pernicious notions about consistency—and to such a degree that the average man has turned the rights and wrongs of things entirely around, and is proud to be consistent unchanging, immovable, fossilized, where it should be his humiliation that he is so.

MARK TWAIN

It is important to recognize that the logical concept of consistency is not the same as, and in some ways is quite at odds with, one everyday notion of consistency—that of constancy or unchangeability. This is the concept that Mark Twain is attacking above.

and the other who didn't. But when we specify that we are talking about the proposition expressed by a sentence that is being used at a specific time in a specific context, that proposition is that specific fixed meaning and can be nothing else. The proposition that is about the Pat who did in fact get an A in logic is true; the proposition concerning the Pat who did not get an A is false. These are two different propositions (which may have been expressed by the same sentence being used in different contexts), one of which is true and the other of which is false. It is *not* the case that there is only one proposition that is true at one time and false at another time.

Logicians traditionally have placed a high value on consistency, and it is widely accepted that if an individual holds two beliefs that are logically inconsistent, one or the other must ultimately be rejected. Some people argue, however, that nothing is wrong with inconsistencies and that they must not only be tolerated but must be recognized as accurately reflecting the "nature of reality." Although such a view has recently been presented as a "new contribution" to Western cultures from Oriental traditions, the significance and value of strict adherence to consistency has been critically questioned throughout the history of the Western intellectual tradition.

In contrast to the everyday concept, the logical concept of consistency requires flexibility and change. Whenever two statements are determined to be logically inconsistent, one of them must be rejected as false, as the King of Id is asserting in the cartoon. People who do not adhere to the logical concept of consistency never have to change their positions, since they are willing to accept both a proposition and its denial. Nothing can require such persons to reconsider any of their beliefs, since they are all simultaneously acceptable. Such persons can never even become involved in disagreements with other people, because they would have no real grounds for challenging any other position. Few people, if any, actually place *no* value on the concept of logical consistency.

Many situations in everyday life that are thought of as involving other logical relations such as deduction or implication often are actually concerned

"The Wizard of Id" by permission of Johnny Hart and Creators Syndicate, Inc.

"Freddy" by Rupe. Copyright 1974 by Field Enterprises, Inc. Courtesy of Field Newspaper Syndicate.

The inconsistency in this cartoon is grounded in the fact about the world that it is impossible to press down and pull up on something simultaneously. It is not clear that the situation involves a *logical* inconsistency or impossibility.

primarily with consistency. When jurors are deliberating about the guilt or innocence of a defendant, they usually are sorting out statements made by various witnesses to determine which are consistent with one another and which are inconsistent. Doctors who are making medical diagnoses are usually trying to determine which diseases are consistent or inconsistent with particular sets of symptoms. And business people try to determine which strategies (marketing, finance, personnel, etc.) are most consistent with a set of statements specifying the goals and economic constraints within which their businesses operate.

Due to space limitations, most of our study of consistency is restricted to pairs of propositions. However, the tools and techniques provided for determining whether two statements are consistent also can be used for the larger numbers of statements that we deal with most of the time in everyday life.

EXERCISE 1–9

Indicate which of the following pairs of statements are logically consistent and which are logically inconsistent.

1. A: Either Tally's on the porch or she's not on the porch.
   B: Either Tally's not on the porch or she's not on the porch.

2. A: The phaser is in Mr. Spock's right hand.
   B: The phaser is in Mr. Spock's left hand.

3. A: Pat loves to eat alfalfa sprouts.
   B: Jan loves to eat alfalfa sprouts.

4. A: This van Gogh painting of sunflowers is a famous piece of modern art.
   B: This van Gogh painting of sunflowers is famous but it's not modern.

5. A: This zebra is more white than black.
   B: This zebra is more black than white.

6. A: Binkie scrubbed, rinsed, and brushed.
   B: Binkie never brushed.

7. A: Whenever it rains, it always pours.
   B. Sometimes it rains without pouring.

8. A: Rick is a patriot or a bartender.
   B: If Rick is not a bartender, then he's not a patriot.

9. A: If Ramona is the queen, then Harvey's in trouble.
   B: Harvey's not in trouble, but Ramona is the queen.

10. A: Taylor left his shoes at the party.
    B: There were no shoes left at the party.

1.8 Real versus Apparent Disagreements

It is a basic fact of life that we find ourselves involved in disagreements with other persons from time to time and also experience "inner conflicts" within ourselves. Therefore, it is important for us to be able to distinguish between real disagreements and conflict situations resulting from various kinds of misunderstanding.

The first thing that must be done in trying to analyze, evaluate, and resolve disagreements in ordinary language is to agree on what is really being said. Otherwise, we are likely to waste time, energy, and tempers in knocking down claims our opponent never intended to make or in passionately defending a position that is not the one being attacked. Such a procedure may score us points for verbal cleverness, but it probably will not be very effective in convincing our opponent that we are right.

To begin with, then, we need to formulate the positions of both (or all) disputants as fully, clearly, and sympathetically as possible. Once the position of each disputant is accurately stated, it is possible to determine whether the disagreement is real or only apparent. A **real disagreement** is one in which *the statements of the disputants' positions are logically inconsistent*—that is, one in which it is logically impossible for both to be true. For example, assume that persons A and B make the following assertions:

A: The moon is made of green cheese.
B: The moon is not made of green cheese.

If the words 'moon,' 'made of,' and 'green cheese' have the same meanings in both sentences, then if one of these statements is true, the other must be false. Therefore, this is a case of real disagreement between A and B.

On the other hand, if *the statements of the disputants are not logically inconsistent*—if it is possible for both of them to be true—we have an **apparent disagreement** or **pseudodisagreement**. For instance, if person A meant by 'moon' the moon of the earth while person B meant by 'moon' one of the moons of Jupiter, they would not be talking about the same thing and thus would not really be in disagreement.

Now consider the following statements by A and B, that are similar to, but logically very different from, the previous two statements.

A: I believe the moon is made of cheese.
B: I don't believe the moon is made of cheese.

Here the statements might or might not be logically inconsistent, depending on how we interpret expressions such as "I believe that . . . ". If we interpret such sentences as expressing statements about the speakers' subjective states of belief, then A's and B's statements are consistent since it is possible for A to actually believe one thing and for B to believe the opposite (just as it is possible for A to feel happy and B to feel unhappy). However, in many situations we simply use expressions such as "I know that . . ." and "I believe that . . . " to emphasize or qualify a statement that we intend to be about something other than our psychological state. On this interpretation, A is saying essentially the same thing as is normally expressed using sentences such as 'The moon is made of green cheese,' in which case A is really disagreeing with B.

Because of the ambiguity of expressions such as 'I believe that . . .' and 'I know that . . .', we need to stipulate how *we* interpret such expressions. In this book, *we interpret expressions such as 'I think that . . .' as stating something about the psychological state of the speaker* (that is, as expressing something like 'I am in the psychological state of believing that . . .') unless it is explicitly indicated that such an expression is *not* being used in this way in a specific context.

Even when we interpret 'I believe . . . ' expressions as saying something about the speakers' psychological states, this does not mean that A and B are necessarily in perfect harmony. The objects of their belief-states are diametrically opposed to one another, so they are clearly in conflict over the matter. But so long as two parties merely describe their states of mind, and their utterances are not interpreted as saying anything about any factual states of affairs outside of their minds, the conflict is not one that can be dealt with logically. This is what we mean by calling it an apparent disagreement or pseudodisagreement.

It *is* possible to have a real disagreement about a particular individual's psychological belief-state as in the following two statements:

A: I believe the moon is made of cheese.
B: A does not really believe the moon is made of cheese.

Here we have two logically inconsistent statements about the same person's state of mind, and hence they involve a real disagreement.

Some of life's more useless arguments are waged over statements that can appear on the surface to be logically inconsistent but which on more careful consideration can be seen to be consistent, as in the following case:

A–1: That ball is red.
B–1: That ball is blue.

A request for clarification could result in reformulations such as the following:

A–2: I am having a sensation of a red spherical object now.
B–2: I am having a sensation of a blue spherical object now.

Since we now are talking about sensations received by two individuals, it is easier to see that the argument might be a pseudodisagreement, because these statements deal with individual perceptions and not with assertions of external states of affairs. It is when each party draws, from his or her sensations of different parts of the ball, an inference about the "real" color of the *whole* ball that a genuine disagreement arises.

In a situation such as this, when two inconsistent statements (A–1 and B–1) are inferred from two consistent statements (A–2 and B–2), something must be wrong with the mode of inference, and the logician might be able to help by pointing out the error in reasoning. In the present case, a more correct pair of inferences would be from A–2 and B–2 to the following:

A–3: The part of the ball that I see is red.
B–3: The part of the ball that I see is blue.

These statements *are* logically consistent, and they suggest a solution to the "disagreement"—that the ball is half red and half blue and person A and person B are on opposite sides of it.

The distinction between perception and reality is especially important in the area of group dynamics and interpersonal communication. For example, consider the following:

A–4: B is always trying to pick a fight.
B–4: That's not so! I never try to pick a fight.

If A and B can be induced to examine the matter from a different perspective, they might restate their positions as follows:

A–5: I perceive B's behavior as an attempt to pick a fight.
B–5: I do not intend my behavior as an attempt to pick a fight.

The statements expressed by these sentences, unlike the originals, are not logically inconsistent. What appeared to be a real, and rather nasty, disagreement about B's intentions has been revealed as a pseudodisagreement stemming from two different perceptions of B's behavior. We cannot yet determine why these perceptions differ—perhaps A and B come from two different cultural backgrounds that put different interpretations on certain kinds of language and gesture. But once both parties recognize that what A perceives might not be what B intends, it becomes possible that each can at least learn to understand more accurately what the other is trying to say.

EXERCISE 1–10

Indicate which of the following pairs of statements are logically consistent and which are logically inconsistent. Assume A and B are expressed by different persons.

1. A: I like strawberry better than any other flavor of ice cream.
   B: I like chocolate better than any other flavor of ice cream.

2. A: I think zebras are white.
   B: I think zebras are black.

3. Fred: I am a careful, conscientious worker.
   John: Fred is neurotically fussy about his work.

4. A: Thoreau's book *Walden* is interesting.
   B: Thoreau's book *Walden* is boring.

5. [Police getting descriptions of a robber from two witnesses]
   Six-foot-eight teenager: He was a short, chubby, middle-aged man.
   Five-foot-two 80-year-old: He was a big, fat, youngish man.

6. [Around a campfire at night in the woods]
   A: I saw a bear moving in the woods!
   B: You only saw the moving shadows cast by the campfire.

7. [Campfire again]
   A: There's a bear out there in the woods!
   B: There are no bears in these woods!

8. A: I hate Tom! How could he do a thing like that to me?
   B: You don't really mean it; you're just very upset right now.

9. A: If Alex is blue, he's at the Salty Tire.
   B: Alex is blue, but he's not at the Salty Tire.

10. A: I think Ike is at the Tea House.
    B: You know very well that Ike is not at the Tea House.

1.9 Verbal Disagreements

As with all logical analyses, it is important to make sure in any dispute that the words are being used with the same meaning by both sides. The disagreement grounded in A and B meaning different things by 'moon' is one example of what happens when words are not used with the same meanings. Consider also the following:

> A–6: Exactly half the people in the United States are poor.
> B–6: Exactly one-fifth of the people in the United States are poor.

This might not be a real disagreement. If it turns out that A interprets 'poor' to mean 'receiving less than the median income,' and B interprets it to mean 'receiving less than $10,000 per person per year,' it is possible that both statements are true. Logicians have given this kind of *pseudodisagreement—one in which a key word or phrase is being used with different meanings*—the name **merely verbal disagreement.**

A merely verbal disagreement is resolved—or dissolved—as soon as it is recognized that the two parties are using a key word or phrase with different meanings. However, the recognition of such a merely verbal dispute can lead to another sort of dispute—this time over the meanings themselves. Notice the difference between the following pairs of statements:

> A–7: I am using the word 'poor' to mean 'receiving less than the median income.'
>
> B–7: I am using the word 'poor' to mean 'receiving less than $10,000 per person per year.'

> A–8: The word 'poor' means 'receiving less than the median income.'
>
> B–8: The word 'poor' means 'receiving less than $10,000 per person per year.'

The first case is a pseudodisagreement, for both A–7 and B–7 can be true; but the second case is a real disagreement, if A–8 and B–8 are assertions that the respective definitions are factual reports of the meanings that most native English-speakers associate with the word 'poor.' (But since the word 'means' itself has several meanings, even this could still be a merely verbal dispute.)

EXERCISE 1–11

Indicate whether each of the following pairs of sentences exemplifies a real or apparent disagreement, and if apparent, whether the disagreement is merely verbal. If you regard a disagreement as apparent rather than real, explain why.

1. Mike: I have strong opinions about politics.
   Pete: I am not very interested in politics.

2. A: I think *60 Minutes* is a boring show.
   B: I think *60 Minutes* is a very entertaining show.

3. A: The Smiths are a poor family.
   B: The Smiths are not a poor family.
   (A and B agree that the total income of the Smith family is $22,800 per year.)

4. A: President Nixon was impeached, since charges were brought against him by the House Judiciary Committee.
   B: President Nixon was not impeached, since he was not tried in the Senate and found guilty of the charges against him.

5. A: YOYO is a long and boring book.
   B: YOYO is a short and thrilling book.

6. Father: Please shut off that blasting radio. I can't think with all that noise.
   Son: That's not noise, dad. That's the number-one rock music hit.

7. A: A straw looks bent when it is placed in a glass of water.
   B: No, the straw isn't bent. It's just as straight as it was before.

8. A: I saw Fred with Marsha last night.
   B: You saw Bob, Fred's identical twin, with Marsha last night.

9. A: Cairn terriers are the smallest dogs.
   B: Scotties are the smallest dogs.

10. A: I saw a strange object in the sky; it was a flying saucer.
    B: What you saw was a space satellite.

11. A: There was a flying saucer in the sky five minutes ago; I saw it.
    B: You did not see a flying saucer; there are no such things.

12. A: Duchamp's painting *Nude Descending a Staircase* is a masterpiece.
    B: It's not a masterpiece; it's not even a hundred years old.

13. A: The sun looks like it revolves around the earth.
    B: No, the earth revolves around the sun.

14. A: Mercury is smaller than Venus in circumference.
    B: Mercury is larger than Venus in circumference.

15. A: John is an excellent student; he got an A in English last semester.
    B: John is a terrible student; he got a D in Biology last semester.

1.10 Implication

A second fundamental logical relation between statements, and one that is as important as consistency, is that of **implication.** In logic, *one statement is said to imply another if and only if it is **impossible** for the first statement to be true and the second false.* To illustrate this relation, let's consider the following two statements:

1. **All dogs are beagles.**

2. **Some dogs are beagles.**

A moment's thought should make it clear that if statement 1 is true, then statement 2 must also be true. That is, it is *impossible* for it to be true that all dogs are beagles and false that some dogs are beagles. Thus, the first statement implies the second statement. However, the second statement does not imply the first statement, because it is possible for it to be true that some dogs are beagles and also for it to be false that all dogs are beagles.

Implication is a much stronger relationship than consistency. While the vast majority of statements are consistent with one another, most statements directly imply very few other statements. If we know that two statements are consistent, this does not tell us whether one implies the other or not.

To use our analogy with personal relationships, implication is similar to one person feeling a strong attraction to another; being attracted to someone involves more than not disliking them. Also, one person can be attracted to another regardless of whether the second person is attracted to the first or not. Or using the analogy to magnets, the fact that a magnet exerts an attractive force on another object does not necessarily mean that the other object exerts an attractive force on the magnet; if the object is a piece of iron, it does not exert an attractive force. Also, knowing that two objects do not exert repulsive forces on one another is not sufficient for knowing that either exerts an attractive force on the other. Similarly, most statements imply only a few of the many statements that they are consistent with.

Sometimes we can look at two statements and determine whether one implies the other or not. However, like syntactical analyticity, implication cannot usually be identified by means of casual observation or intuition. Many statements are such that if they are true then it is very likely—but *not* absolutely necessary—that certain other statements are true, and our intuitions are not able to determine when a particular statement makes the truth of another statement very probable from a statement that makes the truth of another absolutely certain. Fortunately, logicians have developed several formal methods to help us to determine whether or not one statement implies another. Some of these methods are presented in later chapters. Implication is the fundamental logical relation in one kind of argument known as a 'deductive argument.' Thus this concept is discussed in more detail in the next chapter, which is devoted entirely to arguments.

Consistency is what is known as a **symmetrical relation**; that is, *if A is consistent with B, then B must be consistent with A*. Implication, in contrast, is **asymmetrical**; *if A implies B, it does not necessarily follow that B implies A*. This does not mean that B cannot imply A. B might imply A, but it doesn't necessarily have to. The next relation to be presented, logical equivalence, is essentially what results when implication is made symmetrical.

1.11 Logical Equivalence

In our example in the previous section, the first statement implies the second but the second does not imply the first. It is also possible for two statements to imply one another, as in the following example.

No cats are dogs.
No dogs are cats.

These statements are such that it is impossible for either one to be true while the other is false, and vice versa. One definition of **logical equivalence** is that *two statements are logically equivalent if and only if they are such that, whenever one is true then the other must be true, and whenever one is false then the other must be false.*

It is important to recognize that two logically equivalent statements do not necessarily have exactly the same meaning. This concept refers only to certain similarities in logical structure between the two statements. Thus, for example, the following two statements are logically equivalent, but they clearly do not have the same meanings.

This animal is either a horse or not a horse.
Tom did not both get an A in logic and not get an A in logic.

The reason that these two statements are logically equivalent is that they are both syntactically analytically true. This of course means that it is impossible for either to be false, which in turn means that it is impossible for one to be false while the other is true (since neither can ever be false).

Using our analogies, logically equivalent statements are similar to two persons who are mutually strongly attracted to each other; they are also similar to two magnets with their poles reversed which are very strongly attracted to each other. Logically equivalent statements are always consistent with each other except for the special case in which they are both syntactically analytically false, in which case it is of course impossible for both to be true (since neither can be true). Logical equivalence is related to implication in this way: if A is logically equivalent to B, then A implies B *and* B implies A. Also, as mentioned in the previous section, logical equivalence is a symmetrical relation; that is, if A is logically equivalent to B, then B must be logically equivalent to A.

1.12 Independence

A final significant logical relation that can hold between two statements is that of independence. Two statements are logically **independent** of one another if and only if the truth or falsity of one has no relation whatsoever to the truth or falsity of the other. Thus, knowledge that one statement is true tells us nothing about the truth or falsity of the other. And knowledge that one is false reveals nothing about the truth or falsity of the other.

This animal is not a horse.
Tom got an A in logic.

The two preceding statements are logically independent. Like all logically independent statements, they are such that neither implies the other and they are consistent.

Using our analogies, logical independence is similar to cases in which two people are neither attracted to nor repulsed by one another; it is also similar to having substances like wood and granite that normally have neither attractive nor repulsive forces between them.

All the logical relations between statements discussed above are dealt with again in later chapters.

EXERCISE 1–12

Determine for each of the following pairs of statements whether A implies B, B implies A, A is logically equivalent to B, or A and B are independent.

1. A: All students share the spirit of learning.
   B: Some students share the spirit of learning.

2. A: All sailboats are powered by the wind.
   B: Some boats are powered by outboard motors.

3. A: That equation is not a physical law.
   B: Calculus is useful when expressing physical laws.

4. A: All dogs are mammals or not mammals.
   B: All autos are four-wheeled or not four-wheeled.

5. A: Some nonprofessionals are dedicated.
   B: All nonprofessionals are dedicated.

6. A: That tire is brand-new.
   B: That tire is flat.

7. A: All atoms have protons.
   B: Some atoms have electrons.

8. A: No elements are chemical compounds.
   B: No chemical compounds are elements.

9. A: No existential philosophers are people who dismiss the notion of Being.
   B: Some existential philosophers are not people who dismiss the notion of Being.

10. A: Snowshoes are designed only for walking on snow.
    B: Snowshoes are made much larger than the average foot.

11. A: No poems are prose.
    B: No prose is a poem.

12. A: All sports activities have had increased participation.
    B: Sales of new hockey equipment have increased sharply.

13. A: If Harv is a Wurlitzer then Harv is a Wurlitzer.
    B: Syd spooked the grunts or Syd didn't spook the grunts.

EXERCISE 1–13

For each of the following pairs of statements

a. assume that A is true and determine whether B *must* be true, B *must* be false, or B is undetermined.

b. assume that B is true and determine whether A *must* be true, A *must* be false, or A is undetermined.

c. assume that A is false and determine whether B *must* be false, B *must* be true, or B is undetermined.

    d. assume that B is false and determine whether A *must* be false, A *must* be true, or A is undetermined.

1. A: Boggs is a hog.
   B: Boggs is a hog.

2. A: Federico is a philanthropist or a philanderer.
   B: Federico is a philanthropist.

3. A: If June is a darling then David is joyful.
   B: If David is not joyful, then June is not a darling.

4. A: Hal was the brains and Van was the brawn.
   B: Hal was the brains.

5. A: All laureates are languid.
   B: Some laureates are not languid.

6. A: Some otorhinolaryngologists are obstreperous.
   B: No otorhinolaryngologists are obstreperous.

7. A: Some mavens are morose.
   B: All mavens are morose.

8. A: Some physicists are not fickle.
   B: Some physicists are fickle.

9. A: No vicars are vindictive.
   B: All vicars are vindictive.

10. A: If Zogmann is zealous then Huypers is hogtied.
    B: Zogmann is zealous and Huypers is hogtied.

EXERCISE 1–14

Consider and discuss the following statements with other students in your class. In particular, try to determine which statements are analytic and which are synthetic. Also discuss how you might prove the truth of each of the synthetic statements, and, finally, construct an argument you believe is the most reasonable that can be given in support of each statement.

1. The real difference between democracy and oligarchy is poverty and wealth. Wherever men rule by reason of their wealth, whether they be few or many, that is an oligarchy, and where the poor rule, that is a democracy. (Aristotle)

2. When a white man governs himself, that is self-government. But when he governs himself and also governs some other men, that is worse than self-government—that is despotism. What I do mean to say is that no man is good enough to govern another man without that other's consent. (Abraham Lincoln)

3. Enslave the liberty of but one human being and the liberties of the world are put in peril. (William Lloyd Garrison)

4. To be governed is to be watched, inspected, spied, directed, law-ridden, regulated, penned up, indoctrinated, preached at, checked, appraised, seized, censured, commanded by beings who have neither title nor knowledge nor virtue. (Pierre Joseph Proudhon)

5. Every great advance in natural knowledge has involved the absolute rejection of authority. (Thomas Huxley)

6. If the poor man is not able to support his suit according to the vexations and expensive manner established in civilized countries, has not the rich as great an advantage over him as the strong has over the weak in a state of nature? (Edmund Burke)

7. When great changes occur in history, when great principles are involved, as a rule the majority are wrong. The minority are right. (Eugene V. Debs)

8. If Negro freedom is taken away, or that of any minority group, the freedom of all the people is taken away. (Paul Robeson)

9. If the welfare of the living majority is paramount, it can only be on the ground that the majority have the power in their hands. (Oliver Wendell Holmes)

10. Homo sapiens, the only creature endowed with reason, is also the only creature to pin its existence on things unreasonable. (Henri Bergson)

11. The ignorance of the working class and the superior intelligence of the privileged class are superstitions—are superstitions fostered by intellectual mercenaries, by universities and churches, and by all the centers of privilege. (George D. Herron)

12. You can always get the truth from an American statesman after he has turned seventy, or given up all hope of the presidency. (Wendell Phillips)

13. All life is an experiment. (Oliver Wendell Holmes)

14. He who is unable to live in society, or who has no need because he is sufficient for himself, must be either a beast or a god; he is no part of a state. (Aristotle)

15. Freedom is the absolute right of all adult men and women to seek permission for their action only from their own conscience and reason, and to be determined in their actions only by their own will, and consequently to be responsible only to themselves, and then to the society to which they belong, but only insofar as they have made a free decision to belong to it. (Mikhail A. Bakunin)

16. If reason is a universal faculty, the decision of the common mind is the nearest criterion of truth. (George Bancroft)

17. For I do not seek to understand that I may believe, but I believe in order to understand. For this I believe—that unless I believe, I should not understand. (Saint Anselm)

18. Wages is a cunning device of the devil, for the benefit of tender consciences, who would retain all the advantages of the slave system, without

the expense, trouble, and odium of being slave-holders. (Orestes A. Brownson)

19. The history of mankind is a history of repeated injuries and usurpations on the part of man toward woman, having in direct object the establishment of a tyranny over her. (Women's Rights Convention, Manifesto, Seneca Falls, N.Y., 1848)

Summary

1. A **sentence** is a physical and linguistic entity that can be used to convey meaning and perform a variety of tasks in different contexts.

2. A sentence is **cognitive** when it is being used to express a meaning about which it is appropriate to say that it is true or false. Cognitive uses of language in everyday contexts include explaining, classifying, asserting, and so on. Statements of personal beliefs, attitudes, and feelings can also involve a cognitive use of language. A sentence is said to be **noncognitive** when it is used to do something other than express a statement or proposition. Noncognitive uses of language involve such acts as issuing commands or giving orders, making requests, asking questions, and arousing emotions.

3. The context in which a sentence is used is the most important criterion for determining whether or not it is being used to express a statement and is, therefore, logically analyzable. However, a sentence can have mixed uses within a particular context. A **statement** or **proposition** is an assertion, description, or piece of information about which it can properly be said that it is true or false. A statement can be expressed by certain sentences in certain contexts; different statements can be expressed by the same sentence; and different sentences can express the same statement. Logical analysis is useful for identifying special kinds of statements the truth or falsity of which are determined entirely by their internal logical structure.

4. **Supported statements** are statements that require evidence in their support. Statements that require no additional proof are **self-evident statements;** the burden of proof concerning such statements falls on persons challenging their truth. Axioms are self-evident statements.

5. **Analytic statements** are an important kind of self-evident statement. The two types of analytic statement are: **syntactically analytic propositions,** which are true or false by virtue of their logical form; and **semantically analytic propositions,** which are true or false by definition (that is, by virtue of the meanings of the words expressing the statements). A statement that is neither syntactically nor semantically analytic is called a **synthetic** or **contingent proposition.** Such statements are statements about the world, and their truth or falsity is usually ascertained through empirical observation.

6. Several significant logical relations can hold between two statements. Two statements are **consistent** when it is possible for both of them to be true; if it is impossible for both to be true, then they are **inconsistent.** One statement logically **implies** another statement if and only if it is impossible for the first statement to be true and the second false. Two statements are **logically equivalent** if and only if each implies the other; that is, if one is true then the other must be true and if one is false then the other must be false. Two statements are logically **independent** of one another if and only if the truth or falsity of either statement implies nothing about the truth or falsity of the other.

7. A **real disagreement** is one in which the statements of the disputants' positions are logically inconsistent—that is, one in which it is logically impossible for both to be true at the same time. An **apparent disagreement** or **pseudodisagreement** is one in which the statements of the disputants' positions are not logically inconsistent—that is, one in which it is logically possible for both to be true at the same time. A **merely verbal disagreement** is a type of pseudodisagreement in which a key word or phrase is being used with different meanings.

Chapter 2

Informal Analysis of Arguments

> If you are reading this page, you are probably taking a logic course, and if you are taking such a course you will probably get a grade in it. Since you are reading this page, you will probably get a grade in a logic course.

These two sentences express an argument. In addition to the study of the logical structures of individual statements and the many different logical relationships that hold among two or more propositions, logic involves the study of the special class of groups of propositions that constitute arguments.

To get a sense of how common arguments are in everyday life, let's construct some others concerning the logic course you are taking. You probably have some idea now, even before you have gotten very far into it, what grade you will ultimately receive in the course. Even if you're one of the exceptional few who has not thought at all about your possible grade, for the purposes of this exercise, plug some letter into the blank in the following sentence.

I will get a(n) _____ in this logic course.

Judgments such as this normally can be supported by *reasons* of one sort or another. Certainly all kinds of reasons could be given in support of such a prediction about a grade in a logic course. For example, it might be the case that the grading in the course is going to be based on a system that will permit you to retake each test as often as is necessary to get the grade you want, and also that you are determined to retake the tests until you get a B. Or it might be that you have learned from other students that while the person who is teaching the course gives very few As, this instructor also never gives less than a C to anyone who attends all class sessions and takes all the exams. Or it might be that you are basically quite intelligent and hard-working, with high verbal and quantitative aptitude scores and a straight-A average to date, and you intend to work hard to get an A in this course. Or you might have a "foolproof" plan for cheating in this course, or you might want to fail it for some reason, or. . . . The list of possible reasons that support the judgment that a certain person will get a specific grade in this course could be extended indefinitely, but enough possibilities have been offered to give you an idea as to how to construct your own argument.

A second argument related to the one above is:

> **If you are taking a logic course for a grade, then you will have to take at least one exam. You are taking a logic course for a grade. Thus, you will have to take at least one exam.**

It is to be hoped that, if you are indeed in such a situation, you will not find yourself in the predicament of the student in the "Mad Morality" cartoon.

Although it might appear at first glance that the father is presenting an argument, a more careful analysis indicates that he is probably only making an assertion or command to the effect that the son should spend more time studying for the exam (and perhaps also less time worrying about it) so that he will do better on it. In contrast, it might appear at first as if the son is only asking questions, whereas reconsideration makes it seem likely that he is expressing an argument that might be reformulated as

> **If I'm very upset, then I can't study for my exam.**
> **I'm very upset.**
> **Therefore, I can't study for my exam.**

These examples should be sufficient to suggest that it is important to spend more time developing our skills for identifying arguments, which is the primary objective of this chapter.

In the most general sense of the term in logic, an **argument** is *any set of statements such that one or more of them support or provide evidence for the truth of another statement.* To better understand this definition, it is helpful to consider some senses of the term 'argument' with which you are probably already familiar and that are quite distinct and different from the sense of the term as it is used in logic.

When two persons assert logically inconsistent statements, that is, when they are involved in a real disagreement as discussed at the end of Chapter 1, it would be quite proper in ordinary English to say that they are involved in an argument. Thus, if person A were to assert that 'The government should pay for abortions for women on welfare who want them,' and person B asserted that 'The government should not pay for abortions for anyone,' we could correctly say that they were arguing. However, in the context of this book, we do *not* use the term 'argument' to refer to such disagreements.

In pursuing their disagreement, persons A and B might each give reasons in support of their positions. For example, person A might state that the government should pay for abortions for women on welfare *because* women who can afford them can have them at will, and *thus* women on welfare are victims of economic discrimination if they can't afford abortions. Person B might assert that the government should not pay for abortions for women on welfare *because* abortion is morally wrong and, in paying for them, the state would be supporting an immoral practice. In providing reasons in support of their conflicting statements, the two can be said to be presenting arguments. The sense in which we use the term 'argument' in this text is closely related but not identical to this everyday notion of an argument.

A slightly more detailed specification of the ordinary everyday definition of 'argument' is that given in *The American Heritage Dictionary*, that states that it is "a course of reasoning aimed at demonstrating the truth or falsity of something." This definition certainly qualifies our examples above as arguments, insofar as reasons were being given to support or prove the truth or falsity of the position that the government should pay for abortions for women on welfare. But this definition needs several refinements to fit the use of the term 'argument' in formal logic, as we are studying it in this book.

As was explained in the Introduction, logic is not concerned with reasoning processes in general, for much of the study of reasoning is the domain of psychology. Logicians are not concerned with the psychological process of reasoning; rather, they are concerned with relations among statements. However, definite connections exist between the psychological processes and the relations among statements, which we will discuss in more detail here.

2.1 Inferences and Arguments

Notice that the dictionary definition of 'argument' above specifies that an argument is "aimed at" proving something or other. It is important to recognize right away that arguments themselves don't aim at anything. Arguments are sets of statements that can be used by persons toward a variety of ends. The definition does not say that the argument aims at anything; it states quite clearly that an argument is aimed *by someone*. You or I or any other person can intend (or believe or hope) that a particular argument does prove something. The argument, as a set of statements, can*not* intend (or believe or hope) anything.

The dictionary definition states that an argument is "a course of reasoning." Although this might sound okay at first hearing, it is as mistaken as saying that an argument intends or hopes or believes something. This point can be understood better by considering an example. While walking from her apartment to the library, Susan looks at her watch and notices that it shows the same time as it did when she looked at it earlier in the day. Let us also assume that Susan, having made this observation, reacts by saying to herself, "Oh, my watch needs a new battery." She then stops at a store, buys a battery, puts it in her watch and is pleased to observe that the second hand begins to move. She adjusts the time and continues on her way to the library.

In this instance, Susan made an inference. **Inference** is *the psychological process of moving from one thought to another presumably related thought*; Susan inferred from the observation that the hands had not moved to the belief that her watch needed a new battery. An inference is not in itself an argument, but an argument can be constructed that corresponds to any good inference.[1] For example, the following argument corresponds to Susan's inference:

> **In all instances in the past, if my watch hands did not move, then my watch needed a new battery.**
> **The hands of my watch are not moving.**
> **Therefore, my watch needs a new battery.**

Strictly speaking—and logicians try to speak as strictly and precisely as possible—it is only correct to say that persons (or rational beings—possibly chimpanzees, dolphins, and others) make inferences. It is technically incorrect to say that the premises of an argument infer its conclusion. It is correct to say that the premises of an argument imply or support its conclusion. When we say in everyday conversation that a person implied X, we usually are saying that she expressed a statement from which she expected the audience to infer X.

An argument can be constructed that corresponds to every legitimate inference, and the inference is only as good as its corresponding argument. The

---

[1]If a person makes a completely *bad* inference, no corresponding argument can be constructed.

preceding example is a good inference and its corresponding argument is equally good.

Remember!

Persons make inferences; they don't imply anything.
Premises imply or support conclusions; they don't infer anything.

We make inferences almost continually in everyday life. The techniques of formal logic presented in this text can be very helpful for determining whether our reasoning processes are good or bad. One common kind of inference made by students occurs in the context of answering multiple-choice questions on exams (including logic exams!). One of the kinds of reasoning that is often used in answering multiple-choice questions is the process of elimination. Consider how you might think your way through the following multiple-choice question.

Sentences
   1. are always true.
   2. sometimes are used to express premises of arguments.
   3. can never contain more than three words.
   4. can each express only one specific proposition.

Assuming that we can't at this point directly recognize the correct answer, there are a number of ways we might try to infer the right answer. For example, we might know that one and only one of the four answers can be correct. Further, we know from Chapter 1 that sentences are never true or false, that they can contain many words, and that one sentence can be used to express more than one proposition. Therefore, we can reasonably infer that the correct answer is 2. The argument corresponding to this inference is as follows:

One and only one of the four answers can be correct.
Answer 1 can't be correct because . . .
Answer 3 can't be correct because . . .
Answer 4 can't be correct because . . .
Therefore, answer 2 must be correct.

If you have not studied Chapter 1 carefully enough to know immediately that 1, 3, and 4 are false, you might reason in a somewhat different way. For example, you might consider that, in your past experience, 'all' and 'never' statements (known in logic as 'universal generalizations') are true less often than 'sometimes' statements (known as 'particular statements'). You could then infer from this that since 1, 3, and 4 are universal generalizations, the correct answer is probably 2. The argument corresponding to this inference is:

One and only one answer can be correct.
Universal generalizations are usually true less often than particular statements.
Answers 1, 3, and 4 are universal generalizations, and 2 is a particular statement.
Therefore, 2 is most probably the correct answer.

A third way of trying to select the correct answer would be to formulate some kind of hypothesis about the pattern of answers in the test as a whole. We might, for example, feel fairly confident that our answers to all of the other questions are correct, and we might also notice that of the other twenty-four answers, ten are 1s, six are 2s, two are 3s, and six are 4s. We might then reason that, insofar as the person who made up the exam should have tried to distribute the answers as evenly as possible among the four numbers, the correct answer should be 3. However, we could also reason that the person who made up the exam had a preference (conscious or unconscious) for 1s and infer from this that the correct answer is most likely 1. The arguments corresponding to these inferences or reasoning processes would be as follows:

One and only one answer can be correct.
The correct answers should be distributed fairly evenly among the four possible numbers.
All of the other questions have been answered—presumably correctly—and there are disproportionately few 3s among them.
Therefore, it is probable that the remaining answer is 3.

One and only one answer can be correct.
All of the other questions have been answered—presumably correctly—and there are disproportionately more 1s among them.
The person who made up the exam apparently had a conscious or unconscious tendency to make 1 the correct answer.
Thus, it is most likely that the answer to this question is 1.

We study methods for evaluating the quality of such arguments (and their corresponding inferences) in much of the rest of this book.

EXERCISE 2–1

Construct arguments by giving at least three reasons (premises) in support of each of the following judgments (conclusions).

1. I will probably enjoy this logic course.

2. This logic course will probably be my least interesting course this semester.

3. I will never be involved in an automobile accident.

4. I will get a good job when I graduate from college.

5. I am as intelligent as most of the other students in this class.

EXERCISE 2–2

In each of the following problems, you are given the premises of an argument. Choose the conclusion or conclusions that are implied by the premises. (*NOTE: These questions are similar to those that are used on a variety of graduate and professional school admissions exams.*)

1. Gabe loves cottage cheese.
   If Gabe loves cottage cheese, then he loves yogurt.

   a. Gabe loves cottage cheese or Camembert.
   b. Gabe loves yogurt.
   c. Gabe loves cottage cheese and yogurt.
   d. Somebody who loves cottage cheese loves yogurt.
   e. All of the above are implied by the premises.

2. Fran is a darling and Phil is a dear.
   Fran is a darling.

   a. Phil is a dear.
   b. Fran is a darling or Phil is a dear.
   c. Phil is a dear or Phil is not a dear.
   d. All of the above are implied by the premises.
   e. None of the above is implied by the premises.

3. Either Bobbie is wealthy or Frankie is a fibber.
   Frankie's no fibber.

   a. Frankie is a fibber.
   b. Bobbie is wealthy.
   c. Bobbie is wealthy and Frankie is a fibber.
   d. All of the above are implied by the premises.
   e. None of the above is implied by the premises.

4. All admirals are admirable.
   Bobo is admirable.

   a. Bobo's not an admiral.
   b. Bobo is admirable.
   c. Bobo is the only admiral.
   d. All of the above are implied by the premises.
   e. None of the above is implied by the premises.

5. Dom is paunchy.
   Some paunchy things are formidable.

   a. Dom is formidable.
   b. Dom is formidable or Dom is not formidable.
   c. If Dom isn't formidable, then Dom's not paunchy.
   d. All of the above are implied by the premises.
   e. None of the above is implied by the premises.

6. Marie is a cobbler.
   All cobblers are lechers or milkmen.

   a. Marie is a milkman.
   b. Marie is a lecher.
   c. If Marie is not a lecher, then she's a milkman.
   d. All of the above are implied by the premises.
   e. None of the above is implied by the premises.

7. Some dancers are exhibitionists.
   Some tailors are exhibitionists.

   a. All dancers are tailors.
   b. Some dancers are tailors.
   c. No dancers are tailors.
   d. All of the above are implied by the premises.
   e. None of the above is implied by the premises.

8. All hypocrisies are damnable fiascos.
   Some damnable fiascos are real human tragedies.

   a. All real human tragedies are hypocrisies.
   b. Some real human tragedies are damnable fiascos.
   c. Some hypocrisies are real human tragedies.
   d. All of the above are implied by the premises.
   e. None of the above is implied by the premises.

9. Some producers are directors.
   Some directors are madmen.

   a. Some madmen are directors.
   b. Some directors are producers.
   c. Either some producers are madmen or no producers are madmen.
   d. All of the above are implied by the premises.
   e. None of the above is implied by the premises.

10. All entrepreneurs are clever or crooked.
    All clever things are crooked or sheepish.

   a. All entrepreneurs are crooked.
   b. Some entrepreneurs are crooked.
   c. All entrepreneurs are crooked or sheepish.
   d. All of the above are implied by the premises.
   e. None of the above is implied by the premises.

11. Either Jan is vigorous and life is rigorous, or if life is rigorous then Jan is tired.
    Jan isn't tired.

   a. If life is rigorous, then Jan is vigorous.
   b. Life is rigorous.
   c. Jan is vigorous.
   d. All of the above are implied by the premises.
   e. None of the above is implied by the premises.

2.2 The Logical Sense of 'Argument'

In the context of logic, an **argument** is defined as *a set of statements that is such that one of them is identified (explicitly or implicitly) as the **conclusion** which is supported or implied by the others (the **premises**).* It is important to recognize that this sense of the term 'argument' differs from the dictionary definition discussed earlier insofar as it involves no psychological factors like "aiming at" or "intending" anything. Any set of statements that satisfies this definition constitutes an argument, even if no one has ever thought of it, let alone intended that it be used to prove something. Similarly, even if someone intends that a certain set of statements be used to prove something, that set of statements does not constitute an argument if it does not satisfy the definition.

We are in a difficult position at the moment because it is not possible to provide an adequate explanation of the formal logical concept of an argument without actually presenting one or more formal logical systems. Just as our understanding of the everyday concept depends on our understanding of and ability to use the whole system of ordinary English (or some other "natural" language), our understanding of the formal concept of an argument depends on our understanding of a system of formal logic. We have given the formal definition above, but you should not expect to understand it fully until after you have studied some of the later chapters in this book. Because the dictionary definition of 'argument' (and presumably also the sense in which most of us use the term in everyday life) is quite different from the logical sense, it will be useful to supply a way for talking about the everyday use without confusing it with the logical sense of 'argument.' We do this by making explicit the distinction between what a person asserts or intends or believes to be an argument and what is, in fact, an argument. We always talk in this book of the former as something that *appears to be* or that is *asserted* or *intended to be* an argument. We shall reserve the term 'argument' in the remainder of this book to refer only to sets of statements that satisfy our formal definition—that is, to sets of statements that are such that one of them is *in fact* supported or implied by the others. Much of what we study in this book are ways of determining whether sets of statements that *appear* to constitute arguments or that are *asserted* to be arguments are *in fact* arguments.

Because of the "looseness" of ordinary languages, it is not always easy to determine when a set of statements is being asserted or intended as an argument in everyday contexts, let alone whether it actually constitutes an argument. We have all encountered situations such as that in the accompanying *Doonesbury* cartoon, where it is not at all clear whether a statement or set of statements are intended to give reasons in support of a conclusion, and where it is even less clear whether they provide any real support. In the cartoon, does the energy administrator's response in any way support or contradict the statement that the energy priority rating system discriminates against the little person? Is it even intended to be an argument? Or is it simply an attempt to avoid the question and change the subject?

While this is certainly an extreme example, each of us encounters situations daily where the connection (intended or actual) between statements is not clear, or where the logical relations are not what we thought they were at first glance. To evaluate adequately whether sets of statements in everyday contexts actually constitute arguments, we must use the methods and concepts of formal logic. But there is no simple and direct process for doing this; it is more an art than a science. What is needed is a basic intuitive "feel" for both ordinary language and for formal logic.

We can develop this "feel" by discussing in some detail the ways in which people assert in ordinary language that sets of statements are arguments. Once we are able to recognize when a set of statements is being asserted as an argument, we go on to study some of the different methods for determining whether a given set of statements in fact constitutes an argument in the formal logical sense.

EXERCISE 2-3

For each of the following multiple-choice questions, (a) choose one answer, and (b) construct an argument that illustrates the inference you used in your choice of answer.

1. Rugged individualism
   a. is one of the qualities that has contributed to the nation's greatness.
   b. is an outmoded characteristic that cannot be found in our current totalitarian regime.
   c. was coined by T. Veblen.
   d. is a strategic play in rugby.
2. New Orleans' increased use of police to control behavior is an indicator of
   a. societal breakdown.
   b. a police state.
   c. an overstaffed police force.
   d. a likelihood of disorder during the festivities.

3. Future nuclear energy policies will be best determined by
   a. the public and legislators.
   b. an elitist team of experts.
   c. big business interests.
   d. a combination of the above.

4. Nuclear power as a source of energy
   a. is dead.
   b. is an issue that remains debatable.
   c. is unquestionably hazardous.
   d. is the only viable answer to the energy shortage.

5. The split-brain theory
   a. is a well-proven scientific fact.
   b. is used to explain the differences between males and females.
   c. explains the duality in humans.
   d. is simply an interpretive metaphor.

6. Chemotherapy
   a. is a recognized cure for cancer.
   b. is recognized by the AMA as a viable treatment for cancer.
   c. is used as an immunosuppressant to cure cancerous growth.
   d. all of the above.

7. Vitamin supplements are
   a. essential to everyone's health.
   b. necessary when one is body-building.
   c. proven as cancer cures.
   d. none of the above.

8. The ecosystem
   a. is limited in its ability to remain stable.
   b. can absorb all pollutants with little repercussion.
   c. does not include rational beings, such as humans as its denizens.
   d. all but one of the above.

2.3 Premises and Conclusions

It follows directly from our definition of 'argument' that every argument contains one and only one conclusion. So it is reasonable to expect that any set of statements that someone intends or offers as an argument in everyday contexts should also have exactly one conclusion. The following sets of statements all satisfy this requirement. How is it possible to determine which statements are intended as the conclusions and which are intended as the premises?

1. **Since Sue has always done well in science courses, she will probably do well in logic.**

2. **The negotiations will probably fail, because neither the union nor management is willing to compromise.**

3. **All mammals nurse their young; hence all giraffes nurse their young, for all giraffes are mammals.**

In 1, the intended conclusion is 'she will probably do well in logic;' in 2, it is 'the negotiations will probably fail;' in 3, it is 'all giraffes nurse their young.' Identifying the intended conclusions in these examples might seem a simple task, but how was it done? Not in terms of the position of the statement, for the first conclusion follows its premise, the second precedes it, and the third sits squarely between two premises. Nor is there anything in the conclusion statements themselves that differentiates them in kind from the other statements or premises. Rather, the conclusion in each case was recognized from the way in which it is used in the purported argument.

The identification of a particular statement as an intended conclusion is relative to the context in which it is being used. The next time we come across the same statement it might be serving a different function:

4. **Given that all giraffes nurse their young, and that a baby giraffe has just been born at the zoo, it follows that the mother giraffe will nurse it.**

The conclusion of 3 has become a premise in 4, showing that the same statement might be a conclusion in one context and a premise in another.

An important clue to the identification of premises and conclusions is sometimes provided by the use of **indicator words.** Not all arguments or purported arguments contain them, but when they are present they are a fairly reliable guide to the intended relationships between statements. The four examples above do contain such words.

1. **Since** Sue has always . . .
2. . . . **because** neither the union. . . .
3. . . . **hence** all giraffes nurse . . . **for** all giraffes are mammals.
4. **Given that** all giraffes . . . **it follows that** the mother . . . .

'Since,' 'because,' 'for,' and 'given that' usually indicate that the statement that follows is a premise; 'hence' and 'it follows that' usually signal that a conclusion follows.

An indicator word, then, is one that tells us the function that the following (and sometimes preceding) statement is intended to serve. There are many other indicator words, of course, in addition to those already mentioned, including the following:

Conclusion indicators: *thus, as a result, hence, consequently, so, accordingly, it follows that, implies that, therefore, can be inferred that*

Premise indicators: *due to, insofar as, inasmuch as, in view of, as shown by, on the assumption that, it follows from, can be inferred from*

EXERCISE 2–4

Identify (a) the conclusion, and (b) the premise(s) of each of the following sets of statements, that you can assume are intended as arguments.

1. Spiders are not insects, because insects have only six legs.
2. $X + Y = 6$ and $X = 4$, therefore $Y = 2$.
3. Frank could never become a policeman. He is only five feet two inches tall and weighs only 120 pounds.
4. This can't be Pinot Chardonnay, for it is a red wine.
5. Tom will never be able to climb the face of that cliff. He has had no training in rock climbing.
6. The defendant is insane. Therefore, he is not guilty.
7. Some mammals can fly, since bats can fly.
8. Since Ms. Scott is a judge, it follows that she is a lawyer.
9. This figure is a pentagon, so the sum of its interior angles is 540 degrees.
10. The Vietnam War was futile, since neither side really won.
11. That is not a good French dictionary, because it does not show how each word should be pronounced.
12. The flu is caused by a virus; consequently it can't be cured with antibiotics.
13. Coffee keeps people awake; hence it must contain a stimulant.
14. Tom will not be able to go to the New Year's Eve party at the club, due to the fact that he is not a member.
15. It will take two seconds for that rock to fall, since it is going to fall a distance of sixty-four feet.
16. The housing bill will never come to a vote on the floor of Congress, since the opposition has enough votes to kill it in committee.
17. That this solution is an acid can be inferred from the fact that it turns litmus paper red.
18. Composers do not have to be able to hear music in order to write it, as can be shown by the fact that Beethoven was deaf.
19. Starvation will inevitably occur somewhere in the world, inasmuch as the expanding world population will eventually increase beyond the capacity of the total world agricultural resources to feed it.
20. This flint knife we found at our excavation site has to predate 2500 B.C., for it was found three layers below the layer we dated at 2500 B.C.
21. The functioning of an expanding industrial system depends on an abundance of raw materials; hence our industrial system will eventually cease to expand since raw materials are running out.
22. A square circle is a logical contradiction; thus, not even an infinitely powerful being could make one.
23. Given that the defendant was not present at the scene of the crime, it can clearly be inferred that he did not commit the crime.

24. We can expect the home opener to be canceled, due to the fact that it is raining and has been for the past two days.

25. The fact that individuals are free implies that they are responsible.

26. Oil is becoming more expensive and plastics are made from oil; therefore, plastics are becoming more expensive.

27. It takes three seconds to operate the bolt of this rifle; consequently, no one could have gotten off three shots in a span of five seconds, as it has been alleged the defendant did.

28. Oak is a coarse-grained wood. Walnut is a dark-colored wood. Willow is not a very strong wood. Therefore, since this chair is strong and made of light-colored, fine-grained wood, it is not made of oak, walnut, or willow.

29. No statement can be proven with absolute certitude. Therefore, the statement, 'No statement can be proven with absolute certitude' cannot be proved with absolute certitude.

30. As a body approaches the speed of light, its mass becomes infinite. Therefore, it cannot travel faster than the speed of light, since an infinite force would be needed to accelerate it.

2.4 Problems in Recognizing Intended Arguments

Senator links death penalty, Christianity

ALBANY, N.Y. (AP — "Where would Christianity be if Jesus got eight to 15 years, with time off for good behavior?"

That question was posed by state Sen. James Donovan, an advocate of the death penalty, in a letter to a religious group which had written him that it was opposed to capital punishment "as a matter of faith."

"There would be no Christianity if it were not for the death penalty, which gave us the cross and the resurrection," Donovan replied.

The senator, a Republican from Oneida County, made his comment in a March 1 letter to the Council of Churches of the Mohawk Valley Area, which is opposed to the death penalty.

Copies of Donovan's letter were sent to news organizations, along with a handwritten note saying "local churches are shocked at Donovan's logic." The note was not signed.

Donovan confirmed Tuesday that he had written the letter.

Courtesy The Associated Press.

Even when a person definitely intends to be offering an argument, it is not always easy for us to recognize that this is the case or to determine precisely what the intended argument is. Thus, for example, New York State Senator Donovan apparently intended to give an argument in support of the death penalty in the letter cited in the news report opposite, but it is not at all clear what the intended argument, particularly the premises, might be. The problem in this case is probably careless wording or simply bad logic on the part of the senator, but in other cases (as in the *Doonesbury* cartoon in the previous section) the intentions of the speaker (or author) might be intentionally disguised or obscured. It is also possible that in some cases the intention is to make it appear that there is an argument when, in fact, none is really being presented at all.

It is important to recognize that not every set of statements is offered as an argument. Some, for example, are presented only as descriptions of states of affairs with no intention of using them as support for any conclusion.

> **The school was built in 1890. It is of red brick, with a columned portico in front. The main door and the first-floor windows are arched. A limestone cornice creates a horizontal line to balance the vertical thrust of the white columns.**

Here there are several statements, but none of them is offered as a conclusion or as evidence in support of a conclusion. Such a series of statements constitutes exposition rather than argument.

The absence of indicator words is not sufficient for us to conclude that a particular set of statements is being intended as an exposition rather than an argument. In such cases, we have to look for other clues, such as the ways in which the various statements are expressed or presented in relation to each other.

> **That movie is going to be a great commercial success. It has plenty of sex and violence.**

> **High-rise apartments would destroy the character of our town. The rezoning plan ought to be rejected.**

In both of these cases, it is reasonable to assume that an argument is being intended, for a connection is certainly suggested between sex, violence, and commercial success, and between high-rise apartments, civic destruction, and the proper fate of the rezoning plan. Likewise, our knowledge of the context— of the speaker, the audience, the motivation, the background, the previous discussion—all might help us in determining whether a conclusion and supporting premises are being offered.

Conditionals, or *'if . . . then . . . ' sentences*, often appear at first glance to express arguments. Careful consideration of such sentences shows why they do not. Consider the example

> **If Tom studies hard, then he will get an A in logic.**

This sentence does *not* assert either that Tom studies hard or that Tom will get an A in logic; it only asserts that there is a connection between the two states of affairs such that *if* the first holds, *then* the second will hold. Notice that this sentence does not say the same thing as the following sentence, that expresses an argument.

> **Tom studies hard, so he will get an A in logic.**

This sentence asserts two statements, the premise that Tom studies hard and the conclusion that Tom will get an A in logic.

Although the conditional sentences do not express arguments, they do express statements that could be either premises or conclusions of arguments. For example, if the 'If . . . then . . .' statement above were added as a premise to the argument expressed by the second sentence, the resulting argument would be valid.

One other factor that makes identification of intended arguments difficult is the fact that some indicator words have other functions. 'Since' is particularly tricky, for it can indicate temporal sequence as well as logical relation, and it is not always easy to determine which of these possible meanings is intended in a context. "We have not heard from her since she went away" is probably not intended as an argument, but what about "Since he left the company, many things must have changed"? For this, some knowledge of the context is needed.

'Because' is another tricky term because it is often used to indicate a causal relation between two events rather than a premise-conclusion relation between two statements. For example, "Senator Jones was reelected because of her positions on school busing and abortion" is a proposition explaining the cause of Senator Jones' reelection; it is probably not intended as an argument.

No definitive formal rules or procedures can be given that will guarantee that we will always make a correct judgment as to whether a set of statements is being offered as an argument. However, practice and thoughtful consideration of specific cases can definitely improve our ability to identify intended arguments when they are given.

EXERCISE 2–5

Examine each sentence or group of sentences carefully. (a) Assuming ordinary contexts, would each sentence or group normally be used to express an argument? (b) If not, why not? (c) If so, identify the conclusion and premises.

1. If a rock is quartz, it will scratch glass.
2. That could not have been Helen you met last night. Helen has short brown hair.
3. If you want a ride to Chicago for Thanksgiving, give Joan a call.
4. Take your umbrella, because it's raining.
5. Since his company went bankrupt, he has never been the same.
6. Since his company went bankrupt, he lost all his money.
7. Please don't pick the flowers. They are for all who use the park to enjoy.
8. Spiders are not insects, because insects have only six legs.
9. Of course, you are an idealist. All Sagittarians are idealists.
10. Lee Harvey Oswald must have been crazy to shoot President Kennedy.
11. Since the fall of the Roman Empire, there has never been a single government for most of Western Europe.
12. A rolling stone gathers no moss.
13. All humans are mortal. Socrates is a human. Therefore, Socrates is mortal.
14. If sugar is placed in water, it will dissolve.
15. All our citizens must be allowed to express their opinions freely; otherwise, their freedom of speech will be violated.
16. If sugar is placed in water, it will dissolve. This white crystalline substance is not sugar, since it did not dissolve when I placed it in water.
17. Hydrofluoric acid dissolves glass; consequently, it is stored in lead containers.
18. Logic is distinct from psychology for logic deals with prescriptive laws whereas psychology deals with descriptive laws.
19. Nothing interesting has happened since you went away.

20. It could not have rained, because the streets are completely dry.

21. If I pass today's examination, I will graduate.

22. President Nixon was impeachable because he was involved in obstruction of justice.

23. French is called a romance language because it is derived from Latin.

24. Your car was losing power because one of the spark plug wires had come loose.

25. The United States has always been governed by a president, Congress, and Supreme Court since it first came into existence as a nation.

26. No dimes made since 1964 are made of silver.

27. Don't use that book when you write your paper because Professor Brown doesn't agree with the person who wrote it.

28. If a rock is quartz, it will scratch glass. This rock is made of quartz. Therefore, it will scratch glass.

29. If a rock is quartz, it will scratch glass. This rock will not scratch glass, so it can't be quartz.

30. The United States has always been governed by a president, Congress, and Supreme Court, as that is the form of the government specified in the Constitution.

31. B. F. Skinner is a determinist, so I don't think you will agree with his conclusions in *Beyond Freedom and Dignity*.

32. Lake Erie died in the late 1960s. People kept pouring pollutants into it, without thinking about the long-range consequences of their actions.

33. Since the turn of the century, commencement exercises were held on Wednesdays. In 1995, they were changed to Saturday because of a desire for better attendance.

34. Scientific method, although it might seem complicated, is in essence remarkably simple. It consists of observing such facts as will enable the observer to discover general laws governing facts of the kind in question.

2.5 Supplying Missing Statements

Many, and perhaps most, sets of statements intended as arguments are not expressed in a fully explicit way. The intended conclusion and/or one or more of the premises might not be stated. *Such arguments, with parts only implicitly suggested,* are known as **enthymemes.** If a series of statements clearly tends toward a certain conclusion without ever quite getting there, the conclusion can be assumed to be implicitly stated, and we are justified in adding it to complete the intended argument:

> **High-rise apartments will destroy the rural character of our town.**
> **Studies have shown that the presence of such developments tends to**
> **increase the crime rate. Besides, we don't have the facilities to provide**
> **necessary services to such an enlarged population.**

The conclusion, implicit though not stated, is clearly, 'High-rise apartments should not be permitted in our town.'

If premises rather than conclusions are left out, it is often because the intended audience is assumed to be aware of them already. Thus, almost anyone can supply the implicit premises in the preceding example—'Anything that will destroy the rural character of our town should not be permitted,' 'Nothing that tends to increase the crime rate should be permitted in our town,' and 'If facilities to provide necessary services to such an enlarged population are unavailable, then high-rise apartments should not be permitted.'

A general rule of thumb for supplying missing statements is to *add whatever statements are needed to make the intended argument as good as possible.* This rule is sometimes referred to as the **principle of charity,** and we will discuss it in more detail after discussing what constitutes a good argument.

To illustrate the importance of knowledge of context for identifying arguments, let's consider these three sentences:

> **The sun is shining today.**
> **Today is Wednesday.**
> **Tom will get an A in logic.**

Assuming that these sentences do express propositions, we do not have sufficient information to determine whether they might be intended as part of an argument. To make even an educated guess, we should know who is making these statements, where, when, to whom, and for what purpose. Let's consider two possible sets of circumstances in which these statements might be made.

In the first set of circumstances, Linda wakes up on Monday, looks out the window, and says, "Oh, good, the sun is shining today"; two days later Professor Piffle looks at his calendar and says, "That's right, today is Wednesday"; and on Friday Bob, Tom's roommate, relaxes in the dorm and assures a friend, "Oh, yeah, Tom'll get an A in logic. I don't dare start an argument with him any more." In this case, we can safely conclude that there is no argument.

In the second set of circumstances, Linda, who is Tom's girlfriend, meets Bob in the library on Wednesday morning and makes all three of these statements, and both of them already know certain other facts. In this case, there might be an argument intended after all. With the missing premises added in brackets, it might look like this:

> **The sun is shining today.**
> **Today is Wednesday.**
> **[The final exam in logic is on Wednesday.]**
> **[The exam counts for 10 percent of the final grade.]**
> **[Tom has a 90 average going into the exam.]**

[Tom has always done well on sunny days.]
[The cutoff point for an A is 89.5 percent.]
Therefore, Tom will get an A in logic.

Knowing Tom and knowing the school—that is, knowing the relevant context—Linda and Bob can take all but the first two premises and the conclusion for granted, and perceive that these three original statements could be intended as part of such an argument.

Common Problems in Identifying Arguments

1. A set of sentences each of which expresses a proposition may constitute an exposition rather than an argument.

2. Indicator words may be missing from an argument, in which case the premises and conclusion can often be recognized by other linguistic cues or by knowledge of the context.

3. Indicator words may be present when there is no argument.

4. The conclusion may be implicit rather than stated.

5. Premises may be omitted, in which case it may be necessary to examine the context to determine exactly which premise(s) should be supplied.

2.6 Deductive and Inductive Arguments

We have already seen that it is not always easy to determine whether a person intends a particular set of statements to function as an argument or not. It is even more difficult, and often impossible, to make even an educated guess as to how strong an argument might be intended in any given case. Given that an argument is intended, the premises could be offered as providing anything from very weak support to very strong or even absolute support for the conclusion. Because the basic distinction between inductive and deductive arguments depends entirely on the degree of support that the premises provide for the conclusion, and since it is so difficult to determine what degree of support is intended in specific cases, we will focus our discussion of the inductive/deductive distinction on actual arguments (i.e., those in which the premises in fact support the conclusion) rather than on sets of statements intended or offered as arguments.

The distinction between inductive and deductive can be grasped quite quickly at an intuitive level by considering a few examples. Returning to the argument about Tom and his logic grade, it should be clear that the premises offer only partial support for the conclusion. It is certainly possible, even though improbable, that Tom could get an 80 or less on the final exam and thus not get an A in the course. This is an example of an inductive argument.

For the moment, let us consider the effect of changing one of the premises. If instead of a 90 average, Tom had achieved a 100 average, the argument would read as follows:

> **The sun is shining today.**
> **Today is Wednesday.**
> **The final exam in logic is on Wednesday.**
> **The exam counts for 10 percent of the final grade.**
> **Tom has a 100 average going into the exam.**
> **Tom always does well on sunny days.**
> **The cutoff point for an A is 89.5 percent.**
> **Therefore, Tom will get an A in logic.**

Assuming that all the premises are true, is it possible for the conclusion to be false? Obviously not. Given the mathematics of the situation as stated, Tom is sure to end up with a final grade of 90 even if he gets a 0 on the exam. This is an example of what is known as a deductive argument.

The relation between inductive and deductive arguments can be graphically represented as follows:

Degree of Premises' Support of Conclusion

Nonarguments	**Inductive Arguments**			**Deductive Arguments**
none	weak	moderate	strong	absolute

In a deductive argument, the premises must give absolute support for the conclusion. Any argument in which the premises provide anything less than absolute support is by definition an inductive argument. Any set of statements that is such that none of them provide any support at all for any of the others is not an argument at all—either inductive or deductive.

2.6.1 Deductive Arguments

Validity is an important concept in deductive logic. It is not the same thing as truth, though in ordinary speech we sometimes assert that a particular statement or belief is valid—meaning that it is true. We have already seen that in logic a statement is defined as that which can be properly said to be true or false. Likewise, logicians have stipulated that the term **valid** is to be applied only to those *arguments that are such that if the premises are true, the conclusion must also be true.*

NOTE ! ! !

All valid arguments are deductive,
and
All deductive arguments are valid.

Consider the following examples. Are the premises true or false? The conclusions? Which arguments are valid, that is, in which cases do the premises provide *absolute* support for the conclusion?

1. The Eiffel Tower is in London. London is in Germany. Germany is in Africa. Therefore, the Eiffel Tower is in Africa.

2. Plato was a Greek. Plato was a philosopher. Therefore, all Greeks are philosophers.

3. If Bill Clinton's name was on the ballot in the 1992 presidential election, then John voted for him. Bill Clinton's name was on the ballot in the 1992 presidential election. Therefore, John voted for Bill Clinton.

4. Dolphins are a kind of shark. Sharks have breathing holes. Therefore, dolphins have breathing holes.

5. Either the moon is made of green cheese, or it is not. Therefore, Hawaii was the fiftieth state admitted to the Union.

The only arguments that are invalid are 2 and 5. It is easy to see that even though the premises of 2 are true—Plato really was a Greek and a philosopher—this does not imply or necessitate that all his fellow Greeks were also philosophers. In example 5, the premise about the moon is syntactically analytically true, and the conclusion about Hawaii also happens to be true; but the premise does not in itself lend any support for the conclusion. By definition, it is impossible to have a valid argument in which true premises lead to a false conclusion. But, as example 5 illustrates, having true premises and a true conclusion is no guarantee that an intended argument is valid (or even that it is an argument at all).

The other three examples have a logical structure that is such that *if* the premises were true, *then* necessarily the conclusion would be true. That is, if the Eiffel Tower were really in London, and London were really in Germany, and Germany were really in Africa, then it would necessarily follow that the Eiffel Tower is in Africa. Similarly, we know that dolphins are not sharks, and sharks do not have breathing holes; but *if* they were sharks and *if* sharks did have breathing holes, *then* the conclusion that dolphins have breathing holes would have to be true. So it is possible to have a valid argument in which one or more of the premises are false or even one in which all the premises and the conclusion are false. It is also possible to have an intended argument with true premises and a true conclusion that is invalid. The point is that in a valid argument the premises necessarily imply the conclusion. As long as this is so, you can be certain that if the premises are true, the conclusion will be true as well.

Valid arguments have an additional significant characteristic. Look again at argument 4. Suppose a few more premises were added—'Dolphins communicate by means of a system similar to radar,' 'Dolphins were considered omens of good luck by ancient sailors,' 'Sharks have fusiform bodies,' and

'Sharks are carnivorous.' These additional premises neither increase nor decrease the support for the conclusion, because the original premises already guarantee the truth of the conclusion no matter what additional information might be provided. Similarly, no premises we add to the other two valid arguments (1 and 3) will make them any stronger; absolute support is as strong as is possible. Thus, for any deductive argument, given that the original premises are true, the addition of any information whatever to this set of premises will not affect the truth of the conclusion.

In summary, a deductive argument (or, synonymously, a valid argument) can be defined in a number of different ways, including the following.

A deductive (or valid) argument is such that:

If its premises are true, then its conclusion must be true.

or

It is impossible for all of the premises to be true and the conclusion false.

or

The premises imply the conclusion.

or

The premises provide absolute support for the conclusion.

or

The information contained in the conclusion is completely contained in the premises.

Although the wording is different, each of these definitions says essentially the same thing. Unfortunately, even with so many alternative definitions, it is doubtful that you (or anyone else) could have a very clear understanding of the exact nature of a deductive (or valid) argument simply from reading and thinking about the definitions. The best way to gain an understanding of this concept is to study numerous examples of arguments that are and are not deductive, and to learn some of the formal methods that can be used to determine whether particular arguments are deductive or not. For now it is sufficient to memorize the words of the definitions; their meanings will become increasingly clear as you go through the rest of this book.

EXERCISE 2–6

Each of the following arguments is valid. (I) Use blanks to display the logical form of the argument. (II) Construct an argument with the same form in which all of the premises are false and the conclusion is false.

1. The sparrow is a petite bird.
   Some snakes weigh more than 10 pounds.

So, the sparrow is a petite bird and some snakes weigh more than 10 pounds.

2. There are Amish in Pennsylvania.
   Spanish moss flourishes on live oaks in Georgia.
   So, there are Amish in Pennsylvania or Jack Dempsey is a bishop.

3. All octopi are mollusks.
   All mollusks are animals.
   So, all octopi are animals.

4. All cliff divers know how to swim.
   No bananas know how to swim.
   So, no cliff divers are bananas.

5. Some lightbulbs are fluorescent.
   Some fluorescent things are fish.
   So, some fluorescent things are fish or some fluorescent things are cabbages.

6. Some elms are trees.
   All trees are plants.
   So, some elms are plants.

7. Some students are moustached and bespectacled.
   Nothing moustached and bespectacled is a fungus.
   So some students are not fungi.

8. No pickles are six feet long.
   All things six feet long are less than ten feet long.
   So, some things less than ten feet long are not pickles.

9. No mules are mathematicians.
   Some mules are overworked.
   So, some overworked things are not mathematicians.

10. All pineapples are fruits.
    Some staples are not fruits.
    So, some staples are not pineapples.

EXERCISE 2–7

In the following exercises you are given a conclusion. Use your intuitions to help you choose the set of premises from which it can be validly deduced. (These questions are similar to those on various graduate and professional school admissions tests.)

1. Sal changed the diaper.
   a. If Sal heard the crying, then Sal changed the diaper.
   b. If Sal changed the diaper, then the baby stopped crying; what's more, the baby stopped crying.

    c. If Jo's calmed down, then Sal changed the diaper; and Jo's calmed down.

    d. The conclusion is deducible from each of the above statements.

    e. The conclusion is deducible from none of the above statements.

2. Horace sliced the pumpkin.

    a. Everything grinning sliced the pumpkin, and Horace is grinning.

    b. The pumpkin is sliced, and Horace is the only person in the room.

    c. If Horace didn't slice the pumpkin, then the pumpkin isn't sliced.

    d. The conclusion is deducible from each of the above statements.

    e. The conclusion is deducible from none of the above statements.

3. Janice licked the stamp.

    a. If Janice sealed the envelope, then she licked the stamp.

    b. Janice is always licking stamps.

    c. Janice licked the stamp and sealed the envelope.

    d. The conclusion is deducible from each of the above statements.

    e. The conclusion is deducible from none of the above statements.

4. Pip fell in the mud.

    a. All the scouts fell in the mud, and Pip is a scout.

    b. Everything that fell in the mud is a scout, and Pip is a scout.

    c. If Pip didn't fall in the mud, then Chet did.

    d. The conclusion is deducible from each of the above statements.

    e. The conclusion is deducible from none of the above statements.

5. All the dancers squeezed their partners.

    a. Those dancers that don't squeeze their partners are ostracized.

    b. The only dancers that didn't squeeze their partners ate peanut butter, and all dancers that ate peanut butter had strong breath; but none of the dancers had strong breath.

    c. All of the dancers are notorious squeezers.

    d. The conclusion is deducible from each of the above statements.

    e. The conclusion is deducible from none of the above statements.

6. Some of the ruffians tasted the batter.

    a. All of the ruffians tasted the batter or panicked.

    b. Some of the ruffians did not taste the batter.

    c. All of the ruffians tasted the batter or shot the ball, and Sal, who is a ruffian, didn't shoot the ball.

    d. The conclusion is deducible from each of the above statements.

    e. The conclusion is deducible from none of the above statements.

7. If Jules peeled the grapefruit, then Cory washed the dog.

    a. Jules didn't peel the grapefruit.

    b. Cory washed the dog.

    c. Jules only peels the grapefruit if Cory washes the dog.

    d. The conclusion is deducible from each of the above statements.

    e. The conclusion is deducible from none of the above statements.

8. All of the British flossed their teeth.
    a. None of the British did not floss their teeth.
    b. Some of the British did floss their teeth.
    c. The Kernseys, who are British, flossed their teeth.
    d. The conclusion is deducible from each of the above statements.
    e. The conclusion is deducible from none of the above statements.

9. Liza stood on her head.
    a. All of the gymnasts stood on their heads.
    b. Liza is from New York.
    c. Either Liza stood on her head, or she's a gymnast; and she's not a gymnast.
    d. The conclusion is deducible from each of the above statements.
    e. The conclusion is deducible from none of the above statements.

10. None of the hackers sat on the cat.
    a. If a hacker sat on the cat, then Bob licked the fence.
    b. Sally Habspat sat on the cat, but she's not a hacker. [Imagine that!]
    c. Only Sally sat on the cat, but she's not a hacker.
    d. The conclusion is deducible from each of the above statements.
    e. The conclusion is deducible from none of the above statements.

2.6.2 Logical Form and Counterexamples

Let us consider two more arguments.

> **All silamons are wistacious.**
> **Piliute is a silamon.**
> **Therefore, piliute is wistacious.**

> **If carnips are tumbulous, then iliks are quirkles.**
> **Carnips are tumbulous.**
> **Therefore, iliks are quirkles.**

Both these examples contain nonsense words; yet the logical form of each is deductive. If all silamons (whatever they might be) are wistacious (whatever that is), and if piliute is a silamon, it follows that piliute is wistacious. Likewise if the conditional statement 'If carnips are tumbulous, then iliks are quirkles' is true and if carnips are in fact tumbulous, then it necessarily follows that iliks are quirkles. In each example, a logical relationship exists between the premises and the conclusion that is independent of the content of these statements; it is a relationship that is based on the *form* of the argument. This is what we mean when we say that it is possible to evaluate the validity of any argument solely on the basis of its logical form.

Consider now these two examples:

> **Some furnaps are spenels.**
> **Tursid is a furnap.**
> **Thus, Tursid is a spenel.**

All surpids are rustids.
All turnfers are rustids.
Thus, all surpids are turnfers.

Although it might not be intuitively obvious, neither of these two examples is a valid argument. One way to prove that these examples are not valid is to provide counterexamples that are sufficient to prove that it is *possible* for a particular argument form to have true premises and a false conclusion. In constructing a **counterexample,** *one keeps the same argument form but changes the factual content in such a way as to make the premises of the argument true and the conclusion false.* Thus, we can provide the following counterexamples for the arguments above by first identifying their logical form and then filling in terms that make the premises true and the conclusion false:

Some _____ are *****.	Some automobiles are Fords.
_____ is _____.	That Neon is an automobile.
Thus, _____ is *****.	Thus, that Neon is a Ford.
All _____ are *****.	All flies are insects.
All _____ are *****.	All ants are insects.
Thus, all _____ are _____.	Thus, all flies are ants.

Once again, the counterexamples provide concrete evidence that for these argument forms it is possible to have all of the premises true and the conclusion false; this violates the definition of validity. Although providing a counterexample is sufficient to prove that an argument is invalid, the failure to construct an appropriate counterexample for a particular argument is not sufficient to prove that an argument is valid. The fact that we have been unable to think of a way to make the premises true and the conclusion false for a specific argument form does not permit us to conclude that it is *impossible* for anyone to ever think of such a counterexample. Other procedures are necessary for proving that arguments are valid.

EXERCISE 2–8

Each of the following intended arguments is invalid. Provide a counterexample for each.

1. If humans are mortal, then they must eat food to survive. Humans must eat food to survive. Therefore, humans are mortal.

2. Some women are courageous. Some women are considerate. Therefore, some women are courageous and considerate.

3. All paramecia are single-celled organisms. No sea urchins are paramecia. Therefore, no sea urchins are single-celled organisms.

4. All marigolds are plants. All flowers are plants. Therefore, all marigolds are flowers.

5. All cats are felines. A polar bear is not a cat. Therefore, a polar bear is not a feline.

6. Some Englishmen are Protestants. Winston Churchill was a Protestant. Therefore, Winston Churchill was an Englishman.

7. Orange juice is a delicious drink. Pineapple juice is a delicious drink. Therefore, orange-pineapple juice is a delicious drink.

8. All industrialists are rich. Henry Ford was rich. Therefore, Henry Ford was an industrialist.

9. No cats are dogs. No cats are canines. Therefore, all dogs are canines.

10. If an animal is a mammal, then it bears its young live. A gorilla bears its young live. Therefore, a gorilla is a mammal.

11. If an animal is a mammal, then it bears its young live. A bluebird is not a mammal. Therefore, a bluebird does not bear its young live.

12. If you studied hard, then you got an A in logic. You did not study hard. Therefore, you did not get an A in logic.

13. All humans are mortal creatures. Some mortal creatures are toolmakers. Therefore, some humans are toolmakers.

14. Some Greeks are philosophers. Socrates was a Greek. Therefore, Socrates was a philosopher.

15. Bronze is a metal. Bronze is made of copper and tin. Therefore, copper is a metal and tin is a metal.

2.6.3 Inductive Arguments

Now let us return to the original version of the Tale of Tom, in which he had a 90 average going into the last exam. Given these premises, the conclusion that he will get an A in the course does not follow necessarily: with a 90 average, Tom needs an 85 on the final exam to get an 89.5 in the course. Even if all of the original premises are true, it is still possible for the conclusion to be false. The premises do not provide absolute support for it. Thus, this is not a deductive argument. However, the premises do provide *some* support for the conclusion. That is, given the truth of the premises, a reasonable person would be more justified in accepting the truth of the conclusion than he or she would be without the premises. *Any argument whose premises provide some, but not absolute, support for the conclusion* is known as an **inductive argument.**

The concept of an inductive argument covers a broad range of arguments—from those that provide very strong (but not absolute) support for their conclusions to those whose premises provide very little support for their conclusions. Remember, a set of statements that does not provide any support whatsoever for another statement does not constitute an argument at all in the formal logical sense. Any set of statements that does not constitute a deductive argument is either an inductive argument or not an argument at all (in the formal logical sense).

REMEMBER ! ! !

Even if someone asserts that a set of statements does support some conclusion, if the premises do not in fact provide any support for the conclusion, this is neither a deductive nor an inductive argument.

As stated earlier, there is no simple method for determining on direct inspection whether a set of statements constitutes an argument in the formal logical sense, let alone whether it is an inductive or deductive argument. The only methods that can be used with absolute certainty are several formal techniques for determining whether certain sets of statements constitute a valid argument. Thus, it is necessary to develop the ability to make intuitive or educated guesses as to whether a set of statements constitutes an inductive or deductive argument, and, whenever there is some doubt, to assume that it might be a deductive argument and test it using the methods to be presented in later chapters. If a set of statements is explicitly asserted to be a deductive argument, we can proceed directly to testing it, using the formal procedures, and we might be able to prove that it is or is not valid.

We will now look at a few examples of deductive and inductive arguments in order to develop your ability to make informal, but educated, guesses as to whether an argument is deductive (i.e., valid) or inductive.

It often has been said that in deductive arguments we reason from general to particular, whereas in inductive arguments we reason from particular to general. A typical example that is offered of a deductive argument is:

All mammals have eyes.
Flipper is a mammal.
Therefore, Flipper has eyes.

And one pattern for an inductive argument is:

Animal A is a swan and is white.
Animal B is a swan and is white.
Animal C is a swan and is white.
Animal D is a swan and is white.
Therefore, probably all swans are white.

In the deductive argument, we began with the universal statement 'All mammals have eyes' and concluded with a particular statement, 'Flipper has eyes.' In the inductive argument, each premise was particular, but the conclusion was general. However, it is quite possible to have arguments that do not fit these patterns. For example, consider the following:

1. **All mammals have eyes.**
   All dolphins are mammals.
   Therefore, all dolphins have eyes.

2. **If Flipper is a mammal, then he has eyes.**
   Flipper is a mammal.
   Therefore, Flipper has eyes.

3. **All robins are birds and build nests.**
   All sparrows are birds and build nests.
   All bluejays are birds and build nests.
   All pigeons are birds and build nests.
   Therefore, all birds build nests.

4. **Senator Jones is a politician and a liar.**
   Representative Smith is a politician and a liar.
   Mayor Great is a politician and a liar.
   Vice-President Padook is a politician.
   Therefore, Vice-President Padook is a liar.

Arguments 1 and 2 above are deductive, for if the premises are true, the conclusion must also be true. Yet, in both these examples, the reasoning is not from general to particular: in argument 1 the reasoning goes from general premises to a general conclusion, and in argument 2 from particular premises to a particular conclusion. Arguments 3 and 4 are inductive, since the premises provide some but not absolute support for the conclusion, but in both examples the reasoning is not from particular premises to general conclusions. In argument 3, the premises and conclusion are all general, and, in argument 4, both the premises and the conclusion are particular. Consequently, it is evident that the general/particular rule is unreliable in practice as a way of distinguishing between deductive and inductive arguments.

EXERCISE 2-9

Examine each argument below, assuming that each premise is true. (a) Is the argument deductive or inductive? (b) Explain.

1. All birds can fly. I've never seen one that can't.
2. $A = B$ and $B = C$; therefore, $A = C$
3. No Vulcans are Klingons. Mr. Spock is a Vulcan. Therefore, he is not a Klingon.
4. My three swans are white; therefore, some swans are white.
5. My three swans are white; therefore, all swans are white.
6. Bill is a Sagittarian, so his birthday is in December.
7. Bill is a Sagittarian; therefore, he is impulsive.
8. John must have a toothache again. He is not looking very cheerful.
9. Even numbers cannot be odd. Eight is an even number, so it is not odd.

10. One of these statements must be false, because if two statements contradict each other, they cannot both be true, and these two statements do contradict each other.

11. The average college-educated person has a higher yearly income than the national average. Helen has a college education, so her yearly income is above the national average.

12. According to the polls, 54 percent of the voters favor Senator Erskine. Therefore, Senator Erskine will win the election.

13. Today is Wednesday. You came four days ago, so that means you came on Saturday, which was four days ago.

14. I sent her the letter three weeks ago and still have received no answer; therefore, my letter must have been lost in the mail.

15. All human choices are determined, since all events in the universe are determined and all human choices are events in the universe.

16. Spot always comes home by dark. It's dark and he hasn't come home yet. Therefore, he must have been run over by a car.

17. Bob and Kay both have blue eyes. Therefore, the child they are expecting will have blue eyes.

18. Rick must be a conservative, since most supporters of Jack Kemp are conservatives and Rick is a Kemp supporter.

19. If J. Paul Getty had written *Love Story*, he would have been rich. J. Paul Getty was rich, so he wrote *Love Story*.

20. The game will be canceled, since if it rains the game must be canceled, and it's raining.

21. Among the suspects, only the butler and Sir Chisholm knew how to shoot accurately at a distance with a .38 revolver. Lady Lawford was shot at a distance of one hundred feet at nine o'clock Tuesday night. Sir Chisholm was a hundred miles away from the scene of the crime at nine o'clock Tuesday night. Therefore, the butler did it.

22. The electric company says that, if the demand for electricity continues to grow at the present rate, a new power station must be operational by 2000. The company predicts that demand will continue to grow at the present rate. Therefore, construction must start immediately.

23. No species of animal observed to date except the human species is capable of rational thought. Therefore, humans are the only rational animals.

24. The United States, England, France, and Germany all underwent great cultural change during industrialization. Consequently, China will undergo great cultural change as it industrializes.

25. The sea painter is now toggled at the thwart. Only one thing can be toggled at the thwart at one time. Therefore, nothing else is toggled at the thwart.

2.7 Criteria for Good Arguments

So far, we have discussed what an argument is, ways to recognize arguments, and the two different types of argument; we have not touched on the subject of what constitutes a good deductive or inductive argument. It is to this subject that we now turn.

2.7.1 Good Deductive Arguments

The best possible argument—one whose conclusion can be trusted to be true—is called a **sound argument.** To be sound, an argument must satisfy two conditions: *it must be valid,* **and** *the truth of all its premises must be reasonably established.* It was noted earlier that a deductive argument might contain false premises and a true conclusion as well as false premises and a false conclusion. Consider again two valid arguments offered earlier:

> **Dolphins are a kind of shark.**
> **Sharks have breathing holes.**
> **Therefore, dolphins have breathing holes.**

> **The Eiffel Tower is in London.**
> **London is in Germany.**
> **Germany is in Africa.**
> **Therefore, the Eiffel Tower is in Africa.**

In the first example, both premises are false, yet the conclusion is true. In the second, all of the premises and the conclusion are false. Both arguments are valid, though neither one is sound. Soundness refers to only one type of deductive argument: one that contains premises whose truth is well established. In such instances, the truth of the conclusion must necessarily be well established, since a valid argument is such that, if its premises are true, its conclusion must be true, and we are told that the premises are in fact well established.

Let us consider now a valid argument with more problematic premises.

> **Any person who smokes cigarettes runs a higher risk of developing lung**
> **cancer than a person who does not smoke.**
> **Tom smokes two packs of cigarettes a day and Bill does not smoke.**
> **Therefore, Tom is running a higher risk of developing lung cancer than**
> **Bill.**

Determining the truth value of the second premise to a reasonable degree of certainty is a relatively simple task: One could ask Tom and Bill if they smoke, or one could directly observe their behavior for several days. To determine the truth value of the first premise, one might consult a medical specialist or a reliable text. Logicians are not usually concerned with soundness because ordinarily they have no special qualifications to decide if a premise is true or false. The logician's primary concern when examining a set of statements is determining whether it constitutes a deductive argument, an inductive argument, or no argument at all.

A final criterion for determining whether a deductive argument is good is that of noncircularity. A **circular argument** is *one whose conclusion merely restates, in different words, something that is already stated explicitly in the premises.* In one sense, every valid argument is circular, since its conclusion must be contained in the premises. However, the term 'circular' is reserved for arguments such as the following, that we will assume is being presented by a native English speaker to an audience of native English speakers:

All bachelors are unhappy.
Therefore, all unmarried men are unhappy.

Assuming that we already know that a bachelor is by definition an unmarried man, the conclusion of this argument is essentially a restatement of the premise. We are left just where we began. The circularity of an argument is not as easily established as its validity, since it depends on what the hearer already knows. Consequently, an argument might be circular for one person and not for another. If the above argument about bachelors and unmarried men were presented to a Russian with a limited knowledge of English, it would not be circular to him if he was not aware that 'bachelor' means 'unmarried man.' In fact, he might not perceive that any argument existed until someone supplied him with the missing definition.

EXERCISE 2–10

Each of these deductive arguments is valid. (a) Is the truth of each premise well established? (b) Is the argument sound?

1. All flowers are plants. All roses are flowers. Therefore, all roses are plants.

2. All birds can fly. Some fish are birds. Therefore, some fish can fly.

3. All rectangles are four-sided figures. All squares are rectangular. Therefore, all squares are four-sided figures.

4. No apes can write novels. All orangutans are apes. Therefore, no orangutans can write novels.

5. All skyscrapers are tall buildings. The Empire State Building is a skyscraper. Therefore, the Empire State Building is a tall building.

6. All conservatives are wealthy. Some Republicans are conservatives. Therefore, some Republicans are wealthy.

7. All women are wise. Dr. Smith is a woman. Therefore, Dr. Smith is wise.

8. Either all insects have wings or all ants are insects. It is not the case that all ants are insects. Therefore, all insects have wings.

9. If humans are animals, then they must eat food to survive. Humans are animals. Therefore they must eat food to survive.

10. Either all dogs are canines or all cats are canines. It is not the case that all cats are canines. Therefore, all dogs are canines.

2.7.2 Good Inductive Arguments

As with deductive arguments, inductive arguments, to be good, should have premises whose truth is well established. Beyond that, it is necessary to consider the relative strength of support that the premises provide for the truth of the conclusion.

Because its premises do not provide absolute support for its conclusion, an inductive argument, unlike a deductive one, can be strengthened or weakened by the addition of new premises. In the original version of the inductive argument about Tom and his 90 average, we saw that he still has a reasonable chance to get his A. If we now add that Tom has studied hard for this exam and that he had a good night's sleep, the conclusion becomes even more likely. The new argument is stronger than the original. On the other hand, if we were to add the information that only two of the twenty exams Tom has taken thus far in college were taken on sunny days and that the harder Tom studies the more he tends to "go blank" on an exam, the premises now give less support for the truth of the conclusion.

It is important to recognize that while we use only the single name 'inductive argument' to refer to all arguments in which the premises provide less than absolute support for the conclusion, there is not just a single type of inductive argument. Some of these arguments involve the drawing of analogies among a number of particular cases, while others involve drawing generalizations from a limited number of observations. Still other inductive arguments involve the identification of causal relations between two or more events, and still others involve statistical analyses. But each kind allows for arguments in which the premises provide different degrees of support for the conclusions, ranging from almost none to almost (but not quite) absolute. We study the nature of some of the kinds of inductive arguments in more detail in Chapters 9 and 10.

With regard to terminology, neither the term 'sound' nor the term 'valid' are applied to inductive arguments in this book. Instead, we usually say that an inductive argument is stronger or weaker than some other argument. When we assert that an inductive argument is strong (or weak), it should be interpreted as an assertion that of all possible arguments that could be given in support of this conclusion, this particular argument is stronger (or weaker) than most.

2.8 Dealing with Enthymemes

We saw in our discussion of the problems of recognizing which sets of statements are intended as arguments that, in everyday contexts, not all of the parts of intended arguments are stated explicitly. It was also explained that such an argument (or set of statements intended as an argument) is known as an enthymeme. We further indicated that we should adhere to the principle of charity when we supply the missing premises—that is, we should add whatever premises are needed to make the argument as good as possible. We can now elaborate further on this by indicating that the "best" argument is a sound argument, a valid argument with premises whose truth is well established.

This is an example of an enthymeme:

If Paris is in France, then Paris is in Europe.
Therefore, Paris is in Europe.

Although this set of statements does not constitute a valid argument as stated, it seems reasonable to assume that it was intended as an argument, and we should thus try to find other well-established truths that might be added as premises that would result in a valid (and sound) argument. For this example, the obvious missing premise (in brackets) can be supplied to give a valid argument as follows.

If Paris is in France, then Paris is in Europe.
[Paris is in France.]
Therefore, Paris is in Europe.

In this example, the truth of the added premise seems to be quite well established, and it also makes the argument valid.

Although everything worked out simply and well in this example, in many cases adherence to the principle of charity cannot result in a sound argument. Consider, for example, the following:

Shakespeare was an Englishman; consequently, all Englishmen are great playwrights.

If we add the well-established truth, 'Shakespeare was a great playwright,' as a premise, we still do not have a valid argument; at best, the resulting argument is a weak inductive argument.

Shakespeare was an Englishman.
[Shakespeare was a great playwright.]
Therefore, all Englishmen are great playwrights.

It is not at all clear what additional premises would have to be added to make the argument valid, but they would have to be highly questionable statements such as 'If one Englishman has ever been a great playwright, then all Englishmen must be great playwrights.'

In cases such as this, where one must choose between adding well-established, true premises that will produce an invalid argument (with a relatively high degree of inductive strength) and adding questionable premises that will make the argument valid, logicians usually prefer to try to make the argument valid, since their expertise is in determining validity rather than in establishing factual truth. However, in some situations where the only premises that would make the argument valid are obviously false, it might be preferable to add a premise whose truth is well established even though it results in a strong inductive argument.

Assuming ordinary contexts, examine each of the following purported arguments. (a) Identify the conclusion. (b) Identify the stated premises. (c) Add a premise that will make the argument stronger. (d) Add a premise that will make the argument weaker, assuming that the premise for (c) has not been added.

1. That is not a rose bush because it doesn't have thorns.
2. There is no reason to vote, since all politicians are corrupt.
3. The end of a thing is the perfection of that thing, so death is the perfection of life.
4. Bats are not birds, because birds have feathers.
5. This wine is not Chablis, for it is red wine.
6. Gregory is not a Turkish Cypriot; therefore, he is a Greek Cypriot.
7. The baseball game was dull, since both teams played poorly.
8. Susan will not get the job. She has no experience.
9. All metaphysicians are eccentric, so Karl is eccentric.
10. All trees are plants and all oaks are trees. Therefore, all oaks are living things.
11. Mr. Poindexter did not work for the company, so he could not have stolen the money.
12. Since he just received a pay raise, he must be competent at his job.
13. All men make mistakes; consequently, so does John.
14. Peter is not my friend, because he told lies about me.
15. He passed the examination; therefore, he must have lied.
16. This liquid is not acid, for the litmus paper we placed in it did not turn red.
17. Senator Brandt is a major party candidate and he is not a Republican. Therefore, he is a Democrat.
18. If the demand for sugar exceeds the supply, the price of sugar will go up. Therefore, the price of sugar will go up.

2.9 Complex Argument Structures

In all of the examples and exercises with which we have worked up to this point, there has been a single conclusion with one set of premises in direct support of it. But the arguments we encounter in everyday contexts are often more complex than this. For example, it is not uncommon to have two or more quite distinct sets of premises offered in support of a single conclusion, or to have a "chain" of arguments in which several premises support a conclusion and that conclusion is in turn used as a premise in support of some other conclusion. Both inductive and deductive arguments can be incorporated into a single complex argument.

The logical analysis of complex arguments is essentially the same as the analysis of simple arguments, since each of the component subarguments of a complex argument structure can be evaluated as a simple argument in and of itself. But it is still important to be prepared to recognize complex arguments when they do occur so that they can be correctly identified and broken into their subcomponents before a formal analysis is attempted. Let us look briefly at several examples of not-too-complex arguments now; we will consider more of these in Chapter 14.

To analyze complex arguments it is useful to draw a schematic diagram showing the relationship of the component statements. This same method can be used for simple arguments, that is, arguments with a single conclusion supported by a single set of premises. So let's begin with a simple argument.

> **Ed is going to study hard in his logic course because he is rational and he wants to go to a good law school.**

The first step in schematizing any argument is to list each of the explicitly stated component statements and label them as shown below.

A. Ed is going to study hard in his logic course.

B. Ed is rational.

C. Ed wants to go to a good law school.

We should also list any premises that are not explicitly stated but that it is reasonable to assume in the context of the argument. To show that these are being supplied by us (and thus might possibly not have been intended by the original author of the argument), we put the letters identifying such statements in brackets.

[D]. Ed believes that studying hard in logic will help him get into a good law school.

[E]. All rational persons who believe that doing a specific thing will get them something they want will do that thing.

We can now construct a diagram showing that the four premises, taken together, will provide support for the conclusion. We do this by putting the letters representing the premises that go together on a single horizontal line, and then draw a vertical arrow from this line down to the letter representing the conclusion as follows.

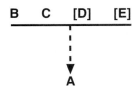

Note that the vertical line with the arrow at the bottom is broken. This signifies that the argument is inductive, that is, the premises provide only partial support for the conclusion. If we know that an argument is valid, then we should draw a solid line connecting the premises to the conclusion. We operate on the general principle that *unless a definite proof of the validity of an argument has been constructed* (using a formal method for proving validity such as one of those presented later in this book), *we should remain on the cautious side and always use the broken line to indicate that the argument has not been proven to be valid.*

One other point deserves mention, although we cannot develop it adequately until Chapter 14. This point is that a complex argument can have subarguments, some of which are deductive and some of which are inductive. The diagram of such an argument would have both solid and broken vertical arrow lines.

Let us now consider a somewhat more complex argument.

At least one student will get an A in this logic course because at least one student in this course is either lucky or works hard. All students who are lucky get As and all students who work hard also get As.

The first step in the analysis is to list the explicitly stated components and assign them letters as follows:

A. At least one student will get an A in this logic course.

B. At least one student in this logic course is lucky or works hard.

C. All students who work hard get As.

D. All students who are lucky get As.

The next step is to list any statements that are not explicitly stated but that it would be reasonable to assume; however, no such statements seem obvious for this argument. The connections among the premises and between the premises and the conclusion can be drawn as follows.

Note that the lines between C and B and between D and B do not have arrows at either end, because neither statement in either pair implies or provides support for the other statement; rather, the line without an arrow shows that these must be connected together to provide support for the conclusion A, and this support is shown by the arrow at the bottom of the line from B to A.

Let us now look at one more example.

> **Students who are caught cheating are always punished in a way that hurts them. Not all students who cheat are caught. However, students who cheat and are not caught are weakening their characters, and this hurts them as much as any punishment. So all students who cheat will be hurt.**

The component statements that are explicitly stated are as follows:

A. Students who are caught cheating are always punished in a way that hurts them.

B. Not all students who cheat are caught.

C. Students who cheat and are not caught are weakening their characters.

D. All persons whose character is weakened are hurt as much as by punishment.

E. All students who cheat will be hurt.

The meaning of B can be expressed more clearly and explicitly by the following sentence:

[B1]. Every student who cheats is either caught or is not caught.

The basic structure of the argument is displayed by the following diagram.

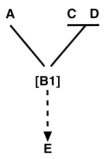

We might be tempted to diagram this argument in other possible ways. For example, the B1 premise could be placed before the other premises and the conclusion, or we might choose to leave B1 out completely. However, it should be intuitively apparent that this premise placed between the other premises and the conclusion provides a "glue" that ties the expressed premises together and connects them with the intended conclusion. If premise B1 is placed before the other premises, its function of tying them together with the conclusion is obscured. If B1 is left out, the argument is weakened considerably.

2.10 Analyzing Sample Arguments

Although logic can be studied as an abstract set of rules and procedures no more closely related to other aspects of human interest and activity than games such as chess or bridge, it does have useful applications, and we are concerned in this book to focus as much as possible on these applications. In addition to being useful in helping us to understand the logical structure of statements and to identify logical relations among two or more statements (as discussed in Chapter 1), logic is also useful for helping us to determine which sets of statements that are *asserted* to support or imply conclusions *in fact* provide absolute or partial support for the conclusion. We have now introduced enough basic concepts to be able to present a general preliminary procedure for analyzing arguments in the ordinary language sense as they appear in everyday contexts to determine whether they are good arguments in the formal logical sense.

Let us begin with a relatively simple example:

> **Susan should do well in this logic course, because she always does well in science courses.**

It is reasonable to interpret this sentence as asserting that the statement 'she always does well in science courses' supports in some way the apparent conclusion that 'Susan will do well in this logic course.' We should be able to see intuitively that the one statement does not imply the other, although it does seem to provide some support for it. As a second step in our analysis, therefore, let us see if there are any other statements that could be added as premises that might make this a valid argument. A likely candidate might be 'This logic course is a science course.' (*Webster's Twentieth Century Dictionary* defines 'logic' as 'the science of correct reasoning,' so this premise can reasonably be said to be well supported.) Adding this premise, the argument now reads:

> [This logic course is a science course.]
> Susan always does well in science courses.
> Therefore, Susan will do well in this logic course.

Although it is stronger than the original version, this argument is still not valid, as can be seen by considering what would happen if we were to add another premise, such as 'Susan is not taking this logic course.' If this statement were true, it would imply that the conclusion is false (since a person cannot do well in a course she is not taking), and by definition an argument for which it is possible to have true premises and a false conclusion is invalid. Thus, we should try to find at least one more premise that would make the argument stronger, and, we hope, make it valid. Stating explicitly that Susan is indeed taking this course (even though we don't know whether it is factually true or false) should make the argument *logically* stronger, so we will add it.

> [A]. [This logic course is a science course.]
>
> [B]. [Susan is taking this logic course.]

    C. **Susan always does well in science courses.**

    D. **Therefore, Susan will do well in this logic course.**

In this form, the argument is actually valid, but since we can't prove this now, we can only say that it appears to be quite strong. If we label the components of the argument as shown, we can display its relatively simple structure as follows:

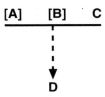

This is about as far as we can go in analyzing the original argument without using any of the techniques of formal logic to test the argument for validity. However, we could also have pursued the analysis along a somewhat different route.

    Instead of interpreting the sentence 'Susan always does well in science courses' in its broadest sense as applying to all courses—past, present, and future—that Susan might ever take, we could interpret it in the narrower sense as referring only to courses that Susan has taken in the past. Such a statement could be easily verified, whereas a statement about present and future courses could never be established as absolutely true (at least not until after Susan dies, in which case it would still be only about past courses that she has already taken). On this interpretation, the argument would now read:

    [A]. **[This logic course is a science course.]**

    [B]. **[Susan is taking this logic course.]**

    E. **Susan has always done well in science courses in the past.**

    D. **Therefore, Susan will do well in this logic course.**

In this form, the argument is now an inductive argument, but its third premise is more likely to be true than the third premise in the deductive version of this argument. We won't be able to evaluate its strength until we have studied the general principles of induction in Chapters 9 and 10.

    One other possible analysis of this example is worth noting. The addition of one more premise to the version just presented could turn that inductive argument into a deductive argument as follows:

    [A]. **[This logic course is a science course.]**

    [B]. **[Susan is taking this logic course.]**

    E. **Susan has always done well in science courses in the past.**

    [F]. **[If Susan has always done well in science courses in the past, she will always do well in them in the future.]**

    D. **Therefore, Susan will do well in this logic course.**

While the additional premise, [F], makes the argument logically stronger, the new argument is not necessarily "better," since the new premise is not at all obviously true, and in fact many people would say that its truth is doubtful indeed. This is another illustration of the general principle that most if not all inductive arguments can be changed into valid arguments with the addition of certain premises, but often at the cost of adding something whose truth is questionable.

The analyses given here are but three of many possible analyses that could be given of the same initial statements that constituted an intended argument. Each of the three is plausible, but it might be difficult to arrive at a consensus even among professional logicians as to which of them, if any, is/are more plausible or reasonable. Such a judgment depends in part on assumptions about the relative value of such things as induction versus deduction and true versus probable premises. No set of generally accepted formal criteria exists that can be appealed to if there is disagreement as to which of several analyses of an argument is "best." Such agreement, if it is to be attained at all, must be the result of open-minded discussion and negotiation among all of the parties.

Not only are many different analyses possible besides those given above, but these are only preliminary analyses. These analyses are only sufficient for preparing the original intended argument to be analyzed further, using the techniques of formal logic, to determine whether it is valid or inductively weak or strong. Although we can't explain this any further here, we return to this example in Chapter 14 to show some of the different kinds of formal analysis that could be done on it.

Let us look at a completely different kind of example to see that the basic method of logical analysis is essentially the same.

In October 1977, the World Health Organization announced that the last "natural" case of smallpox had been treated and declared that this highly infectious disease had been eliminated from the earth. In August 1978, Mrs. Janet Parker, an employee in the Medical School of Birmingham, England, died of what was diagnosed as smallpox. An investigation was launched immediately to try to determine how she had contracted this apparently extinct disease.

The investigators concluded that Mrs. Parker had been infected by a virus transmitted through the air from a laboratory in the building where she worked. Their conclusion was based on the following evidence: Medical examiners isolated the smallpox virus from Mrs. Parker's body and identified it as a strain known as 'Abid.' It was determined that stocks of this strain were being kept and studied in a laboratory directly below the office where Mrs. Parker worked. Although it had long been believed that the smallpox virus could not be transmitted by any means other than direct physical contact, one case occurred in 1970 in a German hospital where it was concluded that smallpox had been transmitted by airborne viruses. Thus, even though Mrs. Parker had no known physical contact with anyone from the lab in which the smallpox virus was being kept, it was considered possible that the virus could have been transmitted through the air to her office. Since no other possible source existed of the virus from which she died, the investigators were certain that it must have come from the lab beneath her office. The tragedy was compounded when the director of that lab committed suicide a short time later.

The argument representing the reasoning of the investigators in this case could be expressed as follows:

A. Mrs. Parker was infected with the 'Abid' strain of smallpox virus.

B. A quantity of the 'Abid' smallpox virus was being stored and studied in the lab directly below Mrs. Parker's office.

C. There was no possible source of the virus other than the downstairs lab.

D. Therefore, the source of the smallpox virus must have been the downstairs lab.

E. It is possible for smallpox virus to be transmitted through the air.

F. The virus was transmitted from the downstairs lab either by air or by a person or object from the lab.

G. Mrs. Parker had not been in contact with any person or object from the lab.

H. Therefore, Mrs. Parker must have been infected by a virus transmitted through the air from the downstairs lab.

The basic structure of this argument is shown in the following diagram:

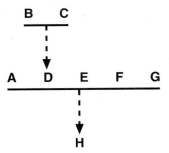

The argument in this form might appear intuitively to be valid. That is, it should be apparent that, if the premises are all true, then the conclusion must be true. In other words, no information could be added to the premises—other than an assertion that at least one of the premises is false—that would make it possible for the conclusion to be false.

It would not be implausible to extract a somewhat different argument from the same case. For example, consider the following version:

The medical examiner reported that Mrs. Parker was infected with the 'Abid' strain of smallpox virus.

A quantity of the 'Abid' strain of smallpox virus was being stored in the lab directly below Mrs. Parker's office.

Of all of the millions of cases of smallpox examined over the years, there was only one in which it appeared that the virus was transmitted through the air.

Mrs. Parker was not known to have been in contact with any person or object from the downstairs lab.

The investigators could find no other source of the 'Abid' virus than the downstairs lab.

Therefore, Mrs. Parker must have been infected by a virus transmitted through the air from the downstairs lab.

It should be apparent that on this interpretation the argument is not valid. Numerous premises could be added that would not challenge the truth of the given premises but that would make the conclusion false or at least doubtful. For example, Mrs. Parker might have been in physical contact with someone from the downstairs lab, even though the investigators had no knowledge of this. Or the medical examiner might have made a mistake. It would still be true that the medical examiner had diagnosed the case as one of 'Abid' smallpox, but it would be false that Mrs. Parker in fact had 'Abid' smallpox.

This kind of example helps us to see the extent to which our individual judgments affect the ways in which arguments are interpreted. It reminds us once again that almost every argument can be qualified to a greater or lesser degree in such a way as to make it deductive or inductive. Thus, all generalizations about the world can be formulated as assertions about the beliefs of specific individuals or groups. For example, we can choose to formulate the third premise in the smallpox argument to say something about the transmittability of the virus through the air, but we can also formulate it as a statement describing the beliefs of medical experts.

Rather than pursue the theoretical limits of analysis of these examples, let us do a partial preliminary analysis of one more complex example, turning to the argument raised by Edwin A. Roberts, Jr.

The apparent conclusion of Roberts' argument is that resort motel operators are among the ten greatest liars. However, since nothing is said about how the comparison is made between resort motel operators and other groups concerning their reliability, no support seems to be given for the conclusion in this form. Reconsideration of this example might lead us to suspect that the reference to the "List of the 10 Greatest Liars" is a literary or rhetorical device that should not be taken literally. On this interpretation, the conclusion would read something like 'Resort motel operators lie a lot about their business.' Taking the statements presented that are relevant to this conclusion, we have the following:

A. All of the resort motel operators interviewed in one Florida town said that their business was fine.

B. The parking lots of these motels were practically empty.

C. The local bank reported that it had cashed many fewer travelers' checks than in the previous year.

D. Therefore, resort motel operators lie a lot about their business.

To have a valid deductive argument, we must add a number of presumably suppressed premises. The following version is more complete but still not valid.

Mainstreams

. . . Thoughts on the 10 Greatest Liars

By Edwin A. Roberts, Jr.

It fell to me the other week, in connection with a story assignment, to ask a dozen or so motel operators in a Florida town how business was. They all said business was just fine, the gasoline shortage wasn't hurting them at all, and if they were making any more money the local bank couldn't accommodate their deposits.

Oddly under such happy circumstances, the motel parking lots were practically empty. So I asked an officer of the local bank how the cashing of travelers' checks this year compared to last. As a matter of fact, said the banker, such check cashings were "way below" 1973. This information suggested that the motel operators

---

Comment

---

were dissembling, and so I am putting motel owners in resort towns on my list of The 10 Greatest Liars.

National Observer, April 6, 1974.

A. All of the resort motel operators interviewed in one Florida town said that their business was fine.

B. The parking lots of these motels were practically empty.

C. The local bank reported that it had cashed many fewer travelers checks than in the previous year.

[E]. If a motel's parking lot is almost empty, then the motel's business is not good.

[F]. If the local bank cashed many fewer travelers' checks than in the previous year, then there must not be many travelers.

[G]. Therefore, there are not many travelers.

[H]. If there are not many travelers, then the motels' business is not good.

[I]. Therefore, the motels' business is not good.

[J]. Anyone who says business is good when it is not is lying.

[K]. Therefore, all of the motel operators interviewed in one Florida town were lying.

[L]. If all of the resort motel operators interviewed in one Florida town lied about their business, then all resort motel operators lie about their business.

D. Therefore, all resort motel operators lie about their business.

The diagram of the basic structure of this argument is quite complex when compared to the other diagrams we have drawn up to this point, but it is still relatively simple in comparison with many arguments that we encounter in everyday situations. As indicated by the 'therefores' included in the list of added statements, this argument has a number of subarguments, the conclusion of each of which becomes a premise of a subsequent argument in the chain of reasoning. One of these subconclusions is also supported by two separate sub-arguments as shown in the diagram.

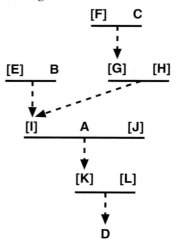

Making all these premises explicit, or supplying all of the premises necessary to make the argument valid, brings out some new difficulties. One difficulty is that it is no longer entirely clear what the conclusion asserts. Does it say that all (that is, each and every one) of the resort motel owners in the country (or world) are liars, or only that as a group they are liars? Certainly it is a very strong claim that all of them are liars. To apply the principle of charity to this example, it would probably be fair to interpret the conclusion as referring to resort motel owners as a group rather than as individuals.

One other direction in which an analysis of this example could go is worth mentioning. Up to this point we have been interpreting the sentence expressing the intended conclusion more or less literally. This might not, however, be a fair reading of the intentions of the author. The sentence, 'I am putting motel owners in resort towns on my List of the 10 Greatest Liars' might instead be read as a recommendation or command, similar to that expressed by a sentence like 'Take statements by motel owners in resort towns with a grain of salt,' or 'Don't always believe everything you are told by motel owners in resort towns.' Such an interpretation would put this argument outside the scope of the methods of formal logical analysis to be discussed in this book, although it could still be further analyzed using other methods. It certainly would not be unreasonable to take this as the most plausible interpretation, even though we would not be able to deal with it further in this book. However, we shall still consider the alternative interpretations as not unreasonable, so we can use this example to illustrate certain features of the various systems of logic to be presented in later chapters.

2.11 Some Basic Elements of Argument Analysis

The following listing of factors to be considered in the analysis and evaluation of arguments is in no way intended to be complete either in substance or in detail. These are at most some of the more important and significant factors, and it must be recognized that many other factors are more or less relevant to the evaluation of particular arguments. It is also hoped that the preceding discussion of the sample arguments has made it clear that a simple task description does not always mean that the task is simple. For example, it is easy to stipulate that the main conclusion should be identified and clearly and precisely formulated; it is all too often the case in dealing with actual arguments that this can be a very lengthy and complex task. In part, this complexity is the result of the requirement to adhere to the principle of charity, that is, to always try to interpret and formulate an argument in its strongest possible form. Since the strength of an argument is a function of the relationship between the premises and the conclusion, we cannot really know which formulation of a conclusion will make an argument stronger or weaker unless we already have some idea what the premises are. This also serves, therefore, as a reminder that the following list should not be understood to represent any kind of a fixed, necessary order for considering the specified factors. In actual practice it is not uncommon and often is even necessary to consider several factors simultaneously and to go from one to another and then back again to the first in some kind of cyclic pattern. With these disclaimers and warnings, we now present the following list of significant factors in the analysis and evaluation of arguments.

Guidelines for Analyzing Arguments

1. Identify and reformulate as necessary the main conclusion of the argument.
2. Identify and reformulate as necessary the premises of the argument, making explicit any implicit premises.
3. Determine whether the argument is most appropriately and strongly formulated in an inductive or deductive form.
4. Identify and evaluate (using these same procedures) any subarguments offered in support of premises.
5. Test the main argument for validity or inductive strength.
6. Identify the different kinds of premises, that is, those that are definitions, those that are statements of scientific fact or theory, metaphysical theory, ethical theory, and so on.
7. Determine the degree of truth or plausibility of each of the premises.

EXERCISE 2–12

Identify the conclusion in each of the following intended arguments and specify all explicitly stated premises. Add whatever premises you think are necessary to put the argument into its strongest form—whether inductive or deductive. Diagram the basic structure of the argument. Compare your analyses with those of other students in your class. Save these analyses! You will need to use them later.

1. We are here to claim our rights as women, not only to be free, but to fight for freedom. It is our privilege, as well as our pride and our joy, to take some part in this militant movement, which, as we believe, means the regeneration of all humanity. Nothing but contempt is due to those people who ask us to submit to unmerited oppression. We shall not do it. (Christabel Pankhurst)

2. An aggressive war is the great crime against everything good in the world. A defensive war, that must necessarily turn to aggressive at the earliest moment, is the necessary great counter-crime. But never think that war, no matter how necessary, nor how justified, is not a crime. Ask the infantry and ask the dead. (Ernest Hemingway)

3. If I were a factory employee, a working man on the railroads, or a wage earner of any sort, I would undoubtedly join the union of my trade. If I disapproved of its policy, I would join in order to fight that policy; if the union leaders were dishonest, I would join in order to put them out. I believe in the union and I believe that all men who are benefitted by the union are morally bound to help to the extent of their powers in the common interests advanced by the union. (Theodore Roosevelt)

4. Our government rests on public opinion. Whoever can change public opinion can change the government practically as such. (Abraham Lincoln)

5. From this arises the question whether it is better to be loved rather than feared, or feared rather than loved. It might perhaps be answered that we should wish to be both; but since love and fear can hardly exist together, if we must choose between them, it is far safer to be feared than loved. (Niccolo Machiavelli)

6. I would like to see the proletariat rule for a while. . . . Through all the past this world has been ruled by property, and if there can ever come a time when the working man can rule it, I will say he ought to have that chance to see what he can do; and yet to tell you that is to believe in the "dictatorship of the proletariat"—well, why not? (Clarence Darrow)

7. All amassing of wealth or hoarding of wealth above and beyond one's legitimate needs is theft. There would be no occasion for theft and no thieves if there were wise regulations of wealth, and social justice. (Mohandas Karamchana Gandhi)

8. All censorships exist to prevent any one from challenging current conceptions and existing institutions. All progress is initiated by challenging current conceptions, and executed by supplanting existing institutions. Consequently the first condition of progress is the removal of censorships. (George Bernard Shaw)

9. There are but three ways for the populace to escape its wretched lot. The first two are by the route of the wine-shop or the church; the third is by that of the social revolution. (Mikhail A. Bakunin)

10. The root problem is very simply stated: if there were no sovereign independent states, if the states of the civilized world were organized in some sort of federalism as the states of the American Union, for instance, are organized, there would be no international war as we know it. . . . (Sir Norman Angell)

11. Freedom is not worth fighting for if it means no more than license for everyone to get as much as he can for himself. And freedom is worth fighting for. Because it does mean more than unrestricted grabbing. (Dorothy Canfield Fisher)

12. There is no safety where there is no strength; no strength without Union; no Union without justice; no justice where faith and truth are wanting. The right to be free is a truth planted in the hearts of men. (William Lloyd Garrison)

13. Marx predicted that the great industrial countries would be the first to advance, or collapse, into communistic socialism. His success as an economist in Russia was, in effect, his annihilation as a prophet. (Gilbert Seldes)

14. No reform, moral or intellectual, ever came from the upper class of society. Each and all came from the protest of martyr and victim. The emancipation of the working people must be achieved by the working people themselves. (Wendell Phillips)

15. Conventionality is not morality. Self-righteousness is not religion. To attack the first is not to assail the last. (Charlotte Brontë)

16. The truth is, as everyone knows, that the great artists of the world are never puritans, and seldom even ordinarily respectable. No virtuous man— that is, virtuous in the YMCA sense—has ever painted a picture worth looking at, or written a symphony worth hearing, or a book worth reading, and it is highly improbable that the thing has ever been done by a virtuous woman. (H. L. Mencken)

17. The dictum that truth always triumphs over persecution is one of those pleasant falsehoods which men repeat after one another till they pass into commonplaces, but which all experience refutes. History teems with instances of truth put down by persecution. If not suppressed forever, it may be thrown back for centuries. (John Stuart Mill)

18. The Industrial Union grasps the principle: "No Government, no organization; no organization, no cooperative labor; no cooperative labor, no abundance for all without arduous toil, hence, no freedom." (Daniel DeLeon)

19. The chief end of man is to frame general propositions and no general proposition is worth a damn. (Oliver Wendell Holmes)

20. It is proof of a base and low mind for one to wish to think with the masses or majority, merely because the majority is the majority. Truth does not change because it is, or is not, believed by a majority of the people. (Giordano Bruno)

EXERCISE 2–13

Return to the arguments that you analyzed in Exercise I–5 of the Introduction and reanalyze them according to the instructions in Exercise 2–12. Compare your new analyses with those you did originally in the Introduction to determine the extent to which the concepts of logic that you learned in Chapters 1 and 2 have enabled you to make more sophisticated analyses. Save all of these answers for comparison with analyses you will be asked to do later.

Summary

1. In the context of logic, an **argument** is defined as a set of statements that is such that one of them (the **conclusion**) is supported or implied by the others (the **premises**). Although an argument is quite distinct from the psychological process (known as **inference**) of moving from one thought to another, an argument can be constructed that corresponds to every good inference. Not all sets of statements that are asserted or intended to be arguments are in fact arguments; that is, the apparent premises do not provide any actual support for the conclusion.

2. Every argument or intended argument by definition contains one and only one conclusion, but it can have any number of premises. Words such as 'since,' 'because,' 'for,' and 'given that' indicate that the statement that follows is intended as a premise. Identification of a conclusion might be facilitated by the presence of conclusion indicators such as 'therefore,' 'hence,' and 'it can be inferred.' In the absence of such **indicator words,** the function of a statement in a given argument often must be determined from its contextual use, since conclusion and premise statements in themselves are not inherently different (a conclusion in one argument might serve as a premise in another), nor do they occupy fixed positions in an argument (a conclusion might precede, follow, or come between premises).

3. Intended arguments might be difficult to identify for several reasons. A series of statements might be asserted as true but might not offer a conclusion or

provide support for any other statement. Indicator words are sometimes present when no argument is intended, or they might serve functions other than that of signifying the logical relationship between a given set of statements. We are then obliged to search for other linguistic clues or to examine the context in order to determine whether an argument is intended or not.

4. It is possible that a series of statements intended as an argument might lack a conclusion and/or one or more premises but would qualify as an argument if the missing propositions were supplied. **Enthymemes,** as such intended arguments are called, might strongly imply a certain conclusion or they might take for granted that the missing premises are already known by the intended audience. In such cases, we are justified in providing the missing statements, as long as we apply the **principle of charity,** that stipulates that whatever statements we add to the argument should make the argument as good as possible.

5. There are two types of argument: deductive and inductive. In a **deductive** (or **valid**) argument, the premises provide absolute support for the conclusion, whether or not they themselves are true. That is, *if* the premises were true, the conclusion would necessarily be true. The validity of an argument, therefore, can be evaluated on the basis of its logical form, rather than its content. An argument that is not deductive must be inductive. The premises of an **inductive** argument provide some, but not absolute, support for the conclusion. A set of statements asserted or intended as a deductive argument might in fact be inductive (or not an argument at all) and vice versa.

6. In order to qualify as a good argument of its type, a deductive argument must be **sound,** that is, the truth of all its premises must be well established. However, since determining the truth value of a given proposition often requires specialized knowledge of a subject, the logician is primarily concerned with evaluating the validity, rather than the soundness, of an argument. A good deductive argument is *not* **circular:** its premises imply (and thus in effect contain) the conclusion, but its conclusion does not simply give an alternate wording of a statement that has already been expressed in the premises.

7. Soundness, validity, and other absolute terms cannot be used in evaluating an inductive argument. In determining whether or not such an argument is good, we must consider the truth of its premises and the probability of its conclusion. We can say that an inductive argument is strong (or weak) if, compared with all possible arguments that could be given in support of its conclusion, this particular argument is stronger (or weaker) than most. Unlike a deductive argument, an inductive argument can be strengthened or weakened by additional information.

8. In dealing with enthymemes (intended arguments with one or more statements implicit), it is usually possible to add statements that will result in a

valid (but possibly not sound) argument and also to add different statements that will make it a (strong or weak) inductive argument.

9. Many factors must be considered in analyzing intended arguments in everyday contexts, including identifying and reformulating the premises and conclusion, identifying and evaluating subarguments, and testing for validity or inductive strength.

Chapter 3

Aristotelian Logic: Statements

We noted in the Introduction that we can introduce in this book only a few of the many different systems of logic that have been developed over the years. The system of logic we discuss in this chapter and the next is significant not only because it was developed as the first comprehensive system more than 2,000 years ago, but also because it is still a useful system for analyzing a certain type of statements and arguments—even in comparison to most of the more "modern" theories!

This system is named after the Greek philosopher Aristotle (384–322 B.C.) who originally formalized it. It was for all practical purposes the only system of formal logic in the Western world for more than two thousand years. Certainly most of the systems of logic developed in the twentieth century are more powerful and sophisticated, but Aristotelian logic is still as good or even better than any of these systems for dealing with certain kinds of statements and arguments because it is easier to use. It is a generally accurate rule of thumb that there is a direct correlation between the power of a logical system and its complexity and difficulty; in other words, the more powerful and sophisticated a logical system is, the harder it is to use.

The ease of use of Aristotelian logic results from its being restricted to only one basic type of statement. The main limitation of Aristotelian logic is that it can deal only with the special class of statements known as categorical statements.

Aristotle

3.1 Categorical Statements

All statements can be expressed by sentences consisting at least of subject and predicate terms. In the sentence 'Tom will do well in logic,' 'Tom' is the subject term and 'will do well in logic' is the predicate term. It is possible to interpret any declarative sentence with a subject and predicate as expressing a relation between two classes of objects—one class named by the subject term and the other class designated by the predicate term. In our example, the subject term 'Tom' can be interpreted as naming the class that has as its only member the person Tom, and the predicate term refers to the class consisting of all of the people who will do well in logic. To take another example, the sentence 'All students are intelligent' expresses a relation between the members of the class of students and the members of the class of intelligent beings.

Classes of things can be related to each other in several ways, and categorical statements clearly distinguish these kinds of relationships. The statement expressed by the sentence 'All human beings are primates' asserts that all the members of the class of human beings are *included in* the class of primates. The statement 'No politicians are honest persons' asserts that all members of the class of things referred to by the subject term 'politicians' are *excluded from* the class of things referred to by the predicate term 'honest persons.' Both these statements make assertions about *all* members of the class referred to by the subject term and their inclusion in or exclusion from the class referred to by the predicate term. Categorical statements can also make assertions about *some* of the members of the class referred to by the subject term and their inclusion in or exclusion from the predicate class. For instance, the statement 'Some persons in this room are politicians' asserts that some of the members of the class of persons in this room are included in the class of politicians. Likewise, the statement 'Some persons in this room are not honest persons' excludes some of the members of the class of persons in this room from the class of honest persons.

Categorical propositions are *statements that assert that some or all of the class of things named by the subject term are included in or excluded from the class of things named by the predicate term.* For reasons that will be presented later, we also stipulate that *the class referred to by the subject term must contain at least one member* for a statement to qualify as categorical. According to this additional criterion, the sentence 'Gremlins are never more than four feet tall' does not express a categorical statement, since the class of gremlins has no members. Similarly, 'Pegasus is a flying horse' does not express a categorical statement because Pegasus does not and never has existed. It is important not to confuse such things as pictures or ideas of gremlins with the members of the class of gremlins. The class of gremlins has no members, but the class of pictures of gremlins does have members, as does the class of ideas of gremlins.

3.1.1 Quality

Each categorical proposition is said to possess a certain **quality,** the characteristic of asserting that some or all of the members of the subject class are included in or excluded from the predicate class. When a statement asserts that all or part of the subject class are *included* in the predicate class, it is said to be **affirmative** in quality. For instance, the statements 'All students are hard workers' and 'Some singers are dancers' are affirmative categorical statements. Categorical statements that assert that all or part of the subject class are *excluded* from the predicate class are said to be **negative** in quality. Categorical statements such as 'No birds are mammals' and 'Some paintings are not works of art' are negative.

3.1.2 Quantity

Categorical statements or propositions also are said to possess **quantity**; they refer to all or some of the members of the subject class. Terms such as 'all,' 'some,' 'few,' 'every,' and 'none' *indicate the quantity of a categorical statement* and are, for this reason, called **quantifiers**. Categorical statements that refer to all the members of the subject class are said to be **universal** in quantity. Statements such as 'All professors are college graduates' and 'No murderers are decent human beings' are examples of universal categorical statements.

Categorical statements that *only make assertions about some of the members of the subject class*—for instance, 'Some corporation executives are embezzlers' and 'Many first novels are not good'—are called **particular** categorical statements. The term 'some' in ordinary discourse is sometimes used as a synonym for 'several' and sometimes implies 'not all.' However, in logic, 'some' is always interpreted to mean 'at least one,' and it does not exclude the possibility that the subject of the statement might refer to the entire class. In logic, the statement expressed by the sentence 'Some officers of the student government are women' does not imply that some officers of the student government are not women; some might be men, but it is also possible that all are women. The particular statement only asserts that at least one member of the class of officers of the student government is a woman; it could be that two, three, or more of them are women.

To understand this more clearly, let us consider a class that contains exactly five members—Sam, Mary, Pat, Ed, and Kay. We will give this class the name 'quint.' Any time we state 'All members of the class quint are students,' we mean that Sam, Mary, Pat, Ed, and Kay are each students. Thus, 'All members of the class quint are students' is true only if Sam is a student and Mary is a student and Pat is a student and Ed is a student and Kay is a student. If any one of the five is not a student, then 'All members of the class quint are students' is false. Likewise, 'No members of the class quint are students' is true only in the event that none of the five members of the class is a student, that is, if neither Sam nor Mary nor Pat nor Ed nor Kay is a student.

But what does it mean to say 'Some members of the class quint are students'? It means that *at least one* of the five is a student. That is, if any one of the five members of the class quint is a student, 'Some members of the class quint are students' is true. And the statement will also be true if two members of the class quint are students, if three are students, if four are students, and even if all five are students. In other words, even if all of the members of the class quint are students, it is still true that at least one member is a student.

Similarly, when we say 'Some members of the class quint are not students,' this means that at least one member of the class quint is not a student. This statement would be true even in the extreme case in which no members of the class quint are students. It is false only in the case in which all five members of the class are students.

The following diagram displays the meanings of the categorical quantifiers 'all,' 'no,' and 'some' as they are interpreted in Aristotelian logic.

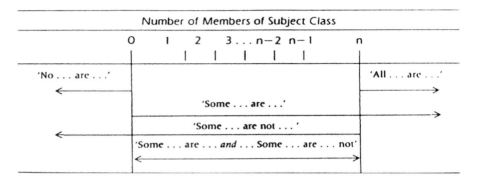

Statements about one individual person or thing—such as 'Jonathan got into a terrible mess today' or 'Greenland is not a nice place to live'—are called singular statements. The subject of a sentence expressing a singular statement may be a proper name, such as 'Jonathan' or 'Greenland,' or it may be a descriptive phrase, such as 'the present mayor of Chicago' or 'this five-dollar bill'; the point to be emphasized is that the subject term makes reference to exactly one individual entity. Logicians have developed a variety of ways to deal with such statements.

While working in the context of Aristotelian logic, we shall interpret a **singular statement** as *a universal statement that asserts that the only member of the one-member class named by the subject is included in or excluded from the predicate class.* The statement 'Jonathan did his logic assignment today' asserts that the class whose only member is Jonathan is included in the predicate class named by 'those who did their logic assignment today,' a class that might have a good many members. On the other hand, in the statement 'Greenland is not a nice place to live,' the subject class whose only member is Greenland is excluded from the predicate class of nice places to live. It is important to remember that since the subjects of singular statements are to be interpreted as referring to all members of single-member classes, these statements are treated in this chapter (and the next) as universal statements.

Singular terms generally should not appear in the predicate of a categorial proposition; they only appear as naming the subject class. Sometimes sentences expressing categorical propositions do contain a singular term or expression in the predicate position, but such sentences can always be rewritten so that the singular term is in the subject position. For example,

The best player on the team is Pat.

can be rewritten so that the singular term 'Pat' appears in the subject position, namely

Pat is the best player on the team.

3.1.3 The Four Types of Categorical Proposition

Categorical statements can be either affirmative or negative in quality and particular or universal in quantity. These characteristics of quality and quantity can be combined to form four different types of categorical statements or propositions, as shown in Table 3–1.

Table 3–1

Quality \ Quantity	Universal (Including Singular)	Particular
Affirmative	Universal Affirmative **A**	Particular Affirmative **I**
Negative	Universal Negative **E**	Particular Negative **O**

Universal affirmative statements, also called **A statements,** affirm that all members of the subject class are included in the predicate class. The following are examples of sentences that can be used to express universal affirmative statements:

Everyone in the room heard the piercing scream.
All rises in prices are due to increased manufacturing costs.
My cat, Dolly, will eat nothing but fish.

Particular affirmative statements, also known as **I statements,** affirm that at least one member of the subject class is included in the predicate class, as in the following examples:

Some professors are inclined to play politics.
Half of the households surveyed own a pickup truck.
Many students at this university live at home.

Universal negative statements, or **E statements,** affirm that all members of the subject class are excluded from the predicate class. The following are examples of sentences that can be used to express universal negative statements:

None of the candidates for mayor had campaigned before.
Marcia is not in the best of spirits this morning.
Mammals never have feathers.

Particular negative statements, or **O statements,** affirm that at least one member of the subject class is excluded from the predicate class, as in the following examples:

Most women are not willing to accept inequality with men.
Some vegetarians do not eat eggs.
Nearly all the students in my dorm do not sleep eight hours.

EXERCISE 3–1

Indicate whether each of the following sentences expresses an **A, E, I,** or **O** statement.

1. All typewriters are noisy.
2. Some doctors are surgeons.
3. Some dodos are not extinct.
4. No newspapers are red.
5. Some Toyotas get thirty miles to the gallon.
6. All triangles have three sides.
7. Yon Cassius has a lean and hungry look.
8. No guitar has more than twelve strings.
9. Some cars do not have pollution-control devices.
10. Some Italians are Neapolitans.
11. No one is an island.
12. All seals have a smooth coat of fur.
13. No seals have a smooth coat of fur.
14. Some dolphins are not cetaceans.
15. Nobody waved good-by.

3.1.4 Standard-Form Sentences

The examples of the four types of categorical statement show that each type can be expressed in a variety of ways. In 'Everyone in the room heard the piercing scream,' 'everyone' refers to all members of the class of persons-in-the-room, just as 'all' in the statement 'All rises in prices are due to increased manufacturing costs' refers to all members of the class of rises-in-prices. Also, we have stipulated that singular statements, such as 'My cat, Dolly, will eat nothing but fish,' are to be treated as universal categorical statements that refer to all members of a class containing exactly one member. These are only some of the many ways in which universal affirmative statements are expressed in ordinary language. And there is as much variety in the other three types of categorical statement, as the examples show.

In compliance with the well-known principle known as KISS (Keep It Simple Stupid), logicians have agreed to use a single form of sentence to express each of the four different types of categorical statement. Categorical statements are easier to work with when each type is always expressed by what is known as its **standard-form sentence**.

A standard-form sentence must

1. begin with one of the three quantifiers—'all,' 'no,' or 'some';
2. have a noun, qualified noun (e.g., 'carnivorous animals'), or noun phrase (e.g., 'rises in prices') as its subject and as its predicate; and
3. have as its principal verb a present-tense form of the verb 'to be' (which is referred to in logic as the copula).

   A sentence that does not satisfy all of these requirements must be put into this form in order to be treated in syllogistic logic.

The following are examples of standard-form sentences expressing the four types of categorical statement:

A—**All cats are carnivorous animals.**

E—**No cats are carnivorous animals.**

I—**Some cats are carnivorous animals.**

O—**Some cats are not carnivorous animals.**

Standard-form sentences expressing universal affirmative or **A** statements can be referred to as **A sentences.** Similarly, standard-form sentences expressing **E, I,** and **O** propositions will be referred to as **E, I,** and **O sentences,** respectively.

When translating ordinary sentences into standard form, one should be particularly careful to make certain that the predicate term is translated into a noun or noun clause. Frequently, ordinary-language sentences containing predicate terms expressed by adjectives are mistakenly assumed to be in standard form. For example, on superficial examination the **A** sentence 'All Republicans are conservative' may seem to be in standard form, but in fact it is not, because the predicate term is an adjective, not a noun. This sentence can be translated into standard form as 'All Republicans are conservative persons' or 'All Republicans are persons who are conservative.' Likewise, when dealing with ordinary-language sentences that contain predicate terms consisting of verb phrases, one might be tempted to think they are in standard form. Consider the following examples:

Original: **All 1960 Bentleys are still running.**
Standard-form: **All 1960 Bentleys are autos that are still running.**

Original: **All students are studying.**
Standard-form: **All students are persons who are studying.**

Notice, too, that it is possible to construct noun phrases in many ways when translating sentences into standard form. For example, the last sentence, 'All students are studying,' might have been translated as 'All students are things that are studying' or as 'All students are animals that are studying.' All these translations are correct, but when dealing with an argument in which several sentences express categorical statements, it is important to make certain that the translation is the same throughout.

For reasons that will soon become clear, it is also generally advisable to avoid having a negation embedded inside a complex subject or predicate term. For example, it is tempting to translate the sentence 'All humans are featherless' as the **A** proposition 'All humans are things that do not have feathers.' However, the 'not' in the middle of the predicate term could cause serious problems. So it is best to get it out of the predicate by translating the sentence as the logically equivalent **E** statement 'No humans are things that have feathers.'

EXERCISE 3–2

As necessary, translate the sentences in Exercise 3–1 into standard form.

3.2 Abbreviations

As in everyday writing, it is often useful in logic to use abbreviations whenever possible, rather than write out entire words and clauses again and again when this is not necessary. Logicians have developed a variety of standard abbreviations. In this chapter and the next, we are particularly concerned with abbreviating subject and predicate terms in sentences expressing categorical propositions. We use the convention that such sentences can be **abbreviated** by replacing the subject and predicate terms with capitals of the first letter of one of the principal words in each term. Thus, 'All required courses are introductory surveys' can be abbreviated 'All C are S,' in which 'C' stands for 'required courses,' and 'S' stands for 'introductory surveys.'

Of course, it is possible for the key words in the subject and predicate terms to begin with the same letter, causing some problems in abbreviating the sentence. For instance, the **A** sentence expressing the universal affirmative statement 'All cats are carnivores' could theoretically be abbreviated 'All C are C.' To avoid the obvious confusion that might result from such an abbreviation, we follow the basic rule that words with two different meanings should not be abbreviated by the same letter. Several alternative kinds of abbreviation can be used when one is confronted with such cases. One possibility is to use more than one letter from a given word; for example, the preceding **A** sentence can be abbreviated 'All C are Car.' Another possibility is to use a letter other than the first to represent the term. Thus, the sentence 'All cats are carnivores' might be abbreviated as 'All C are V,' where 'V' represents the term 'carnivores.' One should use common sense when faced with such abbreviating problems.

Whenever abbreviating sentences, one should provide a "dictionary" indicating the term that a particular letter represents. One handy method is to underscore the letter or letters being used to represent the term as it appears in the actual statement. For example, in the **A** sentence, 'All licensed doctors are medical school graduates,' the letters 'd' in 'doctor' and 'm' in 'medical' are underscored to indicate that they will be used to represent these terms in the abbreviation 'All D are M.' Such a convention is particularly helpful when abbreviating troublesome sentences such as 'All Persians are procrastinators.' In this case, by underscoring the 'P' in 'Persians' and the 'c' in 'procrastinators,' we can abbreviate the sentence as 'All P are C' and avoid confusion. This convention is used throughout this book.

3.3 Schemas

Each type of categorical statement also has its own **schema**, which is *used to exhibit its logical form*. The schema of a proposition is formed by replacing both the subject and predicate terms in its standard-form sentence with blanks. Thus, for example, the schema for universal affirmative statements is

> All _____ are ....

This notation is somewhat awkward and lengthy, so we use symbols to represent the blanks rather than using blanks themselves. We indicate the subject term blank with an 'S' and the predicate term blank with a 'P.'

> **All S are P.**

The lines under the letters indicate that these letters are not being used to abbreviate a particular subject or predicate term.

This is a very important distinction! Abbreviations and schemas are two quite different things. An abbreviation is a shortened sentence, and thus abbreviations express statements that are true or false just as the original sentences do. However, schemata are not shortened sentences and consequently do not express statements; schemata only display the logical form of statements. The underscored letters only represent blanks into which any noun or noun phrase can be placed to form a sentence. The single schema for a given type of proposition will fit any proposition of that type expressed in standard sentence form. Any nouns (or noun phrases) can be inserted into the blanks of a schema. Once terms have been placed into the blanks in a schema, it is no longer a schema; it is now a sentence expressing a specific statement.

3.3.1 Universal Affirmative Statements

The following are examples of standard-form sentences used to express **A** or universal affirmative statements:

> **All drugs are complex organic compounds.**
> **All required courses are introductory surveys.**

It is quite easy to recognize a sentence expressing a universal affirmative statement if it is in standard form. It is more difficult to recognize such a sentence in everyday situations when it is not in standard form, and it is not always easy to convert a sentence from nonstandard form into standard form, even when we know that it expresses an **A** statement. It requires some thought and practice to develop a facility for translating ordinary sentences into standard-form sentences. Consider the following examples:

> Original: **Every actor in the play is well chosen for the part.**
> Standard-form: **All actors in the play are people well-chosen for their parts.**
> Abbreviation: **All A are W.**

> Original: **Anyone who is late for work will be demoted.**
> Standard-form: **All persons who are late for work are persons who will be demoted.**
> Abbreviation: **All L are D.**

Sentences expressing *singular* affirmative statements also are translated as universal affirmatives. Singular propositions can be abbreviated in the normal way, beginning with the quantifier 'All.' For example:

> Original: **Prudence believes in extrasensory perception.**
> Standard-form: **All persons who are members of the class of which Prudence is the only member are persons who believe in extrasensory perception.**

However, singular affirmative statements are often easy to work with as they stand. For our purposes, we stipulate that such sentences can be written with the simpler form for the subject term, such as 'Prudence is a person who believes in extrasensory perception.'

The sentence 'Logic students argue with facility' lacks a quantifier, and it is not clear whether the subject term refers to all or some members of the subject class. Usually the context in which such a sentence is found tells us whether it is expressing an **I** statement or an **A** statement. When the context provides no clues, one should use the weaker interpretation. In this case, the **I** sentence, which refers to some of the students, is weaker than the **A** sentence, which refers to all of them. Thus, provided that no contextual clues indicate otherwise, the sentence 'Logic students argue with facility' should be translated as follows:

Original: **Logic students argue with facility.**
Standard-form: **Some logic students are people who argue with facility.**
Abbreviation: **Some L are A.**

It is also generally advisable to avoid having a negation embedded inside a complex subject or predicate term. Thus, sentences that might appear at first to be expressing **A** statements, such as 'All humans are featherless,' are best translated as **E** statements, e.g., 'No humans are things that have feathers.'

3.3.2 Universal Negative Statements

The following are examples of standard-form sentences used to express universal negative statements or **E** statements:

No courses numbered 300 or above are courses open to freshmen.
No employees who work here are commuters.

Every standard-form **E** sentence begins with the term 'No,' has a subject and a predicate consisting of a noun, qualified noun, or noun phrase, and contains a present-tense form of the verb 'to be,' its copula. Each sentence should be interpreted as expressing a universal negative statement, affirming that all the members of the subject class are excluded from the predicate class.

The standard-form **E** sentence 'No employees who work here are commuters' may be abbreviated as 'No E are C.' As with universal affirmative statements, universal negative statements, or **E** propositions, have a schema that can be shown in one of two ways:

No _____ are ....
            or
No S are P.

It is important to remember that the 'S' and 'P' represent blanks and are not abbreviations for specific nouns or noun phrases. When nouns or noun phrases are substituted in both blanks, the schema becomes a sentence.

Translation of ordinary English sentences into standard-form **E** sentences must be done carefully so that the meaning is not changed. For example, a person is likely to interpret a sentence such as 'Employees who work here are not commuters' as expressing a universal negative statement. However, the correctness of this interpretation depends on the context. Notice that the quantity of the subject is not clearly specified. The sentence could express either the **E** statement 'No employees who work here are commuters' or the **O** statement 'Some employees who work here are not commuters.'

Likewise the sentence 'All students are not lazy persons' at first might appear to express a universal negative statement. With a little thought, however, it should be clear that this sentence is not necessarily expressing the statement 'No students are lazy persons.' More likely, the sentence is expressing the **O** statement 'Some students are not lazy.' Here again, the context in which the sentence is used will be the important factor in determining what statement is being expressed. If the context gives no adequate clues, we must interpret it in the weakest sense, that is, as a particular statement. In general, sentences with the form

> All _____ are not ....

should be translated into standard-form sentences expressing **O** statements unless the context clearly indicates otherwise. Thus, the sentence 'All students are not religious' should be translated into the **O** sentence 'Some students are not religious persons,' when sufficient contextual information is not available to justify any stronger interpretation. *Never use "All _____ are not .... " sentences for expressing your own thoughts*, unless you intend to be ambiguous or confusing.

Sentences expressing singular negative statements should be translated into **E** sentences, since we have chosen to interpret them as affirming that the only member of a one-member class named by the subject term is excluded from the class named by the predicate term. As with sentences expressing singular affirmative statements, sentences expressing singular negative statements usually present no significant translation or abbreviation problems. We again permit them to be abbreviated without the quantifier. For example:

> Original: **This is not a universal affirmative statement.**
> Standard-form: **No statements that are members of the class of which**
>   **this statement is the only member are universal affirmative statements.**
>   *or*
> **This statement is not a universal affirmative statement.**
> Abbreviation: **No S are U.**

3.3.3 Particular Affirmative Statements

The following particular affirmative statements are expressed by standard-form sentences, or **I** sentences:

> **Some affirmative statements are particular statements.**
> **Some facial expressions are signs of emotions.**
> **Some floods are disasters that cause much human suffering.**

Each of these **I** sentences begins with the quantifier 'some,' has a subject and predicate consisting of a noun, qualified noun, or noun phrase, and contains a form of the verb 'to be.' Each sentence should be interpreted as expressing an **I** statement, or proposition that affirms the inclusion of part of the subject class in the predicate class. The method for abbreviating standard-form **I** sentences is the same as that for **A** and **O** sentences. Thus, the sentence 'Some affirmative statements are particular statements' may be abbreviated as 'Some A are P.' All particular affirmative statements have the following schema:

Some _____ are ....
                   or
Some S̲ are P̲.

Just as with **A** and **E** sentences, one must be careful when translating ordinary sentences into standard **I** form.

Original: **Students were among those joining in the festivities.**
Standard-form: **Some s̲tudents are people who joined in the f̲estivities.**
Abbreviation: **Some S are F.**

Although the original sentence has no quantifiers, it is clear that in most contexts it would not be used to refer to all students. However, the phrase 'among those' also makes it possible in appropriate contexts to translate the sentence as: 'Some students are people who joined in the festivities and some nonstudents are people who joined in the festivities.'

Notice what happens to the following ordinary sentences when they are translated into standard-form **I** sentences:

Original: **Many Americans earn less than $50,000 per year.**
Standard-form: **Some A̲mericans are persons who e̲arn less than $50,000 per year.**
Abbreviation: **Some A are E.**

Original: **At least 90 percent of all families own a television.**
Standard-form: **Some f̲amilies are things that own a t̲elevision.**
Abbreviation: **Some F are T.**

Clearly, each of these standard-form sentences is less precise than the original. This is particularly evident when we remember that the word 'some' in **I** sentences must be interpreted as meaning 'at least one.' This loss of meaning cannot be avoided in the system of logic we are now studying, and it is one of the reasons logicians have developed alternative systems that can deal with such statements without so much loss of meaning.

3.3.4 Particular Negative Statements

The following are examples of standard-form sentences expressing particular negative or **O** statements:

Some riots are not student protests.
Some negative statements are not particular statements.
Some houses are not buildings that are made of brick.

Each of these **O** sentences begins with the quantifier 'some,' has a subject and a predicate consisting of nouns, qualified nouns, or noun phrases, and contains a copula consisting of some form of the verb 'to be.' **O** sentences also may be abbreviated. For example, the sentence 'Some <u>a</u>utos are not <u>p</u>owerful' may be shortened to 'Some A are not P.' The schema for particular negative propositions is:

> **Some** _____ **are not ....**
> *or*
> **Some <u>S</u> are not <u>P</u>.**

The following examples provide insight into the ways ordinary sentences that express **O** propositions may be translated into standard sentence form.

> Original: **Many Protestants are not Baptists.**
> Standard-form: **Some <u>P</u>rotestants are not <u>B</u>aptists.**
> Abbreviation: **Some P are not B.**

> Original: **Certain experiences in life are not pleasant.**
> Standard-form: **Some <u>e</u>xperiences in life are not <u>p</u>leasant events.**
> Abbreviation: **Some E are not P.**

Another common way of expressing an **O** proposition is by placing a negation in front of sentence expressing an **A** statement. For example, if we start with 'All students will get an A in logic,' that clearly expresses an **A** statement, and then put a 'Not' in front of it, the resulting sentence expresses an **O** statement.

> Original: **Not all students will get an A in logic.**
> Standard form: **Some students are not persons who will get an A in logic.**

One common problem in dealing with negations in particular statements is positioning the negative qualifier. In converting the sentence 'Some students are not going to graduate in four years' into a standard-form sentence it is quite natural to put it in the form 'Some students are persons who are not going to graduate in four years.' This sentence is definitely in standard form—but it is a standard-form **I** statement, not an **O**. Strictly speaking, there is nothing wrong with this formulation and there are some logical rules that would permit its conversion into an **O** statement. But, for reasons that we can't go into right now, it is almost always preferable to put the negative qualifier with the copula, which makes it an **O** statement.

> Original: **Some students are not going to graduate in four years.**
> Standard-form: **Some students are not persons who are going to graduate in four years.**

In translating such sentences, be careful not to place the negation in the predicate rather than with the copula. 'Some students are persons who are not going to graduate in four years' expresses an **I** statement with a "buried" negation. As mentioned earlier, this could cause problems and thus should be avoided.

As noted in the discussion of universal negative (**E**) propositions, sentences with the form 'All _____ are not ....' are usually ambiguous. Although in some contexts such sentences may express **E** statements, they often express **O** statements. Thus, unless there is additional information available that makes it explicitly clear that an **E** statement is intended, sentences like the following should be interpreted as expressing **O** statements.

> Original: **All students are not going to get an A in logic.**
> Standard-form: **Some students are not persons who will get an A in logic.**

When expressing your own thoughts, you should *always* avoid using "All _____ are not ...." sentences; their ambiguousness can lead to serious misunderstandings. It is not necessary to use standard-form sentences in everyday situations, but whatever sentences you use need to be clear and unambiguous as to whether they are expressing **E** or **O** statements.

3.3.5 Exceptive and Exclusive Statements

Two kinds of statements are particularly tricky and deceptive, and therefore require a bit of special attention.

3.3.5.1 Exceptive Statements One might assume that sentences such as 'Almost all of the students were at the game' or 'Not quite all his money was spent on women' express particular affirmative statements. But such **exceptive statements** expressed by sentences with quantifiers such as 'most,' 'almost all,' 'not quite all,'[1] 'hardly any,' and 'almost everyone' are actually complex propositions that in ordinary contexts usually make two assertions rather than one. In most contexts, 'Almost all of the students were at the game' expresses a *conjunction* of an **I** and an **O** statement that should be expressed in standard form as 'Some students were at the game *and* Some students were not at the game.'

Percentage terms, such as '80 percent' and 'one-third,' often identify sentences expressing exceptive statements. In some contexts sentences beginning with these quantifiers express a conjunction of two propositions. Thus, the sentence 'Forty percent of students are hard workers' expresses both the **I** statement 'Some students are hard workers' and the **O** statement 'Some students are not hard workers.' Likewise, the sentence 'Half of the club members attended the meeting' normally translates into 'Some club members are persons who attended the meeting and some club members are not persons who attended the meeting.' Sentences with such quantifiers do not express one categorical statement but rather the conjunction of two categorical statements.

Not all exceptive statements are conjunctions of particular (**I** and **O**) statements: some of them involve conjunctions of two universal propositions. For example, when quantifiers such as 'all but,' 'all except,' or 'alone' are used in a sentence, it is necessary to translate the original sentence into a conjunction

---

[1]Don't confuse 'not *quite* all' with 'not all.' As indicated in the previous section, 'Not all . . . ' sentences are normally used to express **O** statements.

of **A** and **E** standard-form sentences. Thus, 'All but seniors are eligible for the scholarship' expresses both the **A** statement 'All nonseniors are persons eligible for the scholarship' and the **E** statement 'No seniors are persons eligible for the scholarship.'

3.3.5.2 Exclusive Statements   Exceptive statements should not be confused with a linguistically similar but logically quite different kind of statement known as an **exclusive statement.** Statements expressed by sentences containing qualifiers such as 'only' or 'none but' often are exclusive statements. The following are examples:

> **Only friends are invited to my party.**
> **None but licensed doctors may perform surgery.**

The term 'exclusive' is used to describe such statements, since they usually affirm that the predicate applies exclusively to the subject. Thus, when translating such sentences into standard-form **A** sentences, *it is necessary to reverse the subject and predicate,* as the following examples show:

> Original: **Only friends are invited to my party.**
> Standard-form: **All persons invited to my party are friends.**
> Abbreviation: **All I are F.**

> Original: **None but licensed doctors may perform surgery.**
> Standard-form: **All persons who may perform surgery are licensed doctors.**
> Abbreviation: **All S are D.**

One potentially confusing point needs to be noted. Statements expressed by sentences beginning with the expression '*the* only' are not exclusive; therefore, do not reverse the subject and predicate terms when translating them into standard form. Consider the following example:

> Original: **The only people invited to my party are friends.**
> Standard-form: **All people invited to my party are friends.**
> Abbreviation: **All I are F.**

EXERCISE 3–3

(a) If necessary, translate the following sentences into standard form. (b) Indicate whether each expresses an **A, E, I,** or **O** statement. (c) Write an abbreviation for each sentence, indicating which term each letter represents. (d) Write the schema for each statement.

1. All Italians are Europeans.

2. Lassie is not a cocker spaniel.

3. Some sailors are swarthy.

4. Most CDs cost more than ten dollars.

5. No ponderosas are shrubs.

6. Some hives do not have bees.

7. Rappers are musicians.

8. Panama hats are made in Ecuador.

9. Many dogs are not beagles.

10. Not all animals are primates.

11. All politicians are not dishonest.

12. No mussels are mammals.

13. Many European families do not own an automobile.

14. B. F. Skinner is a behavioral scientist.

15. Almost all paperbacks are inexpensive.

16. War is not healthy for children.

17. Only members of the club are invited.

18. All but automotive unions have settled.

19. Seventy percent of all college students work part time to pay for their education.

20. Blessed are the peacemakers.

21. Almost all professional basketball players are over six feet four inches tall.

22. The only road to success is hard work.

23. None but his friends were invited to the party.

24. Nothing is certain except death and taxes.

25. Only those who bought tickets in advance were able to get seats.

3.4 Venn Diagrams and Categorical Statements

Each of the four types of categorical statement has a schema that displays the logical form of that particular kind of proposition. It is also possible to display the logical form of categorical statements by means of diagrams. One of the most frequently used methods for doing this is the Venn diagram technique, named after John Venn, the nineteenth-century British logician who developed it.

Before showing how the different types of categorical statements can be diagrammed, it is necessary to explicate some of the principles of the method.

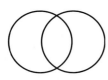

Figure 3–1a

1. Two overlapping circles are used to represent the classes of things referred to by the subject and predicate terms of the categorical statement (see Figure 3–1a).

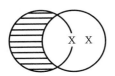

Figure 3–1b

2. Shading in an area of a circle indicates that the area is empty, that is, the class that it represents contains no members.

3. If an X appears in an area of a circle, then the designated class contains *at least one* member.

4. If an X appears on a line between two circles, this indicates that one or the other of the designated classes contains at least one member, but it is undetermined which class contains this member. An X on a line does *not* mean that both classes contain members, although it does not rule out this possibility.

5. If an area is completely blank, that is, if it is *not* shaded and it does *not* contain an X or part of an X, this means that we have *no information* about that area. It does *not* mean that the class represented by the area has no members.

6. Since we are operating on the principle that the subject term of a categorical proposition must name a class that has at least one member, there must be an X in some area of the circle representing the subject class in the Venn diagram for every categorical proposition.

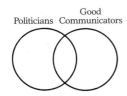

Figure 3–2

Using these principles, let us proceed to diagram the **A** statement 'All politicians are good communicators.' The first thing that must be done is to label each circle to indicate the class it represents, as in Figure 3–2. The circle on the left represents the class of politicians and the circle on the right represents the class of good communicators; the area common to both circles represents the class of things that are both politicians and good communicators. The area outside the circles represents everything else that is neither a politician nor a good communicator. It is also possible to label circles with abbreviations, using letters to represent the full names of the classes. When doing this, follow the rules for abbreviation presented in the first part of this chapter.

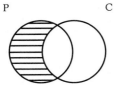

Figure 3–3

In our example, we know that the class of politicians contains at least one member, so an X must be placed somewhere inside the circle representing this class. There are three possibilities: the X could be placed in the area common to P and C, or in the area of P outside of C, or on the line between them. We have to wait to place the X until we get more information. If it is true that all politicians are good communicators, then *no* members of the class of politicians are *not* contained in the class of good communicators; thus, the area of the P circle that is outside of C can be shaded to indicate that the class it represents contains no members, as in Figure 3–3.

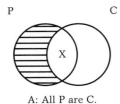

A: All P are C.

Figure 3–4

When the area of P outside of C is shaded, the only remaining area in which an X can be placed to indicate that the class of politicians contains a member is the area that is common to both P and C, as shown in Figure 3–4.

This example shows that sometimes we cannot determine exactly where an X should be placed until *after* shading has been done. For this reason we introduce the following rule for filling in Venn diagrams.

> **Whenever Venn diagrams are used to represent categorical statements, the area(s) that are explicitly identified as containing no members should be shaded before placing Xs where needed.**

In Figure 3–4, an X was placed in the area common to both P and C to show that at least one politician exists. Note that by its location, this X also signifies that at least one crook exists, because all of the members of the class of politicians named by the subject term also happen to be good communicators. The **A** proposition 'All politicians are good communicators' does *not* assert that there are any members in the class of good communicators that are not politicians, but neither does it rule out this possibility; it tells us nothing about the class of politicians that are not good communicators. Good communicators who are not politicians might very well exist, but the proposition says nothing about them. Therefore, it would be incorrect to place an X in the area of C outside the area common to both P and C.

The diagram in Figure 3–4 is a complete representation of all of the information contained in the **A** proposition 'All politicians are good communicators.'

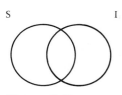

Figure 3–5

Let us diagram another **A** proposition, for example, 'All spiders are insects.' Once again, we begin with two overlapping circles, of which one represents the class of things referred to by the subject term, 'spiders,' and the other represents the class of things that are referred to by the predicate term, 'insects' (Figure 3–5).

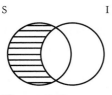

Figure 3–6

Since the statement 'All spiders are insects' asserts that there are no spiders that do not belong to the class of insects, the area of the S circle that is outside the I circle is shaded, as shown in Figure 3–6.

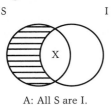

A: All S are I.

Figure 3–7

Next, an X should be placed in the area common to both S and I to indicate that the class of spiders contains at least one member, as in Figure 3–7. This X also indicates that the class of insects contains a member. As in the first **A** proposition that was diagrammed, it would be incorrect to place another X in the area of the I circle that is outside the area common to both the S and I circles. Clearly, the proposition 'All spiders are insects' says nothing about the class of insects that are not spiders; it might contain members or it might be empty—we are not told which is the case.

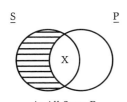

A: All S̲ are P̲.

Figure 3–8

Figures 3–4 and 3–7 are clearly very similar. The only difference between them is the labels on the circles, since each refers to a different class of things. If we were to relabel the circles using the schema symbols 'S̲' and 'P̲' the two diagrams would be identical. The fact that the Venn diagrams for the schemas of two different **A** propositions look the same should come as no great surprise. Venn diagrams are a method for representing the *logical structure* of a categorical statement, and it has already been shown that all **A** statements have the same logical form. For this reason, it is possible to provide a diagram analogous to the schema of any **A** statement (see Figure 3–8). The labels S̲ and P̲ are again

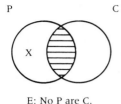

E: No P are C.

Figure 3–9

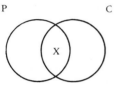

I: Some P are C.

Figure 3–10

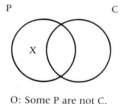

O: Some P are not C.

Figure 3–11

used as "blanks" for which any nouns or noun phrases can be substituted to create a diagram representing an **A** proposition.

The Venn diagram that represents the universal negative, or **E**, statement 'No politicians are good communicators' is shown in Figure 3–9. Since this statement asserts that no members of the class of politicians are members of the class of good communicators, the area common to both classes is shaded to indicate that it contains no members. Also, since the subject class must contain at least one member, an X is placed in the remaining area of the P circle. No X is needed in the C circle, since the proposition asserts nothing about the existence of a member in the predicate class. *All* universal negative (**E**) statements are diagrammed in the same way.

The Venn diagram for **I**, or particular affirmative, statements such as 'Some politicians are good communicators' is shown in Figure 3–10. The X in the area that is common to both circles indicates that at least one member of the class of politicians is included in the class of good communicators. This proposition says nothing about the parts of the subject and predicate classes that are outside of the area where they overlap; that is, it does not assert that there are any politicians who are not good communicators, nor that there are any good communicators who are not politicians. Therefore, no Xs should be placed in these areas of the circles. Notice that no shading is required for diagramming **I** propositions, because we are not told that any areas are definitely empty. *All* particular affirmative, or **I**, propositions are diagrammed in this manner.

Particular negative, or **O**, statements such as 'Some politicians are not good communicators' are represented by the Venn diagram shown in Figure 3–11. An X is placed in the area of P outside of C to indicate that at least one member of the class of politicians is excluded from the class of good communicators; in other words, at least one politician exists who is not a good communicator. This **O** statement does not say that at least one good communicator exists, so we do not need to place an X in either part of the C circle. Once again, no shading is needed when diagramming **O** statements. All particular negative, or **O**, statements are diagrammed in the same way.

EXERCISE 3–4

(a) If necessary, translate each of the following sentences into standard form. (b) Write an abbreviation for each sentence. (c) Write the schema for each. (d) Draw a Venn diagram to represent the categorical statement.

1. Some wine is made from dandelions.
2. No Beatles are bugs.
3. All beetles are bugs.
4. All oaks are hardwoods.
5. No termites are ants.
6. Some nebulae are not galaxies.

7. Not all Arabs are Moslems.
8. All harpies are mythological.
9. Some dancers can do the Charleston.
10. Many people in the world do not have enough to eat.
11. The only persons who do well in logic are those who have good study habits.
12. No behaviorists tolerate idle speculation.
13. No one scored higher than 90 on the test.
14. Almost everyone can do well in logic.
15. Only citizens can vote.
16. None but the staff are invited to the picnic.
17. Lightning never strikes twice in the same place.
18. Almost all exceptive statements are tricky to translate into standard form.
19. Most art collectors are rich.
20. Some areas do not have bugs.

EXERCISE 3–5

Draw Venn diagrams for the statements in Exercise 3–1 and for 1 through 17 in Exercise 3–3.

3.5 Logical Relations between Categorical Propositions

As with statements in general, several logical relationships hold between different categorical propositions. We are now in a position to examine some of the more common and important of these relationships.

3.5.1 Independence

The easiest relationship to recognize in syllogistic logic is that of independence. As explained in Chapter 1, two statements are logically **independent** if knowledge of the truth or falsity of one tells us nothing about the truth or falsity of the other and vice versa. It should be intuitively clear that two propositions that are about different classes of things generally will be logically independent. For example, knowing that the class of apples contains things that are also members of the class of edible things tells us nothing about the class of turtles.

In the context of syllogistic logic, one test for determining whether two categorical propositions are logically independent is to see if at least one of the classes specified in one proposition is in no way specified in the other proposition.

To understand the concept of logical independence better, let us consider these two **I** statements:

1. **Some horses are stallions.**
2. **Some horses are pintos.**

If we know only that statement 1 is true, we can infer nothing about the truth value of statement 2; and if we know only that statement 1 is false, then the truth value of statement 2 still remains undetermined. Likewise, if we know only that statement 2 is true, then we know nothing about the truth value of statement 1; and if we know only that statement 2 is false, then the truth value of statement 1 is still undetermined. Thus, the statements are logically independent, since the truth value of each tells us nothing about the truth value of the other.

It follows from the above that it is impossible for any of the four types of categorical statement that have the same subject and predicate terms to be logically independent.

3.5.2 Consistency

Another important basic logical relationship between statements is consistency. As explained in Chapter 1, two statements are **consistent** if and only if it is possible for both of them to be true.[2] Let us look at the four kinds of categorical propositions to determine which are consistent with one another.

The **A** statement 'All dogs are canines' and the **I** statement 'Some dogs are canines' are consistent because it is *possible* for both to be true. The **E** statement 'No flowers are animals' and the **O** statement 'Some flowers are not animals' are also logically consistent. Likewise, the **I** statement 'Some students are scholarship holders' and the **O** statement 'Some students are not scholarship holders' can both be true. By giving just one example of each, we have shown that *all* **A** and **I** statements with the same subject and predicate terms, *all* **E** and **O** statements with the same subject and predicate terms, and *all* **I** and **O** statements with the same subject and predicate terms are logically consistent. Other pairs of categorical statements are inconsistent. To give just one example, the **A** statement 'All wines are alcoholic beverages' is not consistent with the **E** statement 'No wines are alcoholic beverages,' because it is impossible for both statements to be true.

Venn diagrams can also be used to determine whether two propositions are consistent or not. The circles should be labeled using abbreviations, not the <u>S</u> and <u>P</u> for schemas, since the inconsistencies often result from the specific content of the statements, not just the forms. After drawing the Venn diagrams

---

[2]These definitions of 'consistency' and 'independence' are quite general and can be applied to any type of statement; they are not restricted to categorical propositions.

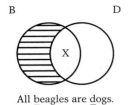

All b̲eagles are d̲ogs.

Figure 3–12

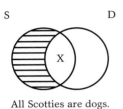

All S̲cotties are d̲ogs.

Figure 3–13

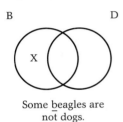

Some b̲eagles are
no̲t d̲ogs.

Figure 3–14

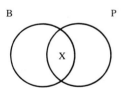

I: Some B are P.

Figure 3–15

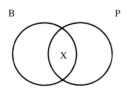

I: Some P are B.

Figure 3–16

for any two statements, you only need to look to see if one diagram contains shading in exactly the same area where the other diagram contains a complete X (not just an X on the line). If shading exists in exactly the same area of one diagram where an X exists in the other, then the two statements are inconsistent. When we specify that the shading and the X must be in exactly the same areas, this means that the areas must have exactly the same labeling, that is, they must represent the same classes. Thus Figures 3–12 and 3–13 both represent **A** propositions, but only the first is inconsistent with the statement represented by Figure 3–14 since the left-hand circle in Figure 3–13 represents a different class than the left-hand circle in Figure 3–14.

If two statements are inconsistent, then if one is true, the other must be false; but this means that inconsistent statements are not independent. From this we can conclude that if two statements are independent, they must be consistent.

3.5.3 Logical Equivalence

Another important relationship between categorical propositions is that of logical equivalence. Two categorical propositions are **logically equivalent** *if and only if they both necessarily have the same truth value*; that is, if one statement is true, the other statement must be true, and if one statement is false, the other must be false. For example, if 'Some bus drivers are poets' is true, then 'Some poets are bus drivers' must be true, and vice versa. And if 'Some bus drivers are poets' is false, then 'Some poets are bus drivers' must also be false, and vice versa. Thus, the two **I** propositions 'Some bus drivers are poets' and 'Some poets are bus drivers' are logically equivalent.

The logical equivalence of two categorical propositions can also be tested by means of Venn diagrams. If the Venn diagrams of two categorical propositions are identical, including the labeling of the circles (using abbreviations, not schema symbols), then the propositions are logically equivalent. The Venn diagram for the statement 'Some bus drivers are poets' is shown in Figure 3–15, and it is clearly identical to the diagram in Figure 3–16 which represents the proposition 'Some poets are bus drivers.' Thus the Venn diagrams confirm that these two statements are logically equivalent. Note that the circle on the left is labeled 'B' for both statements. We could have labeled the left circle 'P' for both instead of 'B.' The important thing is that the labeling must be the same in *both* diagrams.

Knowing that two statements are logically equivalent is important because it enables us to make inferences about the truth value of one statement from the truth value of the other statement. Thus, if we know that two statements are logically equivalent and that one statement is true, then we can immediately infer that the other must be true. Or, if we know that one statement is false, then we can infer that any logically equivalent statement must be false.

Examine each pair of statements. Then (a) indicate whether they are logically dependent or independent; (b) use Venn diagrams to determine whether the statements are logically consistent or inconsistent; and (c) use Venn diagrams to determine whether they are logically equivalent or not.

1. All machines are devices. Some machines are devices.
2. Some devices are machines. Some machines are devices.
3. Some devices are machines. Some devices are clocks.
4. No chimpanzees are animals. Some chimpanzees are animals.
5. All cigarettes are harmful things. No cigarettes are harmful things.
6. All cats are felines. Some lions are felines.
7. All factories are buildings. All dogs are pets.
8. Some Chinese are great athletes. Some Chinese are not great athletes.
9. No Americans are vegetarians. Some Americans are not vegetarians.
10. Some minors are voters. No minors are voters.
11. No dogs are cats. No cats are dogs.
12. All winners are losers. All losers are winners.

3.6 Immediate Inferences

Assuming that each of the four types of categorical statement has the same subject and predicate classes, certain relations exist among them, such that if we know the truth or falsity of a given statement, then we can directly infer the truth or falsity of certain other statements. Because they permit us to make direct inferences from one statement to another (without the "mediation" of any other statements), these relationships are known as **immediate inferences.**

3.6.1 Contradiction

Contradictory propositions are statements that are related in such a way that if one is true, the other must be false, and if one is false, the other must be true. Contradictory propositions cannot both be true; nor can they both be false. Consider the following pair of statements:

All senators are women.
Some senators are not women.

If the **A** statement 'All senators are women' is true, then the **O** statement 'Some senators are not women' must be false. If 'All senators are women' is false, then the statement 'Some senators are not women' must be true. Likewise, given the truth of 'Some senators are not women,' it must be false that all senators are women. If it is false that some senators are not women, then 'All senators are women' must be true. In brief, knowing the truth or falsity of either statement, we can always directly determine the truth or falsity of the other. If we know that one is true, we can validly infer that the other is false; and if we know that one is false, we can infer that the other is true. All **A** and **O** propositions with the same subjects and predicates are contradictories, since it is impossible for both to be true or for both to be false, and, therefore, we can make immediate inferences from the truth or falsity of one to the truth or falsity of the other.

Like **A** and **O** statements, all **E** and **I** statements with the same subject and predicate terms are also contradictories. Consider, for example, the following pair of statements:

No senators are women.
Some senators are women.

If the **E** statement 'No senators are women' is true, then the **I** statement 'Some senators are women' must be false. If the **E** statement is false, then the **I** statement must be true. If the **I** proposition is true, then the **E** proposition must be false, and if the **I** proposition is false, then the **E** must be true.

3.6.2 Contrariety

At first glance, the **A** statement 'All senators are women' might appear to be the contradictory of the **E** statement 'No senators are women,' but further consideration will show this not to be the case. Although it is impossible for both statements to be true, it *is* possible for both to be false, as in the cases where only one senator is a woman or exactly half of the senators are women. Such statements are known as **contraries**. Two statements with the same subject and predicate classes are contraries *if and only if they are related in such a way that both cannot be true, but both can be false.*

Let us consider another example:

All students are logicians.
No students are logicians.

If the **A** statement 'All students are logicians' is true, then the **E** statement 'No students are logicians' must be false, given our assumption that the class of students contains at least one member. If it is true that every single student is included in the class of logicians, then obviously it must be false that no member of the class of students is included in the class of logicians. Likewise, if the **E** statement 'No students are logicians' is true, then the **A** statement must be false. These statements cannot both be true. However, if the **A** statement 'All students are logicians' is false, what can be inferred about the truth or falsity of the **E** statement 'No students are logicians'? Knowing only that it is not the case that every student is a logician, can we validly infer that not even one student is a logician? Obviously not, for knowing that it is false that all students are logicians does not tell us how many are not logicians—it is possible that only half of the students are not logicians, although it is also *possible* that not even one of the students is a logician. Thus, if the **A** statement is false, then the truth or falsity of the **E** statement cannot be determined. Similarly, if we know only that the **E** statement 'No students are logicians' is false, then the truth or falsity of the **A** statement also is undetermined.

3.6.3 Subcontraries

A and **E** propositions have the same quantity, but they differ in quality, one being affirmative and the other being negative. **I** and **O** propositions also have the same quantity and differ in quality. Are **I** and **O** propositions contraries? Consider the following pair of statements:

> **Some dogs are terriers.**
> **Some dogs are not terriers.**

If the **I** statement 'Some dogs are terriers' is true, it is still possible for the **O** statement 'Some dogs are not terriers' to be true. Contrary statements, however, cannot both be true; therefore **I** and **O** propositions are not contraries. Another logical relationship, known as subcontrariety, exists between **I** and **O** statements. Two categorical propositions with the same subject and predicate classes are **subcontraries** if *both cannot be false, but both can be true*. Consider the following pair of statements:

> **Some women are ambitious persons.**
> **Some women are not ambitious persons.**

The two statements cannot both be false, given our assumption that at least one woman exists. If the **I** statement 'Some women are ambitious persons' is false, then the **O** statement 'Some women are not ambitious persons' must be true, and if the **O** statement is false, then the **I** statement must be true. However, if the statement 'Some women are ambitious persons' is true, then the truth or falsity of the **O** statement 'Some women are not ambitious persons' is undetermined. Knowing only that some members of the class of women are members of the class of ambitious persons, we cannot know whether some women are excluded from the class of ambitious persons; it is possible that all women are ambitious. In a similar way, knowing only that 'Some women are not ambitious persons' is true, we cannot infer anything about the truth or falsity of the **I** statement 'Some women are ambitious persons'; it is still possible that no women are ambitious. Both statements cannot be false, but both may be true; this relationship of subcontrariety holds between all **I** and **O** propositions with the same subject and predicate classes.

3.6.4 Subimplication and Superimplication

The logical relationships of contradiction, contrariety, and subcontrariety involve immediate inferences in which the truth of one statement implies the falsity of the other statement, or the falsity of one statement implies the truth of the other statement. In none of the immediate inferences discussed so far could we infer the truth of one statement from the truth of the other, or the falsity of one statement from the falsity of the other. Such immediate inferences can be made with certain types of categorical statements through the relations of subimplication and superimplication.

Before explaining the immediate inferences of subimplication and superimplication, it is necessary to define some terms. Universal statements, both **A** and **E**, are called **superimplicants,** and particular statements, both **I** and **O**, are called **subimplicants.** Strictly speaking, the **A** proposition is the superimplicant of the **I** proposition with the same subject and predicate terms, and the **I** is the subimplicant of the **A**. Likewise, the **E** proposition is the superimplicant of the **O** with the same subject and predicate terms, and the **O** is the subimplicant of the **E**.

Subimplication is the relation in which *the truth of a particular statement is implied by the truth of its corresponding universal statement.* Thus, given the assumption that at least one corporation president exists, if the **A** statement 'All corporation presidents are millionaires' is true, then the **I** statement 'Some corporation presidents are millionaires' must be true. Likewise, if the **E** statement 'No corporation presidents are millionaires' is true, then the **O** statement 'Some corporation presidents are not millionaires' is also true. However, if the **A** statement is false, then the truth value of the **I** statement is undetermined; it is possible that some corporation presidents are millionaires or that none of them are millionaires. If the **E** statement 'No corporation presidents are millionaires' is false, then it is also impossible to determine the truth value of its corresponding **O** statement.

The immediate inference called 'superimplication' is the reverse of subimplication. In **superimplication,** *the falsity of the universal statement is implied by the falsity of its corresponding particular statement.* Thus, assuming at least one corporation president exists and knowing only that the **I** statement 'Some corporation presidents are millionaires' is false, we can infer that the **A** statement 'All corporation presidents are millionaires' must be false. If it is false that even one member of the class of corporation presidents is contained in the class of millionaires, then it must be false that every member of the class of corporation presidents is contained in the class of millionaires. Similarly, if the **O** statement 'Some corporation presidents are not millionaires' is false, then the **E** statement 'No corporation presidents are millionaires' must be false. But if we know only that the **I** statement 'Some corporation presidents are millionaires' is true, then the truth value of the **A** statement 'All corporation presidents are millionaires' is undetermined. In this instance, it is possible that all members of the class of corporation presidents are members of the class of millionaires and it is also possible that only some of them are members of the class of millionaires. Then too, if the **O** statement 'Some corporation presidents are not millionaires' is true, then the truth value of the corresponding **E** statement 'No corporation presidents are millionaires' is also undetermined.

EXERCISE 3–7

Below you will find pairs of categorical statements. (a) Identify the relationship between each pair as contradiction, contrariety, subcontrariety, subimplication, or superimplication. (b) Assuming that the first statement of each pair is true, what can be inferred about the truth value of the second statement? (c) Assuming that the first statement is false, what can be inferred about the truth value of the second statement?

1. All judges are lawyers. No judges are lawyers.
2. Some judges are lawyers. Some judges are not lawyers.
3. Some books are not dictionaries. No books are dictionaries.
4. Some wagons are not motor vehicles. All wagons are motor vehicles.
5. Some diseases are not fatal. No diseases are fatal.
6. No shrews are rodents. Some shrews are rodents.
7. No shrews are rodents. All shrews are rodents.
8. Some newspapers are biased things. All newspapers are biased things.
9. All butterflies are mortal beings. No butterflies are mortal beings.
10. All city police are city residents. Some city police are city residents.
11. No satellites are planets. Some satellites are not planets.
12. Some geniuses are women. Some geniuses are not women.
13. No members of the club are boys. Some members of the club are boys.
14. All Germans are beer drinkers. Some Germans are beer drinkers.
15. No logicians are musicians. All logicians are musicians.

3.7 The Traditional Square of Opposition

Medieval logicians developed what is known as the traditional square of opposition to display these logical relationships. The four different categorical statements were arranged as shown in Figure 3–17. Assuming that the class named by the subject term of a categorical statement contains at least one member, one can use the square of opposition to exhibit a variety of kinds of immediate inference. The logical relations that exist between certain pairs of categorical statements with the same subject and predicate terms can be displayed in the completed traditional square of opposition.

All of the immediate inferences on the square of opposition that can be made from any given categorical statement, such as an **A** statement, can now be brought together. For example, what can be immediately inferred from the statement 'All diamonds are precious gems'? If this **A** statement is true, then, its contradiction, the **O** statement 'Some diamonds are not precious gems' is false; its contrary, the **E** statement 'No diamonds are precious gems,' is false;

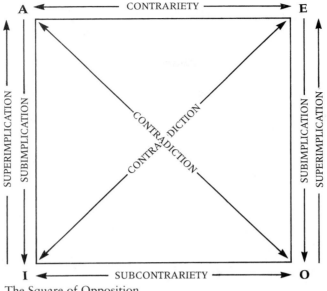

The Square of Opposition

Figure 3–17

and its subimplicant, the **I** statement 'Some diamonds are precious gems,' is true. If the **A** statement is false, then its contradictory 'Some diamonds are not precious gems' is true; the truth or falsity of its contrary 'No diamonds are precious gems' is undetermined; and the truth value of its subimplicant 'Some diamonds are precious gems' is also undetermined.

Immediate Inferences on the Square of Opposition

If **A** *is true*	If **E** *is true*	If **I** *is true*	If **O** *is true*
E is false	A is false	E is false	A is false
I is true	I is false	A is undetermined	E is undetermined
O is false	O is true	O is undetermined	I is undetermined

If **A** *is false*	If **E** *is false*	If **I** *is false*	If **O** *is false*
O is true	I is true	A is false	E is false
E is undetermined	A is undetermined	E is true	A is true
I is undetermined	O is undetermined	O is true	I is true

EXERCISE 3–8

Below are several sets of categorical statements. (a) What is the relationship between each statement and the original? (b) Assuming that the first is true, what can you infer about the truth value of the other statements? (c) Assuming that the first is false, what can you infer about the truth value of the other statements?

1. All straight-A students are women.
    a. No straight-A students are women.
    b. Some straight-A students are women.
    c. Some straight-A students are not women.

2. No computers are humans.
    a. Some computers are humans.
    b. Some computers are not humans.
    c. All computers are humans.

3. Some horses are thoroughbreds.
    a. Some horses are not thoroughbreds.
    b. No horses are thoroughbreds
    c. All horses are thoroughbreds.

4. Some desserts are not fattening foods.
    a. All desserts are fattening foods.
    b. No desserts are fattening foods.
    c. Some desserts are fattening foods.

5. All believers are martyrs.
    a. No believers are martyrs.
    b. Some believers are martyrs.
    c. Some believers are not martyrs.

6. No toothless piranhas are threats.
    a. Some toothless piranhas are threats.
    b. Some toothless piranhas are not threats.
    c. All toothless piranhas are threats.

7. Some people are hard workers.
    a. Some people are not hard workers.
    b. All people are hard workers.
    c. No people are hard workers.

3.8 The Boolean Interpretation

At the beginning of this chapter, we stipulated that we would consider only propositions that are such that the class named by the subject term contains at least one member. The reasons for this policy are both subtle and complex. Logicians have studied and argued over the pros and cons of several ways of dealing with these issues, and although no single policy has been unanimously accepted as the only way, it is generally agreed today that the policy we have followed is one of the two best. We now turn briefly to the second preferred policy; it is the policy we will use in the remainder of this chapter and throughout Chapters 7 and 8.

Instead of requiring that only the subject term must refer to a class that has at least one member, we could require that both the subject and predicate terms refer to classes with at least one member each. We could also remove the requirement completely so that both the subject and the predicate terms can refer to classes with no members. The first option, requiring both classes to have members, makes the process of drawing Venn diagrams quite a bit more complex, and the advantages to be gained for the extra effort are quite small. The second option is simpler to diagram, but it trivializes the entire system, because it makes the diagrams for both the **I** and **O** propositions completely empty of any markings.

The second option has been refined by logicians so that the **I** and **O** propositions are not trivialized. With this refinement, *the classes referred to by the subject and predicate terms in any categorical proposition are not required to have any members, but the **I** and **O** propositions are then interpreted as being compound propositions that include the assertion that at least one member of the subject class exists.* To be specific, the **I** proposition is interpreted as asserting that some members of the subject class are members of the predicate class *and* that at least one member of the subject class exists. For example, 'Some dogs are boxers' is interpreted as stating that some members of the class of dogs are members of the class of boxers and also that at least one dog exists. In other words, the simple sentence 'Some dogs are boxers' is interpreted as saying the same thing as the compound sentence 'Some dogs are boxers *and* at least one dog exists.'

Similarly, **O** propositions are interpreted as asserting that some members of the subject class are excluded from the predicate class and that at least one member of the subject class does exist. Thus, the sentence 'Some dogs are not boxers' is interpreted as saying the same thing as the compound sentence 'Some dogs are not boxers *and* at least one dog exists.'

This refinement of the second option, called the **Boolean interpretation,** has the same Venn diagrams for **I** and **O** propositions as does the method (known as the 'traditional interpretation') we have been using up to now. But *it requires different Venn diagrams for **A** and **E** propositions.* Since the Boolean interpretation does not require that the subject terms refer to classes having members, the diagrams for **A** and **E** propositions on this interpretation do not have any Xs. That is, the diagrams on the Boolean interpretation look like those in Figure 3–18.

Although the Boolean interpretation is easier to diagram and has certain other advantages that we cannot go into here, it also has the significant drawback of eliminating a significant number of immediate inferences, particularly most of the inferences in the square of opposition. Because the **I** and **O** propositions are interpreted as asserting that at least one member of the subject class exists, if the subject class in fact contains no members, the proposition must be false. Thus, on the Boolean interpretation, 'Some unicorns live in Greece' is false, insofar as it is false that at least one unicorn exists. But 'Some unicorns do not live in Greece' also is false for the same reason. Thus, **I** and **O** propositions are not subcontraries since it is possible for both to be false.

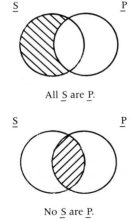

All <u>S</u> are <u>P</u>.

No <u>S</u> are <u>P</u>.

Figure 3–18

Logicians consider the relation of contradictoriness to be very important. So they have chosen to say that it still holds between **A** and **O** propositions and between **E** and **I** propositions on the Boolean interpretation—even though there is no clear intuitive basis for this assumption. (If 'Some unicorns do not live in Greece' is false because no unicorns exist, why must 'All unicorns live in Greece' be true?) Since the **I** and **O** statements can both be false, then their contradictories (the **A** and **E** respectively) can both be true, which means that they are not contraries. And since the **A** and **E** do not assert the existence of any members in their subject classes, they cannot imply the **I** and **O** respectively, since the latter do assert the existence of a member in the subject class. This means that subimplication does not hold on the Boolean interpretation; for similar reasons, it can be shown that superimplication does not hold either. In brief, *the only part of the square of opposition that exists on the Boolean interpretation is the diagonal relation of contradictoriness*, and this holds only for somewhat arbitrary reasons.

To provide a bit of practice in using this alternative to the traditional interpretation of categorical propositions, we will use the Boolean interpretation in our discussion of several more immediate inferences that are not significantly different on the two interpretations.

EXERCISE 3–9

Refer to the pairs of statements in Exercise 3–7 and use the Boolean interpretation for the following: (a) Assuming that the first statement of each pair is true, what can be inferred about the truth value of the second statement? (b) Assuming that the first statement is false, what can be inferred about the truth value of the second statement?

3.8.1 Complementarity

Another important concept in Aristotelian logic is that of complementary classes. The **complement of a class** is *the class of all things or beings in the universe that do not belong to the original class*. Thus, the complement of the class of lovers is the class of all those things that are not lovers. The complement of any class is expressed by joining the prefix 'non' to the name of the class, so the complement of the class of lovers is referred to as the class of nonlovers. The complement of the class of lovers is not the class of haters, for people who are nonlovers are not necessarily haters—just because they don't love anyone does not mean that they hate someone. Furthermore, the complements of terms such as 'nonlovers' and 'nonhaters' are simply expressed as 'lovers' and 'haters,' respectively, to avoid having more than one prefix (such as 'nonnonlovers'). One must be particularly careful when dealing with qualified terms, that is, those containing adjectives or adverb phrases. For example, the complement of the term 'lazy student' is not 'nonlazy students' but 'non(lazy students).' The class referred to by the term 'nonlazy students' contains only students (specifically those who are not lazy), whereas the class referred to by the complementary term 'non(lazy students)' contains all things in the universe that are not lazy students. When forming the complement of any qualified term, always enclose the entire expression in parentheses and then add the 'non' in front of the parentheses.

To deal most simply with the equivalence relations that we will be introducing shortly, we will use the Boolean interpretation's requirement that **I** and **O** statements assert that at least one member of the subject class exists, and *add* the new requirement that *I and O statements also assert that the **complements** of their **subject** classes have at least one member as well.* This is actually a very plausible assumption, because the only class whose complementary class is empty is the class that is identical to all of the things which are being considered in the context of a given statement (known as the 'universe of discourse'), a situation that is generally quite trivial and uninteresting. This new stipulation must be taken into account in drawing Venn diagrams for the remainder of this chapter.

3.8.2 Obversion

Having defined the concepts of logical equivalence and complementary class, we can now consider obversion. **Obversion** is *the mechanical process of changing the quality of a categorical statement and replacing the predicate term with its complement.* Is the obverse of a categorical statement logically equivalent to its original statement? That is, is one true whenever the other is true and false whenever the other is false? Consider, for example, the following statements:

> All senators are lawyers.
> ↓
> *No* senators are *lawyers.*
> ↓
> No senators are nonlawyers.

Here, the first statement, or **obvertend,** is a universal affirmative statement. By changing the quality of this proposition from affirmative to negative and then replacing the predicate term with its complementary term, we arrive at its **obverse,** which is a universal negative proposition.

To see whether these two statements are logically equivalent, examine Figure 3–19, which shows the Venn diagrams for both propositions. The Venn diagrams for both propositions are exactly the same. The **E** statement asserts that no members of the subject class are members of the predicate class. In this instance, the **E** statement 'No senators are nonlawyers' asserts that no members of the class of senators are also members of the class of nonlawyers. The class of nonlawyers is represented by the area outside the L circle, so the area outside the L circle and inside the S circle must be empty. Since all **A** statements and their obverses have the same form, which can be represented by the same schema, the Venn diagrams for **A** statements and their obverses are all the same

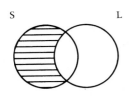

A: All S are L.

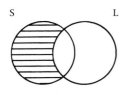

E: No S are nonL.

Figure 3–19

S   L

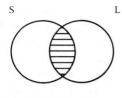

E: No S are L.

S   L

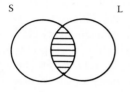

A: All S are nonL.

Figure 3–20

(with the exception of the labels on the circles). Thus, the obverse of any **A** statement is logically equivalent to its original statement. This means that the **A** statement implies its obverse, and the obverse implies the **A** statement. Now let us consider whether the obverses of **E**, **I**, and **O** propositions also are logically equivalent to their original statements.

The obverse of the **E** statement 'No senators are lawyers' is the **A** statement 'All senators are nonlawyers.' The Venn diagrams representing these statements are shown in Figure 3–20. Because their Venn diagrams are identical, the obverse of this **E** statement is logically equivalent to its original statement. Again, because all **E** statements and their obverses have the same logical form and, therefore, are represented by the same Venn diagrams, we can say that all **E** statements are logically equivalent to their obverses.

The obverse of the **I** statement 'Some senators are lawyers' is the **O** statement 'Some senators are not nonlawyers.' The Venn diagrams for these propositions appear in Figure 3–21 and are clearly identical to each other. Therefore, the obverse of this **I** statement and, of course, of any **I** statement, is logically equivalent to its original statement.

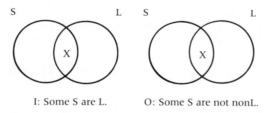

I: Some S are L.   O: Some S are not nonL.

Figure 3–21

Similarly, the obverse of the **O** statement 'Some senators are not lawyers' is the **I** statement 'Some senators are nonlawyers.' The Venn diagrams for these statements, shown in Figure 3–22, make it evident that these statements are also logically equivalent. Thus, *the obverses of all four types of categorical propositions are logically equivalent to their original statements.*

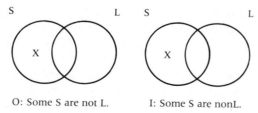

O: Some S are not L.   I: Some S are nonL.

Figure 3–22

EXERCISE 3-10

(a) Write the obverse of each of the following statements. (b) Determine whether the original statement and its obverse are logically equivalent, using Venn diagrams to test for equivalence.

1. No oaks are maples.
2. Some books are dictionaries.
3. All madrigal singers are musicians.
4. Some of Shakespeare's works are not plays.
5. Some gifts are expensive things.
6. All senators are politicians.
7. No biscuits are muffins.
8. Some vampire bats are dangerous animals.
9. Some members are not lawyers.
10. No numbers are integers.

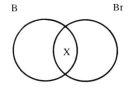

I: Some B are Br.

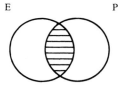

I: Some Br are B.

Figure 3–23

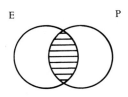

E: No E are P.

Figure 3–24

E: No P are E.

Figure 3–25

3.8.3 Conversion

Conversion is *the mechanical process of interchanging the subject and predicate terms of a categorical proposition.* For example, applying conversion to the **I** proposition 'Some buildings are things designed by Marcel Breuer' results in another **I** proposition, 'Some things designed by Marcel Breuer are buildings.' The original statement is called the **convertend,** and the statement formed from it by the process of conversion is called the **converse.** Thus, in the example above, the **I** statement 'Some buildings are things designed by Marcel Breuer' is the convertend, and the **I** statement 'Some things designed by Marcel Breuer are buildings' is the converse. The Venn diagrams representing these two propositions are presented in Figure 3–23; they show that the original and its converse are logically equivalent.

Since all **I** propositions and their converses have the same logical form, they can be represented by the same Venn diagrams as those shown, except for a change in the letters that abbreviate the subject and predicate terms. Hence, all **I** statements and their converses are logically equivalent statements.

Likewise, all **E** propositions are logically equivalent to their converses. Consider, for example, the **E** statement 'No executives are poets' which is represented by the Venn diagram in Figure 3–24. This **E** statement is converted by interchanging the subject and predicate terms, giving us another **E** proposition 'No poets are executives,' which is represented by the Venn diagram in Figure 3–25.

Since the Venn diagrams in Figures 3–24 and 3–25 are exactly the same, and since we know that all **E** statements have the same form, the Venn diagrams for these statements demonstrate that any **E** statement is logically equivalent to its converse.

A propositions, however, are *not* logically equivalent to their converses. Consider, for example, the **A** statement 'All gorillas are primates.' By interchanging the subject and predicate terms, we obtain its converse, 'All primates are gorillas.' Clearly, these two statements are not logically equivalent, since the original **A** statement is true, whereas its converse is obviously false. The Venn diagrams for these two propositions, shown in Figure 3–26, are different, thereby demonstrating that the propositions are not logically equivalent. This single example is sufficient to prove that no **A** statement is logically equivalent to its converse, since it shows that it is possible for an **A** statement to be true and its converse false.

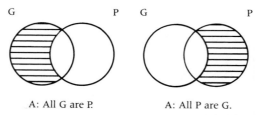

A: All G are P.   A: All P are G.

Figure 3–26

An **O** statement also is *not* logically equivalent to its converse for similar reasons. For example, the converse of 'Some trees are not oaks' is 'Some oaks are not trees,' and, although the first is true, the second is false. The Venn diagrams for these statements are also different, as shown in Figure 3–27.

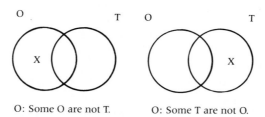

O: Some O are not T.   O: Some T are not O.

Figure 3–27

In summary, we have shown that *all **E** and **I** propositions are logically equivalent to their converses, but no **A** or **O** propositions are logically equivalent to their converses.*

EXERCISE 3–11

(a) Write the converse of each of the following statements. (b) Determine whether the converse is logically equivalent to the original statement by using Venn diagrams.

1. All salmon are fish.
2. No gnus are auks.
3. Some Americans are Californians.
4. Some songs are not ballads.
5. All pens are writing instruments.
6. All asps are vipers.
7. No women are fools.
8. Some tables are marble.
9. Some representatives are not elected persons.
10. No pollutants are beneficial things.

3.8.4 Contraposition

The last immediate inference involving logically equivalent statements is contraposition. **Contraposition** is *the mechanical process of interchanging the subject and predicate terms of a categorical statement and then replacing each with its complement.* In other words, the subject term of the original statement is replaced by the complement of the predicate term, and the predicate term of the original is replaced by the complement of the subject term. Thus, the contrapositive of the **A** statement 'All bass are fish' is the **A** statement 'All nonfish are nonbass.'

All bass are fish.

All fish are bass.

All nonfish are nonbass.

Contraposition can also be considered in light of our discussion of obversion and conversion. For example, examine the following steps:

Original statement: **All bass are fish.**
By obversion: **No bass are nonfish.**
By conversion: **No nonfish are bass.**
By obversion: **All nonfish are nonbass.**

Thus, contraposition is not actually a new process, since we can obtain the contrapositive of a statement by obverting the original, then converting the resulting statement, and then obverting the resulting statement.

Of course, our main concern is whether the contrapositive of a statement is logically equivalent to the original statement. In the case of the **A** statement in the preceding example, this seems to be the case, since each step produces a statement that is logically equivalent to the previous statement. It is possible to check whether the contrapositive of an **A** statement is logically equivalent to

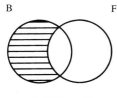

A: All B are F.

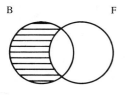

A: All nonF are nonB.

Figure 3–28

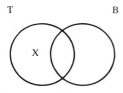

O: Some T are not B.

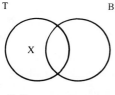

O: Some nonB are not nonT.

Figure 3–29

the original statement by means of Venn diagrams. The Venn diagrams representing the original **A** statement 'All bass are fish' and its contrapositive 'All nonfish are nonbass' are shown in Figure 3–28.

Since the Venn diagrams for the two statements are identical, they demonstrate that this **A** statement and its contrapositive—and therefore that any **A** statement and its contrapositive—are logically equivalent.

Any **O** statement and its contrapositive also are logically equivalent. For example, consider the **O** statement 'Some teachers are not bachelors' and its contrapositive 'Some nonbachelors are not nonteachers.' The Venn diagrams representing both these statements are shown in Figure 3–29.

Clearly, both diagrams are identical, so every **O** statement is logically equivalent to its contrapositive. The logical equivalence of the **O** statement and its contrapositive also can be seen in the following series of operations:

Original statement: **Some teachers are not bachelors.**
By obversion: **Some teachers are nonbachelors.**
By conversion: **Some nonbachelors are teachers.**
By obversion: **Some nonbachelors are not nonteachers.**

Because the statement derived by each operation is logically equivalent to the preceding statement, the original **O** statement 'Some teachers are not bachelors' is logically equivalent to its contrapositive 'Some nonbachelors are not nonteachers.'

An **I** statement is *not* logically equivalent to its contrapositive. Consider, for example, the **I** statement 'Some squares are circles' and its contrapositive 'Some noncircles are nonsquares.' The original statement is clearly false, but its contrapositive is clearly true, which proves that it is not the case that if an **I** statement is false then its contrapositive must be false. This one counterexample shows that the contrapositive of an **I** statement is not logically equivalent to its original statement.

The contrapositive of an **E** statement also is not logically equivalent to its original. Consider, for example, the **E** statement 'No dogs are cats,' which is clearly true, and its contrapositive 'No noncats are nondogs,' which is clearly false (an elephant is a noncat but is also a nondog). This one counterexample proves that no **E** statement is logically equivalent to its contrapositive.

EXERCISE 3–12

(a) Write the contrapositive of each of the following statements. (b) State whether or not this contrapositive is logically equivalent to the original statement.

1. All hammers are tools.

2. No pencils are pens.

3. Some drinks are beverages.

4. Some cars are not Fords.

5. No mice are men

6. All members are students.

7. No elephants are carnivores.

8. Some vehicles are bicycles.

9. Some tools are not hammers.

10. Some women are geniuses.

Summary of Equivalences on the Boolean Interpretation

Obversion

Original Statement		Obverse
A: All S̲ are P̲.	*equivalent*	**E:** No S̲ are nonP̲.
E: No S̲ are P̲.	*equivalent*	**A:** All S̲ are nonP̲.
I: Some S̲ are P̲.	*equivalent*	**O:** Some S̲ are not nonP̲.
O: Some S̲ are not P̲.	*equivalent*	**I:** Some S̲ are nonP̲.

Conversion

Original Statement		Converse
A: All S̲ are P̲.	*not equivalent*	**A:** All P̲ are S̲.
E: No S̲ are P̲.	*equivalent*	**E:** No P̲ are S̲.
I: Some S̲ are P̲.	*equivalent*	**I:** Some P̲ are S̲.
O: Some S̲ are not P̲.	*not equivalent*	**O:** Some P̲ are not S̲.

Contraposition

Original Statement		Contrapositive
A: All S̲ are P̲.	*equivalent*	**A:** All nonP̲ are nonS̲.
E: No S̲ are P̲.	*not equivalent*	**E:** No nonP̲ are nonS̲.
I: Some S̲ are P̲.	*not equivalent*	**I:** Some nonP̲ are nonS̲.
O: Some S̲ are not P̲.	*equivalent*	**O:** Some nonP̲ are not nonS̲.

EXERCISE 3–13

I. (a) How is each of the statements below related in terms of logical equivalences and the square of opposition on the Boolean interpretation to 'All dinosaurs are reptiles'? (b) If the original statement in (a) is true, what can be validly inferred about the truth value of each statement below? Is it true, false, or undetermined?

1. No dinosaurs are nonreptiles.
2. No dinosaurs are reptiles.
3. Some dinosaurs are not reptiles.
4. Some dinosaurs are reptiles.
5. All reptiles are dinosaurs.
6. All nonreptiles are nondinosaurs.

II. (a) How is each of the following statements related in terms of logical equivalences and the square of opposition on the Boolean interpretation to 'No Navahos are Apaches'? (b) If the original statement in (a) is true, what can be validly inferred about the truth value of each statement below? Is it true, false, or undetermined?

1. All Navahos are nonApaches.
2. All Navahos are Apaches.
3. Some Navahos are Apaches.
4. Some Navahos are not Apaches.
5. No Apaches are Navahos.
6. No nonApaches are nonNavahos.

III. (a) How is each of the following statements related in terms of logical equivalences and the square of opposition on the Boolean interpretation to 'Some Englishmen are women'? (b) If the original statement in (a) is *false*, what can be validly inferred about the truth value of each statement below? Is it true, false, or undetermined?

1. Some Tanzanians are not nonwomen.
2. Some Tanzanians are not women.
3. No Tanzanians are women.
4. All Tanzanians are women.
5. Some women are Tanzanians.
6. Some nonwomen are nonTanzanians.

Summary

1. **Categorical propositions** are statements that *assert that part or all of the class of things named by the subject term are included in or excluded from the class of things named by the predicate term.* The class referred to by the subject term must contain at least one member in order for a statement to qualify as categorical. Categorical propositions can be either **affirmative** or **negative** in quality and **particular** or **universal** in quantity.

2. **Universal affirmative** statements, also called **A** statements, affirm that all members of the subject class are included in the predicate class. **Particular affirmative** statements, also known as **I** statements, affirm that at least one member of the subject class is included in the predicate class. **Universal negative** statements, or **E** statements, affirm that all members of the subject class are excluded from the predicate class. **Particular negative** statements, or **O** statements, affirm that at least one member of the subject class is excluded from the predicate class.

3. Although categorical propositions can be expressed in a variety of ways, it is helpful to use a standard-form sentence to express each of the four types. Standard-form sentences can be referred to as **A, E, I,** or **O** sentences, depending on the type of categorical statement being expressed. **Abbreviations** of standard-form sentences express statements that are true or false. Although they look similar, **schemata** are not abbreviations and do not express statements. Schemata *only exhibit the logical form of statements.*

The schema of each type of categorical statement is formed by removing both the subject and predicate terms and retaining only the quantifier and copula; then the letters S and P (underscored to indicate that each represents a blank for which a noun or noun phrase may be substituted) are appropriately inserted. Thus the schema for any **A** proposition is 'All S are P,' for any **I** proposition 'Some S are P,' for any **E** proposition 'No S are P,' and for any **O** proposition 'Some S are not P.'

4. Translating sentences into standard form can present problems. One should make certain that the predicate term is translated into a noun or noun phrase and that the same noun phrase construction is used throughout a given context. Sentences expressing singular statements are translated as universals. Sentences with the form 'All _____ are not ...... ' are usually ambiguous and should be translated as **O** statements unless other information is provided that makes it clear that an **E** statement is intended.

5. When translating sentences expressed in ordinary language, context is often an important factor in determining which type of statement is being expressed. When context provides no clues, use the translation that provides less information. In ordinary contexts, an **exceptive statement** usually expresses two propositions, both of which are either universal or particular, and therefore must be translated into a conjunction of **A** and **E**, or **I** and **O**, standard sentence forms. When translating **exclusive statements** into standard **A** sentences, it is necessary to reverse the subject and predicate terms; but sentences beginning with '*the* only' do not express exclusive statements and therefore do not require a reversal of subject and predicate terms.

6. Two statements are said to be **consistent** if *it is possible for both to be true*. All **A** and **I** statements with the same subject and predicate terms, **E** and **O** statements with the same subject and predicate terms, and **I** and **O** statements with the same subject and predicate terms are logically consistent. Two statements are said to be **logically independent** if *knowledge of the truth value of one (either true or false) tells us nothing about the truth value of the other, and vice versa*. It is impossible for the four types of categorical statement with the same subject and predicate terms to be logically independent.

7. The traditional square of opposition exhibits a variety of types of immediate inference and illustrates the logical relationships that exist among the four types of categorical statements. **Contradictory** propositions are *categorical statements with the same subject and predicate terms that cannot both be true nor both false*. All **A** and **O** propositions and all **E** and **I** propositions with the same subject and predicate terms are contradictories. Two categorical statements are **contraries** if they are related in such a way that *both cannot be true, but both can be false*. All **A** and **E** propositions with the same subject and predicate terms are contraries. **Subcontraries** are

statements with the same subject and predicate terms that are such that *both cannot be false, but both can be true.* All **I** and **O** statements with the same subject and predicate terms are subcontraries. **Subimplication** is the process by which *the truth of a particular statement is inferred from the truth of its corresponding universal statement.* **I** and **O** statements are sub-implicants of **A** and **E** propositions (respectively) with the same subject and predicate terms. **Superimplication** is the process by which *the falsity of the universal statement is inferred from the falsity of its corresponding particular statement.* **A** and **E** propositions are superimplicants of **I** and **O** propositions (respectively) with the same subject and predicate terms.

8. Two propositions are **logically equivalent** if *the truth of one statement necessitates the truth of the other, and vice versa,* **and** *the falsity of one statement necessitates the falsity of the other, and vice versa.*

9. In contrast to the traditional interpretation that the subject terms of categorical propositions must be about classes that contain at least one member, on the **Boolean interpretation** *the classes referred to by the subject and predicate terms are not required to have any members.* However, on this interpretation, the **I** and **O** propositions are interpreted as being compound propositions that include the assertion that at least one member of the subject class exists. The Boolean interpretation has the same Venn diagrams for **I** and **O** propositions as does the traditional interpretation, but since it does not require that the subject terms refer to classes having members, the diagrams for **A** and **E** propositions on this interpretation do not have any Xs. The only part of the square of opposition that exists on the Boolean interpretation is the diagonal relation of contradictoriness.

10. **Obversion** is *the mechanical process of changing the quality of a categorical statement and replacing the predicate term with its complement.* (The **complement of a class** is *the class of all things or beings in the universe of discourse that do not belong to the class* and is expressed by joining the prefix 'non' to the name of the class.) The obverses of all four types of categorical proposition are logically equivalent to their original statements on the Boolean interpretation.

11. **Conversion** is *the mechanical process of interchanging the subject and predicate terms of a categorical proposition.* All **E** and **I** propositions—but no **A** or **O** propositions—are logically equivalent to their converses on the Boolean interpretation.

12. **Contraposition** is *the process of interchanging the subject and predicate terms of a categorical statement and then replacing each with its complement.* Any **O** statement is logically equivalent to its contrapositive, and any **A** statement is logically equivalent to its contrapositive. No **I** or **E** statements are logically equivalent to their contrapositives on the Boolean interpretation.

Chapter 4

Aristotelian Logic: Arguments

Each group below contains three sentences, each of which expresses a categorical statement or proposition.[1] Examine each set of statements carefully to determine whether it is an argument, and, if it is an argument, whether it is valid. As specified in Chapter 2, an argument is a group of statements, one of which (the conclusion) is identified as being supported by the other statements. An argument is valid when the truth of the premises necessitates the truth of the conclusion; that is, it is such that it is impossible for all of the premises to be true and the conclusion false.

1. All college graduates are educated persons. All employees of this company are college graduates. Therefore, all employees of this company are educated persons.

2. No students who are on the Dean's List are lazy, since no students on the Dean's List have poor grades, and all lazy students have poor grades.

3. Some physical exercises are not dangerous activities. All physical exercises are sports, so some sports are not dangerous activities.

4. All humans make mistakes. Perfect teachers never make mistakes. Thus, no humans are perfect teachers.

Each of these groups of sentences expresses an intended argument; each has an indicator word ('therefore,' 'so,' 'since,' and 'thus') which enables us to

---

[1] We continue to follow the two stipulations previously specified. When no specific context is given for a sentence, the reader should interpret it as expressing the statement that it would normally be used to express in ordinary usage. Also, we usually abbreviate the technically accurate expression 'The statement expressed by the sentence "such and such" ' simply as 'The statement "such and such." '

distinguish the premises from the intended conclusion, and the premises do provide support for the conclusion in each case. For example, in the second group, the word 'since' indicates that the second and third statements are being offered in support of the first statement, which is the conclusion. Intended arguments presented in everyday contexts are often formulated in this way.

Your logical intuition guided you correctly if you concluded that each of these groups of statements is a valid argument. Each argument is such that, if all of the premises are true, then the conclusion must be true. In this chapter, we present several methods for testing arguments of this kind for validity, methods that are more reliable than intuition.

In Chapter 3 we were concerned only with logical relations between pairs of statements, some of which were such that, from the truth or falsity of one of the statements, we could directly infer the truth or falsity of the other. Such inferences are *immediate* inferences. In this chapter we shall be concerned with arguments, such as those above which consist of exactly three logically interconnected statements, of a form known as the 'syllogism.' In arguments such as these, which involve **mediated inferences,** the conclusion is drawn from the two premises through a "mediating" term which appears in both premises. In each of the arguments above, the two premises have a term in common, such as 'college graduates' in the first argument and 'physical exercises' in the third.

4.1 The Categorical Syllogism

The **categorical syllogism** is defined in terms of logical form.[2] It is an argument or intended argument

1. *composed of exactly three categorical statements,*
2. *containing three different terms,*
3. *each of which appears twice, but*
4. *each appears only once in any one statement.*

Using this definition, we can determine whether the arguments presented at the beginning of this chapter are categorical syllogisms. Each argument does consist of three statements, but are they all categorical statements? Examine them carefully, identifying each as an **A, E, I,** or **O** categorical statement. Do the arguments fit the requirements concerning the number of terms, their placement within the argument, and their appearance within each statement? Consider the first argument. Its three categorical statements contain only three terms: 'employees of this company,' 'college graduates,' and 'educated persons.' Each

---

[2]Most syllogisms are invalid; fewer than ten percent are valid. Many of the invalid syllogisms are such that their premises provide no support for the conclusion. Thus, many syllogisms are not arguments in the strict sense of the term as it was defined in Chapter 2. Because all syllogisms bear a striking resemblance to each other due to their common form, those that are in fact nonarguments are often assumed (mistakenly) to be arguments.

term appears only twice in the argument, and only once in any one statement. Because the first argument is composed of three categorical statements, and because it also satisfies the requirements concerning the number and location of terms, it is a categorical syllogism. The other arguments presented above also can be shown to be categorical syllogisms.

We will again use the traditional interpretation that *all categorical statements require the existence of at least one member in the classes referred to by the subject terms.*

EXERCISE 4-1

Determine whether each of the following sets of statements is a categorical syllogism.

1. All bees can sting.
   Some bees are insects.
   Therefore, some insects can sting.

2. All Vulcans are completely logical persons.
   Mr. Spock is a Vulcan.
   Therefore, Mr. Spock is a completely logical person.

3. No fluorescent lights are incandescent lights.
   Some electric lights are incandescent lights.
   Therefore, some electric lights are not incandescent lights.

4. No sloops are airplanes.
   All hydroplanes are motorboats.
   Therefore, no hydroplanes are sloops.

5. Some drinkers are drunkards. All drunkards are alcoholics. Therefore, some drinkers are alcoholics.

6. All documentaries are educational. Some films are documentaries. Therefore, some films are educational.

7. All cats are mammals. All mammals are vertebrates. All vertebrates are animals. Therefore, all cats are animals.

8. If this painting is a Rembrandt, then it must be expensive. This painting is a Rembrandt. Therefore, this painting must be expensive.

9. No politicians are dishonest; therefore, no dishonest persons are politicians.

10. No hyperbolas are squares, since all hyperbolas are conic sections, but no squares are conic sections.

11. Some revolutionaries are not Marxists, but all communists are Marxists, so some revolutionaries are not communists.

12. Some food additives should not be allowed, because some food additives are dangerous to human health, and no substances dangerous to human health should be allowed.

13. No generals are kangaroos, since all generals are soldiers, and no kangaroos are soldiers.

14. Some insects are bees; therefore, some insects can sting, since all bees can sting.

15. Some coaches are teachers, so some teachers are coaches.

16. No toadstools are edible things, so some mushrooms are not toadstools, for some edible things are mushrooms.

17. If there is no God, then there is no order in the universe. There is order in the universe. Therefore, God exists.

18. Some respectable citizens are not Democrats, because all mayors are respectable citizens, but some mayors are not Democrats.

19. All Senators are citizens, so all non-citizens are non-Senators.

20. Some people do not have the use of reason; therefore, some rational animals do not have the use of reason, since all people are rational animals.

4.2 Standard-Form Syllogisms

We found in Chapter 3 that using a standard form for the sentences expressing each type of categorical statement is quite useful when studying immediate inferences. This is also true when dealing with categorical syllogisms. When a syllogism is composed of three categorical statements expressed by standard-form sentences and when these statements are presented in a given order, then the syllogism is said to be in standard form. For obvious reasons, when a syllogism is in standard form, the conclusion follows the two premises. The order of the premises is determined by the subject and predicate terms of the conclusion.

The *predicate term of the conclusion* is called the **major term,** and the *subject term of the conclusion* is called the **minor term.** The *term that appears in both premises but not in the conclusion* is called the **middle term** of the syllogism. The premise containing the major term is called the **major premise;** the premise containing the minor term is called the **minor premise.** By definition, a syllogism is in **standard form** when *its three categorical statements, expressed by standard-form sentences, follow the order of major premise, minor premise, and conclusion.*

Standard-Form Syllogism

Major premise—contains predicate term of the conclusion.

Minor premise—contains subject term of the conclusion.

Therefore, the conclusion.

Let us return to the first argument presented at the beginning of this chapter to determine whether it is in standard form.

All college graduates are educated persons.
All employees of this company are college graduates.
Therefore, all employees of this company are educated persons.

All three statements are expressed by standard-form sentences. The predicate term of the conclusion, 'educated persons,' is by definition the major term, and thus the premise containing it (the major premise) should appear first in the syllogism, as it does. 'Employees of this company' is the minor term, since it is

"If the coach and horses and the footmen and the beautiful clothes all turned back into the pumpkin and the mice and the rags, then how come the glass slipper didn't turn back, too?"

Drawing by H. Martin; © *1974 The New Yorker Magazine, Inc.*

Has the child in this cartoon formulated a valid syllogism that punches a hole in the classic fairy tale about Cinderella? The methods to be presented in this chapter will help you to evaluate this intended argument.

the subject of the conclusion, and the premise containing it (the minor premise) appears second, followed by the conclusion. The middle term in this example is 'college graduates,' which appears once in each premise, as it should. Therefore, this categorical syllogism is in standard form.

We have already indicated that the second argument is not in standard form:

No students who are on the Dean's List are lazy, since no students on the Dean's List have poor grades, and all lazy students have poor grades.

The first thing that must be done is to put each sentence into standard form, making certain that each subject and predicate term contains a noun or a noun phrase. Thus, the first sentence, 'No students who are on the Dean's List are lazy' should be translated into something like 'No students who are on the Dean's List are lazy students.' The second sentence can be translated into 'No students who are on the Dean's List are students with poor grades,' in which case the third sentence must read 'All lazy students are students with poor grades.' If the second premise had been translated as 'No students who are on the Dean's List are *persons* with poor grades,' then the third premise would have to be translated as 'All lazy students are *persons* with poor grades' in order to adhere to the requirement that a standard-form syllogism have only three terms.

Of course, merely translating each sentence into standard form does not make this argument a standard-form syllogism. Its conclusion, 'No students who are on the Dean's List are lazy students,' comes first, but it should come last. The predicate term of the conclusion, 'lazy students,' makes the statement 'All lazy students are students with poor grades' the major premise, which should come first. This should be followed by 'No students on the Dean's List are students with poor grades,' the minor premise since it contains the minor term 'students on the Dean's List,' which is the subject term of the conclusion. Written in standard form, the argument should read as follows:

All lazy students are students with poor grades.
No students on the Dean's List are students with poor grades.
Therefore, no students on the Dean's List are lazy students.

The third argument is already in standard form, but the fourth argument must be rewritten.

All humans make mistakes.
Perfect teachers never make mistakes.
Therefore, no humans are perfect teachers.

The premise that is now first does not have a copula and the predicate does not contain a noun; its standard form is 'All humans are persons who make mistakes.' The sentence 'Perfect teachers never make mistakes' also must be translated into standard form, keeping in mind that its subject and predicate terms should be expressed in the same way as the corresponding terms in the other sentences. Consequently, this sentence would be translated as 'No perfect teachers are persons who make mistakes.' (Notice that we had to be careful not to embed the negation in the predicate; it would have been a problem if we had translated this as the **A** statement 'All perfect teachers are persons who never make mistakes.') The predicate term of the conclusion, 'perfect teachers,' is the major term, and 'humans,' the subject term, is the minor term. Therefore, 'No perfect teachers are persons who make mistakes' is the major premise and should come first, not second. 'All humans are persons who make mistakes' is the minor premise, since it contains the minor term, 'humans.' In standard form, the argument now reads:

No perfect teachers are persons who make mistakes.
All humans are persons who make mistakes.
Therefore, no humans are perfect teachers.

When putting a categorical syllogism in standard form, follow this procedure:

1. Translate its three sentences into standard categorical form, if they are not already so, making sure that the subject and predicate terms are worded in exactly the same way in both occurrences.

2. Determine which sentence expresses the conclusion and place it third.

3. Find the premise that contains the predicate term of the conclusion and place that premise first.

4. Make sure that the minor premise (containing the subject term of the conclusion) now comes second.

EXERCISE 4–2

For each of the sets of statements in Exercise 4–1 that is a categorical syllogism, determine whether it is in standard form. If it is not, put it in standard form.

4.2.1 Abbreviating Syllogisms

Syllogisms can be represented in shortened form by using the methods of abbreviation presented in the previous chapter. In addition, the symbol '∴' should be used as an abbreviation of the word 'therefore' or any other conclusion indicator. Thus, the third argument presented at the beginning of this chapter,

> Some physical exercises are not dangerous activities.
> All physical exercises are sports.
> It follows that some sports are not dangerous activities.

can be abbreviated as follows:

> Some E are not D.
> All E are S.
> ∴ Some S are not D.

Consider another categorical syllogism:

> No well-illustrated books are dull books.
> Some textbooks are well-illustrated books.
> Therefore, some textbooks are not dull books.

This syllogism can be abbreviated in the following way, which also makes it easier to see that the syllogism is in standard form.

> No W are D.
> Some T are W.
> ∴ Some T are not D.

4.2.2 Syllogistic Schemas

As we saw in Chapter 3, each type of categorical proposition has a logical form, which can be represented by a schema. The logical form of a categorical syllogism also can be represented by a schema. Let us consider the preceding example about textbooks. As with all categorical syllogisms, it contains three terms: a major term, a minor term, and a middle term. If we remove the terms and fill the remaining blanks with different symbols, we have the following:

> No ******* are . . . .
> Some _____ are *******
> ∴ Some _____ are not . . . .

We have presented a schema for each proposition, substituting the same symbol for each term when it appears. Thus, any three nouns or noun phrases can be substituted in the above schema to produce a syllogism with the same form as the preceding syllogism about textbooks. For the sake of clarification, let us consider for a moment the following example:

> No friends are enemies.
> Some relatives are friends.
> ∴ Some relatives are not enemies.

For the remainder of this chapter we will use the symbol '<u>P</u>' (for predicate) to represent the major term in the schema of any syllogism, '<u>S</u>' (for subject) to represent the minor term, and '<u>M</u>' to signify the position of the middle term.

The standard-form syllogism can be outlined as follows:

Major premise—must contain <u>P</u> and <u>M</u>.
Minor premise—must contain <u>S</u> and <u>M</u>.
Conclusion—<u>S</u> must be the subject and <u>P</u> must be the predicate.

Using the symbols '<u>S</u>,' '<u>P</u>,' and '<u>M</u>' as stipulated above to represent the minor, major, and middle terms, respectively, the schema of any syllogism can be presented concisely. It should be recognized that these symbols are *not* abbreviations; rather they function as blanks into which any noun or noun phrase can be inserted to produce sentences expressing categorical statements. Thus, the following schema,

> No <u>M</u> are <u>P</u>.
> Some <u>S</u> are <u>M</u>.
> ∴ Some <u>S</u> are not <u>P</u>.

displays the logical form of these syllogisms:

> **No well-illustrated books are dull books.**
> **Some textbooks are well-illustrated books.**
> **Therefore, some textbooks are not dull books.**

> **No friends are enemies.**
> **Some relatives are friends.**
> **Therefore, some relatives are not enemies.**

and any other syllogisms with the same logical form.

The process of substituting nouns or noun phrases for the symbols (or blanks) in a schema to produce a syllogism is called the **interpretation** of the schema. For example, consider the following schema:

> No <u>P</u> are <u>M</u>.
> Some <u>M</u> are <u>S</u>.
> ∴ Some <u>S</u> are not <u>P</u>.

Suppose the term 'poets' is substituted for '<u>P</u>,' 'students' for '<u>S</u>,' and 'manipulative people' for '<u>M</u>' in the schema above. This interpretation (that is, substitution of nouns or noun phrases) would produce the following categorical syllogism:

> **No poets are manipulative people.**
> **Some manipulative people are students.**
> **Therefore, some students are not poets.**

Write (a) an abbreviation of the syllogism and (b) its corresponding schema for each of the arguments in Exercise 4–1 that is a categorical syllogism. Make certain the syllogism is in standard form before writing an abbreviation and schema for it.

4.3 Mood and Figure

Notice that each of the last three categorical syllogisms in Section 4.2.2 and the two following schemas has an **E** statement for the major premise, an **I** statement for the minor premise, and an **O** statement for the conclusion. This, of course, does not hold true for all syllogisms in standard form. Look back at the arguments at the beginning of the chapter. The first consists of three **A** statements, and the third argument has an **O** statement for the major premise, an **A** statement for the minor premise, and an **O** statement for the conclusion. Thus, standard-form categorical syllogisms can be composed of various combinations of categorical statements.

Although the last two examples in the previous section have similar schemas, a careful examination shows that they are not exactly the same. These syllogisms have different schemas because the middle term is in a different position in the respective premises. Such similarities and differences between syllogisms are identified in terms of the concepts of mood and figure.

The **mood** of a standard-form syllogism is *the particular combination of categorical statements of which the syllogism is composed,* expressed in terms of the statement names **A, E, I,** and **O.** The first letter in the mood description indicates the form of the major premise, the second that of the minor premise, and the third that of the conclusion. Thus, the mood of the first argument at the beginning of this chapter is expressed as **AAA,** and the mood of the third as **OAO.** The three syllogisms for which schemas were given at the end of the previous section all have the same mood, namely, **EIO.**

Syllogisms having the same mood do not necessarily have the same logical form. Therefore, the description of the mood of a syllogism is not sufficient for revealing its exact form. The following two schemas have the same mood, **EIO;** can you identify the way in which they are different?

No <u>M</u> are <u>P</u>.   No <u>P</u> are <u>M</u>.
Some <u>S</u> are <u>M</u>.   Some <u>M</u> are <u>S</u>.
∴ Some <u>S</u> are not <u>P</u>.   ∴ Some <u>S</u> are not <u>P</u>.

How do these two schemas differ? The difference is in the placement of the middle term. In the schema on the left, the middle term is the subject of the major premise and the predicate of the minor premise. In the schema on the right, the middle term is the predicate of the major premise and the subject of the minor premise. The **figure** of a standard-form categorical syllogism is determined by the placement of the middle term in the two premises of the syllogism.

Two other locations are possible for the middle term besides those given. The middle term could also be the subject of both premises, or it could be the predicate of both premises. These four arrangements of the middle term are the only figures possible for categorical syllogisms; they have traditionally been numbered as follows:

Figure 1	All observant people are expert drivers.	M–P
	All students are observant people.	S–M
	Therefore, some students are expert drivers.	
Figure 2	All expert drivers are observant people.	P–M
	All students are observant people.	S–M
	Therefore, some students are expert drivers.	
Figure 3	All observant people are expert drivers.	M–P
	All observant people are students.	M–S
	Therefore, some students are expert drivers.	
Figure 4	All expert drivers are observant people.	P–M
	All observant people are students.	M–S
	Therefore, some students are expert drivers.	

Observe that the placement of the middle term affects the figure of the syllogism but not its mood.

The **form** of a syllogism *is determined by the combination of its figure and its mood.* It is conventional to express the form of a syllogism by placing the number of its figure after the letters that state its mood. Thus the form of the figure 1 syllogism above is **AAA-1.** For the figure 2 syllogism, the form is **AOO-2.** For the figure 3 syllogism, the form is **IAI-3,** and for the figure 4 syllogism, **EIO-4.** (Notice that the form of a syllogism symbolized in this way is actually an abbreviation of the schema.)

A standard mnemonic, or memory-aiding, device will help you relate the placement of the middle term to the proper number of the figure of a syllogism. A line is drawn through the middle terms with the figures arranged in order, as follows:

Figure 1	Figure 2	Figure 3	Figure 4
M P	P M	M P	P M
S M	S M	M S	M S

Memorizing this pattern might help you to determine the figure of a syllogism or to construct a syllogism in any given figure.

Give the form (the mood and figure) of each of the categorical syllogisms in Exercise 4–2.

Write out the schemas for the arguments with the following forms.

1. **AIA-3**   5. **EAO-4**   9. **III-4**
2. **EOI-1**   6. **IOO-2**   10. **EII-3**
3. **OIE-4**   7. **AAA-3**   11. **AII-1**
4. **IEO-2**   8. **EEO-1**   12. **IAI-2**

4.4 Testing the Validity of Syllogisms

The form of a categorical syllogism is completely specified when its mood and figure are given. Since syllogisms are defined solely in terms of logical form, not all syllogisms are valid arguments. In fact, as mentioned earlier, fewer than ten percent of the 256 different syllogistic forms are valid, and many of them are not even arguments (i.e., the premises provide *no* logical support for the conclusion).

The validity or invalidity of a syllogism does not depend on the terms used in it, that is, on its content, but solely on its form. Syllogisms with certain forms are valid, whereas those with other forms are invalid. This is true regardless of the actual terms in the statements and regardless of the truth or falsity of the statements composing the syllogisms. Consider, for example, the following syllogisms:

All primates are vertebrates.	All $\underline{P}$ are $\underline{M}$.
No insects are vertebrates.	No $\underline{S}$ are $\underline{M}$.
Therefore, no insects are primates.	$\therefore$ No $\underline{S}$ are $\underline{P}$.

All primates are invertebrates.	All $\underline{P}$ are $\underline{M}$.
No insects are invertebrates.	No $\underline{S}$ are $\underline{M}$.
Therefore, no insects are primates.	$\therefore$ No $\underline{S}$ are $\underline{P}$.

Both syllogisms have the same form, **AEE-2**. Since primates, in fact, are vertebrates and insects are not vertebrates, the premises of the first syllogism are both true; the conclusion is also true, for insects are distinct from primates. But the premises of the second syllogism are both false, for primates, in fact, are not invertebrates, but insects are invertebrates. However, the conclusion of the second syllogism, the same as that for the first, is true. Thus, the same true conclusion was drawn in the first syllogism from true premises and in the second syllogism from false premises by use of syllogisms of exactly the same form.

Both syllogisms above are valid, since their logical form is such that for any argument with this form, *if* its premises are true, *then* its conclusion *must* be true. In other words, an argument is valid if and only if *no* argument with that form can have true premises and a false conclusion—that is, the truth of the conclusion follows necessarily from the truth of the premises.

The schema of a statement or proposition cannot properly be said to be true or false; only the statement itself can be so described. Thus, the schema of the true statement, 'All primates are vertebrates,' is 'All S̲ are P̲,' which is not true or false until terms are inserted into the blanks represented by the symbols 'S̲' and 'P̲.' However, an argument schema that shows the form of a syllogism can be characterized as valid or invalid.

A **valid argument schema** is an argument schema for which *there is no possible interpretation—that is, no substitution of terms—that would create an argument with true premises and a false conclusion.* For example, no terms substituted for the symbols in the valid argument schema

> All P̲ are M̲.
> No S̲ are M̲.
> ∴ No S̲ are P̲.

would produce a syllogism with true premises and a false conclusion. An argument is valid if and only if its schema is valid. Consequently, the two syllogisms at the beginning of this section are valid because the argument schema which they share in common is valid.

If a schema is not valid, then no syllogism that is an interpretation of that schema can be valid either. Several methods have been developed for testing the validity and/or invalidity of syllogisms. One such method involves the use of counterexamples.

4.5 Testing by Counterexamples

A **counterexample** is *an interpretation of an argument schema that makes all the premises true and the conclusion false.* An interpretation is the substitution of terms (nouns or noun phrases) for the blanks S̲, P̲, and M̲ of the argument schema. Therefore, this method of testing syllogisms involves constructing a syllogism with a particular logical form that can be seen to be clearly invalid. Let us consider the following syllogism on the understanding that both premises and the conclusion are true.

> All women are good administrators.   All P̲ are M̲.
> Some employees are good administrators.   Some S̲ are M̲.
> Therefore, some employees are women.   ∴ Some S̲ are P̲.

You might have a gut-feeling that something is wrong with this syllogism. You may suspect that it is not valid. But can you *prove* that it is invalid? If you can construct a counterexample—that is, if you can find an argument with the same logical form (i.e., an interpretation of the same schema) that makes both premises true and the conclusion false—then you will have proved that the schema (and *all* arguments with this form) are invalid. The following argument provides such a counterexample:

All apples are fruits.	All $\underline{P}$ are $\underline{M}$.
Some berries are fruits.	Some $\underline{S}$ are $\underline{M}$.
Therefore, some berries are apples.	∴ Some $\underline{S}$ are $\underline{P}$.

Because the conclusion of this interpretation of the schema is false while the two premises are true, the schema has been shown to be invalid. Therefore, the original syllogism also must be invalid, as are all other syllogisms of this form (**AII-2**).

Providing a counterexample with true premises and a false conclusion proves the invalidity of a particular syllogistic form, *but failing to provide a counterexample, or providing an example with true premises and a true conclusion, does **not** prove the **validity** of a syllogistic form.* Examine the following syllogisms:

All Rolls Royces are large cars.
No Rolls Royces are cars that get good mileage.
Therefore, no cars that get good mileage are large cars.

All cats are felines.
No cats are canines.
Therefore, no canines are felines.

Both syllogisms have true premises and true conclusions and both have the form **AEE-3.** Many more examples of syllogisms of this form with true premises and true conclusions could be given, but they would not prove that there is *no* interpretation of the **AEE-3** schema that results in true premises and a false conclusion. As a matter of fact, the substitution of 'Neons' for '$\underline{S}$,' 'Fords' for '$\underline{P}$,' and 'automobiles' for '$\underline{M}$' does produce such a counterexample:

All Fords are automobiles.
No Fords are Neons.
Therefore, no Neons are automobiles.

Both premises are true, but the conclusion, 'No Neons are automobiles,' is false, since all Neons *are* automobiles. This single counterexample shows that *all* syllogisms of the form **AEE-3** are invalid, because it shows that it is *possible* for a syllogism with this form to have true premises and a false conclusion. A thousand examples of arguments of this form with true premises and true conclusions would not prove its validity.

Counterexamples can be used *only* to prove the invalidity of an argument schema. Even at this task the method of looking for counterexamples is not always effective, since counterexamples are often difficult to think up. There is also the problem that the truth or falsity of most specific statements can be challenged in one way or another. Thus, few counterexamples can be taken as absolute, since someone could usually argue that an apparently true premise is possibly false, or a seemingly false conclusion is really true.

What we really need is a **decision procedure,** a *mechanical procedure that can be used to prove the validity or invalidity of any particular syllogism in a finite number of steps.* An ideal decision procedure also would avoid the problem of determining the actual truth or falsity of specific statements, as is necessary in the method of counterexamples. Two other techniques, one using Venn diagrams and the other a set of rules, provide such "ideal" decision procedures.

EXERCISE 4–6

Write counterexamples for each of the following invalid syllogisms, all of which are in standard form.

1. All Nigerians are Africans.
   Some Africans are college-educated persons.
   Therefore, some college-educated persons are Nigerians.

2. Some conservatives are Republicans.
   No Republicans are Democrats.
   Therefore, some Democrats are not conservatives.

3. No lions are tigers.
   No tigers are cheetahs.
   Therefore, no cheetahs are lions.

4. Some humans are not musicians.
   All New Yorkers are humans.
   Therefore, some New Yorkers are not musicians.

5. All Chicagoans are citizens.
   Some citizens are beer drinkers.
   Therefore, some beer drinkers are Chicagoans.

6. All flowers are plants.
   All roses are plants.
   Therefore, all roses are flowers.

7. No captains are generals.
   All captains are officers.
   Therefore, no officers are generals.

8. All falcons are hawks.
   Some birds are hawks.
   Therefore, some birds are falcons.

9. All primates are mammals.
   No primates are egg-bearing animals.
   Therefore, no egg-bearing animals are mammals.

10. All addicts are persons to be pitied.
    All addicts are unhappy persons.
    Therefore, all unhappy persons are persons to be pitied.

11. No rocks are intelligent things.
    No clouds are rocks.
    Therefore, no clouds are intelligent things.

12. Some animals are extinct species.
    No animals are perennial flowers.
    Therefore, some perennial flowers are not extinct species.

13. Some animals are stray animals.
    All dogs are animals.
    Therefore, some dogs are stray animals.

14. All Nazis are culpable persons.
    Some Germans are not Nazis.
    Therefore, some Germans are not culpable persons.

4.6 Testing with Venn Diagrams

Venn diagrams were used in Chapter 3 to exhibit the logical forms of **A, E, I,** and **O** statements and to test whether two categorical statements are logically equivalent. One circle was used to represent each of the two terms of every statement. Venn diagrams also can be used to represent categorical *syllogisms* and to test for their validity or invalidity. Because the standard-form syllogism has three terms—subject, predicate, and middle term—each of which designates a different class of things, three overlapping circles are required to represent the classes to which the three terms refer.

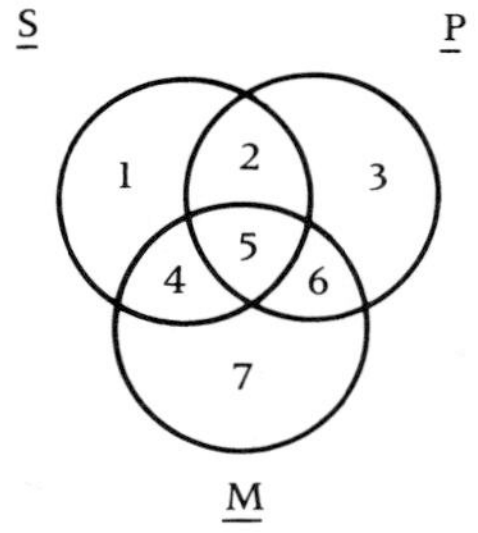

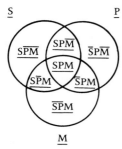

Figure 4–1

4.6.1 Venn Diagrams and Syllogistic Schemas

The three terms of the standard-form syllogism are conventionally diagrammed using the symbols S̲, P̲ and M̲ to stand for the blanks to be filled in by the minor term, the major term, and the middle terms respectively, as shown in Figure 4–1, with the labels placed outside the circles. The S̲ circle represents the class of things referred to by whichever minor term might be supplied; the P̲ circle represents the class of things referred to by the major term; and the M̲ circle represents the class of things referred to by the middle term.

Each of the distinct areas in the circles represents a distinct class, as shown in Figure 4–2. The line above a letter indicates a negation. In other words 'M̄' indicates that no members of the M̲ class are contained in the area designated by 'M̄.'

The center area labeled S̲PM̲ contains all those things that are members of all three classes whose names might be substituted for S̲, P̲, and M̲. Since a bar above a symbol in a section indicates that anything contained in that section is *not* a member of the class signified by that symbol, the area labeled S̲PM̄ contains all those things that are members of the S̲ class (without a bar), but that

Figure 4–2

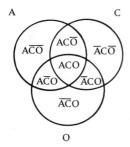

Figure 4–3

are *not* members of the P̲ and M̲ classes, since the P̲ and M̲ circles do not overlap this section of the S̲ circle.

The substitution of nouns or noun phrases for S̲, P̲, and M̲ in the diagram of an argument schema gives us the diagram of a specific argument. Let us provide an interpretation of an argument schema by substituting the term 'artists' for S̲, the term 'creators' for P̲, and the term 'original thinkers' for M̲. In this instance, the various areas of the Venn diagram shown in Figure 4–3 represent the following classes:

ACO is the class of things that are artists, creators, and original thinkers.

ACO̅ is the class of things that are both artists and creators but are not original thinkers.

AC̅O is the class of things that are both artists and original thinkers but are not creators.

A̅CO is the class of things that are both creators and original thinkers but are not artists.

A̅C̅O is the class of things that are original thinkers but are neither artists nor creators.

AC̅O̅ is the class of things that are artists but are neither creators nor original thinkers.

A̅CO̅ is the class of things that are creators but are neither artists nor original thinkers.

A̅C̅O̅ is the class of things that are neither artists, creators nor original thinkers.

EXERCISE 4–7

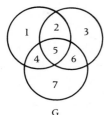

Figure 4–4

Using the Venn diagram in Figure 4–4, indicate which sections (at least one, possibly several) satisfy the conditions specified.

1. Something that is only red.
2. Something that is only blue.
3. Something that is only green.
4. Something that is red and blue but not green.
5. Something that is blue and green but not red.
6. Something that is green and red but not blue.
7. Something that is red and green and blue.
8. Something that is red or blue or green or any combination of them.

4.6.2 Diagramming Categorical Syllogisms

In using Venn diagrams to represent standard-form syllogisms, we will continue to require that the class named by the subject term in every statement must contain at least one member. However, we cannot simply apply the methods used for diagramming individual statements in Chapter 3. The diagrams in

Chapter 3 were for individual categorical statements; the diagrams we must draw now are for logically interconnected pairs of statements. Thus, it is necessary to use a more complex procedure for diagramming that takes account of the interconnections between the major and minor premises of an argument. The rules for diagramming a syllogism are summarized in the following box.

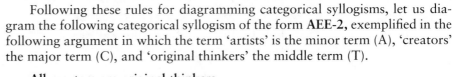

Rules for Diagramming Categorical Syllogisms

The steps should be followed in the sequence specified below.

1. If the major premise states that one (or more) specific area(s) is(are) empty, shade the appropriate area(s).
2. If the minor premise states that one (or more) specific area(s) is(are) empty, shade the appropriate area(s).
3. If the major premise states that at least one thing exists in one specific unshaded area, place an X in that area.
4. If the minor premise states that at least one thing exists in one specific unshaded area, place an X in that area if no X is already there.
5. If the major premise states that at least one thing exists in one or the other of two adjacent unshaded areas, *neither* of which already contains an X, place an X on the line between those areas.
6. If the minor premise states that at least one thing exists in one or the other of two adjacent unshaded areas, *neither* of which already contains an X, place an X on the line between those areas.
7. Do *NOT* draw the conclusion on the diagram.
   a. If anything needs to be added to the diagram of the premises in order to represent the information in the conclusion, then the syllogism is invalid.
   b. If nothing needs to be added to the diagram of the premises in order to represent the information in the conclusion, then the syllogism is valid.

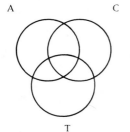

Figure 4–5

Following these rules for diagramming categorical syllogisms, let us diagram the following categorical syllogism of the form **AEE-2,** exemplified in the following argument in which the term 'artists' is the minor term (A), 'creators' the major term (C), and 'original thinkers' the middle term (T).

All creators are original thinkers.
No artists are original thinkers.
Therefore, no artists are creators.

This form is valid, even though one might consider all the statements in this particular interpretation to be false.

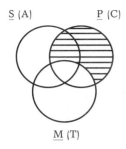

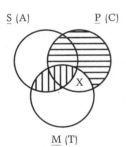

Figure 4–6

First, draw a Venn diagram representing the three terms of this syllogism. The circle representing the class of things referred to by the minor term is labeled 'A'; the circle representing the major term class is labeled 'C'; and the circle representing the middle term class is labeled 'T,' as shown in Figure 4–5.

Step 1 The major premise, 'All creators are original thinkers,' tells us that all members of the class of creators are included in the class of original thinkers, that is, the part of the C circle outside the T circle contains no members. Therefore, these sections of the C circle are shaded as shown in Figure 4–6.

Figure 4–7

Step 2 The minor premise, 'No artists are original thinkers,' tells us that all sections of the A circle that are inside the T circle are empty and thus should be shaded as is shown in Figure 4–7. This is all the shading that needs to be done for the premises. In using Venn diagrams to test a syllogism for validity, we never diagram the conclusion, so we don't add any shading for the conclusion.

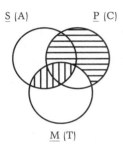

Step 3 Going back to the major premise, we can see that it also tells us that all members of the class of creators are also members of the class of original thinkers. Thus, when we place the X that shows that there is at least one member in its subject class of creators, we must make sure that this X also is inside the circle representing the class of original thinkers. Only one area satisfies this condition so we should put an X there now, as shown in Figure 4–8.

Step 4 With regard to the subject class of the minor premise, artists, only one section of the A circle is not shaded, so we must put an X in that section to indicate that at least one artist exists, as shown in Figure 4–9.

No further information is provided by the premises, so we do not need to do anything for Steps 5 and 6 of the procedure. The filling in of the diagram is now completed.

Figure 4–8

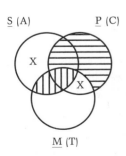

Step 7 Figure 4–9 displays all of the information contained in both the major and minor premises of the syllogism. To test the validity of this syllogism, we must determine whether the diagram of the conclusion is *already* contained in the diagram of the premises. The conclusion, 'No artists are creators,' asserts that all members of the class of artists are *excluded* from the class of creators. In terms of the diagram, 'No A are C' tells us explicitly that there is nothing inside the A circle that is also inside the C circle. The diagram in Figure 4–9 has shading in both of the sections where the A circle and the C circle overlap, and there is an X in the area of the A circle that is outside the C circle. Therefore, the diagram of the premises tells us that no artists are creators. Nothing more needs to be added to the diagram for the conclusion to be shown. The information in conclusion is already contained in the premises, as it must be in a valid syllogism.

Figure 4–9

A   C

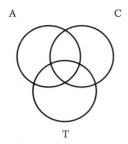

Figure 4–10

A   C

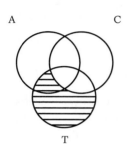

Figure 4–11

A   C

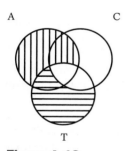

Figure 4–12

A   C

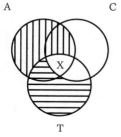

Figure 4–13

Let's use our procedure for diagramming another valid syllogism, this one with the form **AAA-1.**

> **All original thinkers are creators.**
> **All artists are original thinkers.**
> **Therefore, all artists are creators.**

First, draw a Venn diagram representing the three terms of this syllogism. The circle representing the class of things referred to by the minor term is labeled 'A'; the circle representing the major term class is labeled 'C'; and the circle representing the middle term class is labeled 'T,' as shown in Figure 4–10.

Step 1   The major premise, 'All original thinkers are creators,' since it is universal, should have its shading drawn into the diagram first. All of the T circle that is not within the C circle should be shaded to indicate that these parts are empty, since all members of T must also be in the class C, as shown in Figure 4–11.

Step 2   The minor premise, 'All artists are original thinkers,' asserts that all of the members of the class of artists are contained in the class of original thinkers, so we must shade all sections of the A circle outside the T circle to show that they are empty, as shown in Figure 4–12.

Step 3   We can now begin to place the Xs in the diagram for the premises to indicate the existence of at least one member in each of the subject classes of the major and minor premises, original thinkers (T) and artists (A), respectively. The major premise requires that its subject class have at least one member that is also a creator, but it does not specify whether this original thinker should be *inside* the class of artists or *outside* the class of artists. We do not yet have enough information to permit us put an X completely inside either one of the two areas where T and C overlap, so we must go on to the next step.

Step 4   The minor premise requires that there be an X somewhere in the A circle. Since only one area of the A circle is not shaded, the X must be placed in that area, as shown in Figure 4–13.

Step 5   Because the X we have just placed in the only nonshaded part of the A circle also happens to be in the T circle, this now also satisfies Step 3 and we have finished the diagram for the premises of this syllogism; the diagram now displays all of the information provided in the premises, so no additional Xs should be added for Step 5 or Step 6.

Step 7   Figure 4–13 displays all of the information contained in both the major and the minor premises of the syllogism. To test the validity of this syllogism, we must determine whether the diagram of the conclusion is *already* contained in the diagram of the premises. The conclusion, 'All artists are creators,' asserts that all members of the class of artists are also members of the class of creators. In terms of the diagram, 'All A are C' tells us that there is nothing inside the A circle that is not also inside the C circle. All of the sections of the A circle outside of the C circle are already shaded in Figure 4–13, and there is an X in the area of overlap between the A circle and the C circle. Therefore, the diagram of the premises contains all of the information in the conclusion, namely that all artists are creators. Nothing more needs to be added to the diagram for the conclusion to be shown, which proves that the syllogism is valid.

Let us consider another valid syllogism, also with the form **AAA-1**:

All <u>s</u>cientists are <u>e</u>xperimenters.
All <u>p</u>hysicists are scientists.
Therefore all physicists are experimenters.

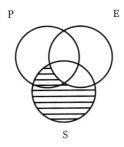

Figure 4–14

Step 1 The major premise, 'All scientists are experimenters,' tells us that the area of the S circle outside the E circle must be empty. Thus, the sections of the S circle outside the E circle are shaded, as shown in Figure 4–14.

Step 2 The minor premise, 'All physicists are scientists,' tells us that the areas of the P circle outside the S circle are also empty, so they should be shaded, as shown in Figure 4–15.

Figure 4–15

Step 3 The major premise requires that its subject class (scientists) have at least one member who is also in the major class (experimenters). But it doesn't specify whether the scientist must be a physicist or not. Thus, we do not know whether we should put the X for the major premise inside the P circle or outside of it or on the line, so we should not draw in any X at this time.

Step 4 Since the subject class of the minor premise must contain at least one member, and there is only one unshaded part of the P circle, we must place an X in that area of P as shown in Figure 4–16.

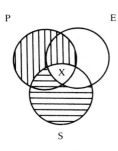

Figure 4–16

Step 5 The X that we placed in the diagram for the minor premise is in the P circle, so we don't need to add another one anywhere else in P. The diagram now contains all of the information contained in the two premises.

The Venn diagrams in Figures 4–13 and 4–16 are identical except for the labeling of the circles. This is not surprising, for we already know that all arguments with the same form (in this case, both are **AAA-1**) have the same schema, and we know that the Venn diagram displays the form of the argument. Consequently, all arguments that are interpretations of the same schema must have the same diagram.

We have seen also that an argument is valid if and only if its schema is valid. Thus, the validity or invalidity of an argument can be tested by testing its schema. However, when testing an argument schema, one must use the symbols <u>S</u>, <u>P</u>, and <u>M</u> to represent the minor, major, and middle terms, respectively. We next use a Venn diagram to display the form of the *schema* of a specific syllogism. In this example we put the abbreviations of the specific terms in parentheses to make it easier to read the diagram, although this is not necessary for persons who are experienced with this method.

A third valid form of syllogism is **OAO-3**, which can be illustrated by the following syllogism and schema:

Some politicians are not communicators.	**Some M̲ are not P̲.**
All politicians are lawyers.	**All M̲ are S̲.**
∴ **Some lawyers are not communicators.**	∴ **Some S̲ are not P̲.**

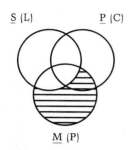

S̲ (L)   P̲ (C)

M̲ (P)

Figure 4–17

Step 1   The major premise is a particular (an **O**) statement and thus requires no shading; we can go to Step 2.

Step 2   'All politicians are lawyers' asserts that there are no politicians who are not also lawyers, so the sections of the M̲ circle not in the S̲ circle are shaded, as shown in Figure 4–17.

Step 3   The particular major premise, 'Some politicians are not communicators,' requires that at least one politician exists who is not a communicator. This can be shown in the diagram by placing an X in the section of the M̲ circle outside of the P̲ circle, as has been done in Figure 4–18. This X is also in the S̲ circle.

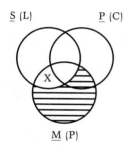

S̲ (L)   P̲ (C)

M̲ (P)

Figure 4–18

Step 4   The minor premise requires an X in a part of the M̲ circle that overlaps the S̲ circle. The X that we put in the diagram for the major premise already satisfies this requirement, so we don't need to do anything more for Step 4.

Step 7   All of the information provided by the premises has been drawn into the diagram, so we can skip Steps 5 and 6. Is all of the information in the conclusion already contained in the diagram of the premises? When we examine Figure 4–18 we can see that there is an X in a part of the S̲ circle that is outside of the P̲ circle, which indicates that there is at least one lawyer who is not a communicator, which is exactly what the conclusion says. Thus, the Venn diagram proves that *all* **OAO-3** syllogisms are valid.

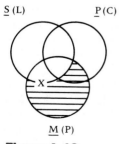

S̲ (L)   P̲ (C)

M̲ (P)

Figure 4–19

What would have happened if the particular major premise had been diagrammed before the universal minor premise? In this instance, the X representing the subject term in the major premise, 'Some M̲ are not P̲,' would have been placed directly on the line of the S̲ circle separating the two sections of the M̲ circle outside of the P̲ circle, as in Figure 4–19. The X would be placed on the line because the major premise does not specify in which section it belongs; it could be either of the two areas or both. Then, in diagramming the universal minor premise, 'All M̲ are S̲,' one of the sections containing the X on the line would have been shaded, thus covering half of the X. This, in effect, tells us that there is no X in the shaded area and that the half-X in the unshaded area should be replaced by a full X. This is why our procedure requires that we complete all shading before drawing any Xs into the diagram.

Another valid syllogistic form is **IAI-4**, illustrated by the following syllogism and schema:

Some mammals are sharks.   Some **P** are **M**.
All sharks are dangerous animals.   All **M** are **S**.
∴ **Some dangerous animals are mammals.**   ∴ Some **S** are **P**.

S (A)   P (M)

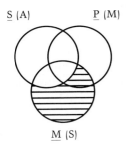

M (S)

Figure 4–20

Step 1   The major premise requires no shading.

Step 2   The universal minor premise, 'All sharks are dangerous animals,' asserts that there are no sharks that are not dangerous animals, so the sections of the M circle outside the S circle are shaded, as shown in Figure 4–20.

Step 3   The major premise 'Some mammals are sharks' tells us that there is at least one member of the shark class which is also a member of the mammal class. Since only one area of the diagram that represents mammals that are also sharks is not shaded, we must put an X there as shown in Figure 4–21.

S (A)   P (M)

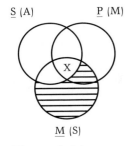

M (S)

Figure 4–21

Step 4   The minor premise also tells us that anything that is a member of the shark class is also a member of the class of dangerous animals. Since the X for the major premise is in one of the areas that represent classes of sharks which are also dangerous animals, we do not need to add another X. We should not place an X in the other unshaded area common to S and M or on the line between them, for this would indicate that this class has at least two members, but our premises do not tell us this.

Once again, we have drawn all of the information from the premises into the diagram, so we can skip Steps 5 and 6.

Step 7   We can now look to see whether all of the information in the conclusion is already contained in the diagram of the premises. The conclusion states that there is at least one thing that is both a dangerous animal and a mammal. The X in the diagram is in one of the areas common to S and P, so the argument is proven valid.

So far we have drawn diagrams only for valid syllogisms. In each example, once the premises had been diagrammed, all of the information in the conclusions was already contained in the diagrams of their two premises. This proved the validity of each of the forms discussed, for the conclusion of a valid argument is contained in the premises of that argument.

If the conclusion of a syllogism is not completely represented in the diagram of the premises, then the argument is invalid. Thus, this Venn diagram technique provides a decision procedure for determining the validity or invalidity of a syllogism. The seven steps of our diagramming procedure are sufficient to determine whether the argument is valid or invalid. Let us now show how Venn diagrams can be used to prove that certain syllogistic forms are invalid.

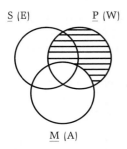

S (E)   P (W)

M (A)

Figure 4–22

Let's consider the following **AII-2** syllogism, which we put into standard form earlier in the chapter. The argument and its schema appear below.

All women are good administrators.	All P̲ are M̲.
Some employees are good administrators.	Some S̲ are M̲.
∴ Some employees are women.	∴ Some S̲ are P̲.

Step 1   The major premise, 'All women are good administrators,' tells us that all sections of the P̲ circle outside the M̲ circle are to be shaded, as shown in Figure 4–22.

Step 2   No shading is necessary for the minor premise.

Step 3   The major premise specifies that all members of the class of women are also in the class of good administrators, but it does not tell us whether they are included in or excluded from the class of employees. This means that we do not know whether the X should be inside or outside of the area common to the S̲, P̲, and M̲ circles. Thus, we must go to the minor premise to see if it gives any information that is more specific.

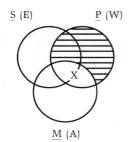

S (E)   P (W)

M (A)

Figure 4–23

Step 4   The minor premise only states that the class of employees contains at least one member that is also a member of the class of good administrators, which can be represented by an X in the area common to the P̲ and M̲ circles. But it does not specify whether this X should be inside or outside of the S̲ circle. Thus, neither premise clarifies the location of the X for the other premise and we must go on to Step 5.

Step 5   The additional information from the minor premise still does not clarify whether the member of the major class is inside or outside the S̲ class. Thus, we must place the X on the line of the S̲ circle inside the P̲ circle as shown in Figure 4–23.

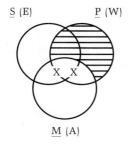

S (E)   P (W)

M (A)

Figure 4–24

Step 6   Finally, all of the information in the premises still does not specify whether the X for the subject class of the minor premise should go inside or outside of the P̲ circle, so this X must be placed on the line of the P̲ circle in the area where the S̲ and M̲ circles overlap as shown in Figure 4–24.

Step 7   Having completed the diagram of the premises, we can now check to see whether the information in the conclusion is contained in this diagram of the premises. The conclusion specifies that there must be an X entirely inside the area common to the S̲ and P̲ circles. The X on the line of the S̲ circle indicates that there *might* be one member in the section of the S̲ circle inside the P̲ circle, but it also might be entirely outside of the S̲ circle. Similarly, the X on the line of the P̲ circle indicates that there *might* be one member in the section of the P̲ circle inside the S̲ circle, but it also might be entirely outside of the P̲ circle.

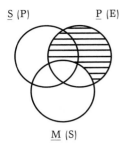

S (P)   P (E)

M (S)

Figure 4–25

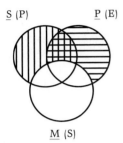

S (P)   P (E)

M (S)

Figure 4–26

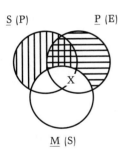

S (P)   P (E)

M (S)

Figure 4–27

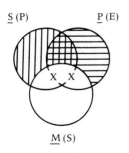

S (P)   P (E)

M (S)

Figure 4–28

Only an X completely inside the single area where all three circles overlap would represent the information in the conclusion, and this is not shown in the diagram, so all syllogisms with the form **AII-2** are invalid.

We have already demonstrated that a syllogism with the form **AAA-1** is valid. Let us examine another syllogism with the same mood but with a different figure. In the following example, we are dealing with a syllogism with the form **AAA-2**:

All experimenters are scientists.	All P are M.
All physicists are scientists.	All S are M.
∴ All physicists are experimenters.	∴ All S are P.

Step 1   The major premise, 'All experimenters are scientists,' tells us to shade all areas of the P circle that are not included within the M circle, as shown in Figure 4–25.

Step 2   The minor premise, indicating that all physicists are included in the class of scientists, tells us to shade all sections of the S circle outside of the M circle, as shown in Figure 4–26.

Step 3   The major premise requires an X in the P circle to indicate that at least one experimenter exists. Since the premises do not tell us whether this experimenter is a member of the class of physicists or not, we must go on to the next step before adding an X to the diagram.

Step 4   The minor premise requires an X somewhere in the S circle, but also fails to specify whether it is inside or outside the P circle. We must thus go on to the next step without adding an X to the diagram.

Step 5   Since the premises do not tell us whether the X in the P circle should be inside or outside the S circle, we must place the X on the line of the S circle, as shown in Figure 4–27.

Step 6   The X added in Step 5 is necessarily also completely contained in the M circle, but there is still no X completely contained in the S circle so we must put one there. Since the premises don't tell us whether this physicist is or is not an experimenter, we must put the X on the line of the P circle, as shown in Figure 4–28.

Step 7   Looking at the resulting diagram in terms of the conclusion, 'All physicists are experimenters,' we can see that it is not contained in the diagram of the premises, for one section of the S circle outside of the P circle remains unshaded. Therefore, although the **AAA** mood is valid for figure 1, it is invalid for figure 2, and *all* syllogisms of the form **AAA-2** must be invalid.

Let us consider another syllogism and its schema, this one with the form **EAE-4**:

No elephants are primates.	No <u>P</u> are <u>M</u>.
All primates are bipeds.	All <u>M</u> are <u>S</u>.
∴ No bipeds are elephants.	∴ No <u>S</u> are <u>P</u>.

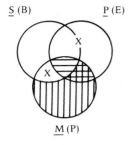

Figure 4–29

The Venn diagram that represents this syllogistic form appears in Figure 4–29. The shading in the area common to the <u>M</u> and <u>P</u> circles indicates, of course, that nothing exists that is both <u>P</u> and <u>M</u>; that is, no elephants are primates. The shading in the <u>M</u> circle outside <u>S</u> tells us that all primates are bipeds. A section of the <u>S</u> circle common to the <u>P</u> circle is still unshaded; even though there is no X completely contained in it that would indicate that at least one biped is definitely an elephant, the lack of shading is sufficient to tell us that it is *possible* that at least one biped is an elephant. Therefore, all **EAE-4** syllogisms are invalid.

"GEE, YOU'RE LOTS OF FUN ! ARE YOU SURE YOU'RE A GIRL?"

"Dennis the Menace" ® *used by permission of*
Hank Ketcham and © *by North America Syndicate.*

Formulate Dennis' argument as a syllogism and test it for validity using Venn diagrams.

Consider one final syllogism and its schema, this one with the form **AOO-1**.

All bears are mammals.	All <u>M</u> are <u>P</u>.
Some animals are not bears.	Some <u>S</u> are not <u>M</u>.
∴ Some animals are not mammals.	∴ Some <u>S</u> are not <u>P</u>.

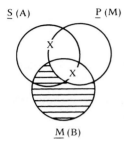

<u>S</u> (A)   <u>P</u> (M)

<u>M</u> (B)

Figure 4–30

Step 1 The major premise requires that all sections of the <u>M</u> circle outside the <u>P</u> circle must be shaded, as shown in Figure 4–30.

Step 2 The minor premise requires no shading.

Step 3 The subject term of the major premise requires an X somewhere in <u>M</u> but does not specify whether it is inside <u>S</u> or outside it, so we cannot draw the X at this time.

Step 4 The minor premise requires an X inside the <u>S</u> circle but outside the <u>M</u> circle; however, it does not specify whether the animal that is not a bear is or is not a mammal, so we still can't draw the X yet.

Step 5 Since we still don't know whether the member of the <u>M</u> class is inside or outside of <u>S</u>, we must now draw an X on the line of the <u>S</u> circle in the unshaded area of <u>M</u>.

Step 6 Finally, an X should be placed on the line between the two sections of the <u>S</u> circle outside the <u>M</u> circle, for the premises do not specify whether the animal that is not a bear is or is not a mammal.

Step 7 The conclusion, 'Some animals are not mammals,' is not completely diagrammed in Figure 4–30. It requires an X completely inside <u>S</u> and completely outside <u>P</u>, but in the diagram of the premises, one X is completely inside the <u>P</u> circle and the other X is inside <u>S</u> but is on the line of the <u>P</u> circle. Thus, the information given by the two premises does not specify that at least one thing exists in the area inside <u>S</u> but outside <u>P</u>, so all **AOO-1** syllogisms are invalid.

EXERCISE 4–8

Test the validity of the following categorical syllogisms with Venn diagrams. Where the syllogisms are not in standard form, put them in standard form first.

1. No pot smokers are law-abiding citizens.
   All hippies are pot smokers.
   Therefore no hippies are law-abiding citizens.

2. All hippies are pot smokers.
   No pot smokers are law-abiding citizens.
   Therefore some law-abiding citizens are hippies.

3. All hallucinogens are dangerous things.
   Some drugs are hallucinogens.
   Therefore, some drugs are dangerous things.

4. All hallucinogens are dangerous.
   All hallucinogens are drugs.
   Therefore, all drugs are dangerous.

5. All hallucinogens are dangerous. All hallucinogens are drugs. Therefore, some drugs are dangerous.

6. Some reactionaries are powerful. All dictators are powerful. Therefore, some dictators are reactionaries.

7. Some dictators are reactionaries. All dictators are powerful. Therefore, some powerful persons are reactionaries.

8. Some actors are rich. Some actors are egotists. Therefore, some rich persons are egotists.

9. Some Buddhists are monks, so some Buddhists are ascetics, since all monks are ascetics.

10. Some Buddhists are not ascetics, because some Buddhists are not monks and all monks are ascetics.

11. No oaks are pines, so no conifers are oaks, since all pines are conifers.

12. All zinnias are roses, since all zinnias are flowers, and all roses are flowers.

13. No cats are canines; so some wolves are canines, since no cats are wolves.

14. Some mushrooms are edible things, but no edible things are toadstools; therefore, some mushrooms are not toadstools.

15. Some mushrooms are not toadstools, because no edible things are toadstools, but some edible things are mushrooms.

EXERCISE 4–9

Test the validity of the following syllogistic schemas with Venn diagrams.

1. **AEE-3**	6. **AEE-1**	11. **AOO-2**
2. **EAE-2**	7. **IAI-2**	12. **III-1**
3. **EAE-3**	8. **IAI-3**	13. **III-2**
4. **EIO-3**	9. **AII-1**	14. **EIO-4**
5. **IEO-4**	10. **AOO-4**	15. **OOE-2**

4.7 Testing by Rules

The form of a categorical syllogism can be specified completely by giving its mood and its figure. Neither mood alone, such as **AAA**, nor figure alone, such as figure 1, will give the precise form of a syllogism. However, together, as in

AAA-1, the mood and figure do provide a complete specification of the form of a syllogism. With this in mind, one can determine the number of possible syllogistic forms. Each change in mood and each change in figure yields a different form of syllogism. There are sixty-four possible moods and four different figures for each mood, resulting in two hundred and fifty-six different possible forms of syllogism. Only twenty-four of these are valid on the interpretation we are presently using.

Although the Venn diagram technique provides a simple and effective decision procedure for determining the validity and invalidity of syllogisms, it does require the use of writing materials and can, therefore, be inconvenient. An alternative decision procedure enables us to determine the validity or invalidity of any syllogism in three steps or fewer and can be performed by direct inspection of the syllogism without the need for writing materials.

An examination of the valid forms of the syllogism—as determined by using the Venn diagram test, for example—shows that they have three characteristics in common that distinguish them from the invalid forms. Any syllogisms that satisfy all three criteria are valid, and any syllogisms that fail to satisfy one or more of these three criteria are invalid.

These three criteria can be formulated as syllogistic rules. It must be emphasized that these rules apply only to standard-form categorical syllogisms. Thus, any argument that has a different form cannot be tested for validity using these rules. In particular, no argument that contains more than three terms can be tested because, by our definition, a categorical syllogism must contain exactly three terms. Sometimes an argument might seem to contain only three terms when, in fact, it contains more. Consider, for example, the following:

> **All criminal actions are morally wrong acts.**
> **All trials for crimes are criminal actions.**
> **Therefore, all trials for crimes are morally wrong acts.**

The surprising conclusion in this argument is caused by the ambiguous middle term, 'criminal actions.' In the major premise, this term means 'behavior of criminals,' but in the minor premise it has shifted in meaning to 'court process dealing with those charged with crimes.' Because the argument actually has four terms it is not a standard-form syllogism and so cannot be tested for validity by Venn diagrams or by the rules we are about to present.

4.7.1 Distribution of Terms

Because two of the rules used to distinguish valid from invalid syllogistic forms are dependent on an understanding of the concept of the distribution of terms, we must first introduce this concept.

The subject and predicate terms of a categorical proposition are not distributed in and of themselves; rather, terms are distributed by the propositions in which they occur. A term is **distributed** if *it occurs in a position in a categorical statement such that every term that appears in that position in every* *statement of that form refers to all members of the class named by the term.* Thus, the subject of any **A** statement is distributed, since, in every **A** statement whatsoever, the subject term refers to every member of the class named. However, the predicate term in an **A** proposition is not distributed. Although 'unmarried males' in the statement 'All bachelors are unmarried males' happens to refer to all of the members of the class it names, the term is not distributed by the proposition, since terms appearing in the same position in other **A** statements do not refer to all members of the class named. For example, 'dogs' in the **A** statement 'All terriers are dogs' does not refer to the entire class of dogs.

Both subject and predicate terms are distributed in **E** statements such as 'No pens are musical instruments.' In excluding all of the class of pens from the class of musical instruments, this **E** statement must refer to the whole class of pens as well as to the whole class of musical instruments. In contrast, both subject and predicate terms of **I** statements are always undistributed. In the statement, 'Some pens are black things,' the whole class of pens is not referred to, for many pens are colors other than black, nor is the entire class of black things referred to, for many black things exist that are not pens. In 'Some terriers are dogs,' 'terriers' in fact happens to refer to the entire class of terriers, but, since in other **I** statements the subject term does not refer to all members of the class named, 'terriers' is not distributed by this **I** statement.

The subjects of **O** statements are always undistributed, but the predicate terms of **O** statements always refer to every member of the class named and therefore are distributed. In the **O** statement, 'Some pens are not black things,' the subject term 'pens' refers to only a part of the whole class of pens, so it is undistributed. However, the proposition excludes these pens from the entire class of black things, thus distributing the predicate term. The subject term in 'Some dogs are not cats' happens to refer to the entire class of dogs, but it is not distributed by the proposition, since the subject terms in some **O** propositions do not refer to every member of the class named.

A summary of the distribution of terms in the four types of categorical proposition is presented in the following table:

Distribution of Terms		
Schema	**Subject Term**	**Predicate Term**
A All S are P.	distributed	undistributed
E No S̄ are P̄.	distributed	distributed
I Some S are P.	undistributed	undistributed
O Some S̄ are not P̄.	undistributed	distributed

4.7.2 Rules for Valid Syllogisms

Having explained the concept of distribution, we can state the characteristics or criteria that distinguish valid and invalid syllogisms in terms of three rules that syllogisms must satisfy to be valid. An argument that violates any one of these rules is said to be **fallacious,** and a fallacious syllogism is invalid. When a syllogism satisfies all the rules, it is valid.

Rule 1 *The middle term of a valid standard-form syllogism must be distributed in at least one premise.* A violation of this rule is known as the **fallacy of the undistributed middle.**

The middle term, 'persons with long hair,' is distributed once in the following syllogism with the form **AAA-1:**

> **All persons with long hair are radicals.**
> **Ed is a person with long hair.**
> **Therefore, Ed is a radical.**

Since the middle term, 'persons with long hair,' is distributed in the major premise, although it is undistributed in the minor premise, this syllogism satisfies Rule 1 and does not commit the fallacy of the undistributed middle.

The two terms of the conclusion of any valid syllogism are related to each other through the middle term in the premises. If *all* the members of the class named by the middle term are not related to some or all of the members of one of the other classes referred to by the premises, then it is possible that the major and minor classes may be related to different members of the class named by the middle term and, consequently, they might not be related to each other at all. Since a term must be distributed by a proposition for us to be certain that it refers to all the members of a class, the middle term of a syllogism must be distributed at least once. The major premise of the above syllogism asserts that all the members of the class named by the middle term, 'persons with long hair,' are contained in the class named by the predicate term, 'radicals.' The minor premise asserts that all members of the class of which Ed is the only member are contained in the class of persons with long hair. Since all the members of the class of persons with long hair are contained within the class of radicals, Ed must also be a member of the class of radicals.

The following invalid syllogism with the form **AAA-2** illustrates what happens when the middle term is undistributed in both premises:

> **All radicals are people with long hair.**   All P̲ are M̲.
> **Ed is a person with long hair.**   All S̲ are M̲.
> **Therefore, Ed is a radical.**   ∴ All S̲ are P̲.

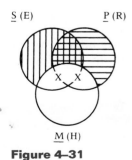

S (E)   P (R)

M (H)

Figure 4–31

In this syllogism, the middle term, 'people with long hair,' is undistributed in both premises, since in both it is the predicate term of an **A** statement. Both the major and the minor terms are related to the middle term in the premises, but neither the major nor the minor class is related to the *entire* class referred to by the middle term, so their relationship to each other is not known. The first premise does not rule out the possibility that the class of people with long hair contains members who are not radicals, and the second premise would permit Ed to be such a person. The Venn diagram representing an **AAA-2** syllogism is shown in Figure 4–31. The diagram visually displays the invalidity of this syllogistic form, since it is possible that something exists inside <u>S</u> but outside <u>P</u>.

Rule 2   *A term that is distributed in the conclusion of a valid categorical syllogism must also be distributed in the premise in which the term occurs.* Breaking this rule involves committing what is known as the **fallacy of the illicit major** or **the fallacy of the illicit minor,** depending on which term is not distributed in its premise. When a term is distributed in the conclusion, it refers to the whole class, and generalization to a whole class cannot be made from statements that refer to only part of the class, since it is possible that something that is true of part of the class might not be true of the entire class. Thus, any term that is distributed in a conclusion also must be distributed in its premise.

The following **AEE-1** syllogism illustrates the fallacy of the illicit major:

All lawyers are logicians.	**All <u>M</u> are <u>P</u>.**
No engineers are lawyers.	**No <u>S</u> are <u>M</u>.**
Therefore, no engineers are logicians.	**∴ No <u>S</u> are <u>P</u>.**

In the conclusion, 'No engineers are logicians,' both terms are distributed—each referring to all members of its class. The minor term, 'engineers,' is also distributed in the minor premise, in which it is again the subject term of an **E** statement. However, the major term, 'logicians,' is not distributed in the major premise, in which it appears as the predicate of an **A** statement. Since the undistributed term occurs in the major premise, the fallacy being committed is that of illicit major. The invalidity of this syllogism is demonstrated by the Venn diagram in Figure 4–32, since the unshaded area common to both <u>S</u> and <u>P</u> indicates that some engineers could be logicians. Thus, all syllogisms of the form **AEE-1** are invalid.

The following **AAA-3** categorical syllogism exemplifies the fallacy of the illicit minor.

All lawyers are well-paid people.	**All <u>M</u> are <u>P</u>.**
All lawyers are logicians.	**All <u>M</u> are <u>S</u>.**
∴ All logicians are well-paid people.	**∴ All <u>S</u> are <u>P</u>.**

In the conclusion of this syllogism, the subject term, 'logicians,' is distributed, but 'logicians' is undistributed as the predicate term of an **A** statement in the minor premise. This invalid syllogism is diagrammed in Figure 4–33. The unshaded section in the <u>S</u> circle outside the <u>P</u> circle leaves open the possibility that at least one logician might not be a well-paid person. Therefore, the information contained in the conclusion is not contained in the diagram of the premises, and all syllogisms of the form **AAA-3** are invalid.

Rule 3   *A valid standard-form categorical syllogism cannot have a negative premise unless it has a negative conclusion, in which case it must have exactly one negative premise.* Violating this rule involves committing one of three different fallacies.

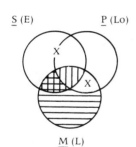

Figure 4–32

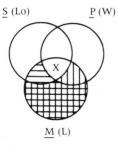

Figure 4–33

The **fallacy of two negative premises** is exemplified by the following syllogism.

No Sundays are good days to study logic.
No Sundays are weekdays.
Therefore, no weekdays are good days to study logic.

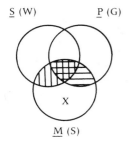

S̲ (W)   P̲ (G)

M̲ (S)

Figure 4–34

Notice first that this argument does not violate either Rule 1 or Rule 2, but its Venn diagram shows it to be invalid (see Figure 4–34). Because negative premises simply affirm the *exclusion* of the members of one class from another class, the major premise here excludes all Sundays from the class of good days to study logic, and the minor premise excludes all Sundays from the class of weekdays. But these exclusions do not in any way specifically relate the members of the class of weekdays to the class of good days to study logic. The way members of the S̲ class (weekdays) and members of the P̲ class (good days to study logic) are related, whether by partial or total inclusion or exclusion, is not specified in the premises. Thus, the premises do not support the conclusion that no members of the S̲ class are contained in the P̲ class.

The following syllogism with the form **OAI-2** also breaks Rule 3, but in a different way which is known as committing the **fallacy of affirmative conclusion from a negative premise.**

Some men are not good athletes.	**Some P̲ are not M̲.**
All baseball players are good athletes.	**All S̲ are M̲.**
∴ **Some baseball players are men.**	∴ **Some S̲ are P̲.**

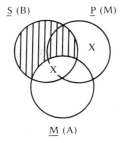

S̲ (B)   P̲ (M)

M̲ (A)

Figure 4–35

This argument violates neither of the first two rules, but its Venn diagram (Figure 4–35) shows that it is indeed invalid. The conclusion, 'Some baseball players are men,' is not shown in the diagram of the two premises, since there is no X completely contained in the unshaded area common to the S̲ and P̲ circles, thus leaving open the possibility that the class of men baseball players may be empty.

The third fallacy that can be committed under Rule 3 is the **fallacy of a negative conclusion from affirmative premises,** illustrated by the following syllogism with the form **AAO-4.**

All gorillas are primates.	**All P̲ are M̲.**
All primates are mammals.	**All M̲ are S̲.**
∴ **Some mammals are not gorillas.**	∴ **Some S̲ are not P̲.**

This syllogism does not violate Rule 1, since the middle term, 'primates,' is distributed in the minor premise. Nor does it violate Rule 2; although the term 'gorilla' is distributed in the conclusion, it is also distributed in the major premise, and the minor term is not distributed in the conclusion. The syllogism also does not have any negative premises, so it doesn't violate either of the first two conditions of Rule 3. However, this syllogism does violate Rule 3 since it has a negative conclusion but has no negative premise. The invalidity of *all* **AAO-4** syllogisms is confirmed by the Venn diagram of its schema, since the

Construct a syllogism corresponding to the reasoning Mark's mother used to trick him into a position where he could not get angry at her for damaging his motorcycle, and test it for validity using the three rules.

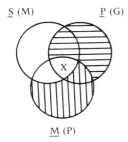

Figure 4–36

diagram of its premises does not contain the diagram of its conclusion (see Figure 4–36). For the conclusion to be represented by the Venn diagram, there must be an X inside the S circle but outside the P circle.

These three rules are sufficient for providing a decision procedure for testing all categorical syllogisms for validity. It is possible to add other rules—in fact, some other texts do—but any such additional rules would be redundant. For example, one could stipulate as a rule that no valid syllogism can have two **I** statements as premises. However, any argument that violates this rule would also violate Rule 1, since both the subject and predicate terms of **I** statements are undistributed, and the middle term appears only in the premises. It is also possible to stipulate that no syllogism can have two **O** premises, but any such syllogism would violate Rule 3, since a syllogism with two **O** premises would have two negative premises. One additional rule commonly found in other texts is that a categorical syllogism can contain only three terms. This rule is unnecessary, since it is part of our definition of a categorical syllogism. Having shown that only three rules are needed, let us test the validity of some additional sample syllogisms, using this decision procedure.

4.7.3 Testing Syllogisms Using the Rules

Let us apply the three rules to the following intended argument:

> Some connoisseurs of food are men.
> All good cooks are connoisseurs of food.
> Therefore, all men are good cooks.

The first step is to check to see whether we are dealing with a categorical syllogism that is in standard form. There are three categorical statements and three terms, each of which appears once in two of the statements. But the premise containing the subject term of the conclusion (the minor premise) appears first and the major premise second. Thus, this syllogism must be recast into standard form as an **AIA-4** syllogism:

All good cooks are connoisseurs of food.	All <u>P</u> are <u>M</u>.
Some connoisseurs of food are men.	Some <u>M</u> are <u>S</u>.
∴ All men are good cooks.	∴ All <u>S</u> are <u>P</u>.

Now we can check to see if one or more of the three rules have been violated. Rule 1 requires that the middle term be distributed in at least one of the premises. The middle term is undistributed in the major premise, for it is the predicate term of an **A** statement. The middle term is also undistributed in the minor premise, since both terms are undistributed in **I** statements. This syllogism thus commits the fallacy of the undistributed middle term. This is sufficient to show that the argument is invalid, but for practice let us proceed through the rest of the rules. According to Rule 2, any term distributed in the conclusion of the argument also must be distributed in the premises. The predicate term of the conclusion, 'good cooks,' is undistributed, but the subject term, 'men,' is distributed. Since the term 'men' is undistributed in the minor premise, where it appears as the predicate of an **I** statement, this syllogism also commits the fallacy of the illicit minor, and is thus invalid on two counts. The syllogism does not violate Rule 3, since it contains no negative propositions at all.

Let us consider one more argument to practice using the three rules.

No common stocks are good investments.	No <u>P</u> are <u>M</u>.
All bonds are good investments.	All <u>S</u> are <u>M</u>.
∴ No bonds are common stocks.	∴ No <u>S</u> are <u>P</u>.

Is this a standard-form syllogism? There are three statements and three terms. Each term appears only once in two statements. Furthermore, the major premise, containing the predicate term of the conclusion, appears first, followed by the minor premise and the conclusion. The argument is a standard-form categorical syllogism of the form **EAE-2**.

The middle term, 'good investments,' is distributed in the major premise, so the syllogism does not violate Rule 1. Both the subject and predicate terms of the conclusion are distributed; consequently, both these terms must be distributed in the premises to satisfy Rule 2. The term 'bonds' appears as the subject term of the minor premise, an **A** statement. Since the subject terms of **A** statements are distributed, the syllogism does not commit the fallacy of the illicit minor. The predicate term of the conclusion, 'common stocks,' appears as the subject term of the major premise, an **E** statement. Because the subject term of an **E** statement is distributed, the syllogism also does not commit the fallacy of the illicit major and thus does not violate Rule 2. The syllogism also satisfies Rule 3, for it has exactly one negative premise to go with its negative conclusion. Because none of the three rules is violated, it follows that this argument, and thus all **EAE-2** syllogisms, are valid. A Venn diagram would confirm this result.

Valid Syllogistic Forms*

Figure 1	Figure 2	Figure 3	Figure 4
AAA	AEE	AII	AEE[†]
EAE	EAE	IAI	IAI
AII	AOO	EIO	EIO
EIO	EIO	OAO	AEO[†]
AAI	AEO	AAI	EAO
EAO	EAO	EAO	AAI

*Each class referred to by the subject term of each premise must contain at least one member.
[†]These two forms require an added assumption that their predicate classes contain at least one member in order to give a result of valid on the Venn diagram test. They are valid according to the three rules without any special assumptions.

EXERCISE 4–10

Identify which rules, if any, are violated by each of the syllogisms in Exercises 4–8 and 4–9.

EXERCISE 4–11

Test the validity of each of the following categorical syllogisms by determining which rules, if any, it violates. Where the syllogism is not in standard form, put it in standard form.

1. All basketball players are athletes.
   Some men are not basketball players.
   Therefore, some men are not athletes.

2. All drunkards are alcoholics.
   Some drinkers are drunkards.
   Therefore, some drinkers are alcoholics.

3. All falcons are hawks.
   All hawks are birds.
   Therefore, some birds are not falcons.

4. All addicts are persons to be pitied.
   All addicts are unhappy persons.
   Therefore, all unhappy persons are persons to be pitied.

5. All dictators are powerful persons. Some reactionaries are powerful persons. Therefore, some dictators are reactionaries.

6. Some conservatives are Republicans. No Republicans are Democrats. Therefore, some Democrats are not conservatives.

7. All interpreters are bilingual persons. Some bilingual persons are persons with good memories. Therefore, all persons with good memories are interpreters.

8. All guppies are fish. No fish are animals with lungs. Therefore, some guppies are not animals with lungs.

9. Some students are not poets. All students are studious. Therefore, some poets are not studious.

10. No friends are enemies. No relatives are enemies. Therefore, some relatives are not friends.

11. No maples have gangrenous limbs, because all maples are trees, and no trees have gangrenous limbs.

12. All amoebae are unicellular organisms, so some amoebae are not primates, since no primates are unicellular organisms.

13. Some intelligent people are sensitive people who will, therefore, suffer a lot in life.

14. Tom is fallible because he is a human being, and everybody makes mistakes.

4.8 The Boolean Interpretation

As explained in Chapter 3, the traditional interpretation which requires that the subject terms of categorical propositions must be about classes that contain at least one member is not perfect. An alternative approach, known as the **Boolean interpretation,** *does not require that any class have members, but the* **I** *and* **O** *propositions are interpreted as being compound propositions that include the assertion that at least one member of the subject class exists.* The Boolean interpretation has the same Venn diagrams for **I** and **O** propositions as does the traditional interpretation. However, the diagrams for **A** and **E** propositions on this interpretation do not have any Xs because these universal statements do not assert that anything exists. As shown in Chapter 3, this system affects the kinds of immediate inferences that can be made; for example, the only part of the Square of Opposition that exists on the Boolean interpretation is the diagonal relation of contradictoriness.

It should not be surprising to learn now that the Boolean interpretation affects the validity of arguments. Insofar as the universal (**A** and **E**) categorical propositions do not assert the existence of any members in their subject classes, while the particular (**I** and **O**) propositions do assert the existence of members in the subject class, on the Boolean interpretation we must add a **Rule 4,** which specifies that *a particular conclusion cannot be validly deduced from two universal premises.* Any syllogism that violates this rule is said to commit the **existential fallacy.** The following **AAI-4** argument is valid on the traditional interpretation, but on the Boolean interpretation it is invalid because it violates Rule 4 and commits the existential fallacy.

All beagles are dogs.	All <u>P</u> are <u>M</u>.
All dogs are mammals.	All <u>M</u> are <u>S</u>.
∴ **Some mammals are beagles.**	∴ Some <u>S</u> are <u>P</u>.

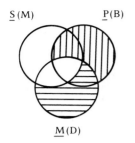

Figure 4-37

The invalidity of this syllogistic form becomes more apparent when we make the Boolean interpretation of the conclusion explicit—it actually asserts that some mammals are beagles ***and*** that at least one beagle exists. But on the Boolean interpretation, the major premise neither assumes nor asserts that the class of beagles contains any members at all. Figure 4–37 shows that the Venn diagram of these premises does not contain even one X, whereas the conclusion requires an X.

The addition of Rule 4 on the Boolean interpretation changes nine of the twenty-four valid syllogisms that are valid on the traditional interpretation so that they are invalid on the Boolean interpretation. One of the primary reasons for using the traditional interpretation is that it gives us nine more valid argument schemas at the relatively small cost of not allowing us to test arguments about unicorns, gremlins, and other nonexistent beings.

EXERCISE 4–12

Using Rule 4 and the Boolean interpretation, reevaluate the arguments that were found to be valid in Exercises 4–10 and 4–11 to determine which ones are still valid.

4.9 Syllogistic Arguments in Ordinary Language

Some of the problems of translating sentences in ordinary language into standard-form sentences are discussed in Chapter 3, where it is shown how the context in which a sentence is uttered or written often provides a clue as to its interpretation. For example, with no contextual clues, 'Cars are a good investment' is ambiguous since it lacks a quantifier. It may be taken to express either the statement, 'All cars are good investments,' or 'Some cars are good investments,' depending on the context. Uttered in the context of the sales pitch of a used-car dealer, in conjunction with the following statements, it probably is being used to express a *universal* affirmative statement:

> **Cars are good investments. After all, no car owner has to pay transportation fares, and the time a driver saves going from one place to another is also worth money.**

However, the same statement appearing in the context of a consumer publication, in conjunction with the following statements, is probably being used to express a *particular* affirmative statement:

> **Considering the average lifespan of cars such as the Mercedes-Benz, Rolls Royce, and Volvo, and the minimal repairs they require, it is obvious that cars are good investments.**

The way statements are translated can make a difference in whether the argument is valid or invalid. Consider, for example, the following argument, uttered at a college track meet:

> Pat is a real athlete, for all persons who run here are real athletes, and
>   Pat runs here.

This argument may be translated into the following standard-form syllogism:

> **All persons who run here are real athletes.**
> **Pat is a person who runs here.**
> **Therefore, Pat is a real athlete.**

The only statement that requires translation into standard form is 'Pat runs here,' since its predicate term is a verb instead of a noun or noun phrase. Of course, it is necessary to place each statement within the syllogism in its proper order, with the major premise first and the minor premise next, followed by the conclusion.

Now let us consider another argument expressed in ordinary language. This one is being uttered by a tour guide who is taking visitors through a completely automated factory in which robots are used on the assembly line:

> **Pat is a machine, for all things that run here are machines, and Pat runs**
>   **here.**

Translated into standard form, this argument would read as follows:

> **All things that run here are machines.**
> **Pat is a thing that runs here.**
> **Therefore, Pat is a machine.**

Now, if the original formulation of the argument is uttered by the guide as she points to a robot labeled Pat, the premises of the argument would seem to be reasonably true, and the truth of its conclusion follows validly from the premises. However, if the guide utters the comment while pointing to the plant superintendent who happens to be a person named Pat and who also happens to be running, then it would be incorrect for us to translate the statement, 'Pat runs here,' as 'Pat is a thing that is running.' In this rather bizarre context, such a translation produces an argument with four terms, since in the major premise 'things that are running here' means 'things operating here,' whereas in the minor premise 'thing that is running here' means 'person who is moving rapidly on foot.' In this last instance, we are not even dealing with a syllogism.

While the example above might seem a bit outrageous, do not assume that translating ordinary language arguments is a simple task. Translation can be tricky, especially when we must supply missing premises for syllogistic arguments expressed in ordinary language.

4.9.1 Enthymemes

As noted in Chapter 2, an enthymeme is an argument in which one or more of the premises and/or the conclusion are not explicitly stated. In everyday discourse, syllogisms are sometimes expressed enthymematically. People seldom state explicitly all of the premises they are assuming as true and as providing support for their conclusions. When we speak or argue with others, we assume that the other people possess a considerable body of knowledge that will enable them to fill in the gaps in our abbreviated arguments. Any type of argument can be expressed as an enthymeme, but our concern in this chapter is only with syllogistic arguments.

When supplying missing premise or conclusion statements in a syllogism, you should adhere to the **principle of charity,** which stipulates that you should *supply statements that make the argument as good as possible.* When possible, the supplied statements should make the argument valid *and* their truth should be reasonably well established.

For the moment, let us consider the following intended argument:

> **Children cannot be expected to know when to be quiet, for they do not possess a wide range of social experiences.**

The conclusion of the argument is explicitly stated: 'Children cannot be expected to know when to be quiet.' However, this sentence is not in standard form. A reasonable translation is 'No children are persons who can be expected to know when to be quiet.' The expressed premise, 'they do not possess a wide range of social experiences,' may be reasonably translated as 'No children are persons who possess a wide range of social experiences.' Since the term 'children' appears as the subject term of the conclusion, we know that this statement is the minor premise.

To complete the argument we must supply the missing major premise. From the context, one reasonable premise that might be added is 'All persons who have a wide range of social experiences are persons who know when to be quiet.' With this major premise, the argument, expressed in standard form, would be:

> **[All persons who possess a wide range of social experiences are persons who can be expected to know when to keep quiet.]**
> **No children are persons who possess a wide range of social experiences.**
> **Therefore, no children are persons who can be expected to know when to keep quiet.**

Expressed in this way, this argument has the form **AEE-1.** However, this formulation makes the argument invalid. The term 'persons who can be expected to know when to keep quiet' is distributed in the conclusion, but it is not distributed in the major premise, a violation of Rule 2, which requires that any term that is distributed in the conclusion of a syllogism must be distributed in the premise in which it occurs.

However, adding a different suppressed premise can make the argument valid. Consider this formulation of the original argument:

> **[All persons who can be expected to know when to keep quiet are persons who possess a wide range of social experiences.]**
> **No children are persons who possess a wide range of social experiences.**

> **Therefore, no children are persons who can be expected to know when to keep quiet.**

The new major premise does not seem any less reasonable than the first one we tried, which made the argument invalid. But, formulated in this new way, the argument has the form **AEE-2,** which is valid. In this new formulation, the term 'persons who can be expected to know when to keep quiet' is distributed in the conclusion and also in the supplied major premise.[3]

Sometimes the minor premise of a syllogism is suppressed. For example, consider the following argument:

> **Since all cats are felines, so are all tigers.**

The conclusion of this argument may be translated as the standard-form sentence, 'All tigers are felines.' The premise, 'All cats are felines,' is already in standard form; since the predicate term of the conclusion is 'felines,' we know that this must be the major premise. The minor premise must be supplied to complete this argument. One premise whose truth is well established and that also makes the argument valid is 'All tigers are cats.' In standard form, the syllogism now reads:

> **All cats are felines.**
> **[All tigers are cats.]**
> **Therefore, all tigers are felines.**

It is also possible for the conclusion of a syllogistic argument to be suppressed. For example, consider the following argument, spoken by a lawyer who is summing up a case for the jury in a trial for theft:

> **Only a person who knew the combination to the safe could have stolen the bonds, and only Mr. Snodgrass knew the combination.**

The conclusion, although unstated, is clearly 'Only Mr. Snodgrass could have stolen the bonds.' However, this statement is not in standard form. The word 'only' indicates that it is an exclusive statement that is expressing a universal affirmative proposition. This proposition may be expressed in standard form as 'All persons who could have stolen the bonds are members of the class of which Mr. Snodgrass is the only member.'

The premise, 'Only a person who knew the combination to the safe could have stolen the bonds,' is also an exclusive statement, which may be translated reasonably as 'All persons who could have stolen the bonds are persons who knew the combination to the safe.' The other premise, 'Only Mr. Snodgrass knew the combination,' is also exclusive. Given these formulations of the

---

[3]Remember that there is no single "correct" way to deal with an enthymeme. In the case of this example, one could also apply the principle of charity by adding a premise whose truth is better established than that of the premise added in the example and that makes the argument inductively strong (rather than valid).

God is Mind and God is infinite; hence all is Mind.

MARY BAKER EDDY

This argument provides the foundation of the religion of Christian Science. Discuss what assumptions must be made about the meanings of the terms in it for it to be interpreted as a syllogism. Test the syllogistic form of this argument for validity using the three rules and also using Venn diagrams. Could this argument be treated as an enthymeme and would doing so make it any stronger?

conclusion and the premises, the major term is 'members of the class of which Mr. Snodgrass is the only member' and the middle term is 'persons who knew the combination to the safe.' This means that 'All persons who knew the combination to the safe are members of the class of which Mr. Snodgrass is the only member' is the major premise. In standard form, this **AAA-1** argument reads as

> All persons who knew the combination to the safe are members of the class of which Mr. Snodgrass is the only member.
> All persons who could have stolen the bonds are persons who knew the combination to the safe.
> [Therefore, all persons who could have stolen the bonds are members of the class of which Mr. Snodgrass is the only member.]

EXERCISE 4–13

Each of the arguments below is an enthymeme. (a) Supply the missing premise or conclusion that would make the enthymeme a valid categorical syllogism. (b) Translate the syllogism into standard form.

1. All mushrooms are fungi; therefore all toadstools are fungi.
2. Some judges are not elected officials, because some judges are appointed.
3. Some mushrooms are not edible; some are poisonous.
4. No soaps are cleansing agents, although all detergents are cleansing agents.
5. Soybeans are nutritious; they contain a lot of protein.
6. All whiskeys are liquors; therefore some whiskeys are bourbons.
7. No operas are understandable, because they're all written in foreign languages.
8. Some people jog five miles every day, and all people who jog five miles every day are in good physical condition.
9. All foreign-language dictionaries are reference books, and no reference books can be taken out of the library.

10. Cyclamates should not be used as food additives, since they may cause cancer.

11. All her students always get good grades; therefore she must be a terrific teacher.

12. Since diamonds are rare, they must be valuable.

13. That movie is sure to make a lot of money; it has plenty of violence and sex.

14. Jack cannot practice law; he never passed the bar examination.

15. All members of the American Bar Association must be college graduates, since all lawyers are college graduates.

16. Ed cooks well, so he must be a connoisseur of good food.

17. Mary is a very intelligent person; after all, she is a member of Phi Beta Kappa.

18. Some paintings are good investments since some of them increase in value.

19. There must be fire, for I smell smoke.

20. Pat is a basketball player, so she must be over six feet tall.

21. There must be water near here; there's grass growing.

22. John can't own a car because he doesn't have a driver's license.

23. Many countries aren't democratic, since some of their citizens can't vote.

24. Most handmade items are expensive because they require so much labor.

4.9.2 Sorites

Many of the intended arguments we encounter in everyday contexts are composed of three or more premises and a single conclusion. The syllogistic method clearly cannot be used directly to test such arguments, since a syllogism, by definition, must have exactly two premises. For example, the following premises

> **All dancers are agile persons.**
> **Some secretaries are dancers.**
> **All secretaries are good typists.**

will not, by a single syllogistic inference, yield the conclusion

> **Some good typists are agile persons.**

Although this is not a single syllogism, it can be treated as *a chain of interlocking syllogisms*. If we combine two of the premises and derive a conclusion from them, then combine this result with the remaining premise, we can validly derive the final conclusion:

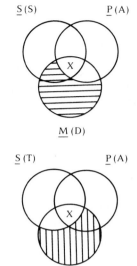

S(S) P(A)

M(D)

S(T) P(A)

M(S)

Figure 4–38

All dancers are agile persons.
Some secretaries are dancers.
[Therefore, some secretaries are agile persons.]

[Some secretaries are agile persons.]
All secretaries are good typists.
Therefore, some good typists are agile persons.

A set of more than three categorical statements, one of which is designated as the conclusion, is known as a **sorites** (from the Greek word for 'pile'—presumably a pile of propositions). Although special kinds of Venn diagrams can be constructed for dealing with arguments having four or more terms (that is, Venn diagrams with four or more circles), the construction of such diagrams can be very tricky; thus, it is wise to test sorites by constructing separate three-circle diagrams for each of the component syllogisms. A sorites is invalid if any one component syllogism is invalid. Venn diagrams for the preceding sorites are shown in Figure 4–38.

The premises, of course, might not be in standard form or in the most useful order. Thus:

Dogs cannot reason.
Anyone who can read can get into college.
Creatures that cannot reason cannot get into college.
Therefore, dogs cannot read.

To have a syllogism, we need a middle term, and the first two premises do not provide one. So we must rearrange the premises to form the following chain of valid syllogisms:

All creatures that can read are creatures that can get into college.
No creature that cannot reason is a creature that can get into college.
[Therefore, no creature that cannot reason is a creature that can read.]

[No creature that cannot reason is a creature that can read.]
All dogs are creatures that cannot reason.
Therefore, no dogs are creatures that can read.

EXERCISE 4–14

The following groups of sentences[4] are sorites. Determine whether each argument is valid by constructing a chain of syllogisms, supplying the intermediate conclusions, and testing each component syllogism by the method of rules or Venn diagrams.

1. All comets are wanderers in the zodiac.
   No terriers are wanderers in the zodiac.

---

[4]These examples are adapted from Lewis Carroll, *Symbolic Logic* (Dover Publications, Inc.), pp. 112–120.

All curly-tailed creatures are terriers.
Therefore, no curly-tailed creatures are comets.

2. All my poultry are ducks.
Some officers are not creatures that waltz.
No ducks are creatures that waltz.
Therefore, none of my poultry are officers.

3. All shade-grown fruit is unripe fruit.
No wholesome fruit is unripe fruit.
All apples in this basket are wholesome fruit.
Therefore, no apples in this basket are shade-grown fruit.

4. All really well-informed people are good company.
All showy talkers are people who think too much of themselves.
No people who think too much of themselves are good company.
Therefore, no showy talkers are really well-informed people.

Summary

1. A **categorical syllogism** is an argument composed of exactly three categorical statements and containing three terms, each of which appears twice in the argument but only once in any one statement. The predicate term of the conclusion of a syllogism is called the **major term,** and the subject term of the conclusion is called the **minor term.** The **middle term** does not appear in the conclusion but appears once in each premise. The premise containing the major term is called the **major premise,** and the premise containing the minor term is called the **minor premise.**

2. A syllogism is in **standard form** when it is composed of three categorical statements expressed by standard-form sentences *and* when these statements follow the order of major premise, minor premise, and conclusion. When abbreviating syllogisms, one should use the methods discussed in Chapter 3 and the following additional procedures: (1) place a line between the minor premise and the conclusion to separate them; (2) use the symbol '∴' as an abbreviation of the word 'therefore' or any other conclusion indicator.

3. The logical form of a categorical syllogism can be represented by an **argument schema** using the symbols $\underline{S}$, $\underline{P}$, and $\underline{M}$, which represent the major term, minor term, and middle term, respectively. These three symbols function as blanks in which nouns or noun phrases may be substituted to produce sentences expressing categorical statements. When such substitutions are made in an argument schema to produce an argument, the process is called the **interpretation** of the argument schema.

4. The **mood** of a standard-form syllogism is the particular combination of statements of which the syllogism is composed, expressed in terms of the

letters **A, E, I,** or **O,** which signify the different types of categorical statement. The first letter in the mood indicates the form of the major premise, the second that of the minor premise, and the third that of the conclusion. Syllogisms having the same mood do not necessarily have the same form. The **figure** of a standard-form syllogism is determined by the placement of the middle term in the two premises of the syllogism. Four arrangements are possible, traditionally numbered as follows: **figure 1,** in which the middle term appears as the subject term of the major premise and the predicate term of the minor premise; **figure 2,** in which the middle term appears as the predicate term in both the major and the minor premises; **figure 3,** in which the middle term appears as the subject term in both the major and the minor premises; and **figure 4,** in which the middle term appears as the predicate term in the major premise and the subject term in the minor premise. The **form** of a syllogism is determined by the combination of its mood and figure, and is usually expressed by placing the number of the figure after the letters that state the mood.

5. The validity of a syllogism depends neither on its terms nor on the truth or falsity of its statements, but solely on its form. A **valid argument schema** is one for which there is no possible interpretation or substitution of terms that would create an argument with true premises and a false conclusion. Accordingly, a valid argument is one with a valid schema. A **counterexample** is an interpretation of an argument schema that makes all the premises true and the conclusion false. Counterexamples can be used only to prove the invalidity of an argument schema. More useful are two techniques—one using Venn diagrams and the other syllogistic rules—that provide definite decision procedures, that is, mechanical procedures that can be used to prove the validity or invalidity of any particular argument schema or argument in a finite number of steps.

6. **Venn diagrams** display the form of an argument and thus can be used to test syllogisms for their validity or invalidity. All arguments with the same form have the same schema, and all arguments that are interpretations of the same schema have the same Venn diagrams (except for the abbreviation labels on the circles). A syllogism is valid if and only if the diagram of its conclusion is already contained in the diagram of its two premises.

7. A term of a categorical proposition is **distributed** if it occurs in a position in the proposition such that every term that appears in that position in every statement of that form refers to all members of the class named by the term. The subject term is distributed in any **A** statement, but the predicate term is not; both subject and predicate terms are distributed in **E** statements; both subject and predicate terms are undistributed in **I** statements; and the predicate term is distributed in any **O** statement, but the subject term is not.

8. Syllogistic rules provide a three-step decision procedure that can be used to test the validity of standard-form categorical syllogisms. Violation of

any of these rules makes an argument invalid. Rule 1: The middle term of a standard-form syllogism must be distributed in at least one premise. Breaking this rule results in the **fallacy of the undistributed middle.** Rule 2: A term that is distributed in the conclusion of a categorical syllogism must also be distributed in the premise in which the term occurs. Breaking this rule results in the **fallacy of the illicit major** or the **fallacy of the illicit minor,** depending on which term (predicate or subject term of the conclusion) is not distributed in its premise. Rule 3: A standard-form categorical syllogism cannot have a negative premise unless it has a negative conclusion, in which case it must have exactly one negative premise. Violating this rule results in one or more of the following fallacies: (1) **negative conclusion from affirmative premises,** (2) **two negative premises,** or (3) **affirmative conclusion from a negative premise.**

9. On the Boolean interpretation, no requirement is made that the subject class must contain at least one member, but the **I** and **O** propositions are interpreted as including the assertion that at least one member of the subject class exists. This requires that Rule 4 be added to the test for valid syllogisms, namely, that a particular conclusion cannot be validly deduced from two universal premises. Violation of Rule 4 results in **the existential fallacy.** This rule cuts the number of valid syllogisms from twenty-four to fifteen.

10. The manner in which the statements of a syllogism are translated from ordinary discourse into standard form can affect the validity or invalidity of the argument. In translating, one should examine the context to clarify any ambiguous terms. An **enthymeme** is an argument with one or more missing premises and/or a missing conclusion. When supplying missing premises or conclusions in enthymematical syllogisms, one should adhere to the **principle of charity;** that is, the supplied statements should make the argument as good as possible on the Aristotelian interpretation, and their truth should be reasonably well established.

11. In some cases, an apparently single argument is actually a chain of syllogisms, and the conclusion cannot be derived directly from the premises as they are given. An argument of this type, known as a **sorites,** must be put into standard form and the intermediate conclusions drawn. It can be tested with a series of Venn diagrams, one for each syllogism. If any one of the syllogisms proves to be invalid, the sorites is invalid.

Chapter 5

Propositional Logic: Statements

Remember from Chapter 1: (1) a proposition is that about which it makes sense to say that it is true or false, and (2) sentences are not true or false; rather, sentences can be used to express propositions which in turn are true or false. Declarative sentences do not always express propositions; interrogative, imperative, and other sentences can be used to express propositions in certain contexts. In logic we are interested essentially in propositions and in arguments composed of propositions.

Instead of saying that a proposition is that about which it makes sense to say that it is true or false, logicians often make the equivalent assertion that every proposition has a **truth value.** Although this is essentially another way of saying the same thing, it is both shorter and, for our purposes in the next few chapters, more convenient.

5.1 Compound Propositions and Logical Operators

In this chapter and the next, we deal with a particular kind of proposition, known as a truth-functional proposition. A **truth-functional proposition** is a statement such that *if we know (1) the truth value (the truth or falsity) of each of its component statements and (2) the meanings of the logical terms in the sentence expressing the statement, we can determine precisely the truth or falsity of the statement.* In other words, the truth value of the proposition is a function of the truth values of the component statement(s).

Let's look at some examples, beginning with the proposition expressed by the following sentence:

It is not the case that Pat enjoys logic.

This proposition contains within it the simple proposition 'Pat enjoys logic,' which itself has a truth value (that is, it is either true or false). The sentence also contains the expression 'it is not the case that,' which, taken by itself, cannot be used to express a proposition.

Insofar as logical terms such as 'it is not the case that' "operate" on propositions to create new propositions with different logical structures, they are called **logical operators.** A logical operator is thus *an expression such that if it is correctly used with an appropriate number of propositions, a new proposition is produced, with a different logical structure.* No logical operator by itself is or expresses a proposition.

In our example, if we know that 'Pat enjoys logic' is true, we can infer that the resulting compound is false. Similarly, if we know that 'Pat enjoys logic' is false, we can infer that the compound is true. That is, if we know the truth value of the proposition and the meaning of the logical operator 'it is not the case that,' we can determine the truth value of the compound proposition produced by combining them. Thus, it is a truth-functional proposition.

Let's take another example:

Pat enjoys logic and all students find logic useful.

Here, we can separate out 'Pat enjoys logic' and 'All students find logic useful' as each by itself expressing a proposition. The word 'and' functions as a logical operator, because it serves to connect the two propositions in such a way that a new compound proposition is formed—a proposition that has a different logical structure than the component propositions taken by themselves.

In this example, if we know that each of the component propositions is true, and we know the meaning of the logical operator 'and,' we can tell that the compound is true. This example also satisfies our definition of a truth-functional proposition.

5.2 Truth-Functional Operators

Certain logical operators are known as **truth-functional operators.** A truth-functional operator is *a logical operator such that when it is correctly used with the appropriate number of propositions, a truth-functional proposition is produced.* Both logical operators considered so far ('it is not the case that' and 'and') are thus truth-functional operators, at least in some contexts.

Terms that can be used as truth-functional operators can also appear in sentences that do not express truth-functional propositions. For example:

Wash your face and brush your teeth.

This is a compound sentence in which component sentences are connected by the logical operator 'and.' However, the component sentences, 'Wash your face' and 'Brush your teeth,' ordinarily express commands, which are neither true nor false, rather than propositions. Thus, the resulting compound also does not express a truth-functional proposition. Operators such as 'and' and 'it is not the case that' are truth-functional operators only when they are parts of a truth-functional proposition.

There are many other compound propositions that are not truth-functional. The following compounds appear similar to 'It is not the case that Pat enjoys logic'; but are they truth-functional?

> **Tom does not believe that Pat enjoys logic.**
> **Susan ought to know that Pat enjoys logic.**
> **Mary hopes that Pat enjoys logic.**

None of these examples satisfies the definition of a truth-functional proposition. Each is a compound, and each contains one simple proposition, 'Pat enjoys logic.' But none of them contains a truth-functional operator. '. . . does not believe that' is a logical operator, for it does operate to produce a new proposition with a changed logical structure; but it is *not* a truth-functional operator, because knowing what this phrase means and knowing the truth value of 'Pat enjoys logic' is not enough to tell us anything about the truth or falsity of the compound statement 'Tom does not believe that Pat enjoys logic.' We still need to know what Tom in fact believes. Knowledge of the truth value of 'Pat enjoys logic' is not sufficient for determining the truth value of this compound statement, for the statement is no longer about Pat but it is about Tom's belief. Tom might not believe that Pat enjoys logic, even if Pat really does enjoy it. Thus, the compound cannot be a truth-functional proposition. A similar analysis can be made of the other two examples.

Another kind of compound proposition that is not truth-functional is

> **John failed the exam because he did not sleep well last night.**

Here, the component sentences 'John failed the exam' and 'He did not sleep well last night' both express propositions, but the word 'because' that connects them does not function as a truth-functional operator. 'Because' is a logical operator, since its inclusion as part of a compound certainly creates a new

"B.C." by permission of Johnny Hart and Creators Syndicate, Inc.

The basic simple truth-functional proposition in the above cartoon is 'You knew that.' Can you explain why all of the other 'knows' can be considered to be logical operators? Given that they are interpreted as logical operators, are they truth-functional operators? Explain why or why not.

proposition with a different logical structure. However, unlike 'and,' which plays a similar connecting role, 'because' is not truth-functional, since knowing its meaning and the truth value of both propositions does not tell us for certain whether the compound statement is true or false. We might know that it is true both that John failed the exam and that he did not sleep well last night without knowing that he failed *because* he did not sleep well. It is possible that he failed the exam because he did not study for it and would have failed even if he had slept well last night. Thus, the causal relationship asserted by 'because' is not truth-functional.

EXERCISE 5–1

For each of the following sentences, (a) indicate whether it expresses a compound proposition. If so, identify (b) all component propositions and (c) logical operators. (d) Indicate whether the proposition is truth-functional.

1. Pines are evergreens and oaks are hardwoods.
2. Oaks are evergreens and pines are hardwoods.
3. It is not true that the earth is flat.
4. It is not the case that ice melts at 32° Fahrenheit.
5. Do good and avoid evil.
6. The sky is blue and the grass is green.
7. You ought to know that the earth is not flat.
8. It is not true that Thomas Jefferson was the second president of the United States.
9. I don't think that Thomas Jefferson was the second president of the United States.
10. Come on out and help me shovel snow.
11. Joseph came out and helped me shovel snow.
12. Are you a Republican or are you a Democrat?
13. Orrin Hatch is a liberal and Edward Kennedy is a conservative.
14. Orrin Hatch is a Republican or Edward Kennedy is a Conservative.
15. Orrin Hatch is a Republican and Edward Kennedy is a Democrat.
16. The woods are full of rattlesnakes; therefore wear your snake boots.
17. Is Maureen coming to dinner or does she have to stay home and study?
18. Maureen is not coming to dinner because she has to stay home and study.

5.3 Propositional Abbreviations and Schemas

The next four chapters will deal with what is known as **symbolic logic.** A **symbol** is *a sign that can be used to abbreviate or schematize any of the components in a given system,* such as the propositions and logical operators we have been talking about. Any logical system can be reduced to symbolic form. But, mainly for historical reasons, the name 'symbolic logic' is usually reserved for the logical systems developed since the latter part of the nineteenth century.

In symbolic logic, the use of certain abbreviations has become conventional to shorten the space and time necessary to express propositions. By this means, long sentences expressing complicated propositions can be condensed into less than a single line, and their logical structure can be more clearly displayed. These techniques are particularly useful for dealing with arguments composed of several compound propositions.

Before we can present and analyze the various truth-functional operations that are covered in the rest of this chapter, it is necessary to introduce a number of new concepts.

5.3.1 Constants and Abbreviations

A **propositional constant** is essentially *an abbreviation for a sentence expressing a proposition*. Such abbreviations can be used to express the same propositions as are expressed by their corresponding sentences.

Logicians commonly use capital letters as propositional constants.[1] Thus we can abbreviate

It is not the case that Pat enjoys logic.

as

It is not the case that P.

where **P** stands for 'Pat enjoys logic.' Similarly, if we let **J** stand for 'Jan enjoys grammar' we can abbreviate

Pat enjoys logic and Jan enjoys grammar.

as

P and J.

Whenever the component propositions of a compound statement are different, we need to use a different propositional constant for each one. However, if one or more propositions are repeated in the same compound statement or in the same group of compound statements, we should use the same letters for them each time they appear, since the proposition expressed by each constant remains the same each time we use it in a given context.

Thus, in the two compound sentences under consideration, since the prop-

---

[1]There is little danger of confusing capital letters used as abbreviations for propositions with capital letters used as abbreviations for nouns and noun clauses in the syllogistic logic treated in Chapters 3 and 4. In syllogistic logic, the letters occur only in the subject and predicate positions of sentences such as 'All A are B;' propositional constants can never occur in such contexts.

osition[2] 'Pat enjoys logic' is expressed by each one, we can use the same propositional constant 'P' in abbreviating that sentence in each compound. And since the sentence 'Jan enjoys grammar' expresses a different proposition, we use a different propositional constant, 'J,' in the second sentence.

Sometimes, as we saw in Chapter 1, different sentences are used to express the same proposition. For example, the German sentence

Beethoven lebt.

can be used to express the same proposition as the English sentence

Beethoven lives.

We can use the same propositional constant to abbreviate two different sentences, as long as both sentences are being used to express the same proposition. Thus, the propositional constant 'B' can be used to abbreviate both of these sentences.

'P' will not always signify 'Pat enjoys logic' and 'B' will not always signify 'Beethoven lives,' since, if they did, the number of propositions that could be so symbolized would be limited to the number of symbols we could invent. However, in the present context, 'P' and only 'P' should be used as an abbreviation for the sentence 'Pat enjoys logic.' In a different context, we could abbreviate a sentence expressing some other proposition with the letter 'L' and the meaning of that symbol would remain constant throughout that context. (This is why we call a propositional constant a 'constant.')

5.3.2 Variables and Schemas

A **propositional variable** is *a symbol that functions as a blank into which we can insert a sentence expressing any proposition whatever.* Since the blank can be filled in by a sentence expressing any proposition, it has no truth value in itself. We use propositional variables to bring out the logical structure of a compound proposition. A formula containing only propositional variables and logical operators is called a **propositional schema.**

The symbols normally used for propositional variables are the small letters from the middle to the end of the alphabet, starting with p (p, q, r, s, t, and so on). If we need more than these eleven variables, we can use p$'$, q$'$, r$'$ and if necessary, p$''$, q$''$ . . . , p$'''$, etc. Using these symbols, we can display the logical form of the proposition expressed by 'P and J' (and any other propositions with the same logical structure, such as 'A and C' or 'D and E') with the propositional schema

p and q

---

[2]We now resume use of the convention stipulated in Chapter 1 to simplify our discussion by sometimes speaking of 'The statement (or proposition) . . .' instead of the more accurate, but more complicated, 'The statement expressed by the sentence. . . .'

If a man will begin with certainties he will end in doubts; but if he will be content to begin with doubts he will end in certainties.

FRANCIS BACON

This statement is about only two things—doubts and certainties—but it requires four different propositional constants in its symbolization. Can you explain why?

The logical form of all the above abbreviations could also be displayed as:

_ _ _ _ _ and . . . .

However, it is customary to use letters instead of blanks, so that more complex logical operations can be symbolized and handled more easily and with less confusion.

If the blanks or propositional variables are filled in or replaced by sentences expressing propositions, or by their abbreviations, then we have added content to the form. In doing this we have changed a propositional schema into a sentence expressing a proposition. Given that 'P' is an abbreviation of 'Pat enjoys logic' and 'J' is an abbreviation of 'Jan enjoys grammar,' the formula

P and J

expresses a proposition with a specific truth value, whereas the formula

p and q

merely displays the form or logical structure of an infinitely large set of propositions and has no further meaning and no specific truth value. 'P and J' is said to be an interpretation of the schema 'p and q.'

EXERCISE 5-2

Given the formulas 'A and B' and 'p and q':

1. Explain the differences between propositional variables and propositional constants.

2. (a) Which contains propositional variables and (b) which contains propositional constants?

3. (a) Which is normally used to represent a particular compound proposition and (b) which to represent an infinite set of compound propositions?

4. (a) Which normally has a determinate truth value and (b) which normally does not?

5. Explain why one formula has a specific truth value and the other does not.

5.4 Conjunction

A truth-functional proposition has been defined as a compound statement such that, if we know the truth or falsity of each of its component statements and the meanings of the logical terms in the sentence expressing the compound proposition, then we can determine precisely the truth or falsity of the compound proposition. So, to determine the truth value of a compound proposition, we must know not only the truth value of each of its component propositions but also the meaning of the logical operator(s).

We have defined the logical operator which creates a truth-functional proposition as a truth-functional operator, and have given 'and' as an example of such an operator.

It is important to recognize that 'and' is often used in ordinary English in ways that are not truth-functional. For example:

Tom and Mary have been married for three years.

In this case, 'and' is being used to conjoin two subjects in the same sentence rather than to conjoin two separate sentences. If we reformulate the sentence as a conjunction of two sentences, we get

Tom has been married for three years and Mary has been married for three years.

This is not equivalent to the original, since it does not assert, as the original obviously does, that Tom and Mary are married to each other.

Another case in which 'and' is not truth-functional would be

Tom woke up and shut off the alarm.

Here, the 'and' expresses a temporal sequence, meaning that Tom woke up and then shut off the alarm. If the word 'and' were truth-functional here, then reversing the sequence of the conjoined propositions would not affect the meaning of the conjunction. But this would give us

Tom shut off the alarm and woke up.

which normally does not have the same meaning as the original, since in the former he woke up first, whereas in the latter he allegedly shut off the alarm first (in his sleep?). Here, too, the 'and' is not truth-functional.

5.4.1 The Dot Operator

Because the English word 'and' has a variety of different meanings, only one of which is that of a truth-functional operator, logicians have created a special symbol which *always* and *only* is used to express the truth-functional meaning of 'and.' This symbol is '·' and is read simply as 'dot.'

Let's examine the meaning of the dot in the following truth-functional propositions:

> **Anatomy is a science · bugs are insects.**
> **Cats can talk · dogs bark.**
> **Edison invented the electric light bulb · Ben Franklin is still alive.**
> **Grouper are mammals · hyenas are reptiles.**

A truth-functional proposition in which the component statements are connected by the truth-functional operator '·' is called a **conjunction;** the component statements of a conjunction are called **conjuncts.** All four of these truth-functional propositions are thus conjunctions and the respective component statements are their conjuncts.

Each of the preceding compound propositions consists of two component statements connected by the truth-functional operator '·'. In the first, the truth of both components is well established. In the second, it is reasonable to assume that the first component is false and the second true. In the third example, the first component is true and the second false. Finally, in the fourth example, both components are presumably false. The question before us is: What effect does the truth-functional operator '·' have on the truth value of each of these compound propositions?

To simplify analysis, we can use the letter '**A**' as a propositional constant to abbreviate '<u>A</u>natomy is a science' and '**B**' to abbreviate '<u>B</u>ugs are insects.' Thus, the compound proposition 'Anatomy is a science and bugs are insects' can be abbreviated as '**A · B.**'

We can abbreviate the second example by symbolizing '<u>C</u>ats can talk' with the propositional constant '**C**' and '<u>D</u>ogs bark' with '**D.**' The two remaining propositions can be similarly abbreviated:

> <u>E</u>dison invented the electric light bulb · Ben <u>F</u>ranklin is alive.   **E · F**
> <u>G</u>rouper are mammals · <u>h</u>yenas are reptiles.   **G · H**

To determine the truth values of these four compound propositions, we must consider the truth value of each of their components. Since '**A**' is true and '**B**' is true, anyone who understands the meaning of 'and' as it is used in this sentence would probably agree that the compound '**A · B**' is true. Most people would also recognize that since '**C**' is false and '**D**' is true, '**C · D**' is false. By the same reasoning, '**E · F**' is false; and since '**G**' is false and '**H**' is false, '**G · H**' is false as well.

Only the first of our conjunctions, '**A · B,**' in which both conjuncts are true, turns out to be true. The other three, in each of which one or both conjuncts are false, all turn out to be false. By way of an informal definition, then, we can say that conjunction is a logical operation in which an operator is used to connect exactly two propositions in such a way that the resulting compound proposition is true if and only if both component propositions are true, and false if either or both of the conjuncts are false.

5.4.2 The Truth Table Definition of Conjunction

The logical structure of any conjunction can be displayed by the propositional schema 'p · q.' In themselves, the propositional variables 'p' and 'q' have no truth values, since they can be replaced by any proposition whatever.[3] Therefore, the schema for conjunction has several possible truth values, for 'p' can be replaced by either a true or a false proposition, and 'q' can also be replaced by either a true or a false proposition.

If we adopt the convention of using the capital letter 'T' to stand for the truth value 'true' and the capital letter 'F' to stand for the truth value 'false,' we can assign the values 'T' or 'F' to any of the four possible instances of 'p · q' exhibited by our examples.

With these conventions, the truth values of the four conjunctions we have already abbreviated can be represented by replacing each of their component propositions with its respective truth value. This gives us:

$$
\begin{array}{ll}
A \cdot B & T \cdot T \\
C \cdot D & F \cdot T \\
E \cdot F & T \cdot F \\
G \cdot H & F \cdot T
\end{array}
$$

These are *the only possible combinations* of Ts and Fs that a conjunction with the form 'p · q' can have.

We saw earlier that, of these four compound propositions, only the first, both of whose components are true, can be regarded as itself true; the other compounds are always false. We can now summarize all of this information by means of the following table, called a **truth table.**

p	q	p	·	q
T	T		T	
F	T		F	
T	F		F	
F	F		F	

A truth table can be used to *display all possible combinations of truth values of statements that could be substituted for the variables* in a truth-functional compound. That is, if the proposition substituted for 'p' is true and the one substituted for 'q' is also true, then the compound 'p · q' is true; if the proposition substituted for 'p' is true and the one substituted for 'q' is false, the compound 'p · q' is false; and so on. The table defines the dot symbol for conjunction in such a way that a conjunction is true if and only if both conjuncts are true; otherwise it is false. This corresponds with the informal definition we established above.[4]

---

[3]Remember that this is not the same as 'A and B,' which is an abbreviation of a specific conjunction and therefore represents components with definite truth values.

[4]It would be technically wrong to construct a truth table for a proposition such as 'A · B' since 'A' and 'B' and 'A · B' are abbreviations for specific propositions that have definite truth values, and thus correspond to only one particular line of the truth table of the schema 'p · q' (in this case the first line).

5.4.3 Translating from English to the Dot Operator

English sentences such as

> **Babe Ruth and Mickey Mantle were baseball players.**

is merely a shorter way of expressing the conjunction

> **Babe Ruth was a baseball player and Mickey Mantle was a baseball player.**

In such a sentence, 'and' operates truth-functionally, and the dot can be used to symbolize it with no loss of meaning.

Many other words in ordinary English are similar to 'and,' such as 'but,' 'although,' 'yet,' and 'moreover.' In appropriate contexts, these words can operate truth-functionally in the same way as 'and,' and insofar as they do they can be symbolized by the dot in a truth-functional conjunction. But like 'and,' they often carry meaning *in addition to* the meaning of the dot and when they do, we ignore this extra meaning at our own risk.

> **The weather is bad,** *but* **we will go to the game.**
> **The mayor was elected on a reformist platform,** *yet* **the city government is still inefficient and corrupt.**
> **The patient is suffering from severe cramps;** *moreover,* **he has a rash on much of his body.**
> **My parents will help send me to graduate school,** *although* **they would rather have me go into the family business.**

As the examples show, these words commonly carry more meaning than that expressed in the truth-table definition of the dot. When the additional meaning is not too great, it is okay to use the dot operator for symbolizing a sentence as long as we explicitly note whatever meaning is being lost from the original.

Let's consider another example:

> **Shaquille O'Neal is big but fast.**

Here, 'but' is used to indicate both that 'Shaquille O'Neal is big and fast' and that 'Shaquille O'Neal is fast despite being big.' The use of 'but' instead of 'and' serves to emphasize that one would not ordinarily expect a 300 pound person to be fast. If we translate 'but' into '·', the sentence would lose part of its meaning. In some contexts, this would be all right—as, for instance, if one wishes to make a coldly objective assessment of Shaq's ability to guard a small quick guard. However, in other contexts the sentence might carry so much extra meaning that a symbolization using the dot would not be appropriate.

Similarly, if we translate

> **Forego won the Widener Handicap although he carried 130 pounds.**

using the dot, we would still be asserting that he won the race and that he carried 130 pounds, but we would no longer be suggesting that horses that

"B.C." by permission of Johnny Hart and Creators Syndicate, Inc.

Discuss whether any loss of meaning results if the 'but' in the above cartoon is symbolized with the conjunction operator of truth-functional logic—that is, the dot.

carry 130 pounds do not usually win handicaps—a suggestion that is conveyed in the original sentence by the term 'although.'

If an 'and' (or related English word) in an ordinary-language sentence is not being used truth-functionally, or if it also expresses extremely significant information over and above the meaning of the dot, it should not be symbolized with the dot. The decision as to whether or not to translate an 'and' (or a similar expression such as 'but') in terms of the dot symbol must be made on a case-by-case basis, using common sense, our knowledge of the context, and our "feel" for the language. Since there are no rigorous formal criteria on which to base such decisions, cases will arise in which two intelligent persons will disagree about whether or not a proposition can be symbolized using the dot. In any case, whenever we use the dot, we must explicitly note any resulting loss of meaning.

EXERCISE 5–3

In each of the following sentences (a) indicate what meaning, if any, would be lost by translating the 'and' with the dot. If the dot cannot be used, explain why. (b) If the translation is possible, symbolize the sentence using the appropriate propositional constants, and indicate what each constant represents.

1. The gunmen robbed the bank and made their getaway.
2. The gunmen's faces were covered with masks and they wore gloves.
3. Oakland and Los Angeles played in the 1994 World Series.
4. The Oakland Athletics and the Los Angeles Dodgers are baseball teams.
5. The band played rock and roll.
6. The band played Stardust and Moon River.
7. Each prisoner wore a ball and chain.
8. The weather will be cloudy and cool tomorrow.
9. Sam was involved in a hit-and-run accident.

10. Jim mailed a letter and bought some books.

11. Jim climbed out of the water and dried himself off.

12. George and Martha are quarreling again.

13. George and Martha are characters in Albee's *Who's Afraid of Virginia Woolf.*

14. Shaquille O'Neal scored twenty points although he played only half the game.

5.5 Truth Tables

As was illustrated in our discussion of conjunction, truth-functional operators can be defined with the use of truth tables. A truth table is an illustrative device that is used to display all of the possible combinations of truth values of propositions that could be substituted for the propositional variables in a given propositional schema. Once we have displayed all the possible combinations of truth values for the propositions that could be substituted for the variables in a schema containing only a single operator, and have displayed the corresponding truth values for each of the compound statements formed by those propositions, we have provided *a complete definition* of the logical operator that is part of that schema. Truth tables, therefore, can be used to define truth-functional operators in terms of an exhaustive list of the possible combinations of truth values in compound statements using a given truth-functional operation.

If we create a new operation of 'truthation' whose operator we will symbolize by '☺', we could define the symbol by the following truth table:

p	q	p ☺ q
T	T	T
F	T	T
T	F	T
F	F	T

From this truth table, it should be obvious that our truthational operator makes true any compound proposition in which it is the main operator, whatever the truth values of the component propositions. Therefore, any proposition with the form 'p ☺ q' would be true by virtue of the definition of the ☺.

We could just as well have defined the truthation operator in the following way:

p	T	F	T	F
q	T	T	F	F
p ☺ q	T	T	T	T

But it has become conventional to display the various possible combinations of propositions that could be substituted for 'p' and 'q' on a truth table in terms of four rows forming a column under each variable. The order of the Ts and Fs used is also a standard one. The Ts and Fs are alternated under the first variable, and pairs of Ts and Fs are alternated under the second variable. This arrangement shows all possible combinations of T and F for a proposition containing exactly two terms.

5.6 Negation

Negation is the name we give to the logical operator that operates on a given proposition to form a new compound statement that has the opposite truth value from that proposition. The standard abbreviation we use for the negation operator is the curl or tilde symbol, '~'. The propositional schema for the negation of a proposition is '~p'.

We can define the negation operator in terms of the two possible truth values of the propositions that could be substituted for the variable 'p' in the propositional schema '~p' with the following truth table:

p	~p
T	F
F	T

Thus, if a proposition is true, its negation is false, and if a proposition is false, its negation is true.

If we wish to deny, or negate, the truth value of a simple proposition in ordinary English, we can do so by forming a new compound statement attaching the operator 'it is not the case that' to that proposition. In most ordinary contexts, whatever the truth value of the proposition being denied, the new proposition that denies it will have the opposite truth value; in such contexts, the expression 'it is not the case that' has essentially the same meaning as the tilde.

In going from a symbolization involving the tilde to an English sentence, we follow the convention of translating the '~' operator into the English phrase 'it is not the case that.'[5] However, when starting with English sentences, we

---

[5]Strictly speaking, 'it is the case that . . . ' is also a truth-functional operator, but it is unnecessary to use it since when one says 'it is the case that P' one is saying nothing more than what is being said in the mere assertion of 'P.' Thus, it would be redundant to have an additional symbol for the truth-functional operator 'it is the case that . . . ' or 'it is true that . . . ' (e.g., the symbol '@'), for if 'P' has the value true, then '@P' is also true, and if 'P' has the value false, then '@P' is false.

need to be aware that there are various other ways of negating a statement which can be symbolized using the tilde. Take the statement

The wicked witch is dead.

We can negate this statement in any of several ways, including the following:

It is not the case that the wicked witch is dead.
It is false that the wicked witch is dead.
The wicked witch is not dead.
The wicked witch is alive.

Because all four of these sentences can normally be used to express the same proposition, they should all be abbreviated in the same way, and should also have the same schema. The important point is that the "obvious" abbreviation for the first three is '~**D**,' while the "obvious" abbreviation for the last is '**A**.' But since all can be used to express the same proposition, is it not necessary that all be symbolized in the same way? The answer is both yes and no. The basic rule to be followed is that once a particular symbol has been assigned to a sentence *in a given context,* the same symbol must be used for every other sentence that is being used in that context to express the same proposition. Thus, if an argument contains both 'The wicked witch is not dead' and 'The wicked witch is alive' as components, then, if 'The wicked witch is not dead' is symbolized as '~**D**,' 'The wicked witch is alive' must also be symbolized as '~**D**.' Alternatively, if 'The wicked witch is alive' is symbolized as '**A**,' then 'The wicked witch is not dead' must also be symbolized as '**A**,' even though it may appear at first to be expressing a negative proposition. (All of this assumes, of course, that the two sentences are being used to express the same proposition.)

EXERCISE 5-4

(a) Symbolize the truth-functional proposition expressed by each of the following sentences using propositional constants and the symbols for conjunction and negation. (b) Indicate precisely which part of the original sentence each constant symbolizes. (c) Indicate what meaning, if any, is lost in replacing the English word with the logical operator.

1. Tom likes ice cream and Orrin Hatch was president in 1985.

2. Jimmy Carter was not president in 1900 and $2 + 2 = 73$.

3. Tom can't symbolize this problem but Mary can.

4. Mary did not miss this problem although she did not understand it.

5. Sue didn't understand the preceding section so she read it again more carefully.

6. Ed symbolized problem 3 using the tilde and he got it wrong.

7. Bill found this question to be difficult but he didn't give up.

8. Ann got all of these problems right and she had a small celebration.
9. The brakes didn't work and the car crashed.
10. Mary passed the test even though she got this problem wrong.
11. Sue and Bill are engaged to be married.
12. Mary and Pat are guards on the basketball team.

5.7 Disjunction

The symbol for the logical operator known as **inclusive disjunction** is the wedge or 'vee' symbol '∨'. We can define the '∨' operator by means of the following truth table:

p	q	p ∨ q
T	T	T
F	T	T
T	F	T
F	F	F

An inclusive disjunction is thus true if and only if either or both disjuncts are true and is false if and only if both disjuncts are false.

Disjunction is the logical operation that most closely corresponds to the connecting of two sentences by the word 'or' in ordinary English. The two sentences being connected are called disjuncts or alternatives. However, in ordinary usage, the English word 'or' is ambiguous in that it is commonly used to express two different meanings. For example, consider the following sentence:

Pat is going to go without beef next week or Pat is going to go without pork next week.

In this sentence, the word 'or' is being used in what is known as the **inclusive sense**. The inclusive 'or' is *used to assert that either the first disjunct or the second disjunct **or both** disjuncts may be true.* Thus, the above statement is true either if Pat is going to go without beef next week or if Pat is going to go without pork next week, *or* if Pat is going to go without *both*. An inclusive disjunction is true if the first, the second, *or both* disjuncts are true; it is false only if both disjuncts are false.

In contrast, when a customer in a restaurant asks the waiter "What dessert comes with this dinner?" and is told "You can have cake or pie," the waiter almost certainly means that the customer is entitled to either cake or pie for dessert, but not both. In this situation, 'or' is being used in **the exclusive sense**. The exclusive 'or' is used in sentences in which *either the first disjunct, or the second disjunct, but not both, may be true.*

An exclusive disjunction is true if and only if the first disjunct is true and the second is false, or the first disjunct is false and the second is true. An exclusive disjunction differs from an inclusive disjunction insofar as when it is true, both disjuncts cannot be true. If we treat the disjunction

Ann vacationed in Florida or California.

as inclusive, then it would be false only if Ann did not vacation in either Florida or California. If we treat it as an exclusive disjunction, then it would be false if Ann did not vacation in either Florida or California, but it would also be false if she vacationed in both Florida and California. Thus, when we treat a disjunction as exclusive, we are making the extra assumption that both disjuncts cannot be true—an assumption that would be warranted only if the

"AND MAKE MR. WILSON'S ULCER BETTER. OR ME, OR ONE OF US, ANYWAY...."

"Dennis the Menace" ® *used by permission of Hank Ketcham and* © *by North America Syndicate.*

What sense of 'or'—inclusive or exclusive—is being used in this cartoon? Would any significant loss of meaning result if the truth-functional disjunction operator—the wedge—were used in place of the 'or'?

context made perfectly clear that this extra restriction was intended. Therefore, in dealing with English sentences in everyday contexts, logicians *usually interpret every 'or' as an inclusive disjunction, unless strong evidence indicates that the 'or' is being used exclusively.* We will follow the practice, since it is always better to assume too little than too much.

Many disjunctions in ordinary language are vague, and only a thorough analysis of the specific contexts can reveal for certain whether they are intended as inclusive or exclusive. In treating as inclusive all disjunctions that are not clearly exclusive, we are covering at least that part of their meaning that all disjunctions have in common, namely that it is not the case that both disjuncts are false. Again, it is always better to assume too little than to assume too much. Later in this chapter we present the logical tools for dealing with cases in which an exclusive disjunction is clearly stated or intended—tools, that is, to express the extra condition that the disjuncts cannot both be true. In the meantime, we interpret the 'or' of disjunction only in its weaker or inclusive sense.

EXERCISE 5–5

(a) Symbolize the truth-functional proposition expressed by each of the following sentences using propositional constants and the symbols for inclusive disjunction and negation. (b) Indicate precisely which part of the original sentence each constant symbolizes. (c) Indicate what meaning, if any, is lost in replacing the English word with the logical operator.

1. Either Tom likes ice cream or Orrin Hatch was president in 1985.
2. Jimmy Carter was not president in 1900 or 2 + 2 = 73.
3. Tom or Mary can symbolize this problem.
4. Mary missed this problem or else she understood the preceding section.
5. Sue understood the preceding section or she read it very carefully.
6. Ed symbolized problem 3 using the tilde or he got it wrong.
7. Bill found this to be difficult or Mary found it to be easy.
8. Ann or Tom got all of these problems right.
9. The brakes didn't work or the car crashed.
10. Mary got an A or a B on the test.

5.8 Material Implication

For a number of reasons that are too complex to go into in this book, most systems of symbolic logic include a truth-functional operation known as **material implication**. The logical operator for material implication is symbolized by the horseshoe symbol '⊃' and is defined in terms of the following truth table:

p	q	p ⊃ q
T	T	T
F	T	T
T	F	F
F	F	T

From this table we can see that any proposition of the form 'p ⊃ q' is false if and only if the proposition substituted for 'p' is true and the proposition substituted for 'q' is false. In all other cases, a proposition with this form is true. The '⊃' is the only one of the truth-functional operators that we use for which the *sequence* of the component propositions is significant. Notice in this truth table that the second and third rows have opposite values under the horseshoe, whereas in the second and third rows of the truth table for the dot, both have Fs under the dot, and the second and third rows of the truth table for the wedge both have Ts under the wedge.

The symbol '⊃' is usually translated into ordinary English in terms of 'If . . . then . . .' sentences, or sentences with the form 'p implies q.' (The relation of material implication to the notion of valid arguments will be discussed in the next chapter.) Sentences of the 'If . . . then . . .' form are also called **conditionals.** The *term preceding the horseshoe* is known as the **antecedent,** and *the term following it* is known as the **consequent.** The horseshoe's definition specifies that the compound is false *only* in the one case in which the antecedent is true and the consequent is false.

Although logicians follow the convention that every formula containing the horseshoe symbol can be translated into an 'If . . . then . . .' sentence, it must be recognized that most 'If . . . then . . .' sentences in ordinary English carry more meaning than does the horseshoe of material implication. In fact, the truth-functional operator symbolized by the horseshoe has no real counterpart in ordinary English. However, it is sufficiently similar to certain ordinary-language terms that it can be used in the logical analysis of many (but not all) conditional statements. This can best be illustrated by concrete examples.

In the first row of the truth table for material implication, both the antecedent and the consequent are true. This is illustrated by the following interpretation of the schema 'p ⊃ q':

2 + 2 = 4 ⊃ George Washington was the first president of the United States.

On the basis of the truth table definition of the horseshoe, we would have to say that the above sentence expresses a true proposition, since both the antecedent and the consequent are true.

Although the term 'conditional' carries suggestions of some sort of substantial relation between the antecedent and consequent, this is definitely not the case with regard to the horseshoe. The sentence above containing the horseshoe symbol does *not* carry all of the meaning contained in the statement expressed by the following sentence in everyday usage:

If 2 + 2 = 4, then George Washington was the first president of the United States.

This sentence asserts that Washington's having been the first president is in some way conceptually or factually related to the mathematical truth that 2 + 2 = 4. This is a suggestion that we would reject on factual grounds, for the truth of the mathematical statement has nothing to do with the truth of this or any other historical statement. We might even want to say that the 'If . . . then . . .' statement is false, even though the statement expressed using the horseshoe is true (by virtue of the truth table definition of the horseshoe). In short, the expression 'If . . . then . . . ,' when used in the context of ordinary language, almost always carries more meaning[6] than does '⊃.' This is why we prefer calling this relation 'material implication,' a term which does not carry any of the extra meaning of expressions such as 'conditional.'

The meaning of the horseshoe is given entirely in its truth table. Like all truth-functional operators, the horseshoe asserts no relationship between the component propositions other than that specified in its truth table. If 'p' and 'q' are both true, then 'p ⊃ q' is true no matter what other relations hold or do not hold between 'p' and 'q.' Once we know the meaning of the horseshoe symbol as a logical operator, then, to determine precisely the truth value of a material implication, we need ascertain only the truth values of the antecedent and the consequent. Any other relationship between antecedent and consequent is irrelevant from a strictly logical point of view.

Knowing this, we can avoid becoming confused about material implications in which the antecedent and the consequent are not only true but also are asserted (in ordinary language) to be causally related. Take, for example, the sentence:

If you stop breathing, then you will die in a few minutes.

In this case, the antecedent and the consequent do not merely both happen to be true; the sentence asserts that the antecedent is the *cause* of the consequent. But when the same sentence is symbolized using the horseshoe, the assertion of a causal connection disappears.

Sentences expressing causal relations represent a connection that is much stronger than material implication. An exhaustive analysis of such sentences would take us beyond the bounds of truth-functional logic. (This topic is dealt with more fully in Chapter 10.) For our present purposes, it is sufficient to note that, by symbolizing such a statement with the horseshoe symbol, we

---

[6]As seen in our discussion of the two senses of disjunction, statement A carries more meaning than statement B if and only if whenever A is true then B is also true, but when B is true it is possible that A might be false.

communicate at least that part of its meaning that is relevant to analyzing the logical structure of arguments containing such statements.

If we assume that it is true that you stop breathing but false that you will die in a few minutes—that is, if we affirm the antecedent and deny the consequent—then the original sentence expresses an obviously false proposition. We have, therefore, a situation corresponding to line 3 of the truth table: 'p' is true, 'q' is false, and 'p ⊃ q' is false. Even if we do not know that the cessation of breathing is the cause of dying soon, we can still know it to be true that, *if* you stop breathing, *then* you will die shortly thereafter. Only if it were in fact the case that people who stopped breathing did not die shortly thereafter would it be false that a material implication holds between 'You stop breathing' and 'You will die in a few minutes.' Therefore we can treat such conditionals as if they were material implications, even though they are also much more; but we must recognize that, in so treating them, we sacrifice much of their meaning.

Material implication also differs in other ways from our ordinary conception of the meanings of conditional sentences. Consider the following:

If the moon is made of green cheese, then I am Superman.

Here the speaker evidently wants to deny the antecedent and uses a patently false consequent ('I am Superman') to assert that the antecedent ('The moon is made of green cheese') is not only false but even ridiculous. According to the truth table definition of the horseshoe, we would have to accept the compound proposition as true, merely because both component propositions are false (see line 4 of the table), which is a much weaker and less interesting assertion than what was intended. To avoid this, the 'If . . . then . . .' statement might best be reformulated as a simple negation of the antecedent:

It is not the case that the moon is made of green cheese.

Here too, however, some meaning is lost from the original.

Whereas conditionals with false consequents are often used in ordinary language as a means of emphasizing the falsity of the antecedent, there are few, if any, ordinary-language contexts in which one would use a conditional with a false antecedent and a true consequent. To anyone other than a logician, the following assertion

If tigers are reptiles, then *War and Peace* was written by Tolstoy.

would naturally suggest either (a) that the speaker sincerely believes tigers to be reptiles (and probably also regards this fact as good evidence for Tolstoy's authorship of *War and Peace*); or—assuming he or she knows that tigers are not reptiles—(b) that he or she believes Tolstoy did not write *War and Peace*; or (c) that the sentence is nonsensical and is not being used to express a proposition at all. But to the logician, if the 'If . . . then . . .' were symbolized using the horseshoe, it would simply express a truth, by virtue of the truth table definition (line 2 of the table).

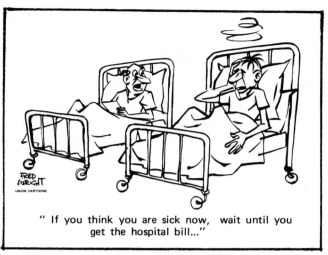

" If you think you are sick now, wait until you get the hospital bill..."

Fred Wright, UE News.

Discuss what meaning is lost when the 'If . . . then . . . ' in this cartoon is symbolized using the horseshoe.

Many conditionals in ordinary language are not truth-functional.[7] But we are here interested only in the one kind of conditional that is. Some material implications seem strange, or even patently absurd, when expressed in ordinary language. Nevertheless, material implication is a legitimate and extremely useful logical operation. Its usefulness will become more evident as we get further into the discussion of propositional logic.

It is always important to remember that the translation of the horseshoe into an ordinary-language 'If . . . then . . .' often results in the addition of new meanings, while the translation of the ordinary-language 'If . . . then . . .' into the horseshoe often results in a significant loss of meaning. Thus, if the form represented by the schema 'p ⊃ q' sometimes sounds very strange when the variables are replaced by ordinary English sentences expressing true or false propositions, we must bear in mind that the horseshoe symbol means only that the compound statement containing it is false if and only if the antecedent is true and the consequent is false.

---

[7]A common type of 'If . . . then . . .' statement in ordinary English that cannot be symbolized with the horseshoe is the **counterfactual conditional,** such as 'If John Kennedy had not been assassinated, then the United States would not have gotten involved in Vietnam' and 'If John Kennedy had not been assassinated, then the United States would have got even more deeply involved in Vietnam.' Clearly, it is impossible for both of these sentences, as we normally interpret them, to express true statements. Yet, since both have a false antecedent, both would be true by definition if symbolized with the horseshoe of material implication. Counterfactuals are generally founded on causal relations, and thus are not discussed here.

Other ordinary English expressions, as well as those of the form 'If . . . then . . . ,' use the term 'if' in such fashion that they can justifiably be symbolized as material implications. For example:

I will go if you will go.

Since the 'if' immediately precedes 'you will go,' this sentence can be symbolized—admittedly with loss of meaning—as

<u>Y</u>ou will go ⊃ <u>I</u> will go.[8]

Its abbreviation and schema display its logical structure directly:

Y ⊃ I   *and*   **q ⊃ p**

The variable 'q' has been substituted for the proposition 'You will go,' and 'p' has been substituted for 'I will go.' If we make the same substitutions in the original proposition, we get 'p if q.'

The slightly different sentence

I will go only if you will go.

can be symbolized as

I will go ⊃ you will go   *or*   **I ⊃ Y**

To understand this more clearly, consider the original sentence as equivalent to the speaker's saying to a third party, "If you see me going, you can be sure Y is going, because if she doesn't go, I won't go either." (Also, look back at the truth table, which shows that in a true 'p ⊃ q' proposition, 'p' can be true *only* if 'q' is true.) Substituting variables for the component sentences, we obtain a schema of the form

p *only if* **q**

which, therefore, can legitimately be symbolized as 'p ⊃ q.'

Still another ordinary English locution using 'if' is

<u>I</u> will go even if <u>y</u>ou go.

This is really a way of asserting simply

I will go.

because in saying, 'I will go even if you go,' I am not only asserting that I will go if you go, but am also asserting that I will go if you do not go. Thus, whether you go or not, I will definitely go. Therefore, statements of the form 'p even if q' can be rendered into statements of the simpler form 'p,' and do not fit the

---

[8]We will continue to identify the letters to be used in abbreviating a sentence by underscoring them in their original context. Thus, in this example, the underscored 'Y' indicates that 'You will go' is to be abbreviated as '<u>Y</u>.'

truth-table definition of material implication (because 'p' may be true even when 'q' is false).

Some General Rules for Translating English into the '⊃'

If p then q	can be symbolized as	p ⊃ q
p if q	can be symbolized as	q ⊃ p
p only if q	can be symbolized as	p ⊃ q
p even if q	can be symbolized as	p
p unless q	can be symbolized as	p ⊃ ~q
when p, q	can be symbolized as	p ⊃ q

Remember, there is almost always some loss of meaning in going from an English expression to the horseshoe.

EXERCISE 5–6

(a) Symbolize the truth-functional proposition expressed by each of the following sentences using propositional constants and the symbols for material implication and negation. (b) Indicate precisely which part of the original sentence each constant symbolizes. (c) Indicate what meaning, if any, is lost in replacing the English word with the logical operator.

1. If you like ice cream, then Ronald Reagan was president in 1985.
2. If Jimmy Carter was president in 1900, then 2 + 2 = 73.
3. If you can't symbolize this problem, then you will get it wrong.
4. You will miss this problem unless you understand the preceding section.
5. If you don't understand the preceding section, you will probably miss this question.
6. If you symbolized problem 3 using the horseshoe, then you got it wrong.
7. It is not helpful to get upset if you find this to be difficult.
8. Tom will celebrate only if he gets all of these problems right.
9. If the brakes don't work, the car will crash.
10. Mary will pass the test even if she gets this problem wrong.

5.9 Material Equivalence

Material equivalence is the name given to *the logical operation that joins two propositions into a compound statement such that, if the the components have the same truth value, the compound statement is true, and if they have different truth values, the compound statement is false.* The logical operator for material equivalence is represented by the symbol '≡'. We can define the '≡' symbol by means of the following truth table:

p	q	p ≡ q
T	T	T
F	T	F
T	F	F
F	F	T

A material equivalence is thus true if both of its component propositions are true or if both are false, and it is false if they have different truth values.[9]

The '≡' symbol for material equivalence can best be rendered into ordinary English as 'if and only if.' Thus, instead of saying

> **'Caesar crossed the Rubicon' is materially equivalent to 'Shakespeare wrote Hamlet,'**

we can say

> **Caesar crossed the Rubicon if and only if Shakespeare wrote Hamlet.**

All we are asserting here is that both components have the same truth value—that either both are true or both are false. The translation of the '≡' into 'if and only if' might sometimes tempt one to read into it more meaning than it is actually intended to bear, just as 'If . . . then . . .' sometimes conveys more meaning than the horseshoe is defined to convey. Thus, it cannot be too strongly emphasized that *the meaning of '≡' is only what is specified in its truth-table definition.*[10]

EXERCISE 5-7

(a) Symbolize the truth-functional proposition expressed by each of the following sentences using propositional constants and the symbols for conjunction, negation, disjunction, material implication, and material equivalence. (b) Indicate precisely which part of the original sentence each constant symbolizes. (c) Indicate what meaning, if any, is lost in replacing the English word with the logical operator.

---

[9]We should not make the mistake of confusing the '≡' for material equivalence with the '=' symbol for identity. Material equivalence says only that both of the component propositions have the same truth value, whereas an identity statement asserts that the two components not only have the same truth value but are identical in every other way as well.

[10]Notice that sometimes, in ordinary English, people use 'If . . . then . . .' sentences to express what is intended as a material equivalence. Thus, the instructor who says to a class, 'If you maintain an average of 90 or better on all your work in the course, then you will get an A,' might in fact be telling the students that they will get As if and only if they maintain a 90 average or better.

1. Roses are red and violets are blue.
2. Roses are red yet violets are blue.
3. It rained today and the mailman was late.
4. If I give you one, then everybody will want one.
5. It is not the case that hickory is a soft wood.
6. It is snowing in Detroit or else the weather report is inaccurate.
7. Joyce needs a kitchen table and some chairs for her apartment.
8. Thoreau was an American or a Frenchman.
9. Athens and Sparta fought in the Peloponnesian War.
10. Athens and Sparta were city-states in ancient Greece.
11. Oil and water will mix if and only if they are emulsified.
12. If a total eclipse of the sun occurs, then the sky darkens.
13. A total eclipse of the sun occurs if and only if the moon is positioned directly between the earth and the sun.
14. His battery went dead and his car wouldn't start.
15. It is not the case that sugar is a protein.
16. If this lump of sugar is placed in water, it will dissolve.
17. This object will float if and only if its specific gravity is less than .10.
18. You left the window open or the thermostat is turned down too low.
19. A geometrical figure is equilateral if and only if all its sides have the same length.
20. It is not true that all triangles are right triangles.
21. I will take the job if it pays well.
22. I will take the job if and only if it pays well.
23. If Pat is late, then the world must be coming to an end.
24. Carl drinks Coke unless Gatorade is available.
25. Most swans are white, although some are gray.
26. It is not true that Plato was Aristotle's disciple.
27. A conjunction is true if and only if both its component propositions are true.
28. If the stock market fails, then many people will lose fortunes.
29. People lose money even if the stock market goes up.
30. Candles can be made of tallow or beeswax.
31. Either he came after I left or he didn't come at all.
32. You will pass this exam if you study hard.
33. You will pass this exam only if you study hard.
34. You will pass this exam if and only if you study hard.
35. It did not rain although the clouds were dark and ominous.

5.10 Propositions with More Than One Logical Operator

Many of the arguments with which we frequently wish to deal contain statements that include more than one logical operator—that is, they are compound statements whose components include other compound statements. For instance, the following compound might appear as either a premise or a conclusion in different arguments:

> **Either the Democrats will not win the election or, if they do, they will not have a very large majority.**

This proposition contains both a disjunction and a conditional (which can be treated as a material implication). Therefore, we must discuss the ways of dealing with truth-functional propositions containing two or more logical operators.

5.10.1 Grouping

When symbolizing compound statements that are parts of larger compound statements, we use additional symbols to group together the components to which a particular operator applies. **Grouping** is *the setting off of compound propositions within a larger compound (usually by means of parentheses) in such a way that it is made clear to which variable or variables a particular operator applies.*

Grouping is a familiar technique in mathematics, where parentheses are used to clarify ambiguous statements such as

> 3 × 5 + 4

which can mean either

> 3 × (5 + 4)

which is equal to 27, or

> (3 × 5) + 4

which is equal to 19.

Certain words and punctuation marks (commas, semicolons, and so on) can serve the same purpose as such parentheses. In English, the ambiguity of the sentence

> **It is not true that Chris will win or I will get sick.**

can be avoided by the appropriate use of the word 'either.' We can place 'either' before the operator 'it is not true that,' which gives us

> **Either it is not true that Chris will win or I will get sick.**

or we can place it immediately after the negation operator, which gives

> **It is not true that either Chris will win or I will get sick.**

which expresses a quite different proposition. We could express the first alternative as

(~C) ∨ I

and the second alternative as

~(C ∨ I)

The former is a disjunction, the first component of which is a negation. Here the wedge is what is known as the **main operator.** The latter is a negation with a component compound proposition that is a disjunction. In this case, the tilde is the main operator. In general, a statement with the form

(~p) ∨ q

clearly has a different logical structure than does a statement with the form

~(p ∨ q).

For the sake of simplicity, we will adopt the convention that no parentheses are needed in symbolizing the negation of a simple proposition. That is, when a propositional constant or variable is preceded by the tilde with no parentheses, the tilde should be understood to apply only to that one constant or variable. Thus, we will simply write '~p ∨ q' instead of the equivalent '(~p) ∨ q.'

Commas and other punctuation marks can also be used in ordinary English to clarify ambiguous groupings. Consider the sentence:

Susan will defeat Fran and I will defeat you or I will give up chess.

This could mean either of the following:

1. **Susan will defeat Fran and I will defeat you, or I will give up chess.**
2. **Susan will defeat Fran, and I will defeat you or I will give up chess.**

The first interpretation uses the comma to make a disjunction out of the whole compound (and a conjunction within the first disjunct) and should be symbolized as

(S · D) ∨ G

In this case, the wedge is the main operator. The second interpretation uses the comma to make the whole compound into a conjunction (in which the second conjunct is a disjunction) and should be symbolized as

S · (D ∨ G)

The main operator now is the dot. If Susan does not defeat Fran, but I do defeat you, and I do give up chess (which makes S false, D true, and G true), the first interpretation is true, since a disjunction is true if one or both of its disjuncts is true. However, the second interpretation is false, since a conjunction cannot be true unless both conjuncts are true. This one case is sufficient to demonstrate

Either all of us are going to die together or we are going to learn to live together and if we are to live together we have to talk.

<small>ELEANOR ROOSEVELT</small>

Make sure that you get the grouping right when you symbolize this statement in propositional logic.

---

that the two interpretations are not the same, since the compound is true in one grouping and false in the other.

The expression 'neither . . . nor . . .' can be a bit tricky to symbolize. At first glance, many people are tempted to symbolize

Neither <u>T</u>om nor <u>M</u>ary is going to the game.

as

$\sim T \vee \sim M$

which actually is the symbolization for

Either Tom is not going to the game or Mary is not going to the game.

which is true if just one of them does not go. Instead, expressions involving 'neither . . . nor . . .' must be symbolized with the negation symbol outside of a parenthesis containing a disjunction. Thus our example should be symbolized as

$\sim(T \vee M)$

which states literally that it is not the case that either Tom or Mary is going to the game.

Sometimes we encounter a sentence composed of three or more conjuncts, or three or more disjuncts; for example,

I overslept and it was raining pitchforks and the professor gave a surprise quiz.

Susan is a plumber or Frank is a cook or Phil is a carpenter.

Sentences of this sort are not ambiguous, since it doesn't change the meaning or the truth value if we group the components one way or the other. But such statements must still be grouped, because the definitions of the logical operators '·' and '∨' limit them to two component propositions. For this reason 'p · q · r'

To Take This Credit.—You must file Form 1040, not Form 1040A, and you meet **all** of the conditions listed below.

(1) It was necessary for you to make child and dependent care payments so you (and your spouse if you were married) could work or look for work.

(2) One or more qualifying persons lived in your home.

(3) You (and your spouse if you were married) paid more than half the cost of keeping up your home. This cost includes rent or mortgage payments; utility charges; maintenance and repairs; property taxes and property insurance; and food costs (but not dining out).

(4) You must file a joint return if you were married. There are two exceptions to this rule. You can file a separate return if:

(a) You were legally separated; or

(b) You were living apart and:

● The qualifying person lived in your home for more than 6 months; and

● You paid more than half the cost of keeping up your home; and

● Your spouse did not live in your home during the last 6 months of your tax year.

Child Custody Test.—If you were divorced, legally separated, or separated under a written agreement, your child is a qualifying person if you had custody for the longer period during 1978. The child must also have:

● Received over half of his or her support from the parents, and

● Been in the custody of one or both parents for more than half of 1978, and

● Been under 15, or physically or mentally unable to care for himself or herself.

(5) You paid someone, other than a dependent relative or your spouse, to care for the qualifying person.

You are allowed to pay a relative who was not your dependent if their services are considered employment for social security purposes. However, if the relative is your child, he or she must have been at least 21. If the relative is your parent, both of the following conditions must have been met for 4 continuous weeks during a calendar quarter:

(a) The qualifying person was your child under 18 or whose physical or mental condition required care by an adult.

(b) You were a widow(er) or divorced; or your spouse was physically or mentally unable to care for the child under 18.

Government documents and forms, despite efforts in recent years to simplify them, still contain some of the most complex statements ever formulated by the human mind (although some wags have suggested that they are in fact formulated by inhuman—and inhumane—minds). Can you interpret and then symbolize the two very complex statements reproduced above from U.S. Income Tax Form 2441—Credit for Child and Dependent Care Expenses?

must be grouped as either '(p · q) · r' or as 'p · (q · r)'; and 'p ∨ q ∨ r' must likewise be grouped as '(p ∨ q) ∨ r' or as 'p ∨ (q ∨ r).' The choice of grouping in each case is completely arbitrary.

EXERCISE 5–8

(a) Symbolize each of the following sentences. In all cases this requires using more than one logical operator. Use the underscored letters as propositional constants, and use parentheses where necessary to indicate correct groupings of propositional constants and logical operators. (b) Identify the main operator in each formula by underlining it.

1. I will both eat shrimp and drink root beer, or else I will go on a diet.

2. I will eat shrimp, and either I will drink root beer or I will go on a diet.

3. Either I will eat shrimp, or I will drink root beer and I will go on a diet.

4. Either I will eat shrimp or I will drink root beer, and in either case I will go on a diet.

5. I will eat shrimp, and I will both drink root beer and I will go on a diet.

6. I will eat shrimp and will drink root beer and I will go on a diet.

7. It is not the case that if I am going to win then I will go home.

8. If it is not the case that I am going to win, then I will go home.

9. If I am going to win, then it is not the case that I will go home.

10. If I am going to win, then I will not go home.

11. If I am not going to win, then I will go home.

12. It is not the case that both Lassie is a collie and Spot is a mongrel.

13. Lassie is a collie and Spot is not a mongrel.

14. Lassie is not a collie and Spot is a mongrel.

15. Lassie is not a collie and Spot is not a mongrel.

16. It is not the case that both Lassie is not a collie and Spot is not a mongrel.

17. It is not the case that both Lassie is a collie and Spot is not a mongrel.

18. It is not the case that both Lassie is not a collie and Spot is a mongrel.

19. If it snows and driving will be hazardous, then the Bakers will not come.

20. If it snows, then both the driving will be hazardous and the Bakers will not come.

21. If it snows, then either the driving will be hazardous or the Bakers will not come.

22. If it snows, then either the driving will be hazardous or the Bakers will come.

23. If it snows, then if the driving will be hazardous the Bakers will not come.

24. If it either snows or the driving will be hazardous, then the Bakers will not come.

25. If the band quits, then everyone will go home and complain.

26. If the band quits, then if everyone goes home, they will complain.

27. If the band quits, then either everyone will go home or complain.

28. If the band quits or everyone goes home, then everyone will complain.

29. Either Kurt is Dutch and Mia is French or Hi is English.

30. Kurt is Dutch and either Mia is French or Hi is English.

31. Kurt is Dutch or Mia is French or Hi is English.

32. Kurt is Dutch and it is not the case that either Mia is French or Hi is English.

33. It is not the case that either Kurt is Dutch or both Mia is French and Hi is English.

34. It is not the case both that Kurt is Dutch and that either Mia is French or Hi is English.

35. It is not the case that either Kurt is Dutch and Mia is French, or Hi is English.

36. Kurt is Dutch or it is not the case that both Mia is French and Hi is English.

37. Kurt is Dutch or both Mia is French and Hi is not English.
38. Kurt is Dutch or it is not the case that both Mia is French and Hi is not English.
39. Kurt is not Dutch and either Mia is French or Hi is English.
40. Kurt is not Dutch and it is not the case that either Mia is not French or Hi is not English.

5.11 Truth Table Construction

Having developed the logical punctuation procedures necessary to present propositional schemas with more than one operator, we can develop the techniques for constructing truth tables for those schemas. Three basic rules govern construction of truth tables for schemas with more than one operator.

The first rule follows from our basic requirement of including all possible combinations and permutations of truth values in the truth table for a particular propositional schema. Mathematicians have shown that, for the two truth values **T** and **F**, the number of possible combinations and permutations for a given compound propositional schema containing exactly n propositional variables is 2^n—that is, n 2s connected with a total of $n - 1$ multiplication signs. We have already seen that each grouping of truth values requires a separate row in the truth table. Therefore, our first rule is that the truth table for a propositional schema should contain 2^n rows, where n is the number of propositional variables in the schema.

The cases we have dealt with thus far conform to this: The truth table for negation, with one variable, contains $2^1 = 2$ rows; the others, with two variables, contain $2^2 = 2 \times 2 = 4$ rows. A schema with three variables has $2^3 = 2 \times 2 \times 2 = 8$ possible groupings of Ts and Fs, and thus eight rows in its truth table. Four variables require $2^4 = 2 \times 2 \times 2 \times 2 = 16$ rows; five variables require $2^5 = 2 \times 2 \times 2 \times 2 \times 2 = 32$ rows; and so on.

The second rule is essentially an extension of the procedure we have already established for listing Ts and Fs in the columns under the propositional variables. As before, we alternate Ts and Fs in the first column at the left, and alternate pairs of Ts and Fs in the second column. In addition, when we require three (or more) columns, we will alternate sets of *four* Ts and *four* Fs in the third column. If we need a fourth column for a fourth variable we alternate sets of *eight* Ts and *eight* Fs; if we add a fifth column for a fifth variable, we alternate sets of sixteen; and so on. This guarantees that every possible combination and permutation of Ts and Fs is included.

To discuss the third rule, it is helpful to use the concept of a parenthesis unit. A **parenthesis unit** is *any part of a schema that has a left parenthesis '(' at its beginning and a right parenthesis ')' at its end, and which contains the same number of left parentheses between the beginning and end as it has right parentheses.* Parenthesis units can be described as 'single,' 'double,' 'triple,' and so on, depending on how many pairs of parentheses they include. Consider the *outer set of parentheses* in the following examples:

1. $(p \lor q)$
2. $(p \lor (q \supset r))$
3. $(p \supset q)$
4. $((p \lor q) \equiv r)$
5. $(p \lor ((q \supset p) \supset r))$

Schema 1 is a single parenthesis unit. Schema 2 satisfies the definition of a double parenthesis unit. Schema 3 is not a parenthesis unit because it has one left parenthesis but no right parenthesis to close it off. Schema 4 is a double parenthesis unit, and 5 is a triple parenthesis unit.

The final rule is that the part of the truth table under the operators in the schema should be filled in with the appropriate truth values, beginning from the "inside" of the parentheses and working outward. This can best be explained in terms of the following example, the construction of a truth table for the schema '$\sim((p \lor \sim q) \supset r)$.'

Step 1   Arrange the variables in alphabetical order at the upper left of the truth table. Use the formula 2^n (where **n** = the number of different variables in the schema) to calculate the number of rows for the truth table. Fill in the columns under each of the variables using the procedure specified above.

Step 2   Once the columns under the propositional variables at the left have been filled in, *find any negation operators that are associated with single propositional variables and fill in the columns under them as stipulated in the truth table definition of the tilde* (that is, if 'p' is true, '$\sim$p' is false, and vice versa). In our example, the only tilde associated with a single propositional variable is the one in '$\sim$q.' We will fill in the column under it first.

p	q	r	$\sim$ (($p \lor$	$\sim$	q) $\supset$ r)
T	T	T		F	
F	T	T		F	
T	F	T		T	
F	F	T		T	
T	T	F		F	
F	T	F		F	
T	F	F		T	
F	F	F		T	
				(1)	

Step 3   *Fill in the columns under any operators that connect components that are not separated by parentheses,* using the truth table definitions of those op-

erators. In our example, the wedge connecting 'p' and '~q' is the only such operator. In each row, we use the last value filled in on each side of the operator within the appropriate parenthesis unit; if nothing has been filled in on one side of the operator, then we use the truth value in the column under the variable at the left. In our example, nothing has been filled in to the left of the '∨' so we use the values under the 'p' at the far left together with the values under the tilde on the right. In the first row, we have the T under the 'p' disjoined (with the wedge) with the F under the tilde, which gives a T under the wedge; in the second row we have an F under the 'p' and an F under the tilde, which gives us an F under the wedge; and so on.

p	q	r	~ ((p	∨	~ q) ⊃ r)
T	T	T		T	F
F	T	T		F	F
T	F	T		T	T
F	F	T		T	T
T	T	F		T	F
F	T	F		F	F
T	F	F		T	T
F	F	F		T	T
				(2)	(1)

Step 4 *Fill in the columns under any tildes that precede single parenthesis units* (none of these appear in our example).

Step 5 *Fill in the columns under operators connecting components at least one of which is a single parenthesis unit* but neither of which is a double parenthesis unit. In our example, the horseshoe is such an operator, as it connects 'r' with '(p ∨ ~q).' We apply the truth table definition of the horseshoe to the truth values in the columns under the wedge and under the 'r' at the far left.

p	q	r	~ ((p ∨	~ q)	⊃ r)
T	T	T	T	F	T
F	T	T	F	F	T
T	F	T	T	T	T
F	F	T	T	T	T
T	T	F	T	F	F
F	T	F	F	F	T
T	F	F	T	T	F
F	F	F	T	T	F
			(2)	(1)	(3)

Step 6 *Fill in the columns under any tildes that immediately precede a double parenthesis unit.*

p	q	r	~	((p	∨	~ q)	⊃ r)
T	T	T	F		T	F	T
F	T	T	F		F	F	T
T	F	T	F		T	T	T
F	F	T	F		T	T	T
T	T	F	T		T	F	F
F	T	F	F		F	F	T
T	F	F	T		T	T	F
F	F	F	T		T	T	F
			(4)		(2)	(1)	(3)

After this, fill in the columns under any operators connecting components at least one of which is a double parenthesis unit, then those under any tildes preceding triple-parenthesis units, and so on.

Procedure for Constructing Truth Tables

1. Write out the variables in alphabetical order in a horizontal row at the top left of the work space, and to the right write in the schema to be analyzed. Fill in a column of alternating single Ts and Fs under the first variable at the left, a column of alternating pairs of Ts and Fs under the second variable, a column of alternating fours of Ts and Fs under the third variable, and so on. Each column should contain exactly 2^n rows, where n equals the number of different variables in the schema.

2. Fill in the columns under any and every negation sign (tilde) directly connected to a propositional variable.

3. Fill in the columns under any and all operators that connect two variables neither of which has a parenthesis between it and the operator.

4. Fill in the columns under any and all tildes that precede a single parenthesis unit.

5. Fill in the columns under any and all operators connecting components at least one of which is a single parenthesis unit but neither of which is more than a single parenthesis unit.

6. Fill in the columns under any and all tildes that immediately precede a double parenthesis unit.

7. Fill in the columns under any and all operators connecting components at least one of which is a double parenthesis unit but neither of which is more than a double parenthesis unit.

Continue this process for tildes preceding triple parenthesis units, then for operators connecting triple parenthesis units, then tildes preceding quadruple parenthesis units, and so on until all columns have been filled in.

The *last operator under which the column is filled in* is the **main operator—**in our example, the tilde preceding the double-parenthesis unit. *It is this column that provides the truth table definition of the schema.*

EXERCISE 5–9

Construct truth tables for each of the following propositional schemas.

1. p ⊙ ~q
2. ~p · q
3. p ⊃ ~q
4. ~p ⊃ q
5. ~p · ~q
6. ~(p · q)
7. ~(p ⊃ q)
8. ~(p · ~q)
9. p ∨ ~q
10. ~(p ∨ q)
11. ~(~p ∨ q)
12. ~(~p ∨ ~q)
13. (p · q) ≡ p
14. (p · q) ⊃ p
15. (p · q) ⊃ q
16. (p · q) ⊃ r
17. (p ∨ q) ⊃ r
18. (p ⊃ q) ⊃ r
19. ~(p · q) ⊃ ~r
20. ~(p · ~q) ⊃ ~r
21. ((p ∨ q) · p) ⊃ r
22. ((p ∨ ~ q) · p) ⊃ r
23. (~(p ∨ ~q) · p) ⊃ r
24. ~(~(p ∨ ~q) · p) ⊃ r
25. ((p ⊃ q) · ~q) ⊃ ~p
26. (p ⊃ q) ≡ (~q ⊃ ~ p)
27. ~(p · q) ≡ (~p ∨ ~q)
28. ~(p · q) ≡ (~p · q)
29. ((p · q) ⊃ r) ≡ (p ⊃ (q ⊃ r))
30. ((~p · q) ⊃ ~r) ≡ (~ p ⊃ (q ⊃ ~r))

5.12 Logically Equivalent Statements

Once we have a procedure for constructing truth tables for any truth-functional propositional schema, we can compare the propositional schemas of statements with different logical structures. In a truth table for a schema with more than one operator, the final column filled in (the one under the main operator) is the one that defines that schema. Any two schemas with the same truth table columns under their variables *and* under their main operators are logically equivalent. (Of course, this presupposes that the truth tables for both schemas were constructed in accordance with the rules given in the preceding section.) *Two propositions are logically equivalent if their schemas are logically equivalent.*

5.12.1 Law of Double Negation

An obvious pair of logically equivalent schemas is 'p' and '~~p.' If we set their truth tables side by side, it becomes apparent that they are clearly the same—or, to be more precise, the last column filled in is the same:

p	p	~	~ p
T	T	T	F
F	F	F	T

In the truth table on the left, the truth values of the propositional schema 'p' are displayed. This column constitutes the entire truth table for this schema. In the table on the right, the schema '~~p' is defined by the column under the first tilde, which is the main operator of this schema. Since both of these columns are the same, with a **T** in the first row and an **F** in the second row, the two schemas are therefore logically equivalent.

In demonstrating the logical equivalence between 'p' and '~~p,' we have proved what is known as the **law of double negation.** According to this law, whenever a negative sentence such as

   It is not the case that meat is healthy.

whose abbreviation is

   ~M

is itself negated, as in the sentence

   It is not the case that it is not the case that meat is healthy.

whose abbreviation is

   ~~M

the resulting statement is logically equivalent to the proposition with both negations removed, namely

Meat is healthy.

whose abbreviation is

M.

5.12.2 De Morgan's Rules

Another important pair of logically equivalent schemas is '~(p ∨ q)' and '(~p · ~q).' The truth tables for these are:

p q	~	(p ∨ q)		p q	(~ p	·	~ q)
T T	F	T		T T	F	F	F
F T	F	T		F T	T	F	F
T F	F	T		T F	F	F	T
F F	T	F		F F	T	T	T
	(2)	(1)			(1)	(2)	(1)

This logical equivalence holds, since the columns under the main operators have the same truth values.

Still another pair of logically equivalent schemas is '~(p · q)' and '(~p ∨ ~q).' Their truth tables are:

p q	~	(p · q)		p q	(~ p	∨	~ q)
T T	F	T		T T	F	F	F
F T	T	F		F T	T	T	F
T F	T	F		T F	F	T	T
F F	T	F		F F	T	T	T
	(2)	(1)			(1)	(2)	(1)

These formulae are logically equivalent, since all the truth values under the main operators of the two schemas are the same.

These two equivalences are known as **De Morgan's rules**; they state that

1. The negation of the *disjunction* of two statements is logically equivalent to the *conjunction* of the negations of the statements.
2. The negation of the *conjunction* of two statements is logically equivalent to the *disjunction* of the negations of the two statements.

5.13 Logical Equivalence and Material Equivalence

The concept of logical equivalence we are discussing here is not the same as, but is closely related to, the concept of material equivalence discussed earlier.

Remember that material equivalence is defined in terms of its truth table, which assigns the value **T** to a compound statement in which the two statements joined by the '≡' operator have the same truth values (either both true or both false) and assigns the value **F** in all other cases. Because two logically equivalent statements are such that their schemas have the same truth values in each row under their main operators, it follows that, if we connect the schemas of two logically equivalent statements with the material equivalence operator, the resulting truth table would have all **T**s under the main operator—that is, it would be analytically true. For example, if we so connect the schemas of a proposition and its double negation, we get the following truth table:

p	p	≡	~	~ p
T		T	T	F
F		T	F	T
		(3)	(2)	(1)

Similarly, the truth table of the schemas of De Morgan's rule joined by the material equivalence operator gives us:

p	q	~	(p ∨ q)	≡	(~ p	·	~ q)
T	T	F	T	T	F	F	F
F	T	F	T	T	T	F	F
T	F	F	T	T	F	F	T
F	F	T	F	F	T	T	T
		(3)	(2)	(4)	(1)	(2)	(1)

Another example of a logical equivalence is expressed in the formula

$$(p \equiv q) \equiv ((p \supset q) \cdot (q \supset p))$$

whose truth table is:

p	q	(p ≡ q)	≡	((p ⊃ q)	·	(q ⊃ p))
T	T	T	T	T	T	T
F	T	F	T	T	F	F
T	F	F	T	F	F	T
F	F	T	T	T	T	T
		(1)	(3)	(1)	(2)	(1)

This shows us that a material equivalence—that is, 'p ≡ q'—is logically equivalent to the conjunction of a conditional, '(p ⊃ q),' and its converse '(q ⊃ p).' This fact has led logicians to call it a biconditional. A **biconditional** is *a statement in which the first component materially implies the second, and the second materially implies the first.*

The logical equivalence between material equivalence and the conjunction of the two material implications is also brought out in the English translation of '≡' as 'if and only if.' As pointed out in the section on material implication, 'p if q' should be symbolized as 'q ⊃ p,' and that 'p only if q' should be symbolized as 'p ⊃ q.' Thus it should come as no surprise that 'p if and only if q' can be symbolized as '(p ⊃ q) · (q ⊃ p)' as well as 'p ≡ q.'

Another material equivalence throws further light on material implication.

$$(p \supset q) \equiv \sim(p \cdot \sim q)$$

has all Ts under the main operator of its truth table.

p	q	(p ⊃ q)	≡	~ (p ·	~ q)
T	T	T	T	T F	F
F	T	T	T	T F	F
T	F	F	T	F T	T
F	F	T	T	T F	T
		(2)	(4)	(3) (2)	(1)

The usual set of truth values for material implication, listed in the column under the horseshoe, is obviously the same as the set of truth values in the column under the first tilde, which is the main operator of the second component. Since the '≡' has all Ts under it, this proves that the component on the left is logically equivalent to the component on the right, which is also consistent with the definition of material implication, since one possible English language rendering of

$$\sim(p \cdot \sim q)$$

is

It is not the case both that p is true and q is false.

Although we have only constructed the truth table for the first, all three of the following material equivalences can be shown to have all Ts under their main operators; in other words, the components to the left of the main '≡' are logically equivalent to the components on the right.

$$(p \supset q) \equiv \sim(p \cdot \sim q)$$
$$(p \lor q) \equiv (\sim(\sim p \cdot \sim q))$$
$$(p \equiv q) \equiv (\sim(p \cdot \sim q) \cdot \sim(q \cdot \sim p))$$

Because, in each of these pairs, the two schemas are logically equivalent (i.e., they have the same columns under their main operators), it is possible to symbolize every truth-functional proposition using only the tilde and the dot. Thus, the ' ∨ ,' ' ⊃ ,' and '≡' are theoretically eliminable from our system. However, since it is so much easier to write 'p ≡ q' than '~(p · ~q) · ~(q · ~p)' and so on, we will continue to use the wedge, horseshoe, and triple-line symbols for

I had reasoned this out in my mind: there were two things that I had a right to. Liberty and death. If I could not have one I would have the other for no man should take me alive.

HARRIET TUBMAN

Harriet Tubman's statement eloquently expresses an exclusive disjunction in a logically complex and sophisticated form. Symbolize her formulation using the horseshoe (and any other necessary operators). Also, symbolize the exclusive disjunction without the horseshoe, and then test your two formulations for logical equivalence using truth tables.

the operations of disjunction, material implication, and material equivalence, respectively.

EXERCISE 5–10

Construct truth tables to determine whether the following pairs of propositional schemas are logically equivalent.

1. p · q   ~(~p ∨ ~q)
2. p · ~q   ~(~p ∨ q)
3. ~p · q   ~(p ∨ ~q)
4. ~(p · q)   ~p · ~q
5. ~(p ∨ q)   ~p ∨ q
6. p ≡ q   ~p ≡ ~q
7. p ⊃ q   ~p ∨ q
8. ~(p ≡ q)   ~p ≡ ~q
9. ~p ≡ q   p ≡ ~q
10. ~(p ⊃ q)   ~p ⊃ ~q
11. ~(p ⊃ q)   p · ~q
12. ~(p ⊃ q)   p ∨ ~q
13. ~(p ∨ q)   ~p ∨ ~q
14. p ≡ q   ~(p · ~q) · ~(q · ~p)

5.14 Tautologies

As explained at the end of Chapter 1, some statements are such that their truth or falsity can be determined solely by analyzing their logical structure. Such statements are known in logic as syntactically analytically true and syntactically analytically false statements. Statements that are syntactically analytically true are also known as **tautologies.** In the context of truth-functional logic, a statement is a tautology *if and only if its schema has only Ts under the main connective in its truth table;* that is, it has a truth-functional form such that it is impossible for it to be false. Thus, all the logical equivalences connected by the material equivalence operator in the preceding section are tautologies, because there are only Ts under the main (material equivalence) operator. Many other tautologies also are of special interest to logicians, and we will consider several of them briefly here.

One schema represents a tautology known as the **law of excluded middle.** Its truth table is

p	(p	∨	~ p)
T		T	F
F		T	T
		(2)	(1)

An example of a proposition that shares this schema is the analytic truth

Either Pat got an A in Logic or it is not the case that Pat got an A in Logic.

We can see that it is impossible for a statement of this form to have the value **F,** since there are only Ts under the main operator in the truth table of its schema. It is not necessary to get additional information in order to determine whether or not the compound proposition is true; it *must* be true by virtue of its logical structure.

Any proposition with the schema

$$\sim(p \cdot \sim p)$$

is also a tautology. This schema expresses what is known as the **law of non-contradiction.** Its truth table is

p	~	(p	·	~ p)
T	T		F	F
F	T		F	T
	(3)		(2)	(1)

Propositions with schemas such as these can be recognized as tautologies as soon as their truth tables are constructed, since for each one there are only Ts under the main connective, showing that it is logically impossible for it to be false.

5.15 Contradictions

Certain propositional schemas are the opposite of tautologies insofar as whatever the truth values of the propositions that are substituted for their variables, the resultant compound statements are false. Propositions with such schemas are false by virtue of their logical form and are known as **contradictions**. A contradiction is a statement with a *schema that has only Fs under the main connective in its truth table*—that is, it is a proposition that has a logical form such that it is impossible for it to be true.

The most obvious example of a contradiction is a statement such as

Russell was a logician and Russell was not a logician.

The schema for this is

$p \cdot \sim p$

and the truth table is

p	p	·	~ p
T		F	F
F		F	T
		(2)	(1)

Another contradictory statement is

Homer was blind if and only if Homer was not blind.

The schema for this is

$p \equiv \sim p$

and its truth table is

p	p	≡	~ p
T		F	F
F		F	T
		(2)	(1)

A more complicated contradictory statement is

If it is the case that John is bald if and only if it is not the case that John is not bald, then it is not the case that either Achilles was a hero or Achilles was not a hero.

Here the schema is

$(p \equiv \sim\sim p) \supset \sim(q \vee \sim q)$

and the truth table is

p	q	(p	≡	~	~ p)	⊃	~	(q	∨	~ q)
T	T	T	T	F		F	F	T		F
F	T	T	F	T		F	F	T		F
T	F	T	T	F		F	F	T		T
F	F	T	F	T		F	F	T		T
		(3)	(2)	(1)		(5)	(4)	(3)		(1)

Since there are only **F**s under the main connective in this truth table, the original proposition must be a contradiction.

Contradictions are also known as **analytically false statements** because their falsity can be completely determined by an analysis of their logical form. As with tautologies, there is no need to make any empirical observations to determine their truth values.

5.16 Contingent Statements

Any statement that is neither a tautology nor a contradiction is said to be contingent. A **contingent statement** is one whose *schema has both Ts and Fs under the main connective in its truth table.* For example, take the sentence

The light in the next room is on.

This expresses a simple (not compound) statement whose schema is 'p.' Its truth table is

p
T
F

Since this truth table has both a **T** and an **F**, we cannot determine whether the statement is true or false simply by examining its logical form. We would have to use other means, such as going into the room and looking around.

Let's consider the compound statement expressed by the sentence

If Joan is a physician, then it is not the case that Joan is ten years old.

Its truth table is

p	q	p	⊃	~	q
T	T		F	F	
F	T		T	F	
T	F		T	T	
F	F		T	T	
			(2)	(1)	

If we had keen vision of all that is ordinary in human life it would be like hearing the grass grow or the squirrel's heart beat, and we should die of that roar which is the other side of silence.

GEORGE ELIOT [MARY ANN EVANS]

You should be able to display the logical structure of the above passage from *Middlemarch* quite adequately using the tools of propositional logic, but it would be difficult if not impossible to express in any other way the meanings packed into this single sentence by its creator. Construct a truth table to determine whether it is contingent, a tautology, or a contradiction.

Again, this truth table has at least one **T** and at least one **F** under its main connective, so the mere analysis of its logical form is not sufficient for determining whether the statement is in fact true or false.

Contingent statements are thus neither analytically true nor analytically false; it is always logically possible for them to be either true or false. If a contingent statement turns out to be factually true, it could have been false without violating any logical law, and if it turns out to be false, it could have been true without violating any logical law. To determine the truth value of a contingent statement, it is necessary to do more than subject it to a logical analysis.

EXERCISE 5–11

Construct truth tables for each of the following schemas. Indicate whether each is a tautology, a contradiction, or a contingent statement.

1. p ⊃ q
2. p ⊃ p
3. p ⊃ ~p
4. (p · q) ⊃ p
5. p ⊃ (p ∨ q)
6. (p ∨ ~p) ⊃ (p ∨ q)
7. ((p ⊃ q) · ~q) · p
8. ((p ⊃ q) · ~q) ∨ p
9. (p ⊃ q) ≡ (~p ∨ q)
10. (p ⊃ q) ≡ (~p · q)
11. (p ⊃ q) ≡ (p · ~q)
12. ((p ⊃ q) · p) · ~q

13. $((p \supset q) \cdot p) \cdot \sim q$

14. $((p \supset q) \cdot p) \supset q$

15. $(p \lor \sim p) \supset (p \cdot \sim q)$

16. $(p \lor \sim p) \supset (p \cdot \sim p)$

17. $\sim(p \supset q) \equiv (\sim p \supset q)$

18. $(\sim p \supset q) \equiv (p \lor q)$

EXERCISE 5-12

Reconsider the statements of which you did preliminary analyses in Exercise 1–14. Symbolize each one with as little loss of meaning as possible using the methods of this chapter. Also use the methods of this chapter to try to determine which of the statements (as symbolized) is analytic and which is synthetic.

Summary

1. To say that a proposition is true or false is equivalent to saying that it has a truth value. A **truth-functional proposition** is a compound statement which is such that, if we know (1) the truth value of each of its component statements and (2) the meanings of the logical terms in the sentence expressing the compound statement, we can determine precisely the truth or falsity of the compound statement: in other words, its truth value is a function of the truth values of the component statements.

2. A **logical operator** is an expression such that if it is correctly used with the appropriate number of propositions, a new proposition is produced with a different logical structure. No logical operator by itself is or expresses a proposition. A **truth-functional operator** is a logical operator such that, when it is correctly used with the appropriate number of propositions, a truth-functional proposition is produced.

3. A symbol is a sign that can be used to abbreviate or schematize any of the components in a given system. A **propositional constant** is a symbol used to abbreviate a sentence expressing a proposition; the meaning of the symbol remains constant throughout a given context. A **propositional variable** is a symbol that functions as a blank into which we can insert any sentence expressing a proposition. Like logical operators, propositional variables have no truth values in themselves. A formula containing only propositional variables and logical operators is a **propositional schema;** it displays the form or logical structure of a proposition. Propositional variables are normally symbolized by small letters from the middle to the end of the alphabet, starting with p.

4. A truth-functional proposition whose component statements are connected by the truth-functional operator '·' is called a **conjunction,** and its component statements are called **conjuncts.** Conjunctions are true if and only if both conjuncts are true; otherwise they are false. In appropriate contexts, such words as 'and,' 'but,' 'although,' 'yet,' and 'moreover' can operate truth-functionally, but in other contexts they can operate in ways that are not truth-functional.

5. A **truth table** is a device that is used to display all of the possible combinations of truth values of propositions that could be substituted for the propositional variables in a given propositional schema. Truth tables can be used to define truth-functional operators in terms of an exhaustive list of the possible combinations of truth values in compound statements using a given truth-functional operation.

6. **Negation** is the logical operator that operates on a given proposition to form a new compound statement that has the opposite truth value from that proposition. The standard abbreviation for the negation operator is the curl or tilde symbol, '~'. Sometimes it is possible to symbolize a given proposition as either an affirmative or a negative statement (that is, as either 'p' or '~p'). However, once a particular symbol has been assigned to a sentence in a given argument, the same symbol must be used for every other sentence in the argument that is being used to express the same proposition.

7. **Disjunction,** symbolized by the wedge or vee, '∨', is the logical operation that most closely corresponds to the connecting of two sentences by the word 'or.' The two sentences connected are **disjuncts.** However, 'or' is used in two senses in ordinary English. In the **inclusive sense,** it asserts that either the first disjunct or the second *or both* may be true. An inclusive disjunction is true under all circumstances except when both disjuncts are false. In the **exclusive sense,** the English 'or' asserts that the first or the second disjunct, *but not both* may be true. An exclusive disjunction is true if and only if one disjunct is true and one is false. Because exclusive disjunction is stronger than inclusive disjunction, logicians always assume that 'or' in ordinary English is being used inclusively, unless there is strong evidence to the contrary.

8. **Material implication,** symbolized by the horseshoe symbol, '⊃', is an operation according to which the compound proposition is false if and only if the antecedent is true and the consequent is false. The symbol '⊃' is usually translated in terms of 'If . . . then . . .' sentences, or sentences with the form 'p implies q.' Sentences of the form 'If . . . then . . .' are conditionals, and in ordinary English they often suggest a causal relation that is absent from the horseshoe of material implication. The meaning of the

horseshoe is given entirely in its truth table, and it asserts no relationship between the components other than that specified in the table.

9. **Material equivalence** is the logical operation, symbolized as '≡', that joins two propositions into a compound statement that is true if and only if the two components have the same truth value. The symbol '≡' is best translated as 'if and only if.'

10. **Grouping** is the setting off of compound propositions within a larger compound in such a way that it is made clear to which variable or variables a particular operator applies.

11. There are three basic rules for constructing truth tables for schemas with more than one operator: (1) the truth table for a propositional schema must contain 2^n rows, where n is the number of different propositional variables in the schema; (2) under the variables, Ts and Fs must be alternated in the column under the first variable, pairs of Ts and Fs in the column under the second, sets of four Ts and four Fs in the column under the third, and so on; (3) the part of the truth table under the operators in the schema must be filled in with the appropriate truth values beginning from the inside of the parentheses and working outward. The last operator under which the column is filled in is the **main operator,** and this column provides the truth table definition of the schema.

12. Any two schemas with the same truth table columns under their main operators are said to be **logically equivalent.** According to the **law of double negation,** whenever a negative sentence is itself negated the resulting statement is logically equivalent to the proposition with both negations removed. **De Morgan's rules** state that the negation of the disjunction of two statements is logically equivalent to the conjunction of the negations of the same statements, and that the negation of the conjunction of two statements is logically equivalent to the disjunction of the negations of the same statements.

13. Two statements are **logically equivalent** if and only if, when they are connected by the symbol '≡', the column under that symbol contains only Ts. A sentence expressing a material equivalence is sometimes called a **biconditional** in that its first component materially implies the second, and the second materially implies the first.

14. A proposition is a **tautology** if and only if its schema has only Ts under the main operator in its truth table; that is, its logical form makes it impossible for it to be false. Two tautologies are the schema 'p ∨ ~p,' which expresses the **law of excluded middle,** and the schema '~(p · ~p),' which expresses the **law of noncontradiction.** Tautologies are **analytically true statements** in that their truth can be completely determined by an analysis of their logical form.

15. A **contradiction** is a statement whose schema has only Fs under the main operator in its truth table; that is, its logical form makes it impossible for it to be true. Contradictions are **analytically false statements** in that their falsity can be determined solely by an analysis of their logical form.

16. A **contingent statement** is one whose schema has both Ts and Fs under the main operator in its truth table. Contingent statements are neither analytically true nor analytically false; their truth or falsity must be determined by extralogical means.

Chapter 6

Propositional Logic: Arguments

In the preceding chapter we were concerned only with the logical structure of individual truth-functional propositions. It was noted there that a truth-functional proposition is a compound statement such that if we know the truth value of each of its component statements and the meanings of the logical operators, the truth or falsity of the compound statement can be determined. Thus, the truth-functional proposition 'It is not the case that George Washington was the third president of the United States' consists of the statement 'George Washington was the third president of the United States,' which is a false proposition, and the logical operator 'It is not the case that.' Consequently, we know that this particular truth-functional proposition is true. Similarly, the proposition 'All men are mortal and all women are mortal' qualifies as a truth-functional proposition, since knowing the truth value of its component statements ('All men are mortal'; 'All women are mortal') and the meaning of its logical operator, 'and,' we can determine the truth value of the compound statement.

An individual truth-functional proposition is not an argument, at least not in the sense in which we are using the term 'argument' in this book. Recall from Chapter 2 that an argument is a set of statements such that one of them is implied or supported by the others. It is important to recognize that some sets of statements that are offered or intended in everyday contexts as arguments are not in fact arguments in our formal sense of the term. That is, some sets of statements that are asserted or apparently intended to be valid or inductively strong are such that the supposed premises do not in fact imply or provide any support for the conclusion.

This chapter is concerned primarily with methods for determining which sets of statements do in fact constitute valid arguments—that is, arguments in which the premises imply or provide absolute support for the conclusion. To see why special methods are useful and sometimes even necessary for determining which arguments are valid, consider the following sets of sentences which are being asserted as arguments. Which of these in fact express valid arguments?

1. **Either John is lying or Bill is lying. It is not the case that John is lying. So don't listen to Bill.**

2. **If Juan's car is a Bentley, then it burns a lot of gas. But Juan's car is not a Bentley. Therefore, Juan's car does not burn a lot of gas.**

3. **If Michael passes his exams, then Susan will be happy. If Scott gives Michael his notes, then Michael will pass his exams. Consequently, if Scott gives Michael his notes, Susan will be happy.**

4. **John loves Mary and Tom loves Sue. Either John will marry Mary or Tom will marry Sue.**

The first of these sets of sentences is not an argument on the purely technical ground that its "conclusion" is a command, not a statement. Each of the sentences in the other three sets would normally express statements, but it is not easy to determine by inspection or intuition which, if any of them, expresses a valid argument. In fact, only set 3 is a valid argument, but this can best be demonstrated using methods and concepts of formal logic.

6.1 Truth-Functional Validity

In this chapter, we present two procedures for identifying valid arguments, that is, arguments such that their premises provide absolute support for their conclusions. The basic definition of validity we are using is that an argument is valid if and only if it is such that if the premises are true, then its conclusion must be true. As noted in Chapter 2, a valid argument may have true premises and a true conclusion, false premises and a true conclusion, or false premises and a false conclusion. The only kind of argument excluded by the definition of validity is one that can have true premises and a false conclusion.

Let us consider purported argument 2 from the previous section.

If Juan's car is a Bentley, then it burns a lot of gas.
But Juan's car is not a Bentley.
Therefore, Juan's car does not burn a lot of gas.

This "argument" is not valid, since the truth of the premises does not guarantee the truth of the conclusion. Even if both premises are true, the conclusion could still be false. For example, Juan might own a Jaguar with a V–12 engine, which is even less fuel-efficient than a Bentley, in which case both premises would be true and the conclusion false, making it invalid by our definition.

Let us now reconsider argument 3.

If Michael passes his exams, then Susan will be happy.
If Scott gives Michael his notes, then Michael will pass his exams.
Consequently, if Scott gives Michael his notes, Susan will be happy.

This is a valid argument; *if* its premises are true, then its conclusion *must* be true. Even if it is false that Susan will be happy if Michael passes his exams, and false that Michael will pass his exams if Scott gives Michael his notes, the conclusion logically follows from the premises.

6.2 Contradictory Premises and Tautological Conclusions

Implicit in our discussion of contradictions and tautologies at the end of the preceding chapter are two consequences that relate directly to the concept of validity. Given our definition of validity, any argument in which at least one of the premises is a contradiction is necessarily valid. This is not as peculiar as it might first sound. If one of the premises of an argument is a contradiction (that is, it cannot possibly be true), we can never have the situation in which all the premises are true and the conclusion is false. Thus, the argument must be valid. This is also the case with an argument which is such that the conjunction of two or more of its premises results in a contradiction.

Any *set of premises which is such that it is logically impossible for all of them to be true* is said to be **inconsistent,** and any argument with an inconsistent set of premises must be valid. Consider, for instance, the following:

5. **The Empire State Building is the world's tallest building and the Empire State Building is not the world's tallest building. Therefore, the Sears Tower is the world's tallest building.**

6. **The Empire State Building is the world's tallest building. The Empire State Building is not the world's tallest building. Therefore, the moon is made of green cheese.**

Each of these arguments is valid. In argument 5, we have one contradictory premise; in argument 6, the two premises are inconsistent.

Notice that in a valid argument the premises have to provide support for the conclusion only in a purely formal and very abstract sense. In argument 6, although no conceptual relation whatsoever exists between the premises and the conclusion, the argument still satisfies the formal logical definition of 'valid.'

The other consequence of our discussion at the end of Chapter 5 is related to the concept of a **tautology,** which is defined as *a statement that is always true by virtue of its logical form.* Given our definition of validity, *any argument in which the conclusion is a tautology must be valid.* If the conclusion of an argument can be only true, then it is impossible for its premises to be true and its conclusion false. So the argument must be valid. Consider the following examples of arguments with tautological conclusions:

7. The Hancock Building is the world's tallest building. Therefore, either the Empire State Building is the world's tallest building or the Empire State Building is not the world's tallest building.

8. George Washington had wooden false teeth. Therefore, either the Empire State Building is the world's largest building or the Empire State Building is not the world's largest building.

In argument 7 we have a false premise, whereas in argument 8 we have a true premise. The conclusion cannot possibly be false in either case because it is a tautology. Both arguments are valid since validity is ruled out only by an argument in which it is possible for the premises to be true and the conclusion false. Because an argument with a tautology as a conclusion must always have a true conclusion, it is impossible for the premises to be true and the conclusion false. Such arguments must be valid.

6.3 Abbreviating Truth-Functional Arguments

In Chapter 5, we saw that it was possible to abbreviate truth-functional propositions by using propositional constants and symbols for the various logical operators. For instance, the statement 'Either John will hit a home run or the other team will win the game' can be abbreviated as

$$J \vee O$$

where 'J' stands for the proposition 'John will hit a home run,'[1] '∨' represents the logical operator of disjunction, and 'O' stands for 'The other team will win the game.'

Just as it is possible to abbreviate individual truth-functional propositions, it is also possible to abbreviate a group of statements that constitute an argument. As noted earlier, we must make certain that we use different propositional constants to represent each different proposition and the same propositional constant to represent the same proposition whenever it occurs in the argument. Consider the argument

9. If whales are fish, then cats are herbivorous. Cats are not herbivorous. Therefore, whales are not fish.

which can be abbreviated as:

$$W \supset C$$
$$\sim C$$
$$\therefore \sim W$$

---

[1] Throughout this chapter, we will continue to use the convention introduced in the previous chapter to the effect that the letter to be used in the abbreviation of a given sentence will be indicated by underscoring it in its original occurrence.

In this abbreviation, 'W ⊃ C' stands for the compound proposition 'If whales are fish, then cats are herbivorous.' More specifically, in this first premise, 'W' represents the proposition 'Whales are fish,' '⊃' represents the material implication operator, and 'C' represents the proposition 'Cats are herbivorous.' The second premise, '~C,' is an abbreviation for the compound proposition 'Cats are not herbivorous,' which consists of the negation operator ('It is not the case that') and the statement 'Cats are herbivorous.' The conclusion, '~W,' is the abbreviation for the compound proposition 'Whales are not fish,' which is also composed of the negation operator and a simple proposition, 'Whales are fish.'

6.4 Schematizing Truth-Functional Arguments

Just as it is possible to display the form of a truth-functional compound statement by using propositional variables and symbols for logical operators, so, too, it is possible to schematize a truth-functional argument. Using our example from the previous section, we can remove all the propositional constants and replace them with different symbols in the following way.

$$. . . . . ⊃ \_ \_ \_ \_ \_ \_$$
$$\sim \_ \_ \_ \_ \_ \_$$
$$\therefore \sim . . . .$$

Notice that we have used the same type of blank in place of the same statement each time it appears in the argument, but that we have used different types of blanks in place of each different statement. Together, the schemas for all of the propositions produce an argument schema.

Just as a propositional schema displays the logical structure of a particular truth-functional proposition, an argument schema displays the logical form of an argument composed of several propositions. The symbols used in the preceding argument schema are blanks that are understood to be such that any proposition may be substituted into any blank, so long as the same proposition is substituted into every blank of a certain type. For instance, we can place the proposition 'The money is missing' in each occurrence of the blank symbolized by '. . . . . ,' and the proposition 'John is a crook' into each occurrence of the blank symbolized by '_ _ _ _ _.' Translating the logical operators into English, we get

10. **If the money is missing, then John is a crook.**
    John is not a crook.
    Therefore, the money is not missing.

Argument 10 has exactly the same form as argument 9.

For convenience, propositional variables, such as those used in schematizing particular truth-functional propositions, also are used to schematize truth-functional arguments. The same convention of using small letters, starting with p and working toward the end of the alphabet, is followed. Thus, the following schema represents the logical form of both arguments 9 and 10 and any other argument with the same form:

p ⊃ q
~q
∴ ~p

The propositional variables—'p' and 'q'—represent blanks into which any particular statements can be substituted. The process of substituting actual propositions for the propositional variables results in a substitution instance or an interpretation of the argument schema. When we substituted the propositions 'The money is missing' and 'John is a crook' into the argument schema, we were creating a substitution instance.

We are not restricted to substituting simple propositions for propositional variables. We could just as well substitute compound propositions into these "blanks," as in the following example, which is a substitution instance of the same schema as that of arguments 9 and 10.

> 11. **If either Tom or Ann gets an A in logic, then Sue will be happy and Ed will be angry.**
> **It is not the case that Sue will be happy and Ed will be angry.**
> **Therefore, it is not the case that either Tom or Ann gets an A in logic.**

In this substitution instance, the disjunction 'Tom or Ann gets an A in logic' was put into the blank in the schema represented by the variable 'p.' The conjunction 'Sue will be happy and Ed will be angry' has been substituted for the propositional variable 'q' in the argument schema.

When providing substitution instances of a particular argument schema, we are restricted in two ways. We can substitute only propositions for propositional variables, and we must substitute the same proposition[2] for every occurrence of any given variable in a particular argument schema. Thus, we could even substitute the same proposition for every occurrence of every variable in a given schema. For example, the following is also a substitution instance of the schema we have been using above:

> 12. **If it is raining, then it is raining.**
> **It is not raining.**
> **Therefore, it is not raining.**

As noted in Chapter 5, a contingent propositional schema—for instance 'p ⊃ q,' the first premise in the schema above—has no truth value until we provide a

---

[2]Remember from Chapter 1 that the same proposition can be expressed by different sentences and that the same sentence can be used to express different propositions. You must always be careful when dealing with arguments expressed in ordinary English not to symbolize them simply in terms of similarities among or differences between the sentences involved. It is the propositions being expressed that are of primary interest to the logician in identifying the logical (as opposed to the grammatical) form of arguments.

specific substitution instance for it. However, it is proper to say that an argument schema is valid or invalid. A valid argument is one such that, if the premises are true, then the conclusion must be true. The necessity of the 'must' is best explained in terms of the form of the argument, as displayed by the schema. An argument is valid if and only if no argument with the same form can have true premises and a false conclusion. Consequently, a **valid argument schema** can be defined as *an argument schema for which there is no possible substitution instance (or interpretation) that would result in an argument with true premises and a false conclusion.* Several methods have been devised to test the validity of argument forms in propositional logic. One such method involves a variation of the method of truth tables that was introduced in Chapter 5.

EXERCISE 6–1

(a) Write an abbreviation for each of the following truth-functional arguments. Be sure to provide a dictionary for each abbreviation, indicating the proposition that each propositional constant represents. (b) Write an argument schema for each argument.

1. If it is raining, then the ground is getting wet. It is raining. Therefore, the ground is getting wet.

2. If it is raining, then the ground is getting wet. The ground is not getting wet. Therefore, it is not raining.

3. Either there are clouds in the sky or the sun is shining. The sun is not shining. Therefore, there are clouds in the sky.

4. Either the television set is not plugged in or it is not working. The television set is plugged in. Therefore, it is not working.

5. If that artifact is from the Stone Age, then it is not made of metal. That artifact is made of metal. Therefore, it is not from the Stone Age.

6. If all dogs are carnivores, then Fido is a carnivore. All dogs are carnivores. Therefore, Fido is a carnivore

7. If all dogs are carnivores, then Fido is a carnivore. Fido is not a carnivore. Therefore, it is not the case that all dogs are carnivores.

8. If the law of noncontradiction does not hold, then logical thought is not possible. Logical thought is possible. Therefore, the law of noncontradiction holds.

9. Either this chair is made of walnut or it is made of mahogany or it is made of teakwood. It is not made of walnut. Therefore, it is made of mahogany or teakwood.

10. If the gross national product has decreased for three straight quarters, then the country is in a recession. The gross national product has decreased for three straight quarters and unemployment is high. Therefore, the country is in a recession.

11. If that glass you are holding contains nitroglycerin and you are dropping the glass, then the nitroglycerin will explode. That glass you are holding contains nitroglycerin and you are dropping it. Therefore, the nitroglycerin will explode.

12. If either the fuse blows or there is an electric blackout, then none of the appliances in the kitchen will operate. There is an electric blackout. Therefore, none of the appliances in the kitchen will operate.

13. If we are going to the state park for a picnic, then we will take Johnny or Billy along. We are going to the state park for a picnic. Therefore, we will take Johnny or Billy along.

14. If we are going to the state park for a picnic, then we will take Johnny and Billy along. We are going to the state park for a picnic. Therefore, we will take Johnny and Billy along.

15. If we are going to the state park for a picnic and we are taking Johnny along, then we will take Billy along. We are going to the state park for a picnic and we are taking Johnny along. Therefore, we will take Billy along.

16. If we are going to the state park for a picnic or we are taking Johnny along, then we will take Billy along. We are going to the state park for a picnic. Therefore, we will take Billy along.

17. If we are going to the state park for a picnic or we are taking Johnny along, then we will take Billy along. We are taking Johnny along. Therefore, we will take Billy along.

18. If Harry needs help painting, then either Joan will take time off from work or Tom will postpone writing his paper. Harry needs help painting. Therefore, either Joan will take time off from work or Tom will postpone writing his paper.

19. If you put topspin on the cue ball, then it will follow the six ball into the pocket and you will scratch. You put topspin on the cue ball. Therefore, it will follow the six ball into the pocket and you will scratch

20. Either it is raining, or it is snowing, or sleet is falling. It is not raining. Therefore, either it is snowing or sleet is falling.

21. If we are having a heavy rain, the sewers will be overloaded. If the sewers are overloaded, the basement will flood. We are having a heavy rain. Therefore, the basement will flood.

22. Either it is snowing or sleet is falling. If it is snowing, then we will go sledding. Sleet is not falling. Therefore, we will go sledding.

23. If it is snowing, then we will go sledding. Either it is snowing or sleet is falling. We will not go sledding. Therefore, sleet is falling.

24. If sleet is falling, then we will not go sledding. Either we will go sledding or we will stay at home. Sleet is falling. Therefore, we will stay at home.

25. If it is raining and the wind is blowing, then water will get in the tent. It is raining. The wind is blowing. Therefore, water will get in the tent.

26. If it is raining, then if it is getting cold, my car won't start. It is raining and it is getting cold. Therefore, my car won't start.

27. If snow is falling, then it is getting cold. If it is getting cold, then my car won't start. Snow is falling. Therefore, my car won't start.

28. If Peter is playing piano and Bob is playing bass and Don is playing drums, then our regular combo is here. Peter is playing piano. Bob is playing bass. Don is playing drums. Therefore, our regular combo is here.

29. If Peter is playing piano and Bob is playing bass and Don is playing drums, then our regular combo is here. Our regular combo is not here. Therefore, either Peter is not playing piano, or Bob is not playing bass, or Don is not playing drums.

30. Either Peter is playing piano and Bob is playing bass and Don is playing drums, or else our regular combo is not here. Our regular combo is here. Therefore, Peter is playing piano and Bob is playing bass and Don is playing drums.

31. If the statement under discussion is an equivalence, then it contains an implication. Either the statement under discussion is a disjunction or it is an equivalence. The statement under discussion is not a disjunction. Therefore, the statement under discussion contains an implication

32. Either the statement under discussion is a disjunction or it is an equivalence. If the statement under discussion is an equivalence, then it contains an implication. The statement under discussion does not contain an implication. Therefore, it is a disjunction.

33. The statement under discussion is either a conjunction or it is a disjunction. It is either a conjunction or an implication. If it is a disjunction, then it is not an implication. Therefore, it is a conjunction.

34. The statement under discussion is either a truth-functional proposition or it is a command. If it is a truth-functional proposition, then it is a compound proposition. If it is a compound proposition, then it contains a logical operator. The statement under discussion does not contain a logical operator. Therefore, it is a command.

35. The statement under discussion is either a truth-functional proposition or it is a command. If it is a truth-functional proposition, then it is a compound proposition. If it is a compound proposition, then it contains a logical operator. The statement under discussion is not a command. Therefore, it contains a logical operator.

36. If the Cheshire cat is yellow, it is colored. If it is colored, it is visible. If it is visible, it is real. The Cheshire cat is yellow. Therefore, it is real.

37. If the Cheshire cat is yellow, it is colored. If it is colored, it is visible. If it is visible, it is real. The Cheshire cat is not real. Therefore, it is not yellow.

38. Either the Cheshire cat is real or it is not visible. Either it is visible or it is not colored. Either it is colored or it is not yellow. The Cheshire cat is not real. Therefore, it is not yellow.

39. Either the Cheshire cat is real or it is not visible. Either it is visible or it is not colored. Either it is colored or it is not yellow. The Cheshire cat is yellow. Therefore, it is real.

40. Either Plato was an Athenian or Descartes was a Parisian. If Plato was an Athenian, then he spoke Greek. If Descartes was a Parisian, then he spoke French. Descartes was not a Parisian. Therefore, Plato spoke Greek.

41. If Herb is a Hoosier, he is from Indiana. If Herb is a Buckeye, he is from Ohio. If Herb is from either Indiana or Ohio, he is a U.S. citizen. Herb is either a Hoosier or a Buckeye. Therefore, Herb is a U.S. citizen.

42. If Pete can come tonight, then either Gary or Ralph can come. If Gary can come, then Sam can come. If Sam can come, then Ted can come. If Pete can come, then Ted cannot come. Pete can come. Therefore, Ralph can come.

43. Either we will have red wine for dinner or we will have white wine. If we have roast beef, then we will have red wine. Either we will have roast beef or we will have fillet of sole. If we have fillet of sole then we will have fruit salad for dessert. We will not have red wine for dinner. Therefore, we will have fillet of sole for dinner, and we will have white wine, and we will have fruit salad for dessert.

44. Either Preston or Quincy is a member of the Safari Club. If either Quincy or Randolph is a member, then Stuart is not. Either Stuart is a member or both Trumbull is a member and Randolph is not. Preston is not a member. Therefore, Quincy and Trumbull are both members.

45. If Preston is a member of the Safari Club, then Quincy is a member; or else, if Randolph is a member, then Stuart is a member. If Preston is a member, then Randolph is a member, and if Trumbull is a member, then Stuart is not a member. Preston is a member. Therefore, Quincy, Randolph, and Trumbull are all members.

6.5 Testing Validity by Truth Tables

In Chapter 5 we defined the meanings of particular logical operators by means of truth tables that displayed all possible combinations of truth values that could be substituted for the propositional variables used in propositional schemas containing those operators. We noted there that it is technically incorrect to construct a truth table for a specific proposition (such as 'Chicago is in

Illinois and San Francisco is in California'), since each component proposition in such a compound proposition has a specific truth value, thereby making it inappropriate to display other possible combinations of truth values. For the same reason, it is technically incorrect to construct a truth table for a particular argument or argument abbreviation since each component proposition also has a specific truth value. It is only proper to construct truth tables for argument schemata.

Basically, the truth table method for testing the validity of arguments requires that we construct a truth table for each premise and the conclusion of an argument schema. Let us do this using the argument schema discussed in the last two sections:

$$p \supset q$$
$$\sim q$$
$$\therefore \sim p$$

We begin by setting up the table, providing a column for each propositional variable ('p' and 'q') and for each premise and the conclusion. We then fill in all possible combinations of truth values for the propositional variables, using the rules presented in Chapter 5.

	p	q	(Premise 1) $p \supset q$	(Premise 2) $\sim q$	(Conclusion) $\sim p$
(1)	T	T			
(2)	F	T			
(3)	T	F			
(4)	F	F			

We then fill in each column under the logical operators for each premise and the conclusion.

	p	q	(Premise 1) $p \supset q$	(Premise 2) $\sim q$	(Conclusion) $\sim p$
(1)	T	T	T	F	F
(2)	F	T	T	F	T
(3)	T	F	F	T	F
(4)	F	F	T	T	T

Once we have constructed the truth table, we must check to see if there is any row in which there are Ts under the main operator of each premise and an F under the main operator of the conclusion. If there is such a row, then the argument schema is invalid, since this shows that a possible substitution instance exists in which there are true premises and a false conclusion. In the truth table above, row 4 is the only row in which both premises have **T**s under their main operators, but the conclusion also has a **T** under its main operator in that row. In other words, the truth table demonstrates that it is impossible for any argument with this schema to have all of its premises true and its conclusion false. Thus the schema is valid, as is every argument that is an interpretation of this schema. This particular argument schema is called **modus tollens,** and it is one we will use later when we present a different system for testing validity.

A schema that is strikingly similar to that of the *modus tollens* schema, but which is truth-functionally invalid, is known as the **fallacy of denying the antecedent.** An example of this schema is provided in argument 2 at the beginning of this chapter and in the cartoon on this page.

The intended argument can be formulated as follows:

If the dollar is in trouble, then the dime is in trouble.
The dollar is not in trouble.
Therefore, the dime is not in trouble.

*"I, for one, am glad the dollar's out of trouble, because if the
dollar's in trouble, then the dime is certainly in trouble."*

Drawing by Dana Fradon; © 1971 The New Yorker Magazine, Inc.

This can be proven truth-functionally invalid using the following truth table:

p	q	p ⊃ q	~ p	~ q
T	T	T	F	F
F	T	T	T	F
T	F	F	F	T
F	F	T	T	T

The truth-functional invalidity of this schema is demonstrated in the second row which shows that it is possible for both premises to be true while the conclusion is false.

For practice, let us test the validity of another truth-functional argument:

If John is intelligent, he will know what to do.
John is intelligent.
Therefore, he will know what to do.

The abbreviation and schema for this argument are:

Abbreviation	*Schema*
J ⊃ K	p ⊃ q
J	p
∴ K	∴ q

The truth table for this argument schema follows:

		(Premise 1)	**(Premise 2)**	**(Conclusion)**
p	q	p ⊃ q	p	q
T	T	T	T	T
F	T	T	F	T
T	F	F	T	F
F	F	T	F	F

As we can see by checking the rows, the argument is valid since there is no row in which there are Ts under each premise and an F under the conclusion. This particular argument schema is called **modus ponens.**

Of course, this truth table proves that any substitution instance of this argument schema is valid, even one that involves the substitution of compound propositions for propositional variables, provided our other restrictions have been satisfied. Consider, for example, the following argument:

If Peter bought a new Cadillac and remodeled his home, then either he
got a large bonus at work or his recently deceased uncle left him a
large inheritance.
Peter bought a new Cadillac and remodeled his home.

> **Therefore, either he got a large bonus at work or his recently deceased uncle left him a large inheritance.**

Using our underscored letters as a dictionary, we may abbreviate the above argument as

> (C · H) ⊃ (B ∨ I)
> C · H
> ∴ B ∨ I

Translating the propositional constants in the abbreviation into propositional variables, we get the following schema for the argument:

> (p · q) ⊃ (r ∨ s)
> p · q
> ∴ r ∨ s

The following truth table demonstrates that this argument schema is valid.

				(Premise 1)			**(Premise 2)**	**(Conclusion)**
p	q	r	s	(p · q) ⊃ (r ∨ s)			p · q	r ∨ s
T	T	T	T	T	T	T	T	T
F	T	T	T	F	T	T	F	T
T	F	T	T	F	T	T	F	T
F	F	T	T	F	T	T	F	T
T	T	F	T	T	T	T	T	T
F	T	F	T	F	T	T	F	T
T	F	F	T	F	T	T	F	T
F	F	F	T	F	T	T	F	T
T	T	T	F	T	T	T	T	T
F	T	T	F	F	T	T	F	T
T	F	T	F	F	T	T	F	T
F	F	T	F	F	T	T	F	T
T	T	F	F	T	F	F	T	F
F	T	F	F	F	T	F	F	F
T	F	F	F	F	T	F	F	F
F	F	F	F	F	T	F	F	F

Upon careful examination of the argument schema, it will become evident that it is possible to recognize that it is truth-functionally valid without considering all its component statements. The basic argument schema is the same as *modus ponens*, except that compound statements have been substituted for the propositional variables.

Another valid argument schema is that known as the **hypothetical syllogism**, which appears as follows:

> p ⊃ q
> q ⊃ r
> ∴ p ⊃ r

An example of an argument with this form is:

> **If you study hard, you will get an A on all the exams.**
> **If you get an A on all the exams, you will get an A in this course.**
> **Therefore, if you study hard, you will get an A in this course.**

The validity of this schema, and thus of any argument which has the same logical form, is demonstrated by its truth table, which has no row in which both premises have the value T and the conclusion has the value F. To repeat, this schema represents a general logical rule known as hypothetical syllogism.

			(Premise 1)	(Premise 2)	(Conclusion)
p	q	r	p ⊃ q	q ⊃ r	p ⊃ r
T	T	T	T	T	T
F	T	T	T	T	T
T	F	T	F	T	T
F	F	T	T	T	T
T	T	F	T	F	F
F	T	F	T	F	T
T	F	F	F	T	F
F	F	F	T	T	T

Let us consider the following intended argument and its corresponding schema to deepen our understanding of the truth table method.

> **If George <u>W</u>ashington is a national hero, then Thomas <u>J</u>efferson is a national hero.**
> **If Alexander <u>H</u>amilton is a national hero, then Aaron <u>B</u>urr is a national hero.**
> **Either George Washington is a national hero, or Aaron Burr is a national hero.**
> **Therefore, either Thomas Jefferson is a national hero, or Alexander Hamilton is a national hero.**

The abbreviation and schema are

> W ⊃ J   p ⊃ q
> H ⊃ B   r ⊃ s
> W ∨ B   p ∨ s
> ∴ J ∨ H   ∴ q ∨ r

Examining the truth table below, we can see that this schema is truth-functionally invalid. When the propositional variables 'p,' 'q,' and 'r' are assigned the truth value F and the propositional variable 's' is assigned the truth value T, each of the premises is T and the conclusion is F, as is shown in row 8.

	p	q	r	s	(Premise 1) p ⊃ q	(Premise 2) r ⊃ s	(Premise 3) p ∨ s	(Conclusion) q ∨ r
(1)	T	T	T	T	T	T	T	T
(2)	F	T	T	T	T	T	T	T
(3)	T	F	T	T	F	T	T	T
(4)	F	F	T	T	T	T	T	T
(5)	T	T	F	T	T	T	T	T
(6)	F	T	F	T	T	T	T	T
(7)	T	F	F	T	F	T	T	F
(8)	F	F	F	T	T	T	T	F
(9)	T	T	T	F	T	F	T	T
(10)	F	T	T	F	T	F	F	T
(11)	T	F	T	F	F	F	T	T
(12)	F	F	T	F	T	F	F	T
(13)	T	T	F	F	T	T	T	T
(14)	F	T	F	F	T	T	F	T
(15)	T	F	F	F	F	T	T	F
(16)	F	F	F	F	T	T	F	F

6.5.1 A Limitation on the Truth Table Method

It is of the utmost importance to recognize that the methods of testing arguments for validity in this chapter have one serious limitation. Any arguments that the methods in this chapter prove to be valid are definitely valid. However, if we test an argument using one of these methods and it is not proved to be valid, it is still possible that the argument could be proved to be valid using one of the other methods presented elsewhere in this book. For this reason, it is always necessary to qualify a judgment of invalidity based on a truth table test with the preface 'truth-functional.' If an intended argument is truth-functionally invalid, it might in some cases be proved to be valid using a different logical system. To get a better idea of what this means, let us consider another example, with its truth-functional abbreviation and schema:

All politicians are liars.	P	p
Mayor Jones is a politician.	J	q
Therefore, Mayor Jones is a liar.	∴ L	∴ r

None of the statements in this argument contains any truth-functional operators, so they cannot be broken into any simpler truth-functional components. Also, each premise is a different proposition, and the conclusion is a different proposition. Thus, the abbreviation of this argument in truth-functional logic must consist of three different constants.

Following is a truth table for the above argument schema:

	p	q	r	(Premise 1) p	(Premise 2) q	(Conclusion) r
(1)	T	T	T	T	T	T
(2)	F	T	T	F	T	T
(3)	T	F	T	T	F	T
(4)	F	F	T	F	F	T
(5)	T	T	F	T	T	F
(6)	F	T	F	F	T	F
(7)	T	F	F	T	F	F
(8)	F	F	F	F	F	F

Once again we check the rows to see if there are any in which there are Ts under the main operator of each premise and an F under the main operator of the conclusion. According to the truth table, this argument is invalid. In row 5, there are Ts under the premises and an F under the conclusion. Now if you have already studied the syllogistic logic presented in Chapters 3 and 4, you probably know that the argument presented above ('All politicians are liars . . .') is a valid syllogism. (Its validity also should be apparent on an intuitive level.) Why then does its truth table show it to be invalid?

It might at first seem problematic that one system of logic tells us that an argument is valid, and another system tells us that it is invalid. But the problem disappears as soon as we realize that the different systems of logic are not really dealing with the same argument at all; they are each dealing with different schemas, and there is no reason why one schema cannot be valid and the other invalid. Thus, the distinction that we must draw is between an argument (that is, a set of specific statements) and the different schemas of which it can be an interpretation.

Knowing which system of logic we should use for testing an argument's validity is dependent on a solid knowledge of each of the different systems of logic. Not even complete mastery of everything in this book would be sufficient to guarantee that you are using the right system to determine whether a particular argument is valid or invalid, although Chapter 14 is designed to increase your ability to make such judgments. For the present it is best to use the rule of thumb in the box below to make sure that you do not judge an argument to be invalid when it may in fact be valid.

An argument with a schema proven valid in any one system of logic can be said to be categorically valid. However, an argument with a schema proven invalid in one system should be said to be invalid only for that system of logic.

"B.C." by permission of Johnny Hart and Creators Syndicate, Inc.

This cartoon provides an example of an argument that is valid but which is very difficult to formulate in a way that makes it truth-functionally valid. For example, the following formulation can be proved valid using other methods, but is invalid using the methods of truth-functional logic.

> *If a beautiful woman kisses this frog, it will turn back into a prince.*
> *This woman kissed the frog and it did not turn back into a prince.*
> *Therefore, this woman is not beautiful.*

Can you reformulate this argument in a form which can be shown to be deductively valid using truth tables?

Thus, when we prove that an argument is invalid in truth-functional logic (using truth tables), we should only say that it is *truth-functionally invalid*, and it should be understood that the argument could very well be proven valid in some other system (such as syllogistic logic).

Excercise 6–2

Test the validity of each of the following argument schemas by the truth table method.

1. $\underline{p \cdot q}$
    $\therefore p$

2. $\underline{q \supset p}$
    $\therefore \sim p \supset \sim q$

3. $\underline{q \supset p}$
    $\therefore \sim q \supset \sim p$

4. $\underline{p \supset q}$
    $\therefore p \supset (p \cdot q)$

5. $\underline{(p \supset q) \supset (p \lor q)}$
    $\therefore (p \lor q) \supset (q \lor p)$

6. $\underline{q \supset p}$
    $\therefore p \supset (p \cdot q)$

7. $p \lor q$
    $\underline{\sim p}$
    $\therefore q$

8. $p \lor q$
    $\underline{p}$
    $\therefore \sim q$

9. $\underline{p \lor q}$
    $\therefore q$

10. $\underline{p}$
    $\therefore p \lor q$

11. $\underline{q}$
    $\therefore p \cdot q$

12. $q \lor r$
    $\underline{p \supset q}$
    $\therefore p \supset r$

13. $p \supset q$
    $\underline{p \supset r}$
    $\therefore q \lor r$

14. $p \supset \sim q$
    $\underline{(q \cdot r) \lor p}$
    $\therefore \sim q$

15. $p \supset q$
    $p \lor r$
    $\underline{\sim r}$
    $\therefore q$

16. $p \supset (q \supset r)$
    $\underline{\sim r \lor \sim q}$
    $\therefore p$

17. $p \supset q$
    $\underline{q \supset r}$
    $\therefore p \supset r$

18. $\underline{(p \supset q) \cdot (r \supset s)}$
    $\therefore p \supset q$

19. $p \supset (q \cdot r)$
    $\underline{(q \lor r) \supset \sim p}$
    $\therefore \sim p$

20. $p \supset q$
    $p \supset r$
    $\underline{\sim r}$
    $\therefore \sim q$

21. $p \supset q$
    $p \supset r$
    $\underline{\sim r}$
    $\therefore \sim q$

22. $p \supset q$
    $p \lor r$
    $\underline{\sim p}$
    $\therefore q$

23. $p \supset q$
    $p \lor r$
    $\underline{\sim q}$
    $\therefore r$

24. $p \supset (q \supset r)$
    $\underline{p \supset q}$
    $\therefore r$

25. ~q
    q ⊃ r
    ∴ r

26. (p · q) ⊃ (p ∨ r)
    p ∨ r
    ∴ p · q

27. p ⊃ q
    ~p
    ∴ ~q

28. p ⊃ q
    q ⊃ r
    p
    ∴ r

29. p ⊃ q
    r · p
    ∴ q ∨ r

30. p ⊃ (q ⊃ r)
    q ⊃ (p ⊃ r)
    ∴ (p ∨ q) ⊃ r

31. (p · q) ⊃ r
    p · ~r
    ∴ ~q

32. p ⊃ q
    ~(q · ~r)
    ∴ p ⊃ r

33. p ⊃ (q ⊃ r)
    p ⊃ q
    ∴ q ⊃ r

34. p ⊃ (q ⊃ r)
    p ⊃ q
    ∴ p ⊃ r

35. ~p ⊃ (q · r)
    ~r
    ∴ p

36. p ∨ (~q · r)
    q ⊃ ~p
    ∴ ~q

37. p ⊃ q
    p ⊃ (q ⊃ r)
    q ⊃ (r ⊃ s)
    ∴ p ⊃ s

38. (p ∨ q) ⊃ (p · q)
    ~(p · q)
    ∴ ~(p ∨ q)

39. (~p ∨ q) ⊃ r
    ~r
    ∴ ~p

40. (p · q) ⊃ (r ∨ s)
    r ⊃ p
    ~r ∨ ~s
    q
    ∴ p ⊃ s

6.6 The Short Truth Table Method

Truth tables provide a mechanical decision procedure by which we can test the validity of an argument in a finite number of steps. However, as the number of propositional variables within a particular argument schema increases, the number of rows increases rapidly according to the formula 2^n, as indicated in the previous chapter. An argument with two variables needs four rows (2^2), an argument with three variables needs eight rows (2^3), an argument with four variables needs sixteen rows (2^4), and so on. Of course, as the number of variables and premises in an argument increases, the number of columns necessary for the truth table also increases.

As we have just seen, when using a truth table to test an argument for validity, we check to see if there is a situation in which the conclusion has an

F under its main operator and the premises all have Ts under their main operators. If such a situation exists, then we know that the argument schema is truth-functionally invalid. The short truth table method is based on this concept insofar as it involves an attempt to identify just one row with all true premises and a false conclusion. In using this method, we begin by assigning an F to the conclusion, and then backtrack to see if it is possible to assign the appropriate truth values to the component statements such that all the premises of the argument can be true while the conclusion is false. If we succeed, we have proved that the argument is truth-functionally invalid.

The shortened truth table method saves considerable time and energy since it is no longer necessary to construct elaborate truth tables with numerous rows and columns. However, one person's failure to identify any row that has all true premises and a false conclusion does not necessarily prove that no such row exists. It is still possible, especially when dealing with complex schemas, such as those with sixteen, thirty-two, or even more rows, that this one person for some reason has not found the one row that would prove the truth-functional invalidity of the schema. The only way that we can know for certain that no row with all true premises and a false conclusion exists is to construct a complete truth table and carefully examine every row in it. Thus, we must stipulate the following rule:

WARNING ! ! !

The shortened truth table method should be used *only* to prove the truth-functional *invalidity* of an intended argument.

A complete truth table should be constructed to prove that an argument is valid. (It is also possible to use the method of deductive proof that will be discussed later in this chapter to prove validity.)

Let us reconsider the last example in the preceding section, which had the schema

$$p \supset q$$
$$r \supset s$$
$$p \lor s$$
$$\therefore q \lor r$$

We begin our shortened truth table by laying out columns for each variable, all premises, and the conclusion of the argument as follows:

p	q	r	s	(Premise 1) $p \supset q$	(Premise 2) $r \supset s$	(Premise 3) $p \lor s$	(Conclusion) $q \lor r$

We place an F under the main operator of the conclusion as shown below, since we are seeking to recreate a situation in which the premises are true and the conclusion false, if such a situation exists. For 'q ∨ r' to be false, both its components must be false. We therefore put Fs under each occurrence of the variables 'q' and 'r.'

				(Premise 1)			(Premise 2)			(Premise 3)			(Conclusion)		
p	q	r	s	p	⊃	q	r	⊃	s	p	∨	s	q	∨	r
	F	F				F		F					F	F	F

Given the truth values of 'q' and 'r,' we then seek to assign to the variables 'p' and 's' those truth values which will make all the premises of the argument true. If we assign the truth value F to the variable 'p' and the truth value T to the variable 's,' all the premises of the argument take the value T as shown in the short truth table below.

				(Premise 1)			(Premise 2)			(Premise 3)			(Conclusion)		
p	q	r	s	p	⊃	q	r	⊃	s	p	∨	s	q	∨	r
F	F	F	T	F	T	F	F	T	T	F	T	T	F	F	F

Thus, we have succeeded in proving that the above argument schema is truth-functionally invalid, since we have constructed a case in which all the premises are true and the conclusion is false. We have also done this without having to fill in truth values for sixteen different rows as we did in the preceding section, where we used complete truth tables.

If the conclusion in our example had been a conjunction (e.g., 'q · r'), three different assignments of truth values to 'q' and 'r' would have made the conclusion false. Also, as the number of variables in an argument increases and as the premises and conclusion of an argument become more complex, using the shortened truth table method becomes less practicable. When dealing with such arguments, it might be necessary to "play" with the short truth table method. For instance, you might make some premises true and then determine whether on the basis of the truth values assigned to various component statements it is possible to create a false conclusion. Practice is the only way to learn when it is easier to use the short method and when the regular method would be at least as easy.

EXERCISE 6–3

Using the short truth table method, prove the truth-functional invalidity of each of the following argument schemas.

1. $p \supset q$
    $q \supset r$
    $\therefore q \lor r$

2. $p \supset q$
    $q \supset r$
    $\therefore r \supset p$

3. $p \supset (q \cdot r)$
    $\sim p$
    $\therefore \sim r$

4. $p \supset (q \lor r)$
    $(q \cdot r) \supset s$
    $\therefore p \supset s$

5. $p \cdot q$
    $p \lor r$
    $\therefore r$

6. $p \supset q$
    $p \lor r$
    $\therefore q$

7. $p \supset q$
    $p \lor r$
    $\therefore q \supset \sim r$

8. $p \supset q$
    $p \lor r$
    $\therefore q \lor \sim r$

9. $p \supset (q \lor r)$
    $\sim q$
    $\therefore r \supset p$

10. $p \supset (q \lor r)$
    $(q \cdot r) \supset \sim p$
    $\therefore \sim p$

11. $p \supset (q \lor r)$
    $q \supset s$
    p
    $\therefore r \supset s$

12. $(p \cdot q) \supset r$
    $r \supset s$
    $(p \cdot s) \supset q$
    $\therefore \sim r \lor q$

13. $p \supset (q \supset r)$
    p
    $\therefore r$

14. $p \supset q$
    $q \supset r$
    $\therefore p \cdot r$

15. $(p \supset r) \cdot (s \supset t)$
    $r \lor t$
    $\therefore p \lor s$

16. $(p \supset q) \lor (q \supset r)$
    $p \lor q$
    $\therefore q \cdot r$

17. $p \supset q$
    $r \supset s$
    $\therefore (p \lor q) \supset (r \cdot s)$

18. $p \supset ((q \cdot r) \lor (s \cdot t))$
    $q \supset \sim (s \cdot t)$
    $\therefore p \supset \sim (q \cdot r)$

6.7 Truth-Functional Arguments and Corresponding Conditionals

In this chapter, we have been concerned thus far with testing the validity or truth-functional invalidity of arguments by means of truth tables or short truth tables. An important logical relationship—that between truth-functional arguments and their corresponding conditionals—has not been touched upon, and it is to this subject that we now turn.

For every truth-functional argument, it is possible to construct a corresponding conditional statement. We saw in our discussion of material implication in Chapter 5 that a conditional statement is an 'if . . . then . . .' statement such that it is false if and only if its antecedent is true and its consequent is false. A **corresponding conditional** to a truth-functional argument is defined as *a material implication in which the antecedent consists of the conjunction of the premises of that argument and the consequent is the conclusion of that argument.* For example, consider the following argument:

> **Either Pat will pass this course or she will be ineligible for the varsity basketball team.**
> **Pat will not pass this course.**
> **Therefore, she will be ineligible for the varsity basketball team.**

The schema for this argument is

> p ∨ q
> ~p
> ∴ q

We can create a corresponding conditional for this argument by conjoining its premises to create the antecedent of a conditional statement, and using its conclusion as the consequent of the conditional; the schema of this conditional is

> ((p ∨ q) · ~p) ⊃ q

Using the phrasing of the original argument, its corresponding conditional reads:

> **If either Pat will pass this course or she will be ineligible for the varsity basketball team, and Pat will not pass this course, then she will be ineligible for the varsity basketball team.**

Of course, this corresponding conditional does not say precisely the same thing as the original argument. The corresponding conditional is only one compound statement, whereas the argument is composed of several statements. Also, the conditional is just that—the conclusion is asserted to be true only on the condition that the premises are true. In contrast to the corresponding argument, the conditional only asserts that, *if* the premises are true, then the conclusion is true. In the argument, the premises are asserted to be true; they are not hypothesized.

However, a significant logical relationship exists between any truth-functional argument and its corresponding conditional statement. If a truth-functional argument is valid, then its corresponding conditional is a tautology, and vice versa. Let us first check to see if the argument schema above, known as the **disjunctive syllogism**, is valid by means of its truth table.

		(Premise 1)	**(Premise 2)**	**(Conclusion)**
p	q	p ∨ q	~ p	q
T	T	T	F	T
F	T	T	T	T
T	F	T	F	F
F	F	F	T	F

From the truth table, it is obvious that this schema is valid, since no row contains an **F** under the conclusion and **T**s under both premises. Let us now construct a truth table for the corresponding conditional to this argument schema.

p	q	((p ∨ q)	·	~ p)	⊃	q
T	T	T	F	F	T	
F	T	T	T	T	T	
T	F	T	F	F	T	
F	F	F	F	T	T	

Examining column 4, we can see that there are all **T**s under the horseshoe, indicating that the statement is, in fact, a tautology.

Let us consider another argument schema and test its corresponding conditional to determine whether it is a tautology. If it is not a tautology, we know that the corresponding argument schema is truth-functionally invalid. The argument schema shown below is known as the **constructive dilemma.**

$$(p \supset q) \cdot (r \supset s)$$
$$p \vee r$$
$$\therefore q \vee s$$

The corresponding conditional for this argument schema is

$$(((p \supset q) \cdot (r \supset s)) \cdot (p \vee r)) \supset (q \vee s)$$

and its truth table is

p	q	r	s	(((p ⊃ q)	·	(r ⊃ s))	·	(p ∨ r))	⊃	(q ∨ s)
T	T	T	T	T	T	T	T	T	T	T
F	T	T	T	T	T	T	T	T	T	T
T	F	T	T	F	F	T	F	T	T	T
F	F	T	T	T	T	T	T	T	T	T
T	T	F	T	T	T	T	T	T	T	T
F	T	F	T	T	T	T	F	F	T	T
T	F	F	T	F	F	T	F	T	T	T
F	F	F	T	T	T	T	F	F	T	T
T	T	T	F	T	F	F	F	T	T	T
F	T	T	F	T	F	F	F	T	T	T
T	F	T	F	F	F	F	F	T	T	F
F	F	T	F	T	F	F	F	T	T	F
T	T	F	F	T	T	T	T	T	T	T
F	T	F	F	T	T	T	F	F	T	T
T	F	F	F	F	F	T	F	T	T	F
F	F	F	F	T	T	T	F	F	T	F

We can see that the statement is a tautology, since the column under its main operator contains all **T**s. This means that the argument schema known as the constructive dilemma is valid.

Notice also that if a conditional is not a tautology, it could be either contingent or a contradiction. The argument corresponding to any conditional which is either contingent or a contradiction must be truth-functionally invalid, because in either case it has at least one row in its truth table with a **T** under the conjunction of the premises (the antecendent) and an **F** under the conclusion (the consequent).

EXERCISE 6–4

(a) Construct the corresponding conditional for each of the argument schemas in Exercise 6–2. (b) Construct the complete truth table for each of the resulting schemas. (c) Determine whether the arguments are valid or truth-functionally invalid by determining whether the corresponding conditionals are tautologies or not.

6.8 The Propositional Calculus

As we have seen, the truth table method described above provides a mechanical decision procedure by which to test the validity of an argument. By the use of truth tables, the validity or truth-functional invalidity of any argument can be determined in a finite number of mechanical steps. However, suppose we had to test the validity of the following argument schema:

$$p \supset q$$
$$q \supset r$$
$$r \supset s$$
$$s \supset t$$
$$t \supset u$$
$$u \supset v$$
$$v \supset w$$
$$w \supset x$$
$$x \supset z$$
$$\therefore p \supset z$$

Using a truth table to test this schema requires 1,024 rows (2^{10})—hardly a very practicable arrangement. How might such an argument schema be tested for validity without requiring such an enormous amount of time and energy? The short truth table method could perhaps be tried, but this particular schema is valid and the short truth table method can be used only to prove truth-functional invalidity, so we would not be able to prove anything using it here. But we can use another, simpler method to prove the validity of such arguments or argument schemas; this is called the **method of deductive proof.**

It is possible to construct a deductive proof system consisting of a set of rules and procedures that enable us to prove the validity of a deductive argument schema in a step-by-step fashion. Since such a deductive system, in effect, allows us to "calculate" the validity of an argument at the propositional (truth-functional) level, it is sometimes referred to as a **propositional calculus.**

Most deductive proof systems do not provide a decision procedure; that is, they do not offer a mechanical procedure such that, after a finite number of steps, we are sure to have a proof that a particular argument is valid or truth-functionally invalid. When using a system that does not provide a decision procedure, if we are unsuccessful in proving the validity of an argument, this does not mean that we have proven it to be invalid; it simply means that we have not been successful in proving its validity. Although it is possible to construct a deductive system that does give us a decision procedure for determining whether each argument is valid or truth-functionally invalid, we will not use such a system here. Instead, we shall present a system that provides us with a foundation for later constructing proofs for a more sophisticated type of argument—a type for which it has been shown to be theoretically impossible to provide a decision procedure.

The fundamental procedure underlying any deductive proof system is the use of a small number of rules or axioms, which are such that, when they are used in conjunction with the premises of a valid argument, it can be shown that, if all the premises are true, then the truth of the conclusion logically follows. The basic rules or axioms are such that it is inappropriate to ask that their validity (or, in some cases, their truth) be proved within the system itself.[3] In effect, we are using the rules of the deductive system in conjunction with the premises of a particular valid argument to draw out and make explicit the conclusion that was already implicitly contained in those premises.

6.9 Constructing a Formal Proof

Let us consider how to construct a formal proof, using as our example the complex argument introduced at the beginning of this section. The schema for this argument reappears in slightly altered form below.

1. $p \supset q$		Premise
2. $q \supset r$		Premise
3. $r \supset s$		Premise
4. $s \supset t$		Premise
5. $t \supset u$		Premise
6. $u \supset v$		Premise
7. $v \supset w$		Premise
8. $w \supset x$		Premise
9. $x \supset z \ / \therefore p \supset z$		**Premise/conclusion**

[3]Their validity can be proved using the method of truth tables, although some logicians consider their validity to be "intuitively obvious," and, thus, to not require any proof at all.

Notice that we have listed the schemata in order of their appearance in the original argument, numbering them consecutively and labeling each as a premise in the column on the right. The last line contains the last-premise schema, a slash, the symbol for 'therefore,' and the conclusion; in the right-hand column we have indicated that both a premise and the conclusion appear on this line. In the construction of a formal proof, this procedure for presenting the premises and conclusion of an argument should always be employed.

Earlier, we considered an argument schema known as hypothetical syllogism and proved it valid by means of a truth table. We will now use the hypothetical syllogism as a basic deductive rule or axiom to aid in proving the validity of the argument schema above. It will be recalled that the schema for the rule of hypothetical syllogism is:

$$p \supset q$$
$$\underline{q \supset r}$$
$$\therefore p \supset r$$

Using this schema as a deductive rule, we can deduce from lines l and 2 of the argument schema that 'p ⊃ r.' We write this information beneath line 9, as shown here:

1.	p ⊃ q	Premise
2.	q ⊃ r	Premise
3.	r ⊃ s	Premise
4.	s ⊃ t	Premise
5.	t ⊃ u	Premise
6.	u ⊃ v	Premise
7.	v ⊃ w	Premise
8.	w ⊃ x	Premise
9.	x ⊃ z / ∴ p ⊃ z	Premise/conclusion
10.	p ⊃ r	H.Syll., 1,2

We have numbered line 10, written out the full schema we have deduced, and indicated at the right both the schemas from which this conclusion was deduced and the abbreviation of the rule ('H.Syll.' for 'hypothetical syllogism') by which we justify the deduction. The statement schema on line 10 then becomes part of the proof. We can use it to deduce other schemas, just as we may use any line of the original argument schema. Why is this possible? Since we know that 'p ⊃ r' follows validly from lines 1 and 2, we know that if the premises are true then the statement with the schema 'p ⊃ r' also must be true. In other words, the truth of the original premises is being transmitted to this new statement. Since line 10 follows deductively from lines 1 and 2, the truth of the original premises is necessarily transmitted to the statement with the schema '$p \supset r$.'

We still have not proved this particular argument schema to be valid, although we are clearly on the right track. It should be fairly obvious that using '$p \supset r$' (our deduced schema) and '$r \supset s$' (line 3 of the original argument schema), we can deduce '$p \supset s$,' as

$$\begin{array}{r} p \supset r \\ r \supset s \\ \hline \therefore p \supset s \end{array}$$

One might object that this argument schema is not the same as that represented by the hypothetical syllogism schema four paragraphs back, since the present schema contains the variables 'p,' 'r,' and 's,' whereas the hypothetical syllogism schema has the variables 'p,' 'q,' and 'r.' The objection, however, does not hold. A variable, it will be recalled, functions as a *blank* into which *any* particular statement can be inserted, so long as the same statement is substituted for the same variable every time it appears in a particular argument schema. Thus, if we substituted, in the previous argument schema, the statement 'Mary gets that job' for the variable 'p,' the statement 'She will be happy' for the variable 'r,' and the statement 'Her sister will be happy' for the variable 's,' we would get the following argument:

If Mary gets that job, then she will be happy.
If she will be happy, then her sister will be happy.
Therefore, if Mary gets that job, her sister will be happy.

If we return to our original formulation of the hypothetical syllogism and substitute the statement 'Mary gets that job' for 'p,' 'She will be happy' for 'q,' and 'Her sister will be happy' for 'r,' we will get exactly the same argument. This illustrates how two argument schemas can be logically identical, even if they contain different variables.

To clarify the point, consider the following three argument schemas the third of which uses a new set of symbols as variables.

$$\begin{array}{r} p \supset q \\ r \supset q \\ \hline \therefore p \supset r \end{array} \qquad \begin{array}{r} r \supset s \\ s \supset t \\ \hline \therefore r \supset t \end{array} \qquad \begin{array}{r} ☼ \supset ☺ \\ ☺ \supset \Diamond \\ \hline \therefore ☼ \supset \Diamond \end{array}$$

The schema at the left is not the same as the one we call 'hypothetical syllogism.' Although it contains three material implication schemas and three propositional variables, the variables are not distributed in the same positions as in the hypothetical syllogism schema. However, the variables in the schemas in the middle and to the right are distributed exactly as they are in the hypothetical syllogism schema. The validity of the argument is due to its form, not to the particular variables used to display that form.

To continue constructing our formal proof of the argument schema under discussion, we add this new schema to our list, also providing the justification for it as shown below:

1.	p ⊃ q	Premise
2.	q ⊃ r	Premise
3.	r ⊃ s	Premise
4.	s ⊃ t	Premise
5.	t ⊃ u	Premise
6.	u ⊃ v	Premise
7.	v ⊃ w	Premise
8.	w ⊃ x	Premise
9.	x ⊃ z / ∴ p ⊃ z	Premise/conclusion
10.	p ⊃ r	H.Syll., 1,2
11.	p ⊃ s	H.Syll., 10,3

Notice that for our justification we have used line 10 (a validly deduced intermediary statement) and line 3 (a premise of the original argument) and the inference rule hypothetical syllogism. It should now be obvious that by continuing to use the hypothetical syllogism rule in the same manner, we ultimately reach the conclusion of the original argument. The full proof is shown below:

1.	p ⊃ q	Premise
2.	q ⊃ r	Premise
3.	r ⊃ s	Premise
4.	s ⊃ t	Premise
5.	t ⊃ u	Premise
6.	u ⊃ v	Premise
7.	v ⊃ w	Premise
8.	w ⊃ x	Premise
9.	x ⊃ z / ∴ p ⊃ z	Premise
10.	p ⊃ r	H.Syll., 1,2
11.	p ⊃ s	H.Syll., 10,3
12.	p ⊃ t	H.Syll., 11,4
13.	p ⊃ u	H.Syll., 12,5
14.	p ⊃ v	H.Syll., 13,6
15.	p ⊃ w	H.Syll., 14,7
16.	p ⊃ x	H.Syll., 15,8
17.	p ⊃ z	H.Syll., 16,9

The schema in line 17 ('p ⊃ z') is identical to the conclusion of the original argument schema. The final line of any deductive proof must be the conclusion of the original argument, if the proof is to demonstrate the validity of the argument schema.[4]

We have thus proved the validity of this argument schema in eight steps, using only one rule—a considerable saving of effort when compared to the 20,480 steps that would be required to construct a truth table for this particular schema.

This is an example of what is known as a **formal proof** insofar as it uses *the process whereby the conclusion of an argument can be validly derived from a set of statements, each one of which either is a premise of the original argument or has been validly deduced using the rules of the system from the premises and/or other statements that have themselves been validly deduced using the rules of the system.*

Of course, one rule alone would not provide us with a very useful deductive proof system. In fact, when setting out to construct such a system, we have a multiplicity of options since the number of rules we choose to include within the system is somewhat arbitrary. Logicians have demonstrated that it is theoretically possible to have an adequate system of deductive proof with as few as three rules. However, such a system has its shortcomings since the fewer the rules, the greater the number of steps necessary to prove the validity of most argument schemas. On the other hand, it would be possible to construct a system with a thousand or more rules, enabling us to test the validity of many complex arguments in a single step. However, such a system would be as inconvenient as one consisting of only three rules since we would be required to have facility with all the rules and would sometimes have to go through literally hundreds of rules to find the appropriate one for a particular proof. Consequently, we are faced with something of a pragmatic dilemma. The obvious solution is to compromise. The system we will employ has been found over the years to be one of the easiest to use. It is also deductively complete: that is, any argument that can be proven valid using truth tables can be proven valid using this system's rules and procedures.

6.10 Inference Rules

The rules of our system are known as **rules of inference**. Rules of inference are essentially basic argument schemas that can be proved valid using the truth table method. We have already proved four of the inference rules in this

---

[4]It is important to note that although it is inappropriate to construct truth tables for arguments or argument abbreviations (truth tables should only be constructed for schemas), it is permissible to construct deductive proofs using abbreviations rather than schemas. This is because our rules are applicable to all substitution instances of a given schema. It is only for reasons of stylistic consistency that all of the deductive proofs in this chapter are presented in terms of schemas rather than abbreviations. The use of abbreviations in the proofs would have been just as appropriate from a logical standpoint.

way—*modus tollens*, *modus ponens*, hypothetical syllogism, and constructive dilemma.

Each rule by itself is quite simple. But that doesn't mean that you can just memorize them and assume this is enough. The skill of using these rules to construct proofs is dependent on having a *working* familiarity with them; it is not sufficient to simply memorize their schemas. The only way to acquire a working familiarity with these rules is to actually use them—over and over and over, in different forms and contexts. The exercises presented in the remainder of this chapter are designed to provide the kind of practice that is most helpful in mastering the use of the rules.

6.10.1 Conjunction, Addition, and Simplification

The first three rules to be presented are simple and straight-forward. Their schemas are as follows:

Conjunction (Conj.)		*Addition (Add.)*		*Simplification (Simp.)*	
p	p				
q	q	p	q	p · q	p · q
∴ p · q	∴ q · p	∴ p ∨ q	∴ p ∨ q	∴ p	∴ q

The **conjunction** rule tells us that we can take any two propositions that we know to be true from totally independent sources and we can connect them with the dot operator and know that the resulting compound proposition is true. Thus, if we know that it is true that Bill Clinton was elected president of the United States in 1992 and we also know that it is true that some cars are Fords, then we can conjoin the two with the dot and know that the resulting compound is true without having to get any additional information, since this reasoning pattern fits the schema of the conjunction rule.

Bill Clinton was elected president in 1992.	p
Some cars are Fords.	q
∴ Bill Clinton was elected president in 1992 and some cars are Fords.	∴ p · q

The **simplification** rule allows us to go in the opposite direction. If we start with the knowledge that a conjunction is true, we can also infer that each of the conjuncts by itself is true.

Bill Clinton was elected president in 1992 and some cars are Fords.	p · q
∴ Some cars are Fords.	∴ q

Bill Clinton was elected president in 1992 and some cars are Fords.	p · q
∴ Bill Clinton was elected president in 1992.	∴ p

It is important to recognize that neither the conjunction rule nor the simplification rule involves any operator other than the dot. There is no rule that permits a direct simplification of a statement in which the main operator is the wedge, horseshoe, or three-line operator. And two statements cannot be directly combined with either the horseshoe or the three-line operator.

There *is* a similar-looking rule for the wedge, namely the **addition** rule, which permits us to add *any* other statement using the wedge to any statement that we already have as a premise or validly derived step. We can do this because the wedge is logically quite weak. Remember from the truth table definition of the wedge that any disjunction that has at least one true disjunct is itself true; thus, if we already have a true proposition, adding a false one to it will still produce a true compound.

> **Bill Clinton was elected president in 1992.** $\dfrac{p}{\therefore p \lor q}$
> **∴ Either Bill Clinton was elected president**
>   **in 1992 or Madonna is the Queen of England.**

There is no comparable rule for any of the other operators.

Most of the time when we are using the inference rules, we are dealing with **variants** of the basic schemas that are used in the presentations of the rules. Sometimes these variants simply involve the use of different variables. For example, each of the following are variants of the basic schema for the addition rule.

$$\frac{p}{\therefore p \lor t} \qquad\qquad \frac{r}{\therefore r \lor q} \qquad\qquad \frac{s}{\therefore s \lor t}$$

Often, however, the variants may involve replacing one or more of the original variables with compound propositional schemas, as in the following:

$$\frac{p}{\therefore p \lor (t \cdot r)} \qquad \frac{(r \supset s)}{\therefore (r \supset s) \lor q} \qquad \frac{(s \equiv q)}{\therefore (s \equiv q) \lor (t \lor p)}$$

Practice is essential for developing your ability to recognize such variants.

Let's consider one other point before practicing recognizing when and how to use the first three inference rules.

$$\frac{p \cdot q}{\therefore (p \lor r) \cdot q}$$

One might be tempted to say that this is a variant of the addition rule, with the disjunction symbol (the wedge) and the variable 'r' added to the first conjunct of the compound premise. Unfortunately, such a use of the rules is not permissible. These **rules of inference** are valid argument schemas, and therefore *cannot be applied to subcomponents of compound propositional schemas within a single step of an argument*. In other words, the rules so far presented (and the next five to be presented) *can be applied only to the main operators of entire lines of a deductive proof*. It is incorrect to apply any of these rules to only part of a line. Thus, the following proof *misuses* the simplification rule:

1. q · (p · r)   Premise
2. q / ∴ p   Premise/conclusion

    3. q · p   Simp., 1 [error]

    4. p   Simp., 3

In line 3 of this proof, simplification is applied to the second conjunction ('p · r')
of line 1. This is impermissible, since an inference rule can be applied only to
the main operator of an entire line of a deductive proof. A correct deductive
proof for the same argument schema, using simplification properly, is shown
below:

    1. q · (p · r)/ ∴ p   **Premise/conclusion**

    2. p · r   **Simp., 1**

    3. p   **Simp., 2**

In this proof, the inference rules are applied only to the main operators of
complete steps, thus satisfying our rule about their use.

EXERCISE 6-5

Provide justification for each step in the following proofs using only the addition,
conjunction, and simplification rules.

 1. 1. p · q
   2. r · s / ∴ p ∨ t
   3. p
   4. p ∨ t

 2. 1. q
   2. p · s /∴ s · q
   3. s
   4. s · q

 3. 1. s ∨ r
   2. r · q /∴ s ∨ q
   3. q
   4. s ∨ q

 4. 1. (p · q) · r
   2. r · t /∴ t · r
   3. t
   4. r
   5. t · r

 5. 1. r
   2. t ∨ p /∴ ((t ∨ p) · r) · ((t ∨ p) ∨ t)
   3. (t ∨ p) · r
   4. (t ∨ p) ∨ t
   5. ((t ∨ p) · r) · ((t ∨ p) ∨ t)

 6. 1. (p · q) · t
   2. s · p /∴ (s ∨ r) · (p · q)
   3. s
   4. s ∨ r

   5. p · q
   6. (s ∨ r) · (p · q)

7. 1. (r ∨ s) ∨ (p · q)
   2. p ∨ q
   3. r · q / ∴ r · (q · (p ∨ q))
   4. r
   5. q
   6. q · (p ∨ q)
   7. r · (q · (p ∨ q))

8. 1. (q ∨ t) · (q ∨ r)
   2. (p · r) · t / ∴ t · (q ∨ r)
   3. q ∨ r
   4. q ∨ t
   5. p · r
   6. t
   7. t · (q ∨ r)

9. 1. p · s
   2. s · t / ∴ ((s ∨ r) ∨ s) · p
   3. s
   4. p
   5. t
   6. s ∨ r
   7. (s ∨ r) ∨ s
   8. ((s ∨ r) ∨ s) · p

10. 1. (q ∨ s) · p
   2. (~p ∨ r) / ∴ ((q ∨ s) ∨ (t · ~t)) · (p · (~p ∨ r))
   3. p
   4. p · (~p ∨ r)
   5. q ∨ s
   6. (q ∨ s) ∨ (t · ~t)
   7. ((q ∨ s) ∨ (t · ~t)) · (p · (~p ∨ r))

EXERCISE 6–6

Construct proofs from the premises to the conclusions given. Provide justification for each step using only addition, conjunction, and simplification.

1.   p · r
   ∴ (r ∨ s) · (p · r)

2.   s
   ∴ (s ∨ (t · p)) · (s ∨ r)

3.   t · r
   (q ∨ p) · s
   ∴ (q ∨ p) · t

4.   (q · t) · r
   ∴ (q · t) ∨ r

5.   p
   t · p
   ∴ ((p · t) · (t · p)) · t

6.   r ∨ t
   ~(r · p)
   ~t
   ∴ p ∨ ((r ∨ t) · (r ∨ ~t))

7. p
    q · (r · s)
    t · (s ∨ (p ∨ t))
    ∴ r · (s ∨ (p ∨ t))

8. p
    s
    ∴ (s ∨ t) · (r ∨ (p ∨ t))

9. (((q · r) · s) · r)
    (t · u) · (p · t)
    ∴ ((p · u) ∨ t) · ((q · r) · s)

10. p · (p ∨ t)
    q · (t · (p · p))
    ∴ ((p · p) ∨ ~p) · ((p ∨ t) ∨ r)

6.10.2 Modus Ponens and Modus Tollens

The horseshoe operator (material implication) is widely used in constructing arguments, so it is essential to have rules for dealing with it. Two of these rules were discussed and they were shown to be valid using truth tables in Section 6.5.

Modus Ponens (M.P.)	*Modus Tollens (M.T.)*
p ⊃ q	p ⊃ q
p	~q
∴ q	∴ ~p

It is easy to confuse these two valid inference rules with several others that look very similar but which are not valid. The two most frequently confused schemas are

p ⊃ q   p ⊃ q
~p   q
∴ ~q   **ERROR!!!**   ∴ p   **ERROR!!!**

As pointed out in the previous section, the inference rules most often appear in variant forms, so it is important to develop the skills needed for recognizing them in these different manifestations. All of the following are examples of the two rules under discussion.

Modus Ponens (M.P.)

(p · r) ⊃ q   p ⊃ (q ∨ t)   (p · r) ⊃ (q ∨ t)
(p · r)   p   (p · r)
∴ q   ∴ (q ∨ t)   ∴ (q ∨ t)

Modus Tollens (M.T.)

p ⊃ (q ≡ r)   (p ⊃ s) ⊃ q   (p ⊃ s) ⊃ (q ≡ r)
~(q ≡ r)   ~q   ~(q ≡ r)
∴ ~p   ∴ ~(p ⊃ s)   ∴ ~(p ⊃ s)

Of course, variants of the inference rule argument schemas can be even more complex than these. For example, consider the following:

(p ∨ (t ⊃ q)) ⊃ (r · (p ≡ ~s))
~(r · (p ≡ ~s))
∴ ~(p ∨ (t ⊃ q))

Although at first glance this might not resemble in any obvious way any of the basic inference rules introduced so far, more careful examination reveals that the schema involves a conditional as the main operator in the first step, the consequent of which is negated in the second step, with the conclusion being the negation of the antecedent. So this is a variant of the inference rule known as *modus tollens*.

To see the form of a schema for the purposes of using the first five rules (and also the next three to be introduced), it is usually sufficient to look only at the main operators of each step, and in some cases at the entire step. Thus, for the example above, we need to see only that the main operator of the first premise is the horseshoe and that the second premise is the negation of the consequent of the horseshoe in the first step. Whatever complexities there might be in the subcomponents (that is, inside the antecedent or consequent of the horseshoe) is relevant to the identification of the rule of inference only insofar

"I DON'T CHEW BUBBLE-GUM, AND *YOU* DON'T CHEW BUBBLE-GUM......"

"Dennis the Menace" ® *used by permission of Hank Ketcham and* © *by North America Syndicate.*

Mr. Wilson's reasoning in this cartoon can be expressed in an argument involving only a substitution instance of the inference rule, disjunctive syllogism. Write out the full argument, abbreviate it, and give its schema.

as we need to recognize that the component following the negation sign in the conclusion is the antecedent of the horseshoe.

Provide justification for each step in the following proofs.

1. 1. p ⊃ q   prem.
   2. q ⊃ r   prem.
   3. ~r /∴ ~p   prem./concl.
   4. ~q
   5. ~p

2. 1. r ⊃ t   prem.
   2. t ⊃ s   prem.
   3. r /∴ s   prem./concl.
   4. t
   5. s

3. 1. t ⊃ p   prem.
   2. ~t ⊃ q   prem.
   3. ~p /∴ q   prem./concl.
   4. ~t
   5. q

4. 1. ~p   prem.
   2. r ⊃ p   prem.
   3. ~r ⊃ ~t /∴ ~t prem./concl.
   4. ~r
   5. ~t

5. 1. ~r ⊃ t   prem.
   2. r ⊃ s   prem.
   3. s ⊃ q   prem.
   4. ~q /∴ t   prem./concl.
   5. ~s
   6. ~r
   7. t

6. 1. p ⊃ (q · t)   prem.
   2. s ⊃ r   prem.
   3. r ⊃ p   prem.
   4. s /∴ q · t   prem./concl.
   5. r
   6. p
   7. q · t

Construct proofs from the premises to the conclusions given, using only *modus ponens* and *modus tollens*. Provide justification for each step.

1. $p \supset q$
    $q \supset r$
    $r \supset s$
    $\underline{p}$
    ∴ s

4. $t \supset r$
    $p \supset s$
    $r \supset {\sim}s$
    $\underline{t}$
    ∴ ${\sim}p$

2. $t \supset p$
    ${\sim}t \supset r$
    $\underline{{\sim}p}$
    ∴ r

5. $q \supset p$
    $p \supset t$
    $t \supset s$
    $\underline{{\sim}s}$
    ∴ ${\sim}q$

3. ${\sim}r \supset s$
    $r \supset {\sim}t$
    $\underline{{\sim}{\sim}t}$
    ∴ s

6. ${\sim}q \supset p$
    $q \supset r$
    $\underline{{\sim}r}$
    ∴ p

EXERCISE 6–9

Provide justification for each step in the following proofs, using only the five rules used in Exercises 6–5 through 6–8.

1. 1. $(r \cdot s) \supset p$ prem.
   2. $(r \vee s) \supset q$ prem.
   3. ${\sim}p \cdot {\sim}q$ /∴ ${\sim}(r \vee s)$ prem./concl.
   4. ${\sim}p$
   5. ${\sim}(r \cdot s)$
   6. ${\sim}q$
   7. ${\sim}(r \vee s)$

2. 1. $t \supset (p \cdot {\sim}q)$ prem.
   2. $(r \cdot s) \supset q$ prem.
   3. t /∴ ${\sim}(r \cdot s)$ prem./concl.
   4. $p \cdot {\sim}q$
   5. ${\sim}q$
   6. ${\sim}(r \cdot s)$

3. 1. $p \cdot s$ prem.
   2. $s \supset q$ /∴ $q \vee s$ prem./concl.
   3. s
   4. q
   5. $q \vee s$

4. 1. $(p \vee r) \supset q$ prem.
   2. ${\sim}q$ prem.
   3. ${\sim}q \supset s$ /∴ $s \cdot {\sim}(p \vee r)$ prem./concl.
   4. s
   5. ${\sim}(p \vee r)$
   6. $s \cdot {\sim}(p \vee r)$

EXERCISE 6–10

Construct proofs from the premises to the conclusion, using only the five rules used in Exercise 6–9.

1. p · q
    (p ∨ r) ⊃ s
    ∴ s

2. p ⊃ (r ∨ s)
    q ⊃ (p · t)
    q
    ∴ r ∨ s

3. ~(p ∨ q) ⊃ (r · t)
    (p ∨ q) ⊃ s
    ~s
    ∴ (r · ~s) · (t ∨ p)

4. (t · s) · (p ⊃ q)
    (r · t) · ~q
    ∴ s · ~p

6.10.3 Disjunctive Syllogism, Hypothetical Syllogism, and Constructive Dilemma

Three other rules are not absolutely essential, but once learned they can make the construction of proofs much simpler. You have already seen truth table proofs that these are valid schemas.

Hypothetical Syllogism (H.Syll.)
  p ⊃ q
  q ⊃ r
∴ p ⊃ r

Constructive Dilemma (Dil.)
  (p ⊃ q) · (r ⊃ s)
  p ∨ r
∴ q ∨ s

Disjunctive Syllogism (D.Syll.)
  p ∨ q   p ∨ q
  ~p   ~q
∴ q   ∴ p

As pointed out previously, the inference rules most often appear in variant forms, so it is important to develop the skills needed for recognizing them in these different manifestations. The exercises following this section are designed to provide practice in recognizing variants of these rules.

With one exception, to recognize any of the schemas introduced thus far, it is sufficient to look only at the main operator of each step, and in some cases at the entire step. The sole exception is the rule of constructive dilemma, which *does* involve the inner structure of the two main subcomponents (both are horseshoes).

Let's look at one final example.

  ((p · q) ⊃ r) ∨ (s · (p ≡ t))
  ~((p · q) ⊃ r)
∴ (s · (p ≡ t))

By focusing on the main operator of its most complex step—the wedge in the first premise—we should be able to see that this is a variant of the rule of inference known as disjunctive syllogism. The first premise is a disjunctive statement, both disjuncts of which are compound statements; the second premise, although complex, is merely the negation of the compound statement that forms the first disjunct of the first premise.

EXERCISE 6-11

Provide justification for each step in the following proofs, appealing only to disjunctive syllogism and hypothetical syllogism.

1. 1. p ⊃ q   prem.
   2. q ⊃ t   prem.
   3. t ⊃ r /∴ p ⊃ r   prem./concl.
   4. p ⊃ t
   5. p ⊃ r

2. 1. (p ∨ r) ∨ (q ∨ s)   prem.
   2. ~(q ∨ s)   prem.
   3. ~p /∴ r   prem./concl.
   4. p ∨ r
   5. r

3. 1. (p ⊃ q) ∨ (r ⊃ s)   prem.
   2. ~(r ⊃ s)   prem.
   3. q ⊃ r /∴ p ⊃ r   prem./concl.
   4. p ⊃ q
   5. p ⊃ r

4. 1. (p ∨ q) ⊃ (r ∨ s)   prem.
   2. (r ∨ s) ⊃ (t ∨ s)   prem.
   3. (t ∨ s) ⊃ (p ∨ r) /∴ (r ∨ s) ⊃ (p ∨ r)   prem./concl.
   4. (p ∨ q) ⊃ (t ∨ s)
   5. (r ∨ s) ⊃ (p ∨ r)

5. 1. (p ∨ q) ∨ ~(r ∨ s)   prem.
   2. ~(r ∨ s) ⊃ (t ∨ u)   prem.
   3. (t ∨ u) ⊃ ~(p ⊃ q)   prem.
   4. ~(p ∨ q)   prem.
   5. (r ∨ s) ∨ (p ∨ t) /∴ p ∨ t   prem./concl.
   6. ~(r ∨ s) ⊃ ~(p ⊃ q)
   7. ~(r ∨ s)
   8. p ∨ t

6. 1. (p ∨ q) ∨ ((r ∨ s) ∨ (t ∨ u))   prem.
   2. ~(p ∨ q)   prem.
   3. ~(r ∨ s)   prem.
   4. ~u /∴ t   prem./concl.
   5. (r ∨ s) ∨ (t ∨ u)
   6. t ∨ u
   7. t

EXERCISE 6–12

Construct proofs from the premises to the conclusions given. Provide justification, using only MT, MP, D.Syll., and H.Syll.

1.   p ⊃ r
    r ⊃ s
    s ⊃ t
    t ⊃ u
  ∴ p ⊃ u

2.   (p ∨ q) ∨ (t ∨ u)
    ~(p ∨ q)
    ~t
  ∴ u

3.   (p ⊃ q) ∨ (t ⊃ u)
    (t ⊃ u) ∨ (q ⊃ s)
    ~(t ⊃ u)
  ∴ p ⊃ s

4.   (p ⊃ q) ∨ ((r ⊃ s) ∨ t)
    s ⊃ u
    u ⊃ (t · u)
    ~(p ⊃ q)
    ~t
  ∴ r ⊃ (t · u)

5.   p ⊃ q
    q ⊃ r
    r ∨ (s ∨ t)
    ~r
    ~t
  ∴ s

6.   p ∨ (q ∨ (r ∨ (s ∨ t)))
    ~p
    ~q
    ~r
  ∴ s ∨ t

EXERCISE 6–13

Provide justification for each step of the following proofs, using only MP, MT, D.Syll., and H.Syll.

1. 1. (p ∨ q) ⊃ ~t   prem.
  2. p ⊃ (~t ⊃ r)   prem.
  3. p ∨ q   prem.
  4. ~q   prem.
  5. ~~t /∴ ~(p ∨ q)   prem./concl.
  6. p
  7. ~t ⊃ r
  8. (p ∨ q) ⊃ r
  9. ~(p ∨ q)

2. 1. (p ⊃ r) ∨ t   prem.
  2. t ⊃ (q ∨ u)   prem.
  3. (p ⊃ r) ⊃ (r ⊃ t)   prem.
  4. ~(q ∨ u) /∴ p ⊃ t   prem./concl.
  5. ~t
  6. p ⊃ r
  7. r ⊃ t
  8. p ⊃ t

3. 1. (r ⊃ p) ∨ (p ⊃ t)   prem.
  2. (p ⊃ t) ⊃ (t ⊃ (r ⊃ p))   prem.
  3. ~(r ⊃ p) /∴ ~p   prem./concl.

4. p ⊃ t
5. t ⊃ (r ⊃ p)
6. p ⊃ (r ⊃ p)
7. ~p

4. 1. (~q ⊃ p) ∨ q   prem.
   2. ~q   prem.
   3. p ⊃ q /∴ ~~q   prem./concl.
   4. ~q ⊃ p
   5. ~q ⊃ q
   6. p
   7. ~~q

Construct proofs from the premises to the conclusions given, using only MT, MP, D.Syll., and H.Syll.

1.   p ∨ (q ⊃ r)
      r ⊃ (s ⊃ p)
      r
      ~p
      ∴ ~s

2.   (p ⊃ t) ∨ (q ⊃ r)
      (q ⊃ r) ⊃ (t ⊃ s)
      ~(t ⊃ s)
      t ⊃ q
      t
      ∴ q

3.   (s · r) ∨ (t ⊃ (p ⊃ q))
      t
      q ⊃ (s · r)
      ~(s · r)
      ∴ p ⊃ (s · r)

4.   (p ⊃ (q ⊃ r)) ∨ (p ⊃ (r ⊃ q))
      (p ⊃ (q ⊃ r)) ⊃ (t · s)
      ~(t · s)
      q ⊃ t
      p
      ∴ r ⊃ t

6.10.4 A Sample Proof

The number of rules and steps required to prove the validity of a particular argument schema varies with the complexity of the argument and the skill of the person doing the proof. Consider, for example, the following schema:

      (p ∨ q) · r
      ~p
      ∴ q

One possible deductive proof for this argument schema is

   1. (p ∨ q) · r   Prem.
   2. ~p /∴ q   Prem./conclusion
   3. ((p ∨ q) · r) · ~p   Conj., 1,2
   4. (p ∨ q) · r   Simp., 3
   5. p ∨ q   Simp., 4
   6. q   D.Syll., 5,2

In step 3, premises 1 and 2 are conjoined using the conjunction rule. Then the '~p' is removed from '((p ∨ q) · r) · ~p' by using the simplification rule. Employing the simplification rule again, the 'r' is removed from '(p ∨ q) · r.' Then, using the disjunctive syllogism rule with the deduced statement 'p ∨ q' and the second premise ('~p'), the conclusion is derived, proving that the schema is valid.

As shown below, it is also possible to prove the validity of this argument schema by means of a deductive proof that contains only two steps instead of four, and uses only two rules instead of three:

1.	(p ∨ q) · r	Premise
2.	~ p /∴ q	Premise/conclusion
3.	p ∨ q	Simp., 1
4.	q	D.Syll., 2,3

Both of these proofs demonstrate the validity of the argument schema. The second proof is certainly simpler than the first, since it employs fewer rules and steps, but both are equally "good" from a logical point of view, since both prove that the argument schema is valid. A person who is thoroughly familiar with the rules of inference is probably less likely than a novice to begin the proof using conjunction as was done in the first proof above; but both can reach the desired conclusion.

These examples highlight several features of our formal deductive proof system. First, an infinite number of correct formal deductive proofs can theoretically be constructed for any valid truth-functional argument. Second, given such an argument, the ability to construct a formal deductive proof is dependent on many subjective factors, such as knowledge of the rules, experience with using them, logical intuition, and psychological and physical state at the moment.

These are some of the reasons why failing to construct a formal deductive proof for a particular argument schema is not sufficient to prove that the schema is truth-functionally invalid; at most, it simply indicates that a specific person has failed to prove it valid at a specific time. The fact that a person has just learned the rules, or had only two hours of sleep the night before, may be the cause of her or his inability to construct a formal deductive proof of the validity of an argument. And it cannot be too strongly emphasized that there is no substitute for practice in constructing formal proofs. Consequently, it is worthwhile to present several more samples and, while doing so, to point out some generally helpful rules of thumb.

6.11 Rules of Thumb for Proof Construction

The most obvious and easily applied procedure for figuring out how to construct a proof for a particular schema is to go through each of the rules mentally to determine which ones can be applied to the various premises with what results. The more you work with the rules, the more familiar they become. Fairly soon you will find that the appropriate rules for each step will immediately come to mind at first glance.

Some rules are particularly useful for *eliminating variables* that appear in the premises but not in the conclusion. For example, hypothetical syllogism is helpful in removing middle terms when we have a sequence such as 'p ⊃ q' and 'q ⊃ r.' Similarly, simplification is helpful as a means of eliminating variables that appear as conjuncts in one or more premises of an argument but do not appear at all in the conclusion.

Sometimes we need to add variables that appear in the conclusion but are not present in the premises. The following argument schema presents such a situation.

$$
\begin{array}{l}
p \vee q \\
\underline{\sim p} \\
\therefore q \vee (r \cdot s)
\end{array}
$$

Because the last line of any formal deductive proof must be identical to the conclusion of the original argument schema, we must somehow add 'r · s,' which appears in the conclusion but not in the premises. The addition rule permits this. Thus, we can prove the validity of this particular argument schema by means of the following proof:

1. p ∨ q	Premise
2. ∼p /∴ q ∨ (r · s)	Premise/conclusion
3. q	D.Syll., 1,2
4. q ∨ (r · s)	Add., 3

Remember that addition permits us to add a variable (or a compound) *only* as a disjunct; it does not permit adding anything by means of the dot or any other operator.

Sometimes it is helpful in working out a proof to examine the conclusion of a particular argument schema and use the rules to work backward from it to the premises. For example, consider the following:

$$
\begin{array}{l}
\sim p \\
(q \vee p) \supset r \\
p \vee s \\
\underline{(s \vee t) \supset q} \\
\therefore r
\end{array}
$$

Starting from the conclusion, we look back to see if there are any premises from which this statement can be directly deduced. We find that there are none; and we also see that 'r' appears only in premise 2. We know that we could deduce 'r' from '(q ∨ p) ⊃ r' by means of *modus ponens* if we had the premise 'q ∨ p.'

Looking again at the premises, we can see that 'q ∨ p' appears only in the material implication of line 2. However, we know that we could derive 'q ∨ p' by addition if we had the premise 'q.' Examining the premises again, we see that 'q' appears in the material implication of line 4. We could derive 'q' from line 4 by means of *modus ponens,* if we could assert 's ∨ t.' However, 's ∨ t' appears only in line 4, but we could derive 's ∨ t' from 's' by means of addition if we had 's' by itself. And, by means of disjunctive syllogism, we can derive 's' from premises 3 and 1 ('p ∨ s' and '~p'). Thus, our entire deductive proof falls into place, as shown here

1. ~ p	Premise
2. (q ∨ p) ⊃ r	Premise
3. p ∨ s	Premise
4. (s ∨ t) ⊃ q /∴ r	Premise/conclusion
5. s	D.Syll., 3,1
6. s ∨ t	Add., 5
7. q	M.P., 4,6
8. q ∨ p	Add., 7
9. r	M.P., 2,8

6.12 The Rule of Rigor

A final procedural principle, sometimes referred to as the **rule of rigor** (or sometimes, more feelingly, as the "pain-in-the-neck principle"), requires that we *use only one rule in each step of a deductive proof, and that we use the rules only in the form in which they are given in the system.* The following proof violates the rule of rigor in line 3:

1. p ∨ (q · r)	Premise
2. ~p /∴ r · q	Premise/conclusion
3. r · q	D.Syll., 1,2 [error]

Although the schema 'r · q' in line 3 might appear to be the same as the schema 'q · r' in the second disjunct of line 1, the two are different in that the two component variables appear in opposite sequence; thus the proof violates the rule concerning the use of rules in their stated form.

One might try to get around this by using the following proof:

1. p ∨ (q · r)	Premise
2. ~ p /∴ r · q	Premise/conclusion
3. q · r	D.Syll., 1,2
4. r · q	Simp., Simp., Conj., 3 [error]

Here, in line 4, we deduce the statement 'r · q' from 'q · r' by employing simplification twice and then conjunction. In fact, we *can* derive 'r · q' from 'q · r' by using these rules, but only one rule may be used in each step. Thus, an acceptable proof for this argument schema is:

1. p ∨ (q · r)	Premise
2. ~p /∴ r · q	Premise/conclusion
3. q · r	D.Syll., 1,2
4. r	Simp., 3
5. q	Simp., 3
6. r · q	Conj., 4,5

The rule of rigor might indeed seem like nothing more than a pain in the neck. Nevertheless, it should be adhered to, particularly by the novice, so that errors can be avoided in the construction of formal deductive proofs for complex argument schemas.

EXERCISE 6–15

Provide justification for each step in the following proofs, using the eight inference rules.

1. 1. p · (q ⊃ r)   prem.
    2. q ∨ s   prem.
    3. r ⊃ (t · p)   prem.
    4. ~(t · p) /∴ p · s   prem./concl.
    5. ~r
    6. q ⊃ r
    7. ~q
    8. s
    9. p
    10. p · s

2. 1. r ⊃ (q ⊃ s)   prem.
    2. p · r   prem.
    3. t ⊃ p   prem.
    4. t ∨ q /∴ s ∨ p   prem./concl.
    5. r
    6. q ⊃ s
    7. (t ⊃ p) · (q ⊃ s)
    8. s ∨ p

3. 1. p ⊃ (s · r)   prem.
    2. ((s · r) ∨ p) ⊃ ~t   prem.
    3. p · (t ∨ ~~r) /∴ ~~r · (s · r)   prem./concl.
    4. p
    5. s · r

  6. (s · r) ∨ p
  7. ~t
  8. t ∨ ~~r
  9. ~~r
  10. ~~r · (s · r)

4. 1. s ⊃ (r · (p ⊃ (q ⊃ t)))   prem.
    2. (q ⊃ t) ⊃ ~t   prem.
    3. s · p /∴ ~t · ~q   prem./concl.
    4. s   simp 3
    5. r · (p ⊃ (q ⊃ t))   mp 1,4
    6. p ⊃ (q ⊃ t)   simp 5
    7. p   simp 3
    8. q ⊃ t   mp 6,7
    9. ~t   mp 2,8
    10. ~q   mt 8,9
    11. ~t · ~q   conj 9,10

5. 1. (p ⊃ q) ⊃ (p · (s ∨ r))   prem.
    2. p ∨ (t · r)   prem.
    3. (t · r) ⊃ s   prem.
    4. ~s · (p ⊃ q) /∴ q ∨ s   prem./concl.
    5. p ⊃ q
    6. p · (s ∨ r)
    7. p
    8. q
    9. s ∨ r
    10. ~s
    11. r
    12. (p ⊃ q) · ((t · r) ⊃ s)
    13. p ∨ (t · r)
    14. q ∨ s

6. 1. (p ⊃ t) · p   prem.
    2. (t ∨ s) ⊃ (t ⊃ r) /∴ (t · p) · r   prem./concl.
    3. p
    4. p ⊃ t
    5. t
    6. t ∨ s
    7. t ⊃ r
    8. p ⊃ r
    9. r
    10. t · p
    11. (t · p) · r

7. 1. ((p ∨ s) ∨ t) ∨ r   prem.
    2. ~(p ∨ s) · ~r   prem.
    3. (t ∨ (r · p)) ⊃ q /∴ q   prem./concl.

   4. ~r
   5. (p ∨ s) ∨ t
   6. ~(p ∨ s)
   7. t
   8. t ∨ (r · p)
   9. q

8.   1. (s ∨ p) ⊃ ((r ⊃ s) ⊃ (t ⊃ p))   prem.
     2. r ⊃ s   prem.
     3. s · (r ∨ t) /∴ (s ∨ p) · (r ∨ t)   prem./concl.
     4. s
     5. s ∨ p
     6. (r ⊃ s) ⊃ (t ⊃ p)
     7. t ⊃ p
     8. (r ⊃ s) · (t ⊃ p)
     9. r ∨ t
    10. (s ∨ p) · (r ∨ t)

9.   1. p ⊃ (t · r)   prem.
     2. (t · r) ⊃ (s ∨ p)   prem.
     3. p ⊃ (s ∨ p)   prem.
     4. ~s · ~(s ∨ p) /∴ ~p · (p ⊃ (s ∨ p))   prem./concl.
     5. ~(s ∨ p)
     6. ~p
     7. ~(t · r)
     8. p ⊃ (s ∨ p)
     9. ~p · (p ⊃ (s ∨ p))

10. 1. p ∨ (q ⊃ (r · s))   prem.
     2. p ⊃ (t · q)   prem.
     3. ~s · ((t · q) ⊃ s) /∴ q ⊃ (r · s)   prem./concl.
     4. ~s
     5. (t · q) ⊃ s
     6. ~(t · q)
     7. ~p
     8. q ⊃ (r · s)

EXERCISE 6–16

Construct proofs from the premises to the conclusions given, using the eight inference rules.

1.   ~p · (q ⊃ r)
     r ⊃ ~t
     s ⊃ t
     s ∨ p
     ∴ ~t ∨ t

2.   s ∨ (r ⊃ (t ⊃ p))
     s ⊃ (q · t)
     ~(q · t) · r
     ∴ (t ⊃ p) ∨ p

3.   p · (q ⊃ (r ∨ t))
      ~s ∨ ~r
      ~~r · (s ∨ ~(r ∨ t))
    ∴ ~q

4.   ~t
      t ∨ (~t ⊃ (p · (r ∨ s)))
    ∴ ~t · ((r ∨ s) · p)

5.   p ∨ (q ⊃ r)
      s ⊃ (p · (t ∨ q))
      ~p · (q ∨ s)
    ∴ r ∨ (p · (t ∨ q))

6.   p · ~r
      ~s ∨ (p ⊃ t)
      t ⊃ q
      q ⊃ r
    ∴ (t ∨ (~t · ~r)) · (t ⊃ r)

7.   r ⊃ (s · ~t)
      r ∨ ~(s · ~t)
      ~~(s · t)
    ∴ (p ⊃ q) ∨ (r · s)

8.   (p ⊃ q) · ((q ⊃ r) ∨ (q ⊃ t))
      (q ⊃ r) ⊃ (s ⊃ t)
      ((s ⊃ t) ⊃ t) · ~ t
    ∴ q ⊃ t

9.   ((p · t) ∨ (s · r)) ⊃ q
      t
      (q ∨ (s · r)) ⊃ p
    ∴ p

10.   t · (s ⊃ (r · ~p))
      (p ∨ t) ⊃ s
    ∴ r

6.13 The Replacement Rule

The proof discussed at the end of the previous section requires three steps to deduce 'r · q' from 'q · r.' These two schemas are, of course, logically equivalent. As we saw at the end of Chapter 5, we can test any two propositional schemas for logical equivalence by connecting them with the biconditional (three-line) operator and then using the truth table method. If we find all Ts under the material equivalence operator, then the two schemas are logically equivalent. This is shown in the following truth table:

q	r	(q · r)	≡	(r · q)
T	T	T	T	T
F	T	F	T	F
T	F	F	T	F
F	F	F	T	F

If we had an inference rule that allowed us to substitute logically equivalent statements in a deductive proof, we could save a considerable number of steps in arguments such as the previous one. Fortunately, we do have such a rule, which we will introduce now to our deductive proof system. The rule of **replacement** is much more complex than the previous eight inference rules. In symbolic language, it states:

The two following schemata are valid inference forms:

$$\ldots \Phi \ldots$$
$$\underline{\Phi \equiv \Psi} \qquad or \qquad \underline{\Phi \equiv \Psi}$$
$$\therefore \ldots \Psi \ldots \qquad\qquad \therefore \ldots \Psi \ldots$$

where '$\Phi \equiv \Psi$' is one of the equivalences listed below:

De Morgan's rules (DeM.): $\sim(p \cdot q) \equiv (\sim p \vee \sim q)$
$\sim(p \vee q) \equiv (\sim p \cdot \sim q)$

Commutation (Comm.): $(p \vee q) \equiv (q \vee p)$
$(p \cdot q) \equiv (q \cdot p)$

Association (Assoc.): $(p \vee (q \vee r)) \equiv ((p \vee q) \vee r)$
$(p \cdot (q \cdot r)) \equiv ((p \cdot q) \cdot r)$

Distribution (Dist.): $(p \cdot (q \vee r)) \equiv ((p \cdot q) \vee (p \cdot r))$
$(p \vee (q \cdot r)) \equiv ((p \vee q) \cdot (p \vee r))$

Double Negation (D.N.): $p \equiv \sim\sim p$

Transportation (Trans.): $(p \supset q) \equiv (\sim q \supset \sim p)$

Material Implication (Impl.): $(p \supset q) \equiv (\sim p \vee q)$
$(p \supset q) \equiv \sim(p \cdot \sim q))$

Material Equivalence (Equiv.): $(p \equiv q) \equiv ((p \supset q) \cdot (q \supset p))$
$(p \equiv q) \equiv ((p \cdot q) \vee (\sim p \cdot \sim q))$

Exportation (Exp.): $((p \cdot q) \supset r) \equiv (p \supset (q \supset r))$

Tautology (Taut.): $p \equiv (p \vee p)$
$p \equiv (p \cdot p)$

Five of the basic logical equivalences—double negation, De Morgan's rules, material implication, material equivalence, and tautology—were introduced and proven to be equivalences in Chapter 5. The other five can also be proved to be logical equivalences by using truth tables.

Simply stated, the rule of replacement asserts that any propositional schema that is produced by replacing all or part of another schema with a schema that is equivalent to the replaced portion, according to one of the listed equivalences, is validly derivable from the original schema. This should not be surprising, since two statements that are logically equivalent have the same truth value in the same instances. If one statement is true in the original premises, then its logically equivalent statement is also true, and vice versa. Thus, *a statement can be substituted for a logically equivalent statement anywhere in a proof, even in the middle of a line. It is not necessary to replace only whole lines with equivalent statements.*

Although we are formally introducing the rule of replacement as a single inference rule, we shall treat it—for reasons that should soon become obvious—as ten distinct rules in constructing proofs. Each of these rules consists of the original general formula, with Φ and Ψ, plus one of the ten equivalence statements. In our proofs, we shall use the names of the equivalences to identify the justifications of steps. This is considerably more convenient and helpful than simply referring to the general rule of replacement.

Returning to the argument schema in the section on the rule of rigor, we can see that these additional rules can save us a number of steps, as shown in the following proof:

1.	p ∨ (q · r)	Premise
2.	~p /∴ r · q	Premise/conclusion
3.	q · r	D.Syll., 1,2
4.	r · q	Comm., 3

In this proof, we justified deducing 'r · q' from 'q · r' by the commutation rule. Technically speaking, we employed a part of the inference rule of replacement, but we gave only the name of the appropriate equivalence as a justification. From this point on we shall refer to the ten forms of the rule of replacement as **equivalence rules** and we shall identify them by their specific names (for example, 'commutation') or abbreviations (e.g., 'Comm.') when we use them in a step of a proof.

As with the first eight inference rules, it is not enough to merely memorize the ten equivalence rules; it is necessary to practice using them until one can quickly and accurately recognize when one is being used or should be used in the context of a particular proof.

6.13.1 Commutation, Association, Double Negation, and Tautology

Some of the equivalence rules are very similar to rules that are taught in elementary arithmetic, so it should not be hard to memorize their basic schemata. But practice is still important to ensure that one will be able to recognize the many variant forms in which they can appear in the contexts of proofs.

Double negation is probably the most familiar and also the simplest to recognize.

Double Negation (D.N.): $\qquad$ p ≡ ~~p

Each of the following is a legitimate use of the rule in the context of a proof (where 'm' is a premise or a legitimately derived step in a proof and 'm+n' is some subsequent step):

m.	~~p · ~~q	
m + n.	p · ~~q	D.N., m
m.	(q ∨ p) · r	
m + n.	(q ∨ ~~p) · r	D.N., m

m.	$r \cdot (s \cdot (\sim t \cdot q))$	
m + n.	$\sim\sim r \cdot (s \cdot (\sim t \cdot q))$	D.N., m

Remember that the rule of rigor requires that we must apply even the double negation rule in a step by itself, even if it might seem too obvious and simple to require such an effort.

Although you might not have ever seen the rule of **tautology** written out as a separate rule, its truth should be intuitively obvious. It is usually fairly easy to identify in most variant forms and in most contexts.

Tautology (Taut.): $p \equiv (p \vee p)$
$p \equiv (p \cdot p)$

Each of the following is a legitimate use of this rule in the context of a proof.

m.	$\sim\sim(p \vee (r \cdot s))$	
m + n.	$\sim\sim((p \vee p) \vee (r \cdot s))$	Taut., m

m.	$p \cdot (q \vee (r \cdot \sim r))$	
m + n.	$(p \cdot p) \cdot (q \vee (r \cdot \sim r))$	Taut., m

The rule of **commutation** is very useful for reversing the sequence of variables in conjunctions and disjunctions, but it is important to remember that it cannot be used with the horseshoe.

Commutation (Comm.): $(p \vee q) \equiv (q \vee p)$
$(p \cdot q) \equiv (q \cdot p)$

Each of the following is a legitimate use of this rule in the context of a proof.

m.	$\sim\sim(p \vee (s \cdot r))$	
m + n.	$\sim\sim(p \vee (r \cdot s))$	Comm., m

m.	$(\sim\sim p \supset q) \cdot (p \vee \sim\sim p)$	
m + n.	$(p \vee \sim\sim p) \cdot (\sim\sim p \supset q)$	Comm., m

The **association** rule is useful for regrouping parentheses. It can be used with groupings involving only the dot and it can also be used with groupings involving only the wedge. There is no form of the association rule for the horseshoe or three-line operator.

Association (Assoc.): $(p \vee (q \vee r)) \equiv ((p \vee q) \vee r)$
$(p \cdot (q \cdot r)) \equiv ((p \cdot q) \cdot r)$

Each of the following is a legitimate use of this rule in the context of a proof.

m.	$p \vee ((p \cdot q) \vee \sim\sim r)$	
m + n.	$(p \vee (p \cdot q)) \vee \sim\sim r$	Assoc., m

m.	$(r \vee s) \cdot ((q \cdot p) \cdot (q \supset p))$	
m + n.	$((r \vee s) \cdot (q \cdot p)) \cdot (q \supset p)$	Assoc., m

EXERCISE 6–17

Provide justification for each step in the following proofs, using only commutation, association, double negation, and tautology.

1. 1. p · (q · r)
    2. t · ~~s /∴ s · t
    3. (p · q) · r
    4. ~~s · t
    5. s · t

2. 1. ~~p · ~~q
    2. (p ∨ q) ∨ r /∴ p · q
    3. p ∨ (q ∨ r)
    4. p · ~~q
    5. p · q

3. 1. (p ∨ q) · r
       /∴ (q ∨ ~~p) · (r · r)
    2. (q ∨ p) · r
    3. (q ∨ ~~p) · r
    4. (q ∨ ~~p) · (r · r)

4. 1. p ∨ (s · r)
       /∴ ~~((p ∨ p) ∨ (r · s))
    2. ~~(p ∨ (s · r))
    3. ~~(p ∨ (r · s))
    4. ~~((p ∨ p) ∨ (r · s))

5. 1. p ∨ ((p · q) ∨ ~~r)
       /∴ r ∨ (p ∨ ((q · p) · (p · q)))
    2. (p ∨ (p · q)) ∨ ~~r
    3. ~~r ∨ (p ∨ (p · q))
    4. r ∨ (p ∨ (p · q))

5. r ∨ (p ∨ (q · p))
6. r ∨ (p ∨ ((q · p) · (q · p)))
7. r ∨ (p ∨ ((q · p) · (p · q)))

6. 1. (p ⊃ q) · ~~p
       /∴ (p ∨ ~~p) · ((p ∨ ~~p) ⊃ q)
    2. (~~p ⊃ q) · ~~p
    3. (~~p ⊃ q) · (~~p ∨ ~~p)
    4. (~~p ⊃ q) · (p ∨ ~~p)
    5. (p ∨ ~~p) · (~~p ⊃ q)
    6. (p ∨ ~~p) · ((~~p ∨ ~~p) ⊃ q)
    7. (p ∨ ~~p) · ((p ∨ ~~p) ⊃ q)

7. 1. (p · q) · (s · (r · t))
       /∴ (s · (r · (~~ t · t))) · (q · p)
    2. (s · (r · t)) · (p · q)
    3. (s · (r · ~~t)) · (p · q)
    4. (s · (r · (~~t · ~~t))) · (p · q)
    5. (s · (r · (~~ t · t))) · (p · q)
    6. (s · (r · (~~ t · t))) · (q · p)

8. 1. ~~((p · q) · (r ∨ s))
       /∴ ((r ∨ s) · (q · p)) · (q · p)
    2. (p · q) · (r ∨ s)
    3. (q · p) · (r ∨ s)
    4. (r ∨ s) · (q · p)
    5. (r ∨ s) · ((q · p) · (q · p))
    6. ((r ∨ s) · (q · p)) · (q · p)

EXERCISE 6–18

Construct proofs from the premises to the given conclusions, using only commutation, double negation, association and tautology.

1. (p · q) · (s · r)
    ∴ (r · s) · (q · p)

2. p ∨ (q ∨ r)
    ~~p ∨ (q ∨ r)
    (q ∨ r) ∨ ~~p
    ∴ q ∨ (r ∨ ~~p)

3. s · (r · ~t)
    ∴ ~~~t · (s · r)

4. p · s
    ∴ p · (s · ~~(p · s))

5. $((p \cdot q) \cdot s) \cdot r$
      $\therefore ((q \cdot (\sim\sim s \cdot \sim\sim s)) \cdot r) \cdot (p \vee p)$

6. $p \vee (q \vee (r \vee s))$
      $\therefore (q \vee r) \vee ((s \vee p) \vee ((q \vee r) \vee (s \vee p)))$

7. $p \vee q$
      $\therefore (p \vee q) \vee (\sim\sim(p \vee q) \vee (p \vee q))$

8. $s \vee (r \vee t)$
      $\therefore ((s \vee (r \vee t)) \vee \sim\sim s) \vee (\sim\sim r \vee \sim\sim t)$

9. p
      $\therefore ((p \vee p) \vee (p \cdot p)) \vee (p \cdot p)$

10. $(q \cdot r) \cdot ((s \cdot t) \cdot u)$
      $\therefore \sim\sim q \cdot ((u \vee u) \cdot ((t \cdot s) \cdot r))$

6.13.2 De Morgan's Rules and Distribution

The two rules discussed in this section can be difficult to recognize, especially when the schema is in a variant form. People also tend to apply these rules incorrectly, so extra caution is advised.

De Morgan's rules are very useful for removing a negation sign from in front of a parenthesis that has a dot or wedge as the main operator inside of it. There is no comparable rule for the horseshoe or three-line operator. Notice that when the tilde is moved from in front of the parenthesis to in front of each of the two main components following it, the dot changes to a wedge and the wedge changes to a dot.

De Morgan's rules (DeM.): $\sim(p \cdot q) \equiv (\sim p \vee \sim q)$
                                  $\sim(p \vee q) \equiv (\sim p \cdot \sim q)$

Each of the following is a legitimate use of this rule in the context of a proof.

m.	$\sim\sim(p \cdot q) \cdot \sim(\sim s \vee \sim r)$	
m + n.	$\sim\sim(p \cdot q) \cdot (\sim\sim s \cdot \sim\sim r)$	DeM., m

m.	$\sim(r \vee s) \vee (\sim r \cdot \sim t)$	
m + n.	$\sim(r \vee s) \vee \sim(r \vee t)$	DeM., m

Many students find the **distribution** rule to be the most difficult to remember and also the most difficult to recognize in the context of a proof. It is worth giving it special attention.

Distribution (Dist.): $(p \cdot (q \vee r)) \equiv ((p \cdot q) \vee (p \cdot r))$
                              $(p \vee (q \cdot r)) \equiv ((p \vee q) \cdot (p \vee r))$

Each of the following is a legitimate use of this rule in the context of a proof.

m.	$(s \cdot t) \cdot (r \vee p)$	
m + n.	$((s \cdot t) \cdot r) \vee ((s \cdot t) \cdot p)$	Dist., m

m.	$\sim((p \vee q) \cdot r) \vee (\sim t \cdot (s \vee t))$	
m + n.	$\sim(((p \vee q) \cdot r) \vee \sim t) \cdot (((p \vee q) \cdot r) \vee (s \vee t))$	Dist., m

EXERCISE 6-19

Provide justification for each step in the following proofs, appealing only to De Morgan's rule and distribution.

1. 1. ~(p · q)   prem.
    2. ~(p ∨ q) /∴ (~p · ~q)   prem./concl.
    3. (~p ∨ ~q)
    4. (~p · ~q)

2. 1. ~(~(p · q) ∨ (~s ∨ ~r))
        /∴ ~(~p ∨ ~q) · (~~s · ~~r)   prem./concl.
    2. ~~(p · q) · ~(~s ∨ ~r)
    3. ~~(p · q) · (~~s · ~~r)
    4. ~(~p ∨ ~q) · (~~s · ~~r)

3. 1. p · (q ∨ r)   prem.
    2. p ∨ (q · r) /∴ (p ∨ q) · (p ∨ r)   prem./concl.
    3. (p · q) ∨ (p · r)
    4. (p ∨ q) · (p ∨ r)

4. 1. (s · t) · (r ∨ p)   prem.
    2. (p ⊃ q) ∨ (t · p) /∴ ((p ⊃ q) ∨ t) · ((p ⊃ q) ∨ p)   prem./concl.
    3. ((s · t) · r) ∨ ((s · t) · p)
    4. ((p ⊃ q) ∨ t) · ((p ⊃ q) ∨ p)

5. 1. ~r · (~s ∨ ~t)   prem.
    2. ~((p ∨ q) · (p ∨ r)) /∴ ~p · ~(q · r)   prem./concl.
    3. (~r · ~s) ∨ (~r · ~t)
    4. ~(r ∨ s) ∨ (~r · ~t)
    5. ~(r ∨ s) ∨ ~(r ∨ t)
    6. ~(p ∨ (q · r))
    7. ~p · ~(q · r)

6. 1. ~((~p ∨ ~q) ∨ ~(t ∨ r))   prem.
    2. ~((p ∨ q) · r) ∨ (~t · (s ∨ t))
        /∴ ~(((p ∨ q) · r) ∨ ~t) · (((p ∨ q) · r) ∨ (s ∨ t))   prem./concl.
    3. ~(~(p · q) ∨ ~(t ∨ r))
    4. ~(~(p · q) ∨ (~t · ~r))
    5. ~~(p · q) · ~(~t · ~r)
    6. ~(((p ∨ q) · r) ∨ ~t) · (((p ∨ q) · r) ∨ (s ∨ t))

EXERCISE 6-20

Construct proofs from the premises to the conclusions given, using only distribution and De Morgan's rules.

1.   ~(p ∨ q)
    ∴ ~p · ~q

2.   ~((~p ∨ ~q) · ~(p ∨ q))
    ∴ ~~(p · q) ∨ ~(~p · ~q)

3. $(\sim(\sim p \cdot \sim q) \cdot \sim(\sim s \vee \sim r))$
    $\therefore \sim(\sim(p \vee q) \vee \sim(s \cdot r))$

4. $(p \vee q) \cdot (p \vee r)$
    $\therefore p \vee (q \cdot r)$

5. $p \cdot (q \vee (r \cdot (s \vee t)))$
    $\therefore ((p \cdot q) \vee p) \cdot ((p \cdot q) \vee ((r \cdot s) \vee (r \cdot t)))$

6. $p \vee \sim(r \vee q)$
    $\therefore (((p \vee \sim r) \cdot p) \vee (p \vee \sim r)) \cdot (((p \vee \sim r) \cdot p) \vee \sim q)$

EXERCISE 6–21

Provide justification for each step in the following proofs, using only association, commutation, De Morgan's, distribution, double negation and tautology.

1. 1. $(\sim q \vee \sim r) \cdot \sim\sim t$ /$\therefore \sim((\sim t \vee q) \cdot (\sim t \vee r))$ prem./concl.
    2. $\sim\sim t \cdot (\sim q \vee \sim r)$
    3. $(\sim\sim t \cdot \sim q) \vee (\sim\sim t \cdot \sim r)$
    4. $\sim(\sim t \vee q) \vee (\sim\sim t \cdot \sim r)$
    5. $\sim(\sim t \vee q) \vee \sim(\sim t \vee r)$
    6. $\sim((\sim t \vee q) \cdot (\sim t \vee r))$

2. 1. $\sim(s \cdot \sim r) \cdot \sim(t \vee p)$
        /$\therefore \sim((s \vee \sim r) \cdot (s \vee \sim r)) \cdot \sim(t \vee p)$ prem./concl.
    2. $\sim((s \cdot \sim r) \vee (t \vee p))$
    3. $\sim((s \cdot (\sim r \vee \sim r)) \vee (t \vee p))$
    4. $\sim(((s \cdot \sim r) \vee (s \cdot \sim r)) \vee (t \vee p))$
    5. $\sim((s \cdot \sim r) \vee (s \cdot \sim r)) \cdot \sim(t \vee p)$

3. 1. $\sim(s \vee r)$ /$\therefore \sim(s \vee r)$ prem./concl.
    2. $\sim s \cdot \sim r$
    3. $(\sim s \cdot \sim s) \cdot \sim r$
    4. $\sim s \cdot (\sim s \cdot \sim r)$
    5. $\sim s \cdot \sim(s \vee r)$
    6. $\sim(s \vee (s \vee r))$
    7. $\sim((s \vee s) \vee r)$
    8. $\sim(s \vee r)$

4. 1. $(\sim p \cdot \sim q) \cdot \sim(t \vee r)$ /$\therefore \sim(p \vee q) \cdot (\sim t \cdot \sim r)$ prem./concl.
    2. $\sim\sim((\sim p \cdot \sim q) \cdot \sim(t \vee r))$
    3. $\sim(\sim(\sim p \cdot \sim q) \vee \sim\sim(t \vee r))$
    4. $\sim(\sim\sim(p \vee q) \vee \sim\sim(t \vee r))$
    5. $\sim((p \vee q) \vee \sim\sim(t \vee r))$
    6. $\sim((p \vee q) \vee (t \vee r))$
    7. $\sim(p \vee q) \cdot \sim(t \vee r)$
    8. $\sim(p \vee q) \cdot (\sim t \cdot \sim r)$

EXERCISE 6–22

Construct proofs from the premises to the conclusions given, using only the six rules used in the previous exercise.

1. $\underline{(\sim\sim p \cdot \sim\sim q) \vee (\sim\sim p \cdot \sim\sim r)}$
   $\therefore \sim(\sim q \cdot \sim r) \cdot p$

2. $\underline{\sim\sim\sim p \vee (\sim\sim q \cdot \sim r)}$
   $\therefore(\sim\sim\sim p \vee \sim\sim q) \cdot (\sim\sim\sim p \vee \sim r)$

3. $\underline{\sim p \vee (\sim q \cdot \sim r)}$
   $\therefore ((\sim r \cdot \sim p) \vee (\sim r \cdot \sim q)) \vee (\sim p \cdot \sim(p \cdot q))$

4. $\underline{\sim r \cdot (\sim s \cdot \sim(t \vee u))}$
   $\therefore \sim((s \vee t) \vee (u \vee r))$

6.13.3 Transportation and Exportation

Two other rules that are commonly confused both involve the horseshoe. **Transportation** is similar to commutation, but it is significantly different insofar as a tilde must be added in front of the antecedent and in front of the consequent after they have been reversed.

> **Transportation (Trans.):** $(p \supset q) \equiv (\sim q \supset \sim p)$

Each of the following is a legitimate use of this rule in the context of a proof.

m.	$(p \cdot q) \supset r$	
m + n.	$\sim r \supset \sim(p \cdot q)$	Trans., m

m.	$(p \supset (\sim r \supset \sim q)) \supset (q \supset (\sim t \supset \sim r))$	
m + n.	$(\sim(\sim r \supset \sim q) \supset \sim p) \supset (q \supset (\sim t \supset \sim r))$	Trans., m

The **exportation** rule is similar to the transportation rule mainly in that it involves the horseshoe, but many people have a mental picture that connects the operation involved in one rule with the name of the other rule. It is thus important to keep these names straight as well as to be able to recognize variants of both. The exportation rule is used to move parentheses in a schema with a horseshoe as follows:

> **Exportation (Exp.):** $((p \cdot q) \supset r) \equiv (p \supset (q \supset r))$

Each of the following is a legitimate use of this rule in the context of a proof.

m.	$(\sim q \cdot r) \supset (r \supset s)$	
m + n.	$((\sim q \cdot r) \cdot r) \supset s$	Exp., m

m.	$(p \cdot q) \supset ((r \cdot s) \supset t)$	
m + n.	$(p \cdot q) \supset (r \supset (s \supset t))$	Exp., m

EXERCISE 6–23

Provide justifications for each step of the following proofs, using only transportation and exportation.

1. 1. p ⊃ (q ⊃ r) /∴ ~r ⊃ ~(p · q)   prem./ concl.
   2. (p · q) ⊃ r
   3. ~r ⊃ ~(p · q)

2. 1. (p ⊃ q) ⊃ (r ⊃ s)
         /∴ ~~~s ⊃ ~~~((p ⊃ q) · r)   prem./ concl.
   2. ((p ⊃ q) · r) ⊃ s
   3. ~s ⊃ ~((p ⊃ q) · r)
   4. ~~((p ⊃ q) · r) ⊃ ~~s
   5. ~~~s ⊃ ~~~((p ⊃ q) · r)

3. 1. ~q ⊃ (r ⊃ (r ⊃ s))
         /∴ ~s ⊃ ~(~q ⊃ (r · r))   prem./concl.
   2. (~q · r) ⊃ (r ⊃ s)
   3. ((~q · r) · r) ⊃ s
   4. ~s ⊃ ~((~q · r) · r)
   5. ~s ⊃ ~(~q ⊃ (r · r))

4. 1. ((p · q) ⊃ r) ⊃ ((q · r) ⊃ t)
         /∴ (~(~r ⊃ ~q) ⊃ ~p) ⊃ ((q · ~t) ⊃ ~r)   prem./ concl.
   2. (p ⊃ (q ⊃ r)) ⊃ ((q · r) ⊃ t)
   3. (p ⊃ (q ⊃ r)) ⊃ (q ⊃ (r ⊃ t))
   4. (p ⊃ (~r ⊃ ~q)) ⊃ (q ⊃ (r ⊃ t))
   5. (p ⊃ (~r ⊃ ~q)) ⊃ (q ⊃ (~t ⊃ ~r))
   6. (~(~r ⊃ ~q) ⊃ ~p) ⊃ (q ⊃ (~t ⊃ ~r))
   7. (~(~r ⊃ ~q) ⊃ ~p) ⊃ ((q · ~t) ⊃ ~r)

5. 1. p ⊃ (q ⊃ ((r · s) ⊃ t))
         /∴ ~((r · ~~s) ⊃ ~~t) ⊃ ~(p · q)   prem./ concl.
   2. (p · q) ⊃ ((r · s) ⊃ t)
   3. (p · q) ⊃ (r ⊃ (s ⊃ t))
   4. (p · q) ⊃ (r ⊃ (~t ⊃ ~s))
   5. (p · q) ⊃ (r ⊃ (~~s ⊃ ~~t))
   6. ~(r ⊃ (~~s ⊃ ~~t)) ⊃ ~(p · q)
   7. ~((r · ~~s) ⊃ ~~t) ⊃ ~(p · q)

6. 1. (((p · t) ⊃ s) · ~q) ⊃ ((r · s) ⊃ t)
         /∴ ~((~q · ~(s ⊃ t)) ⊃ ~r) ⊃ ~(~(t ⊃ s) ⊃ ~p) prem./ concl.
   2. ((p · t) ⊃ s) ⊃ (~q ⊃ ((r · s) ⊃ t))
   3. ((p · t) ⊃ s) ⊃ (~q ⊃ (r ⊃ (s ⊃ t)))
   4. (p ⊃ (t ⊃ s)) ⊃ (~q ⊃ (r ⊃ (s ⊃ t)))
   5. (~(t ⊃ s) ⊃ ~p) ⊃ (~q ⊃ (r ⊃ (s ⊃ t)))
   6. (~(t ⊃ s) ⊃ ~p) ⊃ (~q ⊃ (~(s ⊃ t) ⊃ ~r))

7. (~(t ⊃ s) ⊃ ~p) ⊃ ((~q · ~(s ⊃ t)) ⊃ ~r)
8. ~((~q · ~(s ⊃ t)) ⊃ ~r) ⊃ ~(~(t ⊃ s) ⊃ ~p)

EXERCISE 6–24

Construct proofs from the premises to the conclusions given, using only transportation and exportation.

1. (p · q) ⊃ (r ⊃ s)
   ∴ ~(~s ⊃ ~(q · r)) ⊃ ~p

2. ~t ⊃ (r ⊃ (r ⊃ p))
   ∴ (~t · r) ⊃ (~p ⊃ ~r)

3. ((r ⊃ t) · (s ⊃ p)) ⊃ (r ⊃ q)
   ∴ (r ⊃ t) ⊃ (~q ⊃ ~((~p ⊃ ~s) · r))

4. q ⊃ (p ⊃ ((t · s) ⊃ r))
   ∴ ~(~(t ⊃ (s ⊃ ~~r)) ⊃ ~p) ⊃ ~q

5. (((r · p) ⊃ s) · ~q) ⊃ ((r · s) ⊃ p)
   ∴ (~(p ⊃ s) ⊃ ~r) ⊃ (~q ⊃ ((r · ~p) ⊃ ~s))

6. (((p · q) · (r · s)) · t) ⊃ u
   ∴ ~~(p · q) ⊃ ~~(r ⊃ (s ⊃ (~u ⊃ ~t)))

EXERCISE 6–25

Provide justifications for each step in the following proofs, using only transportation, exportation, De Morgan's, and distribution. The first step of each is the premise and the last step is the conclusion.

1. 1. ~(p ⊃ q) · ~(t ⊃ r)   prem.
   2. ~((p ⊃ q) ∨ (t ⊃ r))
   3. ~((~q ⊃ ~p) ∨ (t ⊃ r))
   4. ~((~q ⊃ ~p) ∨ (~r ⊃ ~t))
   5. ~(~q ⊃ ~p) · ~(~r ⊃ ~t)

2. 1. (p ∨ (q · r)) ⊃ t   prem.
   2. ((p ∨ q) · (p ∨ r)) ⊃ t
   3. (p ∨ q) ⊃ ((p ∨ r) ⊃ t)
   4. ~((p ∨ r) ⊃ t) ⊃ ~(p ∨ q)
   5. ~((p ∨ r) ⊃ t) ⊃ (~p · ~q)

3. 1. (s · p) ⊃ (r ⊃ (~t · ~s))   prem.
   2. (s · p) ⊃ (r ⊃ ~(t ∨ s))
   3. ((s · p) · r) ⊃ ~(t ∨ s)
   4. ~~(t ∨ s) ⊃ ~((s · p) · r)
   5. ~~(t ∨ s) ⊃ (~(s · p) ∨ ~r)

4. 1. ((p · q) ⊃ s) ∨ (t · r)   prem.
   2. (((p · q) ⊃ s) ∨ t) · (((p · q) ⊃ s) ∨ r)
   3. ((p ⊃ (q ⊃ s)) ∨ t) · (((p · q) ⊃ s) ∨ r)
   4. ((p ⊃ (q ⊃ s)) ∨ t) · ((p ⊃ (q ⊃ s)) ∨ r)

5. $((\sim(q \supset s) \supset \sim p) \lor t) \cdot ((p \supset (q \supset s)) \lor r)$
6. $((\sim(\sim s \supset \sim q) \supset \sim p) \lor t) \cdot ((p \supset (q \supset s)) \lor r)$
7. $((\sim(\sim s \supset \sim q) \supset \sim p) \lor t) \cdot ((p \supset (\sim s \supset \sim q)) \lor r)$
8. $((\sim(\sim s \supset \sim q) \supset \sim p) \lor t) \cdot (((p \cdot \sim s) \supset \sim q) \lor r)$

EXERCISE 6–26

Construct proofs from the premises to the conclusions given.

1. $\dfrac{\sim((p \cdot u) \supset r) \supset \sim(t \lor p)}{\therefore \; \sim r \supset \sim(((t \lor p) \cdot p) \cdot u)}$

2. $\dfrac{\sim(\sim(u \cdot s) \supset \sim p) \cdot \sim(\sim r \supset \sim p)}{\therefore \; \sim(p \supset (u \cdot s)) \cdot \sim(p \supset r)}$

3. $\dfrac{\sim((t \lor (\sim s \supset \sim r)) \supset p) \supset (\sim t \cdot \sim q)}{\therefore \; (t \lor (q \cdot (r \supset s))) \supset p}$

4. $\dfrac{(\sim(p \supset (q \supset s)) \lor \sim t) \cdot (\sim(p \supset (q \supset s)) \lor \sim r)}{\therefore \; \sim((\sim s \supset \sim(p \cdot q)) \cdot (t \lor r))}$

6.13.4 Material Implication and Material Equivalence

The final two equivalence rules are essentially alternative definitions of the three-line and horseshoe operators. The **material implication** rule, especially the dot version of it, will be extremely useful in the system of quantificational logic that is presented in the next chapter.

Material Implication (Impl.): $(p \supset q) \equiv (\sim p \lor q)$
$(p \supset q) \equiv \sim(p \cdot \sim q)$

Each of the following is a legitimate use of this rule in the context of a proof.

m.	$((p \cdot q) \supset \sim t) \cdot (\sim t \supset (p \cdot q))$	
m + n.	$(\sim(p \cdot q) \lor \sim t) \cdot (\sim t \supset (p \cdot q))$	Impl., m
m.	$((p \supset q) \supset (r \equiv s)) \supset (t \supset p)$	
m + n.	$((p \supset q) \supset (r \equiv s)) \supset \sim(t \cdot \sim p)$	Impl., m

Careful consideration of the **material equivalence** rule is not only helpful for developing skills needed for constructing proofs; it will also increase your understanding of this sometimes obscure operator.

Material Equivalence (Equiv.): $(p \equiv q) \equiv ((p \supset q) \cdot (q \supset p))$
$(p \equiv q) \equiv ((p \cdot q) \lor (\sim p \cdot \sim q))$

Each of the following is a legitimate use of this rule in the context of a proof.

m.	$(\sim(p \cdot q) \lor r) \equiv s$	
m + n.	$((\sim(p \cdot q) \lor r) \supset s) \cdot (s \supset (\sim(p \cdot q) \lor r))$	Equiv., m
m.	$((p \supset q) \supset (r \equiv s)) \supset \sim(t \cdot \sim p)$	
m + n.	$((p \supset q) \supset ((r \supset s) \cdot (s \supset r))) \supset \sim(t \cdot \sim p)$	Equiv., m

Provide justification for each step in the following proofs, using only material implication and material equivalence. The first step of each is the premise and the last step is the conclusion.

1. 1. p ≡ q   prem.
   2. (p ⊃ q) · (q ⊃ p)
   3. (~p ∨ q) · (q ⊃ p)
   4. (~p ∨ q) · ~(q · ~p)

2. 1. ((p · q) · ~t) ∨ (~(p · q) · ~~t)   prem.
   2. (p · q) ≡ ~t
   3. ((p · q) ⊃ ~t) · (~t ⊃ (p · q))
   4. (~(p · q) ∨ ~t) · (~t ⊃ (p · q))
   5. (~(p · q) ∨ ~t) · ~(~t · ~(p · q))

3. 1. (p ⊃ q) ≡ (t ⊃ r)   prem.
   2. ((p ⊃ q) · (t ⊃ r)) ∨ (~(p ⊃ q) · ~(t ⊃ r))
   3. ((~p ∨ q) · (t ⊃ r)) ∨ (~(p ⊃ q) · ~(t ⊃ r))
   4. ((~p ∨ q) · ~(t · ~r)) ∨ (~(p ⊃ q) · ~(t ⊃ r))
   5. ((~p ∨ q) · ~(t · ~r)) ∨ (~~(p · ~q) · ~(t ⊃ r))
   6. ((~p ∨ q) · ~(t · ~r)) ∨ (~~(p · ~q) · ~(~t ∨ r))

4. 1. (((p · q) ⊃ r) ⊃ s) · (s ⊃ ((p · q) ⊃ r))   prem.
   2. ((p · q) ⊃ r) ≡ s
   3. (~(p · q) ∨ r) ≡ s
   4. ((~(p · q) ∨ r) ⊃ s) · (s ⊃ (~(p · q) ∨ r))
   5. ((~(p · q) ∨ r) ⊃ s) · ~(s · ~(~(p · q) ∨ r))
   6. (~(~(p · q) ∨ r) ∨ s) · ~(s · ~(~(p · q) ∨ r))

5. 1. ((p ⊃ q) ⊃ (r ≡ s)) ⊃ (t ⊃ p)   prem.
   2. ((p ⊃ q) ⊃ (r ≡ s)) ⊃ ~(t · ~p)
   3. ((p ⊃ q) ⊃ ((r ⊃ s) · (s ⊃ r))) ⊃ ~(t · ~p)
   4. ((p ⊃ q) ⊃ ((r ⊃ s) · (~s ∨ r))) ⊃ ~(t · ~p)
   5. ((p ⊃ q) ⊃ ((~r ∨ s) · (~s ∨ r))) ⊃ ~(t · ~p)
   6. (~(p · ~q) ⊃ ((~r ∨ s) · (~s ∨ r))) ⊃ ~(t · ~p)
   7. (~~(p · ~q) ∨ ((~r ∨ s) · (~s ∨ r))) ⊃ ~(t · ~p)
   8. ~((~~(p · ~q) ∨ ((~r ∨ s) · (~s ∨ r))) · ~~(t · ~p))

Construct proofs from the premises to the conclusions given, using only material implication, material equivalence, and double negation.

1.   (~r ∨ (p · q)) · ~((p · q) · ~r)
   ∴ (r · (p · q)) ∨ (~r · ~(p · q))

2.   ((~p ∨ s) · ~(t · ~q)) ∨ (~~(p · ~s) · ~(~t ∨ q))
   ∴ (p ⊃ s) ≡ (t ⊃ q)

3. $(\sim q \lor \sim(t \lor p)) \cdot \sim(\sim(t \lor p) \cdot \sim q)$
    ∴ $\overline{(q \cdot \sim(t \lor p)) \lor (\sim q \cdot \sim\sim(t \lor p))}$

4. $(\sim(\sim q \lor r) \lor s) \cdot \sim(s \cdot \sim(\sim q \lor r))$
    ∴ $\overline{((q \supset r) \supset s) \cdot \sim\sim(s \supset (q \supset r))}$

5. $((p \equiv q) \supset t) \equiv (\sim(s \cdot \sim t) \supset u)$
    ∴ $\overline{((\sim((\sim p \lor q) \supset (q \cdot \sim p)) \supset t) \supset (\sim(s \cdot \sim t) \supset u))}$
    $\cdot (((\sim(s \cdot \sim t) \supset u) \supset (((\sim p \lor q) \cdot \sim(q \cdot \sim p)) \supset t))$

6. $((q \supset u) \supset ((p \cdot r) \equiv s)) \supset (t \supset q)$
    ∴ $\overline{(\sim(q \cdot \sim u) \supset ((\sim(p \cdot r) \lor s) \cdot (\sim s \lor (p \cdot r)))) \supset \sim(t \cdot \sim q)}$

EXERCISE 6–29

Provide justification for each step in the following proofs, using only material implication, material equivalence, transportation, exportation, and double negation. The first step of each is the premise and the last step is the conclusion.

1. 1. $p \equiv q$ prem.
    2. $(p \supset q) \cdot (q \supset p)$
    3. $(\sim p \lor q) \cdot (q \supset p)$
    4. $(\sim p \lor q) \cdot (\sim p \supset \sim q)$

2. 1. $((p \supset q) \cdot r) \lor (\sim(p \supset q) \cdot \sim r)$ prem.
    2. $(p \supset q) \equiv r$
    3. $((p \supset q) \supset r) \cdot (r \supset (p \supset q))$
    4. $((p \supset q) \supset r) \cdot ((r \cdot p) \supset q)$
    5. $((p \supset q) \supset r) \cdot (\sim q \supset \sim(r \cdot p))$

3. 1. $(p \supset (s \supset t)) \equiv r$ prem.
    2. $((p \supset (s \supset t)) \supset r) \cdot (r \supset (p \supset (s \supset t)))$
    3. $((p \supset (\sim t \supset \sim s)) \supset r) \cdot (r \supset (p \supset (s \supset t)))$
    4. $((p \supset (\sim t \supset \sim s)) \supset r) \cdot ((r \cdot p) \supset (s \supset t))$
    5. $((\sim p \lor (\sim t \supset \sim s)) \supset r) \cdot ((r \cdot p) \supset (s \supset t))$
    6. $((\sim p \lor (\sim t \supset \sim s)) \supset r) \cdot (((r \cdot p) \cdot s) \supset t)$
    7. $((\sim p \lor \sim(\sim t \cdot \sim\sim s)) \supset r) \cdot (((r \cdot p) \cdot s) \supset t)$

4. 1. $(p \equiv q) \supset (q \equiv r)$ prem.
    2. $((p \supset q) \cdot (q \supset p)) \supset (q \equiv r)$
    3. $((p \supset q) \cdot (q \supset p)) \supset ((q \cdot r) \lor (\sim q \cdot \sim r))$
    4. $((\sim q \supset \sim p) \cdot (q \supset p)) \supset ((q \cdot r) \lor (\sim q \cdot \sim r))$
    5. $((\sim q \supset \sim p) \cdot \sim(q \cdot \sim p)) \supset ((q \cdot r) \lor (\sim q \cdot \sim r))$
    6. $\sim((\sim q \supset \sim p) \supset (q \cdot \sim p)) \supset ((q \cdot r) \lor (\sim q \cdot \sim r))$
    7. $\sim\sim((\sim q \supset \sim p) \supset (q \cdot \sim p)) \lor ((q \cdot r) \lor (\sim q \cdot \sim r))$
    8. $\sim\sim(\sim(\sim q \supset \sim p) \lor (q \cdot \sim p)) \lor ((q \cdot r) \lor (\sim q \cdot \sim r))$

5. 1. $(p \equiv r) \cdot \sim r$ prem.
    2. $((p \supset r) \cdot (r \supset p)) \cdot \sim r$
    3. $\sim\sim(((p \supset r) \cdot (r \supset p)) \cdot \sim r)$
    4. $\sim(((p \supset r) \cdot (r \supset p)) \supset r)$

5. ~((p ⊃ r) ⊃ ((r ⊃ p) ⊃ r))
6. ~((p ⊃ r) ⊃ (~r ⊃ ~(r ⊃ p)))
7. ~((p ⊃ r) ⊃ (~r ⊃ ~(~r ∨ p)))
8. ~(~(p ⊃ r) ∨ (~r ⊃ ~(~r ∨ p)))

6. 1. ~(~p ∨ q) ≡ (t ≡ r)   prem.
   2. ~(p ⊃ q) ≡ (t ≡ r)
   3. ~(p ⊃ q) ≡ ((t · r) ∨ (~t · ~r))
   4. ~~(p · ~q) ≡ ((t · r) ∨ (~t · ~r))
   5. (~~(p · ~q) · ((t · r) ∨ (~t · ~r))) ∨ ~(~~(p · ~q) · ~ ((t · r) ∨ (~t · ~r)))

EXERCISE 6–30

Construct proofs from the premises to the conclusions given, using only material implication, material equivalence, transportation, and exportation.

1. (~s ∨ t) · (~s ⊃ ~t)
    ∴ (s · t) ∨ (~s · ~t)

2. (t ⊃ (p ⊃ r)) · (~t ⊃ ~(p ⊃ r))
    ∴ (t · (p ⊃ r)) ∨ (~t · ~(p ⊃ r))

3. ((~q ∨ ~(~s · ~~t)) ⊃ p) · (((p · q) · t) ⊃ s)
    ∴ (q ⊃ (t ⊃ s)) ≡ p

4. ((t ⊃ q) · (q ⊃ t)) ⊃ ((q · r) ∨ (~q · ~r))
    ∴ ((t · q) ∨ (~t · ~q)) ⊃ ((~r ⊃ ~q) · ~(r · ~q))

5. ((p ⊃ s) ⊃ (~s ⊃ ~(~s ∨ p)))
    ∴ ~((p ≡ s) · ~s)

6. (~p ∨ t) ≡ (t ≡ s)
    ∴ (~(p · ~t) · ((t · s) ∨ (~t · ~s))) ∨ (~~(p · ~t) · ~((t · s) ∨ (~t · ~s)))

EXERCISE 6–31

Provide justification for each step in the following proofs, using any of the ten equivalence rules. The first step of each is the premise and the last step is the conclusion.

1. 1. ~~~p ≡ (p · (t ⊃ s))   prem.
   2. ~~~p ≡ ((t ⊃ s) · p)
   3. ~~~p ≡ ((~t ∨ s) · p)
   4. ~~~p ≡ ((~t ∨ (s ∨ s)) · p)
   5. p ≡ ((~t ∨ (s ∨ s)) · p)

2. 1. ~(p · ~q) ⊃ (r · (~s ∨ t))   prem.
   2. ~(p · ~q) ⊃ (r · (s ⊃ t))
   3. (~p ∨ ~~q) ⊃ (r · (s ⊃ t))
   4. (p ⊃ ~~q) ⊃ (r · (s ⊃ t))
   5. (p ⊃ q) ⊃ (r · (s ⊃ t))
   6. ~(r · (s ⊃ t)) ⊃ ~(p ⊃ q)

3. 1. p ≡ q   prem.
   2. (p ⊃ q) · (q ⊃ p)
   3. (~q ⊃ ~p) · (q ⊃ p)
   4. (~~p ⊃ ~~q) · (q ⊃ p)
   5. (p ⊃ ~~q) · (q ⊃ p)

4. 1. s · (r · (t ∨ p))   prem.
   2. s · ((r · t) ∨ (r · p))
   3. (s · s) · ((r · t) ∨ (r · p))
   4. (s · s) · ((r · p) ∨ (r · t))
   5. (s · (s · ((r · p) ∨ (r · t)))

5. 1. (p · (q · r)) · (p ∨ (q · r))   prem.
   2. ((p · q) · r) · (p ∨ (q · r))
   3. ((p · q) · r) · ((p ∨ q) · (p ∨ r))
   4. ((q · p) · r) · ((p ∨ q) · (p ∨ r))
   5. ~~((q · p) · r) · ((p ∨ q) · (p ∨ r))
   6. ~~((q · p) · ~~r) · ((p ∨ q) · (p ∨ r))
   7. ~((q · p) ⊃ ~r) · ((p ∨ q) · (p ∨ r))

6. 1. ~~p ≡ (p · (t ⊃ s))   prem.
   2. ~~p ≡ ((t ⊃ s) · p)
   3. ~~p ≡ ((~t ∨ s) · p)
   4. ~~p ≡ ((~t ∨ (s ∨ s)) · p)
   5. p ≡ ((~t ∨ (s ∨ s)) · p)
   6. (p ⊃ ((~t ∨ (s ∨ s)) · p)) · (((~t ∨ (s ∨ s)) · p)) ⊃ p)

7. 1. p ≡ (s ⊃ t)   prem.
   2. (p ⊃ (s ⊃ t)) · ((s ⊃ t) ⊃ p)
   3. ((p · s) ⊃ t) · ((s ⊃ t) ⊃ p)
   4. ((s ⊃ t) ⊃ p) · ((p · s) ⊃ t)
   5. (~p ⊃ ~(s ⊃ t)) · ((p · s) ⊃ t)
   6. (~p ⊃ ~~(s · ~t)) · ((p · s) ⊃ t)
   7. (~p ⊃ (s · ~t)) · ((p · s) ⊃ t)
   8. (~p ⊃ (s · ~t)) · (~t ⊃ ~(p · s))

8. 1. (p · t) ⊃ (r · s)   prem.
   2. p ⊃ (t ⊃ (r · s))
   3. p ⊃ (~(r · s) ⊃ ~t)
   4. p ⊃ ~(~(r · s) · ~~t)
   5. p ⊃ (~~(r · s) ∨ ~~~t)
   6. p ⊃ ((r · s) ∨ ~~~t)
   7. p ⊃ ((r · s) ∨ ~t)
   8. p ⊃ (~t ∨ (r · s))
   9. p ⊃ (t ⊃ (r · s))

9. 1. (t · s) ∨ (r · ~p)   prem.
   2. (t · s) ∨ ~~(r · ~p)

    3. (t · s) ∨ ~(r ⊃ p)
    4. ~~(t · s) ∨ ~(r ⊃ p)
    5. ~(~(t · s) · (r ⊃ p))
    6. ~(~(t · s) · ~(r · ~p))
    7. ~(~(t · s) · (~r ∨ ~~p))
    8. ~(~(t · s) · (~r ∨ p))

10. 1. ~(s ∨ (p · q)) ⊃ p   prem.
       2. (~s · ~(p · q)) ⊃ p
       3. ~(~s · ~(p · q)) ∨ p
       4. ~(~s · ~(q · p)) ∨ p
       5. ~(~s · ~(q · p)) ∨ (p · p)
       6. (~~s ∨ ~~(q · p)) ∨ (p · p)
       7. (~s ⊃ ~~(q · p)) ∨ (p · p)
       8. (~s ⊃ (q · p)) ∨ (p · p)
       9. ~~(~s ⊃ (q · p)) ∨ (p · p)
    10. ~(~s ⊃ (q · p)) ⊃ (p · p)

EXERCISE 6–32

Construct proofs from the premises to the conclusions given, using only the ten equivalence rules.

1.   (p · (s · t)) ⊃ t
   ∴ (t ∨ ~(s · t)) ∨ ~p

2.   (t · (s ∨ r)) ⊃ p
   ∴ p ∨ (~(t · s) · ~(t · r))

3.   (s ∨ t) ≡ (p · q)
   ∴ (~(s ∨ t) ⊃ ~(p · q)) · (~(s ∨ t) ∨ (p · q))

4.   t ⊃ ((p · s) ⊃ r)
   ∴ r ∨ (~t ∨ (~p ∨ ~s))

5.   t · ((s ⊃ p) ∨ (r ⊃ u))
   ∴ (t · (p ∨ ~s)) ∨ ((t · ~r) ∨ (t · u))

6.   (p ∨ (q ⊃ s)) · (p ∨ (r ⊃ t))
   ∴ p ∨ ~(~(~q ∨ s) ∨ ~(~t ⊃ ~r))

7.   ~(t ⊃ s) · ~(~(p · q) ⊃ r)
   ∴ ~((~s ⊃ ~t) ∨ ((~p ∨ ~q) ⊃ (r · r)))

8.   ((~s ∨ r) · ~(t ∨ p)) ⊃ (~q ∨ ~u)
   ∴ ~((~t · ~p) ⊃ ~(q · u)) ⊃ (s · ~r)

9.   ((p · q) · (r · s)) ⊃ t
   ∴ ~(~(r ⊃ (~~t ∨ ~s)) ⊃ ~q) ⊃ ~p

10. (p · q) ⊃ r
   ∴ (~p ∨ (~q ∨ r)) · (p ⊃ (q ⊃ r))

EXERCISE 6–33

Identify which inference rule can be used to justify the inference from step n to step n+1 in each of the following argument schemas. Identify the various forms of the rule of replacement by their specific names. In the event that a particular inference cannot be justified by any of the rules, identify it as 'error.'

1. n. $p \supset (q \vee r)$
    n + 1. $\sim(q \vee r) \supset \sim p$

2. n. $r \supset s$
    n + 1. $(r \supset s) \vee q$

3. n. $s \vee q$
    n + 1. $\sim(\sim s \cdot \sim q)$

4. n. $(s \vee q) \cdot (p \supset r)$
    n + 1. $(s \vee q) \cdot (\sim p \vee r)$

5. n. $p \cdot (q \vee s)$
    n + 1. $q \vee s$

6. n. $(p \cdot \sim(t \supset \sim r))$
    n + 1. $(p \cdot (t \supset r))$

7. n. $r \supset \sim q$
    n + 1. $(r \vee s) \supset \sim q$

8. n. $(u \supset r) \cdot (\sim s \vee v)$
    n + 1. $(u \supset r) \cdot (s \supset v)$

9. n. $(s \equiv r) \vee (p \supset (q \supset u))$
    n + 1. $(s \equiv r) \vee ((p \cdot q) \supset u)$

10. n. $(p \equiv t) \cdot (r \vee (s \supset q))$
    n + 1. $((p \supset t) \cdot (t \supset p)) \cdot (r \vee (s \supset q))$

11. n. $\sim(p \vee \sim t) \cdot (s \equiv u)$
    n + 1. $(\sim p \cdot \sim\sim t) \cdot (s \equiv u)$

12. n. $\sim r \vee (s \cdot q)$
    n + 1. $\sim r \vee q$

13. n. $(r \supset s) \vee (t \cdot \sim u)$
    n + 1. $((r \supset s) \cdot t) \vee ((r \supset s) \cdot \sim u)$

14. n. $(\sim s \equiv (t \vee q)) \supset r$
    n + 1. $((\sim s \equiv (t \vee q)) \supset r) \vee (p \cdot \sim r)$

6.13.5 Some Sample Proofs

The equivalence rules not only simplify some proofs, they also enable us to prove the validity of some argument schemas that cannot be proved valid using only the eight original rules of inference, although such schemas can be shown to be valid using the truth table method. The following is such an argument:

If John is Peter's brother, then Mary is Peter's sister.
If Mary is John's sister, then Mary is not Peter's sister.
Therefore, if John is Peter's brother, then Mary is not John's sister.

The abbreviation and schema for this intended argument are

$$J \supset P \qquad\qquad\qquad\qquad p \supset q$$
$$M \supset \sim P \qquad\qquad\qquad\qquad r \supset \sim q$$
$$\therefore \overline{J \supset \sim M} \qquad\qquad\qquad\qquad \therefore \overline{p \supset \sim r}$$

By using the equivalence rules as well as our eight original rules, we can prove the validity of this argument schema:

1. p ⊃ q	Premise
2. r ⊃ ~q /∴ p ⊃ ~ r	Premise/conclusion
3. ~~q ⊃ ~r	Trans., 2
4. q ⊃ ~r	D.N., 3
5. p ⊃ ~r	H.Syll., 1,4

Notice that on line 4 we justify the schema 'q ⊃ ~r' by double negation, even though we apply it to only a subcomponent of the schema in line 3 ('~~q ⊃ ~r'). As indicated earlier, when using the replacement rule, we may substitute logically equivalent schemas whenever they occur, either as a whole step or as part of a step—as cannot be done with the eight original inference rules.

Consider one more example:

$$(p \supset q) \cdot (r \supset s)$$
$$p \vee r$$
$$\underline{(p \supset \sim s) \cdot (r \supset \sim q)}$$
$$\therefore s \equiv \sim q$$

Examining this schema to formulate a strategy, we can see that only the variables 's' and 'q' appear in the conclusion, thereby indicating that we must eliminate 'p' and 'r' which appear in the premises but not the conclusion. This can be accomplished most simply by using constructive dilemma as shown below:

1. (p ⊃ q) · (r ⊃ s)	premise
2. p ∨ r	premise
3. (p ⊃ ~s) · (r ⊃ ~q) /∴ s ≡ ~q	premise/conclusion
4. q ∨ s	Dil., 1,2
5. ~s ∨ ~q	Dil., 3,2

Working backward from the conclusion of the original argument schema ('s ≡ ~q'), we can see that it is a biconditional. In our list of equivalences, only the material equivalence rule has a component that is itself a biconditional, so we need to find a way to use the equivalence rule in the proof. But this rule can be used only with a conjunction of two material implications—(p ≡ q) ≡ ((p ⊃ q) · (q ⊃ p))—or with the disjunction of two conjunctions—(p ≡ q) ≡ ((p · q) ∨ (~p · ~q)). We have reduced our argument to the two variables ('q' and 's') that appear in the conclusion, but they appear in disjunctive propositions (see lines 4 and 5). Consequently, we must somehow transform the disjunctions of lines 4 and 5 into either material implications or conjunctions. The material implication rule—(p ⊃ q) ≡ (~p ∨ q)—permits us to replace a disjunction with its logically equivalent material implication. Thus, we can complete our proof as below:

6.	~~q ∨ s	D.N., 4
7.	s ⊃ ~q	Impl., 5
8.	~q ⊃ s	Impl., 6
9.	(s ⊃ ~q) · (~q ⊃ s)	Conj., 7,8
10.	s ≡ ~q	Equiv., 9

Notice that, since the rule of rigor does not permit us to apply two rules in one step of a proof, it is necessary (in Step 6) to apply double negation to step 4 before using implication in line 8.

This proof is intended as a guide, to show one way to go about constructing a formal deductive proof of the validity of a complex argument schema. Although the strategy used in this proof is a good one, it must be emphasized that there is no one correct formal deductive proof for a particular argument schema. As noted earlier, an infinite number of different logically correct proofs could be constructed for any one schema, using the eighteen rules presented thus far—though most of the proofs would be somewhat long and complex. The knowledge of how and when to use particular strategies can come only from extensive practice and experience with constructing such deductive proofs.

Reprinted by permission of UFS, Inc.

Write out the argument given in this cartoon and prove its validity using the rules of the propositional calculus. If you can't construct a proof of its validity, use the short truth table method to see if it's truth functionally invalid. If it's truth-functionally invalid, then reformulate your interpretation of the cartoon so that it becomes valid.

EXERCISE 6–34

Using the rules of inference discussed thus far, including the ten equivalence rules, construct a proof to demonstrate the validity of each of the following argument schemas.

1. ~p
    ∴ ~(p · q)

2. ~p · ~q
    (p ∨ q) ∨ (r ∨ s)
    ∴ r ∨ s

3. p
    ~q ⊃ ~p
    ∴ q

4. p
    ~p ∨ q
    q ≡ r
    ∴ r

5. p
    q ∨ (r · s)
    ~q ∨ ~p
    ∴ s

6. p ∨ q
    (q ∨ p) ⊃ (r ∨ s)
    (s ∨ r) ⊃ ~q
    ∴ p

7. q ⊃ (p · r)
    ~p
    ∴ ~q

8. p ∨ (q ∨ r)
    (p ∨ q) ⊃ ~s
    ~r
    ∴ ~s

9. ~r · ~s
    (p ∨ q) ⊃ (r ∨ s)
    ∴ ~(p ∨ q)

10. ~r · ~s
    (p ∨ q) ⊃ (r ∨ s)
    ∴ ~(p · q)

11. p ⊃ (q ⊃ r)
    ~r
    ∴ ~(p · q)

12. ~p
    ~q
    ~(p ∨ q) ⊃ (p ∨ r)
    ∴ r

13. ~p
    ~(p · q) ⊃ (~p ⊃ r)
    ∴ r

14. ~r
    (p · q) ⊃ (r · s)
    ∴ ~p ∨ ~q

15. ~(p ∨ q)
    r ⊃ p
    s ⊃ q
    ∴ ~(r ∨ s)

16. ~r · ~s
    (p ∨ q) ⊃ (r ∨ s)
    ∴ ~q

17. ~r · ~s
    (p ∨ q) ⊃ (r ∨ s)
    ∴ ~q ∨ t

18. ~r · ~s
    (p ∨ q) ⊃ (r ∨ s)
    ∴ ~q · ~r

19. ~r · ~s
    (p ∨ q) ⊃ (r ∨ s)
    ∴ ~(p · q)

20. ~r ∨ ~s
    ~(r · s) ⊃ (p · q)
    ∴ q ∨ t

21. ~(q ∨ ~p)
    (p · ~q) ⊃ (p ⊃ r)
    r ⊃ s
    ∴ p ⊃ s

22. p ⊃ q
    (r ∨ s) ⊃ p
    (~p ∨ q) ⊃ s
    ∴ q

23.   ~(p ⊃ q)
       p ⊃ r
       s ⊃ q
   ∴ ~(r ⊃ s)

24.   ~(p · q)
       (p ⊃ ~q) ⊃ (~(p · q) ⊃ r)
   ∴ r

25.   p
       q
   ∴ p ≡ q

26.   ~p ∨ q
       (p ⊃ q) ⊃ (p ⊃ r)
   ∴ p ⊃ r

27.   ~p ∨ q
       (p ⊃ q) ⊃ (p ⊃ r)
       p
   ∴ r

28.   ~p ∨ q
       (p ⊃ q) ⊃ (p ⊃ r)
       p
   ∴ q · r

29.   ~(p · ~q)
       (p ⊃ q) ⊃ (p ⊃ r)
   ∴ p ⊃ r

30.   p · ~r
       (p ⊃ q) ⊃ (p ⊃ r)
   ∴ p · ~q

31.   p · (q ∨ r)
       ~(p · r)
   ∴ q

32.   p · (q ∨ r)
       ~p
   ∴ q

33.   (p · q) ⊃ r
       (p · r) ⊃ q
       p
   ∴ r ≡ q

34.   (p · q) ≡ (r ∨ s)
       r
   ∴ p · r

35.   ~p ∨ (q · r)
       r ⊃ p
   ∴ p ≡ r

6.14 Conditional Proof

Not every argument that can be proved valid using truth tables can be proved valid using our eighteen rules of inference. Consider, for example, the following argument:

> John is a doctor or Susan is a doctor.
> Therefore, if John is not a doctor then John is not a doctor and Susan is a doctor.

The abbreviation and schema for this argument are:

    J ∨ S   p ∨ q
∴ ~J ⊃ (~J · S)   ∴ ~p ⊃ (~p · q)

We can show this particular argument schema to be valid by introducing a new rule called the rule of **conditional proof**. Notice that the conclusion of this argument schema is a conditional proposition. Conditional proof is most commonly used in arguments with such conclusions, although it can also be used in other contexts. The method of conditional proof requires assuming an additional premise, which is actually the antecedent of a conditional statement that is necessary in the proof, and then deducing the consequent of the desired statement from the assumption and the original premises.

Let's first present a conditional proof for the above argument schema and then discuss each step:

1. $p \lor q \; / \therefore \; \sim p \supset (\sim p \cdot q)$	Premise/conclusion
2. $\sim p$	Assumption
3. q	D.Syll., 1,2
4. $\sim p \cdot q$	Conj., 2,3
5. $\sim p \supset (\sim p \cdot q)$	C.P., 2–4

We set up the premise and conclusion in line 1 in exactly the same way as in our other deductive proofs. In line 2 we assert our assumed premise, '$\sim p$,' which is the antecedent of the conditional conclusion, and label it as an assumption. In line 3, we deduce the statement 'q' from lines 1 and 2 by means of disjunctive syllogism. In line 4, we use conjunction to deduce the statement '$\sim p \cdot q$,' which is the consequent of the conditional conclusion. Then, in step 5, we deduce the conclusion statement '$\sim p \supset (\sim p \cdot q)$' from lines 2 and 4 by means of the rule of conditional proof (C.P.).

In this proof, premises 2, 3, and 4 are marked off by a line with an arrow pointing to line 2 (the assumed premise), which then extends downward and finally crosses beneath line 4. This line indicates the **scope** of our assumption; that is, lines 3 and 4 can be validly deduced from the premises *only* by assuming '$\sim p$' as an additional premise. As soon as we assert the rule of conditional proof, we end the scope of the assumption, that is, the assumption is said to be **discharged.** Line 5 of the proof is not dependent on our assumed premise; it is dependent only on the original premise of the argument, because what it says is that *if* $\sim p$ is assumed, *then* ($\sim p \cdot q$) is true.

In effect, the rule of conditional proof is a straightforward application of our definition of material implication. A formal statement of this new inference rule is:

> ***The following procedure can be inserted at any point in a proof,*** **provided that none of the formulae derived within the lined-off area are used outside this portion of the proof:**

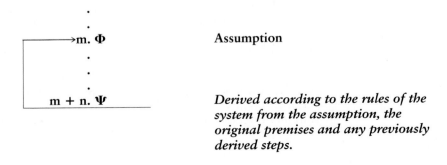

m. Φ	Assumption
m + n. Ψ	*Derived according to the rules of the system from the assumption, the original premises and any previously derived steps.*

$$m + n + 1. \; \Phi \supset \Psi \qquad\qquad C.P., \; m - (m + n)$$
.
.
.

All that is being said in step m + n + 1 is that if Φ is true, then Ψ is also true.

The step ending the conditional proof *must* be a conditional statement with the assumed premise as its antecedent. Also, as the formal statement of the rule indicates, no step from inside the scope of the assumption—that is, from inside the line marking off the conditional proof—can be used *outside* that assumption. Thus, in our example, one could not use step 3 ('q') at any point in the proof after the line between steps 4 and 5, which discharges the assumption. Step 3 could be used after this only if it could be derived again, independently of the assumption '~p'—which, in this particular case, is impossible. Our proof demonstrates that, given 'p ∨ q,' then if '~p' then '~p · q.' In terms of the propositions of our original example, we have shown that given 'John is a doctor or Susan is a doctor,' then *if* 'John is not a doctor' is true, then 'John is not a doctor and Susan is a doctor' is also true.

The rule of conditional proof does more than enable us to prove the validity of arguments whose validity cannot be proved using only the eighteen rules discussed earlier. It is a powerful tool that also enables us to prove in relatively few steps the validity of complex arguments which require numerous steps

---

In other words the argument goes like this: If we don't have CRP, the Soviet Union could evacuate its cities, do something provocative, and dare us to attack, knowing that we couldn't evacuate our cities (except spontaneously and haphazardly in preparation for their counterattack. If we do have CRP, and the Soviet Union evacuates its cities and does something provocative, then we could evacuate our cities, giving the Russians good reason to think we would *dare to attack. However, since the Russians would be well aware that we have CRP and could match their evacuation with our evacuation, they would be less likely to evacuate in the first place, or, for that matter, to do something provocative. Thus, if we have CRP, it is unlikely that we will need it. We need it only if we don't have it. And we don't have it. So we need it.*

Not everyone agrees with this logic. "It's a crazy way to spend money," Representative Aspin says. "If they evacuate, we have them *in a blackmail situation. How long can they sit out in the countryside with their cities and all their industries sitting idle?"*

ED ZUCKERMAN,
"Hiding from the Bomb Again," Harper's, *July, 1979.*

Use the propositional calculus to test the validity of these two arguments from near the end of the "Cold War" period—one in support of and one opposed to the U.S. Defense Department's program called Crisis Relocation Planning (CRP). Consider the extent to which this kind of reasoning might have contributed to the eventual "thawing" of relations between the United States and Russia.

when we use only the eighteen rules. For example, consider the following conditional proof:

1. $(q \lor r) \cdot (s \lor p)$
   $/\therefore \sim s \supset (p \cdot (q \lor r))$ Premise/conclusion
→ 2. $\sim s$ Assumption
3. $s \lor p$ Simp., 1
4. p D.Syll., 2,3
5. $q \lor r$ Simp., 1
6. $p \cdot (q \lor r)$ Conj., 4,5
7. $\sim s \supset p \cdot (q \lor r)$ C.P., 2–6

You might wish to try constructing a formal deductive proof for this same argument schema using only the eighteen rules, without conditional proof. It can be done, but it takes so many steps that the attempt should suffice to demonstrate the great convenience of this additional rule.

Of course, we are not limited to making only one assumption in a proof. Any number of assumptions can be made, provided they are each eventually discharged, leaving the conclusion dependent only on the premise(s) of the original argument schema. Consider, for example, the following conditional proof, which uses two assumed premises:

1. $\sim p \lor (q \supset r)$ Premise
2. $\sim q \lor (r \supset s)$
   $/\therefore p \supset (q \supset s)$ Premise/conclusion
→ 3. p Assumption
→ 4. q Assumption
5. $\sim\sim p$ D.N., 3
6. $q \supset r$ D.Syll., 1,5
7. r M.P., 4,6
8. $\sim\sim q$ D.N., 4
9. $r \supset s$ D.Syll., 2,8
10. s M.P., 7,9
11. $q \supset s$ C.P., 4–10
12. $p \supset (q \supset s)$ C.P., 3–11

Notice that the scope of the second assumption, 'q,' carries through line 10. What we have done in lines 4 through 10 is derive the consequent of the conclusion. The second assumption is contained within the scope of the first assumption, since line 6 is justified by lines 1 and 5, and line 5 is derived from our first assumption. Therefore, line 11, which is justified by lines 4 through 10, cannot be derived without the assumption of line 3 as well.

EXERCISE 6–35

Prove the validity of the following argument schemas using the rules of inference including conditional proof.

1. $p \supset q$
    $\therefore p \supset (p \cdot q)$

2. $(p \supset q) \cdot (r \supset s)$
    $\therefore (p \lor r) \supset (q \lor s)$

3. $(p \lor q) \supset (r \cdot s)$
    $\therefore \sim s \supset \sim q$

4. $(p \lor q) \supset r$
    $\therefore ((r \lor s) \supset t) \supset (p \supset t)$

5. $p \supset (q \supset r)$
    $\therefore (\sim r \cdot s) \supset (q \supset \sim p)$

6. q
    $\therefore p \supset (p \cdot q)$

7. $p \supset (q \supset r)$
    $\therefore (p \cdot q) \supset r$

8. $p \supset (q \supset r)$
    $p \supset q$
    $\therefore p \supset r$

9. $q \supset r$
    $\therefore p \supset (q \supset (r \lor s))$

10. $p \supset r$
    $\therefore p \supset (q \supset (r \lor s))$

11. $(p \lor q) \supset (r \equiv s)$
    $\sim(\sim s \cdot p)$
    $\sim t \supset \sim r$
    $\therefore p \supset (t \cdot r)$

12. $\sim p \lor \sim(q \cdot r)$
    $\therefore q \supset (r \supset \sim p)$

13. $\sim p \supset (q \supset r)$
    $s \supset q$
    $\therefore s \supset (\sim p \supset r)$

14. $p \supset q$
    $\therefore (p \cdot r) \supset q$

15. $(p \cdot q) \supset r$
    $\therefore p \supset (q \supset r)$

16. $(p \cdot q) \lor (r \cdot s)$
    $\therefore \sim p \supset (r \cdot s)$

17. $p \cdot (q \lor r)$
    $\therefore \sim q \supset (p \cdot r)$

18. $r \equiv s$
    $p \lor r$
    $\therefore \sim p \supset (r \cdot s)$

19. s
    $\therefore p \supset (q \supset (r \supset s))$

20. r
    $\therefore p \supset (p \lor q)$

6.15 Indirect Proof

Logicians have found one other procedure to be particularly useful as an alternative when attempts at constructing a deductive proof have failed. The method itself is relatively simple and straightforward; the theoretical reasons why it works are not so simple. We will first show what the procedure is; then we will see why it works. Even if you don't understand clearly why it works, you will still be able to use it.

This final method, known as **indirect proof** (which we abbreviate in proofs as 'I.P.'), *involves assuming the denial of the conclusion of an argument, deriving a contradiction within the scope of the assumption and then directly deriving the original conclusion.* This procedure is also known as the **reductio ad absurdum** proof and is illustrated in the following example.

1. p ⊃ q	Premise
2. p ∨ r	Premise
3. ~q /∴ r	Premise/conclusion
4. ~r	Assumption
5. p	D.Syll., 2,4
6. q	M.P., 1,5
7. q · ~q	Conj., 3,6
8. r	I.P., 4–7

To understand why this method works, it is helpful to see that it is derivative from the method of conditional proof. This should not be a surprise since it involves making and then discharging an assumption. We could proceed in exactly the same way for the first six steps of the previous example. We could then have continued, using conditional proof as follows:

1. p ⊃ q	Premise
2. p ∨ r	Premise
3. ~q /∴ r	Premise/conclusion
4. ~r	Assumption
5. p	D.Syll., 2,4
6. q	M.P., 1,5
7. q ∨ r	Add., 6
8. r	D.Syll., 3,7
9. ~r ⊃ r	C.P., 4–8
10. ~~r ∨ r	Impl., 9
11. r ∨ r	D.N., 10
12. r	Taut., 11

The method of indirect proof simply involves leaving out several steps, which is justified by the fact that all proofs using I.P. share a common pattern. First, we can leave out all of the steps within the scope of the assumption that come after the contradiction in step 7. Our justification for doing this is the fact that *anything whatsoever* can be validly deduced from a contradiction, since it is impossible for all of the premises to be true and the conclusion false (remember, the contradictory step is analytically false).

This pattern holds for every indirect proof where we have been able to derive a contradiction within the scope of the assumption. We know that if we wanted to we could *always* take half of the contradiction ('q' in step 6 of our example) and add our desired conclusion ('r' in our example) to it using the addition rule. Then we could use the disjunctive syllogism rule with the other half of the contradiction '~q' in our example) to derive the desired conclusion as a step by itself. Second, we can leave out the step after the assumption has been discharged, because this is *always* a conditional with the negation of the conclusion as the antecedent and the conclusion as the consequent. And we can leave out the two steps used to derive the conclusion from the conditional, because these are *always* applications of the implication and double negation rules. Leaving out these steps, which are common to every indirect proof beginning with the negation of the conclusion (when the argument is valid), we then have the basic pattern used at the beginning of this section.

Although it is a straightforward variation of the rule of conditional proof, the rule of indirect proof can be formally stated on its own as follows:

> *The following procedure can be inserted at any point in a proof,* provided that none of the formulae derived within the lined-off area are used outside this portion of the proof:

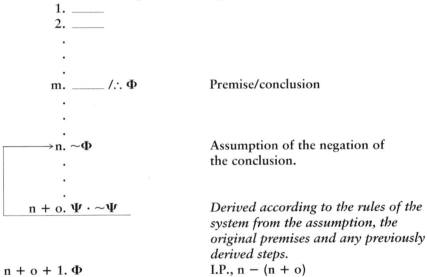

1. ____
2. ____
   .
   .
   .
m. ____ /∴ Φ   Premise/conclusion
   .
   .
   .
n. ~Φ   Assumption of the negation of the conclusion.
   .
   .
   .
n + o. Ψ · ~Ψ   *Derived according to the rules of the system from the assumption, the original premises and any previously derived steps.*
n + o + 1. Φ   I.P., n − (n + o)

Quite obviously, the rule of indirect proof is powerful, since it enables us to prove the validity of some argument schemas in fewer steps than does the rule of conditional proof. As one might expect, since indirect proof is a special case of conditional proof, it too can be used to prove the validity of arguments that cannot be proved using only the eighteen rules of inference and equivalence.

6.16 Deductive Completeness

So far, we have touched on the subject of the **deductive completeness** of our propositional calculus only in an incidental way. A deductive proof system for truth-functional arguments is said to be deductively complete *when any argument schema that can be proved valid using truth tables can be proved valid* *using the system's rules and procedures.* Thus, the original eighteen rules of inference do not in themselves constitute a deductively complete system. As we have seen, certain argument schemas that can be proved valid by truth tables cannot be proved valid using these rules alone. However, the original eighteen rules in conjunction with the rule of conditional proof do constitute a complete deductive system, since any argument schema that can be proved valid using truth tables can be proved valid using one or more of the eighteen rules and the conditional proof rule.

Indirect proof does not add anything to the deductive completeness of our system. Since it is a special case of conditional proof, any argument schema that can be proved valid using indirect proof can be proved valid using conditional proof. However, since both conditional proof and indirect proof are powerful tools for testing truth-functional validity, we include both within our system.

In conclusion, it should be reiterated that the deductive system given in this chapter does not provide a decision procedure. True, it is theoretically possible, using our nineteen rules (or twenty, if we count indirect proof as a separate rule), to construct a proof of validity for every argument that can be proved valid using truth tables. However, these rules do not provide a mechanical method that *guarantees* that after a finite number of steps we will have proved that a given argument is valid or invalid. The system of rules cannot be used at all to prove invalidity. Failure to derive the desired conclusion after a specified number of steps could indicate a failure on the part of the individual to find the proper sequence of steps just as well as it could suggest the invalidity of the argument. Therefore, if, after trying for a reasonable length of time to construct a proof, one has not been able to do it, it would be appropriate to test the argument by the short truth table method, which does enable us to prove invalidity.

EXERCISE 6–36

Prove the validity of each of the following argument schemas using the method of <u>indirect proof</u>.

1. $\sim q \supset (\sim p \cdot r)$
   $\sim r$
   $\therefore q$

2. $p \supset (q \cdot r)$
   $\sim q$
   $\therefore \sim p$

3. $p \lor (q \cdot r)$
   $p \lor t$
   $t \supset \sim(q \cdot r)$
   $\therefore p$

4. $(r \lor q) \supset p$
   $p \supset (s \cdot t)$
   $\sim s \lor \sim t$
   $\therefore \sim(r \lor q)$

5. $(p \supset q) \cdot (r \supset s)$
   $(q \lor s) \supset t$
   $\sim t$
   $\therefore \sim(p \lor r)$

6. $p \lor q$
   $p \lor \sim q$
   $\therefore p$

7.   p ⊃ (q ⊃ r)
      ~s ⊃ (p ∨ r)
      <u>p ⊃ q</u>
    ∴ s ∨ r

8.   ~p ⊃ q
      <u>~(~p · q)</u>
    ∴ p

9.   (p · q) ⊃ r
      ~p ⊃ r
      <u>q</u>
    ∴ r

10.   p ≡ q
      <u>~r ∨ p</u>
    ∴ r ⊃ q

11.   p · q
      <u>~(p ⊃ q)</u>
    ∴ r ⊃ s

12.   ~p ⊃ (q · r)
      <u>~r</u>
    ∴ p

13.   p ⊃ (q ∨ ~(r ∨ s))
      <u>~r ⊃ s</u>
    ∴ ~q ⊃ ~p

14.   (p ∨ q) ⊃ (r ⊃ ~s)
      <u>(s ∨ t) ⊃ (p · r)</u>
    ∴ ~s

Reprinted by permission of UFS, Inc.

Can you do any better than Charlie Brown in finding the error in this argument with the conclusion, "It doesn't matter how I act"? Is the propositional calculus at all helpful in analyzing this apparent argument?

EXERCISES 6–37

> Using all of the inference rules plus conditional proof and indirect proof, attempt to construct a deductive proof of the validity of the arguments in Exercise 6–1. If you have difficulty with a particular argument, use the method of short truth tables to test it for possible truth-functional invalidity.

Summary

1. A **truth-functional proposition** is a compound statement which is such that if we know the truth value of each of its component statements and the meanings of the logical operators, the truth or falsity of the compound statement can be determined.

2. A valid argument is such that, if the premises are true, then the conclusion must be true. Given this definition of validity, two consequences result:

Any argument with an inconsistent set of premises is necessarily valid (because it is impossible for all its premises to be true), and any argument with a conclusion that is a tautology must be valid (because it is impossible for the conclusion to be false, whatever the truth or falsity of the premises).

3. In the same way that it is possible to abbreviate and schematize a truth-functional compound statement by using propositional constants, propositional variables, and symbols for logical operators, so, too, it is possible to abbreviate and schematize a truth-functional argument by means of the same symbols. An **argument schema** displays the logical form of an argument. Once such a schema is set up, either simple or compound propositions may be substituted for the propositional variables in the schema. This produces a **substitution instance,** or an **interpretation** of the argument schema. But two restrictions apply: Only propositions can be substituted for propositional variables, and the same proposition must be substituted for every occurrence of any given variable in a particular argument schema.

4. Unlike a propositional schema, an argument schema is valid or invalid. A **valid argument schema** is one for which there is no possible substitution instance that would result in an argument with true premises and a false conclusion.

5. The truth table method for testing the validity of arguments requires that we construct a truth table for each premise and the conclusion of an argument schema. If, in this table, any row has Ts under the main operator of each premise and an F under the main operator of the conclusion, then the argument schema is **truth-functionally invalid.** An argument with such a schema can, in some cases, be proved valid when tested by the methods of other systems of logic such as the syllogistic and quantificational logic discussed in other chapters of this book.

6. Because using the full truth table method becomes cumbersome as the number of propositional variables in an argument schema increases, a short method can be used in such cases. This method can be used to prove only the truth-functional invalidity, not the validity, of an argument schema. In using it, we begin by assigning an F to the conclusion and then backtrack to see whether it is possible to assign truth values to the component statements, such that all of the premises can be assigned the truth value T. If so, the argument is truth-functionally invalid.

7. For every truth-functional argument, it is possible to construct a **corresponding conditional statement,** that is, a material implication with an antecedent that consists of the conjunction of the premises of the argument and a consequent that is the conclusion of the argument. An argument and its corresponding conditional differ in two respects: First, the argument is composed of several statements, whereas the corresponding conditional is a single compound statement; and second, whereas in the argument the

premises are asserted to be true, they are not so asserted in the conditional. If a truth-functional argument is valid, then its corresponding conditional is a tautology, and vice versa.

8. The method of deductive proof supplies an alternative to the truth table method of proving the validity of argument schemas. A **deductive proof system,** consisting of a set of rules and procedures that make it possible to prove the validity of an argument schema in step-by-step fashion, is known as a **logical calculus.** Most deductive proof systems do not provide a decision procedure, and therefore cannot be used to obtain an unequivocal proof of invalidity; they can be used only to prove validity. Basically, a deductive proof system uses a small number of rules or axioms which are such that when they are used in conjunction with the premises of a valid argument, it can be shown that, if all the premises are true, then the truth of the conclusion logically follows.

9. A deductive proof system for truth-functional arguments is **deductively complete** if any argument that can be proved to be valid using truth tables also can be proved valid using that system's rules and procedures. The number of rules contained in such a system may vary from as few as three to infinitely many. A system of convenient size and substantial utility can be constructed with about twenty rules, and such a system is used in this book.

10. Each of the rules of this system is a **rule of inference,** that is, a basic argument schema that can be proven valid by the truth table method, and that can be used in constructing a formal proof for other, more complex truth-functional arguments.

11. The first eight rules of inference are **modus tollens, modus ponens, hypothetical syllogism, constructive dilemma, disjunctive syllogism, simplification, conjunction,** and **addition.** Because these rules are valid argument schemas, not propositional schemas, they can be applied only to entire lines of a proof and not to individual subcomponents of such lines.

12. A **formal proof** is the process whereby the conclusion of an argument can be validly derived, using the rules of the system, from a set of statements, each one of which either is a premise of the original argument or has been validly deduced from the premises and/or other statements that have themselves been validly deduced by means of the rules of the system. Theoretically, an infinite number of correct formal deductive proofs can be constructed for any valid truth-functional argument. The ability to construct a formal deductive proof for a valid argument is dependent on many subjective factors. Thus, failure to construct a formal deductive proof for a particular argument schema is not sufficient to prove that the schema is truth-functionally invalid. Several rules of thumb for constructing proofs are provided in this chapter, but the most effective way to acquire the skills necessary for constructing proofs is continued practice.

13. A procedural rule, called the **rule of rigor,** requires that only one rule be used in each step of a deductive proof and that the rules be used only in the form in which they are given in the system.

14. The **rule of replacement** allows us to substitute logically equivalent statements in a deductive proof. It asserts that any propositional schema that is produced by replacing all or part of another schema with a schema that is equivalent to the replaced portion according to one of the equivalences listed in the following paragraph is validly derivable from the original schema. Unlike the first eight rules of inference, the **equivalence rules** included under the rule of replacement can be applied to parts of lines in a proof as well as to entire lines.

15. The ten equivalences contained in the rule of replacement are **De Morgan's rules, commutation, association, distribution, double negation, transportation, material implication, material equivalence, exportation,** and **tautology.**

16. Not every argument that can be proved valid using truth tables can be proved valid using these eighteen rules of inference. The addition of the rule of **conditional proof** (abbreviated 'C.P.') makes our system deductively complete and enables us to prove the validity of such arguments. The method of conditional proof involves *assuming* an additional premise, which is actually the antecedent of a conditional statement that is necessary in the proof, and then deducing the consequent of the desired statement from the assumption and the original premises. The step ending the conditional proof must be a conditional statement, with the assumed premise as its antecedent.

17. Steps derived from the assumed premise are said to be within the **scope** of the assumption. As soon as the rule of conditional proof is asserted, the scope of the assumption is ended, and the assumption is said to be discharged. No formula that has been derived within the scope of the assumption (and that is therefore dependent on the assumption) may be used outside its scope. This is because conditional proof asserts only that, if the assumption (the antecedent of the conditional) is true, the consequent is also true; it does not assert that the assumption is true. Any number of assumptions can be made, provided they are eventually discharged, leaving the conclusion dependent only on the premise(s) of the original argument schema.

18. **Indirect proof** (abbreviated 'I.P.'), or the *reductio ad absurdum* proof, is a special case of conditional proof. Using I.P., we assert the negation of the conclusion as our assumed premise and then derive a contradiction from it, which then permits us to derive the conclusion of the argument schema.

Chapter 7

Quantificational Logic: Statements

The system of logic to be presented in this and the following chapter is more powerful than either of the two systems presented in the previous chapters. Indeed, this new system enables us to deal with every kind of statement and argument that those systems can, and more. Does this mean that the study of those systems of logic was a waste of time? Some readers probably suspect that anything as old as syllogistic logic could never be worth studying. But the answer to the question is a definite "No," and for several reasons.

The new system of logic, which is known as **quantificational** or **predicate logic**, extracts a price for its increased power. For one thing, it is more complicated, adding several complex rules to those of propositional logic. Also, it does not provide a decision procedure, that is, a procedure—like Venn diagrams or truth tables—that in a finite number of steps gives us a definite judgment that a particular argument is valid or is not valid.

But we must remember that syllogistic logic has the serious limitation of being able to deal only with propositions that are categorical in form. Also, although propositional logic provides a decision procedure, we can never place too much weight on a judgment of invalidity, and in fact must always qualify it so that we only judge arguments to be truth-functionally invalid; that is, we recognize that any argument we prove to be "invalid" using the method of truth tables in propositional logic might really be valid. Thus, although the two previously studied systems have the virtue of being simpler, they have sufficient weaknesses to make it worth our while to learn this new, more difficult, system.

7.1 Predicates and Individuals

Remember that in propositional logic, the basic components are simple propositions and truth-functional operators that "operate" on the simple propositions. The "simple" propositions were those which did not themselves include any of the five truth-functional operators. The following sentences all express what are considered to be simple propositions in propositional logic.

1. **Mark is happy.**
2. **Argus is a dog.**
3. **Amy is going to the store.**
4. **John likes Donna.**
5. **Ann gave James the book.**

The limitations of propositional logic result from the fact that the validity or invalidity of an argument often is determined by the internal structure of "simple" propositions such as these. Thus, to get around these problems, we must devise a way for getting at the internal logical structure of such statements.

Propositions can always be expressed by the type of sentence that grammarians call a 'declarative' sentence. Such sentences always have a subject and a predicate, which can be displayed as follows:

[subject] / [predicate]

The subject term of a declarative sentence always contains a noun or pronoun, which can be modified by adjectives, adverbs, and phrases. In the sentences above, 'Mark,' 'Argus,' 'Amy,' 'John,' and 'Ann' are the subject terms. The predicate always contains a verb and often an object (direct or indirect). Predicates may also contain a variety of different adjectives, adverbs, phrases, and clauses. The predicate of sentence 1 is 'is happy'; the predicate of 2 is 'is a dog'; the predicate of 3 is 'is going to the store'; the predicate of 4 is 'likes Donna'; and the predicate of 5 is 'gave James the book.' Putting any of these terms into the diagram of the subject-predicate form, we get

1. **Mark / is happy**
2. **Argus / is a dog**
3. **Amy / is going to the store**
4. **John / likes Donna**
5. **Ann / gave James the book**

We have indicated that the subject term of a declarative sentence must contain a noun or pronoun and we have given five examples. However, we must note one other distinction—that between a proper noun and a general noun. A **proper noun** is the name of a specific individual person, place, thing (for example, 'Tom,' 'Florida,' 'Empire State Building'), group (for example, 'Chicago Cubs'), or organization (for example, 'IBM'). Proper nouns are not the only grammatical device that can be used to identify such specific persons, places, things, groups, and organizations; this can also be done by qualified nouns or noun clauses (for example, 'my roommate,' 'the building at the corner of Thirty-Fourth Street and Fifth Avenue in Manhattan,' or 'the largest office equipment manufacturer'), which single out particular individuals such as these.

Philosophers have debated for centuries what exactly it is that a general noun names, but for our purposes it is sufficient to give it a negative definition to the effect that a **general noun** is *any noun that is not a proper noun;* it can name a type of individual person (for example, 'man,' 'doctor,' 'athlete'), a kind of thing (for example, 'mammal,' 'building,' 'idea'), a kind of place (for example, 'city,' 'heaven'), a property (for example, 'redness,' 'heaviness'), and so on.

7.2 Variables and Constants

We have seen in the other systems of logic that we have studied that it is very useful to use abbreviations to simplify sentences, and schemas to make more apparent the logical structure of statements. This is also true in quantificational logic. The abbreviations we use here are as follows:

small letters 'a' through 't' $=_{df}$ **abbreviation of proper nouns or any other linguistic expression that names a specific individual.**

capital letters 'A' through 'Z' $=_{df}$ **abbreviation of all predicates.**

As with every system of notation, symbols that function as abbreviations are called 'constants,' so the small letters are called 'individual constants' and the capital letters are called 'predicate constants.' We can provide a "dictionary" indicating the meanings of specific constants in a given context by placing a single line beneath the letter abbreviating the expression identifying a particular individual and by placing a double line beneath the letter abbreviating the expression stating the predicate.

Unfortunately, things are not quite as simple as we might hope when it comes to using this new symbolization, but we will work our way into some of the complications gradually, beginning with the simplest cases.

The abbreviation rules just presented can be applied quite straightforwardly to statement **1**. The proper noun 'Mark' can be abbreviated with the small letter 'm' and the predicate 'is happy' with the capital letter 'H.' To **abbreviate** the sentence we *put the predicate constant first and then attach the individual constant to its right.* The entire sentence is thus reduced to the abbreviation 'Hm.' Sentence **2** can be abbreviated in essentially the same way, using 'a' as the abbreviation for 'Argus' and 'D' for 'is a dog,' which then gives us 'Da.'

Sentence **3** looks equally simple; we can abbreviate 'Amy' as 'a' and the predicate 'is going to the store' as 'G.' The abbreviation of the sentence would then be 'Ga.' But we must note that the expression 'the store' is at best ambiguous; the article 'the' usually indicates that a specific individual is being referred to by the following noun, although in colloquial English, when people say they are 'going to the store' they sometimes mean nothing more specific than that they are going shopping. We could know which is intended in this case only by knowing more about the context in which it is being used. But if the context were to indicate that a specific store is being referred to, then we would have to assign the individual constant 's' to 'the store' and change the predicate abbreviation to apply only to 'is going to,' with the sentence abbreviation then becoming 'Gas' (no pun intended!). If the constants were reversed so that the 's' precedes the 'a' (that is, as 'Gsa'), the abbreviation would be of the sentence 'The store is going to Amy.' A *predicate such as 'is going to' that requires two individual terms to complete its meaning* is known as a **two-place** (or **dyadic**) **relational predicate.**

The fourth sentence should now be quite easy, since it has two obvious proper nouns naming specific individuals. If we abbreviate 'John' by 'j,' 'Donna' by 'd,' and the relational predicate 'likes' by 'L,' the abbreviation of the sentence will be 'Ljd.' If we had a sentence that asserts that Donna likes John, its abbreviation would be 'Ldj.'

The fifth sentence looks very similar to **4,** but it is a bit different. Certainly we should abbreviate the proper names 'Ann' and 'James' with the individual constants 'a' and 'j' respectively. It is not quite so clear what we should do about the predicate, but it seems plausible to change it around slightly to something like 'gave the book to' which could simply be abbreviated as 'G.' But if 'the book' is taken as referring to a specific individual book, then we have to abbreviate it with an individual constant such as 'b' and change the predicate to 'gave _____ to'; which would then result in the abbreviation 'Gabj.'

As with any kind of symbolization in logic, any abbreviation can be transformed into a schema by replacing one or more of the constants with variables. Remember, a variable is simply a blank into which we can insert any constant of a certain kind. Remember also that schemas only display logical forms; they cannot assert anything true or false because they contain blanks or "holes" and thus do not express propositions. One way of schematizing statement **1** is to actually use a blank, as '_____ is happy' or 'H__.' But of course it is simpler, especially when we begin to need a number of different kinds of blanks, to use some other kind of symbol. In quantificational logic we will use the *small letters from 'u' through 'z'* to serve as **individual variables,** that is, as *blanks into which we can substitute any individual constant* (or any noun, qualified noun, or noun phrase that names a specific individual) whatever. The schema for the statement expressed by sentence **1** is thus 'Hx.' Because the individual variable is a blank, 'Hx' does not express a statement; such expressions are called **open sentences.**

When using individual variables, it is important to use a different variable as a replacement for every different individual constant in a particular context. (Obviously, since there are so few individual variables, we can and must use the same variables to replace different constants as long as this is done in different contexts.) Thus, for example, in writing the schema of the abbreviation of sentence **4** we should substitute different variables for 'j' and 'd,' which gives us 'Lxy.' It is also possible to schematize abbreviations further by replacing the predicate constants with predicate variables; however, we will not go to this level of complication in this book.

Things are probably beginning to look a bit confusing, but several other complications haven't even been touched on yet. This is a good place to stop to take time to develop a working familiarity with individual constants and variables and predicate constants, and to polish your skills at applying these concepts to actual sentences and statements.

EXERCISE 7–1

(a) Abbreviate the following sentences expressing propositions using predicate and individual constants. (b) Indicate precisely which part of the original sentence each constant symbolizes. (c) Convert each abbreviation into a schema by replacing each individual constant with an individual variable.

1. Ed is tall.
2. Mary is studying hard.
3. The Sears Tower is the tallest building in the world.
4. Chicago, Illinois, is a city.
5. Sue is taller than Pat.
6. Al got out of his car.
7. Washington, D.C., is the capital of the United States.
8. Kim won the NCAA tennis singles championship.
9. Ted likes Professor Allen better than Professor Nella.
10. Wendy took her pet boa constrictor to Dr. Vet.

7.3 Compound Propositions

Since sentences that we symbolize in quantificational logic all express propositions, we can connect them using the truth-functional operators from propositional logic. In doing this, we must remember that the simplest propositional unit consists of a predicate constant followed immediately by the appropriate number of individual constants. Thus, it is incorrect to use any of the operators inside such a unit. This will become clear if we look at several examples.

Consider the following statement.

6. M̲ark is not h̲appy.

Although we might be tempted to interpret the predicate as 'is not happy,' this would not acknowledge the presence of the negation operator. To indicate clearly the presence of the negation operator, it is necessary to give the positive form of the predicate as 'is happy' and to abbreviate the sentence using the tilde as '~Hm.'

It is not always obvious how to symbolize negative adjectives such as 'unhappy.' Sometimes it is possible to symbolize them as negations of their positive antonyms, so that 'Mark is unhappy' would be symbolized in the same way as 'Mark is not happy.' But it is important to be aware that this can be done only if we are reasonably certain that the same proposition is expressed by both sentences. However, in most contexts, 'Mark is unhappy' does not mean exactly the same thing as 'Mark is not happy.' 'Happy' and 'unhappy' are both adjectives that can be used to describe ranges of emotions, and there is an area between them in which neither applies. This can be seen more clearly if we display it as follows.

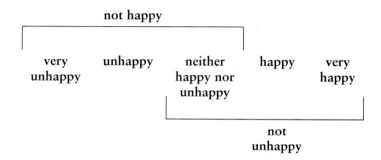

Thus, it is possible for someone to be not happy without being unhappy (and also to be not unhappy without being happy). This one example hopefully makes it clear why we need to be careful, relying on our native intuition, when deciding how to symbolize predicate terms involving negations.

The other truth-functional operators can be also used in symbolizing statements in quantificational logic. Thus, if we want to abbreviate 'Mark and John are happy,' we can do this by using the dot operator to symbolize the relation between the simple propositions 'Mark is happy' and 'John is happy' as

Hm · Hj.

Similarly, 'Mark and John are both not happy' can be abbreviated as the conjunction of two negations,

~Hm · ~Hj.

The conjunction of more than two terms simply requires that we group the components with parentheses so that there is no ambiguity as to which components a particular operator is operating on. Thus, 'Mark, John, and Amy are all happy' can be abbreviated as

(Hm · Hj) · Ha.

Similar procedures hold for the other truth-functional operators. Thus, 'Either Mark or John or Amy will go to Washington, D.C.' can be abbreviated as

'(Gmw ∨ Gjw) ∨ Gaw' where 'G' is the abbreviation of 'will go to.' 'If John is happy then Mark is not happy' can be abbreviated as 'Hj ⊃ ~Hm,' where it is understood that any suggestion of a causal connection being expressed by the original 'If . . . then . . .' is lost in the translation to the horseshoe, just as in propositional logic.

EXERCISE 7–2

(a) Abbreviate the following sentences expressing propositions using predicate and individual constants, together with the truth-functional operators from propositional logic. (b) Indicate precisely which part of the original sentence each constant symbolizes. (c) Convert each abbreviation into a schema by replacing each individual constant with an individual variable.

1. Ed and Sue are not tall.
2. Mary and Tom are studying hard.
3. The Sears Tower and the Empire State Building are both tall buildings.
4. Chicago and San Francisco are both cities.
5. Either Sue or Tony is taller than Pat.
6. Al and Dawn got out of Ed's car
7. Neither New York nor Los Angeles is the capital of the United States.
8. If Kim won the NCAA tennis singles championship, then her coach is pleased.
9. Ted likes Professor Allen better than either Professor Nella or Professor Lean.
10. Mike will pass logic if and only if Wendy is a good tutor.

7.4 Existential Quantifiers

Perceptive readers might have noticed that we have not yet provided any means for dealing with subjects of statements that do not involve specific individual beings, places, things, organizations, or groups. These subjects are usually expressed by what are called 'general nouns,' examples of which are 'teachers,' 'cities,' 'trees,' 'corporations,' and 'clubs.' The following are representative sentences using general nouns.

7. **Some trees are tall.**
8. **All teachers are intelligent.**
9. **Most students work hard.**
10. **No cats are beagles.**

Because the subjects of these sentences do not name or refer to specific individuals, we cannot use individual constants to abbreviate them. But if we abbreviate them with predicate constants, we have nothing to attach to them, and a predicate constant by itself does not express a proposition. Thus, we must come up with a new device for symbolizing propositions such as those expressed by sentences 7 through 10. (Observe that 10 also has a general noun in the predicate position. Our method for dealing with general nouns in the subject place also provides for general nouns in the predicate, as we will see when we apply it to sentence 10.)

The clue for a way to symbolize propositions with general terms in the subject position is to note that all sentences expressing such statements must also include, tacitly or explicitly, an expression such as 'all,' 'some,' 'no,' 'most,' 'several,' or 'many.' Such expressions (as was noted in the chapters on syllogistic logic) are called **quantifiers** in recognition of the fact that *such terms specify something* (more or less precisely) *about the quantity of things referred to by the general noun in the subject position.* Quantificational logic deals with general nouns in the subject position by adding two new operators that function in a way that is similar to certain quantifiers in ordinary English.

One of these new operators, the **existential quantifier** is symbolized by a reversed capital E connected to an individual variable, with all of this contained in parentheses. Despite this complicated description, it really looks quite simple: '(∃x).'

The symbol for the existential quantifier is usually read in English as 'some,' but its most precise and complete English expression is 'There exists at least one thing such that. . . .' This is intended to include a broad range of possibilities, from the assertion of the existence of just one thing up to the existence of all but one of everything. In other words, all quantifying expressions other than those such as 'all,' 'every,' and 'no' are normally to be symbolized using the existential quantifier. Although it is intended to apply to cases ranging from a single (unidentified) individual to all individuals but one, it also leaves open the possibility that the predicate applies to all members of the subject class. This can be displayed as follows.

None	One	Several	A few	Many	Most	All
	← - - - - - - - - - - - - - (∃x) - - - - - - - - - - - - →					

Thus, as with some of the truth-functional operators studied in Chapter 5, the existential quantifier can often be used only at the cost of a significant loss of meaning. Once we have translated an English sentence into symbolism using the existential quantifier, we have lost whatever meaning there was in the English quantifier over and above the basic sense of 'at least one.' However problematic it might seem, in the system we are using here, all of the following sentences are to be translated using the existential quantifier.

At least one dog is brown.
Some dogs are brown.

Several dogs are brown.
A few dogs are brown.
A number of dogs are brown.
Hundreds of dogs are brown.
More than half of all dogs are brown.
Many dogs are brown.
Millions of dogs are brown.
Most dogs are brown.

The loss of meaning occurs because we cannot translate back from the symbolic form into any of the above wordings except for the first two. Even if we start with 'Most dogs are brown' and translate it into symbolism using the existential quantifier, when we translate it from the symbolism into English it can only be into 'At least one dog is brown' or 'Some dogs are brown.' This will become more clear when we look at some examples shortly. (Special logical systems, known as "fuzzy logics," can distinguish among some of these statements, but we cannot discuss them in this book.)

This system of quantificational logic does provide a way for specifying exact numbers of things (as in 'Exactly three dogs are brown'), but it provides no means for being more precise about statements such as those above.

The English term 'some' is often used in ways intended to convey that something is true of at least one thing while it is not true of others. For example, if a professor stands in front of a class and says, 'Some of you will not pass this course' with a strong emphasis on the word 'some,' students would not be seriously mistaken to understand him as also saying that some students will pass. But *the existential quantifier* can never be interpreted as conveying such a meaning; it *always leaves open the possibility that whatever is being asserted of at least one thing might be true of everything,* unless it is conjoined with another expression that explicitly asserts that it is not true of everything.

The existential quantifier does not express a proposition by itself. In order to express a complete statement, the existential quantifier must be followed by at least one schema consisting of a predicate constant attached to at least one individual variable of the same kind as that included in the existential quantifier. This might be easier to see in examples rather than in an abstract definition. Given that 'Hx' means 'x is happy,' we can translate the following symbolizations that use the existential quantifier.

11. $(\exists x)Hx$ = There exists at least one thing such that it is happy.   *or*
    = Something is happy.

12. $(\exists y)Hy$ = There exists at least one thing such that it is happy.   *or*
    = Something is happy.

13. $(\exists z)Hz$ = There exists at least one thing such that it is happy.   *or*
    = Something is happy.

14. $(\exists x)Hy$ = *does not express a proposition.*

Notice in these examples that since each individual variable represents a blank into which any individual constant whatever can be inserted, it does not make any difference (at this point in our development of this system, at least) which individual variable we use, as long as the same variable is inside the quantifier *and* also is attached to the predicate constant. (Sentence **14** does not express a proposition because the variable in the quantifier does not match the variable attached to the predicate constant.)

It is particularly important to notice that the existential quantifier is so unspecific that it might refer to any possible thing in the universe. Our instinct is to assume that if something is said to be happy, that thing must be a human being, or at least some other species that we consider to be capable of feeling emotions. But when using logical symbols, we must make a special effort to set such assumptions aside and to interpret the symbols strictly in accordance with their stipulated definitions. Thus, it would be *wrong* to translate **11, 12,** or **13** as 'Some*body* is happy' or as 'Some*one* is happy.' We will see how to express statements such as these shortly.

Nothing is different about using the existential quantifier with predicates that have two or more individual terms connected with them. If we assume that 'Hxy' means 'x is happier than y' and that 'm' means 'Mark,' the following symbolizations can be translated as shown.

15. (∃x)Hxm = There exists at least one thing such that it is happier than Mark.   *or*
    = Something is happier than Mark.

16. (∃y)Hym = There exists at least one thing such that it is happier than Mark.   *or*
    = Something is happier than Mark.

17. (∃x)Hmx = There exists at least one thing such that Mark is happier than it.   *or*
    = Mark is happier than something.

Notice again that a change in variables does not result in any change in meaning; a blank by any name is a blank. But observe in **15** and **17** that a change in the sequence of the two individual terms following the predicate constant results in a very definite change in meaning. Also, these examples serve to remind us that the existential quantifier must always be interpreted as asserting the existence of at least one thing; it cannot be translated as asserting the existence of a person (except under special conditions that we are not invoking here). Thus, we must continue to resist our instinct to translate **16** as 'Some*body* is happier than Mark' or **17** as 'Mark is happier than some*one*.'

EXERCISE 7–3

(a) Abbreviate the following sentences expressing propositions using the existential quantifier, individual variables, and predicate and individual constants as necessary. (b) Indicate precisely which part of the original sentence each constant symbolizes. (c) Finally, translate your symbolized expression back into English, noting what meaning, if any, has been lost from the original.

1. Something is tall.
2. At least one thing works.
3. Something is a tall building.
4. Several things are cities.
5. Many things are taller than Pat.
6. Al's car is faster than a few things.
7. Some things got broken.
8. More than half of the things are on sale.
9. Something likes Mary better than George.
10. Wendy has several things.

7.4.1 Existentially Quantified Compound Propositions

Very few propositions occur in the very simple form of a single subject and predicate. Thus, we need to have a procedure for dealing with those propositions that require the existential quantifier and that are more complex than those discussed thus far. Let us begin with 'Somebody is happy,' which we found in the last section to be one that we cannot symbolize using a single predicate. When we try to symbolize this as '$(\exists x)Hx$' we find that this says that 'At least one thing is happy.' What we need to do then is to add the qualification that the thing being talked about happens in this case to be a person. To express this symbolically, we can conjoin an expression specifying this to the original symbolization as follows.

> 18. $(\exists x)(Px \cdot Hx)$ = **There exists at least one thing such that it is a person and it is happy.**
> = **Somebody is happy.**

7.4.2 Scope of Quantifiers

The meaning of the symbolization in **18** would be changed significantly if we didn't use the parentheses around '$Px \cdot Hx$.' The expression

> 19. $(\exists x)Px \cdot Hx$

says literally 'Something is a person and _____ is happy' which because of the blank does not even express a proposition. The *parenthesis immediately following the existential quantifier* designates what is known as the **scope** of the quantifier. That is, *it indicates that every individual variable of the kind in the quantifier should be read in conjunction with the quantifier every time it occurs until that parenthesis is closed out* (that is, the right-hand parenthesis that matches the original left-hand one is supplied). When a variable is within the scope of its quantifier, we say that it is **bound** by that quantifier; when a variable is not within the scope of its quantifier, we say that it is **free.** By definition, then, any symbolization that contains a free variable cannot express a proposition. In **18**, both the first 'x' and second 'x' are bound by the existential quantifier. In **19**, the first 'x' is bound, but the second 'x' is free.

Example **18** shows that we must be sensitive to rather subtle aspects of language when formulating symbolizations. Theoretically, in addition to every general noun, every adjective, adverb, and other modifying expression and most components of the predicate can be expressed by separate predicate constants, as demonstrated by the following examples.

20. $(\exists x)((Sx \cdot Ix) \cdot Ax)$ = Some intelligent students get A's in logic.

21. $(\exists x)(Lx \cdot Hxe)$ = Some logic problems are harder than example 20.

22. $(\exists x)((((Ex \cdot Bx) \cdot Sx) \cdot Px) \cdot Dx)$ = Some blue-eyed, blond, slender people are Danes.

It is not always necessary to express each and every component with a separate constant or variable, but this is usually dependent on a number of contextual considerations that are discussed in Chapter 14. For the purposes of this chapter, you should always provide a separate term for every different component of a proposition. We do stipulate, however, that it is normally unnecessary to use separate predicate constants to indicate that things that are students are also persons, that things that are dogs are also animals, and so on. In other words, we consider it to be sufficient in most situations simply to indicate that some students work hard without conjoining a 'Px' to further indicate that these students are also people.

Since symbolizations with all of the individual variables bound by a quantifier express propositions, we can also use the truth-functional operators to connect bound expressions as follows.

23. $(\exists x)(Sx \cdot \sim Tx) \cdot (\exists x)(Sx \cdot Fx)$ = Some students don't study and at least one student will fail.

Notice that this is quite different in a number of ways from

24. $(\exists x)((Sx \cdot \sim Tx) \cdot Fx)$ = At least one student who does not study will fail.

Statement **24** tells us that at least one student does in fact exist who is not studying and who will fail, whereas **23** says that at least one student does not study and at least one student will fail. Also, **24** tells us that it is the student(s) who does (do) not study who will fail, while **23** does not make this connection. In other words, in **23** the student who fails does not have to be the same student who does not study. Even though we have used the individual variable 'x' in both quantifiers in **23**, since a blank is a blank whatever variable we use for it, we cannot assume that the same individual(s) is (are) being referred to by each component. Thus, **23** would be true if Mary did not study and Tom failed the course. But for **24** to be true, the same person who does not study must also be the one who fails, because all of the variables are bound by the same quantifier.

(a) Translate the following formulas into English using the dictionary provided. (b) Translate your symbolized expression in (b) into English to check to see whether it has the same meaning as the original.

Dictionary:

t	= Tom	l	= Tom's logic book
m	= Mary	Px	= x is a person
Hx	= x is happy	Tx	= x passes the test
Fxy	= x is faster than y	Fx	= x is fast
Bxy	= x borrowed y	Nx	= x is nocturnal
Lxyz	= x likes y better than z	Lxy	= x is more logical than y

1. (∃x)Ftx
2. (∃x)Hx
3. (∃y)Py
4. (∃y)Fy
5. (∃x)Bxl
6. (∃x)Ltxm
7. (∃x)(Px · Hx)
8. (∃x)Fxt
9. (∃y)Bmy
10. (∃y)(Py · Fmy)
11. (∃x)(Px · Bxl)
12. ~(∃x)(Tm · Lmx)
13. (∃x)((Px · Tx) · Lxm)
14. (∃y)(Px · ~Hy)
15. (∃y)(Ny · Lyt)
16. (∃x)(Nx · Lmx)
17. Bml
18. (∃y)Lmyt
19. (∃x)(Px · Hx)
20. (∃x)(Px · Lmxt)

(a) Abbreviate the following sentences expressing propositions using the existential quantifier, individual variables, predicate and individual constants, and truth-functional operators as necessary. (b) Indicate precisely which part of the original sentence each constant symbolizes. (c) Finally, translate your symbolized expression back into English, noting what meaning, if any, has been lost from the original.

1. Somebody is tall.
2. At least one student works.
3. Some people are tall and heavy.
4. Several cities have populations of more than a million.
5. Many women are shorter than Pat.
6. Some students are fast and some are slow.
7. Al's car is faster than some dogs and horses.
8. Some fragile things were dropped and got broken.
9. Most valuable things do not cost much or are free.
10. Somebody likes Mary better than George.
11. Some smart people study logic and math.
12. Some smart people study logic and some smart people study math.

7.5 Universal Quantifiers

The propositions 'All teachers are intelligent' and 'No cats are beagles' cannot be symbolized using the existential quantifier because they are not about only some of the things being referred to. The first is about *all* teachers, not just some of them, and the second is about *no* cats, not even one. Both of these propositions and any others that are about all or none of the things being referred to can be symbolized by using one additional quantifier known as the 'universal quantifier.'

The **universal quantifier** is symbolized by an individual variable contained

Try to symbolize the statements in frames 3 and 4 using quantificational logic. The trickiest part is deciding what to do with expressions such as 'means' and 'it don't mean.'

in parentheses, '(x).' The symbol for the universal quantifier is usually read in English as 'For any thing whatsoever. . . ,' and it can be used to symbolize only the relatively small number of quantifiers in English that are used to designate all of a certain kind of thing. Unlike the situation with the existential quantifier, there is usually little if any loss of meaning when the universal quantifier is used to replace English words such as 'all,' 'every,' 'any,' and 'no.'

As with the existential quantifier, the universal quantifier does not express a proposition by itself. In order to express a complete statement, the universal quantifier must be followed by at least one schema composed of a predicate constant attached to at least one individual variable of the same kind as included in the quantifier. This may be easier to see in examples rather than in an abstract definition. Given that 'Hx' means 'x is happy,' we can translate the following symbolizations which use the universal quantifier.

25. (x)Hx = **For any thing whatsoever, it is happy.**   *or*
        = **Everything is happy.**

26. (y)Hy = **For any thing whatsoever, it is happy.**   *or*
        = **Everything is happy.**

27. (z)Hz = **For any thing whatsoever, it is happy.**   *or*
        = **Everything is happy.**

28. (x)Hy = *does not express a proposition.*

Notice from these examples that since each individual variable represents a blank into which any individual constant whatever can be inserted, it does not make any difference (at this point in our development of this system, at least) which individual variable we use, as long as the same variable that is inside the quantifier is also attached to the predicate constant.

It is particularly important to notice that the universal quantifier is so general as to refer to *all possible things in the universe.* We must again resist our instinct to assume that if something is said to be happy, that thing must be a human being (or a member of some other species that we consider to be capable of feeling emotions). Thus, it would be wrong to translate **25, 26,** or **27** as 'Every*body* is happy' or as 'Every*one* is happy.' We will see how to express statements such as these shortly.

A special problem arises when we use the universal quantifier with relational predicates, that is, predicates that have two or more individual terms connected to them. We need some new logical tools to deal with this problem, so we will have to wait until we have these tools before we try to use the universal quantifier with simple relational predicates.

EXERCISE 7–6

(a) Abbreviate the following sentences expressing propositions using the universal quantifier, individual variables, and predicate and individual constants as necessary. (b) Indicate precisely which part of the original sentence each constant symbolizes. (c) Finally, translate your symbolized expression back into English, noting what meaning, if any, has been lost from the original.

1. Everything is tall.
2. Everything works.
3. Everything is round.
4. All things are elephants.
5. All things have mass.
6. Everything can move.
7. All things get broken.
8. All things are alive.

7.5.1 Universally Quantified Compound Propositions

We have commented before that very few propositions occur in the very simple form of a single subject and predicate. Thus, we also need a procedure for dealing with those propositions that require the universal quantifier and that are more complex than those discussed thus far. Let us begin with 'Everybody is happy.' When we tried in the previous section to symbolize this as '(x)Hx' we found that it actually says 'Everything is happy.' What we need to do is to add something that indicates that the things being talked about are persons. Let us begin by first trying to symbolize this as we would with an existential quantifier, except that we will use the new universal quantifier instead. If we do this we will get

> 29. $(x)(Px \cdot Hx)$ = **For any thing whatsoever, it is a person and it is happy.**   *or*
> = **Everything is a happy person.**

This is obviously a very strong, and quite absurd, claim. We do not want to say that every tree, rock, book, and molecule of water in the universe is a happy person! But how can we avoid making such statements with the universal quantifier?

The solution is not intuitively obvious, but it is relatively simple and straightforward. To express this universal proposition symbolically, we must use the horseshoe rather than the dot, as shown below:

> 30. $(x)(Px \supset Hx)$ = **For any thing whatsoever, if that thing is a person, then it is happy.**   *or*
> = **Everybody is happy.**

Notice that the horseshoe works for us because it does not assert that every thing is in fact a person; it only says that for any thing that we choose from the entire universe, *if* that thing is a person, *then* it is also happy. And this is exactly what the original universal proposition says.

The meaning of the symbolization in **30** changes significantly if we don't use the parentheses around 'Px ⊃ Hx.' The expression '(x)Px ⊃ Hx' says literally 'If everything is a person then _____ is happy,' which because of the blank does not even express a proposition.

The parenthesis immediately following the universal quantifier designates its scope. To review this concept, the first parenthesis indicates that every individual variable of the kind in the quantifier should be read in conjunction with the quantifier each time it occurs until that parenthesis is closed out (that is, the right-hand parenthesis that matches the original left-hand one is supplied). *When a variable is within the scope of its quantifier,* it is **bound;** *when a variable is not within the scope of its quantifier,* it is **free.** In **29** and **30,** both the first 'x' and second 'x' are bound by the universal quantifier. In '(x)Px ⊃ Hx' the first 'x' is bound by the universal quantifier, but the second 'x' is free.

As with the existential quantifier, when using the universal quantifier we must be careful to notice every adjective, adverb, and other modifying expressions, as well as most components of the predicate, that can be expressed by separate predicate constants, as demonstrated by the following examples.

31. **(x)((Sx · Ix) ⊃ Ax) = All intelligent students get A's in logic.**

32. **(x)(Lx ⊃ Hxm) = All logic problems are harder than this mathematics problem.**

33. **(x)((((Ex · Bx) · Sx) · Px) ⊃ Dx) = All blue-eyed, blond, slender people are Danes.**

Although it is not always necessary to express each and every component with a separate constant or variable, this is usually dependent on a number of contextual considerations that are discussed in Chapter 14. For the purposes of this chapter, you should always provide a separate term for every different component of a proposition, except that we will consider it to be sufficient in most situations to simply indicate, for example, that all students work hard without conjoining a 'Px' to further indicate that these students are also people.

We mentioned at the end of the previous section that there is a particular problem in using the universal quantifier with relational predicates, that is, predicates that connect two or more individual terms. We are now able to consider this problem. If we assume that 'Hxy' means 'x is happier than y' and that 'm' means 'Mark,' the following symbolizations can be translated as shown.

34. **(x)(Px ⊃ Hxm) = For any thing whatsoever, if it is a person, then it is happier than Mark.** *or*
   = Everybody is happier than Mark.

35. **(x)(Px ⊃ Hmx) = For any thing whatsoever, if it is a person, then Mark is happier than it.** *or*
   = Mark is happier than everybody.

The problem, which might not be obvious at first glance, is that insofar as the universal quantifier refers to everything in the universe, it must also be referring to Mark. If we make this explicit, we can see that **34** asserts that every person, including Mark, is happier than Mark, which of course means that Mark must be happier than himself! Similarly, **35** says that Mark is happier than every person, including himself.

This problem does not normally arise in English because native speakers understand that 'is happier than' is a relation such that it necessarily excludes the members of the group named by the first term from being members of the second group. But in symbolizing this in a formal system of logic as we are doing here, we must make this assumption explicit. The simplest way to indicate that Mark is not one of the things that can be substituted for the individual variable 'x' is to use the predicate 'is identical to' (symbolized by the predicate constant 'I') as follows.

34a. (x)((Px · ~Ixm) ⊃ Hxm) = For any thing whatsoever, if it is a person and it is not identical to Mark, then it is happier than Mark.

35a. (x)((Px · ~Ixm) ⊃ Hmx) = For any thing whatsoever, if it is a person and it is not identical to Mark, then Mark is happier than it.

It is important to recognize that not all relations are like 'is happier than.' In fact, many relations are such that a thing *can* stand in that relation to itself. For example, 'likes' is a relation for which it would make as much sense to say that 'Mark likes himself' as it does to say that 'Mark likes ice cream.' Relations such as these are known as **reflexive** relations.

Relations such as 'is happier than' that do not permit anything to stand in that relation to itself are said to be **nonreflexive.** Propositions involving reflexive relations can be symbolized using a universal quantifier without having to use the identity predicate 'is identical to.'

The Drabble cartoon illustrates a slightly different problem resulting from

"The Wizard of Id" by permission of Johnny Hart and Creators Syndicate, Inc.

Here may be a case where the self-referential nature of unrestricted universal generalizations can sometimes have unintended results. Symbolize the wizard's statement as it is expressed in frame 2. Then, modify the statement so that it is no longer self-referential and symbolize this second form. Which do you think the wizard *intended?*

DRABBLE

Reprinted by permission of UFS, Inc.

the inclusiveness of the universal quantifier. The reason that it is difficult to throw away one's trash can is that it is generally understood that the policy of trash collectors is that everything left at the curb, *except* the trash can, is to be taken away. How can this be symbolized? Since 'trash can' is used here as a general noun rather than as a term referring to a specific individual, we should represent it with a predicate constant and we do not need to use the identity predicate. The trash collectors' policy can then be expressed as follows.

> **36. (x)((Lx · ~Cx) ⊃ Hx) = For any thing whatsoever, if that thing is left at the curb and it is not a trash can, then it is to be hauled away.**

While this solves the problem of how to express the policy in quantificational logic, it does not solve the problem of how to get an old trash can hauled away. You might want to figure out how the policy statement needs to be modified in order to make this possible.

Before doing the following exercises, notice again that a change in variables does not result in any change in meaning; a blank by any name is a blank. But observe in **34** and **35** that *a change in the sequence of the two individual terms following the predicate constant results in a very definite change in meaning.* Also, these examples serve to remind us that quantifiers must always be interpreted as making assertions about *things*; they should not be interpreted as saying anything about persons (except under special conditions that we are not invoking here). Thus, we must continue to use the predicate 'P' for 'is a person' whenever we want to symbolize a statement involving references to 'every*body*' or 'every*one*.'

EXERCISE 7–7

(a) Abbreviate the following sentences expressing propositions using the universal quantifier, individual variables, predicate and individual constants, and truth-functional operators as necessary. (b) Indicate precisely which part of the original sentence each constant symbolizes. (c) Finally, translate your symbolized expression back into English, noting what meaning, if any, has been lost from the original.

1. Everybody is tall.
2. All students work.
3. Everyone is tall and heavy.
4. All cities have populations of more than a million.
5. All tall people are heavy.
6. All women are shorter than Pat.
7. Every student studies.
8. Al's car is faster than all dogs and horses.
9. All fragile things break easily.
10. All valuable things ought to be insured.

7.6 Negation and Quantifier Exchange

Although we have indicated that 'no' and 'none' are quantifiers, we have not yet discussed any examples involving them. This is because negations are one of the trickiest aspects of using quantifiers and they deserve special attention. The English terms 'no' and 'none' are not really 'pure' quantifiers and they do not require new symbols. These terms combine both a quantificational meaning and a qualitative sense of negation. Thus, they can be symbolized using either the universal or existential quantifier together with the truth-functional negation operator. And this is where things can be tricky.

It should be intuitively apparent that when we say 'Nothing is big' we are talking about all things, and we are making a negative statement about them. But it might seem equally intuitively clear at first glance that the symbolization of such a statement requires us to use the negation operator in front of the universal quantifier, as in '$\sim(x)Bx$.' We need to give this a closer look, for what it says literally is that it is not the case that all things are big, which is the same as saying that at least one thing is not big, while leaving open the possibility that some things are big. Thus, the correct translation into English is

37. $\sim(x)Bx$ = **It is not the case that all things are big.** *or*
    = **At least one thing is not big.** *or*
    = **Something is not big.**

To say that no things are big is actually to say that all things are such that they are not big. In other words, what we must do is to separate the quantifying function of the words 'no' and 'none' from their negating function and express the quantificational meaning first, which then gives us

38. $(x)\sim Bx$ = **For any thing whatsoever, it is not big.** *or*
    = **Nothing is big.**

If we think of the English expression of this proposition further, we can see that saying that nothing is big is identical to saying that there is not one thing in the universe that is big, or to put this into its most verbose (but also most precise) form, that it is not the case that there exists even one thing that is big. And if we symbolize this last expression we get the interesting result shown as **39**.

> **39.** ~(∃x)Bx = **It is not the case that there exists one thing that is big.**
> *or*
> = **Not even one big thing exists.** *or*
> = **Nothing is big.**

Insofar as **38** and **39** both can be translated into English as 'Nothing is big,' this gives us a basis for making the following connection.

> **40.** (x)~Bx ≡ **Nothing is big.** ≡ ~(∃x)Bx *or*
> (x)~Bx ≡ ~(∃x)Bx

If we look again at **37** we can see that the original negation of the universal quantifier can be translated into an English expression that we know can be translated into an existentially quantified expression, which gives us another connection as follows.

> **41.** ~(x)Bx ≡ **Something is not big.** ≡ (∃x)~Bx *or*
> ~(x)Bx ≡ (∃x)~Bx

The identities expressed by **40** and **41** display an interesting and important pattern associated with the use of the negation sign and quantifiers. This pattern is summarized in the **quantifier exchange** rule, which states that *we can change any universal quantifier to an existential quantifier and any existential quantifier to a universal quantifier if at the same time we add exactly one negation sign immediately preceding and one negation sign immediately following the quantifier.* When used in a step of a proof, we abbreviate it as 'QE.' No changes should be made in the symbolization within the scope of the quantifier. In any case in which the addition of a negation sign results in a double negation, we can remove this using the equivalence rule of double negation. The quantifier exchange rule can be applied in only four possible ways, as listed in the box. Since the rule does not affect anything in the scope of the quantifier, we will simply symbolize the scope with a set of parentheses enclosing a broken line.

Quantifier Exchange Rule

(x)(---) ≡   ~(∃x)~(---)
~(x)(---) ≡ ~~(∃x)~(---) ≡ (∃x)~(---)
(x)~(---) ≡ ~(∃x)~~(---) ≡ ~(∃x)(---)
~(x)~(---) ≡ ~~(∃x)~~(---) ≡ (∃x)(---)

Since these are logical equivalences, we can go from right to left as well as from left to right. That is, we can use these same formulas for beginning with an existential quantifier and exchanging it for a universal quantifier.

Reprinted by permission of The Austin American-Statesman.

Although the statement in the second frame might appear to be outrageously (and intuitively) false, it is quite likely that your first attempt to symbolize it in quantificational logic will put it in a form that is analytically true. This is due more to an ambiguity in the English sentence than to your symbolization. Keep working at this until you can get it in a form that is not analytically true. Then translate it back into English to see if this eliminates the ambiguity.

EXERCISE 7–8

For each of the following formulas, use the quantifier exchange rule to replace each universal quantifier with an existential quantifier and each existential quantifier with a universal quantifier.

1. $(x)Tx$
2. $(\exists x)Gx$
3. $(\exists x){\sim}Dx$
4. ${\sim}(\exists x)(Fx \cdot Bx)$
5. ${\sim}(x)(Px \supset Jx)$
6. $(x){\sim}(Qx \cdot Px)$
7. ${\sim}(\exists x){\sim}(Dx \cdot Kx)$
8. ${\sim}(x){\sim}(Fx \supset Tx)$
9. $(\exists x){\sim}(Px \cdot Qx)$
10. $(x)(Kx \cdot Nx)$

7.6.1 Negation and Multiple Predicates

The examples and exercises in the previous section did not include certain kinds of statements, most notably negative statements involving two or more predicates, such as 'No beagles are cats' and 'Some dogs are not beagles.' To understand how such statements should be symbolized in quantificational logic, it is helpful to use several equivalence rules and the new quantifier exchange rule.

Let's begin with the negative statement 'No beagles are cats.' If we were simply to follow the pattern that we use for single predicate statements such as 'No things are cats' and our rule of thumb that the main operator in the scope of a universal quantifier is usually the horseshoe, we might symbolize it as

42. (x)~(Bx ⊃ Cx) = **For any thing whatsoever, it is not the case that if it is a beagle, then it is a cat.**

The English translation of this formulation is so complicated that it is not intuitively obvious whether or not it says the same thing as 'No beagles are cats.' So let's try the symbolization using the existential quantifier, which gives us the following.

43. ~(∃x)(Bx · Cx) = **It is not the case that there exists at least one thing such that it is a beagle and it is also a cat.**

The English translation here seems intuitively to be the same as 'No beagles are cats.' Now let us convert the existential quantifier into a universal quantifier using the rule of quantifier exchange (abbreviated 'QE'), which will give us

44. ~(∃x)(Bx · Cx) ≡ (x)~(Bx · Cx)   **QE**

We can see immediately that although the universally quantified schema on the right is similar to **42**, it is different insofar as the main operator in the parentheses after the universal quantifier is the horseshoe in **42** while it is the dot in **44**. Let us apply the equivalence rule of material implication to the second half of **44**. (We must use double negation once first, in order to comply with the rule of rigor.)

44a. ~(∃x)(Bx · Cx) ≡ (x)~(Bx · Cx)   **QE**
 ≡ (x)~(Bx · ~~Cx)   **D.N.**
 ≡ (x)(Bx ⊃ ~Cx)   **Impl.**

The final formula can be directly translated into English as 'For any thing whatsoever, if that thing is a beagle then it is not a cat.' And it should be intuitively clear that this says the same thing as 'No beagles are cats,' and that **42** is *not* a correct symbolization of such a universal negative proposition.

We therefore recommend as a basic rule of thumb that statements expressed by *sentences of the general form 'No D are G' should be symbolized starting with the tilde preceding the existential quantifier*. We can then apply the quantifier exchange rule and the various equivalence rules to change it into a formula with the universal quantifier and a horseshoe if this is desired. This procedure also allows us to deal with statements with more than two predicates such as 'Nobody who studies hard and is intelligent will fail this logic course,' as is shown below.

45. ~(∃x)(((Px · Sx) · Ix) · Fx) ≡ (x)~(((Px · Sx) · Ix) · Fx)   **QE**
 ≡ (x)(~((Px · Sx) · Ix) ∨ ~Fx)   **DeM.**
 ≡ (x)(((Px · Sx) · Ix) ⊃ ~Fx)   **Impl.**

What about statements such as 'Some dogs are not beagles'? If we were to try to follow the same pattern as we did for statements such as 'Something is not a beagle' (which we symbolized as '(∃x)~Bx') and then apply De Morgan's rule to it, we would get

46. (∃x)~(Dx · Bx) ≡ (∃x)(~Dx ∨ ~Bx)

which translates into English as

> **There exists at least one thing such that it is either not a dog or not a beagle.**

This symbolization expresses a true proposition if at least one thing exists that is not a dog; for example, it is proven true by the fact that this book exists and is not a dog (nor is it a beagle). But this is not what 'Some dogs are not beagles' says. Thus, we need to try a different formulation. It should be intuitively apparent that 'Some dogs are not beagles' is normally used to express essentially the same statement as 'It is not the case that all dogs are beagles,' which can be symbolized as

47. ~(x)(Dx ⊃ Bx)

We can transform this formula using the rules of quantifier exchange, material implication and double negation into an equivalent formula with an existential quantifier as follows.

47. ~(x)(Dx ⊃ Bx) ≡ (∃x)~(Dx ⊃ Bx)   QE
  ≡ (∃x)~~(Dx · ~Bx)   Impl.
  ≡ (∃x)(Dx · ~Bx)   D.N.

The final formula can be translated into English as

> **There exists at least one thing that is a dog and is not a beagle.**

which is true if and only if at least one dog that is not a beagle exists. The existence of things such as this book cannot make **47** true because they do not satisfy the requirement that at least one dog exists.

In the United States there is more space where nobody is than where anybody is.

Gertrude Stein

This deceptively simple statement is trickier to symbolize than it might at first appear to be. Be careful!

It is important to recognize that the formulas in **47** are quite different from the following.

48. $(\exists x)(\sim Dx \cdot Bx)$

Statement **48** asserts that at least one thing exists that is not a dog but is a beagle—in other words, that some beagles are not dogs. This makes it clear that we cannot simply use the existential quantifier and put a tilde in front of either of the predicates that we might arbitrarily choose. The placement of the tilde *does* make a very big difference. If you are in doubt as to where to put the tilde, it might be wise to symbolize statements of the form 'Some D are not G' with a negation in front of the universal quantifier and then transform this into an existentially quantified statement. The horseshoe in the universally quantified form guarantees that the predicates are in the proper sequence.

EXERCISE 7–9

(a) Abbreviate the following sentences expressing propositions using the universal quantifier, individual variables, predicate and individual constants, and truth-functional operators as necessary. (b) Indicate precisely which part of the original sentence each constant symbolizes. (c) Use the rule of quantifier exchange and the equivalence rules from propositional logic to transform the abbreviation from one with a universal quantifier into one with an existential quantifier or vice versa. (d) Finally, translate your symbolized expression in (c) into English to check to see whether it has the same meaning as the original.

1. Nobody is tall.
2. Some students do not work.
3. Someone is not both tall and heavy.
4. No cities have populations of more than a million.
5. No tall students are heavy.
6. Not every student wants to do well.
7. Some imported cars are not fast.
8. No fragile things are tough.
9. Some valuable things are not insured.
10. Some tall people are not basketball players.

7.7 Multiple Quantifiers

Thus far we have only considered statements that do not have quantifiers inside the scope of other quantifiers. This means that we cannot yet symbolize statements such as 'Something is faster than something else' or 'Nothing is bigger than everything.' We have all of the necessary symbols for doing this, but we must learn to deal with a number of complications.

The first principle for dealing with statements that require one quantifier to have one or more other quantifiers in its scope is that we must use a different variable in each quantifier so that we can identify which of the subsequent variables belong to each quantifier.

Using a universal quantifier within the scope of another universal quantifier can be done quite straightforwardly as can be seen in the following symbolization.

49. (x)(y)Sxy = Everything is s̲imilar to everything.

This reads awkwardly if we try to interpret it literally; it says 'For any thing whatsoever, it is similar to any thing whatsoever.' Although we might have an instinctive urge to add to the end of this sentence the phrase 'other than itself,' we must not do so. Remember from our discussion of formulas **34** and **35** that the universal quantifier tells us that absolutely anything in the universe can be put in the place of the second variable, including the same thing that was substituted for the first variable. Thus if we are to add anything to our English translation at all, we must add at the end 'including itself,' however absurd this may in fact be.

Since the predicate 'similar' represents a reflexive relation, its correct symbolization is given by **49**. But nonreflexive predicates such as 'is bigger than' and 'is next to' cannot be symbolized in this way.

In order to eliminate the reflexive element of the symbolization in **49**, we must use the identity predicate 'I,' which we introduced earlier to perform a similar function when we were using single quantifiers. We need to state explicitly that the individual substituted for the variable 'x' cannot be the same as the individual substituted for the variable 'y.' We can express this as '~Ixy,' which means simply that whatever individual is inserted into the 'x' blank must be different than the individual inserted into the 'y' blank. We can now symbolize a nonreflexive relation as

50. (x)(y)(~Ixy ⊃ Nxy) = Everything is n̲ext to everything except itself.

Similarly, using existential quantifiers, we can symbolize 'Something is faster than something else' as

51. (∃x)(∃y)(~Ixy · Fxy) = **There exists at least one thing that is not i̲dentical to some other thing and it is f̲aster than that thing.**

If we had left out the '~Ixy,' the formula would have asserted that something is faster than something—possibly itself, which is not what we wanted to say! This might not be obvious because the use of the two different individual variables seems to indicate that the two things being referred to must be different. But because a variable is merely a blank into which the name of any individual

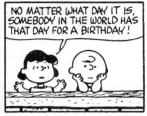

Reprinted by permission of UFS, Inc.

Symbolize Lucy's statements in frames 1 and 2 using quantificational logic. Although the English sentences are quite different, it is possible that they express identical propositions. Did you symbolize the two in the same way? If not, what accounts for the difference between your two formulations?

whatsoever can be inserted, it is in fact possible that the same individual could be referred to by both the 'x' and the 'y' unless this possibility is explicitly ruled out. And the only way we have at this point to rule out the possibility that the same term is substituted for both 'x' and 'y' is to explicitly assert that the individual in the x blank cannot be identical to the individual in the y blank.

When we are using two or more instances of the same quantifier (that is, all universal quantifiers or all existential quantifiers) at the beginning of a formula, it does not make any difference which one we put first, which second, and so on. But when we are using at least one of each kind, the sequence affects the meaning in very significant ways. We can see this clearly if we take a single two-place relational predicate—let us say 'Bxy' = 'x is bigger than y'—and use one universal quantifier and one existential quantifier and two individual variables in different sequences.

52. $(x)(\exists y)Bxy$

53. $(x)(\exists y)Byx$

54. $(\exists y)(x)Byx$

55. $(\exists y)(x)Bxy$

Notice that all four of these formulas have the same quantifiers and the same individual variables; only one change in order is made in going from one formula to the next. But each of them has a very different meaning from each of the others, as we shall see when we translate them into English.

It is a bit difficult to translate these formulas, so we rely on some simple diagrams to help. Formula **52** can be translated literally into something like 'For every thing whatsoever, there exists at least one thing such that the first is bigger than the second,' or more simply (but not necessarily more clearly), 'Everything is bigger than something or other.' To really understand what this means, consider the diagram in Figure 7–1, in which each number represents a particular individual in the universe, and an arrow between two numbers indicates that the thing referred to by the number at the "tail" is bigger than the thing referred to by the number at the point of the arrow. For example, if

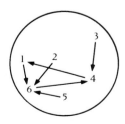

Figure 7–1

we have '1 → 5,' this means that the specific individual named by '1' is bigger than the specific individual named by '5.'

Given these meanings, Figure 7–1 displays the meaning of **52** in a universe consisting of exactly six individuals, namely that whichever individual we select out of the universe, it is bigger than at least one other individual. Notice that this requires that we have the absurd situation that some things—in this case 1, 6, and 4—must also be bigger than themselves, again because of the sweeping inclusiveness of the universal quantifier. Our choice of a universe with six members is entirely arbitrary; the same concept can be illustrated by a diagram of a universe with any finite number of individual members whatsoever. But no matter what size the universe might be, there has to exist at least one string of arrows that ultimately go in a circle, indicating that each object in the string is bigger than itself. (This situation can be avoided only if we add an additional component asserting that at least one individual exists that is not bigger than anything else—but this involves complications that we can't go into here.)

Formula **53** can be translated literally as 'For every thing whatsoever, there exists at least one thing such that the second is bigger than the first.' An equivalent but simpler formulation is 'Everything is such that something is bigger than it.' Again, the meaning is made more clear by a diagrammatic representation of the universe, this time one with the arbitrarily chosen number of eight individuals shown in Figure 7–2. Given that the numbers and arrows have the same meaning as in Figure 7–1, this diagram shows that for whichever individual we choose from this universe, there exists at least one other individual that is bigger than the first. Notice that only some of the individuals need to be such that they are also bigger than at least one other individual. But as with **52**, this formula does not rule out the possibility that some individuals (in Figure 7–2 they are numbered 1, 4, and 8) are bigger than themselves.

Formula **54** translates literally into an English sentence that is at least as awkward as those for **52** and **53**, but it has an equivalent interpretation that is quite simple and comprehensible. The literal translation is 'There exists at least one thing such that for any thing whatsoever, the first is bigger than the second.' The simple version is 'There exists at least one thing that is bigger than everything,' or even simpler, 'A biggest thing exists.' This is shown clearly in the diagram in Figure 7–3, which is of a universe with the arbitrarily chosen numbers of ten individuals. Notice that we had to include an arrow that begins with individual 8 and that loops around and points at 8, thus indicating that individual 8 is bigger than itself. Although we know commonsensically that this is impossible, it is what **54** says for any finite universe. To eliminate this absurdity, we would have to add a component that specifies that any individual substituted for the x variable must not be identical to any individual substituted for the y variable, that is,

$$(\exists y)(x)(\sim Iyx \supset Byx)$$

Finally, **55** also has a complex literal translation as well as a simple version. The literal English translation is 'There exists at least one thing such that for

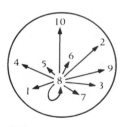

Figure 7–2

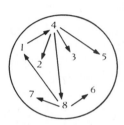

Figure 7–3

We have put quite a bit of emphasis on the need to look out for statements in which the use of a quantifier adds a self-reference that was not intended in the original English expression. But what does one do with an explicitly self-referential statement such as the sign in the photograph? What would you do if you drove by and saw it? Would you be ignoring the sign or not?

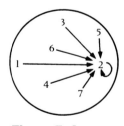

Figure 7–4

any thing whatsoever the second is bigger than the first.' The simpler, but equivalent, translation is 'There exists at least one thing such that everything is bigger than it,' or even more simply, 'A smallest thing exists.' This is shown in the diagram of an arbitrarily chosen universe of seven individuals in Figure 7–4. Notice again that the individual than which every individual is bigger (that is, the smallest individual) must also be bigger than itself. This can be avoided if we add a component that stipulates that the individual substituted for the x variable cannot be identical to the individual substituted for the y variable, that is,

$$(\exists y)(x)(\sim Iyx \supset Bxy).$$

EXERCISE 7–10

(a) Translate the following formulas into English using the dictionary provided. (b) Use the rule of quantifier exchange and the equivalence rules from propositional logic to transform the formula from one with a universal quantifier and horseshoe operator into one with an existential quantifier and dot operator or vice versa. (c) Finally, translate your symbolized expression in (b) into English to check to see whether it has the same meaning as the original.

Dictionary:

t	= Tom	Px	= x is a person
m	= Mary	Hxy	= x is happier than y
Hx	= x is happy	Ixy	= x is identical to y
Fx	= x is fast	Fxy	= x is faster than y
Tx	= x passes the test	Lxyz	= x likes y better than z

1. (x)Ftx
2. (x)(∃y)Fxy
3. (x)(∃y)Fyx
4. (∃x)(∃y)Fxy
5. ~(∃x)(y)Hxy
6. (∃x)~Ltxm
7. (∃x)(y)Hxy
8. (y)(∃x)Hxy
9. (x)((Px · Hx) ⊃ Fx)
10. (x)(∃y)((Px · Py) ⊃ Hxy)
11. (x)(∃y)(~Ixy ⊃ Fyx)
12. (∃x)(y)(((Px · Py) · ~Ixy) · Hyx)
13. ~(x)(y)((Tx · ~Ty) ⊃ Hxy)
14. (x)((Px · Tx) ⊃ Hxm)
15. (x)(y)(((Px · Hx) · (Py · ~Hy)) ⊃ Ltxy)

EXERCISE 7–11

Translate each of the following quantified propositions into English. (Use the provided dictionary.)

Dictionary:

Px	= x is a person	Nx	= x is nocturnal
Lx	= x is a librarian	Vx	= x is a violinist
Ax	= x will earn an A in logic	Qx	= x is quarantined
Bxy	= x borrowed y	Lxy	= x is more logical than y
Hxy	= x studies harder than y	Dxy	= x drank y

1. (∃x)(y)Hxy
2. (∃x)(y)Hyx
3. (y)(∃x)Hyx
4. (y)(∃x)Hxy
5. (x)(Px · Vx)
6. (x)(∃y)(Nx ⊃ Lxy)
7. (∃x)(y)(Nx · Lxy)

8. (y)(∃x)(Hyx ⊃ Ay)

9. (x)(∃y)(Px ⊃ Bxy)

10. (∃x)(y)(Lx · Lxy)

11. (∃y)(x)(Lxy · ~Ly)

12. (x)(∃y)(Lyx ⊃ ~Ax)

13. (y)(∃x)(Lyx ⊃ Ax)

14. (∃y)(x)(Qy · Ax)

15. (x)(∃y)(Px · Bxy)

16. (y)(∃x)(Px · Bxy)

17. (x)(∃y)((Px · Py) ⊃ ~Lxy)

18. (y)(∃x) ((Px · Py) ⊃ Lxy)

19. (∃x)(Px ⊃ Vx)

20. (∃x)(y)(Px ⊃ Dxy)

21. (∃x)(y)((Px · Py) · Hxy)

22. (∃y)(Py · (x)(Px ⊃ Hxy))

23. (∃x)(y)(Px ⊃ Hxy)

24. (∃x)(y)((Px · Py) · Lxy)

25. (∃y)(x)((Px · ~Ixy) ⊃ Lxy)

26. (∃x)(y)((Px · ~Ixy) · Byx)

27. (x)(∃y)(((Px · Py) · ~Ixy) ⊃ Lxy)

28. (∃x)(∃y)(((Py · Px) · ~Ixy) · (Vx · Vy))

Although we are now closing our discussion of symbolizing statements in quantificational logic, we are far from having covered the entire topic. As a matter of fact, we have only begun to scratch the surface. As indicated at the beginning of the chapter, this is a particularly sophisticated and powerful system of logic. It is hoped that enough has been shown of it to convince you of the truth of this claim and also to convey a basic understanding of the fundamental concepts of quantificational logic. Anyone who is truly interested in learning more about this system should seek out an opportunity to take an advanced course in logic that will go into it in greater depth.

We must also recognize that we have not done enough to allow anyone to claim mastery even of the aspects of quantificational logic discussed in this chapter. The fact of the matter is that the process of translating statements expressed in everyday English into the symbolism of quantificational logic is as much an art as it is a technical skill. Ordinary English usage is so rich, so full of subtlety and complexity, and all too often so vague and ambiguous, that no set of rules or mechanical translating techniques can guarantee complete and accurate translations from English into quantificational symbolism. Some additional opportunities to do more sophisticated translations from English are

If blood be shed, let it be our blood. Cultivate the quiet courage of dying without killing. For man lives freely only by his readiness to die, if need be, at the hands of his brother, never by killing him.

MOHANDAS KARAMCHAND GANDHI

Use the principle of charity to add the suppressed premises and conclusion to this argument. Then symbolize each statement in quantificational logic.

provided in Chapter 14. Continual practice over a sustained period of time, together with discussions and arguments with others working on the same statements, is most likely to help you develop your abilities in this area.

With these qualifying comments in mind, we present the following rules of thumb for translating statements from ordinary English into quantificational logic. While they should be helpful in many cases, these rules might not always lead to the desired results. Even practice probably will not make you a perfect translator, but it will certainly make you a better one.

Rules for Symbolizing English Statements in Quantificational Logic

1. The main operator inside the scope of a universal quantifier is usually the horseshoe (material implication).

2. The main operator inside the scope of an existential quantifier is usually the dot (conjunction).

3. The negation operator does not always capture the precise meaning of the antonym of a term.

4. Make certain that all individual variables are bound by a quantifier.

5. Use a predicate constant (usually 'P') if persons are being referred to (e.g., 'some*one*', 'every*body*').

6. Use the negated identity operator (e.g., '~Ixy') to explicitly rule out the possibility that an individual has a relation to itself (e.g., is larger than itself).

EXERCISE 7–12

(a) Abbreviate the following sentences expressing propositions, using the universal and existential quantifiers, individual variables, predicate and individual constants, and truth-functional operators as necessary. (b) Indicate precisely what part of the original sentence each constant symbolizes. (c) Finally, translate your symbolized expression back into English, noting what meaning has been lost from the original.

1. Emil is in the tournament and there is at least one player in the tournament whom Emil can beat.
2. All members of the chess team are friends of George.
3. George's friends are all members of the chess team.
4. Everyone has at least one friend.
5. If some residents of Dorm A are women, then not all residents of Dorm A are men.
6. Whatever is greater than something is neither less than nor equal to that thing.
7. All members of the L family greet everyone they meet.
8. Something is identical to something.
9. Nothing is identical to everything.
10. If Sally is older than Winifred, then Winifred is not older than Sally.
11. George is always late for class.
12. Everyone who knows German knows at least one foreign language.
13. Most cigar smokers prefer a mild tobacco.
14. Old wines are not always the best wines.
15. All members of the Dean's List are students with good grades.
16. All members of the L family greet everyone they meet, if they remember their names.

EXERCISE 7-13

Quantificational treatment might, or might not, make the logic of the following statements clearer. Symbolize them and compare your symbolizations with those of other students. Discuss any differences.

1. No great advance has ever been made in science, politics, or religion, without controversy. (Lyman Beecher)
2. If you do not tell the truth about yourself you cannot tell it about other people. (Virginia Woolf)
3. We affirm, as a fundamental principle, that labor, the creator of wealth, is entitled to all it creates. (Wendell Phillips)
4. If my theory of relativity is proven successful, Germany will claim me as a German and France will declare that I am a citizen of the world. Should my theory prove untrue, France will say that I am a German, and Germany will declare that I am a Jew. (Albert Einstein)
5. All law has for its object to confirm and exalt into a system the exploitation of the workers by a ruling class. (Mikhail A. Bakunin)

6. If the thing believed is incredible, it is also incredible that the incredible should have been so believed. (Saint Augustine)

Summary

1. Quantificational logic is more powerful and sophisticated than either syllogistic logic or propositional logic, but it does not provide a decision procedure—such as Venn diagrams or truth tables—that would enable us to always determine in a finite number of steps whether a particular argument is valid or invalid.

2. Quantificational logic deals with the internal structure of both simple and compound propositions. It distinguishes between proper nouns (that is, names of specific individual persons, places, things, groups, and organizations) and general nouns (any nouns that are not proper nouns). Proper nouns are abbreviated using small letters from 'a' through 't' and general nouns are abbreviated with capital letters from 'A' through 'Z.' The small letters are called **individual constants** and the capital letters are called **predicate constants.** A simple sentence can be abbreviated using an individual constant for its subject term and a predicate constant for its predicate term; for example, 'Pat is tall' can be abbreviated as 'Tp.'

3. Any abbreviation can be transformed into a schema by replacing one or more of its constants with variables. Only individual variables, represented by the small letters 'u' through 'z,' are used in this chapter. These individual variables function as blanks into which we can substitute any individual constant (or proper noun).

4. The five truth-functional operators can be used in quantificational logic. The negation operator is particularly tricky. Placing a tilde in front of a predicate constant does not always accurately represent the meaning of the original English expression. For example, symbolizing 'Mark is unhappy' as '~Hm' leaves open the possibility (ruled out by 'unhappy') that Mark is neither happy nor unhappy.

5. The **existential quantifier,** represented by a reversed capital E connected to an individual variable, all contained in parentheses, '(∃x),' means 'There exists at least one thing such that. . . .' Its meaning is close to that of 'some' in everyday English, but it can also be used to symbolize expressions such as 'several,' 'more,' and 'most,' even though using it for these latter terms results in considerable loss of meaning.

6. To express a complete statement, the existential quantifier must be followed by at least one schema consisting of a predicate constant attached to at least one individual variable of the same kind as that included in the quantifier. The quantifier '(∃x)' refers to at least one of all possible things in the universe; it is wrong to translate it as referring to a person or a

member of some other subclass of all things. To symbolize 'Some*body* is happy' it is necessary to add a term that states explicitly that the thing that is happy is also a person, for example, '(∃x)(Px · Hx).'

7. When using two or more predicate constants with a single quantifier, it is important to be aware of the scope of the quantifier. The **scope** of a quantifier begins with the first parenthesis following it and ends when that parenthesis is closed off, that is, where the right-hand parenthesis paired with it appears. When a variable is within the scope of its quantifier, it is **bound;** when it is outside the scope of its quantifier, it is **free.**

8. The **universal quantifier,** represented by an individual variable contained in parentheses, for example, '(x),' means 'For any thing whatsoever. . . .' Its meaning is close to that of 'all,' 'any,' and 'every' in everyday English.

9. To express a complete statement, the universal quantifier must be followed by at least one schema consisting of a predicate constant attached to at least one individual variable of the same kind as that included in the quantifier. The quantifier '(x)' refers to all possible things in the universe; it is wrong to translate it as referring to persons or some other subclass of all things. To symbolize 'Every*body* is happy' it is necessary to add a term that states explicitly that the thing that is happy is also a person, for example '(x)(Px ⊃ Hx).'

10. When symbolizing a proposition involving more than one predicate term with a universal quantifier, it is usually necessary to use the horseshoe rather than the dot as the main operator within the scope of the quantifier.

11. When using a quantifier with a two-place (or larger) predicate, it is important to be aware of the **reflexive** characteristic of such expressions, that is, that they keep open the possibility that a thing may have that relation to itself. If the original statement does not say that a thing stands in a relation to itself (e.g., that a thing is larger than itself), then it is necessary to use the predicate '~Ixy' (= 'x is not identical to y') to make it explicit that it does not stand in that relation to itself.

12. The **quantifier exchange** rule (abbreviated '**QE**') states that we can change any universal quantifier to an existential quantifier and any existential quantifier to a universal quantifier if at the same time we add exactly one negation sign immediately preceding and following the new quantifier.

Chapter 8

Quantificational Logic: Arguments

One of the most important values of any logical system is its usefulness in proving the validity of arguments. And one of our main reasons for going beyond the two systems of logic introduced earlier in this book (syllogistic and propositional) is that they are inadequate for proving many valid arguments to be in fact valid.

We saw in Chapter 7 that the equivalence rules of propositional logic can be used anywhere including inside the scope of quantifiers, but the first eight inference rules of propositional logic can be used *only* on the main operator of a step if it is *outside* the scope of any quantifiers. We also introduced a new equivalence rule for quantifiers, the rule of quantifier exchange. Even with this new rule, because of the limitation on the use of the eight inference rules, we are not able to construct proofs of the validity of relatively simple valid arguments such as

All humans are mortal.	$(x)(Hx \supset Mx)$
Socrates is a human.	Hs
Therefore, Socrates is mortal.	$\therefore Ms$

It is intuitively obvious that if it is true that all humans are mortal, then it must also be true that any specific human such as Socrates must be mortal, but we have as yet no inference rule that enables us to do anything with our quantified first premise that will in turn connect it with the second premise to give us the conclusion. We must therefore introduce such inference rules now.

8.1 Universal Instantiation

The first new inference rule for quantifiers is relatively simple and straight-forward; it can even be described as intuitively obvious. This rule permits us to remove a universal quantifier that is the main operator of a step (including a premise) of a proof. This is particularly valuable because it permits us in many cases to apply one or more of the first eight inference rules to the "interior" of the step. The only complication here is that we cannot merely delete the quantifier, for this would give us an open sentence—that is, a sentence with one or more "holes" in it where it has unbound individual variables. Thus, *the rule that permits us to remove the universal quantifier also stipulates that we must change each occurrence of the individual variable in the quantifier to an individual constant—more specifically, to the* same *individual constant at each occurrence*. This rule of inference is called **universal instantiation,** and it is abbreviated as **UI.**

Although the rule of universal instantiation is relatively straightforward, you must respect several restrictions when using it. These restrictions are as follows.

Restrictions on Universal Instantiation

1. **UI** can be applied only to a universal quantifier that is the main logical operator in a step of a proof. Thus '(x)Px ⊃ Fa / ∴ Pa ⊃ Fa' is not a valid instance of **UI,** because the horseshoe, rather than the universal quantifier, is the main operator in the original step. Likewise, '(∃y)(x)Kxy / ∴ (∃y)Kay' is not a correct application of **UI,** since the existential quantifier '(∃y)' is the main operator in the original step. And '(∃y)(Gy · (x)Byx) / ∴ (∃y)(Gy · Byn)' is not a correct use of **UI,** again because the universal quantifier is not the main operator in the original step.

2. If **UI** is applied at all in a step, every occurrence in that step of the variable in the universal quantifier must be replaced by the same constant. Thus, '(x)(Px ⊃ Fx) / ∴ Pa ⊃ Fx' is not a correct application of **UI** because no constant has been substituted for the variable 'x' in the second term 'Fx.' And '(x)(Px ⊃ Fx) / ∴ Pa ⊃ Pb' violates this restriction on **UI** because the same constant has not been substituted for the variable in the quantifier in every occurrence.

Since the universal quantifier refers literally to *every* thing in the universe, it is permissible to substitute *any* individual constant whatsoever for the variable in the quantifier being removed. The decision as to which specific constant to use in a given application of the rule is entirely dependent on what is needed in that particular context. If the constant **j** appears in other steps to which the universally quantified step needs to be connected, then we can use **j** as the constant when we apply **UI** to the step. But if we need a **q** for our proof, we can use **q** when we apply **UI**. In fact, if it is necessary, we can apply **UI** several different times to the same universally quantified expression to get formulas with different individual constants, as in the proof of the valid argument 'All students work hard. Tom and Sue are students, so they must work hard.' The proof of the validity of this argument goes as follows.

1.	(x)(Sx ⊃ Wx)	Premise
2.	St · Ss / ∴ Wt · Ws	Premise/conclusion
3.	St ⊃ Wt	UI, 1
4.	St	Simp., 2
5.	Wt	M.P., 3,4
6.	Ss ⊃ Ws	UI, 1
7.	Ss	Simp., 2
8.	Ws	M.P., 6,7
9.	Wt · Ws	Conj., 5,8

Once again, the only restriction on the substitution of individual constants is that the **same** constant must be substituted for **every** instance of the variable in the universal quantifier that is being removed, in the step where **UI** is being applied.

The following are all examples of the application of the rule of universal instantiation:

1. (x)Fx / ∴ Fc
2. (x)(Px ⊃ Fx) / ∴ Pg ⊃ Fg
3. (x)(∃y)Kxy / ∴ (∃y)Kay
4. (x)(Gx ⊃ (∃y)Byx) / ∴ Gn ⊃ (∃y)Byn

Each of these four inferences meets the requirements of the rule of universal instantiation.

Although **UI** can be used only when the universal quantifier is the main operator in a step, other rules sometimes can be used to translate a formula into an equivalent form to which **UI** can be correctly applied, as can be seen in the following example.

1.	~(∃x)(Px ∨ Rx) / ∴ ~ Rg	Premise/conclusion
2.	(x)~(Px ∨ Rx)	QE, 1
3.	~(Pg ∨ Rg)	UI, 2
4.	~Pg · ~Rg	DeM., 3
5.	~ Rg	Simp., 4

Reprinted by permission of UFS, Inc.

Charlie Brown presents an argument (in enthymematic form) in frame 2. State the implicit premise(s) and then symbolize the argument as a whole. Try to construct a proof of the argument (it will require the use of **UI**). Charlie then tries to amplify his argument in frame 3. Symbolize the statement that he makes there and think about how it might relate to the argument in frame 2. Is Charlie correct when he says that it doesn't make sense?

EXERCISE 8–1

Explain why each of the following is not a correct application of the rule of universal instantiation.

1. (x)Tx ⊃ (y)Dy / ∴ Tc ⊃ (y)Dy
2. (x)(Gx ⊃ Mx) / ∴ Gx ⊃ Mx
3. (x)~Dx ≡ (x)Bx / ∴ (x)~Dx ≡ Bp
4. (x)(Fx ⊃ Bx) / ∴ Fa ⊃ Bx
5. (x)Px ⊃ Jx / ∴ Pn ⊃ Jn
6. (x)~(Qx ⊃ ~Px) / ∴ ~Qd ⊃ (x)~Px
7. ~(x)(~Dx ⊃ Kx) / ∴ ~(~Dg ⊃ Kg)
8. (x)(~Fx ∨ (y)Ry) / ∴ ~Fj ∨ Rj
9. (x)(y)~(Px · Py) / ∴ ~(Pf · Pk)
10. (y)(x)((Py ∨ Kx) · Ny) / ∴ (y)((Py ∨ Kr) · Ny)

EXERCISE 8–2

For each of the following formulas, apply the rule of universal instantiation to any quantifiers to which its application is permissible. In those cases where UI cannot be correctly used, explain why it cannot be used.

1. (x)Tx
2. (x)(Gx ⊃ (Mx · Rx))
3. (∃x)~Dx ≡ (x)Bx
4. (x)(Fx ⊃ Bx)
5. (x)Px ⊃ Jx
6. (x)~(Qx ⊃ ~Px)

7. ~(x)(~Dx ⊃ Kx)

8. (x)(~Fx ⊃ (Ta ∨ (∃y)Ry))

9. (x)(∃y)~((Px · Py) ⊃ Gxy)

10. (∃y)(x)((Py ∨ Kx) · Ny)

8.2 Existential Generalization

The next new inference rule for quantifiers is also relatively simple and straightforward. In nontechnical terms, it says that if we know that something is true of a particular individual, then we can say that the same thing is true of at least one thing. This rule permits us to make inferences that are intuitively valid but that cannot be proven valid using the rules that we have introduced so far. 'Everything has mass, therefore something has mass' is an example of an intuitively valid argument that cannot be proven valid without this new rule.

(x)Mx / ∴ (∃x)Mx

We can use **UI** to remove the universal quantifier in the premise to get 'Ma' (or 'M' with any other individual variable), but then we are at a dead end. We do not have a formal rule in our logical system that lets us take the next, intuitively obvious, step of *going from the step that asserts that a specific individual* **a** *is an* **M** *to the conclusion that at least one thing is an* **M**. To make such inferences possible in our system of logic, we introduce a rule that enables us to do precisely this; this rule is known as **existential generalization**, and it is abbreviated as **EG**. We can now complete the proof using **EG** as follows.

1.	(x)Mx / ∴ (∃x)Mx	Premise/conclusion
2.	Ma	UI, 1
3.	(∃x)Mx	EG, 2

The restrictions on the use of the rule of existential generalization are simple and straightforward. We can use it on any step that contains at least one individual constant, as long as we do not violate any of the following restrictions.

Restrictions on Existential Generalization

1. **EG** can be applied only when the new existential quantifier is the main operator in a step. It follows from this that **EG** cannot be used within the scope of another quantifier; for example, we cannot use **EG** to go directly from '(x)(Px ⊃ Jxm)' to '(x)(∃y)(Px ⊃ Jxy)' because the new existential quantifier is inside the scope of the universal quantifier.

2. We cannot apply a single quantifier to more than one kind of individual constant. Thus, we cannot use **EG** to go from 'Fc ∨ Gk' to '(∃x)(Fx ∨ Gx).' We can go from 'Fc ∨ Gk' to '(∃x)(Fx ∨ Gx).'

3. We must apply **EG** to all occurrences of a particular constant in a step. In other words, it would be incorrect to go from 'Hr · Lr' to '(∃y)Hy · Lr.'

Within these restrictions, all of the following are legitimate applications of **EG.**

5. **Kc / ∴ (∃x)Kx**

6. **(Pb ∨ Fb) / ∴ (∃y)(Py ∨ Fy)**

7. **Hg · Rn / ∴ (∃x)(Hg · Rx)**

8. **(x)Axr · Bd / ∴ (∃y)((x)Axr · By)**

9. **(∃x)((Px · Pq) · Mqx) / ∴ (∃y)(∃x)((Px · Py) · Myx)**

Notice that we do not have to be concerned about going from a true universal statement about nonexistent things to a false statement with the existential quantifier asserting that at least one of those nonexistent things exists. For example, we cannot use **UI** and **EG** to prove valid an argument such as 'All unicorns have a single horn in the middle of their foreheads, so at least one unicorn with a single horn in the middle of its forehead exists.' This is because a formula with the universal quantifier as its main operator normally needs to have the horseshoe as the main operator in its scope. We can see why the inference to the existence of a unicorn can't be proved valid with **UI** and **EG** if we try to construct such a proof.

"The Wizard of ID" by permission of Johnny Hart and Creators Syndicate, Inc.

Construct an argument that reflects the peasant's reasoning process that led to his response to the knight's question. Then symbolize the argument in quantificational logic and try to construct a proof of its validity.

1. (x)(Ux ⊃ Hx) / ∴ (∃x)(Ux · Hx)   Premise/conclusion
2. Ua ⊃ Ha   UI, 1
3. (∃x)(Ux ⊃ Hx)   EG, 2

Step 3 does *not* say that at least one unicorn with a single horn in the middle of its forehead exists; it *does* say that *if* at least one thing exists such that it is a unicorn then it has a single horn in the middle of its forehead. This is even more clear when we recognize that step 3 is equivalent (by the rule of material implication) to '(∃x)(~Ux ∨ Hx).' This says that at least one thing exists such that it is either *not* a unicorn *or* it has a horn in the middle of its forehead, and it is confirmed as true by the existence of this book (which is not a unicorn).

EXERCISE 8–3

Explain why each of the following is not a correct application of the rule of existential generalization.

1. Ta · (y)Dy / ∴ (∃x)Tx · (y)Dy
2. Gf · Mc / ∴ (∃y)(Gy · My)
3. ~Dm ≡ (x)Bx / ∴ (∃y)~Dy ≡ (x)Bx
4. Fa · Ba / ∴ (∃y)Fy · Ba
5. Pn · Jd / ∴ (∃y)(Py · Jy)
6. ~(Qm · ~Pm) / ∴ ~(∃x)(Qx · ~Px)
7. ~(x)(~Dg ⊃ Kx) / ∴ ~(x)(∃y)(~Dy ⊃ Kx)
8. (x)(~Fx ∨ Rb) / ∴ (x)(∃y)(~Fx ∨ Ry)
9. ~(Pf · Pq) / ∴ (∃x)(∃y)~(Px · Py)
10. (x)((Px ∨ Kh) ⊃ Nx) / ∴ (x)(∃y)((Px ∨ Ky) ⊃ Nx)

EXERCISE 8–4

For each of the following formulas, apply the rule of existential generalization to any individual constants to which its application is allowed. In those cases where EG cannot be correctly used, explain why it cannot be used.

1. Ta
2. (Gc · (Mc · Rc))
3. ~Dm ≡ (x)Bx
4. (Fr · Bf)
5. (x)Px · Jh
6. (x)~(Qp ⊃ ~Px)
7. ~(De · Kn)
8. (x)(~Fx · (Ta ∨ Rb))
9. (x)~((Px · Pg) ⊃ Gxg)
10. (Pf ∨ Kd) · Nf

EXERCISE 8–5

Use quantifier exchange, universal instantiation, and existential generalization in addition to the rules of propositional logic to construct proofs of the validity of the following arguments. (All are valid.)

1. (y)Dy / ∴ (∃y)Dy

2. (x)(Gx ⊃ Mc) / ∴ (∃y)(~Gy ∨ My)

3. ~(∃x)Bx / ∴ ~Bf

4. ~(y)(Fy ⊃ By) / ∴ (∃y)(Fy · ~By)

5. Pn ∨ (x)Jx
   ~Pn / ∴ (∃y)Jy

6. ~(x)~Qx ⊃ ~Pm
   Pm / ∴ (∃x)~(Qx · Rx)

7. ~(∃x)(Dx · ~Kx)
   ~ Kr / ∴ ~(x)(Dx · Kx)

8. (y)(Fy ⊃ Ry) / ∴ (∃y)(~Fy ∨ Ry)

9. ~(Pf · Pq) ∨ ~(∃x)Qx
   (x)(Pf · Rx)
   ~Pq ⊃ ~Rj / ∴ (∃y)~Qy

10. (x)((Px ∨ Kh) ⊃ Nx)
    Kh / ∴ ~(x)(~Jx · ~Nx)

8.3 Existential Instantiation

The next new inference rule for quantifiers is not as intuitively obvious as the rules of **UI** and **EG,** and it requires a rather strong restriction on it to guarantee that only valid inferences are permitted. This new rule *permits us to remove an existential quantifier* and thus is known as the rule of **existential instantiation** (abbreviated as **EI**). The rule of existential instantiation has all of the basic restrictions that hold for **UI**, namely that the rule can be applied only to a quantifier that is the main logical operator in a given step, and when the quantifier is removed, each and every occurrence in that step of the variable in the quantifier must be replaced by the same individual constant. In addition, **EI** *has one strong restriction that does not apply to* **UI,** *namely that the individual constant that is used to replace the individual variables cannot have appeared in any previous step of the proof and cannot appear in the conclusion.* It is helpful to understand *why* such a restriction is needed.

If we are told that at least one thing exists that has a certain property, we do not know for which specific individual (or individuals) this is true. Certainly, unlike the case for the universal quantifier, we cannot merely remove an existential quantifier and replace it with any individual constant we might wish to use. For example, if a professor is told that at least one student cheated on the last logic exam, she cannot validly infer from this information alone that it was Tom (or Mary or Ann) or any other specific individual who is the cheater. In other words, we cannot validly move from the premise '(∃x)(Sx · Cx)' to a statement about Tom's (or any other specific individual's) cheating.

This might lead us to think that we should never instantiate from an existential quantifier to a specific individual. However, there are times when we have a statement with an existential quantifier as part of a proof, and we need to drop the quantifier in order to do something that is essential for completing that proof. Thus, we need to have some way of removing the existential quantifier without using an individual constant that requires more information than is provided in the premises of the argument. We do this simply by stipulating that *we can remove an existential quantifier only if we replace each occurrence in that step of the variable in the quantifier with an individual constant that does* not *occur in any previous step of the proof or in the conclusion.*

The restriction on which constant(s) we can substitute for the variable in the removed quantifier keeps us from knowing (on the basis of the information provided in the premises) which specific individual is being talked about. To understand this better, let us consider an example. Let us assume that we have instantiated the existential quantifier in the formula '(∃x)(Sx · Ax)' according to the rule **EI** and replaced the occurrences of the variable with the individual constant **t**. Now, if someone asks us what specific individual is being referred to by **t**, we would have to answer that we know nothing whatsoever about this individual other than what is stated in this step itself, namely that **t** is a student and **t** cheated on the logic exam. If our questioner persists and asks if **t** is Tom L. Smith or Tom D. Wilson or Tom S. Jefferson, who are the only students named 'Tom' in the logic class, we would have to say that we do not know which of the three is being referred to by the **t**. As a matter of fact we do not even know that these three persons are in the course or that they are the only three students named 'Tom' because that information is not included in the premises. If it had been included in the premises and one of the three Toms had been assigned the constant **t**, we would not be able to use the constant **t** when applying **EI** because that would violate the restriction against using a constant that appears in an earlier step.

In summary, the restrictions on our rule of existential instantiation are as follows.

Restrictions on Existential Instantiation

1. **EI** cannot be applied to an existential quantifier that is not the main operator of a step. '(∃x)Mx · (∃y)Qy / ∴ Ma · (∃y)Qy' violates this restriction since the main operator is the dot. Also, '(x)(∃y)Kxy / ∴ (x)Kxa' is not a correct application of **EI**, since the universal quantifier '~(x)' is the main operator in the original step.

2. If **EI** is applied at all in a step, every instance of the variable in the existential quantifier that is in the scope of the quantifier must be replaced by the same constant. Thus, '(∃x)(Px · Fx) / ∴ Pa · Fx' is not a correct application of **EI** because no constant is substituted for the variable 'x' in the second term 'Fx.' And '(∃x)(Px · Fx) / ∴ Pa · Pb' violates this restriction on **EI** because the same constant is not substituted for the variable in the quantifier in every occurrence.

3. In any application of **EI**, the individual constant used to replace the occurrences of the variable in the quantifier must be one that has not appeared in any previous step of the proof and is not in the conclusion. To see what this means, let us assume that we have a proof with the premises '(∃x)~Px' and 'Pb ∨ (x)Fxr,' and the conclusion '(∃y)Fgy.' If at some point in the proof we find that it is necessary to remove the existential quantifier in the first premise, we cannot change it to '~Pb' (or to '~Pr') because the individual constant 'b' (and 'r') appears in a previous step (the other premise, to be precise). We also cannot instantiate to '~Pg' because the individual constant 'g' appears in the conclusion.

Given these restrictions, let us look at an example to see what a valid proof using **EI** looks like.

1.	(x)(Px ⊃ (∃y)(Byx)	Premise
2.	(∃y)(Py · ~Qy) / ∴ (∃x)(∃y)Bxy	Premise/conclusion
3.	Pa · ~Qa	EI, 2
4.	Pa ⊃ (∃y)Bya	UI, 1
5.	Pa	Simp., 3
6.	(∃y)Bya	M.P., 4,5
7.	Bca	EI, 6
8.	(∃y)Bcy	EG, 7
9.	(∃x)(∃y)Bxy	EG, 8

This example is helpful because it shows that the *sequence* in which we take steps is of particular importance when using **EI**. If we had started our proof by applying **UI** to the first premise using the individual constant **a**, we would have been prevented by restriction 3 from then applying **EI** to premise 2 using **a**. We could apply **EI** using some other individual constant, but then this would not connect up with anything else in the proof. This provides us with a general rule of thumb, namely, that *we should always use **EI** as early in a proof as possible so that we have maximum flexibility in choosing which constant to use.*

EXERCISE 8–6

Explain why each of the following is not a correct application of the rule of existential instantiation.

1. (∃x)Tx ⊃ (y)Dy / ∴ Tc ⊃ (y)Dy
2. (∃x)(Gx · Mx) / ∴ Gx · Mx
3. (x)~Dx ≡ (∃x)Bx / ∴ (x)~Dx ≡ Bp
4. (∃x)(Fx · Bx) / ∴ Fa · Bx
5. (∃x)Px · Jx / ∴ Pn · Jn
6. (∃x)~(Qx · ~Px) / ∴ ~ Qd · (∃x)~Px
7. ~(∃x)(~Dx · Kx) / ∴ ~(~Dg · Kg)
8. (∃x)(~Fx ∨ (∃y)Ry) / ∴ ~Fj ∨ Rj
9. (∃x)(∃y)~(Px · Py) / ∴ ~(Pf · Pk)
10. (y)(∃x)((Py ∨ Kx) · Ny) / ∴ (y)((Py ∨ Kr) · Ny)
11. (∃x)(Px · Sa) / ∴ (Pa · Sa)
12. (∃x)(Px · Sx) / ∴ Pa · Sa

EXERCISE 8–7

For each of the following formulas, apply the rule of existential instantiation to any quantifiers in the premises to which its application is permissible. It is not necessary to try to complete the proofs; do not even assume that the arguments are valid. The conclusions are provided only as a basis for determining whether restriction 3 applies. In those cases where EI cannot be correctly used, explain why it cannot be used.

1. (∃x)Tx / ∴ (∃y)(Ty ∨ Wy)
2. (∃x)(Gx · (Mx · Rx)) / ∴ (∃x)Rx
3. (∃x)Dx ≡ (x)~Bx / ∴ (x)Dx
4. (∃x)(Fx · Bx) / ∴ Bk
5. (∃x)Px · Jx / ∴ (∃x)(Px · Jx)
6. (∃x)(Qx ∨ ~Px) / ∴ ~(~Qg · Pg)
7. ~(x)(~Dx ∨ Kx) / ∴ (∃x) Kx
8. (∃x)(~Fx · (Ta ∨ (∃y)Ry)) / ∴ Ta ∨ Rf
9. (x)(∃y)~((Px · Py) ⊃ Gxy) / ∴ Gdm
10. (∃y)(x)((Py ∨ Kx) · Ny) / ∴ (∃x)Nx

8.4 Universal Generalization

The final new inference rule for quantifiers is the least simple and straightforward. In nontechnical terms, it says that *if we know that something is true of a randomly selected individual, then we can say that the same thing is true of every thing whatsoever.* This rule is called **universal generalization** and it can be abbreviated as **UG.** The addition of this rule to the other quantification rules and the rules of propositional logic permits us to construct proofs of all valid arguments that can be fully expressed in this system.

This rule is on the surface problematic and appears to go against our basic logical intuitions. It seems obviously false that just because something is true of one individual that it must therefore be true of everything. For example, just because it is true that Mary got an A on the last logic exam, it certainly does not follow that everybody got an A on that exam. It is tempting to reject completely any notion of universally generalizing from an individual constant, but this would then prevent us from being able to construct proofs of some valid arguments such as

$(x)(Px \supset Fx)$, $(x)(Px) / \therefore (x)Fx$

To give ourselves the ability to construct proofs of valid arguments requiring that we universally generalize an individual constant, while at the same time protecting ourselves from using invalid inferences, we must put a very strong restriction on **UG.** This restriction is that we can use **UG** only on an individual constant that was first introduced to the proof by an application of **UI,** *and* we cannot use **UG** on any step that contains an individual constant introduced by **EI,** even if we are not applying **UG** to that constant. Universal generalization also has the same restrictions as **EI;** the full set of restrictions on it are listed in the box.

Restrictions on Universal Generalization

1. **UG** can be used only on a universal quantifier that is the main operator in a step. This means that we cannot use **UG** to go directly from '$(x)(Px \supset Jxm)$' to '$(x)(y)(Px \supset Jxy)$' because the main operator in the second formula is '(x).'

2. We cannot apply a single quantifier to more than one particular constant. Thus, we cannot use **UG** to go from '$Fc \lor Gk$' to '$(x)(Fx \lor Gx)$.'

3. We must apply **UG** to all occurrences of a particular constant in a step. In other words, it is incorrect to go from '$Hr \supset Lr$' to '$(y)(Hy \supset Lr)$.'

4. **UG** cannot be used on any individual constant that has not been introduced to the proof by an application of **UI.** The following proof violates this restriction.

1. $Tc \cdot {\sim}Jn$ /$\therefore (x)(Jx \supset Wx)$	Premise/conclusion
2. ${\sim}Jn$	Simp., 1
3. ${\sim}Jn \lor Wn$	Add., 2
4. $Jn \supset Wn$	Impl., 3
5. $(x)(Jx \supset Wx)$	**Violates restriction 4**

5. **UG** cannot be used in any step that contains an individual constant introduced by **EI**, even if **UG** is not being applied to that constant. The following proof violates this restriction.

1. (y)(My ⊃ Dy)		Premise
2. (∃x)(Px · ~Da) /∴ (y)(~My · Pb)		Premise/conclusion
3. Pb · ~Da		EI, 2
4. Ma ⊃ Da		UI, 1
5. ~Da		Simp., 3
6. ~Ma		M.T., 4,5
7. Pb		Simp., 3
8. ~Ma · Pb		Conj., 6,7
9. (y)(~My · Pb)		**Violates restriction 5**

Within these restrictions, both of the following proofs involve legitimate applications of **UG**.

1. (x)(Wx ⊃ Kx)	Premise
2. Wf /∴ (x)Kx	Premise/conclusion
3. Wf ⊃ Kf	UI, 1
4. Kf	M.P., 2,3
5. (x)Kx	UG, 4

1. (x)(∃y)(Px ⊃ Kxy)	Premise
2. (x)~(∃y)Kyx /∴ (x)~Px	Premise/conclusion
3. (∃y)(Pa ⊃ Kay)	UI, 1
4. Pa ⊃ Kab	EI, 3
5. ~(∃y)Kyb	UI, 2
6. (y)~Kyb	QE, 5
7. ~Kab	UI, 6
8. ~Pa	M.T., 4,7
9. (x)~Px	UG, 8

EXERCISE 8–8

Explain why each of the following is not a correct application of the rule of universal generalization.

1. Ta ⊃ (y)Dy / ∴ (x)Tx ⊃ (y)Dy
2. Gf ⊃ Mc / ∴ (y)(Gy ⊃ My)

3. ~Dm ≡ (x)Bx / ∴ (y)(~Dy) ≡ (x)Bx

4. 1. (x)(Fx ⊃ Bx) / ∴ (y)Fy ⊃ Ba
   2. Fa ⊃ Ba
   3. (y)Fy ⊃ Ba

5. 1. (x)(y)(Px ⊃ Jy) / ∴ (y)(Py ⊃ Jy)
   2. (y)(Pa ⊃ Jy)
   3. Pa ⊃ Jb
   4. (y)(Py ⊃ Jy)

6. 1. (∃x)(y)(Px · Ry) / ∴ (∃x)(Px · Ry)
   2. (y)(Pa · Ry)
   3. Pa · Rb
   4. (∃x)(Px · Rb)
   5. (∃x)(Px · (y)Ry)

7. 1. ~(∃x)(Qx · ~Px) / ∴ (x)~(Qd · ~Px)
   2. (x)~(Qx · ~ Px)
   3. ~(Qd · ~Pd)
   4. (x)~(Qd · ~Px)

8. 1. (x)(∃y)(Px ⊃ Ryx) / ∴ (∃y)(x)(Px ⊃ Ryx)
   2. (∃y)(Pb ⊃ Ryb)
   3. (∃y)(x)(Px ⊃ Ryx)

9. 1. (y)(∃x)(~Fx ∨ Ry) / ∴ (x)(~Fb ∨ Rx)
   2. (∃x)(~Fx ∨ Ra)
   3. ~Fb ∨ Ra
   4. (x)(~Fb ∨ Rx)

10. 1. (x)(∃y)(Px ⊃ Mxy)
    2. Pr / ∴ (∃y)(x)Mxy
    3. (∃y)(Pr ⊃ Mry)
    4. Pr ⊃ Mra
    5. Mra
    6. (x)Mxa
    7. (∃y)(x)Mxy

If there is a human being who is freer than I, then I shall necessarily become his slave. If I am freer than any other, then he will become my slave. Therefore equality is an absolutely necessary condition of freedom.

<small>MIKHAIL A. BAKUNIN</small>

Use the principle of charity to add the suppressed premises to this argument. Consider carefully whether the uses of 'I' are intended to refer to a specific individual, or whether their use is more figurative than literal. Then symbolize each statement in quantificational logic. Finally, try to construct a proof of the validity of the argument in quantificational logic.

For each of the following proofs supply the justifications for each step and apply the rule of universal generalization to any individual constants in the last step provided to which its application is allowed. In those cases where UG cannot be correctly used explain why it cannot be used.

1. 1. (x)Tx / ∴ (y)Ty
    2. Ta
    3.

2. 1. (x)(Gx ⊃ (Mx · Rx))
    2. (x)Gx / ∴ (x)(Mx · Rx)
    3. Ga ⊃ (Ma · Ra)
    4. Ga
    5. Ma · Ra
    6.

3. 1. (x)Bx / ∴ (x)(Bx ∨ Kx)
    2. Ba
    3. Ba ∨ Ka
    4.

4. 1. Fr ∨ (x)Bx
    2. ~(∃x)(Fx ∨ Tx) / ∴ (y)(By ∨ Cy)
    3. (x)~(Fx ∨ Tx)
    4. ~(Fr ∨ Tr)
    5. ~Fr · ~Tr
    6. ~Fr
    7. (x)Bx
    8. Ba
    9. Ba ∨ Ca
    10.

5. 1. (x)Px ∨ (y)Qy
    2. ~Pa · ~Qb / ∴ (x)(Px · Qx)
    3. ~Pa
    4. (∃x)~Px
    5. ~(x)Px
    6. (y)Qy
    7. Qc
    8. ~Qb
    9. (∃y)~Qy
    10. ~(y)Qy
    11. (x)Px
    12. Pc
    13. Pc · Qc
    14.

6. 1. (x)((Rx · Dx) ⊃ (y)Sxy)
    2. (x)~Sxj / ∴ (x)~(Rx · Dx)
    3. ~Saj
    4. (Ra · Da) ⊃ (y)Say
    5. (∃y)~Say
    6. ~(y)Say
    7. ~(Ra · Da)
    8.

EXERCISE 8–10

Write formal proofs of the following. Some of the last eight are most readily solvable by conditional proof.

1. (x)Tx / ∴ (∃x)Tx

2. (x)(Tx ⊃ Nx)
   (∃x)Tx / ∴ (∃x)(Tx · Nx)

3. (x)(Tx ⊃ (Nx ⊃ Cx)) / ∴ (x)((Tx · Nx) ⊃ Cx)

4. (x)(Tx ⊃ Nx) / ∴ (x)(~Tx ∨ Nx)

5. (x)(Tx · Nx) / ∴ (x)Tx · (x)Nx

6. (x)Tx · (x)Nx / ∴ (x)(Tx · Nx)

7. (x)(y)Sxy / ∴ Sdd

8. (x)(y)Sxy / ∴ (∃x)(∃y)Sxy

9. (x)(y)Sxy / ∴ (y)(x)Sxy

10. (∃x)(∃y)Sxy / ∴ (∃x)(∃y)Syx

11. (∃x)Tx / ∴ ~(x)(~Tx · ~Nx)

12. (∃x)(y)Lxy / ∴ (y)(∃x)Lxy

13. (x)(Tx ⊃ Nx) / ∴ (x)Tx ⊃ (x)Nx

14. (x)Tx ∨ (x)Nx / ∴ (x)(Tx ∨ Nx)

15. (∃x)(Tx ∨ Nx) / ∴ (∃x)Tx ∨ (∃x)Nx

16. (x)(Cx ⊃ Hx) ⊃ (∃x)Ux
    (x)~Ux / ∴ (∃x)(Cx · ~Hx)

17. (∃x)(Cx · Hx) ⊃ (x)Ux
    (∃x)~Ux / ∴ (x)(Cx ⊃ ~Hx)

18. (x)(Fx ⊃ Gx)
    (x)(Gx ⊃ Hx) / ∴ (∃x)Fx ⊃ (∃x)Hx

19. (x)(y)(Mxy ⊃ ~Myx) / ∴ (x)~Mxx

20. (x)(y)(Mxy ⊃ ~Myx)
    (x)(y)(Dxy ⊃ Myx) / ∴ (x)(y)(Dxy ⊃ ~Mxy)

We must end our discussion of constructing proofs of validity in quantificational logic as we ended our discussion in the previous chapter, that is, by recognizing that we are very far from having covered the entire topic and that we have really only gotten our toes wet, to borrow a frequently used metaphor. We *have* done enough to show the power and sophistication of this system and also to convey a basic understanding of the fundamental concepts of quantificational logic. But we have not even touched on a number of important aspects of quantificational logic, such as methods for proving invalidity, the question of a decision procedure, and quantifying over predicates. Anyone interested in learning more about this system can do so in an advanced course in logic that will go into it in greater depth.

We have not done enough to allow anyone to claim mastery even of the aspects of quantificational logic discussed in this chapter. As with translation, the process of constructing proofs of validity of arguments in quantificational logic is as much an art as it is a technical skill. Since no set of rules or mechanical procedures exist that can guarantee a proof of the validity of a quantificational argument, we are dependent on repeated and continual practice over a sustained period of time to develop and refine our ability to construct such proofs. An additional opportunity for such practice is provided in Chapter 14. With these qualifying comments in mind, we present the following rules of thumb for constructing proofs in quantificational logic. While they should be helpful in many cases, these rules might not always lead to the desired results. But only practice will improve your ability to construct proofs.

Guidelines for Constructing Proofs in Quantificational Logic

1. Whenever possible, any existentially quantified premises should be instantiated using **EI** before **UI** is used in the proof.
2. The equivalence rules from propositional logic can be used in the scope of any quantifier, and the rule of quantifier exchange can be used on any operator at any time in a proof.
3. The first eight inference rules from propositional logic can be used only on the main operator of a step, which means that the operator cannot be in the scope of any quantifier.

Contending for the rights of women, my main argument is built on this simple principle, that if she be not prepared by education to become the companion of man, she will stop the progress of knowledge, for truth must be common to all, or it will be inefficacious with respect to its influence on general practice.

MARY WOLLSTONECRAFT

Use the principle of charity to add the suppressed premises to this argument. Consider carefully whether the uses of 'she' are intended to refer to a specific individual, or whether their use is more figurative than literal. Then symbolize each statement in quantificational logic. Finally, try to construct a proof of the validity of the argument in quantificational logic.

Go through each of the following proofs carefully looking for possible errors. Identify all errors and explain why they are errors.

1. 1. (x)(Ax ⊃ Bg) / ∴ (x)(Ax ∨ Bx)   Premise/conclusion
   2. Aa   UI, 1
   3. Aa ∨ Ba   Add., 2
   4. (x)(Ax ∨ Bx)   UG, 3

2. 1. (x)(Ax ∨ Bx)   Premise
   2. (Aa ∨ Bg) ⊃ (x)Cx / ∴ (x)(Cx)   Premise/conclusion
   3. Aa ∨ Bg   UI, 1
   4. (x)Cx   M.P., 2,3

3. 1. (x)(Ax ⊃ Bx)   Premise
   2. (∃x)(Cx ⊃ Ax) / ∴ (x)(Cx ⊃ Bx)   Premise/conclusion
   3. Ca ⊃ Aa   EI, 2
   4. Aa ⊃ Ba   UI, 1
   5. Ca ⊃ Ba   H.Syll., 3,4
   6. (x)(Cx ⊃ Bx)   UG, 5

4. 1. (∃x)Ax   Premise
   2. (∃x)Bx / ∴ Aa · Ba   Premise/conclusion
   3. Aa   EI, 1
   4. Ba   EI, 2
   5. Aa · Ba   Conj., 3,4

5. 1. (x)(Ax ⊃ Bg) / ∴ (x)(Ax ⊃ Bx)   Premise/conclusion
   2. Ag ⊃ Bg   UI, 1
   3. (x)(Ax ⊃ Bx)   UG, 2

6. 1. (∃x)Ax ⊃ (y)By   Premise
   2. (x)Ax / ∴ (y)By   Premise/conclusion
   3. Aa   UI, 2
   4. (∃x)Ax   EG, 3
   5. (y)By   M.P., 1,4

7. 1. (∃x)(y)Fxy / ∴ (∃x)Fzz   Premise/conclusion
   2. (y)Fay   EI, 1
   3. Faa   UI, 2
   4. (∃z)Fzz   EG, 3

8. 1. (y)(∃x)Lxy / ∴ (∃x)(y)Lxy   Premise/conclusion
   2. (∃x)Lxa   UI, 1
   3. Lba   EI, 2
   4. (y)Lby   UG, 3
   5. (∃x)(y)Lxy   EG, 4

9. 1. (x)(Ax ⊃ Bx) / ∴ (x)Ax ⊃ (x)Bx   Premise/conclusion
   ┌→2. (x)Ax   Assumption
   │ 3. Aa   UI, 2

4. Aa ⊃ Ba	UI, 1
5. Ba	M.P., 3,4
6. x(Bx)	UG, 5
7. (x)Ax ⊃ (x)Bx	C.P., 2–6

10.
1. (x)(∃y)Sxy	Premise
2. (x)(y)(Sxy ⊃ Syx) / ∴ (∃x)(y)Sxy	Premise/conclusion
3. (∃y)Say	UI, 1
4. Sab	EI, 3
5. (y)(Say ⊃ Sya)	UI, 2
6. Sab ⊃ Sba	UI, 5
7. Sba	M.P., 4,6
8. (y)Sby	UG, 7
9. (∃x)(y)Sxy	EG, 8

EXERCISE 8–12

For the following arguments (a) symbolize the premises and conclusion (indicating abbreviations and what they stand for) and (b) deduce the conclusion from the premises

1. No tomatoes grow on trees and no squash grow on trees. Since acorns grow on trees they are neither squash nor tomatoes.

2. Members of the T family speak to everyone whose name they remember; they also gossip about everyone they speak to. Consequently, if any member of the T family remembers anyone's name they gossip about that person.

3. If someone is injured on the job, every member of group Z is alerted automatically. Felice, who is a member of group Z, has not been alerted. Therefore, no one has been injured on the job.

4. Some three-year-old horses are neither thoroughbreds nor trotters. Only three-year-old thoroughbreds are eligible for the Belmont Stakes. Hence some three-year-old horses are not eligible for the Belmont Stakes.

5. If the horse that finishes first is disqualified, the second horse is placed first unless it is disqualified also. Since we know that Lazy Bill finished first and was disqualified, and Maizy Dae, who finished second, was not placed first we can conclude that Maizy Dae was disqualified also.

6. [For the following argument, which is an enthymeme, a 'transitivity premise' must be added—that is, a premise analogous to 'If anything is larger than a second, and the second is larger than the third, then the first is larger than the third.' Supply such a premise.] Ellen runs faster than Harry and Harry runs faster than Joanne. Therefore, Ellen runs faster than Joanne.

7. All human beings are entitled to equal respect. Sally and John are human beings. Sally, therefore, is entitled to as much respect as John.

8. No farmers are executives. Bill is an executive, so he is not a farmer.

9. All beauty contest queens are beautiful and some college graduates are beauty contest queens. Consequently, some college graduates are beautiful.

10. All politicians are liars. Some women are politicians. Thus it follows that some women are liars.

11. Terriers and poodles are dogs. Cairns are terriers. Therefore, cairns are dogs.

12. Universities are either financially sound or bankrupt. Universities are not all bankrupt. Thus, it follows that there are financially sound universities.

EXERCISE 8–13

The first three of the following arguments need to be reworked with benefit of the principle of charity but you should be able to get them into a valid form. Proof of validity will then be easy. The last two are much trickier.

1. Somebody must not have anteed up. The pot's a dollar short.

2. I'm sure that John won't be in the tournament. To be eligible you have to qualify.

3. When experienced gardeners hear of a frost warning they take precautions. You can count on Jimmy.

4. But I do not think that communism as a belief, apart from overt and illegal actions, can be successfully combatted by police methods, persecution, war or a mere anti spirit. The only force that can overcome an idea and a faith is another and better idea and faith positively and fearlessly upheld. (Dorothy Thompson)

5. A Galileo could no more be elected president of the United States than he could be elected Pope of Rome. Both high posts are reserved for men favored by God with an extraordinary genius for swathing the bitter facts of life in bandages of self-illusion. (H. L. Mencken)

Summary

1. In order to construct deductive proofs in quantificational logic, it is usually necessary to remove one or more quantifiers and also to add quantifiers. Four new inference rules permit us to do this.

2. Several basic restrictions apply to all four new rules. One is that *the quantifier that is being removed or added must be the main operator in that step.* Another shared restriction is that *every individual variable of a specific kind must be replaced in each occurrence by the same constant,* or vice versa, depending on whether a quantifier is being added or removed.

3. The rule of **universal instantiation** permits us to remove a universal quantifier that is the main operator of a step if we replace each instance of the

individual variable in the quantifier with the same individual constant throughout the step. This rule is abbreviated **UI**.

4. The rule of **existential generalization** permits us to add an existential quantifier as the main operator in a step if each occurrence of one specific individual constant in that step is replaced by the individual variable in the quantifier. This rule is abbreviated **EG**.

5. The rule of **existential instantiation** can be used to remove an existential quantifier that is the main operator of a step if we replace each occurrence in that step of the variable in the quantifier with an individual constant that does not occur in any previous step of the proof or in the conclusion. This rule is abbreviated **EI**.

6. The rule of **universal generalization** can be used to add a universal quantifier as the main operator in a step. This rule is abbreviated **UG**. In addition to the basic requirement that every occurrence of one individual constant in the step must be replaced by the variable in the quantifier, **UG** has two other very strong restrictions. One is that it cannot be applied to any individual constant that has not been introduced to the proof by an application of **UI**. The second restriction is that **UG** cannot be used in any step that contains an individual constant introduced by **EI**, even if **UG** is not being applied to that constant.

7. No system of deductive proof in quantificational logic provides a **decision procedure.** That is, there is no mechanical procedure (as with a Venn diagram or truth table) such that after a finite number of steps we can arrive at a definite answer that an argument is or is not valid. If we successfully deduce the conclusion of an argument from the premises using the inference rules (including the four quantificational rules in this chapter), we have proven that the argument is definitely valid. But if we fail to deduce the conclusion, we have not proven that the argument is invalid.

Chapter 9

Inductive Arguments

Examine each of the following sets of sentences. Assuming ordinary context, each set expresses an argument. In terms of the definitions of 'deductive argument' and 'inductive argument' in Chapter 2, determine which of the arguments is deductive and which is inductive.

1. Swan A is white.
   Therefore, some swans are white.

2. Swan A is a white bird.
   Therefore, Swan A is a bird.

3. All swans are white.
   Therefore, swan A is white.

4. Swan A is white.
   Swan B is white.
   Swan C is white.
   Therefore, all swans are white.

5. Swan A is white.
   Swan B is white.
   Swan C is white.
   Therefore, Swan D is white.

6. All swans are birds and can swim.
   All ducks are birds and can swim.
   All seagulls are birds.
   Therefore, all seagulls can swim.

You are correct if you identified arguments 1, 2, and 3 as deductive arguments and 4, 5, and 6 as inductive arguments. Since we will be considering various types of inductive argument in this and the next two chapters, it is worthwhile to reiterate and expand on the characteristics that distinguish the two different types of argument.

It is often said that deductive arguments move from the general to the particular, whereas inductive arguments move from the particular to the general. As noted in Chapter 2, this distinction between the two types of argument is inaccurate. It is possible to have a deductive argument that moves from general premises to a general conclusion, as in the following example:

7. **All fish are animals that live in water.**
All bass are fish.
Therefore, all bass are animals that live in water.

An inductive argument may have particular premises and a particular conclusion, as in argument 5. It is also possible for an inductive argument to have general premises and a general conclusion. For example:

8. **All dogs are mammals and are warm-blooded.**
All chimpanzees are mammals and are warm-blooded.
All lions are mammals and are warm-blooded.
All men are mammals and are warm-blooded.
Therefore, all mammals are warm-blooded.

In Chapter 2, a **deductive argument** was defined as *any argument in which the conclusion follows necessarily from the premises,* that is, any argument which is such that:

If the premises are true, then the conclusion must be true; *or*
The premises provide absolute support for the conclusion; *or*
The conclusion is completely contained in the premises.

In this formal sense of the term, it is redundant to say that an argument is deductively valid; if it is valid, then it must be deductive, and if it is deductive, then it must be valid. Also, remember that an argument is not deductive simply because someone asserts or intends that the premises provide absolute support for the conclusion. One of the primary values of formal logic is that it gives us procedures for determining which of the many sets of statements that people assert or intend to be valid are, in fact, valid.

Another essential characteristic of a deductive argument is that the addition of one or more premises can in no way affect the support that the premises provide for the conclusion. For example, in argument 1, if the premises 'Swan B is black,' 'Swan C is beautiful,' and 'Swan A is dead' were added to the original argument, this would in no way affect the support that the argument provides for the conclusion 'Some swans are white.' In a valid argument, the truth of the premises guarantees the truth of the conclusion, regardless of any additional premises that might be supplied.

Of course, the validity of an argument is not dependent on the actual truth of the premises; rather it is dependent on the *form* of the argument, as was pointed out in Chapter 2. Thus, it is possible to have a deductive argument with a false premise (or premises) and a true conclusion. For instance, the premise of argument 3, 'All swans are white,' is false, for black swans do exist; nevertheless, the conclusion 'Swan A is white' may be true. In other words, the discovery that a premise in a deductive argument is false is not sufficient for proving that the conclusion is false, and it in no way affects the validity of the argument. However, if we know that the conclusion of a deductive argument is false, then one or more of its premises must be false. Taking argument 3 again, if Swan A is actually black, the conclusion is false, and so the premise 'All swans are white' must be false.

It should also be remembered from Chapter 2 that an inductive argument is any argument that is not deductive—or to put it in more positive terms, an inductive argument is any set of statements such that one of them is supported by (but *not* implied by) the others. As with deductive arguments, it is irrelevant from the logical point of view whether a particular set of statements has been asserted or intended as an argument by anyone. The only thing that is relevant is the logical relation that actually holds between the statements. Thus, even if someone asserts that a particular set of statements composes an inductive argument, if the "premises" do not, in fact, provide any support for the "conclusion," then it is not an inductive argument. It is also possible on our definitions for someone to assert that a particular set of statements composes an inductive argument when, in fact, the premises provide absolute (not just partial) support for the conclusion, in which case it is really a deductive argument.

Any argument that is inductive has the basic characteristic that, even if all of its premises are true, it is still possible for the conclusion to be false, because the premises provide only partial support for the conclusion. The partial support that the premises provide for the conclusion can range from almost absolute support at one extreme to almost no support at the other.

Degree of Premises' Support of Conclusion

Nonarguments	Inductive Arguments			Deductive Arguments
none	weak	moderate	strong	absolute

Another characteristic that distinguishes deductive from inductive arguments is that adding new premises to an *inductive* argument might strengthen or weaken the support for the conclusion. For example, if the premise 'Swan D is black' is added to argument 4, then the support that the original premises provide for the conclusion 'All swans are white' is completely destroyed. On the other hand, if the premises 'Swan D is white,' 'Swan E is white,' . . . 'Swan W is white' are added, then the support for the conclusion is somewhat strengthened.

9.1 Enumerative Inductions

In this chapter we are concerned with a kind of inductive argument known as 'enumerative induction.' An **enumerative induction** is *an argument whose premise(s) constitute a listing of cases concerning either individuals or classes* *of individuals to support conclusions about individuals or classes of individuals.* For example, in argument 5, the premises concern individuals (Swans A, B, and C), and the conclusion is about an individual (Swan D). In argument 4, the premises are also about individuals, but the conclusion is about the class of individuals (all swans). In argument 6, all of the premises and the conclusion are about classes of individuals.

9.1.1 Types of Enumerative Induction

Logicians have traditionally made a distinction between two different kinds of enumerative inductive argument. Argument 4 is an example of the first type and is generally referred to as an **inductive generalization.** As its name suggests, an inductive generalization is *an inductive argument whose conclusion is a universal proposition (that is, a statement about all of the members of some class or group),* **and** *at least one of whose premises is such that its falsity* **could** *imply the falsity of the conclusion.* (The reason for this "could" qualification will be explained in the section on inductive generalization.) Argument 4 has a universal proposition as its conclusion—'All swans are white'—and each of the first three premises is such that its falsity implies the falsity of the conclusion (for if Swan A, for instance, is not white, then it follows that not all swans are white).

Any enumerative induction that does not satisfy the criteria for an inductive generalization is commonly referred to as an **induction by analogy.** Argument 5 is clearly an induction by analogy, since its conclusion is not a universal proposition but an individual one about a specific event.

Argument 6 has a universal conclusion: 'All seagulls can swim'; thus it satisfies the first criterion for an inductive generalization. But an examination of the three premises shows that none of them is such that its falsity can possibly imply the falsity of the conclusion. For instance, even if it were shown to be false that all swans can swim, this would at most lessen the probability that all seagulls can swim—it does not prove that it is false that all seagulls can swim.

9.1.2 Induction by Analogy

When we make an *analogy,* we compare two or more different things or ideas by pointing out the ways in which they are similar. Analogies are frequently used by writers to *explain* new and/or difficult concepts by comparing them to more familiar ideas. A relatively simple example is given in a passage in which the founder of psychoanalysis, Sigmund Freud, asserts that "the conscious mind may be compared to a fountain playing in the sun and falling back into the great subterranean pool of the subconscious from which it rises." The analogy here is used for explanatory purposes only; it does not involve an argument, for, although two phenomena are compared, no conclusion is drawn.

In daily life we often make inferences that involve analogical judgments.

In fact, it is possible to view *all* judgments relating two discrete experiences as being grounded in inductions by analogy, if it is argued that we can determine only that our present experience is very similar to, somewhat different from, or very different from previous experiences or abstract concepts that are used as paradigms or models. For instance, suppose Sue asks Beth if she can borrow Beth's biology book overnight. Beth lends Sue the book on the condition that she return it by 9:00 the next morning, telling Sue to leave it near the door to her dormitory room. Beth wakes up at 9:15 the next morning, goes to the door, opens it, and finds a biology book there. How does Beth *know* that it is her book? It looks like her book: her name is in it, it is underlined in places with a blue marker, there is a coffee stain on the pages dealing with reproduction, and so on. In effect, Beth is drawing an analogy; she is saying that this book is her book because it has the same characteristics as her book. Of course, it is highly unlikely that Sue would have replaced Beth's book with a different one, going through all the trouble to make it appear as if it were Beth's. Nevertheless, Beth has no absolute certainty that it is her book. All that Beth can do and does do is make a comparison between the book she has now and her memory of the book she lent to Sue.

Whether it is true that *all* judgments involve the drawing of analogies is open to debate. But certainly many inferences made in daily life are based on analogies between different cases. For instance, a couple might patronize a particular restaurant, inferring that since they had a good meal there the last time, they will have a good meal there this time. A business executive might infer that because a worker was competent at the previous task performed, this same worker will do a good job at the next task. A person might buy the latest album by a certain rock group, assuming that he or she will like it because previously purchased albums by the same group were enjoyable. A farmer who has had previous success with a certain pesticide might infer that the same pesticide will help fight against the insects that are destroying the lettuce crop.

All these instances deal with inferences made by means of analogies. None of these examples involves inductive arguments by analogy; they are merely inferences, although for each inference we can construct such an argument, as was noted in Chapter 2. Considering the importance of inductions by analogy in everyday life, it is worthwhile to examine the form that such arguments take, as well as the criteria for determining the relative strengths of these arguments.

Now let's consider the following argument:

> **Tim, Sue, Mary, and John are philosophy majors who were enrolled in Professor Wilson's metaphysics course last semester and all of them got As. So Tom probably got an A, since he is a philosophy major who was in last semester's metaphysics course taught by Professor Wilson.**

To facilitate discussion, it is helpful to formulate the argument in the following way, making all the premises and the conclusion explicit:

Notice how people obey traffic laws when there's a patrol car in sight?

That's the idea behind NATO.

Nothing maintains order like the presence of authority.

It keeps children from snitching cookies. Adults from running red lights. And it helps keep peace among nations.

The presence of the North Atlantic Treaty Organization (NATO) has provided security in Europe for 25 years. At the same time, this peace force of 15 allied nations has sought to ease tensions and improve relations between East and West.

Today from a foundation of strength and in a climate of stability, the East and West can contemplate mutual and balanced force reductions.

Which means more of NATO's resources can be devoted to advancements in economic affairs, science and cultural relations.

That's the idea behind NATO.

April 4th is NATO's 25th anniversary. This week, McDonnell Douglas personnel are observing NATO's founding with a paid holiday for the 11th consecutive year.

McDonnell Douglas Corporation.

MCDONNELL DOUGLAS

Is the analogy being drawn in this 1974 ad very strong? What weaknesses or disanalogies can you identify? Is there an argument implicit or explicit in the ad? If so, what is it and how good is it? Have the changes in world politics since 1974 made the analogy stronger or weaker?

*"Some man, that Kissinger . . .
Goes day and night."*

Stayskal—Chicago Today.

Richard Nixon's Secretary of State, Henry Kissinger, had a reputation as a person with seemingly unlimited energy. The humor in this cartoon makes us recognize the extent to which all of our judgments involve some degree of analogical reasoning.

9. Tim is a philosophy major who was in Professor Wilson's metaphysics course last semester and got an A.

Sue is a philosophy major who was in Professor Wilson's metaphysics course last semester and got an A.

Mary is a philosophy major who was in Professor Wilson's metaphysics course last semester and got an A.

John is a philosophy major who was in Professor Wilson's metaphysics course last semester and got an A.

Tom is a philosophy major who was in Professor Wilson's metaphysics course last semester.

Therefore, Tom got an A.

Quite clearly, we are dealing with an enumerative induction, for the premises of this argument constitute a listing of cases about individuals. We can also determine that this is an induction by analogy, since the conclusion is not a universal proposition *and* no premise is such that its falsity could necessitate the falsity of the conclusion. For example, if the second premise (about Sue) is false, this means that Sue is not a philosophy major or that Sue was not in Professor Wilson's metaphysics course last semester or that Sue did not get an A in Professor Wilson's metaphysics course. But none of these implies that it is false that Tom got an A in Professor Wilson's course. The same holds for each of the other premises.

The analogy in this particular example involves five persons who are alike in at least two ways: they all (a) are philosophy majors, and (b) were enrolled in Professor Wilson's metaphysics course. Four of them have been observed, and the fifth is being asserted (c) to have received an A grade. If we let *a, b,* and *c* represent the three characteristics respectively, and if we use X_1, X_2, X_3, X_4, and X_5 to stand for Tim, Sue, Mary, John, and Tom, respectively, the argument can be schematized in the following ways:

X_1 has a, b, and c.
X_2 has a, b, and c.
X_3 has a, b, and c.
X_4 has a, b, and c.
X_5 has a and b.
Therefore, X_5 has c.

or

X_1, X_2, X_3, X_4, and X_5 have a and b.
X_1, X_2, X_3, and X_4 have c.
Therefore, X_5 has c.

Notice that characteristics *a* and *b* (philosophy major and enrollment in Professor Wilson's metaphysics course) appear only in the premises of the argument, whereas characteristic *c* (the A grade) appears in both the premises and the conclusion. Furthermore, the premises of the argument assert that five of the persons (X_1 . . . X_5) are alike in two respects (*a* and *b*) and that four of these persons (X_1 . . . X_4) are known to be alike in a third respect (*c*). From the premises, it can be inferred that the fifth person (X_5) also shares the third characteristic (*c*).

Of course, not all enumerative inductions by analogy are concerned only with five cases that share three characteristics, nor do all such inductions contain premises about individuals that support a conclusion about individuals. In the following argument, the premise is about a class of individuals, as is the conclusion, and these classes of individuals share only two characteristics.

10. **All students in Professor Wilson's metaphysics course last semester got As.**
    Therefore, all students in Professor Wilson's metaphysics course this semester will get As.

This argument certainly qualifies as an enumerative induction, even though its premise lists only one case, concerning one class of individuals, to support a conclusion about another class of individuals. It is also an induction by analogy, for the falsity of its premise does not guarantee the falsity of its conclusion. If the premise statement is false—that is, if some students in Professor Wilson's metaphysics course last semester did not get As—it is still possible for all the students in his course this semester to get As.

It is also possible to have an enumerative induction by analogy with premises that are about a class of individuals and a conclusion that is about a particular individual, or vice versa. Furthermore, an induction by analogy might contain premises that involve both a class of individuals and a particular individual, and a conclusion that involves a particular individual. For example, consider the following arguments:

11. **Every student in Professor Wilson's metaphysics course last semester got an A.**
    Therefore, Tom will get an A in Professor Wilson's metaphysics course this semester.

12. **Some students in Professor Wilson's metaphysics course last semester got As.**
    Therefore, all students in Professor Wilson's metaphysics course this semester will get an A.

13. **Every student in Professor Wilson's metaphysics course last semester got an A.**
    Bob is a student in Professor Wilson's metaphysics course this semester.
    Therefore, Bob will get an A this semester.

Notice that, in each of these arguments, the falsity of the premise(s) could not necessitate the falsity of the conclusion. One might, on an intuitive level, sense that certain of the arguments seem stronger than others, but we will put off our discussion of the relative strength of inductions by analogy until after we have discussed the form of the second type of enumerative induction—inductive generalization.

EXERCISE 9-1

Read each passage carefully and determine whether it contains an analogical explanation or an analogical argument.

1. Ants are highly organized creatures which go about their task of tunnel construction in a systematic manner. Similarly, the engineers who built the subway system in New York City manifested a high degree of organization in the systematic manner in which they approached and performed their task.

2. A particularly troublesome manifestation of the pollution problem called "backwash" has recently been brought to the attention of our citizenry. This phenomenon occurs when the level of pollution becomes so high in an inlet area that the tides cannot carry all the waste material to the sea, thereby causing the pollutants to accumulate in the inlet. This situation is similar to the problem faced by home owners when they let too much solid waste go down the drain, thereby causing the waste disposal system to back up.

3. The Watergate scandals in the mid-1970s brought to light erroneous political thinking concerning campaign spending. In the past, politicians—Republicans and Democrats alike—believed that the more money put into a campaign, the better it would turn out. That's like saying that the more sugar I put into my coffee, the better it will be, just because I happen to like sugar in my coffee. However, we all know that too much sugar will make coffee taste lousy. Politicians long ago should have learned from ordinary experience such as this that too much of a good thing often produces a lousy thing.

4. The computer revolution has arrived, but most people still do not know how a computer works. It works by a process of eliminating possibilities until it comes to the right conclusion. The theory behind it reminds me of my friend's theory of how to find a satisfactory conversationalist at a party. He simply goes from person to person, eliminating possibilities until he finds the right one.

5. Many people claim that the scientific method is the basis for all modern technological advances. Using the scientific method, a researcher formulates a hypothesis which conforms to known facts and then devises tests, the results of which either confirm the hypothesis or disconfirm it. In the latter event, the researcher formulates a new hypothesis and tests it. Such a method can be likened to that of a man who pushes a mule to see if this will make it move. If the mule moves, all is well; if not, he tries something else.

6. Some people have claimed that waterbeds provide them with comfortable sleep, likening the experience to floating in a quiet pool of water. Others dislike them, because when you sit on them, you sink in. In this respect, waterbeds are similar to an old couch that has lost the resiliency of its supporting springs.

7. An accident occurred during yesterday's football practice at school. Chuck ran a pattern toward the goal post and, looking back to catch a pass, lost his sense of direction. As he caught the ball, he turned, ran right into the post, and was knocked on his back. It was like the driver who turned around and ran right into the stopped car in front of him.

8. Chimpanzees are the creatures closest to humans in the line of evolution, and for this reason have been the subject of extensive study. It has been observed that when two or more chimpanzees are enclosed in a confined area, the level of tension among the animals increases proportionately to the time element involved; that is, the longer they are confined, the greater the tension. The moral is, don't get stuck in an elevator for any great length of time!

9. In one study, two groups of gorillas were observed. Both were kept in zoos. One group was accessible to the public, whereas the other was kept in a restricted area without access by the public. It was found that the gorillas

to which the public had access had unbalanced diets (a result of additional feeding by the public), were overweight, and tended to be sluggish. This study is analogous to a study of two groups of humans. One group was confined to an institution and had a planned diet. The other group was also confined to an institution but had access to unlimited food. Again, those not restricted from additional eating had unbalanced diets, were overweight, and tended to be sluggish. Consequently, it is evident that strict control of diet is required for any creature to maintain prime physical health and to avoid becoming overweight and sluggish.

10. Pat was a graduate of Xavier High School, and when she sought employment, she got the job she wanted. Peter was a graduate of Central High School, and he also got the job he wanted. Jack was a dropout from an exclusive prep school and he did not get the job he wanted. It should be obvious that no matter what high school people graduate from, so long as they graduate, they will get the jobs they want.

9.1.3 Inductive Generalizations

Let us reconsider the argument concerning the students in Professor Wilson's metaphysics class last semester, modifying the conclusion to read as follows:

> **14.** **Tim was a student enrolled in Professor Wilson's metaphysics course last semester and got an A.**
> **Sue was a student enrolled in Professor Wilson's metaphysics course last semester and got an A.**
> **Mary was a student enrolled in Professor Wilson's metaphysics course last semester and got an A.**
> **John was a student enrolled in Professor Wilson's metaphysics course last semester and got an A.**
> **Therefore, all students enrolled in Professor Wilson's metaphysics courses get As.**

Quite clearly, this is an enumerative inductive argument, for its premises consist of a listing of statements about individual cases. It has a universal proposition as its conclusion. It also is such that if any one of the premises is false because one of the students in question did not get an A in Professor Wilson's metaphysics course—then it necessarily follows that the conclusion of the argument is false. This is an example of an enumerative inductive generalization.

Notice that, if the conclusion had been 'All students enrolled in Professor Wilson's metaphysics course *this semester* will get As,' none of these premises is such that its falsity could imply the falsity of the conclusion, so such an argument would be an induction by analogy. The point is significant because it clarifies the difference between the two kinds of inductive argument. In the induction by analogy, the falsity of none of the premises can guarantee the falsity of the conclusion. In the inductive generalization, at least one premise is such that its falsity *could* imply the falsity of the conclusion.

Why does the definition of 'inductive generalization' assert that 'at least one premise is such that its falsity *could* imply the falsity of the conclusion,' rather than the more definite '. . . *would* imply. . . '? The reason for this qualification is that an observation statement, such as 'A is a swan and is white,' can be false on several different grounds, only one of which is sufficient to falsify a universal conclusion statement such as 'All swans are white.' For example, 'A is a swan and is white' is false if A is not a swan; but if A is not a swan, the fact that A is not white does not imply that the generalization 'All swans are white' is false. Only if A *is* a swan, and is also not white, would it follow that 'All swans are white' is false. Any inductive argument with such a conclusion and at least one such premise qualifies as an inductive generalization, even though the falsity of the premise does not *always* guarantee the falsity of the conclusion.

If we let X_1, X_2, X_3, X_4 represent Tim, Sue, Mary, and John, respectively, and let A stand for being a student enrolled in Professor Wilson's metaphysics course and B stand for getting a grade of A in the course, the argument above can be schematized as follows:

> X_1 is an A and a B.
> X_2 is an A and a B.
> X_3 is an A and a B.
> X_4 is an A and a B.
> Therefore, all As are Bs.

or

> X_1, X_2, X_3, and X_4 are all both As and Bs.
> Therefore, all As are Bs.

This argument contains premises about particular individuals that are used to support a conclusion about a whole class of individuals. It is also possible to have an enumerative generalization that contains premises about classes of individuals that are used to support a conclusion about a class of individuals. For example, consider the following:

15. **All students enrolled in Professor Wilson's metaphysics course last**
      semester got As.
    All students enrolled in Professor Wilson's metaphysics course the
      semester before last got As.
    All students enrolled in Professor Wilson's metaphysics course three
      semesters ago got As.
    Therefore, all students enrolled in Professor Wilson's metaphysics
      course get As.

This, too, is an enumerative generalization, because if it were false that all of the students in one of Professor Wilson's metaphysics courses got As, this would guarantee the falsity of the conclusion. Notice that if the conclusion had read 'All students enrolled in Professor Wilson's metaphysics course next semester will get an A,' the argument would be an induction by analogy. Notice that it is impossible to have an inductive generalization with a particular conclusion.

Some inductive generalizations have considerable predictive value, but they also might have drawbacks, as when someone concludes that all Italians (or Poles, or Jews, or blacks, or whites, or members of any other ethnic or racial group) are stupid or untrustworthy, after having had contact with only a few such people. We must therefore establish criteria for determining which inductive arguments are better than others—in other words, criteria of the relative strengths of enumerative inductions.

EXERCISE 9–2

Determine whether each of the following is an induction by analogy or an inductive generalization.

1. All ants are insects and are social animals. All bees are insects and are social animals. All termites are insects and are social animals. Therefore, all insects must be social animals.

2. All ants are insects and are social animals. All bees are insects and are social animals. All termites are insects and are social animals. All flies are insects. So, all flies are social animals.

3. Rudolf Nureyev was trained by Alexander Pushkin and was a great ballet dancer. So were Mikhail Baryshnikov and Valery Panov, and they were great ballet dancers. Therefore, one may infer that all dancers trained by Alexander Pushkin were great ballet dancers.

4. Susan, Veronica, and Caroline are all intelligent women, and each reads *Science* magazine. Betty Ann is also an intelligent woman, so she also reads *Science*.

5. All past presidents of the United States were men. Therefore, all future presidents will be men.

6. The movie I saw on the late show yesterday was a mystery, and the movie I saw on the late show the night before that was a mystery. Therefore, the movie I will see on tonight's late show will be a mystery.

7. Regina plays football; so do Christine and Judith; so all girls play football at some time in their lives.

8. I have been a Yankee baseball fan for many years and have followed seventeen of their players very closely. All seventeen are great hitters, great fielders, and great throwers. It must be that all Yankees are great hitters, fielders, and throwers.

9. Earth is a planet and revolves in an elliptical orbit around the sun. Mars is a planet and revolves in an elliptical orbit around the sun. Jupiter is a planet and revolves in an elliptical orbit around the sun. Therefore, all planets revolve in elliptical orbits around the sun.

10. *The Mousetrap* and *Murder on the Orient Express* are both by Agatha

Christie. Both are also interesting detective stories. *Murder Ahoy* is by Agatha Christie, so it too must be an interesting detective story.

11. Ann, Frank, Carol, and Mike are all successful business executives and they all read *The Wall Street Journal*. Consequently, one can infer that all successful business executives read *The Wall Street Journal*.

12. John, Peter, Susan, and Frieda are friends of Bob's and graduated from Michigan State, so all of Bob's friends are Michigan State graduates.

13. American, Delta, and United all charge the same coach fare for flights from Chicago to New York. Therefore, all airlines that have flights from Chicago to New York charge the same coach fare.

14. A horse is a mammal and is warm-blooded. A porpoise is a mammal and is warm-blooded. Therefore, all mammals are warm-blooded.

15. Jack couldn't ride the bucking machine at last year's fair. Bill couldn't ride the bucking machine at last year's fair. Therefore, no one will be able to ride the bucking machine at this year's fair.

16. My father always listens to me when I talk to him. My brother, too, always listens to me. My mother always listens to me when I talk to her. Therefore, everybody always listens to me when I talk.

9.2 Relative Strength of Enumerative Inductions

We have seen that one of the basic differences between deductive and inductive arguments is that, in a deductive argument, the premises provide absolute support for the conclusion whereas, in an inductive argument, they provide support that ranges from just less than absolute at one extreme to almost none at the other extreme. Thus, it cannot be said of an inductive argument that it is either good or bad in any absolute sense, as it can be said of an argument that it is either valid or invalid. Instead, inductive arguments can be evaluated only in terms of degrees of strength or weakness. It would be convenient if this could be done by means of a single fixed scale, but so far no such system has been devised. Thus, we must evaluate inductive arguments in terms of their *relative* strengths; that is, we must devise criteria for determining whether one inductive argument is stronger or weaker than another. This can be accomplished by seeing how the strength of the argument is affected when we take a fixed set of premises and change the conclusion, when we take a fixed conclusion and modify the premises, and, finally, when both premises and conclusion are changed in certain ways.

9.2.1 Inductive and Deductive Strength

Consider the following inductive arguments. Try to determine which argument is inductively strongest, which is next strongest, and so on.

16. Every student in Professor Wilson's metaphysics course last semester got an A.

    Therefore, (1) at least one student in Professor Wilson's metaphysics course next semester will get an A.

17. Every student in Professor Wilson's metaphysics course last semester got an A.

    Therefore, (2) Herb will get an A in Professor Wilson's metaphysics course next semester, if he takes the course.

18. Every student in Professor Wilson's metaphysics course last semester got an A.

    Therefore, (3) every student in Professor Wilson's metaphysics course next semester will get an A.

19. Every student in Professor Wilson's metaphysics course last semester got an A.

    Therefore, (4) all students in all of Professor Wilson's metaphysics courses get As.

20. Every student in Professor Wilson's metaphysics course last semester got an A.

    Therefore, (5) being a student in Professor Wilson's metaphysics course causes a student to get an A.

You are correct if you concluded that these arguments are listed in order of *decreasing* inductive strength. That is, the premise of argument 16 gives stronger support for its conclusion than 17 gives for its conclusion, 17 gives more support for its conclusion than 18 gives for its, and so on. On an intuitive level, you can probably see that the argument with statement (1) as its conclusion is stronger (that is, its premises provide stronger support for its conclusion) than the argument with statement (2) as its conclusion. The argument with statement (2) as its conclusion is as strong as, or stronger than, the one with (3) as its conclusion; the one with (3) as its conclusion is stronger than the one with (4) as its conclusion; and the one with (4) as its conclusion is stronger than the one with (5) as its conclusion. The reason for attributing the highest degree of inductive strength to the argument with conclusion (1) is that this conclusion encompasses the broadest range of possibilities. Thus, if any one student in Professor Wilson's metaphysics course next semester gets an A, the conclusion is true. On the basis of the evidence offered in the premise, it is more likely that someone or another of the students in next semester's class will get an A than it is that one specifically named student, such as Herb, will get one; it is at least as likely that Herb will get an A as that *every* student enrolled in Professor Wilson's metaphysics course next semester will get one; and it is more likely that every student in *next* semester's course will get an A than it is that all students in *all* of Professor Wilson's metaphysics courses get As. Finally, it is more likely that all students in Professor Wilson's course get As than it is that being a student in the course *causes* a student to get an A. [Causal statements, such as (5), are discussed in Chapter 10.]

Notice that each of these arguments contains the same premise. Because the premises are identical and the inductive strengths of the arguments are different, the differences in strength must be the result of differences in the conclusions of the arguments. An examination of the conclusion statements in relation to each other will help to clarify the notion of relative strength. Listed without their premises, the conclusion statements are:

(1) **At least one student in Professor Wilson's metaphysics course next semester will get an A.**

(2) **Herb will get an A in Professor Wilson's metaphysics course next semester, if he takes the course.**

(3) **Every student in Professor Wilson's metaphysics course next semester will get an A.**

(4) **All students in all of Professor Wilson's metaphysics courses get As.**

(5) **Being a student in Professor Wilson's metaphysics course causes that student to get an A.**

Now, if conclusion (5) is true,[1] then conclusions (4), (3), (2), and (1) must also be true, for conclusion (5) deductively *implies* conclusions (4), (3), (2), and (1). If being a student in Professor Wilson's metaphysics course causes a student to get an A, then it necessarily follows that 'All students in all of Professor Wilson's metaphysics courses get As' is true, 'Every student in Professor Wilson's metaphysics course next semester will get an A' is true, 'Herb will get an A in Professor Wilson's metaphysics course next semester, if he takes the course' is true, and 'At least one student in Professor Wilson's metaphysics course next semester will get an A' is true. Notice, however, that none of the other conclusions implies conclusion (5). It is possible for any one (or even all) of conclusions (1), (2), (3), and (4) to be true and for conclusion (5) to be false. Similarly, if conclusion (4) is true, the conclusions (3), (2), and (1) must be true, for conclusion (4) implies conclusions (3), (2), and (1). However, conclusion (4) does not imply conclusion (5); that is, it is possible that all students in Professor Wilson's metaphysics classes get As without it being true that being a student in his class causes a student to get an A. The truth of conclusion (3) implies the truth of conclusions (2) and (1), but neither conclusion (4) nor conclusion (5) is validly deducible from conclusion (3). By the same token, if conclusion (2) is true, conclusion (1) must be true, for conclusion (2) implies conclusion (1), but conclusion (2) does not imply conclusions (3), (4), or (5). Finally, conclusion (1) does not imply any of the other conclusions. If at least one student in Professor Wilson's metaphysics course next semester gets an A, this does not

---

[1]As explained in Chapter 2, no statement is a premise or a conclusion in and of itself; it becomes a premise or a conclusion only by being so used in a specific argument. Thus, strictly speaking, we should here talk of the statement being used as the conclusion in such-and-such an argument rather than the conclusion statement. For simplicity, however, we use the shorter phrasing in our discussion, with the specification that it should be understood as a shorthand for the more complicated technically precise wording.

imply that it was Herb who got the A, nor that every student got an A, nor that all students in Professor Wilson's metaphysics course get As, nor that being a student in Professor Wilson's course causes a student to get an A.

All of this can be summed up by saying that the conclusion statements above are arranged in order of *increasing* **deductive strength.** *Statement A is said to be deductively stronger than statement B if and only if statement A implies statement B* **and** *statement B does not imply statement A.* Statement A is said to be *deductively weaker* than statement B if and only if B implies A *and* A does not imply B. Statements A and B are of equal deductive strength if A implies B *and* B implies A. We can now assert the following rule:

> The relative strengths of any two or more inductive arguments with the same set of premises are inversely proportional to the deductive strengths of their conclusions.

Thus, in our arguments above—all of which have the same premise—we can see that as we move from the argument with conclusion (1) to the argument with conclusion (5), the inductive strength of the arguments decreases, whereas the deductive strength of their conclusions increases. Similarly, as we move from the argument with conclusion (5) to the argument with conclusion (1), the inductive strength of the arguments increases, whereas the deductive strength of the conclusions decreases. Notice, too, that of the four enumerative inductions (arguments 17 through 20), the inductive generalization, 20, is inductively weaker than any of the inductions by analogy, 17 through 19.

Thus, one way of evaluating the relative inductive strengths of arguments with the same set of premises is in terms of the relative deductive strengths of their conclusions. Another method requires consideration of what are known as positive and negative analogies. To deal more easily with this method, we must first introduce the notions of observed and unobserved cases.

EXERCISE 9–3

Place the following arguments in order of decreasing inductive strength on the basis of the relative deductive strength of the various conclusions.

1. Standard premise for all conclusions that follow:
   Every stone I found yesterday was precious.
   Conclusions:
   a. ∴ Exactly two of the stones I will find today will be precious.
   b. ∴ Every stone I find today will be precious.
   c. ∴ Some stones I will find today will be precious.
   d. ∴ Every stone I find is a precious stone.
   e. ∴ My finding a stone causes it to be precious.

2. Standard premise for all conclusions that follow:
   All European nations have shown aggressive tendencies in the past.

Conclusions:

a. ∴ Italy will show aggressive tendencies in the future.

b. ∴ Every European country will show aggressive tendencies in the future.

c. ∴ At least one European country will show aggressive tendencies in the future.

d. ∴ Being European causes a country to show aggressive tendencies.

e. ∴ All European countries always show aggressive tendencies.

3. Standard premise for all conclusions that follow:

   Every adult member of the Smith family is a college graduate.

   Conclusions:

   a. ∴ Mr. and Mrs. Smith's eight-year-old son and twelve-year-old daughter will be college graduates.

   b. ∴ All of Mr. and Mrs. Smith's three children will be college graduates.

   c. ∴ At least one of Mr. and Mrs. Smith's children will be a college graduate.

   d. ∴ Mr. and Mrs. Smith's eight-year-old son will be a college graduate.

   e. ∴ Being a member of the Smith family causes a person to be a college graduate.

4. Standard premise for all conclusions that follow:

   All clothing designed by Pierre in the past has been expensive.

   Conclusions:

   a. ∴ Being designed by Pierre causes clothing to be expensive.

   b. ∴ All clothing designed by Pierre is expensive.

   c. ∴ All of Pierre's new evening dresses are expensive.

   d. ∴ Some clothing in Pierre's new lines will be expensive.

   e. ∴ All of Pierre's new evening dresses and coats will be expensive.

5. Standard premise for all conclusions that follow:

   Every member of the Jones family has always voted Republican.

   Conclusions:

   a. ∴ Mr. Jones will vote Republican in the coming election.

   b. ∴ Being a member of the Jones family causes a person to vote Republican.

   c. ∴ At least one member of the Jones family will vote Republican in the coming election.

   d. ∴ All members of the Jones family will vote Republican in the coming election.

   e. ∴ All members of the Jones family will vote Republican in all future elections.

6. Standard premise for all conclusions that follow:

   All persons at Joe's parties in the past have been interesting.

   Conclusions:

   a. ∴ Being at Joe's parties causes a person to be interesting.

   b. ∴ The first person I talk to at Joe's party tonight will be interesting.

   c. ∴ Some persons at Joe's party tonight will be interesting.

   d. ∴ Everyone at Joe's party tonight will be interesting.

   e. ∴ All persons at Joe's parties are interesting.

7. Standard premise for all conclusions that follow:
     All lions observed to date are carnivorous, warm-blooded mammals.
   Conclusions:
   a. ∴ All lions are carnivorous, warm-blooded mammals.
   b. ∴ The next lion to be observed will be a carnivorous, warm-blooded mammal.
   c. ∴ At least one lion that will be observed in the future will be a carnivorous, warm-blooded mammal.
   d. ∴ Being a lion causes an animal to be a carnivorous, warm-blooded mammal.
   e. ∴ The next six lions to be observed will be carnivorous, warm-blooded mammals.

8. Standard premise for all conclusions that follow:
     All South American countries have had at least one coup d'etat in the past fifty years.
   Conclusions:
   a. ∴ Chile will have a coup d'etat in the next fifty years.
   b. ∴ Every South American country will have a coup d'etat in the next fifty years.
   c. ∴ At least one South American country will have a coup d'etat in the next fifty years.
   d. ∴ Being a South American country will cause it to have at least one coup d'etat every fifty years.
   e. ∴ All South American countries have at least one coup d'etat every fifty years.

9.2.2 Observed and Unobserved Cases

In our example of Professor Wilson's metaphysics course, each premise has the characteristic of describing situations that have presumably already been observed to be the case, while the conclusion refers to something that has apparently not yet been observed. However, strictly speaking, logicians do not consider it relevant to distinguish between observed and unobserved cases. Rather, their only concern is with the logical relationship between the statements in an argument that are designated as premises and the statement that is designated as the conclusion. Thus, it is unnecessary to specify whether the situation described by either a premise or conclusion statement in an inductive argument has been actually observed to be the case.

It is a fact that most enumerative inductions, if they are at all interesting, do involve premises that describe observed cases, while the conclusion involves a prediction—that is, a situation that is yet to be observed. Because it is not always appropriate to use the terms 'premise' and 'conclusion' in talking about inductive arguments, we use the terms 'observed cases' and 'unobserved cases' for simplicity in our discussion of these arguments.

9.2.3 Positive and Negative Analogy

The ways in which the particular individuals or classes of individuals cited in an enumerative induction are *alike* is called a **positive analogy,** while the ways in which they are *different* is called a **negative analogy.** Consider the following argument:

21. O_1 Pat's first dog was a male beagle and lived fourteen years.
    O_2 Pat's second dog was a male beagle and lived fourteen years.
    O_3 Pat's third dog was a male beagle and lived fourteen years.
    U   Pat's fourth dog is a male beagle and is presently ten years old.
    ∴ Pat's fourth dog will live fourteen years.

In this example there is a positive analogy among the observed cases (Pat's first three dogs) with regard to breed (beagle), sex (male), and life span (fourteen years). There is also a positive analogy between the first three cases and the observed features of the fourth case (that is, the case in which the life span has not been observed) in terms of breed and sex. It can also be reasonably assumed that there is a negative analogy, possibly among the first three cases and certainly between the first three and the fourth case, with regard to the time of their acquisition by Pat. In this induction by analogy, the premises provide at least some support for the conclusion that Pat's fourth beagle will live to the age of fourteen years.

   If we increase the negative analogy between the observed cases and the unobserved case by making the fourth beagle a female, the resulting inductive argument is somewhat weaker than the original. As a general rule, we can state that *an enumerative induction becomes weaker as the negative analogy between the relevant observed cases and the unobserved case increases, provided everything else remains the same.*

> ENON, Ohio (AP) — Dairyman Earl E. Chapman says if the government is going to tax property to pay for schools, it ought to tax the knowledge a person gets by going to school.
>
> Chapman said educated people should be taxed on knowledge they use to earn a living, just as his farm is taxed.
>
> "They bought their education just like I buy my land and I pay taxes on the land, but they don't have to pay taxes on their knowledge and that irks me," he said. "I use the land to earn my living and they use their knowledge to earn theirs. If the government can tax my investment, then it should tax their knowledge."
>
> Chapman didn't say how this might be accomplished.

Although it is not an enumerative induction, Mr. Chapman's argument clearly involves analogical reasoning. Evaluate the strength of the analogy he makes, identifying both positive and negative analogies between the two cases.

This basic principle can be better understood and used by means of the following method of graphic representation. We begin by drawing a circle, which we will take as representing the universe of all possible things relevant to our argument. It is very important to recognize that the circle does not usually represent everything in the universe, for usually most things that can be observed in the universe are irrelevant to any specific argument. For example, if we have a conclusion dealing with beagles (for example, 'All beagles are mammals weighing less than fifty pounds'), the observations that we must make to support the conclusion only need to be of beagles. It would be a complete waste of our time to weigh collies, boxers, and St. Bernards, for these observations would be irrelevant to our conclusion about beagles. Even though the conclusion is about mammals and things weighing less than fifty pounds, we do not have to examine any mammals that are not beagles. Thus the circle for this argument about beagles should be interpreted as containing all beagles. This point is so basic and commonsensical that we will not belabor it further, and for the most part we will assume it and not explicitly mention it in the discussion of the examples in the remainder of this chapter.

Although we do not want to allow the circle to contain things that are irrelevant to the conclusion, we need to be careful not to define the contents of the circle too narrowly. In argument 21, the conclusion and all of the listed observed cases are about one or another of *Pat's* beagles. But it would be wrong to limit the contents of the circle to Pat's beagles, since the life spans of beagles in general are of some relevance to the conclusion about Pat's next beagle. That is, if the average life span of all beagles is ten years, the likelihood that Pat's next beagle will live fourteen years is less than if the average life span of all beagles is sixteen years, whatever might be the case with Pat's first three beagles. Thus the circle for this argument should be interpreted as representing the class of all beagles, not just beagles owned by Pat; it should not include any non-beagles.

Having drawn the circle representing the class of all beagles, *we then place an O_n inside the circle for each observed case given in the premises of the argument.* (The subscript '$_n$' is simply used to distinguish one observed case from another.) The most important part of this process is the locating of the various Os. We can place the first O anywhere in the circle that we wish, although as a rule of thumb it is usually best to place it away from the exact center. Then, each of the other Os must be placed according to the degree of their similarity (that is, their positive analogy) to the first O and any other Os that have been placed in the diagram. *The greater the positive analogy between two observed cases, the closer they should be placed to each other; the greater the negative analogy the farther apart they should be placed.* Locating the Os on the diagram is an art and a skill that requires practice and the development of a certain intuitive 'feel,' but once learned, it is quite useful in assessing the relative strength of inductive arguments.

Figure 9–1 provides a graphic representation of the premises in argument 21. If we consider the universe represented by the circle to be all of the beagles

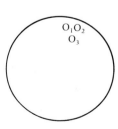

Figure 9–1

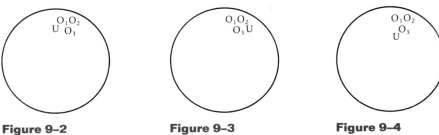

Figure 9–2   Figure 9–3   Figure 9–4

that exist now and those that have ever existed in the past, we can see intuitively that Pat's first three dogs are relatively very similar to each other and that therefore O_1, O_2, and O_3 should be located very close to one another, as is shown on the diagram.

The second step for using diagrams to assess the relative strength of an inductive argument is to *place a 'U' to represent the unobserved case from the conclusion.* As with the observed cases, it should be located in relation to the Os already on the diagram in such a way as to indicate its relative degree of similarity to and/or difference from each of them. There is no single correct location for the unobserved case in the diagram for most arguments. Figures 9–2, 9–3, and 9–4 all represent legitimate locations for the unobserved case for argument 21.

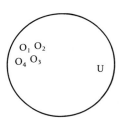

Figure 9–5

To understand how to "read off" from the diagram a judgment of the relative strength of the argument, it is helpful to have an idea of the range of possible diagrams. Figures 9–2, 9–3, and 9–4 display a very strong positive analogy among the observed cases and a very strong positive analogy between the observed cases and the unobserved case. At the other extreme would be an argument with a strong positive analogy among the observed cases but a strong negative analogy between the observed cases and the unobserved case. An illustration of such an argument is provided by Figure 9–5. It should be intuitively clear why such an argument is very weak when Figure 9–5 is contrasted with an argument with a diagram like Figure 9–4, which is clearly strong.

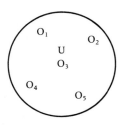

Figure 9–6

It is also possible to have an argument with a strong negative analogy among the observed cases and a strong positive analogy between the observed cases and the unobserved case. An extreme version of this kind of argument is given in Figure 9–6; it should be clear that it is a very strong argument. A bit of thought about this diagram should lead us to understand why there cannot be a strong negative analogy between the observed and unobserved cases if there is a very strong negative analogy among the observed cases: there is no place in the diagram to place a U that is very far from at least one of the observed cases. The *basic rule* for interpreting diagrams is that *the greater the distance between the unobserved case and the nearest observed case, the weaker the argument.* If the distance between the U and the nearest O is small, the argument is relatively strong. If the distance between the U and the nearest O is great, the argument is relatively weak.

The basic principle at work here is essentially the same as that involved in the concept of "random sampling" used by pollsters and others. For instance, in polling voters about their opinions on a particular social, economic, or political issue, opinion research organizations carefully select the people they interview to get a good cross-section of the population in terms of relevant characteristics such as geographical location, annual income, education, age, political and religious affiliations, and occupation. A sample that is restricted to only white, male, blue-collar workers would not provide much support for a conclusion about the preferences of a general population that included such members as women, blacks, and white-collar workers.

Now let us consider the diagrams for the following modified versions of the argument about Pat's dog.

22. O_1 Pat's first dog was a male beagle and lived fourteen years.
    O_2 Pat's second dog was a male beagle and lived fourteen years.
    O_3 Pat's third dog was a male beagle and lived fourteen years.
    U   Pat's fourth dog is a female collie and is now ten years old.
    ∴ Pat's fourth dog will live fourteen years.

23. O_1 Pat's first dog was a male beagle and lived fourteen years.
    O_2 Pat's second dog was a male pointer and lived fourteen years.
    O_3 Pat's third dog was a female setter and lived fourteen years.
    U   Pat's fourth dog is a female collie and is now ten years old.
    ∴ Pat's fourth dog will live fourteen years.

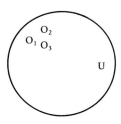

Figure 9–7

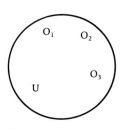

Figure 9–8

The premises in these versions clearly provide stronger support for the conclusion than in argument 21. The diagram for argument 22 is given in Figure 9–7, and the diagram for argument 23 is given in Figure 9–8. Notice that argument 22 has the same observed cases as argument 21, but the unobserved case of 22 has a stronger negative (or weaker positive) analogy with the premises than the unobserved case of 21 has with the same premises. This is displayed in the diagram of 22 by placing the U farther from the Os than in the diagram of 21. The unobserved case in 23 is the same as in 22, but the observed cases have been changed so that there is a greater negative (or weaker positive) analogy among them in 23 than in 22.

A careful look at Figures 9–7 and 9–8 should make it clear that argument 22 is weaker than argument 23, insofar as the unobserved case is farther from any observed cases in 9–7 than in 9–8. It is very hard to move the Os farther away from each other in 9–8 without moving at least some of them closer to the U. This explains why increasing the negative analogy among the observed cases will usually strengthen an inductive argument if the unobserved case remains the same.

Although increasing the number of observed cases can increase the strength of an inductive argument, the reason for the increased strength is that the new observed cases usually increase the negative analogy among the observed cases and/or increase the positive analogy between the observed cases and the

Today, George Allen starts his fifth year with the Washington Redskins. This time, his contract is for seven years instead of five, but that aside there are a number of very striking parallels, both physical and psychological, between his years with the Rams and with the Redskins, parallels which make one think that if year five at Los Angeles was the end for George Allen and the Rams, then year five at Washington will be, at the very least, the beginning of the end for George Allen and the Redskins.

The most concrete parallels exist in won-lost records. With both teams Allen turned losers into immediate, first year winners: the 4-10 Rams bounced to 8-6 in 1966, the 6-8 Redskins were 9-4-1 in 1971. With both teams, his second year was the best: the 1967 Rams were 11-1-2 and almost got to the Super Bowl, while the 1972 Redskins were 11-3 and did get to the Super Bowl, only to lose to the Dolphins. And a case could even be made that in both cities the second-best Allen teams were his fourth year efforts: the 1969 Rams were 11-3 and won their division, while the 1974 Redskins, though finishing with the same 10-4 record as the 1973 bunch, had the advantage of a healthy Sonny Jurgensen for the playoffs, an advantage, many observers feel, that could have gotten the Redskins perhaps as far as the Super Bowl if George Allen had chosen to use it. He did not.

William Gildea and Kenneth Iuran, "Is This the End for George Allen?" Washington Post/Potomac, 7/21/75.

The prediction in this induction by analogy turned out to be quite accurate: George Allen's contract with the Washington Redskins was not renewed. Was this just a lucky guess on the part of the authors, or is the argument a good one?

unobserved case. The effect of adding premises can usually be seen in a carefully drawn diagram. We will discuss this in more detail later.

It is possible for an induction by analogy to have a universal conclusion, as in the following example.

24. O_1 Pat's first dog was a male beagle and lived fourteen years.
      O_2 Pat's second dog was a male beagle and lived fourteen years.
      O_3 Pat's third dog was a male beagle and lived fourteen years.
      U $\therefore$ All dogs that Pat may have in the future will live fourteen years.

Rather than being about a single specific unobserved case, this conclusion is about an indeterminate class of possible individuals. It cannot be diagrammed using the single letter 'U,' which represents a specific individual, but must be represented by a dotted circle that indicates the possible range of individual dogs that could be Pat's pets in the future. We must expand the definition of the original circle to include the possible dogs that do not now exist but that may exist at any future point in Pat's life. The diagram could then look like Figures 9–9, 9–10, or 9–11, or any similar diagram, since all indicate essentially the same logical relationships.

If we make the conclusion deductively stronger than that in argument 24, the argument becomes weaker, as shown in 25.

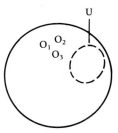

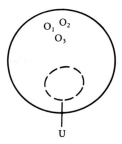

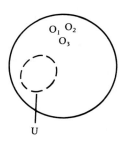

| Figure 9–9 | Figure 9–10 | Figure 9–11 |

25. O_1 Pat's first dog was a male beagle and lived fourteen years.
    O_2 Pat's second dog was a male beagle and lived fourteen years.
    O_3 Pat's third dog was a male beagle and lived fourteen years.
    U   ∴ All dogs in the future will live fourteen years.

This argument's structure is represented in Figures 9–12, 9–13, and 9–14, or any other similar diagram.

Inductions by analogy can have universal propositions as their premises as well as their conclusions. The following is an example of such an argument.

26. O_1 All of Pat's dogs have lived fourteen years.
    O_2 All of Mary's dogs have lived fourteen years.
    O_3 All of Bill's dogs have lived fourteen years.
    U   ∴ All of Sue's dogs will live fourteen years.

This can also be accommodated in the diagrams by using circles to represent the classes of things referred to by the universal terms. If we designate the large circle as representing the class of all dogs, we can use smaller solid circles to represent Pat's, Mary's, and Bill's dogs. We can also use a broken circle to represent Sue's dogs. If we knew that all of the dogs were beagles from the same litters, or were similar in some other ways, we would be justified in placing some of the circles closer to one another. However, since we are given no other specific details about the dogs, we are not justified in placing the circles very

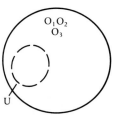

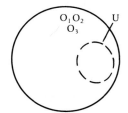

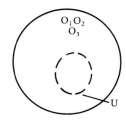

| Figure 9–12 | Figure 9–13 | Figure 9–14 |

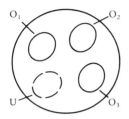

Figure 9–15

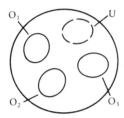

Figure 9–16

close together, and the diagram should look something like those in Figures 9–15 and 9–16.

If we make the conclusions of argument 25 or 26 deductively stronger by including references to all previously or currently existing dogs, the arguments would possibly become inductive generalizations, so we will stop first to summarize the basic concepts for evaluating the strength of inductions by analogy.

The following principles generally hold for inductions by analogy, although exceptions exist for each principle.

1. If two inductions by analogy have the same conclusion, the argument that has the strongest negative analogy (or weakest positive analogy) among the relevant observed cases is usually inductively stronger.

2. If two inductions by analogy have the same set of observed cases, the argument that has the strongest positive analogy (or the weakest negative analogy) between the observed cases and the unobserved case is usually inductively stronger.

3. If two inductions by analogy have the same set of observed cases, the argument with the deductively weaker conclusion is usually inductively stronger.

EXERCISE 9–4

Draw a diagram for each of the following arguments labeling the observed cases using the notation provided. Then add each of the new observed cases (given in a through d) and determine for each whether its addition makes the argument inductively stronger or weaker. Finally, replace the conclusion with each of the unobserved cases (given in e and f), locate these cases on the diagram, and determine whether the argument containing each is stronger or weaker than the original argument.

1. O_1 Ed's car is a 1988 Buick, is insured by State Farm, and is red.
      O_2 Sue's car is a 1988 Buick, is insured by State Farm, and is red.
      O_3 Tom's car is a 1988 Buick, is insured by State Farm, and is red.
      O_4 Mary's car is a 1988 Buick, is insured by State Farm, and is red.
    ∴ U_1 Al's car, which is a 1988 Buick and is insured by State Farm, is red.

    a. O_5 Ann's car is a 1988 Buick, is insured by State Farm, and is red.
    b. O_6 Bill's car is a 1988 Buick, is insured by Allstate, and is red.
    c. O_7 Pat's car is a 1985 Buick, is insured by Nationwide, and is red.
    d. O_8 Ken's car is a 1985 Toyota, is insured by Allstate, and is red.
    e. U_2 Al's car, which is a 1985 Buick and is insured by State Farm, is red.
    f. U_3 Al's car, which is a 1985 Toyota and is insured by Allstate, is red.

2. O_1 Ed is a senior who got 750 on the math SATs and an A on the logic exam.

   O_2 Sue is a senior who got 765 on the math SATs and an A on the logic exam.

   O_3 Tom is a junior who got 740 on the math SATs and an A on the logic exam.

   O_4 Mary, a sophomore, got 700 on the math SATs and an A on the logic exam.

   ∴ U_1 Al, a junior who got a 745 on the math SATs, got an A on the logic exam.

   a. O_5 Ann is a freshman who got 760 on the math SATs and an A on the logic exam.

   b. O_6 Bill is a junior who got 600 on the math SATs and an A on the logic exam.

   c. O_7 Pat is a sophomore who got 450 on the math SATs and an A on the logic exam.

   d. O_8 Ken is a freshman who got 500 on the math SATs and a C on the logic exam.

   e. U_2 Jan, who is a freshman who got 735 on the math SATs, got an A on the logic exam.

   f. U_3 Chris, a junior who got 400 on the math SATs, got an A on the logic exam.

9.2.4 Analogy in Inductive Generalizations

If we took any of arguments 22 through 26 and changed the conclusion to ' ∴ All of Pat's dogs will live fourteen years,' this new argument could not be inductively stronger than the original, since its conclusion would be deductively stronger than the conclusion of any of the original arguments. In terms of the relative strengths of inductive generalizations, the same relationships obtain regarding positive and negative analogies among observed cases and between observed and unobserved cases. To clarify this, consider the following:

27. O_1 **Pat's first dog was a male beagle and lived fourteen years.**

    O_2 **Pat's second dog was a male beagle and lived fourteen years.**

    O_3 **Pat's third dog was a male beagle and lived fourteen years.**

    U ∴ **All of Pat's dogs live fourteen years.**

This argument is an inductive generalization insofar as at least one of the premises is such that its falsity *could* imply the falsity of the conclusion. In diagramming this argument, the original circle should be defined as including all dogs that might have been or will be alive during Pat's lifetime. Since its conclusion is about an indeterminate class of possible individuals (including dogs that Pat might acquire in the future), it cannot be diagrammed using the single letter 'U' (which represents a specific, individual unobserved case), but must be represented by a dotted circle (or oval) that indicates the possible range of

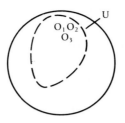

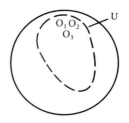

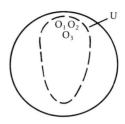

Figure 9–17   **Figure 9–18**   **Figure 9–19**

individual dogs that could belong to Pat in the past, present, or future. The diagram could then look like Figures 9–17, 9–18, or 9–19, or any similar diagram, since all indicate essentially the same logical relationships.

This argument is relatively weak because there is a relatively strong positive analogy among the observed cases. The argument can be made stronger by increasing the negative analogy among the observed cases, for example, as shown below.

28. O_1 Pat's first dog was a male beagle and lived fourteen years.
    O_2 Pat's second dog was a male pointer and lived fourteen years.
    O_3 Pat's third dog was a female setter and lived fourteen years.
    U   ∴ All of Pat's dogs live fourteen years.

This argument's structure is represented in Figures 9–20, 9–21, and 9–22, or any other similar diagram. The diagram helps to show that *increasing the negative analogy among the observed cases also usually results in an increase in the positive analogy between the observed cases and the unobserved case* (that is, the generalization in the conclusion).

The analogy between the observed and unobserved cases also can be changed by making the conclusion deductively stronger or weaker. As we indicated earlier, if the conclusion is replaced by one that is deductively stronger, the new argument is usually inductively weaker. This can be seen when argument 29 is compared to argument 28.

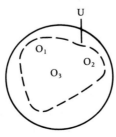

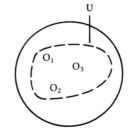

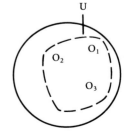

Figure 9–20   **Figure 9–21**   **Figure 9–22**

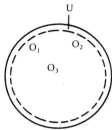

Figure 9–23

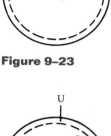

Figure 9–24

29. O₁ Pat's first dog was a male beagle and lived fourteen years.
    O₂ Pat's second dog was a male pointer and lived fourteen years.
    O₃ Pat's third dog was a female setter and lived fourteen years.
    U ∴ All dogs live fourteen years.

The diagram for argument 29 should look something like Figures 9–23 and 9–24.

The basic principles for evaluating the relative strengths of inductive generalizations are essentially the same as those for evaluating inductions by analogy. It is worthwhile to repeat them again here before going on to some exercises.

The following principles generally hold for inductive generalizations, although exceptions exist for each principle.

1. If two inductive generalizations have the same conclusion, the argument that has the strongest negative analogy (or weakest positive analogy) among the relevant observed cases is usually inductively stronger.

2. If two inductive generalizations have the same set of observed cases, the argument that has the strongest positive analogy between the observed cases and the unobserved case is usually inductively stronger.

3. If two inductive generalizations have the same set of observed cases, the argument with the conclusion that is deductively weaker is usually inductively stronger.

EXERCISE 9–5

Draw a diagram for each of the following arguments labeling the observed sets using the notation provided. Then add each of the new observed sets (given in a through d) and determine for each whether its addition makes the argument inductively stronger or weaker. Finally, replace the conclusion with each of the unobserved cases (given in e and f), locate these cases on the diagram, and determine whether the argument containing each is stronger or weaker than the original argument.

1. O₁ Ed's car is a 1988 Buick, is insured by State Farm, and is red.
    O₂ Sue's car is a 1988 Buick, is insured by State Farm, and is red.
    O₃ Tom's car is a 1988 Buick, is insured by State Farm, and is red.
    O₄ Mary's car is a 1988 Buick, is insured by State Farm, and is red.
    ∴ U₁ All 1988 Buicks are red.

    a. O₅ Ann's car is a 1988 Buick, is insured by State Farm, and is red.
    b. O₆ Bill's car is a 1988 Buick, is insured by Allstate, and is red.
    c. O₇ Pat's car is a 1985 Buick, is insured by Nationwide, and is red.
    d. O₈ Ken's car is a 1985 Toyota, is insured by Allstate, and is red.

  e. U_2 All Buicks are red.

  f. U_3 All cars are red.

2. O_1 Ed is a senior who got 750 on the math SATs and an A on the logic exam.

  O_2 Sue is a senior who got 765 on the math SATs and an A on the logic exam.

  O_3 Tom is a junior who got 740 on the math SATs and an A on the logic exam.

  O_4 Mary, a sophomore, got 700 on the math SATs and an A on the logic exam.

$\therefore$ U_1 All seniors who got above 700 on the math SATs got an A on the logic exam.

  a. O_5 Ann is a freshman who got 760 on the math SATs and an A on the logic exam.

  b. O_6 Bill is a junior who got 600 on the math SATs and an A on the logic exam.

  c. O_7 Pat is a sophomore who got 450 on the math SATs and an A on the logic exam.

  d. O_8 Ken is a freshman who got 500 on the math SATs and a C on the logic exam.

  e. U_2 All students who got above 600 on the math SATs got A's on the logic exam.

  f. U_3 All seniors got an As on the logic exam.

9.2.5 Number of Observed Cases

Although the intuitively "obvious" principle is generally correct that *the more cases that are observed to support a conclusion, the stronger an inductive argument will be,* some significant qualifications of this principle have to be recognized. One qualification is that, as the number of *relevant positive* observed cases increases, the inductive support given by *each* additional relevant positive observed case decreases. For instance, if we are dealing with an argument in which five observed cases are offered in support of the conclusion, and then one hundred more relevant positive observed cases are added, the strength of the inductive argument increases greatly. But if we are considering an argument with one thousand relevant positive observed cases cited in the premises, then an additional one hundred cases do not add as much support to the conclusion as did the additional one hundred cases in the example which has only five observed cases in the original set of premises.

It must also be recognized that in some cases, an enumerative induction with just a few observed cases, or even one, is not necessarily a weak argument. For instance, suppose you place a magnet near a pile of iron filings and observe that the filings are attracted to the magnet. You might infer, from your observation, that in all instances in which a magnet is placed near iron, the iron will be attracted to the magnet. An argument corresponding to your inference might read as follows:

> **In this instance, when I placed a magnet near iron, the iron was attracted to the magnet.**
> ∴ **In all instances in which a magnet is placed near iron, the iron will be attracted to the magnet.**

As it stands, this is a weak induction. But under the principle of charity, the argument might be treated as an enthymeme—that is, an argument in which not all of the premises are explicitly stated. Thus it might be a strong inductive generalization—even though the premise cites only one observed case—depending on other previous inductions or background information that can be added to the premises. You might know, for instance, that nickel, copper, cobalt, silver, gold, and other pure metals each exhibit uniform behavior in the presence of a magnet, that is, some are attracted to it, whereas others are not. Thus you could reasonably assume that iron, too, will exhibit uniform behavior in the presence of a magnet. When the missing premises based on this background information are supplied, your original argument might read as follows:

> **In past instances, any given pure metal has exhibited uniform behavior whenever a magnet was placed near it.**
> **Iron is a pure metal.**
> **In this instance, when I placed a magnet near iron, the iron was attracted to the magnet.**
> ∴ **In all instances in which a magnet is placed near iron, the iron will be attracted to the magnet.**

The relative strength of this argument can be understood more clearly by comparing it to the argument implicit in the cartoon below, which is essentially as follows:

> **When smaller wheel A collided with larger wheel B, the larger wheel was destroyed.**
> **Smaller wheel C is about to collide with larger wheel A.**
> ∴ **Larger wheel A will be destroyed.**

"B.C." by permission of Johnny Hart and Creators Syndicate, Inc.

In this case, we do not have any theoretical base that can be drawn on to support this induction; indeed, many basic general principles directly contradict the first premise.

This argument really involves a possible rejection of a whole set of scientific (and commonsense) theories and laws associated with our normal expectations that larger objects usually suffer less damage when they collide with smaller objects. Thus, when such an anomalous case appears that conflicts with all reasonable expectations, it is usually wise to examine it more carefully to determine whether some significant disanalogy is involved. For example, in the case of the cartoon, it would be necessary to determine what materials the various wheels might be made of. It could be that, in the first case, the small wheel might be made out of steel and the large one out of brittle rock, while, in the second case, both wheels are made of the same substance.

The weakness of the argument is not the fact that there is only one observed case but that there is a negative analogy between the observed and unobserved cases as shown here:

> **When small steel wheel A collided with large, brittle-rock wheel B, the larger (brittle-rock) wheel was destroyed.**
> **Small steel wheel C is about to collide with larger steel wheel A.**
> **∴ Larger wheel A will be destroyed.**

In this form, with the extra information about the material out of which the wheels are made now explicit, the weakness of the inductive argument is quite clear.

Just as an enumerative induction with one or a few observed cases in the premise(s) is not necessarily a weak argument, one with a large number of observed cases is not necessarily strong. For instance, suppose you are the Commissioner of Parks in Chicago and you want to find out what percentage of Chicagoans use the city's parks. You send one of your bright young assistants out to do a survey. The assistant goes to five parks and speaks with twenty people in each; each interviewee says he or she uses the park. Based on these one hundred interviews, your bright young assistant returns and informs you that 'All Chicagoans use the city's parks.' Dubious of this conclusion, but not inquiring about the method of research, you request another survey. Again, the assistant goes to five parks, this time interviewing fifty people in each, which gives a total sample of two hundred and fifty interviews. Again, all those interviewed report that they use the parks, leading the assistant to conclude again that all Chicagoans use the city's parks.

Since the size of the sample is two and one-half times that of the original, the assistant is even even more confident that the conclusion is true. This time you inquire about the sampling procedures and on finding out what they were, you fire the assistant on the spot. You realize that interviewing a thousand people at each park would have been no more helpful. No number of additional observed cases gathered in this way would strengthen the argument.

Even though the example is a bit absurd, it illustrates that the use of a large

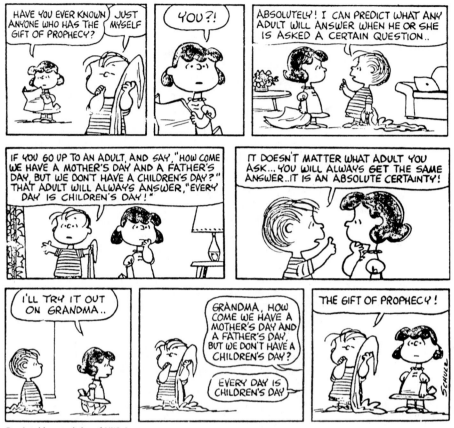

How, if at all, can Linus' act of "prophecy" in this cartoon be interpreted as an induction? What would the inductive argument reflecting his reasoning look like? To what extent, if at all, does Lucy's observation confirm Linus' hypothesis or add strength to his induction?

number of observed cases in the premises of an enumerative induction does not necessarily strengthen the argument. All we can say is that, *generally speaking,* the greater the number of observed cases, the stronger the induction. This is so because *usually,* as we increase the number of observed cases in the premises of an enumerative induction, we also increase the negative analogy among the observed cases. As we noted earlier, the greater the negative analogy among observed cases, the more likely it is that the unobserved case—or generalization—will have a positive analogy to the observed cases, thus increasing the probability of the conclusion and strengthening the enumerative induction.

9.2.6 Relevance

The relevance of the characteristics of the cases being compared or contrasted affects the strength of an enumerative induction, but determining which characteristics are relevant or irrelevant is not a simple task. For instance, in the argument about Pat's dogs, it is possible that the diet of the animals or certain genetic traits might be as relevant or more relevant to their life span as any of the characteristics considered in the argument. No *formal* logical procedure can guarantee that we have considered all and only the relevant factors in any given case. An individual's personal background of experience and theoretical assumptions will certainly influence her or his judgments as to what should and should not be considered relevant in any case. For instance, a person who has bought three dogs from pet shops, each of which died within two years, might consider the place of purchase relevant to the argument. A believer in astrology might consider the date of purchase and the birth date of the purchaser to be relevant. In Chapter 10 we discuss some methods for determining in a more formal way whether a particular factor we think might be relevant is, in fact, relevant.

EXERCISE 9–6

Read each of the following arguments carefully. Determine whether the addition of the suggested premises weakens or strengthens the argument in terms of positive and negative analogy, relevance, and/or the number of observed cases. Use diagrams to assist you as necessary.

1.   All bees are insects and can fly.
       All flies are insects and can fly.
       All wasps are insects and can fly.
    ∴ All insects can fly.

    a. Add the following premise only: All butterflies are insects and can fly.
    b. Add the following premise only: All moths are insects and can fly.
    c. Add the following premise only: All fleas are insects and do not fly.
    d. Add the following premise only: All spiders are insects and do not fly.
    e. Add premises a and b.
    f. Add premises a, b, and c.

2.   The Thomases are Irish Catholic and have always voted Democratic.
       The O'Connors are Irish Catholic and have always voted Democratic.
       The Caseys are Irish Catholic and have always voted Democratic.
       The Flynns are Irish Catholic and have always voted Democratic.
       The Kellys are Irish Catholic.
    ∴ The Kellys have always voted Democratic.

    a. Add the following premise only: Mrs. Kelly's brother was the Republican candidate for mayor last year.
    b. Add the following premise only: The Kellys are registered Democrats.

    c. Add the following premise only: The Kellys are very active in the Democratic party.

    d. Add the following premise only: The Thomases, O'Connors, Caseys, and Flynns are first-generation Americans and the Kellys are fifth-generation Americans.

    e. Add the following premise only: Ninety-five percent of Irish Catholic voters vote Democratic in every election.

    f. Add premises a and d.

    g. Add premises b and e.

    h. Add premises c and d.

3.   All lions I have observed are cats, warm-blooded, mammals, and carnivorous.

    All leopards I have observed are cats, warm-blooded, mammals, and carnivorous.

    All panthers I have observed are cats, warm-blooded, mammals, and carnivorous.

    All cougars I have observed are cats, warm-blooded, and mammals.

    ∴ All cougars are carnivorous.

    a. Add the following premise only: All tigers I have observed are cats, warm-blooded, mammals, and carnivorous.

    b. Add the following premise only: All types of cat I have observed were in the Kenya Wildlife Reserve.

    c. Add the following premise only: I have observed only one of each type of cat.

    d. Add the following premise only: All tabbies I have observed are cats, warm-blooded, mammals, and carnivorous.

    e. Add premises a and d.

    f. Add premises b and c.

4.   All bluejays are birds and can fly.

    All robins are birds and can fly.

    All sparrows are birds and can fly.

    All hawks are birds and can fly.

    ∴ All birds can fly.

    a. Add the following premise only: All seagulls are birds and can fly.

    b. Add the following premise only: All ostriches are birds and cannot fly.

    c. Add the following premise only: All pelicans are birds and can fly.

    d. Add the following premise only: All crows are birds and can fly.

    e. Add the following premise only: All penguins are birds and cannot fly.

    f. Add premises a, c, and d.

    g. Add premises a, c, d, and e.

5.   The Franklins purchased a 1993 Marchtag washer and have had excellent service.

    The Peppers purchased a 1993 Marchtag washer and have had excellent service.

The Goldslags purchased a 1993 Marchtag washer and have had excellent service.

The Corleones purchased a 1993 Marchtag washer.

∴ The Corleones will have excellent service.

a. Add the following premise only: The Franklins', Peppers', and Goldslags' washers hold twenty-four-pound loads, whereas the Corleones' washer holds a sixteen-pound load.

b. Add the following premise only: The Franklins, Peppers, and Goldslags all use White, the detergent recommended by the Marchtag company, whereas the Corleones use Wash, the cheapest brand of detergent.

c. Add the following premise only: The Franklins, Peppers, and Goldslags all use a bleach and fabric softener in addition to detergent, whereas the Corleones do not.

d. Add the following premise only: The Petersons purchased a 1993 Marchtag washer and have had excellent service.

e. Add the following premise only: All the washers were manufactured at the same plant, tested by the same inspector, and bought from the same store.

f. Add the following premise only: The Corleones' washer was a floor model, whereas all the other washers were new, in factory-sealed cartons.

6. Pat went to Excel High School and won a scholarship to college.
Jan went to Excel High School and won a scholarship to college.
Chris went to Excel High School and won a scholarship to college.
Jackie went to Excel High School and won a scholarship to college.
Robin goes to Excel High School.

∴ Robin will win a scholarship to college.

a. Add the following premise only: Pat, Mary, Chris, Jackie, and Robin each have B+ or better averages.

b. Add the following premise only: When Pat, Jan, Chris, and Jackie graduated from Excel High school, the school had a special program preparing students for scholarship examinations; no such program exists now.

c. Add the following premise only: Pat, Jan, Chris, and Jackie won scholarships to the state university; Robin has only applied for a scholarship at private colleges.

d. Add the following premise only: Pat, Jan, and Robin took advanced courses in high school, whereas Chris and Jackie did not take advanced courses.

e. Add the following premise only: Pat, Jan, Chris, and Jackie got between 600 and 650 on their college boards, whereas Robin got between 700 and 750 on her college boards.

f. Add premises a, d, and e.

g. Add premises b and c.

7. The Santiagos bought a 1994 Metro and get about 45 miles to a gallon of gas.

The Prices bought a 1994 Metro and get about 45 miles to a gallon of gas.

The Thomases bought a 1994 Metro and get about 45 miles to a gallon of gas.

The Allens bought a 1994 Metro.

∴ The Allens' car gets at least 45 miles to a gallon of gas.

a. Add the following premise only: The Judds bought a 1994 Metro and get about 50 miles to a gallon of gas.

b. Add the following premise only: The Martinos bought a 1994 Metro and get about 30 miles to a gallon of gas.

c. Add the following premises only: The Santiagos', Prices', and Thomases' cars are red, and the Allens' car is blue.

d. Add the following premise only: All the families bought their cars in the same week from the same dealer.

e. Add the following premises only: The Santiagos', Prices', and Thomases' cars do not have air conditioning and power windows, and the Allens' car has air conditioning and power windows.

f. Add the following premises only: The Santiagos', Prices', and Thomases' cars have automatic transmissions, and the Allens' car has a manual transmission.

g. Add the following premise only: The Santiagos, Prices, and Thomases use high-octane gas in their cars, and the Allens use regular gas in their car.

h. Add premises e and g.

9.3 The Possible Elimination of Inductions by Analogy

Some logicians have suggested that there is no need to make the distinction between inductions by analogy and inductive generalizations. They have argued that it is possible to do away with inductions by analogy as long as deduction and inductive generalization are available. This claim can be illustrated by examples. Consider the following induction by analogy:

Swan A is white
Swan B is white.
Swan C is white.

∴ Swan D is white

Now consider the following two-step argument, which consists of an inductive generalization followed by a deductive argument, using the generalization as a premise:

Swan A is white.
Swan B is white.
Swan C is white.

∴ All swans are white.

> **All swans are white.**
> **D is a swan.**
> ∴ **D is white.**

In the two-step argument, the same conclusion is ultimately derived from the same initial set of premises as in the original single-step induction by analogy. And it should be clear that a similar two-step generalization/deduction argument can be formulated corresponding to every induction by analogy. If the two-step procedure can be shown to provide a stronger connection between the premises and the final conclusion, it certainly would be a better form to use in presenting inductive arguments. And even if it should turn out to be only strictly equivalent to the one-step method, it still might be considered a better form, since it reduces the basic types of argument from three (deduction, induction by analogy, and inductive generalization) to two.

At first glance the one-step and two-step formulations might appear to be at least logically equivalent, or the two-step method might even appear to be the better of the two alternatives. In point of fact, however, the two methods are not equivalent, and the one-step method is at least as good as, if not better than, the two-step. This is because, insofar as the conclusion in the two-step method is deduced from a generalization that was established by induction, that conclusion can be no more probable than the generalization from which it was deduced. But this means that all conclusions arrived at by means of this method (using the same generalization) are equally probable; that is, the premises provide the same support for a number of different conclusions. For example, we could construct the following argument:

> **Swan A is white.**
> **Swan B is white.**
> **Swan C is white.**
> ∴ **All swans are white.**

> **All swans are white.**
> **At least four swans exist in the universe.**
> ∴ **At least one swan other than A, B, or C is white.**

This new conclusion receives no more support from the premises in this formulation than did the conclusion of the previous argument—'D is white,' because both are exactly as strong as the initial inductive generalization. But it should be intuitively clear that, given that three swans have been observed to be white, it is more probable that at least one additional swan will be observed to be white than that a specific other swan (D) will be white—or that all swans are white.

These are precisely the points recognized by our distinction between induction by analogy and inductive generalization and also by our rule concerning relative inductive and deductive strengths in arguments with the same premises. Thus, the one-step method, in which the premises lead directly to the conclusion by means of an induction by analogy, is not equivalent to but is stronger than the two-step method, which proceeded by way of the weaker inductive generalization. The one-step method is a "better" method insofar as it is also more in line with our basic intuitions about the relative strengths of inductive arguments, and it allows us to formally identify intuitively apparent differences in inductive strength.

EXERCISE 9-7

Reformulate each of the following ordinary-language arguments as (a) a one-step argument—that is, an induction by analogy—and (b) a two-step argument containing an inductive generalization followed by a deductive argument.

1. Frank will win when we play five-card stud [a type of poker]. He's already won at high-low, seven-card stud, and five-card draw [other types of poker].

2. My mother, father, and both sisters have caught the flu, so I will, too.

3. It will rain on Saturday, since it rained on Sunday, Monday, Tuesday, Wednesday, Thursday, and Friday.

4. Swans A, B, C, D, E, F, G, H, I, and J are all white; so Swan K is also white.

5. The flood crested upriver in Pittsburgh and Cincinnati earlier this week, so it will crest here in Louisville this week, too.

6. We will have a big snow storm this year, since we had big snow storms last year, two years ago, three years ago, and four years ago.

7. The Smiths, Parkers, Roberts, Mitchells, and Conners all own Zowie stereos and get excellent performance. So, the Carters, who just bought a Zowie stereo, will get excellent performance.

8. Chimpanzees A, B, C, D, E, and F each engaged in grooming behavior. Consequently, at least one other chimp will engage in grooming behavior.

9. My grandfather, my father, and my older brother went bald before they were thirty years old, so I will, too.

10. *Swan Lake,* composed by Tchaikovsky, is a great ballet score. And *The Nutcracker,* also composed by Tchaikovsky, is a great ballet score. *Sleeping Beauty* was composed by Tchaikovsky, so it too must be a great ballet score.

11. Jan, Hans, Maria, Karl, and Karin are all Swiss and speak German. Therefore Antonio, who is Swiss, must speak German.

12. The Rolls-Royce, Volvo, Mercedes-Benz, and Volkswagen are all European-made cars and perform well. The Fiat is a European-made car; consequently, it performs well, too.

13. John got As in every course he took in his first, second, third, and fourth semesters in college, so he will get As in every course he takes this semester, which is his fifth.

14. The movie I saw on the "Late Show" yesterday was interesting, and the movie I saw on the "Late Show" the night before that was interesting. Thus, at least one movie I will see on the "Late Show" in the future will be interesting.

15. There were interesting people at Joe's last three parties, so undoubtedly there will be interesting people at Joe's party tonight.

9.4 Statistical Inductions

We have distinguished two types of enumerative induction: induction by analogy and inductive generalization. Consider the following arguments:

> **Every student in Professor Wilson's metaphysics class last semester got an A.**
> ∴ **Every student in Professor Wilson's metaphysics class next semester will get an A.**

> **Every student in Professor Wilson's metaphysics class last semester got an A.**
> ∴ **Every student in each of Professor Wilson's metaphysics classes gets an A.**

The first argument is an induction by analogy, since the falsity of its premise cannot guarantee the falsity of its conclusion. The second argument is an inductive generalization, because the falsity of its premise can guarantee the falsity of its conclusion and, of course, its conclusion is a universal proposition.

If we substitute '100%' for 'every' in the premises and conclusions, the arguments would read as

> **100% of the students in Professor Wilson's metaphysics class last semester got As.**
> ∴ **100% of the students in Professor Wilson's metaphysics class next semester will get As.**

> **100% of the students in Professor Wilson's metaphysics class last semester got As.**
> ∴ **100% of the students in each of Professor Wilson's metaphysics classes get As.**

Both versions carry the same sense as the original arguments: we have merely substituted the numerical value '100%' for the word 'every.' The first type of argument above is therefore called a **statistical induction by analogy.** Notice that, as in the inductions by analogy previously discussed, the falsity of its premise cannot guarantee the falsity of its conclusion. The second type is called a **statistical generalization.** As with all inductive generalizations, at least one premise must be such that its falsity could entail the falsity of the conclusion.

We can also say that the statistical generalization is inductively weaker than the statistical induction by analogy, since the conclusion of the statistical generalization is deductively stronger than the conclusion of the statistical induction by analogy.

Of course, most statistical inductions—whether they are statistical inductions by analogy or statistical generalizations—do not draw conclusions about 100% of the cases. For example:

> **All of the students in Professor Wilson's metaphysics class last semester got As.**
> ∴ **Some students in Professor Wilson's metaphysics class next semester will get As.**

This argument is inductively stronger than any of the previous arguments in this section. Its strength is the result of the word *'some'* (which in logic always means 'at least one'). The statement would be true if *any* one student in the class got an A; but it would also be true if two or three or four or even all of the students got As. Clearly, given the premise 'All of the students in Professor Wilson's class last semester got As,' it is more likely that at least one student next semester will get an A than it is that all of the students in next semester's class will get As.

It is possible to remove the vagueness of the word 'some' by replacing it with a number. For example:

> **All of the students in Professor Wilson's metaphysics class last semester got As.**
> ∴ **Exactly two students in Professor Wilson's metaphysics class next semester will get As.**

If we know that only five students are registered for next semester's class, the argument also might be written as follows:

> **All of the students in Professor Wilson's metaphysics class last semester got As.**
> ∴ **Exactly 40% of the students in Professor Wilson's metaphysics class next semester will get As.**

The conclusions of these arguments—'Exactly two students in Professor Wilson's metaphysics class next semester will get As' and 'Exactly 40% of students in Professor Wilson's metaphysics class next semester will get As'—are deductively stronger than the conclusion 'Some students in Professor Wilson's metaphysics class next semester will get As.' This is so because, if two of the students (or 40% of the students) in next semester's class get As, then it must be the case that at least one student next semester will get an A. The conclusions of the two arguments above imply the conclusion 'Some students in Professor Wilson's metaphysics class next semester will get As,' but neither of the numerically precise statements can be deduced from the 'some' statement. Thus, the last two arguments are inductively weaker than the original argument containing the word 'some' in its conclusion because they have the same premises and the conclusions are deductively stronger.

Notice that the conclusion 'Exactly two students in Professor Wilson's metaphysics class next semester will get As' is deductively stronger than the conclusion 'At least two students in Professor Wilson's metaphysics class next semester will get As.' Provided the premise in both arguments remains the same ('100% of the students in Professor Wilson's metaphysics class last semester got As'), the argument with the conclusion 'Exactly two students in next semester's class will get As' is inductively weaker than the argument with the conclusion 'At least two students in next semester's class will get As.' Clearly, the first conclusion encompasses only one possibility, whereas the second conclusion is satisfied if two *or more* students in next semester's class get As. Similarly, the conclusion 'Exactly 40% of the students in Professor Wilson's metaphysics class next semester will get As' is deductively stronger than the conclusion 'At least 40% of the students in Professor Wilson's metaphysics class next semester will get As.' And the argument with the conclusion 'At least 40% . . .' is inductively stronger than the argument with the conclusion 'Exactly 40%. . . .'

If we draw the further conclusion 'Tom and Bill will get As in Professor Wilson's metaphysics class next semester,' this is deductively stronger than the conclusion 'At least two . . .' or 'Exactly two . . . ,' for it implies both of them, but is implied by neither. Therefore, the argument with this conclusion is inductively weaker than the others. The probability that *some* two or more students will get As is clearly greater than that two *specific* students will get As.

Usually when we go to the bother of specifying a particular number or percentage, we are intending it to add precision to our statement. Thus, we will follow the rule that *unless a numerical statement explicitly states something like 'at least _____ ,' we should interpret it as asserting something about the* **exact** *number specified,*

Of course, it is also possible to have statistical generalizations that argue from less than 100% of the cases. For example, consider the following arguments:

> **60% of the students in Professor Wilson's metaphysics class last semester got As.**
> **∴ 60% of all students in each of Professor Wilson's metaphysics classes get As.**

> **Three students in Professor Wilson's metaphysics class last semester got As.**
> **∴ Three students in every metaphysics class taught by Professor Wilson get As.**

> **Tom was enrolled in Professor Wilson's metaphysics class last semester and got an A.**
> **Sue was enrolled in Professor Wilson's metaphysics class last semester and got an A.**

> Ann was enrolled in Professor Wilson's metaphysics class last semester and got a B.
> Al was enrolled in Professor Wilson's metaphysics class last semester and got a C.
> Liz was enrolled in Professor Wilson's metaphysics class last semester and got an A.
> Tom, Sue, Al, Ann, and Liz were the only students in Professor Wilson's metaphysics class last semester.
> ∴ 60% of all students enrolled in each of Professor Wilson's metaphysics classes get As.

From these arguments, we can see that, although the premises of a statistical generalization may be about individuals and/or classes of individuals, the conclusion is always about a class of individuals. We can see also that numerical values in a statistical generalization can occur in the conclusion or in both the premises and the conclusion.

9.4.1 Evaluating Statistical Inductions

The same criteria that are used to evaluate the strength of enumerative inductions are used to evaluate the strength of statistical inductions, since the latter are merely a type of enumerative induction. Thus, the positive and negative analogies among observed cases and between observed and unobserved cases are important, as is the relevance of the characteristics shared by observed and unobserved cases. The number of observed cases cited is also important. As they stand, none of the statistical inductions above about the students in Professor Wilson's metaphysics class is very strong. Let us consider why this is so, using the following argument:

> 60% of the students in Professor Wilson's metaphysics class last semester got As.
> ∴ 60% of the students in Professor Wilson's metaphysics class next semester will get As.

This argument is inductively weak for several reasons. First, the only positive analogy between the observed case and the unobserved case is that the students are enrolled in a metaphysics course taught by Professor Wilson. Other relevant characteristics are unknown. If we knew, for example, that last semester's class contained five students and that the three students who got As were senior philosophy majors with 3.8 grade-point averages and that next semester's class also contains five students, three of whom are senior philosophy majors with 3.8 averages, then the argument would be stronger than the one above. This is so because the positive analogy between observed and unobserved cases has been increased. However, if the three A students in last semester's class were senior philosophy majors with 3.8 averages, and the next semester's class contains twenty students, three of whom are senior philosophy majors with 2.0 to

Carter a one-term president

The United States will have a new president in January 1981.

Ordinarily, we would hesitate to make that flat statement this long before the next presidential election. But all signs point to Jimmy Carter being a one-term president.

Opinion polls show that the major concern of Americans is how far their dollar will go, which isn't very far at all these days. When Carter took office, inflation was at four percent. It's now running at an annual rate of 13 percent.

And the recession that was supposed to have started late last year or early this year, thereby allowing Carter to run as a president who just pulled us out of a recession, is just beginning. and may be worse than predicted. At any rate, it will still be fresh in voters' minds come primary and election days.

Carter's inability to handle inflation and to

program the recession for his political benefit shows in the polls. According to the latest Harris Poll, Carter's rating is 75-24 percent negative, the worst for any president in modern times. Even Nixon at his nadir was more highly regarded by the American people as a president.

Carter gets his highest mark for foreign policy, 38 percent positive. But voters don't elect a president because of his foreign policy. They vote for a man because they think he can help their pocketbook.

And this is where the poll is most damaging to Carter. His two lowest positive ratings are for handling the economy, 14 percent, and his anti-inflation program, 13 percent. Both figures are down from the June poll.

Studying these figures, and taking into consideration the attitude of the American electorate, we can come to only one conclusion.

Jimmy Carter has had it.

The Troy Times Record.

This editorial was published in July 1979, more than a year before the 1980 presidential election. Considering the time at which it was written, was it a good inductive argument or not, regardless of the actual outcome of the primaries and election? Is the actual outcome at all relevant to the evaluation of the argument? Why or why not?

3.0 averages, then the argument would be weaker than the original. In this instance, the negative analogy between observed and unobserved cases has been increased, thereby weakening the argument inductively.

The relevance of the characteristics shared by observed and unobserved cases is also important when evaluating the relative strength of statistical inductions. For instance, if Professor Wilson is a white Anglo-Saxon Protestant, and all of the students in last semester's class were white Anglo-Saxon Protestants, while all the students in next semester's class are members of other ethnic and racial groups, the argument might be weakened. We say *might* be, because, as we noted earlier, there is no formal logical procedure by which to determine which characteristics are relevant to an enumerative or statistical induction. It might be that ethnicity and race do not affect Professor Wilson's grading or that they affect it significantly; other background information would be necessary to determine whether these characteristics are relevant.

Of course, the number of observed cases also affects the strength of a statistical induction. Consider, for example, the following arguments:

40%[2] of the five students in Professor Wilson's metaphysics class last semester got As.

∴ 40% of the students in Professor Wilson's class next semester will get As.

[2]Remember that if no explicit wording is included to indicate that this refers to *at least* 40%, we should interpret it as making an assertion about *exactly* 40% of the students.

> In Professor Wilson's metaphysics class three semesters ago, there were twenty students and 40% of them got As.
> In Professor Wilson's metaphysics class two semesters ago, there were twenty-five students and 40% of them got As.
> In Professor Wilson's metaphysics class last semester, there were ten students and 40% of them got As.
> ∴ In Professor Wilson's metaphysics class next semester, 40% of the students will get As.

Both arguments contain the same conclusion statement, but the number of observed cases offered in support of the conclusion in the second example is significantly greater than the number offered in the first. In this case, the second argument is inductively stronger than the first argument.

Now consider the following:

> 87% of 100 observed Roman Catholics are registered Democrats.
> 84% of another 100 observed Roman Catholics are registered Democrats.
> 87% of another 100 observed Roman Catholics are registered Democrats.
> 73% of another 100 observed Roman Catholics are registered Democrats.
> ∴ 87% of the next group of 100 Roman Catholics observed will be registered Democrats.

An argument such as this is inductively weak, since, in making an inference about a future group of Roman Catholics, it uses the upper limit cited in the observed cases or premises. The following argument based on the same set of premises is inductively stronger, since its conclusion is deductively weaker than the conclusion in the argument above.

> 87% of 100 observed Roman Catholics are registered Democrats.
> 84% of another 100 observed Roman Catholics are registered Democrats.
> 87% of another 100 observed Roman Catholics are registered Democrats.
> 73% of another 100 observed Roman Catholics are registered Democrats.
> ∴ Between 70% and 90% of the next group of 100 Roman Catholics observed will be registered Democrats.

As we can see, this argument is stronger than the first, for the conclusion in the second example is less precise than the conclusion of the first argument; this means that the probability that the conclusion of the second argument is true is greater than the probability that the conclusion of the first argument is true.

The problem, when dealing with statistical inductions such as these, is really one of balancing two extremes. *The less precise the conclusion, the stronger the inductive support for it.* However, very often, when dealing with statistical inductions, we are concerned equally with the precision of the conclusion and the inductive strength of the argument. For instance, a politician would not be very satisfied with a public opinion survey that told him he would receive between 30 and 70% of the vote on election day. Given normal sampling procedures, an argument with this conclusion would certainly be inductively stronger than an argument with the conclusion that the politician would receive between 50 and 55% of the vote, but the politician clearly would be more interested in the argument with the more precise conclusion. Thus, in dealing with statistical inductions that involve percentages about classes, we must find the happy medium; that is, we must seek to determine at which point the argument is sufficiently strong *and* the conclusion is sufficiently precise.

The following rules hold in general for enumerative inductions, statistical as well as absolute, but there are numerous exceptions, as indicated in the text. In general:

- An enumerative induction becomes weaker as the negative analogy between the relevant observed and unobserved cases increases, provided that everything else remains the same.

- The stronger the positive analogy between the relevant observed and unobserved cases, the stronger the enumerative induction.

- Increasing the negative analogy among the relevant observed cases does not usually weaken the argument and can even strengthen it.

- If two arguments have the same observed cases, the argument with the conclusion that is deductively weaker is inductively stronger.

- As the number of positive observed cases cited in the premises of an enumerative induction increases, the argument becomes stronger, but the amount of support given by each additional premise is usually less than for previous premises.

- Irrelevant characteristics, even if shared by all cases, do not affect the strength of an enumerative induction.

EXERCISE 9–8

Place the following arguments in order of decreasing inductive strength

1. Standard premise for all conclusions that follow:
   80% of the 100 fiddler crabs observed dig burrows in the sand.
   Conclusions:
   a. ∴ 80% of all fiddler crabs dig burrows in the sand.
   b. ∴ At least eight of the next ten fiddler crabs I observe will dig burrows in the sand.

c. ∴ Exactly 80% of the next ten fiddler crabs I observe will dig burrows in the sand.

d. ∴ Some of the next ten fiddler crabs I observe will dig burrows in the sand.

2. Standard premises for all conclusions that follow:

60% of 100 observed college graduates earned more than $20,000 a year within two years after graduation.

55% of another 100 observed college graduates earned more than $20,000 a year within two years after graduation.

68% of another 100 observed college graduates earned more than $20,000 a year within two years after graduation.

71% of another 100 observed college graduates earned more than $20,000 a year within two years after graduation.

88% of another 100 observed college graduates earned more than $20,000 a year within two years after graduation.

83% of another 100 observed college graduates earned more than $20,000 a year within two years after graduation.

Conclusions:

a. ∴ At least 55% of the next 100 observed college graduates will earn more than $20,000 a year within two years after graduation.

b. ∴ Exactly 75% of the next 100 observed college graduates will earn more than $20,000 a year within two years after graduation.

c. ∴ Between 55% and 83% of the next 100 observed college graduates will earn more than $20,000 a year within two years after graduation.

d. ∴ Between 50% and 90% of the next 100 observed college graduates will earn more than $20,000 a year within two years after graduation.

e. ∴ Exactly 60% of the next 100 observed college graduates will earn more than $20,000 a year within two years after graduation.

3. Standard premises for all conclusions that follow:

78% of 100 observed students graduating from law school last year passed the bar examination on the first try.

71% of 100 observed students graduating from law school two years ago passed the bar examination on the first try.

73% of 100 observed students graduating from law school three years ago passed the bar examination on the first try.

69% of 100 observed students graduating from law school four years ago passed the bar examination on the first try.

75% of 100 observed students graduating from law school five years ago passed the bar examination on the first try.

Conclusions:

a. ∴ At least 69% of 100 observed students graduating from law school this year will pass the bar examination on the first try.

b. ∴ Some of 100 observed students graduating from law school this year will pass the bar examination on the first try.

c. ∴ Exactly 72% of 100 observed students graduating from law school this year will pass the bar examination on the first try.

d. ∴ Between 65% and 80% of 100 observed students graduating from law school this year will pass the bar examination on the first try.

e. ∴ At least 79% of 100 observed students graduating from law school this year will pass the bar examination on the first try.

4. Standard premise for all conclusions that follow:

    10% of the 200 books published by our company last year sold 10,000 copies or more.

    Conclusions:

    a. ∴ Exactly 10% of the books published by all companies last year sold 10,000 copies or more.

    b. ∴ At least ten of the next 100 books our company publishes this year will sell 10,000 copies or more.

    c. ∴ Some of the next 100 books our company publishes this year will sell 10,000 copies or more.

    d. ∴ Exactly ten of the next 100 books our company publishes this year will sell 10,000 copies or more.

5. Standard premises for all conclusions that follow:

    75% of all students entering the university in 1985 graduated in 1989.
    73% of all students entering the university in 1986 graduated in 1990.
    82% of all students entering the university in 1987 graduated in 1991.
    73% of all students entering the university in 1988 graduated in 1992.
    80% of all students entering the university in 1989 graduated in 1993.
    71% of all students entering the university in 1990 graduated in 1994.
    84% of all students entering the university in 1991 graduated in 1995.

    Conclusions:

    a. ∴ At least 80% of all students entering the university in 1992 graduated in 1996.

    b. ∴ Exactly 70% of all students entering the university in 1992 graduated in 1996.

    c. ∴ At least 70% of all students entering the university in 1992 graduated in 1996.

    d. ∴ Between 60% and 90% of all students entering the university in 1992 graduated in 1996.

    e. ∴ Some students entering the university in 1992 graduated in 1996.

EXERCISE 9–9

Read each argument carefully. Determine whether the addition of the suggested premises weakens or strengthens the argument, in terms of positive and negative analogy, relevance, and/or the number of observed cases.

1. 80% of the 100 fiddler crabs I observed dug burrows in the sand.
   ∴ At least 80% of all fiddler crabs dig burrows in the sand.

a. Add the following premise only: All of the fiddler crabs I observed were from the same location.

b. Add the following premise only: 89% of the next 100 fiddler crabs I observed dug burrows in the sand.

c. Add the following premise only: Of the 100 fiddler crabs I observed, 50% were males and 50% were females.

d. Add the following premise only: Of the 100 fiddler crabs I observed, 10 were from Miami, 10 were from New York, 10 were from Maine, 10 were from California, 10 were from Mexico, 10 from England, 10 from France, 10 from China, 10 from Russia, and 10 from Canada.

e. Add the following premise only: All of the fiddler crabs I observed had a disease and died shortly after digging their burrows.

2. [Use the premises from number 2 in Exercise 9–8]
∴ Between 55% and 83% of the next 100 observed college graduates will earn more than $20,000 a year within two years after graduation.

a. Add the following premise only: Each of the observed college graduates in each group came from different schools.

b. Add the following premise only: All of the observed college graduates in each group came from the same school.

c. Add the following premise only: All of the observed college graduates in each group were graduated with honors.

d. Add the following premise only: Of the observed college graduates in each group, 50 had a C average, 35 had a B average, 10 had a B+ average, and 5 had an A average.

e. Add the following premise only: All of the observed college graduates in each group earned business degrees.

f. Add the following premise only: Of the 100 observed college graduates in each group, 10 were English majors, 10 were history majors, 10 biology majors, 10 philosophy majors, 10 sociology, 10 political science, 10 premedical, 10 business, 10 engineering, and 10 education.

3. 75% of 500 observed students graduating from law school last year passed the bar examination on the first try.
∴ At least 75% of all students graduating from law school pass the bar examination on the first try.

a. Add the following premise only: All of the 500 observed students graduated from the same law school.

b. Add the following premise only: Of the 500 observed students, 100 had A averages, 100 had B+ averages, 100 had B averages, 100 had C+ averages, and 100 had C averages.

c. Add the following premise only: All of the 500 observed students were on their school law review.

d. Add the following premise only: All of the 500 observed students were males.

4. 41% of 100 observed families watched *Roseanne* last week.
39% of 100 observed families watched *Roseanne* two weeks ago.

50% of 100 observed families watched *Roseanne* three weeks ago.

46% of 100 observed families watched *Roseanne* four weeks ago.

∴ Between 39% and 50% of the families to be observed this week will watch *Roseanne*.

a. Of the 100 observed families in each group, all of them had their televisions turned on to *Wheel of Fortune,* which precedes *Roseanne* on the same channel.

b. The same 100 families constituted the sample each week, but this week a new 100 families will be sampled.

c. Of the 100 observed families in each group, all lived in New York City.

d. Of the 100 observed families in each group, 10 lived in New York, 10 lived in Philadelphia, 10 lived in Atlanta, 10 lived in Miami, 10 lived in Chicago, 10 lived in St. Louis, 10 lived in Memphis, 10 lived in Akron, 10 lived in New Orleans, and 10 lived in San Francisco.

e. A new sample of 100 families was used each week.

Summary

1. A **deductive argument** is any argument such that, if the premises are true, then the conclusion must also be true; that is, the premises provide absolute support for the conclusion; or, in other words, the conclusion is completely contained in the premises. The addition of one or more premises in no way affects the support that the premises provide for the conclusion. Deductive arguments are valid by virtue of their form. A false premise in a deductive argument is not sufficient to prove that the conclusion is false, and it in no way affects the validity of the argument.

2. An **inductive argument** is an argument that does not satisfy the definition of a deductive argument. Thus, it is any argument such that, even if all the premises are true, the conclusion may still be false. That is, the premises provide, at most, only partial support for the conclusion; or, in other words, the information in the conclusion is, at most, only partly contained in the premises. The addition of further premises can change the support provided for the conclusion.

3. An **enumerative induction** is an argument with premise(s) that constitute a listing of cases concerning either individuals or classes of individuals to support conclusions about individuals or classes of individuals. Most interesting enumerative inductions involve premises that describe *observed cases* about individuals and/or classes of individuals, and have conclusions concerned with an *unobserved case* about an individual and/or a class of individuals. On the basis of the different relationships between the premises and the conclusion, it is possible to distinguish two types of enumerative inductive argument.

4. An inductive argument with a universal conclusion, in which at least one of the premises is such that its falsity could necessitate the falsity of the

conclusion, is an **inductive generalization.** An inductive generalization may contain premises either about individuals or about classes of individuals, but it cannot possibly have a particular conclusion, regardless of whether the premises are general or particular.

5. Any inductive argument that is not an inductive generalization is an **induction by analogy.**

6. The support the premises provide for the conclusion of an inductive argument can vary from just less than absolute support to no support whatsoever. Inductive arguments can be evaluated only in terms of their *relative* strengths. The relative strengths of inductive arguments *with the same set of premises* are inversely proportional to the deductive strengths of their conclusions. Of two statements, one is **deductively stronger** than another if and only if the first implies the second and the second does not imply the first. Likewise, of two statements, one is **deductively weaker** than another if and only if the second implies the first and the first does not imply the second. Statements are of equal deductive strength if they imply each other.

7. The ways in which the individuals or classes of individuals cited in an enumerative induction are alike is called **positive analogy;** the ways in which they are different is called **negative analogy.**

8. In general, an enumerative induction becomes weaker as the negative analogy between the relevant observed and unobserved cases increases and provided everything else remains the same. In general, the stronger the positive analogy between observed and unobserved cases, the stronger the enumerative induction, assuming that everything else is unchanged. Increasing the negative analogy among the relevant observed cases in an enumerative induction does not usually weaken the argument; in fact, it might strengthen it, since the greater the negative analogy among the relevant observed cases, the greater the number of possible unobserved cases that would have a positive analogy with the observed cases.

9. In general, as the number of relevant positive observed cases mentioned in the premises of an enumerative induction increases, the stronger the argument becomes. But as the number of relevant positive observed cases increases, the inductive support given by *each* additional observed case decreases. However, an enumerative induction with only a few observed cases, or even one, is not necessarily a weak argument. Likewise, an enumerative induction with a large number of observed cases is not necessarily a strong argument.

10. The relevance of the characteristics being compared or contrasted affects the strength of an enumerative induction. But determining which characteristics are relevant is not always easy, since there is no formal logical procedure that enables us to list all of the possible relevant factors. To a

considerable extent, determining what is relevant depends on an individual's perception rather than on some absolute standard.

11. Although the same conclusion can be supported by the same set of premises by using an induction by analogy and by using a two-step inductive generalization combined with a deductive argument, the induction by analogy usually gives *stronger* support for the conclusion than does the two-step argument.

12. A **statistical induction** by analogy is an induction by analogy in which a numerical value appears as the quantifier for the subject term in the premises and/or the conclusion. Similarly, a **statistical generalization** is an inductive generalization in which a numerical value appears as the quantifier for the subject term in the premises and/or the conclusion. Most of the rules that apply to enumerative inductions in general apply also to statistical inductions.

13. The same criteria that are used to evaluate the relative strengths of enumerative inductions are used to evaluate the relative strengths of statistical inductions. The positive and negative analogies among observed cases and between observed and unobserved cases are important, as is the relevance of the characteristics shared by the observed and unobserved cases and the number of observed cases cited. In statistical inductions, the less precise the conclusion, the stronger the inductive support for it. Often a middle point must be reached that provides both a sufficiently strong argument and a sufficiently precise conclusion to be useful for the desired purpose.

Chapter 10

Scientific Method

The methods of induction by analogy and inductive generalization are discussed in Chapter 9 in a relatively abstract and formal way, and the examples and exercises might have seemed a bit artificial or contrived. But these two types of arguments are in fact used regularly, both in everyday life and in scientific research. In this chapter we will look at how the methods of enumerative induction can be applied in the context of scientific research.

It is also noted in Chapter 9 that neither method of enumerative induction is adequate for dealing with certain arguments with deductively very strong conclusions, namely those with conclusions asserting *causal* relations between two phenomena or events. In the latter part of this chapter we shall examine a set of methods that are widely used for dealing with such arguments, particularly in scientific research.

10.1 The Hypothetico-Deductive Method

Although the method of induction by analogy cannot be reduced to the method of inductive generalization, another form of inductive reasoning is essentially equivalent to inductive generalization. This method—known as the **hypothetico-deductive method**—is not equivalent to and cannot be used as an alternative to the method of induction by analogy. The hypothetico-deductive method is claimed by its proponents to reflect more accurately the way in which people do in fact reason, in that it involves a temporal sequence of three distinct steps. These steps are:

1. The formulation of a "hypothetical" generalization.
2. The deduction of particular observation statements from this generalization (sometimes in conjunction with other statements).
3. The testing of the observation statements to determine whether they

are all true (and thus confirm the generalization) or at least one is false (in which case the generalization is considered to be refuted).

10.1.1 Formulating a Generalization

The starting point of the hypothetico-deductive method is the formulation of a generalization as a "working hypothesis." Let us take as an example the generalization 'All sea otters use rocks to crack open seashells.' We are not concerned here with the mental processes by means of which this generalization is reached; our only concern is with the justification that can ultimately be provided for it. In other words, it is essentially irrelevant whether a person formulated the hypothesis after observing a thousand sea otters or after experiencing some strange sensations while eating clams. What is of primary importance to the logician is the degree of support that can ultimately be provided for the generalization. The history of science is rich with cases of hypotheses for which a minimal amount of evidence was available at the time they were formulated but for which overwhelming support was obtained afterward. Such experiences are common in everyday life, as well. The logician, as a logician, is not concerned with how the conclusion was arrived at, but rather with whether or not the evidence that is ultimately acquired adequately supports it.

10.1.2 Deducing Observation Statements

The second step of the hypothetico-deductive method involves the deduction of particular observation statements from the hypothesized generalization. Given the generalization 'All sea otters use rocks to crack open seashells' as one premise, and conjoining it with other premises, such as 'I will observe several sea otters' and 'Hunters will observe thousands of sea otters off the coast of Alaska this year,' a theoretically unlimited number of observation statements can be derived as conclusions, such as the following:

> All sea otters use rocks to crack open seashells.
> Therefore, the next sea otter I observe (X_1) will use rocks to crack open seashells.
> Therefore, the twenty-third male sea otter that will be observed by hunters this year off the coast of Alaska (X_2) uses rocks to crack open seashells.
> Therefore, the last female sea otter observed by Professor Smith last year off the coast of Alaska (X_3) used rocks to crack open seashells.
> Therefore, the next sea otter that will be observed off the coast of Newfoundland (X_4) uses rocks to crack open seashells.

Notice that all of these observation statements are about specific individuals. Although other generalizations are also validly deducible from the original hypothesis (for instance, 'All sea otters living off the coast of Denmark use rocks to crack open seashells'), the hypothetico-deductive method is concerned only with deducing statements about specific individuals such that the truth or falsity of these statements can be determined by direct observation.

EXERCISE 10–1

Indicate what other premise(s) is (are) needed to deduce the specified observation statement from the given generalization.

1. Generalization: Every student who took the logic exam got an A on it.
   Observation statement: Ann got an A on the logic exam.

2. Generalization: All football players are philosophy majors.
   Observation statement: Ed is a philosophy major.

3. Generalization: All American novels are at least one hundred pages long.
   Observation statement: *The Blithedale Romance* is at least one hundred pages long.

4. Generalization: All logicians are exciting lecturers.
   Observation statement: Professor Wilson is an exciting lecturer.

5. Generalization: All men are chauvinists.
   Observation statement: Bill is a chauvinist.

6. Generalization: All planets move in elliptical orbits.
   Observation statement: Jupiter moves in an elliptical orbit.

7. Generalization: All mountains over twenty thousand feet in height are dangerous to climb.
   Observation statement: K-2 is dangerous to climb.

8. Generalization: All logic exercises are easy.
   Observation statement: This is an easy exercise.

9. Generalization: All professional tennis players are in good physical condition.
   Observation statement: Gabriela Sabatini is in good physical condition.

10. Generalization: All philosophers are good logicians.
    Observation statement: W. V. Quine is a good logician.

EXERCISE 10–2

Below are a generalization and a number of observation statements. None of the observation statements are deducible from this generalization alone. What other generalizations or assumptions would be needed, in addition to the one given, before each observation statement could be validly deduced? Compare your answers with those of your classmates, or discuss the exercise in class.

Generalization: The earth is spherical rather than flat.
   Observation statements:

1. When I stood on the shore and watched a ship sail away, I saw its hull disappear first, and then its superstructure.

2. The sun rose in the east this morning and set in the west tonight.

3. In the past in New York City, the day has been longer in summer than in spring or fall, and has been shorter in winter. In Quito, Ecuador, it has been approximately the same length all year round.

4. My brother, who is 5'11'' tall, cast a shadow equal to his own height at noon on September 22 in Venice, Italy. I, who am also 5'11'' tall, cast a shadow only 4' long at noon on September 22 in Cairo, Egypt.

5. A ship that set sail in a westerly direction from the Atlantic coast of Africa was able to return to the same spot, all the while continuing to sail in a basically westerly direction.

10.1.3 Testing the Observation Statements

The third step in the hypothetico-deductive method involves testing the observation statements, that is, making the appropriate observations to determine whether each statement is in fact true or false. In our example above, the person seeking to justify the generalization will note whether the next sea otter observed uses rocks to crack open seashells. If it does not[1], the observer will have discovered a disconfirming instance, which in and of itself is sufficient for proving that the generalization is false. However, if this sea otter is observed to use a rock to crack open a seashell, the person will deduce another observation statement and proceed to test it. In this instance, the observer might check to see whether a particular male sea otter off the coast of Alaska uses rocks. If it does not, then the generalization has been proved false. But if this male sea otter off the coast of Alaska does use rocks to crack open seashells, then the researcher must continue the process, deducing new observation statements and testing them.

How far should this process of deducing and testing observation statements be carried to provide adequate confirmation of the hypothesized generalization? The process obviously ends as soon as any one of the deduced observation statements is found to be false. If no falsifying instance is found, however, the process could be continued indefinitely. The crucial consideration here is not really how far the process should be extended, but rather how it should be applied.

One formulation of a basic rule of thumb for the hypothetico-deductive method is that, the greater the effort that is made to find a falsifying instance of the generalization, the greater the probability of its truth (assuming, of course, that no falsifying instances are found). The notion of *effort* can be made more precise in terms of our example of the sea otter. One person might deduce from the generalization about all sea otters only observation statements about

---

[1]Of course, such an observation would not be very easy to make. The researcher would have to make certain that the particular sea otter is being observed every moment from its birth to its death to be entitled to assert that it *never* used a rock to crack open sea shells. It would be much easier, for example, to test an observation statement such as 'This sea otter has a backbone.'

by bernice bede osol

March 26, 1974

YOUR BIRTHDAY

You'll have an opportunity this year to improve your financial position and get a little salted away. Be careful of who you team up with.

LIBRA (Sept 23-Oct 23) A situation where you share a joint interest requires some adjustments. Bring things out in the open now.

SCORPIO (Oct. 24 - Nov 22) This could be a very trying day workwise. Make some "fun" plans for this evening so your can unwind.

ARIES (March 21-April 19) Materially, things look promising today, but there's another situation that will cause frustration due to a companion's opposition.

CANCER (June 21-July 22) Avoid the company of one in your peer group who is putting pressure on you. This person is much too dictatorial at present.

CAPRICORN Dec 22-Jan 19) Tread lightly early in the day. Domestic pressures will still be heavy. Toward late afternoon they'll begin to lift.

SAGITTARIUS (Nov 23-Dec 21) It's going to take self-discipline to direct your efforts where they belong. Keep your mind on your tasks.

TAURUS (April 20-May 20) You're likely to have to face some heavy obligations not of your making. Try to have others carry their share.

LEO (July 23-Aug 22) Seconday issues could easily sidetrack you today. Concentrate on goals that contribute to your reputation or career.

AQUARIUS (Jan 20-Feb 19) Don't deal in the realm of ideas. They won't show a profit at this time. Something practical you're involved in will.

GEMINI (May 21-June 20) Your interest is not focused where it should be at this time. This could cause future problems. Attend first to priority matters.

VIRGO (Aug 23-Sept 22) This is nt the time to act on financial matter without **expert** outside advice. Don't rely only on your judgment.

PISCES (Feb 20-March 20) Your finances are still up in the air. Your outlay is likely to be greater than your intake. Be very conservative.

Used by permission of Newspaper Enterprise Association, Inc.

Astrology is believed by a surprising number of persons to provide a "scientific" basis for predicting future events. Consider the "predictions" in this horoscope and determine which of them, if any, could possibly be falsified by observations, and discuss ways in which an astrologer might respond to an apparent observational "refutation."

sea otters of a certain kind in a certain location at a certain time. In contrast, a second person might derive observation statements about sea otters of many different kinds at different locations and at different times. Assuming that all of the observation statements were found to be factually true, it seems intuitively evident that the second person has established the probability of the truth of the generalization to a higher degree than has the first, and it appears reasonable to attribute this increased probability to the increased effort made to find a falsifying instance.

When we speak of effort in this context, we are not concerned with either the physical or the psychological effort expended in the attempt to find a falsifying instance. It could have been very difficult and required much psychological effort for the first person in our example to deduce even one observation statement—for instance, if the person had little aptitude for logic or was very tired at the time. Similarly, the second person might have derived the set of diverse observation statements with little or no effort. The same might be true of the testing of the observation statements. It might have taken the first person several weeks of hiking in below-zero weather to reach the one location specified in the observations, while the second person might have simply telephoned colleagues in locations around the world and asked them to make the observations in the areas closest to them. Thus, when we talk of maximizing effort, we are speaking not of physical or psychological effort, but of **logical effort**—which we can define as *the effort to deduce and test those observation statements that are most likely to turn out to be factually false.* This rather vague concept is essentially equivalent to one of the basic concepts discussed in Chapter 9. To see this more clearly, let us examine the extent to which the hypothetico-deductive method is essentially a reformulation of the method of inductive generalization.

EXERCISE 10–3

Describe how each of the following observation statements can be tested for truth or falsity. Compare your answers with those of your classmates.

1. Ann got an A on the logic exam.
2. Ed is a philosophy major.
3. *The Blithedale Romance* is at least one hundred pages long.
4. Professor Wilson is an exciting lecturer.
5. Bill is a chauvinist.
6. Jupiter moves in an elliptical orbit.
7. K-2 is difficult to climb.
8. This is an easy exercise.
9. Gabriela Sabatini is in good physical condition.
10. W. V. Quine is a good logician.

EXERCISE 10–4

Indicate which of the following statements could be confirmed or falsified by direct observation. For those that cannot be, try to suggest observations that could serve to test them. Compare your answers with those of other members of the class.

1. This book has 7,439 pages.
2. The moon is 249,172 miles from the earth.

3. This swan is white.
4. The Declaration of Independence was signed on July 4, 1776.
5. An electric current is flowing through this wire.
6. The last page of *Webster's Ninth New Collegiate Dictionary* is 1562.
7. All of the earth's continents once formed a single land mass.
8. Light travels at 186,000 miles per second.
9. Right now I am having the sensation of seeing a solid blue tie.
10. This sculpture is made of an aluminum alloy.
11. That dog over there is a poodle.
12. I am having a sensation of a red spot here and now.
13. The capital of Corsica is Ajaccio.
14. Most American families own television sets.
15. $2 + 2 = 4$.

10.2 Hypothetico-Deductive Method and Inductive Generalization

Once the generalization has been hypothesized and the observation statements deduced and confirmed by means of the hypothetico-deductive method, an inductive generalization can be constructed, using the confirmed observation statements as premises and the generalization as conclusion. (Of course, if one of the observation statements has been found to be false, there is no need to deal with inductive arguments, since the falsity of the generalization can be validly deduced from the falsity of the observation statement.) Thus we can construct the following inductive argument out of the sea otter example:

> The sea otter I observed in Australia (X_1) used rocks to crack open seashells.
> The twenty-third male sea otter observed by hunters this year off the coast of Alaska (X_2) used rocks to crack open seashells.
> The last female sea otter observed by Professor Smith last year off the coast of Alaska (X_3) used rocks to crack open seashells.
> The sea otter just observed off the coast of Newfoundland (X_4) used rocks to crack open seashells.
> Therefore, all sea otters use rocks to crack open seashells.

This formulation of the argument brings out the important fact that the rule of thumb for the hypothetico-deductive method (to make the greatest possible logical effort to falsify the generalization) corresponds to a basic criterion for evaluating inductive generalizations—that the greater the negative analogy among observed cases (premises), the stronger the support they are likely to provide for a related generalization. If we have deduced, tested, and found true those observation statements that were most likely to have been false, we have in effect provided the material for constructing an inductive generalization[2] in which the premises provide a high degree of support for the conclusion, since, in such a case, there is almost certain to be a significant negative analogy among the premises. As explained in Chapter 9, the greater the negative analogy among observed cases, the greater the likelihood that there will be a strong positive analogy between the observed and unobserved cases, and, therefore, the argument will have greater inductive strength.

To clarify this point, let us examine the example of the sea otters a bit further. Assume that the first researcher deduced and tested observation statements only about sea otters in Nootka Sound in British Columbia and then formulated the following argument:

> **The first male sea otter I observed in Nootka Sound in 1995 used rocks to crack open seashells.**
> **The twenty-third male sea otter I observed in Nootka Sound in 1995 used rocks to crack open seashells.**
> **Therefore, all sea otters use rocks to crack open seashells.**

Clearly, in this argument the premises offer less support for the generalization than do those in the argument cited earlier, which was based on the testing of deduced observation statements about sea otters in a variety of locations at different times. Even if the person in question deduced a hundred or even a thousand more observation statements about sea otters in Nootka Sound using rocks to crack open seashells, tested them, and found them true, the inductive argument that could be constructed on the basis of these tested observation statements would not provide much added support for the generalization, since the negative analogy among the observed cases would not have been significantly increased.

One final comment is called for on the basic nature of the hypothetico-deductive method. The third step of this method has been described in different ways by different philosophers. Some view the essence of this step as being verification or confirmation of the generalization, whereas others view it as directed toward falsification of the generalization. At the level of the present discussion, this is more or less a distinction without a difference. As we have already seen, the crucial consideration should be that of increasing the negative analogy among the observed cases. If we increase the negative analogy and then discover that none of the observation statements is factually false, we have provided some confirmation of the generalization. And, of course, if one or more of the observation statements is determined to be false, then the gener-

---

[2]This example also helps explain why the hypothetico-deductive method has no formal relation to induction by analogy. Because each observation statement is, in effect, a premise whose falsity can imply the falsity of the hypothesis (conclusion), every inductive argument formulated using this procedure must be an inductive generalization.

For Better or For Worse
by Lynn Johnston

Reconstruct young Lizzie's experience with the flagpole as an application of the hypothetico-deductive method.

alization has been falsified. Therefore, for present purposes, we need not be too concerned about the question of whether we are seeking to falsify or verify the generalization, inasmuch as in either case we should be trying to maximize the negative analogy among the observed cases.

EXERCISE 10–5

For each of the generalizations given below, indicate which of the observation statements are such that if they are false, the generalization also must be false.

1. All professors are intelligent, well-informed college graduates.
   a. Professor Baker is intelligent.
   b. Professor Legrand is a college graduate.
   c. Professor Wheelwright is brilliant.
   d. Professor Rodriguez is well informed and a college graduate.
   e. Professor Thompson is intelligent and well informed.
   f. Every professor whose course I will take next semester will be an intelligent, well-informed college graduate.

2. All Sony portable color television sets are trouble-free for the first six months.
   a. The Keanes will have no trouble for at least four more months with the Sony portable color television set they brought two months ago.
   b. Jim will have no trouble before June with the Sony portable color television set he rented early in December.

    c. The De Carlos will have trouble soon with the Sony portable color television set they bought six and a half months ago.

    d. None of the new Sony portable color television sets sold by the Cathode Corner during the last month will need repairs until at least five months from now.

    e. Jay and Laura Wilcox's new Sony console color television set will not have any trouble for at least six months.

3. When fares on any type of public transportation are increased, the number of people using such transportation decreases immediately.

    a. [Assume that taxi fares have just been raised.] Fewer people will ride taxis today than did so just before the increase.

    b. [Assume that airline fares were raised last year.] Lauren will not travel by air the next time she goes east.

    c. [Assume that bus fares are going up tomorrow.] At least one person who rode a bus today will not ride one tomorrow.

    d. [Assume that bus fares are going up tomorrow.] At least one of the people who rode the bus with me today will not do so tomorrow.

    e. [Assume that taxi fares have just been raised.] A lot more people will be riding the buses tomorrow.

4. The area of any rectangle is equal to its length times its width.

    a. This sheet of paper measuring 8 by 11 inches has an area of 88 square inches.

    b. A rectangle 4 inches on each side has an area of 16 square inches.

    c. The Sterns' garden, which is a rectangle measuring 6 by 12 feet, has an area of 8 square yards.

    d. This corner lot, which measures 100 feet along one street and 60 feet along the other, has an area of 6,000 square feet.

    e. Dave's new carpet measures 9 by 12 feet and cost $10 per square yard or $120.

5. All wild chimpanzees use tools, engage in grooming behavior, and live in social groups. [Assume that it is true that A, B, C, D, E, F, G, and H are wild chimps.]

    a. Wild Chimp A engages in grooming behavior.

    b. Wild Chimp B uses twigs to dig out ants from tree bark.

    c. Wild Chimp C uses tools.

    d. Wild Chimps D, E, and F live in the same social group.

    e. Wild Chimp G uses tools for grooming.

    f. Wild Chimp H lives in a social group.

6. Whenever the price of a product increases and the supply decreases, fewer persons buy the product.

    a. The price of televisions increased and the supply decreased six months ago. Fewer people will buy televisions now than before the price increase and supply decrease.

b. The price of electric knives has just increased and the supply just decreased. Mr. Smith will not buy an electric knife.

c. The price of gasoline has increased and the supply decreased. Floridians are buying less gasoline than before the price increased and the supply decreased.

d. The price of milk has increased in New York City. Fewer people in New York City will buy milk than before the price of milk increased.

e. The supply of milk has decreased in New York City. Fewer people in New York City are buying milk than before the supply of milk decreased.

EXERCISE 10–6

Formulate three hypotheses—statements of any sort, so long as they can be supported or disproved by evidence. Then give five observation statements for each, three of which, if true, would support the hypothesis, and two of which, if true, would disprove it.

EXERCISE 10–7

Each of the hypotheses given below is followed by five sets of observation statements, all of which are deducible from the hypothesis (sometimes in conjunction with other premises). Assume that all the observation statements have been confirmed. Construct an inductive argument, using each set of observation statements; then list these arguments in order of decreasing inductive strength.

1. All people can laugh.
   a. *i.* Sergei, a Russian, can laugh. *ii.* Elena, a Spaniard, can laugh. *iii.* Muhammed, a Tunisian, can laugh. *iv.* Vani, a Bantu, can laugh. *v.* Mikako, a Japanese, can laugh.
   b. *i.* Pierre, a Frenchman, can laugh. *ii.* Elena, a Spaniard, can laugh. *iii.* Ahmed, an Algerian, can laugh. *iv.* Muhammed, a Tunisian, can laugh. *v.* Mario, a Maltese, can laugh.
   c. *i.* Hans, a German, can laugh. *ii.* Asfa, an Ethiopian, can laugh. *iii.* Su Mei, a Chinese, can laugh. *iv.* Two Eagles, a Navaho, can laugh. *v.* Kameha, a Hawaiian, can laugh.
   d. *i.* Hans, a German, can laugh. *ii.* Pierre, a Frenchman, can laugh. *iii.* Francesca, an Italian, can laugh. *iv.* Elena, a Spaniard, can laugh. *v.* Fernando, a Portuguese, can laugh.
   e. *i.* Olaf, a Norwegian, can laugh. *ii.* Pierre, a Frenchman, can laugh. *iii.* Ahmed, an Algerian, can laugh. *iv.* Asfa, an Ethiopian, can laugh. *v.* Vani, a Bantu, can laugh.

2. All birds have beaks.
   a. *i.* A bluebird observed in Canada had a beak. *ii.* A pigeon observed in New York had a beak. *iii.* A red robin observed in Ireland had a beak. *iv.* A sparrow observed in England had a beak. *v.* A raven observed in Russia had a beak.

b. *i.* An ostrich observed in Kenya had a beak. *ii.* A bluejay observed in France had a beak. *iii.* A nightingale observed in China had a beak. *iv.* A parrot observed in Argentina had a beak. *v.* A penguin observed in Alaska had a beak.

c. *i.* A crow observed in New York had a beak. *ii.* A pigeon observed in New York had a beak. *iii.* A finch observed in New York had a beak. *iv.* A swallow observed in New York had a beak. *v.* An oriole observed in New York had a beak.

d. *i.* A ptarmigan observed in Alaska had a beak. *ii.* A parrot observed in Argentina had a beak. *iii.* A cockatoo observed in Chile had a beak. *iv.* A penguin observed in Antarctica had a beak. *v.* A seagull observed in Newfoundland had a beak.

e. *i.* A robin observed in Spain had a beak. *ii.* A sparrow observed in France had a beak. *iii.* A pigeon observed in Italy had a beak. *iv.* A bluejay observed in Portugal had a beak. *v.* An oriole observed in Switzerland had a beak.

3. All dogs are carnivores.

a. *i.* Frenchie, a miniature poodle, is a carnivore. *ii.* Natasha, a Russian wolfhound, is a carnivore. *iii.* Pierre, a standard poodle, is a carnivore. *iv.* King, a German shepherd, is a carnivore. *v.* Lassie, a collie, is a carnivore.

b. *i.* Peanut, a Yorkshire terrier, is a carnivore. *ii.* Elizabeth, a cairn terrier, is a carnivore. *iii.* Lad, a Scottish terrier, is a carnivore. *iv.* Charles, a West Highland terrier, is a carnivore. *v.* Sidney, an Australian terrier, is a carnivore.

c. *i.* Friskie, an Alaskan husky, is a carnivore. *ii.* Saber, a malamute, is a carnivore. *iii.* Chico, a chihuahua, is a carnivore. *iv.* Sasha, an afghan, is a carnivore. *v.* Heather, a mixed breed, is a carnivore.

d. *i.* Lassie, a collie, is a carnivore. *ii.* Frenchie, a miniature collie, is a carnivore. *iii.* Lassette, a miniature collie, is a carnivore. *iv.* Pierre, a standard poodle, is a carnivore. *v.* BonBon, a toy poodle, is a carnivore.

e. *i.* King, a German shepherd, is a carnivore. *ii.* Duke, a German shepherd, is a carnivore. *iii.* Duchess, a German shepherd, is a carnivore. *iv.* Princess, a German shepherd, is a carnivore. *v.* Lady, a German shepherd, is a carnivore.

10.3 Crucial Experiments

A variation of the hypothetico-deductive method is sometimes cited to characterize the procedure used for distinguishing between two competing theories or generalizations.[3] We can describe this method briefly as follows:

Given two logically inconsistent generalizations, that is, two generaliza-

[3]We do not have space to give adequate treatment in this text to the concept of a theory. Since it is generally agreed that one component of any theory is a generalization or a set of generalizations, we can simplify our discussion and focus on this one component for the moment.

tions such that it is impossible for both to be true, it is possible to derive observation statements from these generalizations that are such that a single observation will make one statement false and the other true. Thus, a single observation will force the falsification of one of the generalizations and will provide some degree of confirmation of the other.[4] This is sometimes referred to as the **method of crucial experiment** and is often illustrated by examples from the history of science.

10.3.1 Locating the Center of the Universe

One particularly famous and important debate occurred during the sixteenth and seventeenth centuries between the supporters of the "traditional" view

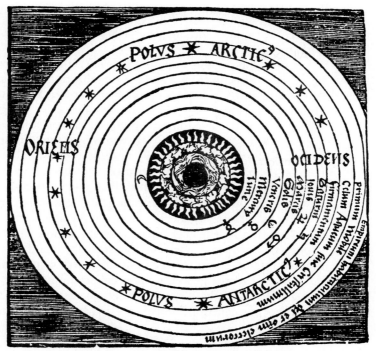

The Aristotelian scheme of the universe, as portrayed in the Middle Ages. From within, outwards, (1) spheres of earth, water, air, and fire; these compose the terrestrial region; (2) the planetary spheres carrying Moon, Mercury, Venus, Sun, Mars, Jupiter, Saturn, and the fixed stars. Then come (3) the crystalline sphere which provided the rotation of the pole; (4) the first mover, which impels the rest, and (5) the realm of God and the Saints.

---

[4]Because the hypothetico-deductive method can often be used to eliminate at least one of two inconsistent generalizations, it is sometimes referred to as a method of eliminative induction, in contrast to the methods of enumerative induction discussed in Chapter 9. Other methods of eliminative induction are discussed later in this chapter.

(associated with the second-century Greek astronomer Ptolemy) that the earth is stationary at the center of the universe, with all other heavenly bodies revolving around it, and the supporters of the "heretical" view of Copernicus, Galileo, and others that it is the sun that is stationary, while all other stars and planets, including the earth, revolve around it.

The historical events surrounding the ultimate acceptance of the Copernican heliocentric theory, and the rejection of the Ptolemaic geocentric account, have sometimes been described as a use of the hypothetico-deductive method to construct a crucial experiment. The two competing hypotheses are essentially the generalizations

All heavenly bodies revolve about a stationary earth,

and

All heavenly bodies (including the earth) revolve about a stationary sun.

Clearly, the generalizations cannot both be true, although it is possible that both are false.

It should be readily apparent that few, if any, observation statements can be deduced directly from a single generalization such as 'All heavenly bodies revolve about the stationary earth.' For example, the statement 'Mars revolves about the stationary earth' can be deduced from the generalization only in conjunction with the additional premise 'Mars is a heavenly body.' And even a specific statement such as 'Mars revolves around the stationary earth' is not really an observation statement, since it cannot be determined to be true or false on the basis of direct observation. However, if we add enough additional assumptions, definitions, generalizations, and other observation statements (all of which are components of the same general theory) as premises in conjunction with our hypothesized generalization, it is possible to deduce an infinite number of observation statements from that generalization. Thus the second step of the hypothetico-deductive method theoretically could have been carried out, though certainly not as easily as was suggested by our example of the sea otters.

The case of the geocentric and heliocentric theories was apparently such that almost all of the observation statements that could be derived from the two competing generalizations and tested at that time were essentially the same.

A seventeenth-century engraving portraying the Ptolemaic system of the second century.

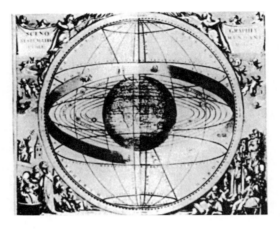

A medieval view of the world.

Most observations that would confirm one hypothesis would also confirm the other, and an observation that would falsify one would falsify the other. For instance, both theories gave essentially the same description of the locations of particular bodies at certain times, specifying that an eclipse of the moon would occur at such and such a time, that Mars and Jupiter would be in conjunction at a specific time, and so forth. Of the pairs of observation statements that were such that one observation would confirm one statement and falsify the other, most were such that it was impossible at that time to make the specified observation.

The invention of the telescope around the beginning of the seventeenth century made it possible to test one pair of observation statements. It could be deduced from the geocentric generalization (in conjunction with other components of the Ptolemaic theory) that the planet Venus, if it could be viewed at sufficiently close range, would never appear to be more than a fairly thin crescent, rather like the Earth's moon shortly before and after the new moon. On the other hand, it was deduced from the heliocentric generalization (in conjunction with other components of the Copernican theory) that Venus should exhibit all of the phases, "growing" from a crescent to a full circle, waning again to a crescent, and finally vanishing in darkness for a time before reappearing as a crescent, just as the moon does. Telescopic observations made by Galileo in 1609 revealed that Venus does, in fact, exhibit the full set of phases. (Of course, what was *directly* observed was not Venus itself, but only an image in a telescope. More will be said about this later.)

Since the heliocentric hypothesis was more and more widely accepted after this time, and the geocentric hypothesis was less and less favored, it would seem that this historical case provides a clear instance of a crucial experiment in which one of two competing generalizations was falsified and the other confirmed by a single observation or set of observations. However, this interpretation of the historical events has been seriously questioned by historians and philosophers of science. They have cited numerous other factors that appear to

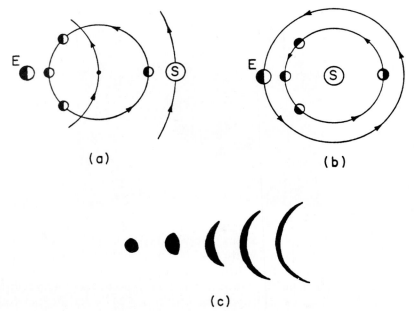

(a)   (b)

(c)

Reprinted by permission of the publishers from The Copernican Revolution: Planetary Astronomy in the Development of Western Thought *by Thomas A. Kuhn, Cambridge, Mass.: Harvard University Press, Copyright © 1957 by the President and Fellows of Harvard College, 1985 by Thomas S. Kuhn.*

The phases of Venus in (a) the Ptolemaic system, (b) the Copernican system, and (c) as observed with a low-power telescope. In (a) an observer on the earth should never see more than a thin crescent of the lighted face. In (b) the observer should see almost the whole face of Venus illuminated just before or after Venus crosses behind the sun. This almost circular silhouette of Venus when it first becomes visible as an evening star is drawn from observations with a low-power telescope on the left of diagram (c). The successive observations drawn on the right show how Venus wanes and simultaneously increases in size as its orbital motion brings it closer to the earth.

have played some role in the actual acceptance of the heliocentric theory and the rejection of the geocentric theory. They emphasize that some people had already rejected the geocentric theory even before Galileo's observations, and others did not reject it until one hundred years or more afterwards.

Some of the additional conditions that have been identified as factors in such cases as this one include psychological factors, religious beliefs, aesthetic considerations, and the relationship between theories of astronomy and physics. For instance, so far as psychological factors were concerned, it was considered an attack on the self-esteem of individuals to be told they were not at the center of the universe. In terms of religious beliefs, those who supported the geocentric theory could point to biblical passages that made reference to the sun's movement, such as prophets who "made the sun stand still." On the other hand, advocates of the heliocentric theory could point to the commonly held beliefs that the sun possessed special powers and was the source of life.

From an aesthetic point of view, the heliocentric theory as a whole was simpler and "more elegant" than the geocentric theory. But the physics of the time was unable to explain how it was possible, or what the mechanisms might be, for the earth and other bodies to move in the orbits attributed to them by the heliocentric hypothesis—although the mechanism suggested for the geocentric system had problems as well.

A logical objection can also be raised against the claim that Galileo's observation was an example of a crucial experiment. This objection is grounded in the fact that the falsification of the observation statement about the appearance of Venus does not necessarily falsify the generalization that the earth is stationary at the center of the universe. The observation statement concerning the phases of Venus could be deduced from the geocentric generalization only in conjunction with a set of other statements; therefore, the fact that the deduced observation statement was false could just as reasonably be attributed to one or more of the other statements. The latter could then be modified in such a way that the geocentric generalization could be retained and the true observation statement about the phases of Venus could be deduced from it in conjunction with the new components of the general theory. Also, one could even claim that the statement about the phases of Venus is not really an observation statement, since Venus was not being "directly" observed. On such a view, the observation statement would be reduced to a series of statements like 'I am having the sensation of a yellow disc on a black background here and now,' which could then be logically connected to the statement about Venus in a very complex way. This allows additional room for explaining away the "apparent" inconsistency between the generalization and the observation statement, again permitting the retention of both statements.

10.3.2 Do Biorhythms Affect Our Lives?

A theory that was very much in vogue in the mid-1970s and that is still heard of from time to time is the theory of biorhythms. This theory holds that every person has three different biorhythm cycles—physical, intellectual, and emotional. The theory asserts that every twenty-three days our physical capacities go through a full cycle from low to high and back again to low. When a person is at a low point on his or her physical cycle, he or she is not capable of performing various acts as well as when at the peak of a cycle. The intellectual cycle is asserted to be thirty-three days long, and the emotional cycle is twenty-eight days in duration. According to the theory, if two or three of the cycles all hit a low point on a given day, then that person will perform even worse in the affected activities, and, if two or three are at a high point simultaneously, the person is supposed to perform exceptionally well in all areas.

A full-page advertisement that appeared in Sunday newspapers across the country provided the following evidence that was asserted to prove the theory. First, the ad reported that an organization known as the Biorhythm Research Association had studied a "group of celebrities." All the celebrities had one thing in common. They were leading ordinary lives when suddenly they were "skyrocketed to wealth, success, and fame." Three "representative" cases are then cited, one of which is that of the late Jacqueline Bouvier Kennedy, whose mental and emotional cycles were both at their peaks on May 8, 1952, the day she first met John F. Kennedy. The ad then cited two cases of noncelebrities who also experienced good luck, including that of the Ohio housewife who had a remarkable string of gambling wins during a week when all three of her cycles were at their high points, including winning her office check pool, a number of Bingo games, the superfecta at the racetrack (for $850), and the trifecta and perfecta (for $950).

These "documented cases" are certainly impressive in terms of the dramatic good fortune of the persons cited, but they do not provide much inductive support for any generalization concerning any possible connection between the events and the biorhythm cycles of the individuals. An article in *Psychology Today* presented a critique of the biorhythm theory, one element of which was the citation of several cases in which predicted results did not occur. One of these cases was that of baseball player Reggie Jackson's performance in the 1977 World Series. Does this example serve as a "crucial experiment" to falsify the biorhythm theory? How might a proponent of the theory attempt to explain away this apparent counterexample?

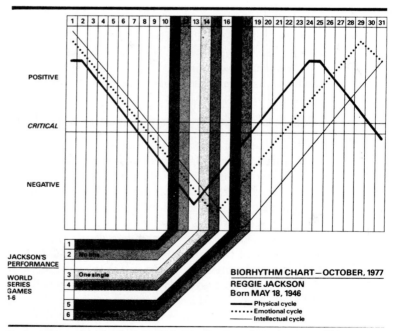

Reprinted with permission from Psychology Today Magazine, *Copyright © 1978 (Sussex Publishers, Inc.)*

If the biorhythm charts are right, why did Reggie Jackson hit five home runs? The chart, based on the Yankee slugger's birth date (May 18, 1946), shows all three of Jackson's cycles plunging to their lowest levels during his World Series hitting spree.

Logically as well as historically, then, Galileo's experiment was probably not "crucial." The factors that are now believed to have led to the rise of the heliocentric theory and the fall of the geocentric theory are very complex and still not fully understood; but it appears that purely logical factors played a relatively minor role in this (and most other) episodes in the history of science.

This is at best a crude oversimplification of the arguments by which philosophers have attempted to relate the hypothetico-deductive method to science. An adequate treatment of the subject would require an entire book or course on the philosophy of science, and any interested reader is urged to pursue either or both alternatives. However, our present characterization is sufficiently detailed and accurate to permit us to discuss some of the basic relations between formal logic and science.

10.4 Scientific Method

There is little need to state the ways in which science has positively and negatively affected the course of human history. Without science, we would probably still face the threat of plagues such as the ones that killed millions in fourteenth- and fifteenth-century Europe, we would probably be unable to provide food for the world's population, we would be unable to travel around the world at our present speeds, and we would never have made it to the moon and back. By extending the human life span, science has increased the world's population, and rapid growth of industrial production has led to environmental problems that have yet to be solved. To understand these historical processes and to have some control over our future, we are well advised to understand, so far as possible, the precise nature of science itself.

Many philosophers and scientists have argued, using concrete historical examples, that the hypothetico-deductive method, or some variation of it, is and should be the "scientific method." They have based their argument in support of this recommendation on what they consider to be an accurate description of the way science has functioned to date. In essence, they have argued that science has been very successful during the past several hundred years and is very successful today; that this success resulted from the use of the hypothetico-deductive method (or some variation of it); that, presumably, if this method were to be used in the future, science would continue to be successful; and that, therefore, science should be based on the hypothetico-deductive method.

As we indicated at the end of the discussion of the geocentric-heliocentric debate, there is good reason to doubt the basic premise of the argument just outlined. The history of science is not a sequence of clear-cut, straightforward applications of the hypothetico-deductive method.

In recent years, support has been growing for alternative theories about the nature of scientific theories, which argue that a scientific theory is much more than a collection of statements of fact and generalizations based on them.

After R. W. Leeper, "A Study of a Neglected Portion of the Field of Learning: The Development of Sensory Organization." Pedagogical Seminary and Journal of Genetic Psychology, *1935, pp. 41–75.*

One such alternative account asserts that, not only are a person's perceptions (in part, at least) determined by his or her theoretical assumptions, but that a person's theoretical assumptions and perceptions are both determined to some extent by the culture in which the individual was raised. Thus, it is considered possible for two different persons who have different cultural and educational backgrounds to literally see different things when presented with what is presumably the "same" stimulus. For instance, look at the drawing in the left margin. Do you see an old woman or a young woman? Or perhaps just a set of black marks on a white background, or black ink on white paper? You might have seen all of these; yet psychologists have found that many people cannot see one or more of them, even though apparently exposed to the same stimuli. These differences in perception have been variously attributed to cultural biases, educational background, and other factors, but they still are not fully understood. In terms of the theories being discussed, such "facts" about perception carry the ultimate implication that "crucial experiments" as described above are impossible, since the proponents of the two competing theories would not necessarily perceive the same things and thus could not even agree as to the truth or falsity of a particular observation statement.

These theories about theories themselves have been the subject of a variety of criticisms and are far from being universally accepted. With regard to the debates over the nature of science and of knowledge in general, the logician can only point out that, since a theory about theories is itself a theory, it must ultimately be a theory about itself. But for the most part, the debates about the nature of science go far beyond the scope of logic and this book. Regardless of which theory about theories in general, and about scientific theories in particular, a person might ultimately accept, there are certain logical relations that will hold in most such theories and that permit—or even require—the use of the techniques of formal logic. We will discuss this point more fully at the end of this chapter.

EXERCISE 10–8

1. Construct five cases (giving the complete relevant context) in which it would be reasonable for a person who is confronted with a generalization and an observation statement that are logically inconsistent to reject the generalization and retain the observation statement.

2. Construct five cases (giving the complete relevant context) in which it would be reasonable for the person in question 1 to reject the observation statement and retain the generalization.

EXERCISE 10–9

For each of the following cases, discuss ways in which (a) the generalized hypothesis could rationally be retained while rejecting the observation statement, and (b) the hypothesis could be rejected while retaining the observation statement. (c) Which strategy seems most reasonable for the given case? Could a crucial experiment be constructed?

1. At one time, it was hoped that a drug known as L-DOPA would cure or at least slow the progression of Parkinson's disease. It had been hypothesized that the disease was caused by a deficiency in the brain of dopamine, a transmitter of nerve messages, and that all persons with a sufficient amount of dopamine would, in effect, not have the disease. L-DOPA has the effect of correcting the dopamine deficiency. The results of recent tests on sixty patients show that the drug does reduce many of the symptoms of the disease, but the patients using it apparently do not live any longer than the patients who do not use it. (The scientists concluded that this meant that they should reject their hypothesis and look for a new cause of the disease.)

2. It has been hypothesized that lecithin is a "cholesterol fighter"—that is, lecithin causes the cholesterol level in the blood to decrease. In one study, fifteen persons were given six tablespoons of lecithin daily, and the average fall in serum cholesterol was 30 percent. Another study showed that every time an average person eats two eggs (which contain lecithin), the cholesterol level in his or her blood increases.

3. Horoscopes are supposed to be deductions from a complex set of general hypotheses concerning causal relations between the stars, planets, and individual persons. Look up your horoscope in yesterday's paper. Do your experiences of yesterday confirm or refute the astrological hypothesis?

4. A lie-detector expert has hypothesized that plants react to the thoughts of human beings in their vicinity. He claims that these reactions can be registered on lie-detector type devices attached to the plants. He has conducted many tests which he says confirm the hypothesis. However, when repeating the tests for a well-known plant physiologist, no such responses were observed. The lie-detector expert explained that nothing registered because the plants had "fainted" when they sensed that the plant physiologist in her studies used the procedure of incinerating plants and otherwise harming and destroying them.

5. One hypothesis concerning the social causes of unrest and aggression is known as the "twenty-five-year itch hypothesis." This hypothesis maintains that every twenty-five to thirty years the memories of social unrest, war, or aggression die with the generation that was involved in these activities. The young generation is then willing to defy institutions and engage once again in these activites. Asked his opinion of the hypothesis, Herman Kahn, a social commentator and think-tank administrator, said: "It is an attractive theory but I don't think it is accurate. I suspect the analogy is drawn from one single instance—the time that elapsed between 1914 and 1939, and I for one would hesitate to generalize from one observation. If one goes further back in history: In the Napoleonic wars, young men in France had been bloodied over and over again but were still willing to go to war. They liked war in some real

sense. In America, on the other hand, twenty-five or thirty years after the Civil War there was no sign of any generational unrest, any thirst for a fresh conflict coming to the surface.''

10.5 Causal Explanations

Somewhere in the folklore of most peoples can be found a story more or less like the following: A proud and handsome rooster made it his daily custom, in the cold gray light of early dawn, to fly up to the tallest post of the barnyard fence and crow melodiously, announcing his own magnificence to the clucking accompaniment of his admiring hens below. One day, as he finished his song and stood, crimson-combed head raised high, regally surveying his domain, he saw the sun come up over the eastern hills. "There!" he said to himself, delicately preening a ruffled feather, "Even the sun comes to listen to my splendid crowing." The next day he watched, and again, just as he finished his crowing, the sun rose. This happened day after day, and at last the rooster announced to the assembled hens, "My dears, you are fortunate to be the wives of so great a personage as I. Have you not noticed that it is I who, by my crowing, make the sun rise each day?" All the hens clucked in admiration, save one, who cackled "Nonsense," and turned away to peck at a worm.

The rooster was angry and flew down from the fencepost to punish her; but she said, "If your crowing really makes the sun rise, then prove it. Tomorrow, do not crow at dawn. If you are right, the sun will not rise, and your glory will then be greater than ever."

The rooster confidently accepted her challenge. The next morning he did not crow, but remained on the ground, strutting about before the hens. The grey light grew as always, and then—just when the rooster, on any other day, would have finished his crowing—the sun rose. A great cackle of laughter burst from the hens, and the humiliated rooster, all his splendid feathers drooping in embarrassment and shame, crept miserably away to hide in the darkest corner of the henhouse.

The rooster in this story fell into an error most of us are prone to. He began with an observation of fact: "I crowed, and the sun came up." After observing that this sequence of events occurred regularly and consistently, he formulated the enumerative generalization: "Every morning I crow, and the sun comes up." So far, he was quite correct. His mistake came when he inferred, on the basis of this observed regularity, a causal relationship between the two events: "It is my crowing that causes the sun to come up." His ensuing public humiliation stemmed from his failure to recognize an important principle of logic: no generalization that is arrived at solely by means of enumerative induction is strong enough to support the inference of a causal connection between two or more associated events. That is to say, the fact that Y has always followed X in the past does not prove that X is the cause of Y.

While some purely enumerative inductions are of interest in certain contexts, what people generally look for in their dealings with the world are stronger connections between events—those which are commonly referred to as causal connections. The process involved in the search for causes can be relatively simple, as when a person decides on the basis of a few simple observations that a houseplant is growing spindly because it is not getting enough sun. On the other hand, the process can be more complex, as when a voter decides to support a particular candidate for office on the basis of her or his belief that the candidate will be able to influence legislation in the right direction; or when a student, desperately needing a good grade, decides to take a course with a teacher who is regarded as undemanding. In all these cases, the person is called upon to make a causal inference, to reason from cause to effect or from effect to cause. We frequently make such inferences without full awareness of the kinds of thought processes we are using. In explanation of our judgments, we might say nothing more than "It must not be getting enough light; I'd better move it closer to the window," or "I'm going to vote for Krumholz; she's the only person who can solve the city's problems," or "I think I'll take Schlumbum's course; he's a pushover."

Often, though, one cannot be satisfied with such intuitive, unsystematic methods of causal inference. This is especially so for scientists, who need to make their methods clear and distinct so that others may repeat their experiments and test their conclusions. It is also important, on occasion, for the average person to be able to reason clearly and explicitly about causes. It is this need that has led scientists and philosophers, from the time of Aristotle and before, to investigate the nature of causality.

10.6 Kinds of Cause

When people seek to determine the causes of events, it is generally so that the events can be repeated, prevented, or at least predicted, in the future. For example, geologists today are seeking to discover the causes and "early warnings" of earthquakes, since the better these are understood, the greater the chance that earthquakes can be predicted and perhaps even controlled, thus reducing the danger they pose to human life and property. Or, to take a more mundane example, if a chef mixes a particularly superb sauce, she will want to know exactly what she did that caused the sauce to turn out so well, so that she can do it again later.

When we ask what "causes" a given occurrence, we might mean a number of different things by the word 'cause.' For example, if a glass is dropped at a cocktail party, what causes it to break? Is it the fact that glass is a brittle material? Is it the force with which the glass strikes the floor? Or is it the person who dropped the glass, or another person who bumped into him, thereby knocking the glass out of his hand? Each of these, in its own way, could reasonably be called a cause of the broken glass; but they are not all causes in the same sense. The different answers involve different notions of causality.

Consider now a more serious matter, the case of the DC-10 airliner that crashed near Paris in 1974, killing all 346 persons on board. At first the cause seemed a mystery. The plane had taken off for London only a few minutes before, with all systems presumably functioning well. The pilot had sent no word of an emergency before the crash. Some observers reported that the landing gear had been momentarily lowered, as if for an emergency landing, then retracted again, as the plane plunged to earth.

The principal hypotheses at first were that the crash had been caused by an explosion on board—perhaps a bomb—or by an engine malfunction. One piece of evidence that seemed to support the explosion hypothesis was that six bodies had been found relatively close together, several miles nearer the airport than the crash site. It was suggested that a sudden decompression of the passenger cabin, such as would occur if an explosion breached the cabin wall,

Firemen stand near the fuselage of the DC-10 jetliner that crashed north of Paris in 1974. All 346 persons aboard were killed in the worst disaster in civil aviation history up to then.

could have sucked them out of the plane before the crash. Some anonymous phone calls also alleged sabotage, and authorities quoted sources that said that certain of the passengers might have been Palestinian guerrillas and guerrilla sympathizers carrying bombs.

The discovery of a cargo-hold door in the same area as the six bodies bolstered the rapid-decompression theory but suggested that the decompression had originated not in the passenger cabin but in the cargo hold. Investigators began examining the door for evidence of burning or chemical deposits, such as might have been left by a bomb. But then it was noted that an earlier incident had occurred, near Windsor, Ontario, in which another DC-10 had lost a cargo door in flight. The resulting sudden decompression of the cargo hold had caused the floor of the passenger cabin to buckle, jamming important control cables. Although in this case the plane had landed safely, it was clear that a similar accident could have resulted in the Paris crash.

Further investigation showed that in the Windsor incident the cargo door had been improperly latched; that after that incident a design change in the latch had been introduced to prevent improper closing; and that this change had never been made on the airliner involved in the Paris crash, although company records erroneously showed that it had been made. Together with evidence gathered at the crash site, this information seemed conclusive: The final report of the investigating commission gave the cargo-latch failure as the "sole cause" of the disaster.

In a sense, it was the sole cause. There had been no bomb nor other sabotage, and no engine failure. But why had the cargo door been improperly latched? Even without the design change, it was possible to close it correctly and safely. Had the baggage handlers been careless? Had the flight crew failed to check as they should have? And why had the company records shown the design change as having been made when in fact it had not? Was this the fault of the worker who should have installed the new mechanism? Of the safety inspector who should have checked the installation? Of the plant supervisor? After the Windsor incident, the federal agency responsible for aviation safety had only recommended, not required, the design change. Who was responsible for that decision? And were not all of these people, and their actions or failures to act, in some sense, "causes" of the crash? One might even claim that the cause of the crash was the fact that the plane was in the air. Had it remained on the ground it would not have crashed.

It should be clear from these two examples that the word 'cause' can be used in a number of different senses. Some possible meanings include (1) *the preceding events that trigger the event* in question (the incorrect closing of the latch, the dropping of the glass, or the bumping-into): this has traditionally been known as the **efficient cause.** It may mean (2) *the material out of which a thing is made* (such as that which constituted the broken cocktail glass)— traditionally known as the **material cause.** Or it may mean (3) *the form of the object involved* in the event (the defective design of the latch, the distinctive shape of the glass)—known as the **formal cause.** Still another kind of cause may be (4) *the aim or goal of an action* (if, as at first suspected, the airliner had been sabotaged, or if the elbow-jogger were trying to embarrass the glass-dropper). This fourth type is known as the **final** or **purposive cause.** The sort of cause we look for will depend on what we are trying to explain, predict, or control. A manufacturer of glassware might note the shape and the chemical composition of the glass; the hostess at the cocktail party would probably be more concerned about the crowding that made it hard for guests to avoid jostling each other. The airplane manufacturer would certainly be interested in the design of the faulty latch, but the airport maintenance supervisor would be more concerned about the carelessness or lack of comprehension on the part of the cargo handler. And these are not the only possible meanings of 'cause.'

10.6.1 Proximate and Remote Causes

Thus we can see that usually many causal factors are associated with any given event. When the causes (in the first sense of the term as described above) occur in a temporal sequence, each event producing the next and leading up at last to the event that is to be explained, a causal chain can be said to exist. The "Peanuts" cartoon provides a good illustration of reasoning involving a causal chain of events.

In this example, Linus is presenting an argument to explain (or defend) his decision to spend his dollar on the salami sandwich instead of the cologne. His primary goal is to make Lucy as happy as possible, and he believes that Lucy would be happier if he were to become a doctor who would help people than if she were to get a bottle of cologne. He then argues that his eating a salami sandwich now is one link in a causal chain that will ultimately lead to his becoming a doctor. His argument also involves an implicit premise to the effect that, if he hadn't bought the sandwich, he would never become a doctor.

Reprinted by permission of UFS, Inc.

The last event in a causal chain (here, Linus, the doctor, helping the people of the world) is commonly referred to as the **proximate cause**—that is, *the one closest in time to the event whose cause is being considered* (in this case, making Lucy happy). It is the proximate cause that is assumed to directly precipitate the caused event. The *other links in the chain* are the more or less **remote causes.**

How far back we go in analyzing a causal chain depends on our reason(s) for investigating the case in the first place. In the case of the airplane crash, the proximate cause was apparently the blowing off of the cargo door. However, the investigators probably would not be satisfied merely with knowing that the cargo door had blown off. It blew off because the latch had failed to lock. The latch had failed to lock because someone had closed it improperly; it was possible to close it improperly because the recommended change in the mechanism had not been made; the failure to make the change had passed unnoticed because the company's records were wrong; the change had been needed because a faulty design had been approved in the first place; and so on. All these elements were parts of a causal chain leading up to the crash, and the investigator would be interested in discovering as many links in the chain as possible, so that steps could be taken to prevent a recurrence of the final tragedy.

EXERCISE 10–10

In each of the following paragraphs, determine the proximate and remote causes of the events specified. (Letters identify sentences.)

1. Event: Judy's forehead gets cut.
   (a) It was a sunny day, the first in two weeks, so Judy decided to take a drive in her new Alfa Romeo convertible. (b) She settled comfortably into the brown leather driver's seat. (c) She started the engine and backed carefully out of the driveway. (d) At first, she drove slowly along the country road, listening to the birds and enjoying the sight of green fields and trees in the late spring sunshine. (e) Gradually, though, her foot pressed more heavily on the accelerator. (f) The car gained speed, and she felt the wind on her face. (g) For a couple of seconds, she closed her eyes and leaned her head back to enjoy the sensation. (h) As she opened her eyes, she saw a moving shape at the edge of the road. (i) Suddenly, a deer dashed in front of the now speeding car. (j) Judy slammed on the brakes and turned the wheel sharply. (k) The car spun halfway round, skidded off the road, and rammed nose-first into a tree. (l) Even though Judy was wearing her seat belt, she was thrown forward and her head hit the steering wheel. (m) When she recovered her wits sufficiently to realize what had happened, she began checking herself for injuries. (n) Her forehead felt sticky when she touched it. (o) When she looked in the mirror, she could see a small, bleeding cut, just below the hairline.

2. Event: Mrs. Miller's glasses get knocked off.
   (a) Sharon Miller sat on the picnic bench in the backyard of her suburban home. (b) She smiled as she watched the goings-on by the sandbox. (c) Her husband was there, playing ball with their five-year-old son, Glenn. (d) Mr.

Miller would gently bounce the big red beach ball on the terrace, and Glenn would spread his arms wide to embrace it. (e) Then Glenn would giggle and, with all the energy of his small body, throw the ball to the ground so it would bounce again for his father to catch. (f) After about five minutes of this, Lou and Alice Porter, the Millers' next-door neighbors, strolled up the driveway with their English sheepdog, Rugg. (g) Sharon waved and called out a greeting. (h) Just at that moment, Rugg spotted the ball and made a dash for it. (i) He made contact with it in midair, but it was much too big for him to get a grip on it. (j) Consequently, it bounced off his nose and hit the corner of the bench where Sharon Miller was sitting. (k) There it bounced again, changed direction, and hit Sharon on the side of the head, knocking her glasses off. (l) Fortunately, the glasses landed on the grass and were undamaged. (m) Sharon laughed, picked them up, and put them back on as she got up to talk with the Porters.

EXERCISE 10–11

The following excerpts are adapted from newspaper reports. Each presents what purports to be a causal chain of events. Try to identify (a) the final event of the causal chain, (b) the proximate cause, and (c) the remote cause(s). Discuss your answers with other members of your class.

1. In 1949, Ivar Hennings, then chairman of the South Bend Bait Company, had a solution to the "threatening" problem of communism. According to Mr. Hennings, "the furnishing of quality tackle would lead to more fishing, which promotes a clean mind, healthy body, and leaves no time for succumbing to communistic or socialist propaganda—simultaneously building for a better America." Lower taxes would also help to solve the problem, he said. (*The New York Times*, May 1, 1974)

2. Discontent has been aggravated by a famine that killed tens of thousands of people last year in rural areas of Ethiopia. This was followed by steep rises in fuel prices caused by the world energy crisis, and by other price increases that have severely pressed both the rural and the urban population. (*The New York Times*, February 27, 1974)

3. A panel of scientists appointed by the National Research Council supported the theory that the proposed Supersonic Transport (SST) would dangerously deplete the ozone layer.

   The panel was created to assess the argument that the introduction of oxides of nitrogen into the stratosphere by exhaust from a fleet of about 500 supersonic transports would initiate a series of ozone-depleting chemical reactions.

   The nitric oxides, this argument goes, would serve as catalysts. That is, they would participate in the reactions but remain afterward to stimulate further reactions in an open-ended manner. The effect would be to convert ozone, whose molecules are formed of three oxygen atoms, into oxygen gas, which consists of paired oxygen atoms. Ozone, in the region between 10 and 30 miles aloft, strongly absorbs the lethal wavelengths of ultraviolet sunlight. The SSTs would operate in the lower part of this region.

[In 1971,] Dr. Harold Johnston, a leading authority on atmospheric chemistry at the University of California in Berkeley, contended that within one year the projected SST fleet might halve the amount of ozone in the atmosphere. This, he said, could blind all animals, including human beings, except those remaining indoors or under water. (*The New York Times*, November 5, 1972)

4. The immediate cause of Jackie Robinson's death at age 53 was apparently a heart attack. But to many doctors a more fundamental process was involved: diabetes and its complications.

The former Brooklyn Dodger's heart attack, which came after a decade of failing health, was his third since 1968. . . . Mr. Robinson had developed most of the conditions that can complicate [diabetes]. . . . The first black major leaguer lost the sight of one eye and was becoming progressively blind in the other. . . . In 1961, his knee, already damaged by arthritis caused by the trauma of sliding around the bases on the playing field, was further injured by a serious infection. The staphylococcal bacteria that caused the knee infection also poisoned his blood system with a near fatal case of septicemia and temporarily threw his diabetes out of control until antibiotics and more insulin helped him recover. Mr. Robinson also suffered from burning sensations and other pains in his legs that had resulted from a combination of diabetic damage to the nerves and arteries in his legs. . . . Also, his blood pressure was abnormally high for many years. (*The New York Times,* October 29, 1972)

10.6.2 Causes as Necessary and Sufficient Conditions

As noted above, the word 'cause' can be understood in a variety of ways—not only as proximate and remote, but as referring to the material or the form of an object, the preceding events, or even the goal or aim of an action.

Unfortunately, the term 'cause' has become too closely associated in most people's minds with only one of the several meanings of the term. People today, on being asked about the cause of something, are apt to think immediately of the proximate efficient cause and fail to go any further. And, indeed, many philosophers believe that, in the proper theoretical context, all causes can ultimately be reduced to proximate and remote efficient causes. However, our discussion thus far should be sufficient to show that other kinds of causal explanation (that is, in terms of material, design, or intent) would normally be regarded as quite legitimate and appropriate in certain contexts without needing to be expressed in terms of efficient causes only.

Because of the tendency to interpret 'cause' as equivalent to 'proximate efficient cause,' logicians and others concerned with accurate reasoning find it helpful to use the more neutral term **condition**. We will follow this usage in most of our discussion in the present chapter, speaking not of the causes of an event, but of the conditions under which it takes place. These conditions might be causally related to the event, or they might not: they might be effects of it, or joint effects with it of some other cause, or simply accidents which happened to occur, for no particular ascertainable reason, at the same time. For instance, if a car skids on an icy road and plows into a telephone pole, several associated factors might be noted by the police officer who investigates the accident. The tire treads are worn down; the front wheels are out of alignment; the driver had just been to see his doctor; he was driving fast; a dog ran into the road; someone screamed; a siren sounded nearby; the road is narrow; there was a gusty wind blowing; it was near sunset; and so on. Whether and in what way any of these factors "caused" the accident remains to be determined; but they are all conditions in the presence of which it occurred.

When, as in this case, we are interested primarily in the determination of causal conditions, we must make a distinction between two important types: necessary and sufficient conditions. For the airliner to crash, it had to be in the air. This was a necessary condition for the crash—that is, the crash could not have happened without it. However, the plane's mere being in the air was not sufficient by itself to cause the crash; many planes take off and land without crashing. Other conditions—including the faulty latch and the difference in air pressure inside and outside the plane—also had to be present to create a sufficient condition for the plane to crash.

A **necessary condition**, then, is *one in the absence of which the event cannot take place.* A **sufficient condition** is *one in the presence of which the event is certain to take place.*

The distinction can be further illustrated by the following example: Without clouds there can be no rain. Therefore, clouds are a necessary condition of rain. If the necessary condition is not present, the event (rain) will certainly not occur. However, even if this necessary condition is present, there is still no guarantee that the event will occur. Although there can be no rain when there are no clouds, there may be clouds without rain. Clouds, therefore, do not by themselves constitute a sufficient condition for the occurrence of rain. Other conditions are also necessary. When clouds are present, and when those clouds are beyond a certain saturation point, and when the temperature of the air is above freezing, then rain occurs. These conditions, which individually are necessary conditions, together make up a sufficient condition for the occurrence of rain.

Charlie Brown's mistake, for which he is being tormented by his classmates in the "Peanuts" cartoon, was that of giving a single proximate necessary condition when the teacher apparently wanted a sufficient (and possibly somewhat remote) condition as the appropriate answer. The "correct" answer probably should have included some consideration of the geographical location of the state of Oregon in terms of its proximity to the Pacific Ocean, some mention

Reprinted by permission of UFS, Inc.

of the major currents and wind patterns, and even some consideration of the mountain systems in the state.

In the case of rain, the sufficient condition is a **conjunction**—that is, a combination, a joining together—of several necessary conditions. There are other cases in which a necessary condition is a **disjunction** of two or more conditions; that is, the presence of one or another (but not all) of several conditions is necessary to produce the caused event. For example, if the police find the dead body of a prominent citizen on the sidewalk below his fifteenth-floor apartment, they are likely to assume that he fell from the window. There are (at least) three possibilities as to the proximate cause of the fall: (1) he fell by accident; (2) he was pushed; (3) he jumped. Any one of these three by itself is a sufficient condition of the fall. The necessary condition is a disjunction of all three (assuming that these three are the *only* possible necessary conditions): The victim could not have fallen unless he either jumped or was pushed or fell by accident.

Whether one looks for the necessary or the sufficient condition(s) in investigating the cause(s) of an event often depends on one's practical aims. If one is trying to prevent a certain occurrence, then one will probably search for the necessary condition(s), whose removal will make the recurrence of the event impossible. Thus, suppose a number of thefts have been committed in an office building, and the thieves are believed to be persons who do not legitimately work in the building. One can say that free access by unauthorized persons is (in this case) a necessary condition of the event (theft), so that by removing the condition the management can prevent the event. The management might thus institute a system of door guards and identification badges to keep unauthorized persons out.

Conversely, if one is seeking to produce a given event, one seeks the sufficient condition(s). If I wish to attract a certain species of bird to my garden, I might provide a suitable nesting site, or scatter food of which this species is particularly fond, or play a recording of the mating call of the species. Assuming that such birds are in the neighborhood, any one of these actions should be sufficient to produce the event I desire.

Of course, if the sufficient condition is conjunctive, the process may be more involved. A cook, for example, must keep a number of conditions in mind when setting out to prepare a given dish. The correct ingredients; their freshness; their combination in the proper amounts, order, and manner; the proper cooking utensils; and the application of the proper amount of heat for the right amount of time are all necessary conditions. The cook must know not just one of these necessary conditions, but all of them; for, together, they constitute the sufficient condition of success in preparing the dish.

The following box summarizes what we mean by necessary and sufficient conditions, and their relationships to one another.

Necessary and Sufficient Conditions

1. When we say that A is a necessary condition of B, we mean that it is possible for B to occur if and only if A is present: that is, if A is absent, B cannot occur.

2. When we say that A is a sufficient condition of B, we mean that whenever A is present, B is certain to occur.

3. A sufficient condition is the conjunction of all of the necessary conditions: that is, if necessary conditions A_1 and A_2 and A_3 are all present together, and they are the only necessary conditions for B, then event B will occur.

4. A necessary condition is sometimes a disjunction of several conditions; that is, unless either condition A_1 or A_2 or A_3 is present, necessary condition A is not present and event B cannot occur.

5. When an event occurs, it follows by definition that all necessary conditions, and thus at least one sufficient condition, for its occurrence are present.

6. Generally, when one is presented with an event and then attempts to reason back to the "cause" to prevent the event, one is looking for a necessary condition. When one is trying to predict whether a given event will occur, or when one is trying to produce the event, one is looking for the sufficient condition.

EXERCISE 10–12

1. Assuming ordinary circumstances:
   a. Is decapitation a sufficient condition for death? A necessary condition for death?
   b. Is oxygen a sufficient condition for life? A necessary condition for life?
   c. Is Zulu parentage a sufficient condition for black skin? A necessary condition for black skin?
   d. Is being female a sufficient condition for having a soprano voice? A necessary condition for having a soprano voice?
   e. Is spilling a bucket of red paint on the floor a sufficient condition for having red paint on the floor? A necessary condition for having red paint on the floor?
   f. Is the conjunction of ground beef, a piece of cheese, and a bun a sufficient condition for the creation of a cheeseburger? A necessary condition for the creation of a cheeseburger?
   g. Is being eighteen years of age or older a necessary condition for being eligible to vote in a national election? A sufficient condition?
   h. Is being a male a sufficient condition for being elected president of the United States? A necessary condition?
   i. Is being a dog a sufficient condition for being a canine? A necessary condition?
   j. Is the disjunction of being a man, or a woman, or a boy, or a girl a sufficient condition for being human? A necessary condition?
   k. Is the presence of clouds a necessary condition for a snowfall? A sufficient condition?
   l. Is being shot with a gun a necessary condition for death? A sufficient condition?

2. Read the following paragraph and identify the necessary and sufficient conditions of the event 'Williams won the top prize for the day.' (Letters identify sentences.) (a) None of the other riders in the rodeo had been able to stay on the fiery little horse, Dynamite, for three minutes; the best time so far was 2:57. (b) In the chute, Williams climbed into Dynamite's saddle. (c) He was announced as the next rider. (d) Williams boasted to the gate attendant, "You just watch—I'll stay on him for at least three minutes." (e) The attendant grinned and said, "Yeah, sure, that's what the rest of 'em said." (f) Williams spat on the ground. (g) "Okay," he said, "let's go!" (h) The gate opened, and the horse plunged into the arena. (i) Williams' wife, sitting in the stands, crossed her fingers and watched tensely. (j) Williams gripped the frantically bucking horse with his knees, waving his hat at the crowd with one hand. (k) Suddenly the horse lowered his head and kicked back fiercely, his hind legs going almost straight up in the air. (l) The crowd roared as the clock passed the three-minute mark. (m) Williams tumbled off, landing hard on the packed dirt floor of the arena. (n) Many of the spectators gasped, sure he must have been hurt. (o) Then Williams got up jauntily, and the crowd

cheered. (p) The judges certified his time, 3:02. (q) Williams won the top prize for the day.

3. Scramblex Communications Systems wanted to hire four new management trainees. Eight people answered the personnel director's advertisement. Their qualifications were as shown in the following table:

Person	Male	Math Major	Engineering Degree	Writing Experience	Computer Experience	Age 23 or Over
1	X	X		X		X
2	X	X	X		X	X
3		X	X		X	X
4	X		X	X		X
5	X	X		X		
6	X				X	X
7	X	X	X			
8				X		X

Persons 1, 2, 3, and 6 were hired. What can you identify as probably necessary condition(s) of getting the job? What are the sufficient conditions for getting the job?

4. Smart University offered five scholarships to seniors majoring in biology. Ten candidates applied. Their qualifications are shown in the chart.

Student	Overall B-Average	A-Average in Biology	Family Income under $20,000	2 Letters of Recommendation	Siblings at the School	Intends to Teach
1	X	X	X	X		X
2	X	X	X	X	X	X
3	X	X				X
4	X		X	X		X
5	X	X	X	X	X	
6	X	X		X	X	
7	X		X	X		X
8	X				X	
9	X	X		X	X	X
10	X		X	X		X

Students 1, 2, 4, 5, and 7 received the scholarships. What can you identify as probably necessary and/or sufficient conditions for receiving the scholarship?

10.7 Mill's Methods

Sherlock Holmes, after brilliantly solving some puzzling crime, used to favor his doctor friend with a superior smile and remark, "Elementary, my dear Wat-

John Stuart Mill

son—elementary!" He would then proceed to unfold a complicated chain of reasoning that, to ordinary mortals, appeared anything but elementary.

The great detective to the contrary, the process of determining the "cause" of anything is rarely "elementary," especially when inductive reasoning is involved. In the following sections we discuss a set of inductive methods frequently used for determining necessary and sufficient conditions. They are known as 'Mill's methods,' after the nineteenth-century British philosopher John Stuart Mill, who did much to popularize them. Mill's own formulations of the methods have been superseded by others, but they are still called by the names he used. As with all inductive methods, these can be used only to establish the probability of a statement, not its absolute certainty.

Of the five methods with which Mill's name has become associated, we shall discuss the four most frequently used. It should be emphasized that what follows is not exactly the way in which Mill presented the methods. We incorporate significant modifications that have been suggested by other logicians in the century since Mill's death. For example, this discussion is based on the distinction between necessary and sufficient conditions, whereas Mill used the ambiguous notion of causes.

Like the hypothetico-deductive method discussed earlier in this chapter, each of Mill's methods involves the formulation of a generalization about what might be necessary and/or sufficient conditions of an event and then the search for disconfirming instances. But, unlike the hypothetico-deductive method, which considers a single generalization, Mill's methods generally require that we begin by hypothesizing *several* possible conditions for the occurrence of the event.

10.7.1 The Method of Agreement

The first (and perhaps most frequently used) of the five methods is the **method of agreement.** This method states that *if, in every case in which an event or phenomenon occurs, a certain condition is present, and no other factor is common to all occurrences, then that condition is probably a necessary condition of the event or phenomenon.* (The event or condition which exists or occurs first is said to be probably the necessary condition of the other.) This method will not by itself aid in the discovery of sufficient conditions.

To take a relatively simple case, suppose the farmers in a particular region all raise stringbeans. Agents of the government agricultural service notice that the yields of different farms fall into two categories: half the farms produce twice as many bushels of stringbeans per acre as the other half. The service wants to determine what caused the success of the more productive farmers so as to advise the others on ways to improve their crops. Rainfall, sunlight, and soil quality are approximately the same throughout the region; so, insofar as they are necessary conditions for the production of good crops, they are present already, both on the high-yield and on the low-yield farms. There must be at least one more necessary condition which is present only on the high-yield farms. Someone suggests that a certain type of fertilizer might be that condition, so the agents interview all the high-yield farmers to find out what fertilizers they use. It turns out that four commercial brands of fertilizer are popular, with most of the growers using a combination of two or more. The findings are summarized in Table 10–1, in which 'P' (present) is used to indicate that a particular farmer uses a particular fertilizer, 'A' (absent) that it is not used by that farmer. The table shows that the only fertilizer used by all of the high-yield farmers is Super-X. It therefore appears probable that Super-X (or one of its ingredients) is a necessary condition for high stringbean production in this region—that is, if Super-X were not present, the high yields would not occur.

Table 10–1 Fertilizer Usage by High-Yield Farmers

	Farmer				
Fertilizer Used	**1**	**2**	**3**	**4**	**5**
Greengro	P	P	A	P	A
Bearwell	A	A	P	P	A
Super-X	P	P	P	P	P
Zippp	P	A	P	P	P

The method of agreement has its limitations. If further research were to establish that another farmer (perhaps Farmer 97) used another brand of fertilizer, Formula Z, and got equally high yields but did not use Super-X, we would have to reject Super-X as a necessary condition in and of itself. However, we could also modify our conclusion to assert that it is probable that a necessary condition is the use of either Super-X or Formula Z. Again, suppose that the five successful farmers had all used Zippp as well as Super-X. It would then be impossible, using the method of agreement alone, to determine whether the high yield had been caused by the Zippp, the Super-X, or a combination of the two. Also, given that a necessary condition can be a disjunction of conditions, one could conclude from Table 10–1 that the disjunction of Greengro or Zippp is a possible necessary condition. Additional tests would have to be run to rule this out. We must always be aware, therefore, that the use of the method of agreement by itself always exposes us to the risk of premature judgment.

A classic story illustrates the pitfalls of the method of agreement. It concerns the drunkard who reasons on Monday afternoon: "Friday night, I drank rye and soda and got drunk; Saturday night, I drank scotch and soda and got drunk; Sunday night, I drank bourbon and soda and got drunk. I must be getting drunk on soda. So tonight, I'll drink straight gin." In this case, the drinker is bound to discover on the morning after that not enough alternative possibilities were considered. But Monday night's experience by itself will have been sufficient to prove, at any rate, that soda is not a necessary condition for getting drunk.

In the case of the string bean farmers, the necessary condition disclosed by the method of agreement was a positive factor—the presence of Super-X. This is a case, therefore, of positive agreement. Agreement can also be negative, when a necessary condition turns out to be not the presence but the absence of something.

An absent factor has been identified as a necessary condition of rickets, a bone disease that once caused widespread crippling, especially among children in northern Europe.[5] The disease was first noticed in England in the 1650s when the use of soft coal was introduced, and it spread through Europe with the Industrial Revolution (see map of England and Scotland on page 478).

Because many of the victims of rickets were poor, dietary deficiency was considered as a possible cause. But a medical study in 1889 made clear that rickets was associated more with city life than with poverty: in the cities, among rich and poor alike, it was more common than in country districts, even though the country diet, at this period, was often poorer.

Confinement was also offered as a tentative explanation. Animals in the London zoo, well cared for and comfortably housed, developed rickets, though wild animals never seemed to. Other observations revealed that German babies born in the fall and dying in the spring were more likely to show skeletal evidence of rickets than those born in the spring and dying in the fall; and it was suggested that this was because spring-born infants had more chance of fresh air and exercise.

It was also found that rickets was almost totally absent among the Japanese, even those who were poor or undernourished; it was also rare or unknown in Manchuria and Mongolia; and in Java, European children who were suffering from rickets when they arrived recovered in a few months' time without medical treatment. In fact, it appeared, rickets was almost completely a northern European malady; the only known occurrence outside of northern Europe was among well-off Moslems and upper-caste Hindus in Bombay, India. Poor Hindus in the same region rarely developed it, despite their poor diet and living conditions.

The common factor in all these cases turned out to be an absence of sunlight. Winter sunlight in northern Europe is relatively weak, days are short, and the soft coal used in the factories created a heavy, smoky overcast that further obscured it. The industrial poor, who constituted the largest group of sufferers, lived in dark, cramped quarters on dark, narrow streets. Zoo animals in London suffered the effects of the smoke pall; zoo animals in cities with better sunlight remained rickets-free. German children whose rickets had seemed to be associated with confinement also suffered, of course, from lack of sunlight; so did caged puppies in whom rickets was experimentally produced. As for the Hindu and Moslem victims in sun-rich India, they were young mothers and their babies who, in accordance with custom, spent virtually all their time indoors, often in semidarkened rooms. The Hindu poor, like people in Manchuria, Mongolia, and Japan and like Europeans living at a distance from smoky

---

[5]The following information is drawn from W. F. Loomis, "Rickets," *Scientific American,* December, 1970.

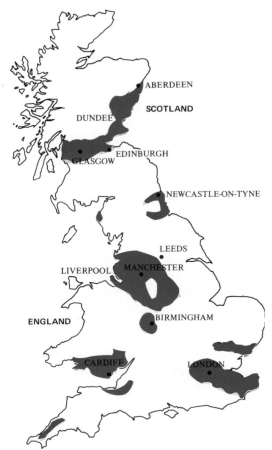

Adapted from Scientific American, *Dec. 1970, p. 79.*

Correlation of rickets with industrial areas and smoke from the burning of coal appeared in data assembled in 1889 by the British Medical Association. The map, which shows in color the principal concentrations of rickets, is based on maps of England and Scotland prepared by the association. Since diets in these areas were in general better than those in poorer surrounding areas, the distribution of rickets is not what one would expect if the disease were of dietary origin. A proximate necessary condition was found to be a lack of sunlight.

industrial towns, were exposed to adequate amounts of sunlight, and did not develop rickets.

A chart of the findings might look like that in Table 10–2. As can be seen, the only condition that remained constant for all of the high-rickets groups was the absence of sunlight, which could therefore be regarded as a probable necessary condition of the disease. Once this conclusion was reached, steps were taken to eliminate the condition, and the incidence of rickets thereupon decreased, giving proximate additional support to the conclusion.

Table 10–2 Conditions Associated with High Incidence of Rickets

High-Rickets Group	Factors		
	Confinement	Malnutrition	Sunlight
English city poor	A	P	A
English city non-poor	A	A	A
German fall-born babies	P	A	A
Upper-class Indian Moslems	P	A	A
Upper-caste Indian Hindus	P	A	A
Caged puppies	P	A	A
London zoo animals	P	A	A

Actually, the "cause" (in this case, the relevant necessary condition) of the disease has now been more precisely determined to be the lack of the hormone calciferol, which is needed for proper bone formation. The human body cannot synthesize calciferol without the aid of ultraviolet radiation, which it normally receives from sunlight. Strictly speaking, therefore, the necessary (and coincidentally, the sufficient) condition of rickets is lack of calciferol, and lack of sunlight is a more remote cause, a link in the causal chain. But it was the discovery of the role of sunlight, through the method of agreement, that pointed the way to fuller knowledge.

Although the method of agreement, when used correctly, can lead to the identification of necessary conditions, this is not a guaranteed way to solve

Copyright © Selby Kelly, Ex.

certain kinds of problems. It is true that if we eliminate a necessary condition for an event, that event will not occur; but not all conditions are easily removed. For example, the method of agreement was properly applied in the Pogo cartoon, but the necessary condition so identified is clearly not one that can be eliminated. In fact, the necessary condition identified is part of the problem, since polluted air is considered to be undesirable precisely because it interferes with breathing.

10.7.2 The Method of Difference

The **method of difference** can be stated as follows: *If the conditions in two cases appear to be essentially the same, but the caused event or phenomenon occurs in only one of them, we should look for a condition that exists in this one but not in the other; this condition is the probable sufficient condition of the phenomenon.* (This method is not adequate for identifying necessary conditions.)

To illustrate this method, Mill suggests the case of a man who is shot in the heart and dies. Here the two cases involve the same individual—the man when alive and the man when dead. Having eliminated all other possible causes of death, we assume that the bullet wound is the sufficient condition, because it is the only circumstance that differs significantly from those present when the victim was alive. (Certainly, the time has changed, but, on the basis of other experience, it can be ruled out as a possible causal factor. A small change in time is a necessary condition of the death only in the trivial and uninteresting sense that no person can be both alive and dead at the same moment—it can in no way be a sufficient condition.)

A more complex example of the use of the method of difference to determine a sufficient condition is the experiment carried out by Professors Robert Rosenthal and Lenore Jacobson concerning the effects of teacher expectation on pupil achievement. During the heyday of the War on Poverty in the 1960s, it was noted that children from socioeconomically disadvantaged backgrounds generally did less well in school than children of more affluent families. It was widely assumed that the principal cause (or sufficient condition) of these children's academic failure lay in the cultural deprivation arising from their background and environment and that massive amounts of new funding for programs of remedial instruction, cultural enrichment, and the like could remove the sufficient condition and allow the children to succeed.

Rosenthal and Jacobson hypothesized that "at least some of the deficiencies . . . might be in the schools, and particularly in the attitudes of teachers toward disadvantaged children."[6] They therefore devised an experiment to test this hypothesis.

Since—if they were correct—disadvantaged children who were failing were

---

[6]Robert Rosenthal and Lenore F. Jacobson, "Teacher Expectations for the Disadvantaged." *Scientific American,* April 1968. All information in the following account is drawn from this article.

doing so, not primarily because of cultural deprivation, but because their teachers expected them to fail, it was necessary to change this expectation, in the case of some children, to an expectation of success without changing any of the other relevant conditions. If, in these circumstances, disadvantaged children did succeed, it could reasonably be supposed that the positive expectations of their teachers provided the sufficient condition for their success; and, therefore, it could also be inferred that the former negative expectations had been a sufficient condition of their failure.

In a certain California elementary school (called Oak School in the report), all the children from kindergarten through fifth grade were given a "Test of Inflected Acquisition." Teachers were told that the test was designed to predict which children would show unusual intellectual growth in the next year or two. In fact, the test was an ordinary standardized intelligence test; the important thing was not what it showed, but what the teachers thought it showed.

The test was given in the spring, and was supposedly sent to Harvard for scoring. In the fall, the teachers were told—casually and as if almost by chance—which of the children could be expected to "spurt" ahead academically in the coming year.

In reality, the names of the "spurters" had been chosen randomly, with no reference to the test. There were four or five of them in each classroom, and they included slow, average, and fast-track learners. Nothing special was done for them; the only way in which, as a group, they differed from their schoolmates was that their teachers had been told they were likely to improve more than their classmates.

During the next two years, the children were tested three more times. The results showed, interestingly, that both the experimental group (the spurters) and the control group (those not designated as spurters) had made gains in I.Q. But in some grades—particularly the first and second—the gains shown by the spurters far outdistanced those of the control-group children. In these two grades, nearly 80 percent of the spurters gained at least ten points in I.Q., compared with about 50 percent of the control group; more than 20 percent of the spurters gained at least thirty I.Q. points compared with 5 or 6 percent of the control group. It appeared probable, therefore, that, at least in the early grades, the teacher's expectation that a pupil would improve was a sufficient condition for improvement. And, since the children who improved included some from disadvantaged backgrounds, the experiment seemed to show that, contrary to general opinion, the condition of being socioeconomically disadvantaged was not a sufficient condition for academic failure.

How does this experiment illustrate use of the method of difference? First, the pupils were divided into two groups corresponding to the two cases of the method of difference. The groups were chosen in such a way that, as groups, they were essentially alike in all characteristics thought to be significant for the phenomenon under study (intellectual improvement). Next, one characteristic or condition (teacher expectation) was changed for the experimental group.

The phenomenon of intellectual improvement was then observed to occur to a significantly greater degree in the experimental group than in the control group. This led to the conclusion that the one condition in which the two groups differed was probably a sufficient condition for greater improvement. If, instead, improvement had occurred among the advantaged children and not among the disadvantaged, the socioeconomic difference would have been shown to be a probable sufficient condition.

EXERCISE 10–13

Which method does the following example illustrate? What is the causal condition? Is it a necessary or a sufficient condition, or both? How can you tell?

On the morning of November 1, the Jonesburg police department received phone calls from twelve different local merchants. All reported that plate glass windows in their stores had been cracked or broken during the night. It looked like an outbreak of vandalism. Officer Brody investigated the complaints. He found that, while all the windows were badly cracked, there were only two in which pieces of glass had been knocked out and that no merchandise had been taken from any of the stores. Hence theft did not appear to be a motive. Then he tried to establish some pattern of similarity among the stores. They included two supermarkets, one delicatessen, three pharmacies, one shoe store, two small department stores, one hardware store, a sporting-goods store, and a dry-cleaning establishment. Seven of the proprietors were members of the Rotary Club; one of the seven and one other were Poles (Poles constituted a minority group in Jonesburg, and, in general, were slightly looked down upon). All twelve had been among thirty local merchants who had donated space for a Halloween window-painting competition for local children sponsored by the volunteer fire department. The broken windows were still covered with the colorful pictures, which had been painted directly on the glass.

Officer Brody's wife, a physics teacher at the local high school, finally came up with the solution. There had been a sharp frost on Halloween night. All the affected windows were so located that they had caught the full rays of the early sun the next morning. Because the paint on each was of different colors in different spots, the areas of the glass had expanded at different rates in the sudden warmth, and the strain of the differential expansion had resulted in cracking.

EXERCISE 10–14

Which of Mill's methods is illustrated by the following examples?

1. In ancient times, people noticed that if a substance such as meat was kept around for too long, it became infested with maggots or other such insects. From this, a belief grew up that these creatures were actually produced by

the decaying meat. This theory of spontaneous generation—that living organisms can be produced naturally by inanimate matter—was long accepted, until in the nineteenth century Pasteur decided to test it. He placed meat broth in a flask, boiled it to destroy all bacteria, and sealed the flask. After some time he examined the liquid and found it still free of bacteria. Then he left it exposed to the air for a time. In a few hours it contained bacteria and was beginning to decay. Pasteur concluded that the bacteria had entered the broth from the air rather than being spontaneously generated by the broth itself.

2. An examination of patients suffering from a type of blindness called keratitis showed that they had only one thing in common other than the blindness: a deficiency of riboflavin in their diet. The patients were then given large doses of riboflavin, and the condition soon cleared up. Therefore, a lack of riboflavin must be the cause of keratitis.

EXERCISE 10–15

In the following problem, identify the causal condition, tell whether it is a necessary or a sufficient condition, and indicate the method used to find it.

On October 23, 1999, a large meteor split apart in the sky over the United States, and pieces of it landed in four different areas of the country. Almost immediately, most of the identifiable pieces were picked up by astronomers and amateur collectors. Early in December, doctors in two of these regions began seeing patients afflicted with a new and unidentified disease. The attacks were invariably severe and almost always brought death within three or four days. Whatever the infection was, the human immune system seemed unable to build up a defense against it. Strict quarantine was imposed on the affected regions, and medical researchers hastily began seeking a cure or a preventive.

Because of the timing, location, and virulence of the outbreaks of disease, and the identity of the first victims (all people who had been in direct contact with the meteoric rock), it was generally assumed that the cause must be associated somehow with the rocks. Cautiously, geologists began assessing their content.

Rock from the first of the affected regions turned out to contain about 20 percent carbon compounds, about 20 percent quartz crystal, about 30 percent various common volcanic minerals, and about 30 percent of an unknown substance, provisionally labeled zeroz. Rock from the other affected region was 30 percent iron and manganese, 40 percent zeroz, and 30 percent quartz crystal. Rock from the two unaffected regions was also checked: The first proved to contain about 40 percent iron, 30 percent other common volcanic minerals, and 30 percent zeroz. Rock from the fourth region was about 10 percent carbon compounds, 70 percent iron and manganese, and 20 percent quartz crystal. What was the "cause" of the new disease?

10.7.3 The Joint Method of Agreement and Difference

We have noted that the method of agreement, when used by itself, has a weakness: It may lead us to identify as the necessary condition of an event something which is not really necessary, or it may not give us enough data to allow us to distinguish the necessary condition from accompanying coincidental circumstances. For example, if the successful stringbean farmers had all used Greengro as well as Super-X, we could not be sure, without making additional tests, which fertilizer was responsible for their better crops.

Sometimes we can add the method of difference to the method of agreement by taking away the single circumstance believed to be a necessary condition. If the event then does not occur, our conclusion that we have identified a necessary condition will be strengthened. But it is not always possible to do this. We might not be able to find two instances that are alike in all but this one circumstance, or the circumstance may be one that for some reason cannot be removed. In such a case, we might be able to use what is known as the **joint method of agreement and difference.**

In this method *we first use the method of agreement to find a probable necessary condition. We then look for a number of cases in which the phenomenon under study does not occur. Without worrying about whether they resemble the first group of cases in all other respects (as we would have to do in using the method of difference), we look only to see whether the suspected causal factor is missing. If it is missing from all of them, not only will our belief that this factor is indeed a necessary condition of the phenomenon be further justified, but we will have reason to believe that it may be a sufficient condition as well.*

As an example, let us consider again the matter of rickets and its cause. We have described how the use of the method of agreement indicated lack of sunlight as a probable necessary condition of the disease. Now, it would have been possible to set up a method-of-difference experiment, in which two groups of children would have been maintained in precisely the same way, save that one group would have been exposed to sunlight and the other cut off from it. Such an experiment might well have tended to confirm the previous conclusion, but it would also have deliberately exposed half of the children to high risk of a serious and permanently crippling disease. Some other method of checking the conclusion was clearly preferable.

We have already noted that several population groups had been found to be generally free of rickets. These groups, that is, constituted a set of cases in which the phenomenon did not occur. They included, among others, English rural poor, Japanese poor, low-caste Hindus, Manchurians, Mongolians, puppies raised outdoors, and wild animals. When these were rated on the same factors as the rickets groups, it was found that some of the factors were present for each group, but that the only factor common to all of them was the absence of the lack-of-sunlight factor. That is, all the groups that did not tend to develop rickets had a fairly plentiful exposure to sunlight. A table of the findings would look more or less like Table 10–3.

Table 10–3 Conditions Associated with Low Incidence of Rickets

High-Rickets Group	Factors		
	Confinement	Malnutrition	Sunlight
English rural poor	A	P	P
Japanese poor	A	P	P
Low-caste Indian Hindus	A	P	P
Manchurians	A	P	P
Mongolians	A	A	P
Puppies raised outdoors	A	A	P
Wild animals	A	A	P

If this table is compared with that in Table 10–2, it will be seen that the same factor (sunlight) which was absent for all the high-rickets groups was present for all the low-rickets groups. This not only serves to strengthen the conclusion, already arrived at, that absence of sunlight is a necessary condition of rickets, but implies that it may also be a sufficient condition as well—since, in every group for which absence of sunlight was found, the incidence of rickets was high, and no other significant conditions appear to have been shared by these groups.

10.7.4 The Method of Concomitant Variations

The **method of concomitant variations** is useful when one seeks the cause of changes that occur along a continuum, such as a gradual increase in the divorce rate or an economic decline. It can be stated as follows: *If a change in one phenomenon is found to occur every time a certain change in another phenomenon occurs, and if the degree of change in one phenomenon varies consistently with the degree of change in the other, then either: (1) the change in the first phenomenon is the cause of the change in the second; (2) the change in the second phenomenon is the cause of the change in the first; or (3) a third factor is the cause of the change in both.*

The word 'concomitant' means 'accompanying' or 'corresponding,' and the point of the method of concomitant variations is to find a phenomenon that varies in proportion to changes in the studied phenomenon—either at the same time or with a consistent time lag between them.

Statistical studies rely heavily on the method of concomitant variations. Social scientists use it constantly to show relationships between phenomena—unemployment and marriage breakup, slum housing and crime, amount of education and family size, and so on. Certain economic theories use it in their analyses of the relations among such things as supply, demand, and price. For instance, if the supply of a commodity remains constant and the demand for it goes up, an economist would expect the price to rise along with the demand.

If the demand remains constant but the supply decreases, the price would also be expected to rise. The first of these illustrates positive concomitant variation in which both factors vary in the same direction. The second case demonstrates inverse variation in which one factor increases as the other decreases.

Medical research, too, employs the method, to show the connection between some particular illness and its suggested cause. An excellent illustration of this is the research on the harmful effects of cigarette smoking. A connection between smoking and cancer was suspected as long ago as 1859, when a French physician noticed that nearly all those of his patients who suffered from cancer of the areas around the mouth were smokers. Almost a century later, after cigarette smoking became increasingly popular, Drs. Alton Ochsner and Michael DeBakey in New Orleans observed that most of their growing number of lung cancer patients were cigarette smokers. Other observations sharpened the suspicion, and eventually some full-scale controlled studies were undertaken. In one of these, a study by Hammond and Horn, a total of 187,783 men were questioned about their past and present smoking habits. These men were then kept track of for nearly four years. During this time, 11,870 of them died, and for each of these the cause of death was recorded.

The findings were quite unequivocal. In Hammond's words, "The total death rate (from all causes of death combined) is far higher among men with a history of regular cigarette smoking than among men who never smoked." Furthermore, "Death rates rose progressively with increasing number of cigarettes smoked per day. . . . The death rate of those who smoked two or more packs of cigarettes a day was approximately two and a quarter times higher

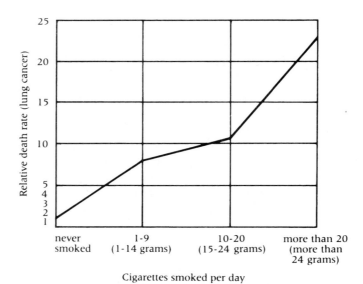

Cigarettes smoked per day

Adapted from "The Effects of Smoking," by E. Cuyler Hammond. Scientific American, *July 1962, p. 42.*

Figure 10–1 Concomitant Variations in Cigarette Smoking and Lung Cancer

than the death rate of men who never smoked." The covariation of cigarette smoking and death rate, as it appeared in this study, is made very clear in Figure 10–1.

The study also showed that the rates of death from certain diseases varied greatly in accordance with smoking habits. The rate for coronary artery disease was 70 percent higher among smokers; that for lung cancer was more than ten times higher. In each case, the death rate rose progressively as the habitual daily number of cigarettes increased; and in each case, also, the death rate for those who had once been smokers but had stopped smoking was lower than that for active smokers but higher than that for those who had never smoked.

In this and similar studies, the method of concomitant variations was used to show a strong probability that cigarette smoking is a cause of certain diseases. Since the frequency of death from such diseases increased as cigarette smoking increased and decreased as cigarette smoking decreased, it was highly likely that one was a cause of the other; and cigarette smoking was more likely to be the cause than the effect. In this case, however, it does not appear that either a necessary or a sufficient condition is involved, since some people with lung cancer and other fatal diseases have never smoked, and some very heavy smokers live very long lives with no such diseases. This is why researchers are looking for more basic "causes" of such deaths—for truly necessary or sufficient conditions.

The relationship between cigarette smoking and lung cancer is a positive one, as the graph shows. In the case of a negative or inverse relationship, such as that of the hypothetical sales estimates shown in Figure 10–2, the line on

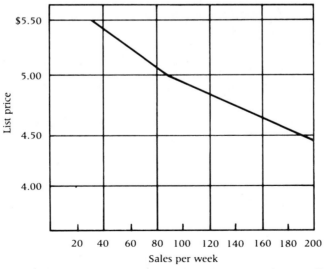

From Robert Dorfman, The Price System. © 1964. Reprinted by permission of Prentice-Hall, Inc., Englewood Cliffs, N.J.

Figure 10–2 Sales of Widgets at Various Prices

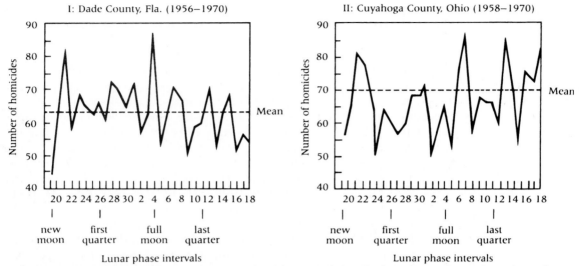

Figure 10–3 Homicides in Two U.S. Counties, Plotted in Relation to the Lunar Cycle

the graph slants in the other direction. Here the sales manager for Superlative Widgets, Inc., has calculated how many widgets the company has sold per week at each of several prices. At a price of $5.50, only about thirty were sold; but when the price was lowered to $4.50, weekly sales increased to nearly two hundred. At a price of $5.00, sales reached about eighty per week. Sales at other prices varied more or less consistently along the curve, so the company can now decide on a price that will bring in the best overall profit.

Sometimes it is hard to tell whether concomitant variations are present or not. For example, psychiatrists Arnold Lieber and Carolyn Sherin conducted a study of possible associations between the cycles of the moon and human emotional disturbance.[7] They obtained homicide records for two counties covering periods of fifteen and thirteen years, respectively, and matched the dates of the homicides against the monthly cycle of the moon—new, first quarter, full, and so on. The results are shown in the two graphs in Figure 10–3.

In this case there is no clear relationship, as there was in the case of smoking and lung cancer. However, in both counties the pattern of homicides seems to

[7]Arnold L. Lieber, M.D., and Carolyn R. Sherin, Ph.D., "Homicides and the Lunar Cycle: Toward a Theory of Lunar Influence on Human Emotional Disturbance," *American Journal of Psychiatry,* July 1972.

reach a peak at or just after the full moon. In other respects the two graphs are somewhat different. It is reasonable to suppose, of course, that so complex an event as homicide would be influenced by many conditioning factors, so we would not expect it to vary consistently with any one of these factors alone. Lieber and Sherin, evaluating the data summarized in these graphs and relating it to findings in other studies, concluded that the pattern of homicide in the two counties did, in fact, support their hypothesis of a relation between homicide and the lunar cycle—that is, that underneath all other influential factors, there is a concomitant variation of homicide and the phases of the moon. Other investigators might have interpreted the results differently; for the scientific community in general, the question remains open.

10.8 Replicability and Controls

Most scientists (and many others) normally adhere to two fundamental requirements in applying any of Mill's methods. The first is **replicability,** that is, the condition that *persons other than the original investigator should be able to carry out the same study in essentially the same way and arrive at the same results.* This is basically a theoretical requirement; it is only necessary that the experiment *can* be done by someone else with the same results. In reality, many experiments never are replicated, due to economic and other restrictions; many simply fit in well with researchers' expectations based on general theory-based principles and related observations by others. But many claims that are made by various individuals and that are claimed to be "scientific" are clearly not repeatable and are also in direct conflict with what are considered to be well-established theories. Although this does not prove that the claims are false, at the very least it puts an additional burden of proof on the persons making these claims.

One example of a nonreplicable experiment is that dealing with the ability of plants to react to thoughts of persons in their vicinity. A researcher claimed that he had attached electronic monitoring devices to the leaves of plants in a special laboratory. He and other persons in the lab would then think either positive thoughts about the plants, or they would think negative thoughts about them (such as about breaking off a leaf or even destroying them). The plants would give off very different electrical signals when the people were thinking bad thoughts than when they were thinking good ones. However, when other researchers tried to do the same experiment, they got the same signals no matter what they were thinking. The original researcher responded that they simply had not replicated his experiment because the people in the lab were not the same ones as when he had run it. He suggested that the plants had sensed that they were genuinely hostile people and that the plants were either too frightened or otherwise upset to give any other responses.

Other claims are not replicable on more basic grounds. For example, claims about UFOs (unidentified flying objects) and miracles are such that there is no way in which they can be controlled or manipulated as required by any observers, and one cannot even arrange to be in a position to observe such events. This is also true of large-scale social phenomena for which it is impossible, for political, practical, and other reasons, to replicate the circumstances surrounding an event, such as a major economic depression, a riot, or a war. This is only one reason it is extremely difficult to provide any kind of a reasonable account of the cause—or necessary and sufficient conditions—of such significant events. Another problem also associated with cases of this kind is the problem of controls.

It is very important in using Mill's methods in most cases to have a considerable degree of confidence that all possible relevant factors are known and are being held constant or are varied as we require in the given case. Thus, for example, in using the method of difference, it is necessary to assume that all the factors in all the cases under consideration are the same except for the specific factors that are being considered as possible sufficient conditions. In some cases, we can only examine the cases as carefully as possible and then hope that the various factors have all been recognized and taken into consideration. But in other cases we can take more definite steps to make sure that what we have identified is really a necessary or sufficient condition. This is well illustrated by a case from the history of science.

Before the nineteenth century, it was widely believed that there was a kind of spontaneous generation of living creatures analogous to what we know today as a spontaneous generation of fires. In brief, it was believed that, by putting together the proper mix of substances, such as water, air, wood, straw, and salt, under proper conditions for certain periods of time, it was possible to cause the creation of all sorts of animals, including geese, lambs, and frogs. The seventeenth-century experimenter, van Helmont, designed an experiment that he believed demonstrated that mice would be spontaneously generated from human sweat (from dirty clothes) and wheat in exactly twenty-one days. He used what appears to be a version of the method of difference, showing that a dirty shirt by itself, and wheat by itself, would not be sufficient, but that the two together are sufficient for producing mice in twenty-one days. What he failed to do was to introduce appropriate controls to rule out other possible factors from coming into play, such as mice being attracted by the wheat and establishing a nest in the dirty shirt. A recent textbook has suggested that appropriate controls would have involved placing the dirty shirt and wheat in a sealed wooden box (see illustration). The control suggested in this illustration is not, however, appropriate. If no mice had been generated in the box after the specified period of time, it could have been argued that other factors such as light and fresh air were also necessary for the spontaneous generation of mice. A better control would have been something like a screen or cage which would not let mice in (or out) but would allow sunlight and air to enter.

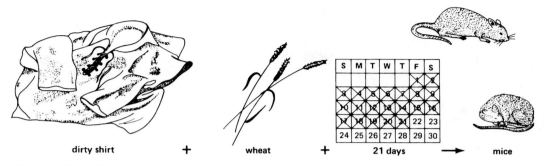

dirty shirt   **+**   wheat   **+**   21 days   **→**   mice

VAN HELMONT'S "RECIPE"

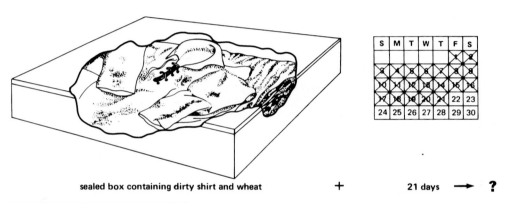

sealed box containing dirty shirt and wheat   **+**   21 days   **→**   **?**

THE CONTROL THAT WASN'T THERE

Adapted from Biological Sciences—Molecules to Man, *Biological Sciences Curriculum Study. Houghton Mifflin, 1963.*

In brief, we must always be as careful as possible to make certain that we have adequately considered all of the possibly relevant factors in applying Mill's methods and to try to set up effective **controls** to keep extraneous factors from influencing the results.

EXERCISE 10–16

Each of the following accounts involves the use of one of Mill's methods. For each, tell (1) which method was used; and (2) whether the causal condition discovered was necessary, sufficient, or both.

1. The Visor Television Company shipped 1,000 television sets to a large department store chain. During the next three months, 115 of the sets were returned. In each case, the picture reception was good, but there was no sound. Examining the first group of ten returned sets, a plant inspection supervisor noticed that, in every set, a certain wire to the speaker was

improperly soldered. She also noticed that the same person—Bill Evans, a fairly new employee—had done the soldering. The supervisor inspected the next group of returned sets and found the same improperly soldered wire in each. She concluded that Bill Evans' faulty soldering was the cause of the problem. She returned the sets to Bill with the necessary instructions; later, as other sets with the same defect were returned, she sent these to him as well.

2. It is now generally accepted that the addition of fluorine to drinking water helps to prevent or reduce tooth decay. One of the experiments by which this fact was established was conducted in two communities on the Hudson River. In each community a group of about 1,000 children was chosen; the children were selected so that each of the two groups had about the same number of cavities. Then, for ten years, a small amount of sodium fluoride was added to the water supply of one community; none was added to that of the other. At the end of the ten-year period, the two study groups were checked again, and the group that had received fluoridated water was found to have significantly fewer cavities than the other group. The fluorine was considered the cause of the difference.

3. A sociologist conducted a survey of ten families to determine the relation, if any, between a family's total income and its expenditures on recreation and entertainment. A summary of the findings appears in the following table:

Family Income	Approximate Total Recreation and Entertainment Expediture	
	In Dollars	Percentage of Total Income
$ 5,000	$ 500	10.0
7,500	650	8.7
12,500	1,100	8.8
17,500	1,450	8.3
22,500	1,600	7.1
27,500	2,000	7.3
32,500	2,300	7.1
42,500	2,800	6.6
75,000	3,600	4.8
100,000	5,500	5.5

4. Professor Stein frowned as he studied the seven Philosophy 104 examination papers spread out on his desk. All seven contained a major error in the third essay question; and all the errors were essentially the same, even to the wording. He examined the papers again. There was a suspicious similarity in some of the correct answers as well. Clearly there had been cheating, either during the examination or before. He looked up his records of the seven students. Two were sophomores, the rest juniors. Furthermore, they were in two different sections of the course, which meant, according to the standard practice at High Rise University, that they had taken the exam in

two different rooms. This seemed to rule out collusion during the time of the exam. Someone must have got hold of the questions beforehand and either studied them with the others or prepared a crib sheet that the rest had used. Professor Stein called the office of the Dean of Students and asked to know the residences of the students involved. He found that all seven were members of the very exclusive X Fraternity and lived in its residence. None of the other students in either section of the course was a member of X Fraternity, and there was no indication in the papers that any others had participated in this particular piece of cheating. The professor still had no idea how the questions had been obtained, but he concluded that they had been, quite deliberately, circulated only within X Fraternity.

5. Researchers at the state agricultural laboratories were seeking a means of immunizing poultry against a new virus disease, and had developed several varieties of a vaccine that looked hopeful. To test them, they isolated 500 newly hatched chicks for six days, one day longer than the usual incubation period of the disease. Because none of the chicks became ill, it was clear that they had not contracted the virus, either since hatching or while still in the egg. The chicks were then separated into five groups of 100 each, and each of the first four groups was inoculated with a different one of the four vaccines being tested. The fifth group was given no inoculation. All groups were given the same diet and living conditions. A week later, all 500 chicks were deliberately exposed to the virus. Within ten days, 90 of the chicks in group 5 were dead; 48 of those in group 4; 6 of those in group 3; 59 of those in group 2; and 62 of those in group 1. The researchers concluded that the vaccine given to group 3 furnished a high degree of protection against the virus.

6. Phil and Doris McCabe had never had any particular trouble with their telephone until one fall it went dead three times in two weeks. On each occasion, it came back on by itself in a couple of days. The phone company repairman could find nothing wrong with the instrument or the interior connection, and no one else on the block was having comparable difficulties. The McCabes did not know what to think. Then, a week later, Doris was in the middle of a business call when the phone went dead again. She glared at the receiver, muttered something unladylike, and hung up. Going to the window, she stared out in disgust at the driving November rain. Suddenly she recalled that on each previous occasion when the phone had gone dead, there had also been heavy, driving rain. "I wonder . . . ," she said aloud, and made a point of noting that the rain was slanting in from the east, on a fairly strong wind. That night she told Phil her idea. The next day, Saturday, Doris got out the ladder and checked the east wall of the house. Sure enough, high up under the eaves, where the telephone wires from outside were led into the wall, a small patch of insulation on the wires was worn thin and cracked, and the area was still damp from yesterday's rain. A call to the local newspaper office on Monday—by then the phone had turned itself on again—confirmed

that on the three earlier occasions the rain had also been driving from the east. Apparently, given the location of the damaged part of the wire, only such a rain could reach the worn spot and penetrate it, thus temporarily short-circuiting the wires.

EXERCISE 10–17

Which of Mill's methods is illustrated by each of the following examples?

1. Two randomly selected groups of people listened to a recorded statement concerning the need for a national compulsory health insurance plan. One group was told that the statement was made by the Surgeon General, and the other group was informed that it was made by a college student. In the former group, the statement was universally considered persuasive; the second group unanimously found it unpersuasive. (F. S. Haiman, "An Experimental Study of the Effects of Ethos in Public Speaking," *Speech Magazine,* 16, 1949, pp.190–202)

2. Scientists were interested in learning why, in some cadavers, rigor mortis sets in soon after death and lasts for a relatively short time, while in others it begins late and lasts for a longer time. Observations showed that, in the cases of late and long rigor mortis, at least one of several conditions was usually present: either the person had been in good health and well nourished at the time of death, or had been well rested, or had been subject to cold temperatures. Early and brief rigor mortis was usually associated with poor nutrition, or physical exhaustion caused by intense exercise, or convulsions brought on by disease. Eventually it was found that the common factor present in all cases of late rigor mortis was a high degree of "muscular irritability"—strong reaction of muscles to an electrical impulse. This irritability seemed to be a result of the other conditions noted. The conditions associated with early rigor mortis all resulted in a low degree of muscular irritability. Thus, high muscular irritability at time of death was established as probably the proximate cause of late and prolonged rigor mortis.

EXERCISE 10–18

1. Which of Mill's methods is most appropriate to the following? On the basis of the evidence: (a) what seems to be the "cause" of Mr. Johnson's insomnia? (b) does it seem to be a necessary condition, a sufficient condition, or both?

   Mr. Johnson, a young stockbroker, was suffering from insomnia. To locate the cause of the sleeplessness, he began keeping a list of all the things he did and all the food he ate after arriving home from work. On Monday, he had a dinner of filet of sole, a baked potato, stringbeans, cole slaw, vanilla ice cream, and coffee with cream. After dinner, he did the dishes and helped his children with their homework. He read part of an exciting novel and then jogged for a mile. Just before going to bed he ate a cream-filled doughnut, kissed his wife, and glanced out the window to notice a brilliant full moon. On Tuesday, he had a meal of steak, mashed potatoes with mushroom gravy, green beans, blueberries and cream, and tea with lemon. After dinner, he did the dishes and helped his children with their homework. He finished reading his novel, watched the late news, kissed his wife, and noticed that the moon was beginning to wane. On Wednesday, he had spaghetti and meatballs, a green salad and beer, skipped dessert, did the dishes and helped his children with their homework. He jogged for a mile, watched a mystery show on television, and had a snack of pretzels and Coke. Before going to bed he kissed his wife and saw that the moon was still waning. On all three occasions he did not sleep. On Thursday, dinner consisted of veal cutlets, yams, asparagus, apple pie, and a bottle of wine. After dinner, he did the dishes and helped his children with their homework. He listened to records, kissed his wife, and saw that the moon was continuing to wane. That night he slept well. On Friday, he ate corned beef and cabbage, mashed potatoes, beets, sliced peaches, and tea with lemon. He washed the dishes while his wife went out to a late meeting, and he went to bed before she returned. He slept as fitfully as before. On Saturday, he worked outdoors all afternoon, and had a cocktail before dinner. The meal was filet of sole, spaghetti, tortoni, and coffee with cream. He read the latest issue of the *National Geographic*, kissed his wife, ate a jelly doughnut, and did not sleep. On Sunday, he took the family out for a day at the beach with some neighbors. He ate potato chips, hot dogs with sauerkraut and mustard, cotton candy, and beer. At home he watched a horror movie on television, kissed his wife, and was too tired to notice the moon. On Monday, he awoke refreshed from a good night's sleep. For dinner that night, he had meat loaf and mashed potatoes with carrots and peas, a green salad and iced tea. After dinner, he did the dishes and helped his children with their homework. Before going to bed he jogged for a mile and kissed his wife. That night he slept well.

2. The table below lists the price-earnings ratio of Dow-Jones Industrial Stocks and the national unemployment rate over a period of nineteen years.

Year	Price-Earnings Ratio	Unemployment Rate
1948	7.7	3.4
1949	8.5	5.5
1950	7.7	5.0
1951	10.1	3.0
1952	11.8	2.7
1953	10.3	2.5
1954	14.4	5.0
1955	13.7	4.0
1956	15.0	3.8
1957	12.1	4.3
1958	20.9	6.8

Year	Price-Earnings Ratio	Unemployment Rate
1959	19.8	5.5
1960	19.1	5.6
1961	22.9	6.7
1962	17.4	5.6
1963	18.5	5.7
1964	18.8	5.2
1965	18.1	4.6
1966	13.6	3.8

Analyze these figures (by means of a graph, if possible) and compare your findings with the following statement.

A relative scarcity of manpower, as indicated by a low unemployment rate, has seemed to go hand-in-hand with low price/earnings ratios, while ratios have been high in years that a high unemployment rate indicated free availability of men for industry to hire. (Alfred L. Malabre, *The Wall Street Journal,* August 29, 1967.)

Do you agree with Malabre's conclusion? If he is correct, which of Mill's methods is demonstrated by these figures?

EXERCISE 10–19

Each of the following illustrates the use of more than one of Mill's methods. Tell which and identify the probable necessary and/or sufficient conditions.

1. An old man was picked up on the streets of Manhattan one morning, clearly in bad shape—rigid with cramps, in a state of shock, and blue around the fingers and lips from a condition known as cyanosis. At the hospital, a tentative diagnosis of gas poisoning was made, and the man was given treatment. After about two hours, his condition began to improve. During the day, ten other men with similar symptoms were admitted at several hospitals in the same area. All were elderly, in poor general health, and semiderelict. All had eaten breakfast that morning at a certain cheap cafeteria, and all but one had oatmeal, rolls, and coffee. The last had ingested only oatmeal. All were heavy drinkers.

The first diagnosis was not wholly convincing, for some of the usual symptoms of gas poisoning were missing. Besides, the cafeteria was the only place in which all the men could have been poisoned, and they had been there at times varying from 7 to 10 A.M. If the cafeteria had been full of gas for three hours, there should have been many more victims.

Because all the men had eaten oatmeal, investigators considered food poisoning, but the symptoms were wrong. For one thing, the trouble had started too soon after eating, and too suddenly. Could a drug be involved? A blood test was made, and it showed that the men had, in fact, consumed some sort of drug.

An investigator visited the cafeteria and took samples of everything that would have been used in preparing the men's breakfast—including dry oatmeal, sugar, salt from the small can on the stove, and salt from the big supply can which was used to refill the small one. He also took some saltpetre (sodium nitrate) from a can which stood alongside the salt supply can. Saltpetre looks very much like regular salt. Tests of all these samples were made, and it was discovered that the "salt" in the small can and the "saltpetre" in the second large can were really sodium nitrite—a substance that is legally used for some of the same purposes as sodium nitrate, but which is poisonous in more than small quantities. Apparently the cook had inadvertently refilled the small can from the wrong large one, and had consequently used sodium nitrite instead of salt in preparing the oatmeal.

But a test batch of oatmeal showed that the amount of nitrite in a single portion was less than a toxic dose. That explained why none of the other people who had eaten oatmeal that morning had been poisoned. How, then, had these eleven men got enough extra nitrite to make up the difference? A check of the salt shakers on the cafeteria tables revealed that one of them contained a high percentage of nitrite. If the men had sat at that table, if they had used salt—as some people do—instead of sugar on their oatmeal, and if they had each used about a full teaspoon, they would have received a toxic dose of the poison.

By now the men were out of the hospitals and could not be traced, but the explanation seemed reasonable. Still—why would they have put so much salt on their oatmeal? Someone remembered that they were all heavy drinkers. Such people usually have a low level of sodium chloride in their blood and tend to eat extra salt to compensate. This seemed to answer the final question. (Adapted from Berton Roueche, *Eleven Blue Men*. N.Y.: Berkley Publishing Corp., 1955)

2. The Peterson Motor Company began distribution of its new compact car, the Qumquat, in April. Within a month, dealers began receiving complaints about rusty radiators. The complaints came from a wide geographical area, but investigation showed that all the defective cars had been purchased west of the Mississippi, which meant that they had been assembled at the company's western plant in California. Cars produced at the eastern plant, in West Virginia, seemed to be unaffected. Company investigators then checked the production procedures at the California plant, but these revealed nothing to account for the problem. Furthermore, identical procedures were being followed in the West Virginia plant. Cars were taken off the California production line at several stages and tested, but no rust or cause of rust appeared. Finally, someone thought of the fact that, in California, completed cars were stored in an outdoor lot near the ocean for periods up to three weeks before being shipped to the dealers. In West Virginia they were stored indoors. Could the damp salt air in the California lot be the answer? Sample rust-free cars fresh from the California production line were stored in the lot for three weeks, then moved into rented indoor quarters for

two months. Other, similar samples were stored indoors for the entire period. Nearly half of the first group developed radiator problems before the end of the testing period, while none of the second group did. The company concluded that the moist salt air in the oceanside lot was indeed the source of the problem, and began making arrangements for indoor storage.

EXERCISE 10-20

Many real-life situations are of such a degree of complexity that Mill's methods can be applied to them only in modified form. The following cases are drawn from newspapers, magazines, and other everyday sources. On the basis of the evidence presented and the conclusions derived: (1) determine which, if any, of Mill's methods was used in that case; (2) indicate what additional evidence, if any, would have (a) strengthened the support for the conclusion, (b) weakened the support for the conclusion, (c) falsified the conclusion; (3) where the term 'cause' is used in the statement of the conclusion, specify whether a necessary or a sufficient condition is more probably meant.

1. Dr. Arthur Klatsky conducted a study in which 197 male cardiac patients, each of whom died within twenty-four hours after a heart attack, were compared with a similar group of cardiac patients who did not die suddenly. There turned out to be significantly more current cigarette smokers in the sudden-death group than in the other. No significant difference was found in coffee drinking, heavy aspirin use, or alcohol. The researchers concluded that current cigarette smokers were at substantially greater risk than non-smokers of sudden death from heart attacks. This would seem to substantiate the contention that cigarette smoking is a cause of sudden cardiac death.

2. Some commentators have argued that the cause of crime is not poverty but wealth. He points out that, whereas poverty has not greatly increased in recent years, both crime and the number of very rich people have increased dramatically. He explains this combination of events by suggesting that crime is especially profitable for the rich, who are often in a position to exercise considerable influence over decisions of business and government agencies and who are seldom punished severely even if they are convicted of crimes. Ambitious members of lower classes, seeing that crime pays for the rich, are led to imitate them as far as they can, thus further increasing the amount of crime. Therefore, concludes Quick, an effective way to reduce crime is to reduce the number of wealthy people.

3. Among British and American troops in North Africa during World War II, the incidence of paralytic poliomyelitis was much higher for officers than for men in the lower ranks. Because none of the obvious hypotheses seemed to explain this discrepancy, some rather wild ones were proposed. One of these took note of the fact that most of the officers drank whiskey, whereas most of the other men drank beer, and suggested that this difference was the cause of the different rates of polio.

(It is now believed that persons who are exposed in infancy to the polio-carrying virus are likely to develop a natural resistance to it, and escape paralysis. Such exposure is more likely in unhygienic surroundings. Since more enlisted men than officers, in the North African group, came from lower-class social backgrounds and were thus likely to have been exposed to such conditions as children, they were less vulnerable to infection in adult life.)

4. Medical researchers have found evidence of a possible correlation between beer drinking and certain types of cancer. They compared the per capita consumption of beer in forty-one states with the mortality rates in those states for twenty types of cancer. They found statistical correlations with at least seven types, of which the strongest was with cancer of the large intestine and rectum.

5. Doctors have long been puzzled by the occurrence of sudden fatal heart attacks in persons who were, until the attack, in apparently good health. One researcher has reported that in one group of twenty-six employees of a single company who died of such sudden heart attacks, nearly all had been suffering a period of depression for some time. This depression was then interrupted by some sudden event, usually unpleasant, which made them anxious or angry or otherwise upset their emotional and physical reactions. Usually the heart attacks and death followed shortly thereafter. The researcher concluded that the combination of depression and sudden arousal probably contributed importantly to the deaths.

6. One of the more common signs of heart trouble is the painful condition known as angina pectoris. This is caused by a shortage of oxygenated blood supply to the heart muscle and can be a forerunner of a damaging or fatal heart attack. The usual treatment for it today is coronary bypass surgery, in which the circulation is shunted around the obstruction in the coronary artery that is directly causing the trouble. Some cardiologists have questioned the value of this, believing that surgery itself entails considerable risk and that effective, less-dangerous treatment with drugs is possible. One researcher reported that he treated one group of 102 severe angina patients for six years with a combination of several drugs, and found that their death rate during this period was about the same as that for the general population in the same age range. Citing statistics that showed that those who receive coronary bypass surgery have a higher death rate than the general population as well as a high incidence of major nonfatal postoperative complications, the researcher concluded that drug treatment is safer than surgery and at least as effective.

7. A study of regular marijuana smokers indicated that marijuana use may cause a depression of the body's immune system, rendering the user more susceptible to disease. The pertinent evidence can be summarized as follows: Taking T-lymphocytes, or immunologically active white blood cells, from the pot smokers and from healthy, nonsmoking volunteers, the

doctors mixed the cells in test tubes with substances known to elicit immune responses. Cells from both groups responded to the foreign substances by multiplying, but those taken from the marijuana users reproduced 40 percent less than those from control subjects, a result suggesting that regular marijuana users may be more susceptible to disease.

8. Between 1968 and the end of 1972, 147 attempts were made to hijack United States aircraft, and 91 of these were successful. Thirty-one attempts were made in 1972 alone. In 1973 there was only one hijacking—of an Air Force helicopter—and the hijacker was arrested two days later. What caused this abrupt drop? Did potential hijackers suddenly lose interest? Did some secret organization of hijackers send out the word to "lie low"? Was public outrage a factor?

   Early in 1973, President Nixon ordered establishment of the screening procedures now standard at commercial airports, whereby passengers and all their carry-on luggage and other material pass through special X-ray units before boarding their planes. Some people have objected to this procedure on the grounds that it violates their constitutional right to privacy and constitutes an "unwarranted search and seizure." Proponents of the procedure argue that it is the cause of the virtual elimination of hijackings, and that if it were to be discontinued, hijackings would again occur and people would be more seriously inconvenienced or even killed.

9. A medical researcher has argued that economic recessions cause an increase in deaths from heart disease, kidney failure, and stroke. Statistics over the past sixty-eight years, he says, show that periods of economic downturn are consistently followed by waves of deaths from all these causes, as well as a rise in infant mortality, and that suicides, murders, and traffic deaths increase during a recession. So do the numbers of patients admitted to mental hospitals. He attributes all these phenomena to the increased stress suffered by individuals at these times, whether from unemployment, fear of unemployment, or the struggle to secure basic necessities. He notes that the use of alcohol and tobacco increases during a recession, and holds that these two factors, plus others such as a rise in blood pressure and cholesterol level, are sufficient to cause many of the heart-attack, stroke, and kidney-failure deaths, as well as to increase the number of mothers who give birth to infants unable to survive.

10. Mothers in the United States long ago abandoned breast-feeding of their babies in favor of bottle-feeding. Today, many of them are coming back to the breast. But now mothers in less-developed countries have begun to adopt bottle-feeding, and nutritional experts are concerned about the possible effects on infants' health. In these countries, cow's milk is often expensive, and packaged formulas are even more so, so a mother may dilute the milk—perhaps with impure water—before giving it to her baby. Or she may prepare a formula incorrectly, because she does not understand the

directions on the package. Also, cow's milk does not contain, as human milk does, precisely the right blend of ingredients for the needs of human babies. Thus a baby may need more cow's milk than human milk to achieve equally good nutrition.

Doctors have noted that, as bottle-feeding has increasingly replaced breast-feeding in many less-developed countries, babies have begun showing signs of severe malnutrition at earlier and earlier ages. This appears to support the contention that in poor countries bottle-feeding causes an increased level of infant malnutrition.

10.9 The Role of Logic in Science

Strictly speaking, as we have emphasized throughout this text, logic is essentially concerned with the logical structures of individual statements and with the logical relationships—such as consistency and implication—among two or more statments. If we wish to go beyond this—for instance, to determine the meanings of certain ordinary-language sentences (that might be used to express premises or conclusions of certain arguments), or to determine the truth or falsity of statements whose truth or falsity cannot be determined solely on logical grounds—then we have to resort to extralogical methods and considerations. Within these restrictions, what role can logic play in science?

Given that science is, at least in part, a body of knowledge contained in a set of statements, logic can be used to identify the logical relations among these statements. Many of the statements that constitute the scientific corpus belong to one of two basic types: statements about specific observed or observable individual cases (such as "When dropped from a height of sixteen feet in a vacuum chamber, it took this metal ball precisely 1.004397 seconds to reach the bottom"), and universal generalizations (such as "The distance traversed by a freely falling body is equal to one-half times the gravitational constant times the square of the elapsed time; that is, '$s = 1/2\ gt^2$' ")

Before proceeding with this brief outline of the role of logic in science, it must be pointed out that, although it is adequate for our present purposes, the distinction between generalizations and observation statements should not be interpreted as being a complete or even correct characterization of the types of statements that constitute the scientific corpus. A statement such as 'Mars rotates in a circular orbit around a stationary earth' is about the behavior of a specific individual entity, but its truth or falsity cannot be tested in as direct a way as can that of a statement such as 'Swan D is white.' Also, statements about what are sometimes referred to as "theoretical entities" (such as the electron in a particular hydrogen atom or Rush Limbaugh's id) are not such that their truth or falsity can be determined directly. In brief, the distinction between generalizations and observations certainly does not exhaust the kinds of statement that constitute a body of scientific knowledge. Thus, although the present discussion is restricted to the logical relations between generalizations and observation statements, it should be understood that this is for illustrative purposes only and should not be taken as an adequate description of science in general. As the analysis of the kinds of statements becomes more sophisticated and complex, so also does the description of the logical relations among these statements.

Several things can be determined by the logician about such statements and their relations. For one thing, it can be determined whether or not either an individual statement or a generalization is true or false solely by virtue of its logical form. (It is generally agreed that no observation statement can be true or false solely on logical grounds, and it is widely accepted that few, if any, significant generalizations are true or false on such grounds.) More important, the logician can determine whether one statement is validly deducible from one or more other statements, whether two statements are logically inconsistent (that is, whether it is logically impossible for both to be true), and whether or not one statement provides any inductive support for another.

Perhaps the most significant of these possible contributions by the logician to the scientific enterprise is the determination of the consistency or inconsistency of two or more statements. The question of consistency can arise between generalizations, between a generalization and an observation statement, or even between two observation statements. It can also arise between statements in two different theories.[8]

It is generally agreed that inconsistency is undesirable in any system, since (for reasons explained in Chapter 6) if a system contains just two inconsistent statements, anything whatsoever can be derived within that system, thus rendering the system essentially useless. The problem that arises, however, when a logical inconsistency is identified within a system, is that of deciding which of the two inconsistent statements to reject. Since, at most, only one of the two can be true, we must decide which to hold onto and which to eliminate from the system. But this decision goes beyond the scope of logic proper, and it must be grounded on other, extralogical criteria. Consider two generalizations that are determined to be logically inconsistent—the key generalizations of the Ptolemaic and Copernican theories:

All heavenly bodies (including the sun) move around the stationary earth.

---

[8]A problem has been identified in recent years with respect to determining the consistency or inconsistency of two statements in competing scientific systems (or competing systems of any other kind, for that matter). This is the problem of commensurability of meanings of the two statements—that is, of whether the two statements are such that they can both be translated into the same formal system without distortion of meaning. If they cannot—that is, if different theories are logically incommensurate—then the use of formal logic must be limited to the study of the logical relations of statements within a particular theory. This issue is related to that of the nature of perception, mentioned briefly on page 460.

All heavenly bodies (including the earth) move around the stationary sun.

We might reasonably choose to reject the one whose elimination would cause the least disruption in the rest of the system; but a generally acceptable formal definition of "least disruption" has yet to be formulated. If two observation statements are determined to be inconsistent—for instance, the two statements about the phases of Venus—one might decide which to retain and which to reject on the basis of considerations such as the past reliability of the observers. But this is not an absolute principle. For example, if the observation statement made by a previously reliable observer conflicted with a number of widely held basic beliefs, and the observation statement of an unreliable observer were to support the generally shared beliefs, it would not be unreasonable to accept the unreliable observer's statement, or at least to try to get more information before making a choice. Also, if both observers have been equally reliable, or both observations were made by the same observer, other factors will have to be considered.

Now, if an observation statement is found to be logically inconsistent with a generalization, which should be rejected and why? As we saw in our discussion of the hypothetico-deductive method, the answer is not necessarily "the generalization," although, contrary to the exhortations of some philosophers such as Plato, it probably should not always be "the observation statement" either. Numerous factors should be (and usually are) taken into consideration by scientists in arriving at a decision as to which statement to retain and which to reject. This is equally true in everyday life, for we not infrequently make judgments such as "Gee, I'd have sworn that I saw you at the ball game Thursday, but since you never go to ball games, I must have been mistaken," or "I used to think all college courses were dull and useless, but Dr. Whosit's Logic course sure showed me I was wrong." Thus, again, the question of which of two inconsistent statements to reject and which to retain cannot be answered in terms of purely logical criteria.

These are precisely the kinds of questions philosophers have been trying to answer for more than twenty-five hundred years. The questions themselves have not been adequately formulated in the limited space of this chapter and the possible answers have been barely hinted at. The main point we have attempted to make here is that logic in and of itself cannot provide adequate answers to such questions, but the questions cannot even be reliably identified, much less resolved, without some consideration of basic logical issues.

EXERCISE 10–21

Use any of the concepts of scientific methodology discussed in this chapter to evaluate the research presented in the following account.

Since World War II, increasing numbers of heroin addicts have died suddenly, in a characteristic fashion, which has generally been attributed to an overdose of the drug. These "overdose" deaths occur very suddenly, they occur very soon after injection of the drug (sometimes even before the needle can be withdrawn), and they are usually accompanied by massive pulmonary edema (filling of the lungs with fluid). Some researchers have challenged the belief that these deaths are caused by heroin overdose and have offered an alternative theory. The case against the overdose theory and for this alternative theory was presented by the editors of *Consumer Reports*. Against the overdose theory, they cite the following evidence:

First, the symptoms present in these deaths are not those previously known to be associated with heroin overdose—stupor, lethargy, and prolonged coma, lasting from one to twelve hours before death ensues.

Second, in several studies, heroin addicts have been given quantities of the drug far larger than their usual dosages—in some cases, six to nine times larger—without dying or suffering any serious ill effects.

Third, toxicological examination of tissues and urine from victims, and of syringes and emptied packets found near their bodies, has failed to disclose evidence of abnormally high dosage.

Fourth, other addicts injecting the same dosage at the same time from the same supply are usually unharmed.

Fifth, the victims are usually long-term addicts, who should have a fairly high tolerance for the drug, and not new users, whose tolerance is probably low.

On the basis of such evidence, the authors reject the overdose theory. They then go on to examine other evidence that might suggest an alternative:

First, the timing and increase of these deaths. They were first noted around 1943 and increased fairly slowly at first, then more rapidly, until in 1969 they constituted about 70 percent of all addict deaths in New York City and in 1970 about 80 percent. During the same period, the number of addict deaths from other causes did not significantly increase.

Second, the timing of possibly related events. During World War II, heroin was sometimes unavailable or hard to find; and from this time on, the amount of heroin in a standard New York City bag gradually decreased. Also, after 1939 quinine began to be used to "cut" or adulterate pure heroin; and quinine is capable of producing the symptoms associated with "overdose" deaths.

Third, evidence that the combination of heroin with alcohol or barbiturates can be dangerous. Several deaths (such as that of Janis Joplin) were known to have occurred immediately after an addict injected heroin while under the influence of alcohol or barbiturates. In 1967, toxicological examination revealed the presence of alcohol in about 43 percent of "overdose" deaths in New York City. Hospital personnel were aware that it was dangerous to give standard injections of morphine—which is closely related to heroin—to accident victims who were drunk. British doctors reported that many victims of "overdose" deaths had taken barbiturates with heroin or shortly before.

Fourth, evidence that addicts often use alcohol or barbiturates when they are deprived of heroin. At a clinic in San Francisco, 37 percent of addicts reported using barbiturates during withdrawal; 24 percent reported using alcohol.

Fifth, a 1958 study showing that addicts at that time generally believed it unsafe to combine alcohol or barbiturates with heroin; and the fact that by the 1960s this belief seemed largely to have disappeared.

Sixth, the fact that "overdose" deaths occurred in Britain, where quinine was not used as an adulterant of heroin.

On the basis of this evidence, the authors concluded that it was probable that the "overdose deaths" were caused by an acute shock-type reaction to the combination of heroin with a central nervous system depressant such as alcohol or barbiturates. They reasoned that an addict who was temporarily unable to obtain heroin might take alcohol or barbiturates to ease withdrawal symptoms, then obtain a supply of heroin and inject it while still under the influence of the depressants. This would create a sufficient condition for the typical "overdose" death and would be consistent with all the known conditions of addict behavior.

Summary

1. The **hypothetico-deductive method** differs from the more formal mode of enumerative induction presented in Chapter 9, in that it purports to reflect more accurately how people do in fact reason. It involves a temporal sequence of three steps: (1) formulate a generalization in the form of a "working hypothesis;" (2) validly deduce observation statements (that is, statements whose truth or falsity can be determined by direct observation) from the generalization; and (3) test the observation statements to determine whether each is, in fact, true or false, for the falsity of an observation statement logically implies the falsity of the generalization from which it was derived.

2. The process of deducing and testing observation statements obviously ends when any one of the deduced observation statements is found to be false. If no falsifying instance is found, the process could be continued indefinitely. A basic rule of thumb is that the greater the "logical effort" expended to deduce and test those observation statements which are most likely to be factually false, the greater the probability that, if they prove to be true, the generalization is true as well.

3. The rule of thumb for the hypothetico-deductive method corresponds to a basic criterion for evaluating inductive generalizations—the greater the negative analogy among relevant positive observed cases (premises), the stronger the support they are likely to provide for a related generalization. Some logicians view the second and third steps of this method as being directed toward the *verification* of the generalization, while others view it as being directed toward its *falsification*.

4. A variation of the hypothetico-deductive method, the method of **crucial experiment,** is sometimes cited to characterize the procedure for choosing

between two competing theories. Given two logically inconsistent generalizations, it is possible to derive observation statements from them which are such that a single observation will make one false and the other true. Thus, a single observation will force the falsification of at least one of the generalizations, and might provide some confirmation of the other.

5. Many argue that the hypothetico-deductive method, or some variation of it, is or should be *the* "scientific method." The argument used to justify this claim is subject to criticisms of circularity. Another difficulty with the argument is that a careful examination of the history of science provides little, if any, evidence that science has in fact developed in this way.

6. An even more serious problem in trying to characterize the nature of science is the apparent fact that the statements of science cannot be neatly and simply categorized as either theoretical statements (or generalizations) or observation statements. It is even possible that individuals from different cultures (or with different theoretical training) actually see different things when exposed to the same stimuli. To the extent to which this is true, observations cannot provide a basis for resolving theoretical disputes.

7. No generalization that is arrived at solely by means of an enumerative induction is strong enough to support the inference of a *causal* connection between two or more associated events.

8. The word 'cause' may be used in a number of different senses. The **efficient cause** is the set of preceding events that trigger the event in question. The **material cause** is the material out of which a thing is made. The **formal cause** is the form or structure of the object involved in the event. The **final** or **purposive cause** is the aim or goal of an action.

9. The last event in a causal chain is commonly designated as the **proximate cause**—that is, the one closest to the event whose cause is being sought. It is the proximate cause that is assumed to directly precipitate the caused event. The other links in the causal chain are **remote causes.**

10. Because of the tendency to interpret 'cause' as equivalent to 'proximate efficient cause,' or to assume that association of two events necessarily indicates a causal relationship, the neutral term **condition** is useful. There are two types of condition: necessary and sufficient. A **necessary condition** is one in the absence of which the event cannot take place. A **sufficient condition** is one in the presence of which the event is sure to take place. In some cases, the sufficient condition is a **conjunction**—that is, a combination, a joining together—of several necessary conditions. In other cases, the necessary condition is a **disjunction** of two or more conditions—that is, the presence of one or another (but not necessarily all) of several conditions is necessary to produce the caused event.

11. When an event occurs, it follows by definition that all necessary conditions, and thus at least one sufficient condition, for its occurrence are present. To

prevent an occurrence, we would search for and eliminate at least one necessary condition; to produce it, we would create at least one sufficient condition.

12. Mill's methods are frequently used to determine necessary and sufficient conditions. Each uses a variation of the process of **eliminative induction;** that is, it considers a number of possibilities, and then eliminates most of them in order to arrive at necessary and/or sufficient condition(s). None of these methods establishes the truth of any proposition absolutely. They merely establish a degree of probability.

13. The **method of agreement states** that if, in every case in which an event occurs, a particular condition is present, and no other factor is common to all occurrences, then that condition is probably a necessary condition of the event.

14. The **method of difference states** that if all but one of the conditions in two cases are essentially the same, and the caused phenomenon occurs in only one of them, the condition which exists in this one but not in the other is probably the sufficient condition of the phenomenon.

15. In the **joint method of agreement and difference,** the method of agreement is used to find a probable necessary condition. Then a number of cases in which the phenomenon does not occur are examined (regardless of whether they resemble the first group of cases in other respects). If the suspected causal factor is missing from all of them, then it is probably a necessary condition of the phenomenon and might be a sufficient condition as well.

16. The **method of concomitant variations** is useful when one seeks the cause of changes that occur along a continuum. It states that if a change in one phenomenon is found to occur every time a certain change in another phenomenon occurs, and if the degree of change in one phenomenon varies consistently with the degree of change in the other, then: either (1) the change in the first phenomenon is the cause of the change in the second; or (2) the change in the second phenomenon is the cause of the change in the first; or (3) a third factor is the cause of the change in both. Positive concomitant variation occurs when both factors vary in the same direction. Inverse concomitant variation occurs when the factors vary in opposite directions.

17. Scientists normally apply two additional criteria when using Mill's methods. One is that studies should be **replicable,** that is, repeatable by other persons with the same results. Special efforts also must be made to establish **controls** to make certain that only the factors being considered are, in fact, influencing the outcome of the study.

18. Given that science is, at the least, a body of knowledge contained in a set of statements, logic can be used to identify and evaluate the logical relations among these statements. Many scientific statements belong to one of two

basic types: statements about specific observable cases and universal generalizations. Logic can be used to determine whether a specific statement is true or false solely by virtue of its logical form. More important, the logician can determine whether one statement is validly deducible from one or more other statements, whether two statements are logically inconsistent, and whether one statement provides any inductive support for another. Perhaps the most significant of these is the determination of inconsistency, since it is generally agreed that inconsistency is undesirable in any system. When an inconsistency is found, one must decide which of the two statements to reject, but this decision goes beyond the scope of logic proper. Although logic alone cannot provide adequate answers to many questions concerning what science is and/or should be, the problems cannot be identified, nor adequate solutions provided, without some use of logic.

Chapter 11

Probability

Let's fantasize that you've had the good fortune to have won $1,000 as a door-prize at a party you attended last weekend. You decide that you would like to invest it in the stock market in the hope that it would increase in value so that you could use it as the down payment on a good new car when you graduate from college. As you try to decide which stock to invest in, you realize that it would be helpful if you could assign precise probability figures to each stock. If you had such figures, you could simply choose the four that have the highest probabilities for increasing in value and invest $250 in each. Unfortunately, no single set of such probability figures exists, and the figures that do exist are not necessarily very reliable.

One way of identifying stocks that have the highest probability of increasing the most in value is to ask experts, for example professional stock analysts with good track records. However, such a procedure is far from foolproof. For example, over the last several years *The Wall Street Journal* has been asking "experts" each month for their predictions as to which stocks will increase most in value over the next six months. The *Journal* also used a second method—throwing four darts at a board on which all stocks were printed. During the three-year period from mid-1990 to mid-1993, the stocks selected by the four professionals performed better than the stocks selected by throwing darts only 19 times; the stocks selected by throwing darts performed better than those chosen by experts 17 times! Does this indicate that the two methods of determining probabilities are equally good (or bad)? Is there any better way of determining which stocks have the highest probability of doing well in the next six months? Do probability figures really have any value at all?

Experts versus Darts

	Performance 9/2/92–2/28/93
Stock Picked by Expert 1	−0.7%
Stock Picked by Expert 2	−13.9%
Stock Picked by Expert 3	−44.6%
Stock Picked by Expert 4	−47.5%
Average of 4 Stocks Picked by Experts	−26.7%
Average of 4 Stocks Picked by Darts	+15.6%
Dow Jones Industrial Average	+2.5%

Adapted from The Wall Street Journal, *March 1, 1993*

11.1 Some Basic Terminology

In Chapters 9 and 10, the word 'probable' is used frequently. We have said that in an inductive argument the premises provide some, but not absolute, support for the truth of the conclusion. Thus, having observed fifty randomly selected swans and seen that all of them are white, we can reasonably make an enumerative induction to the conclusion that probably the next swan we observe will be white, or that probably all swans are white.

We are all familiar with other types of probability statements, such as those expressed by the following sentences:

> The probability of a person picking the winning three-digit number in a lottery is 1-in-1,000.
> The chance that a tossed coin will turn up heads is one in two.
> The probability that the Dow-Jones industrial stock average will drop 20 percent next Wednesday is .005.
> The odds that the American League team will win the World Series next year are 7–5.

The statements of probability expressed by these sentences might be quantitatively more precise than the types mentioned in the first paragraph, but the basic concept of probability involved is no more clear. Philosophers and mathematicians have formulated several quite different concepts of the nature of probability and theories about how probabilities should be calculated. Before examining several of these competing theories of the nature of probability, we need to look at some even more fundamental points on which the different theories are in general agreement.

We sometimes talk about the probability that *a statement is true,* while at other times we speak of the probability that *something will happen.* Usually, an assertion that a statement is probably true can be translated into an assertion that something will probably occur, and vice versa. For example, the judgment 'The statement "It will rain tomorrow" is probably true' can be reformulated as the judgment 'It will probably rain tomorrow.' If the first is true, then the second must be true, and vice versa. For the most part, we talk in this chapter of the probability of things happening, even though we could just as well talk about the probability of the truth of statements about these events.

It is also helpful in talking about the probabilities of certain things happening that we distinguish between events and the outcomes of events. We use the term **event** to refer to *a general state of affairs or situation that leads to one or more possible other states or situations,* and we call *the resulting states* the **outcomes** of the event. Thus, we usually consider a game—whether it is a college football game, a tennis match or a lottery—to be an event with several possible outcomes—for example, a team or individual winning or losing or possibly tying. But we will also consider various states of affairs which are not controlled by persons as events—such as the weather or geological states of volcanoes or earthquake faults—to be events in our technical sense of the term. If we define a particular event as the various elements constituting the meteorological conditions in a particular location on a given day, the possible outcomes include rain or clouds with no rain or sunshine, and probabilities can be assigned to each of these possible outcomes.

We usually are interested in knowing the probability of certain outcomes of an event, such as the outcome of getting an A on the next logic exam. We refer to the particular outcome in which we are interested as the **specified outcome.** The specified outcome need not always be desirable or positive, since we are often more interested in knowing what the chances are that an undesirable outcome may occur (for example, what is the probability of an earthquake ocurring in a specific place at a certain time). We represent the probability of a particular outcome in which we are interested with the notation 'P(**specified outcome**) = ____' where the blank contains a number between 0 and 1, or a 0, or a 1. To say that the probability of an outcome is 0 means that that outcome is impossible; for example, P(getting an 8 on one toss of a six-sided die that has the numbers 1 to 6 on the respective sides). To say that the probability of an outcome is 1 means that that outcome is absolutely certain to happen; for example, P(getting a number less than 8 on one toss of a six-sided die that has the numbers 1 to 6 on the respective sides).

Identifying and describing the outcomes of particular events can be quite tricky, and several of the difficulties are discussed later in this chapter. To keep things as simple as possible for now, we stipulate that the outcomes of any event must come at the end of the event. If we take as an event that a famous rock star went into convulsions and died suddenly and unexpectedly, it might seem appropriate for a person to state that it is highly probable that the death was caused by a drug overdose. But this appears to assign a probability to something that *preceded* the event; it also sounds very strange to say that taking a drug overdose was an "outcome" of the rock star's sudden death. We can deal with such problems by expressing the outcome-statements in such a way that they are clearly about possible future events. Thus, the statement about the cause of the rock star's death can be reformulated to be about a future state of affairs, such as "It is highly probable that the coroner will determine that the cause of the rock star's sudden death was a drug overdose." (Notice that this rewording also changes the event to being the coroner's investigation rather than the rock star's death.)

Another difficulty in specifying the outcomes of an event is choosing from among alternative modes of description. For example, if the event we are considering is Pat's taking of a logic exam, we could describe the same outcome in different ways, such as (1) passing or failing, (2) getting an A or B or C or D or F, and (3) getting a score of 100 or 99 or 98 or 97 . . . or 2 or 1 or 0. This is significant because each of these outcome-descriptions result in different probabilities. No one mode of description is the only correct way of describing the outcomes; we must choose the mode that seems to be the most appropriate for the specific situation. Thus, if Pat is only interested in passing the exam, then description 1 would probably be sufficient; if Pat hopes to get a B on the exam, then 2 provides a more appropriate description; and if Pat needs a 93 or higher, mode 3 should be used.

The abilities to recognize the different ways of defining the outcomes of a particular event, and also to describe most if not all of the possible outcomes under a particular mode of description, are clearly critical skills for computing probabilities. We will discuss these issues further in this chapter and provide exercises that will allow you to develop your abilities.

EXERCISE 11–1

Identify at least four possible outcomes for each of the following events. If possible, you should also try to find two or more different ways of defining the outcomes for each type of event.

1. One day's geological activity along the San Andreas fault within ten miles of San Francisco.

2. One day's development of a tropical storm in the Caribbean, which was moving west and had high winds of 55 miles per hour at 6 A.M.

3. A golf tournament with 72 players entered (identify each player with a number).

4. Robin buys one ticket in a 6-number lottery that pays prizes for choosing three or more of the winning numbers.

5. Jan takes a True-False exam with fifty questions.

6. One day's activity on the stock market for IBM common stock, which started the day at $92 per share.

7. Pat takes a commercial airliner from New York to Chicago on a flight scheduled to arrive at 3:50 P.M.

8. The routine operation of a major hospital that has 437 patients at the beginning of the day.

9. Lee's car, which is ten years old and has been breaking down regularly lately, being driven all over town on a variety of errands.

10. Sue's submitting applications to each of the top ten MBA programs in the country.

11.2 Two General Principles of Probability

It is generally agreed by the proponents of all the competing theories of probability that any adequate theory must satisfy at least two basic requirements. First, *a statement that is absolutely true has a probability of 1; a statement that is absolutely false has a probability of 0; and any statement that is neither absolutely true nor absolutely false must have a probability between 0 and 1.* For example, the probability that any human will die before her/his 2,000th birthday is 1, insofar as this is considered to be absolutely certain. But the probability that any human living today died yesterday is 0, insofar as we can agree that this is impossible. And the probability that a person who is living at this moment will survive for another ten years is a fraction between 0 and 1, depending on the person's health, lifestyle, and other factors.

A second requirement for any theory of probability is that *the sum of the probabilities of any logically inconsistent statements* (that is, statements not more than one of which can be true at any given time), *can be no greater than 1.* For example, consider the statements 'The next card to be drawn from this deck will be an ace'; 'The next card to be drawn from this deck will be an eight'; and 'The next card to be drawn from this deck will be a five.' Not more than one of these can be true for any specific draw, although they could all be false. Thus the sum of the probability that the first is true, the probability that the second is true, and the probability that the third is true cannot be more than 1. So far, all logicians agree. But when we try to specify the probability of any stated outcome to any degree of precision beyond that imposed by these generally accepted restrictions, the differences among the competing theories become very apparent.

EXERCISE 11–2

Use your intuitions to "guesstimate" the probability of each of the following outcomes as being 0, 1, or a fraction in between. If in between, would it be about .5, nearer to 1, or nearer to 0?

1. At least one baby will be born tomorrow in New York City.

2. The sun will rise in the west tomorrow morning.

3. There will be no measurable precipitation at your local airport tomorrow.

4. There will be a serious flood on the Mississippi River in July of next year.

5. A particular healthy two-year-old child will die within the next ten years.

6. A particular ninety-two-year-old man will die within the next six years.

7. The Arctic ice cap will completely melt in the next year.

8. Jan, who is a senior with a 4.0 grade-point average, will fail to graduate.

9. A mugging will be committed in New York City next week.

10. The next ball I draw from this box that contains only white balls will be white.

11. It will rain somewhere in the world next month.

12. One of the five tickets I bought this week will win the state lottery jackpot.

13. Someone will win the jackpot in the state lottery this week.

14. Pat, who buys ten tickets each week, will win some kind of prize in the state lottery at some time in the future.

15. Jan, who refuses to buy even one ticket, will never win the lottery jackpot.

EXERCISE 11–3

Can the sum of the probabilities for any of the following pairs of statements be more than 1? Why, or why not?

1. A hurricane will hit Hilton Head tomorrow. It will be clear and calm in Hilton Head for the next 48 hours.

2. The instructor will be late to this class today. The instructor will be on time for this class today.

3. It will rain somewhere tomorrow. It will be sunny somewhere tomorrow.

4. Terry will pass logic this semester. Terry will not pass logic this semester.

5. Sue Smith gave birth to a boy yesterday. Sue Smith gave birth to a girl yesterday.

6. A Republican will lose the next presidential election. A Democrat will lose the next presidential election.

7. The only winning combination in this week's lottery is 6-1-5. The only winning combination in this week's lottery is 0-3-7.

8. Pat will win the lottery this week. Pat will win the lottery next week.

9. The winning number in this week's lottery will contain a 6. Every winning number in the lottery for the next year will contain a 6.

10. Lee will not win the lottery this week. Lee will not win the lottery next week.

11. Pat will never win the lottery. Pat will win the lottery at least once.

12. Jan will guess at least one of the lottery numbers correctly this week. Jan will guess at least two of the lottery numbers correctly this week.

11.3 Three Theories of Probability

How are we to interpret statements of the form 'The probability of X is Y'? The term 'probable' is best defined in terms of the processes by means of which the probability is determined. Many such processes have been suggested over the last several centuries. We shall limit our discussion to three that are among the most frequently discussed and debated. These three theories are quite different from one another, and each has distinct strengths and weaknesses.

11.3.1 The Classical Theory

Consider the situation in which you are taking a multiple-choice test on which every question has four choices and the instructions indicate that you will get no credit (nor will you be penalized) if you mark more than one answer on a question or if you leave it blank. Halfway through the test you encounter a question for which you do not have any idea whatsoever as to which of the four possible answers is the correct one. How would you calculate the probability that answer C is the correct answer?

The **classical theory** can be used to determine such probabilities. The theory requires that you make two assumptions. One assumption—which we call the **principle of omniscience**—is that *all possible outcomes are known;* in the case of the exam question, we can assume from the instructions provided that there are only four outcomes for which you have any chance of getting credit, that is, choosing exactly one of the supplied answers. The second assumption—that the *probabilities of the occurrence of each of the possible outcomes are equal*— is known as the **principle of indifference.** If in a particular case there is good reason to believe that the outcomes are not equally probable, then we cannot use the classical theory for that case.

Given these assumptions, the probability of any particular outcome can be calculated. In the preceding example, it is assumed that students have only four different choices—namely, they can choose answer A, answer B, answer C, or answer D. Of these four events, only one is specified—the one that is correct. By dividing the number of specified events by the total number of equally possible events, we arrive at the probability that the specified event will occur. This can be expressed by the following formula:

$$P(\text{specified outcome}) = \frac{\text{number of possible specified outcomes}}{\text{number of all possible outcomes}}$$

Substituting figures from the example of guessing on the multiple-choice question, the probability of the specified event can be calculated as follows:

$$P(\text{guessing correct answer}) = \frac{\text{number of possible correct answers}}{\text{number of all possible answers}}$$

Using the same formula, we can also calculate the probability of picking the winning number on a lottery of three single-digit numbers (0 to 9). The number of possible specified events is one, since there is only one winning number, and there are exactly 1,000 possible numbers (0 to 999). Using the formula, we can express the probability of choosing the winning number as

$$P(\text{choosing the winning number}) = \frac{1}{1,000}$$

It is necessary to use a certain amount of common sense when applying the principle of indifference. In this case we don't have any information that indicates that the probability of one or more outcomes is significantly greater or lesser than the probability of other outcomes; but this does not mean that such a difference does not exist nor that no one else has any knowledge of such a difference. We should always keep in mind that it is possible that another person has knowledge that we don't have, for example, that a particular coin is weighted to come up heads 75 percent of the time or that a die is loaded to come up 1 or 6 most of the time. A conservative corollary to the principle of indifference is that we should try to avoid assuming that each member of a set of outcomes is equally possible, unless there is good reason to believe this assumption to hold for a particular case or we are forced by circumstances to calculate a probability without having any information concerning the equality of the probability of the possible outcomes. Thus, if someone offers to make a bet that a particular team will win a specific game when we know nothing about either team, it would be prudent to assume that there is a good chance that one of the teams is significantly better and thus more likely to win than the other. Under these circumstances it would be wise to refuse to use the classical theory to calculate the probabilities of the alternative outcomes.

Another type of problematic case for the classical theory is illustrated by the attempt to determine the probability that a randomly selected ten-year-old child in the United States will survive to his or her eleventh birthday. There are only two possible outcomes in this case—the child will either survive or not survive. If the principle of indifference were applied, the probability of survival would be only 1/2. But there is certainly good reason to believe that today the two outcomes are not equally likely, and that a randomly selected ten-year-old has a much better than even chance of living at least one year. The classical theory is simply not applicable to this case. But this is precisely the kind of case with which a second theory is best equipped to deal.

EXERCISE 11-4

Use the classical method to determine the probabilities of each of the following outcomes.

1. Getting heads on one toss of a penny.

2. Winning a raffle in which you have purchased exactly one of the 87 tickets sold.

3. Winning a lottery in which the winning number is an integer from 0 to 99 (inclusive), given that you have purchased exactly one ticket.

4. Getting the correct answer guessing on a true-false question.

5. Getting a 4 or a 5 on one toss of a six-sided die.

6. Winning a lottery in which the winning number will be an integer between 1 and 100, given that you have purchased exactly twelve tickets, each with a different number.

7. Winning a lottery in which the winning number will be an integer between 1 and 1,000, given that you've bought exactly one ticket.

8. Getting either a head or a tail on a single toss of a quarter.

9. Getting the wrong answer on a multiple-choice question with five answers to choose from.

10. Betting on the winning horse in a race with twelve horses in it, when you have bet on exactly seven horses.

11.3.2 The Relative Frequency Theory

The **relative frequency theory** is based not on an abstract assumption like the principle of indifference but on the direct observation of concrete cases. The theory stipulates that the probability of an outcome is based on past observations of similar events and is to be determined by dividing the number of observed instances of the specified outcome(s) by the total number of observed outcomes. This can be expressed by the following formula:

$$\text{P(specified outcome)} = \frac{\text{number of observed specified outcomes}}{\text{number of all observed outcomes}}$$

How would the relative frequency theory be used to determine the probability that a ten-year-old will live to his or her eleventh birthday? The researcher, probably an insurance actuary, would observe a sample of, say, two thousand randomly selected ten-year-olds, and would count the number who survive until their eleventh birthdays. In this instance, let us say that only two die, that is, 1,998 out of the two thousand survive. Dividing the number of observed deaths among ten-year-olds by the total number of observed cases, the researcher would arrive at the probability that a ten-year-old will survive to his or her eleventh birthday.

$$\text{P(ten-year-old surviving to 11)} = \frac{1,998}{2,000}$$

The relative frequency theory can also be used to determine a probability figure for such outcomes as coming up with a head on a flip of a coin or getting a six on one toss of a die. However, this method can be used for such cases only if it is possible to first make a number of observations of similar events so that there will be a significant number of observed outcomes.

There are several different versions of the relative frequency theory. All of them utilize the method outlined above for determining probabilities on the basis of empirical observations; the differences among them result from more subtle technical matters that we cannot go into here. All the versions have weaknesses.

Perhaps the most serious weakness is that no version of the relative frequency theory can normally be used in cases where we have made (or are able to make) relatively few observations. For example, a particular sports team might lose the first three or four games in one season. This means that the number of observed cases of wins is zero, which in turn means that on the relative frequency theory the probability of winning any future games would also be zero. Since a probability of zero means literally that the outcome is impossible, this would not be a particularly helpful (or encouraging) result. But the team and its fans need not give up hope for the remaining games of the season; they simply have to use some other method for calculating the probability that will give a more reasonable chance of winning future games.

One difficulty faced by most versions of the relative frequency theory stems from their assertion that probabilities based on observations of past cases are applicable to future cases only in the long run. That is, they hold that it is not proper—in fact, it is meaningless on many accounts—to assign a probability value to a single outcome, such as getting a head on one particular flip of a coin. To say that the probability of getting a head on the flip of a coin is 1/2, according to these theorists, is only to say that in the long run, or even in an infinite sequence, half of the tosses will come up heads. This interpretation is sometimes used to respond to critics who, for example, might criticize weather forecasters who state every day for a week or more that there is a 20 percent probability of rain and it has not rained at all.

Neither the classical nor the relative frequency theory can deal adequately with complex one-of-a-kind cases, such as the probability that a particular college football team will be ranked number one after the bowl games next year. The classical theory is unsatisfactory because the principle of indifference does not apply in such a case (few people would claim that each of the 100 Division I teams has an equal chance to be ranked number one). The relative frequency theory is also inadequate, because it is not proper to apply this theory to calculating the probability of a particular outcome, especially one that has the complications that are involved in a team sport such as football. The proponents of the subjectivist or personalistic theory claim that it can deal much more reasonably with cases of this kind.

EXERCISE 11–5

Use the relative frequency method to determine the probabilities of each of the following outcomes, given the information provided about previously observed outcomes.

1. Getting heads on one toss of a penny, given that on 20 previous tosses, 15 were tails.

2. Getting the correct answer guessing on a true-false question, given that you guessed correctly on 63 percent of true-false questions in the past.

3. Choosing the winning number in a lottery, given that every one of the 20 numbers you have chosen previously has been a losing number.

4. Getting a 4 or a 5 on one toss of a six-sided die, given that the die has come up 4 thirty-two times and has come up 5 eighteen times on 100 tosses.

5. Getting a heart on a single draw from a standard deck of cards with no jokers (13 hearts, 13 spades, 13 clubs, and 13 diamonds), given that 400 of the last 1,000 draws from this deck have been hearts.

6. That the winning lottery number this week will contain a 3, given that in 80 percent of the previous weeks the winning number has contained a 3.

7. Getting a black card on a single draw from a standard deck, given that 55 percent of the last 170 draws have been red cards.

8. Getting an ace (of any suit) on a single draw from a standard deck, given that 17 of the last 100 cards drawn have been aces.

9. Getting either a head or a tail on a single toss of a quarter, given that 43 of the last 100 tosses have come up tails.

10. That the winning lottery number this week will be 2-4-7, given that last week was the first week of the lottery, and the winning number last week was 2-4-7.

11. Getting the wrong answer on a multiple-choice question with five answers to choose from, given that you have gotten 25 percent of five-answer questions correct on past guesses.

12. Getting the winning ticket for the grand prize in a lottery for which 1,298,174 tickets have been sold, given that you have played the lottery 124 times and have never won a lottery before.

13. Winning the lottery this week, given that you bought 4 tickets for this week's lottery, and that on exactly 2 of the 12 previous occasions on which you bought four tickets for the weekly lottery, you won.

14. Betting on the winning horse in a race with 12 horses in it, given that the horse on which you bet has won 6 of the 8 races in which it has been entered.

15. Choosing the winning number in a lottery, when you won the only previous lottery you ever entered.

16. Choosing at least one correct part of the winning lottery number, given that you have chosen at least one correct part on 20 of the other 50 times you have played.

11.3.3 The Subjectivist Theory

The **subjectivist theory** defines probabilities as being grounded in the beliefs of individual persons. Thus, in contrast to the classical and relative frequency theories, under the subjectivist theory a variety of different probabilities can be assigned to the same specified outcomes of the same event. Although this might seem at first sight to be strange, if not absurd, supporters of the theory see it as a strength insofar as it seems to more closely fit the realities of the way in which people do in fact set probabilities. Usually the coaches, sportswriters, and other "experts" who vote in the polls at the beginning of the football season do not all agree as to which team will be number one at the end of the season, and it is not unusual for only a small minority to have correctly identified the team that eventually does finish first. And the case of the stockbrokers at the beginning of this chapter provides a good example of a situation in which neither the classical nor the relative frequency methods can be used and also in which the "experts" disagreed among themselves (each selected a different stock) and they all were eventually proven to have been very wrong in their predictions.

Although the description thus far of the subjectivist theory might seem to imply that any probability whatsoever can be assigned to a particular outcome—which would certainly justify rejection of the subjectivist theory—in fact, several restrictions significantly limit us in our assignment of probabilities. First, the general rules mentioned earlier still apply. This means that no outcome can have a probability greater than 1 and also that the sum of probabilities of incompatible outcomes cannot be greater than 1. Thus, if a person assigns a probability of 2/3 that a coin will come up heads, that same person cannot also assign a probability of 2/3 that the coin will come up tails on the same toss. Second, the rules of the probability calculus (to be explained in the next section) must also be observed. A significant feature of the subjectivist theory is that it requires that, so far as possible, all of an individual's beliefs be considered in establishing his or her probability for a particular outcome, and the rules of probability calculus provide a means of doing this.

Philosophers and mathematicians have raised numerous technical objections against the subjectivist theory; many critics believe that the mere fact that different probabilities can be assigned to the same outcome by different persons (or by the same person at different times) is a sufficient criticism. Still, the theory has considerable appeal, because it allows one to assign probabilities to many events that other theories cannot deal with at all. And the theory does seem to fit countless facts, such as that the favorite horse (as determined by the millions of wagers placed as well as by the "expert" handicappers) has won Kentucky Derby only once in the last twenty races.

EXERCISE 11–6

Determine which method is most appropriate for determining the probability of each of the following outcomes, given the information provided (if any) about previously observed outcomes, and then calculate the probability of the outcome using that method.

1. Toby enters a lottery in which the winning number will be an integer between 1 and 100. What is the probability that Toby will win?

2. A blindfolded player draws a ball from an urn. What is the probability that a red ball will be drawn if the urn contains: (a) 2 red, 2 white, 2 black, and 2 blue balls? (b) 4 black, 5 white, and 6 red balls?

3. A charity organization raffled off a wrist watch to raise funds. If 512 chances were sold, what is the probability of winning for a person holding: (a) one ticket? (b) 8 tickets?

4. Bo, Jo, and Mo have one ticket each for this week's lottery, in which the winning number will be an integer between 1 and 100. What is the probability that (a) Jo will win? (b) Mo will win? (c) Bo will win?

5. If the average number of male births in the United States per year is 2,180,000 out of a total of 4,258,000 births, what is the probability that the next baby born will be a boy?

6. The winning number for a certain weekly lottery is an integer between 1 and 1,000,000. There has been exactly one winner 70 percent of the weeks, exactly two winners 5 percent of the weeks, and no winner the other weeks. What is the probability that there will be exactly one winner this week?

7. If the federal government outlay this year for veterans' benefits and services is $14,000 million out of total federal expenditures of $300,000 million, what is the probability that the next dollar spent will benefit a veteran?

8. The state you are living in holds a weekly lottery in which each ticket has a different number and exactly one winner is guaranteed. If 525,000 tickets have been sold, what is the probability you will win if you hold exactly one ticket?

9. If the number of plane crashes among domestic airlines in the United States is 156 out of the last 342,576 domestic flights, what is the probability that the next domestic flight you take will crash?

10. If Cat has entered a certain lottery, in which the winning number is an integer between 1 and 100, one-hundred times, but she has never won, what is the probability that she will win the next time she enters?

11. A politician believes that the odds are 5 to 1 that she will win a particular election. (a) What is her probability for winning? (b) What is the probability that she will lose the election?

12. Of 100 juniors who took I.Q. tests at City High School last year, 27 had scores between 110 and 118. The scores of the whole group ranged between 102 and 167. If next year's class is similar to this year's class, what is the probability that a randomly selected junior next year will have an I.Q. between 110 and 118?

13. Three popular racing drivers are among 15 scheduled to compete in today's stock car race. In the past two years, Jan Alpha has won 4 out of 12 races. Ben Beta has won 7 out of 16 in the same period. Gail Gamma has been

having difficulties and has won only 2 out of 10. On the basis of this data alone, what is the probability that each will win today's race?

14. On each of the 50 previous occasions on which Jan has played the lottery, she has chosen a number one of whose digits is 8. What is the probability that the next time she plays the lottery she will choose a number one of whose digits is 8?

15. According to actuarial statistics, out of 100,000 newborn females, 800 do not survive to their third birthday. (a) What is the probability that a newborn female will survive to her third birthday? (b) What is the probability that a newborn female will not survive to her third birthday?

16. In the past 50 turns of a roulette wheel (which has an equal number of red and black slots), the ball has landed on a black slot 35 times and on a red slot 15 times. What is the probability that on the next turn the ball will land in a red slot?

17. A bag contains 50 jellybeans: 20 licorice, 15 cinnamon, and 15 papaya. What is the probability that a blindfolded child who selects one jellybean from the bag will select a licorice one?

11.4 Independent and Mutually Exclusive Outcomes

Thus far we have been discussing only procedures for establishing the probability of a single simple outcome, and we have found that there is no single, generally accepted, and universally applicable method for doing this. But we also wish in certain circumstances to calculate the probabilities of compound outcomes—for example, the probability of getting heads in three consecutive tosses of a coin.

The first type of complex outcome we consider is *one whose component outcomes are such that the occurrence of one has no effect on the occurrence of any of the others*; that is, if one outcome occurs, the probability of the occurrence of the other outcome(s) is not changed. Such outcomes are said to be **independent.** For example, consider how we could calculate the probability of getting heads on two consecutive tosses of a coin. Although at first thought these two outcomes may seem to be dependent, they are in fact independent. In other words, what we get on the first toss of a coin has no effect on what we get on the second toss. (It *does* affect whether we will get *two heads in a row*, insofar as if we get a tail on the first toss, the probability of getting two heads in a row becomes 0. But the probability that we will get a head *on the second toss* is 1/2 whether we got a head or a tail on the first toss.)

The relationship of independent outcomes can also be expressed in the notation of probability theory by introducing the concept of the probability of one outcome occurring *given that* some other outcome has already occurred; we will express this *conditional* probability as **P(y given x).** For outcomes that satisfy the definition of independence specified above, the probability that one will occur given that the other has also occurred is exactly what it would be if the other had not occurred. In our notation,

For any two independent outcomes x and y, P(y given x) = P(y).

Of course, not all complex outcomes have component outcomes that are independent of one another. In many cases, one of the component outcomes affects the circumstances of the second outcome in such a way that the probability of the second is no longer what it would have been if the first outcome had not occurred. Such outcomes are called **dependent** outcomes.

To see the distinction between independent and dependent outcomes more clearly, consider the case of four candidates for student-body president drawing straws to determine who gets to go first in a campaign debate. The moderator holds four straws, the lucky straw being shorter than the rest. They are arranged so that the moderator's fingers hide the lower part of the straws, and the exposed portions are all the same length. At the start of the draw, the probability, as determined under the classical theory, that any particular candidate will receive the short straw is 1/4. Whether the draws are considered to be independent or dependent outcomes depends on the manner in which they are carried out. If each candidate only points to a straw and there is no rule preventing two or more from pointing at the same straw and the moderator reveals the complete straws only after all four candidates have pointed, the outcomes of the candidates' choices are independent. But if each candidate in turn draws a straw and does not replace it, then the composition of the bundle of straws changes as each candidate takes a straw and this changes each remaining candidate's probability of receiving the short straw.

Let P(A) represent the outcome of candidate A receiving the short straw, P(B) the outcome of candidate B receiving it, etc. Then, in the version in which the straws are drawn and not replaced, prior to the first draw the probability of drawing the short straw for each candidate is 1/4. Then, if A draws first and gets the short straw, the probabilities of each of the others getting that straw immediately change to 0. If A goes first and does not draw the short straw, then P(B) = P(C) = P(D) = 1/3. If B draws next and does not get the short straw, then P(C) and P(D) both change to 1/2. And if C draws and does not get the short straw, then P(D) becomes 1.

There is a special kind of set of dependent outcomes which is such that only one of the set can possibly occur: for example, on a given toss a six-sided die can come up 1 or 2 or 3 or 4 or 5 or 6, but it cannot have more than one side up after any one throw. Such outcomes are said to be **mutually exclusive**. Another way of expressing this is that *once one of a set of mutually exclusive outcomes has occurred, it is impossible for any other of these mutually exclusive outcomes to also occur*. This can be expressed in probability notation as

For any two mutually exclusive outcomes x and y, P(x given y) = 0.

It is also the case for mutually exclusive outcomes that it is impossible for two or more to occur, that is, P(x and y) = 0.

11.5 The Probability Calculus

The general procedures for determining the probabilities of compound outcomes have been codified in a formal system of rules known as the **probability calculus.** *Given the probabilities of the occurrence of each of several simple outcomes, the probability calculus enables us to calculate the probability of these outcomes occurring in various combinations.*

Notice that the probability calculus presupposes that we have some independent procedure for establishing the probabilities of individual outcomes before we attempt to calculate the probability of any combination of these outcomes. *The probability of a simple outcome's occurring by itself* is referred to as the **initial probability.** The three theories already discussed are theories for establishing the initial probabilities of individual outcomes. As we have seen, the different theories can establish different initial probabilities for the same simple outcomes. But advocates of all three methods accept essentially the same probability calculus, though with some differences in detail.

In the probability calculus, a complex outcome is viewed as a whole comprising a number of simple outcomes. For example, the complex outcome of a race horse's winning the Triple Crown is a whole of which the component parts are its winning the Kentucky Derby, then the Preakness, and finally the Belmont Stakes. The process of calculating the probability of the whole from the probabilities of its parts depends, as we shall see, on understanding the way in which the parts are related. For the sake of simplicity we use the classical method for determining initial probabilities in the remainder of this chapter.

11.5.1 The Restricted Conjunction Rule

The first rule to be presented is one that applies *only* to independent outcomes. This rule tells us how to calculate the probability that two or more independent outcomes will occur. Let us consider the complex event consisting of two tosses of a coin; four outcomes are possible:

heads and heads
heads and tails
tails and heads
tails and tails

Since we are using the classical theory for establishing the initial probabilities, we must assume that each of these four compound outcomes is equally possible. Thus, the probability of the specified outcome of 'heads and heads' is one out of four, or 1/4.

But this answer can be arrived at in another way that is simpler, especially for more complicated cases. This method involves breaking down the complex outcome into its basic simple components—in this case the outcome of the first toss and the outcome of the second toss. There are two possible outcomes of each toss—heads and tails—and we can calculate the probability of each specified outcome. The probability of heads on the first toss is 1/2, and the probability of heads on the second toss is 1/2. Now we can use these two probabilities in a formula known as the **restricted conjunction rule** which states that

If x and y are independent outcomes, then
P(x and y) = P(x) × P(y).

If we substitute the outcome of a head on the first toss for x and the outcome of a head on the second toss for y, then P(x) and P(y) represent the probabilities of each outcome occurring independently, and P(x and y) represents the probability of their occurring together. Given that the probability of x (heads on the first toss) is 1/2 and the probability of y (heads on the second toss) is 1/2, then

P(heads on 1st toss *and* heads on 2nd toss)
= P(heads on 1st toss) × P(heads on 2nd toss)
= 1/2 × 1/2 = 1/4.

Remember, we are using the classical theory for establishing initial probabilities in these examples only for reasons of simplicity. The restricted conjunction rule can also be used with the other theories for establishing initial probabilities. If we had conducted an empirical study of the coin and determined that it came up heads 3,955 times in 10,000 tosses, then on the relative frequency theory P(x) = P(y) = .3955. The probability of heads on the two tosses would be .3955 × .3955. Or a person might have a "gut-feeling" that heads are luckier than tails today and use the subjective theory to set the probability of heads on one toss at 6/10.

Let us consider a somewhat more complex sample. Sue is quite confident that she knows the correct answer to all of the multiple-choice questions on her logic exam, with the exception of three. Each question has five choices. On one question, Sue is sure that the correct answer must be one of two, so P(correct answer on number 1) = 1/2; on another she has narrowed it down to three, so P(correct answer on number 2) = 1/3; on the third she does not have any idea which of the five answers is the correct one, leaving P(correct answer on number 3) = 1/5. What is the probability that by guessing Sue will get all three of these answers correct? Getting the correct answer on any one question will not affect the correctness of either of the others, so the three outcomes are independent and we can use the restricted conjunction rule. If we allow that she has correctly narrowed the choices on two of the three, we can compute the probability of getting all three correct by inserting the probabilities of the three specified outcomes as follows.

P(x and y and z)
    = P(correct on #1) × P(correct on #2) × P(correct on #3)
    = 1/2 × 1/3 × 1/5 = 1/30.

Notice in both examples that the probability of the complex outcome is smaller than the probability of any one of the independent outcomes. The probability of a complex outcome will always be *less* than the probability of any one of its components (except in the uninteresting case in which each outcome has a probability of 1).

EXERCISE 11–7

Calculate the probabilities of the following conjunct outcomes. Give the following information: (a) the initial probabilities of each of the specified outcomes calculated using the classical theory, and (b) the probability of the conjunct outcome. It is not necessary to multiply out to the final product.

1. If a single six-sided die is tossed three times, what is the probability that a 1 will be up all three times?

2. Tab buys one ticket for each of two different lotteries whose winning number is a three-digit integer between 100 and 999, what is the probability that both are winners?

3. If three six-sided dice are tossed simultaneously, what is the chance that all will come up with 5s?

4. Five business executives are going to a convention in Chicago on the same day. They are all flying from the same airport, but do not know each other. There are three flights they can conveniently take. Assuming that each does in fact take one of these flights, what is the probability that they will all be on the earliest flight?

5. Three nickels are tossed simultaneously. What is the probability of getting heads on all three?

6. Mel bought one ticket for each of two different lotteries; the winning number of the first will be an integer between 1 and 100, and the winning number of the second will be an integer between 1 and 1,000. What is the probability that Mel will win both lotteries?

7. A four-sided die has sides labeled E, F, G, and H. What is the probability that the E side will be up after each of three successive tosses?

11.5.2 The General Conjunction Rule

Since many cases that we encounter involve dependent rather than independent outcomes, we need a rule that will also let us calculate probabilities for dependent outcomes. The rule that is used to calculate probability values of the joint occurrence of a number of simple outcomes (whether they are dependent or independent) is called the **general conjunction rule.** It states that

> **If x and y are any outcomes whatever (either dependent or independent), then**
> **P(x and y) = P(x) × P(y given x).**

As explained in Section 11.4, the notation 'P(y given x)' represents a probability value for the occurrence of the outcome y, given that outcome x has already occurred. Let us consider an example. On the classical theory, we assign the value 1/10 to the initial probability of drawing a red ball from an urn containing 10 balls of 10 different colors, and we also assign 1/10 to the initial probability of drawing a yellow ball. However, once the red ball has been drawn, and not replaced, the probability of drawing the yellow ball—to be precise, P(yellow ball on second draw given red ball on first draw)—becomes 1/9, since only 9 balls remain in the urn. Thus the two outcomes are not independent, since the occurrence of one outcome affects the probability of the occurrence of the other. P(y given x) is the probability of drawing the yellow ball after the red one has been drawn. By substituting the appropriate values in the general conjunction rule, we can compute the probability of drawing a red and a yellow ball in succession as follows:

> P(red on 1st and yellow on 2nd)
> = P(red on 1st) × P(yellow on 2nd given red on first)
> = 1/10 × 1/9 = 1/90.

Consider another example. Suppose there is a jar containing three jellybeans; two are red and one is green. A child sticks his hand into the jar and takes out one jellybean at a time without replacing them. What is the probability that he will pick the two red jellybeans on the first two tries? The probability of getting a red jellybean on the first draw, P(red on 1st try), is 2/3. If a red is drawn on the first try, then there will be only two jellybeans left in the jar, one red and one green. Therefore, the probability of getting a red jellybean on the second draw, given that a red one was drawn on the first try, is 1/2; or, in terms of the formula, P(yellow on 2nd given red on 1st) = 1/2. Using the general conjunction rule, we can calculate that:

> P(red on 1st try and yellow on 2nd try) = 2/3 × 1/2 = 2/6 = 1/3.

Thus the probability that the child will draw two red jellybeans in a row is 1/3.

Notice that if x and y are two independent outcomes, then the probability of y given that x has already occurred is the same as the probability of y itself, since for independent outcomes x and y, P(y given x) = P(y).

Calculate the probabilities of the following conjunct outcomes using the restricted or general conjunction rule as appropriate. Give the following information: (a) Are the simple outcomes dependent or independent? (b) What rule should be used? (c) What are the initial probabilities calculated using the classical theory? (d) What is the probability of the conjoint outcome? It is not necessary to multiply out to the final product.

1. If three six-sided dice are tossed simultaneously, what is the chance that all will come up with 5s?

2. A cloth sack contains 10 balls, each a different color. What is the probability that the first two balls drawn from the sack will be a pink ball and a green ball, in that order, if the first one drawn is *not* returned before the second is drawn?

3. A cloth sack contains 10 balls, each a different color. What is the probability that the first two balls drawn from the sack will be a pink ball and a green ball, in that order, if the first one drawn *is* returned before the second is drawn?

4. Using the same sack (with all 10 balls in it), what is the probability of drawing a pink, a green, a blue, and a white ball, in that order, in four successive selections?

5. Assuming that it is equally probable that a person will be born on any particular date and ignoring the complications of a leap year, what is the probability that two randomly selected people were born on October 20?

6. A ceramic urn contains 10 white, 10 black, and 10 red balls. What is the probability of selecting 3 black balls on the first three draws if each ball drawn is returned before the next is drawn?

7. Using the same urn containing 10 white, 10 black, and 10 red balls, what is the probability of selecting 3 black balls on the first three draws if each ball drawn is *not* returned before the next is drawn?

8. Assuming the same circumstances as in question 6, what is the probability that the person will select a red, a white, and a black ball in that order?

9. Assuming the same circumstances as in question 7, if a person selected three balls just from the urn without returning one before drawing the next, what is the probability she will select a red, a white, and a black ball in that order?

10. The Friendly Finance Corporation has five employees; its offices are on the tenth floor of an office building. There are four elevators in the building that are all equally accessible. What is the probability that each of the five employees of the FFC took elevator number 1 to the offices on a particular morning?

11.5.3 The Restricted Disjunction Rule

All the situations that have been examined so far have involved conjunctions of simple outcomes—complex outcomes whose component outcomes have occurred jointly; that is, the complex outcome was said not to occur unless all of two or more specified outcomes occurred. Other complex outcomes are disjunctions; that is, they may be said to occur when at least one of several specified outcomes occurs. The simplest cases of disjoint outcomes are those in which all of the outcomes are mutually exclusive (i.e., when one occurs, it is impossible for the other(s) to occur).

The rule for calculating the probability of the occurrence of one or another of two or more mutually exclusive outcomes is called the **restricted disjunction rule.** It states that

> **If x and y are mutually exclusive outcomes, then**
> **P(x or y) = P(x) + P(y).**

If we are tossing a six-sided die, we might want to know the probability of getting a 3 *or* a 5 on a particular throw. Since both can't occur on a single throw, they are mutually exclusive. Given that the probability (on the classical theory) of each outcome is 1/6, the probability of getting one or the other is

$$P(3 \text{ or } 5) = P(3) + P(5) = 1/6 + 1/6 = 2/6 = 1/3.$$

Notice that the probability of joint, or conjunct, occurrences is calculated by *multiplying* the probability values of the component outcomes, whereas the probability of disjunct outcomes is calculated by *adding* their probability values. Notice also that the probability of the disjunction of a set of mutually exclusive outcomes cannot exceed 1. Thus, one way to determine whether a set of outcomes is mutually exclusive is to apply the restricted disjunction rule to the disjunction of the entire set of outcomes; if the result is greater than 1, the outcomes are not mutually exclusive.

EXERCISE 11–9

Calculate the probabilities for the following disjunctions of mutually exclusive outcomes, calculating the initial probabilities using the classical theory, when needed.

1. A six-sided die is tossed. What is the probability that it will turn up (a) either a 1 or a 2; (b) either a 1, a 2, or a 3?

2. A cloth sack contains 10 balls, each a different color. What is the probability that the first ball drawn from the sack will be a pink ball or a green ball?

3. Forty percent of the population of a town have gray hair, and 25 percent have blond hair. What is the probability that a randomly selected citizen of the town will have gray hair or blond hair?

4. It is agreed that there is 10 percent chance that the Red Sox will be the league champs this year and a 27 percent chance that the White Sox will be the league champs this year. What is the probability that either the Red Sox or the White Sox will be the league champs this year?

5. A cloth sack contains 10 balls, each a different color and one of which is red. What is the probability that the red ball will be drawn on at least one of the first three draws, if the first one drawn is returned before the second is drawn, and the second is returned before the third is drawn?

6. An urn contains 10 black balls, 5 white balls, 6 blue balls, 5 red balls, and 4 yellow balls. What is the probability that the first ball drawn will be either a white ball or a blue ball?

7. Two coins are flipped simultaneously. What is the probability that exactly one will come up heads?

11.5.4 The General Disjunction Rule

The components of a disjunction of outcomes need not be mutually exclusive; that is, it is possible for many outcomes to occur together. For example, getting a head on one toss of a coin does not make it impossible for the next toss to come up heads. So how do we compute the probability that at least one of two tosses of a coin will come up heads? Obviously, the restricted disjunction rule is inapplicable here. The probability of getting a head on one toss is 1/2, and the probability of getting a head on the second toss is also 1/2. Nevertheless, the probability of getting at least one head in two tries cannot be 1/2 + 1/2 = 1, or certainty, because it is possible to get tails on both tosses. The restricted disjunction rule does not work because the two outcomes are not mutually exclusive. It is possible that both tosses will give heads, or that neither will.

The **general disjunction rule** enables us to calculate the probability of the disjunction of *any* two or more outcomes—that is, it is not restricted to disjunctions of mutually exclusive outcomes. The rule states that

For any outcomes x and y, P(x or y) = P(x) + P(y) − P(x and y)

where P(x and y) can be determined using the general conjunction rule.

To illustrate, let us calculate the probability of either getting a head on the first toss of a coin or getting a head on the second toss of the coin. (The 'or' in the general disjunction rule, and in our example, is to be interpreted in the *inclusive* sense—that is, as 'either x or y *or both*.') Using the classical theory to establish the initial probabilities, we find that P(head on 1st toss) = 1/2 and P(head on 2nd toss) = 1/2. Since the two outcomes are independent, P(head on first toss and head on second toss) = 1/2 × 1/2 = 1/4 (by the general conjunction rule). Substituting these values in the general disjunction rule, we get:

P(head on 1st toss or head on 2nd toss) = 1/2 + 1/2 − 1/4 = 3/4.

This can be checked, using the classical theory, by noting that only four outcomes are possible for the two tosses: heads and heads, heads and tails, tails and heads, and tails and tails. Of the four outcomes, the first three satisfy the specification that at least one toss gives a head. Thus, assuming that all four are equally possible, the probability of obtaining at least one specified outcome is 3/4.

Notice that the restricted disjunction rule can be directly derived from the general rule, by virtue of the definition of mutually exclusive outcomes. Since two outcomes are mutually exclusive if and only if it is impossible for both to occur, it follows that for two mutually exclusive outcomes x and y, P(x and y) = 0. This, then, reduces the general rule to:

P(x or y) = P(x) + P(y) − 0

when x and y are mutually exclusive. And this, in turn, is equivalent to the restricted disjunction rule:

P(x or y) = P(x) + P(y).

For practice, let us consider a situation involving a jellybean fanatic confronted with two nontransparent bags containing jellybeans. One bag contains four green and four red; the other bag contains eight green and four red. If the jellybean addict takes one jellybean randomly from each of the two bags, what is the probability that at least one of the beans will be red? To apply the general disjunction rule, let us take x to be the outcome of drawing a red from the first bag, and take y to be the outcome of drawing a red from the second bag. Since the first bag has four red out of eight jellybeans, P(x) = 4/8 = 1/2. The second bag contains four red out of a total of twelve beans, so P(y) = 4/12 = 1/3. Since x and y are two independent outcomes, we can use the restricted conjunction rule:

P(red from 1st bag and red from 2nd bag)
  = P(red from 1st bag) × P(red from 2nd bag)
  = 1/2 × 1/3 = 1/6.

Applying the general disjunction rule with this value inserted, we have:

P(red from 1st bag or red from 2nd bag)
  = P(red from 1st bag) + P(red from 2nd bag) − P(red from 1st
  and red from 2nd)
  = 1/2 + 1/3 − 1/6 = 4/6 = 2/3.

EXERCISE 11–10

Calculate the probabilities for the following disjunct outcomes. Give the following information for each: (a) Are specified outcomes mutually exclusive? (b) What rule should be applied? (c) What is the initial probability of each specified outcome (calculated using the classical theory)? (d) Where relevant, what is the value of P(x and y)? (e) What is the probability of the disjunct outcome?

1. A six-sided die is tossed. What is the probability that it will turn up (a) either a one or a two? (b) either a one, a two, or a three?

2. One hundred people were asked to sample and rate a new food product. Sixty reported they liked it; 30 said they disliked it; 10 said they had no definite opinion. Two of these people will be randomly selected to do a more in-depth evaluation. What is the probability that at least one of them will be a person who disliked the product?

3. Forty percent of the population of a town have gray hair, and 25 percent have blue eyes. Fifteen percent have both. What is the probability that a randomly selected citizen of the town will have gray hair or blue eyes?

4. In a group of 100 people, 70 are men, and 20 of them smoke. Of the 30 women, 5 smoke. What is the probability that a randomly selected individual will be a woman or a smoker?

5. An urn contains 10 black balls, 5 white balls, 6 blue balls, 5 red balls, and 4 yellow balls. What is the probability that the first ball drawn will be either a white ball or a blue ball?

6. Two coins are flipped simultaneously. What is the probability that both will come up heads or both will come up tails?

7. If the probability that a ten-year-old boy will survive to his twentieth birthday is 97/100 and the probability that his five-year-old sister will survive to her twentieth birthday is 96/100, what is the probability that at least one will survive to age 20?

8. Urn 1 contains 30 balls, of which 10 are black, 10 are white, and 10 are red. Urn 2 contains 30 balls, of which 5 are black, 15 are white, and 10 are red. If one ball is drawn from urn 1, and one ball is drawn from urn 2, what is the probability that at least one of them will be black?

9. Assuming the same circumstances as in question 6, what is the probability that at least one of the balls drawn will be red?

10. An urn contains 50 balls, of which 15 are black, 5 are white, 20 are red, and 10 are yellow. If one ball is selected at random, what is the probability that (a) it will be either white or black? (b) it will be either red or yellow? (c) it will be either black or yellow?

11. Seventy percent of all college students listen to music at a volume that carries easily through the walls in Jackie's apartment complex. At the beginning of the semester, new students moved into the apartments on both sides of Jackie's. What is the probability that Jackie will hear at least one of the new neighbors' music?

12. Jackie finds only 1 percent of all members of the opposite sex to be attractive. Jackie is having two blind dates this weekend. What is the probability that Jackie will find at least one attractive?

11.5.5 Combining the Rules

We must use both conjunction and disjunction rules for calculating the probabilities of some complex outcomes. We will consider just one example to provide at least a brief idea of how this can be done. Assume that we have a cloth bag containing forty beans: 10 red, 10 green, 10 yellow, and 10 black. What is the probability that we will get 5 beans of any one color on the first five tries? The four mutually exclusive specified alternatives here are getting 5 red beans, or 5 green beans, or 5 yellow beans, or 5 black beans. The initial probability of the choice of a red bean, on the classical theory, is 10/40, since there are 10 red among the total of 40 beans. Assuming that the first one chosen is red, there are now 39 beans left from which to choose, only 9 of which represent the specified outcome of another red. So the probability of getting a red on the second draw, after having gotten a red on the first choice, is 9/39. After this there are only 38 beans left, 8 of which are red. Therefore, the probability of getting a red on the third try if the first and second have yielded red is 8/38; the probability of getting a red on the next try is 7/37; and the probability on the fifth try, assuming success in the four previous trials, is 6/36. According to the general conjunction rule, the probability of getting five beans of one particular flavor thus equals:

P(5 beans of one flavor) = 10/40 × 9/39 × 8/38 × 7/37 × 6/36
   = 30,240 / 78,960,960.

Since the other three specified alternatives are mutually exclusive (and are being assumed to be all equally probable), the restricted disjunction rule can be used to calculate the probability of getting five beans of any one color:

P(5 red beans or 5 green or 5 yellow or 5 cinnamon)
   = 30,240/78,960,960 + 30,240/78,960,960
      + 30,240/78,960,960 + 30,240/78,960,960
   = 120,960/78,960,960

In conclusion, it must be emphasized that the preceding discussion barely scratches the surface of the basic subject matter of probability. Not only have we omitted several significant theories concerning the meaning of, and methods for establishing, initial probabilities, but the three theories we have discussed have been presented only in simplified form, with no treatment of the numerous variations of each of the general types. Similarly, we have described only a few of the most basic and simple concepts and rules of the probability calculus. A full treatment of the probability calculus (even without discussion of the alternative techniques for establishing initial probability) would require a whole book.

EXERCISE 11–11

The following problems require the use of more than one method. Give the following information for each: (a) Are specified outcomes mutually exclusive?

(b) What rule should be applied? (c) What is the initial probability of each specified outcome (calculated using the classical theory)? (d) Where relevant, what is the value of P(x and y)? (e) What is the probability of the disjunct outcome?

1. Three six-sided dice are tossed on a single throw. What is the probability of (a) three 2s; (b) either three 2s or three 3s?

2. Four cards are dealt from a well-shuffled deck without a joker. What is the probability of getting an ace, a king, a queen, and a Jack (a) in spades, in the order given; (b) in any one suit, in the order given; (c) in spades, in any order?

3. A coin purse contains two dimes and three nickels. If you reach in to get change to buy a newspaper, what is the probability that (a) the first two coins you draw out will add up to fifteen cents; (b) the first three coins you draw out will add up to fifteen cents; (c) you will get fifteen cents on either the first two or the first three draws?

4. The winning combination in a certain lottery consists of five numbers, between 0 and 9, in any order. No number may be repeated. If Jorge bought one ticket each week for two weeks, what is the probability that he won exactly once?

5. Sheila has entered a lottery in which the winning number consists of four integers, each between 0 and 9, in a particular order. What is the chance that she will either guess all four numbers correctly or guess all four incorrectly?

6. Jo, Pat, Toby, and Mel all enter a lottery in which the winning number is comprised of five numbers, 0 to 29, in any order. No number may be repeated. What is the chance that (a) all four of them will win? (b) exactly three (any three) of them will win? (c) Pat and Mel will win? (d) Pat or Mel will win?

Summary

1. An adequate theory of probability must satisfy at least two requirements. First, a statement that is absolutely true has a probability of 1, while a statement that is absolutely false has a probability of 0, and any statement that is neither absolutely true nor absolutely false has a probability between 0 and 1. A second requirement is that the sum of the probabilities of any logically inconsistent statements (that is, statements not more than one of which can be true at any given time) must be no greater than 1.

2. The **classical theory,** or **a priori theory,** of probability is based on two assumptions. The first is that all possible outcomes are known. The second, called the **principle of indifference,** is that the probability of the occurrence of each outcome is equal to that of the others, unless there is good reason to believe otherwise. The probability that a specified outcome will occur is

determined by dividing the number of possible specified outcomes by the total number of equally possible outcomes. This theory cannot be used when statistical or other evidence indicates that not all possible outcomes are equally probable.

3. All of the several versions of the **relative frequency theory** are based on the direct observation of concrete cases. This theory stipulates that the probability of an outcome is determined by dividing the number of observed specified outcomes by the total number of observed outcomes. One difficulty with most versions of this theory is that of dealing with cases in which no observations have been made of the specified outcome. Another problem with most relative frequency theories stems from their assertion that probabilities based on observations of past cases are applicable to future cases only in the long run. That is, it is improper, or sometimes even meaningless, to assign a probability value to a single outcome.

4. The **subjectivist theory** defines probabilities as being grounded in the beliefs of individual persons. Thus, a variety of different probabilities can be assigned to the same particular outcome. Opponents claim that this is a fatal criticism, but supporters of the theory see it as a strength. This method most closely resembles the way in which many people actually calculate probabilities in everyday life.

5. The procedures for determining the probabilities of compound outcomes have been codified in a formal axiom system known as the **probability calculus.** The **initial probability,** determined by one of the above theories, is the probability of a single outcome's occurring by itself.

6. A **complex outcome** is a whole composed of a number of simple outcomes. **Independent** outcomes are such that the occurrence of one has no effect on the occurrence of the other(s); that is, if one outcome occurs, the probability of the occurrence of the other outcome(s) is not changed. **Dependent** outcomes are such that one affects the circumstances of the other(s) in such a way that, if one occurs, the probability of the other(s) occurring is no longer what it would have been if the first outcome had not occurred. **Mutually exclusive outcomes** are such that only one can occur.

7. The **restricted conjunction rule** states that if x and y are independent outcomes, then the probability of both x and y occurring is equal to the probability of x occurring multiplied by the probability of y occurring.

8. The **general conjunction rule** is used to calculate probability values of the joint occurrence of a number of simple outcomes (whether dependent or independent). This rule states that if x and y are any two outcomes whatever, then the probability of their joint occurrence is equal to the probability of x occurring multiplied by the probability of y occurring, given that x has already occurred. The restricted conjunction rule can be derived from

the general conjunction rule, since if x and y are independent outcomes, then the probability of y, given that x has already occurred, is the same as the probability of y itself.

9. There are some complex outcomes that are disjunctions—those that can be said to occur when one or more of several alternative outcomes occur. The **restricted disjunction rule** is used to calculate the probability of the occurrence of one or another of two or more mutually exclusive outcomes. This rule states that if x and y are mutually exclusive outcomes, then the probability that at least one of them will occur is equal to the probability of x plus the probability of y.

10. The **general disjunction rule** is used to calculate the probability of the disjunction of any two or more outcomes whatsoever; it is not restricted to disjunctions of mutually exclusive outcomes. This rule states that, for any two outcomes x and y, the probability that at least one will occur is equal to the sum of the initial probabilities of x and y minus the probability that both x and y will occur (the probability that both will occur is calculated by the general conjunction rule). The restricted disjunction rule can be derived from the general disjunction rule, since, for mutually exclusive outcomes, the probability that both will occur is 0.

Chapter 12

Informal Fallacies

It was explained in Chapter 2 that a good argument must satisfy three conditions:

1. **It must be valid or, if it is an inductive argument, the premises must provide a reasonable amount of support for the conclusion.**
2. **The truth of the premises must be well established.**
3. **It must not be circular.**

Chapters 3 through 11 present rather rigorous formal procedures, usually grounded on precisely defined concepts, for determining the validity or inductive strength (or weakness) of certain kinds of argument. However, such sophisticated techniques are not always necessary, or even adequate, for identifying many of the bad arguments each of us encounters frequently in everyday life. In this chapter we discuss a variety of kinds of bad argument that can be recognized as such with relatively little reliance on the methods of formal logic.

Logicians traditionally have used the term 'fallacy' as a synonym for 'bad reasoning.' Although some arguments are so blatantly fallacious that at most they can be used to amuse us, many are more subtle and can be difficult to recognize. A conclusion often appears to follow logically and nontrivially from true premises, and only careful examination can reveal the fallaciousness of the argument. This chapter is concerned with such deceptively fallacious arguments, which are often accepted as good by persons in everyday situations—fallacies that are used, knowingly or unknowingly, by writers, advertisers, politicians, lawyers, and all those whose goal is to persuade an audience to accept their conclusions. Such deceptively fallacious arguments, which can be recognized as such with little or no reliance on the methods of formal logic, are known as **informal fallacies.** Logicians and others have identified or defined literally hundreds of informal fallacies in the twenty-three hundred years since

Aristotle wrote the first treatise on logic. We will be able to present here only a small, though representative, sampling of some of the kinds of informal fallacy.

12.1 Disguised Nonarguments

We shall begin by examining several patterns that are commonly used to disguise sets of statements that do not in fact constitute arguments at all, but appear to the casual reader or listener to be arguments. Once you learn these general patterns, it is less likely that you will be taken in by instances of them in everyday contexts.

12.1.1 Begging the Question

As explained in Chapter 2, any argument that is circular is by definition valid—but it is also a bad argument. It was also pointed out that it is difficult, if not impossible, to provide a definition that does not include valid arguments in the class of circular arguments, since one of the features of a valid argument is that its conclusion must be contained in its premises. It was suggested that the definition of 'circular argument' must refer to psychological facts about the knowledge and beliefs of the hearer (or reader) of the argument rather than to any formal features of the argument itself. That is, an argument is circular *if, for its intended audience, the conclusion is merely a restatement of something explicitly stated in the premises.* Any argument that is bad because it is circular is said to commit the fallacy of **begging the question,** or **petitio principii.** It is worth our while to look at several examples of this kind of fallacious reasoning.

Begging the question frequently follows a more circuitous pattern than in the example given in Chapter 2, and is then more aptly called a circular argument. For instance, someone might contend that public television is better than commercial television, the proof being that more-intelligent people prefer it. And when questioned about how it is known that those who watch public television are more intelligent, he or she may reply that they are recognizable by their good taste and critical alertness, and then define people of good taste and critical alertness as those who appreciate the sort of program shown on public television.

> If people with above-average intelligence prefer A over B, then A is better than B.
> People who watch public television are people with good taste and critical alertness.
> People who have good taste and critical alertness are above-average in intelligence.
> People with above-average intelligence prefer public television to commercial television.
> Therefore, public television is better than commercial television.

Reprinted by permission of UFS, Inc.

Although sometimes a circular argument is explicitly circular, it usually involves some attempt to disguise the circularity. The most common method for disguising the circularity is the use of synonyms for key components of the argument. This manner of disguise is used by Lucy in her analysis of the "causes" of Charlie Brown's problem. She does not really provide a causal argument concerning Charlie's problem because the purported causes (weaknesses and failings) are essentially the same things.

The longer the circular argument, the more chance there is that the listener will lose track and be fooled into accepting the conclusion as having been proved true. Such was the strategy effectively employed by Ernst Huber, Nazi political scientist and prolific spokesman for Hitler:

> The Führer is the bearer of the people's will; he is independent of all groups, associations, and interests, but he is bound by laws which are inherent in the nature of his people. . . . The Führer is no representative of a particular group whose wishes he must carry out. . . . He is . . . himself the bearer of the collective will of the people. In his will the will of the people is realized. He transforms the mere feelings of the people into a conscious will. . . . Thus it is possible for him, in the name of the true will of the people which he serves, to go against the subjective opinions and convictions of single individuals within the people if these are not in accord with the objective destiny of the people . . . . He shapes the collective will of the people within himself.[1]

The point is made, but where is the proof? It clearly does not lie in repeating the same thing a half dozen times or more, which is all Huber has really done. In a sense, such a question-begging "argument" as this is not really an argument; it is at best a belabored exposition. But, as history has shown, such nonarguments can be very persuasive.

In brief, "arguments" that commit the fallacy of begging the question are not really arguments at all. They are essentially repetitions of the same

[1]Quoted in Raymond E. Murphy, Francis B. Stevens, Howard Rivers, and Joseph M. Roland, *National Socialism: Basic Principles, Their Application by the Nazi Party's Foreign Organization and the Use of Germans Abroad for Nazi Aims.* U.S. Government Printing Office, 1943, pp. 34–35.

statement often involving an attempt to disguise this fact by expressing the statement using different sentences, all of which express the same thought.

12.1.2 Fallacy of Equivocation

The fallacy of **equivocation** involves disguising a nonargument as an argument using the opposite method of the fallacy of begging the question. Instead of using different words or expressions that have the same meaning, this fallacy *uses the same word which has two or more different meanings in the context of a single argument.* Once the difference in meanings is made explicit, what looks on the surface to be a real argument can be seen for what it actually is— a disguised nonargument.

The fallacy of equivocation is totally dependent on a particular word or set of words having two or more quite different meanings in the context of a single argument as in the following example:

> **Man is an inventor.**
> **No woman is a man.**
> **Therefore, no woman is an inventor.**

The argument appears on the surface to be valid, in part because the repetition of the word 'man' seems to provide a logical link between the two premises. Both premises even seem plausible, so the argument is possibly sound. How, then, could the conclusion possibly be false? The answer is that the word 'man' is used with quite different meanings in the two premises of the argument. 'Man' means 'mankind' or 'the human species' in the first premise; it means 'member of the male sex' in the second. Both meanings are legitimate, but they are not interchangeable.

Some examples of the fallacy of equivocation are patently absurd, such as the following:

> **Somebody arrived at the party at six o'clock.**
> **Somebody left the party at nine o'clock.**
> **Therefore, somebody stayed at the party for three hours.**

The fallacy here lies in ambiguous use of the word 'somebody.' The appearance of validity in this example rests on the false assumption that the term 'somebody' refers to the same person each time it is used.

It is not always as easy to identify a word or phrase being used equivocally as in the preceding examples. Equivocation is often concealed in the manipulation of statistics, as in the following example (which has been made up solely for illustrative purposes here):

> **The war against crime has been highly successful in some areas of the nation. The increase in the number of crimes in Gotham City in 1993 was well below the increase in 1992. In 1992, the number of crimes**

> increased 50 percent over 1991. In 1993, the number increased only 33.3 percent over 1992.

Mathematical substitution can be used to demonstrate that the conclusion cannot be drawn from the facts asserted in the premises. If, for example, there were 1,000 crimes in 1991 and the number of crimes increased by 50 percent in 1992, then there were 1,500 crimes in 1992. If that number increased by 33.3 percent in 1993, there were 2,000 crimes that year. Thus the number of crimes in 1993 increased by 500, just as it did in 1992. The equivocation in this example turns on the false assumption that the phrase '50 percent increase in crime' refers to a larger number than the phrase '33.3 percent increase in crime,' when in fact the two phrases both refer to the same quantity—namely, 500.

A final common form of the fallacy of equivocation involves the use of relative terms—terms of degree that have different meanings in different contexts. All terms that imply a degree of quantitative measurement such as 'heavy,' 'small,' and 'major,' can be sources of equivocation. No one hesitates to pick up a heavy baby on the ground, but it is impossible to lift a heavy car, because we know that 'heavy' means something different when it describes a baby than when it describes a car. But reports of a heavy snowfall in Atlanta might deter a New Englander from driving there until she learned that 'heavy' in the South might mean 'two inches.' Similarly, the fallacy of equivocation can result from imprecise use of such words as 'good,' 'bad,' and 'difficult.' For instance, some people argue that good laws make good citizens, or that a student who is bad in science is a bad student.

The important lesson to be learned from this and similar fallacies is that what sometimes *appears* to be an inductively strong or even valid argument, and what can even be proved to be valid using the techniques of formal logic, is sometimes not even an argument due to the ambiguities inherent in natural languages. We must always be alert for fallacies such as these. Let us now look briefly at a similar fallacy that underlies what appears to be a valid argument.

12.1.3 Fallacy of Amphiboly

An amphibolous statement contains imprecise grammar or syntax that permits two or more interpretations, only one of which is accurate. Dangling modifiers often produce amphiboly, as in the following example;

> The film is about a real person, Frank Serpico, who deals with equally real corruption in the New York City Police Department, and was shot this summer in New York, with full cooperation from the city and the police department.[2]

The fallacy of **amphiboly** occurs *when a person attempts to support a conclusion using a faulty interpretation of a grammatically ambiguous statement.* If

[2]Quoted in *The New Yorker*, Dec. 3, 1973, p. 53. Originally published in the Long Beach (Calif.) *Independent Press-Telegram.* (*The New Yorker*'s comment: "You can't fight City Hall.")

a reader of this movie review concluded that the "real person" Serpico was shot with a gun as part of some official plot, his error would have resulted from the amphiboly of the review.

The real issue with amphiboly—as also with equivocation—is not erroneous reasoning, but erroneous interpretation of arguments presented in informal everyday contexts. Modern advertising is filled with examples of ambiguous statements that the advertiser has intentionally designed to be easily misinterpreted by consumers. For instance, an advertisement might claim that the product comes with a "lifetime guarantee." The consumer assumes that the

"I always promise them the good life. They always re-elect me
and that's exactly what I get — the good life."

Reprinted courtesy of The Boston Globe.

Although it may be debatable whether the politician in this cartoon committed the fallacy of equivocation or the fallacy of amphiboly, it is certainly clear that he intentionally deceived his constituents in his choice of wording for his campaign pledge.

product is guaranteed for as long as she lives, whereas a careful reading of the small print reveals that the guarantee actually refers to the life of the product. Likewise, the manufacturer who claims that "nine out of ten doctors recommend the pain-relieving ingredients in our product" hopes that the consumer will misinterpret the statement to mean "nine out of every ten doctors recommend our product," rather than that they recommend the ingredients—which also are contained in most of the competing brands.

It is sometimes difficult to determine whether a particular bad argument involves the fallacy of amphiboly or the fallacy of equivocation. Take, for instance, the classic tale of Croesus, King of Lydia, who asked the oracle if he could be assured of victory in going to war with Persia. When the oracle replied, "You will destroy a great kingdom," Croesus confidently set off to war, only to learn in the end that the great kingdom to be destroyed was his own. Clearly, he was a victim of fallacious reasoning based on some kind of misinterpretation; but it is not clear whether it rested on the ambiguity in the term 'great kingdom' (in which case it would be the fallacy of equivocation) or on the ambiguity of the entire sentence (in which case it would be the fallacy of amphiboly). For practical purposes (other than taking a logic exam!), what is important is that you are able to recognize that the reasoning is fallacious, even if you can't decide precisely which fallacy it commits.

12.1.4 The Straw Person Fallacy

One of the most commonly used ways of attacking an individual's position on a given matter is to interpret (or perhaps misinterpret) the person's statements in such a way as to make them most susceptible to attack and criticism. In other words, the strategy is to set up what can be called a "straw" person, who can be knocked down much more easily than the "real" person, and who can be counted on not to fight back. In effect, this fallacy is the exact opposite of the principle of charity, the use of which has been advocated throughout this book. Whenever we interpret an opponent's argument in a less than sympathetic way, we are quite possibly committing the **straw person fallacy.** This is a tactic used widely in political campaigns and debates, but it can also be found in advertising and other contexts.

Strictly speaking, the straw person fallacy is not a disguised nonargument; it only occurs when one is purporting to give a counterargument to another argument that has already been given. It might in fact be an argument, even a sound argument, but it does not provide any actual support for the conclusion that some particular other argument is bad. People commit this fallacy to disguise the fact that their counterexamples do not apply to the arguments at which they are targeted.

One of the basic ways of committing the straw person fallacy is to reduce a relatively complex argument to excessively simple form, in the process leaving out some of its key elements. For example, in some recent controversies over the requirements of social order and public safety versus the constitutional rights of prisoners and arrested persons, liberals have sometimes accused conservatives of favoring a repressive police state, while conservatives have accused liberals of wanting to turn hordes of dangerous criminals loose on unprotected communities. Both groups have thus distorted and caricatured the real arguments of their opponents, and have then gone on to refute these "straw" arguments which no one really supports. In doing so, both have avoided coming to grips with the real complexity of the problem and with the many arguments that can reasonably be offered pro and con.

In summary, we are committing the straw person fallacy any time we fail to adhere to the principle of charity in evaluating an argument. We should always make sure, before branding an argument as fallacious, that we have interpreted it in the most favorable way possible, or else we shall be reasoning fallaciously ourselves.

12.1.5 Fallacy of the Irrelevant Conclusion

A young woman has fallen in love with a young man whose family is involved in a long-standing feud with her family. When her father forbids her to see the young man, she passionately defends her love. She argues that although the families have long been enemies, she and her beloved are not. Indeed, they believe they can stop the feud, by marrying and showing their parents that such fighting is unnecessary. When she finishes, her father looks at her coldly and says, "But his grandfather embezzled money from our family's business, and the resulting bankruptcy caused your grandfather to have his fatal heart attack." The father's response is a clear example of the fallacy of **irrelevant conclusion.** He offers as "proof" that his daughter's position is wrong, evidence that actually establishes another conclusion—one that is psychologically related to, but does not refute, the one in question. The young woman argues that feuds are wrong, that she and the young man have no quarrel with each other, and that therefore they should be allowed to marry. Her father cites the bankruptcy of the family business and the death of her grandfather, implicitly concluding that it is justification for continuing the feud into the third generation. Even if this were so, the father has made no attempt to answer the argument that the feud is unnecessary, nor has he really given an argument as to why the two young people should not marry.

Courtroom lawyers sometimes argue toward irrelevant conclusions because, if delivered passionately and cleverly, such arguments are often much more compelling than the relevant ones; they can also be used to obscure the lack of pertinent evidence. In particular, prosecuting attorneys commonly exploit this fallacy to divert a jury's attention from the weakness of evidence of the guilt of the defendant by focusing on photos and other evidence of the brutality of the crime. Many jurors obviously will be impressed by such facts, although the information is not relevant for determining whether the person on trial is the one who actually committed the crime in question.

EXERCISE 12–1

Determine which fallacy is committed in each of the following disguised arguments.

1. The reviewer said that the cooking in this restaurant was especially well done, but he was wrong. I've never seen such a rare steak as this one.

2. They want someone to fill potholes in the office of the Department of Highways. I think I'll apply for the job. I like to work indoors.

3. Allowing people to compete is a necessary condition for high achievement in our society. The technical and economic progress of our free enterprise system is unique in the history of the world and would not be possible without the advances motivated by competition.

4. Tom is a very heavy smoker, so he'd better not sit in that chair—it's not strong enough to hold anything heavy.

5. Diabetics should avoid things containing large amounts of sugar. Sugar maple trees are things containing large amounts of sugar. Therefore, diabetics should avoid sugar maple trees.

6. There is no reason to enact new inheritance laws. The advocates of new inheritance laws believe that without laws to prevent children from inheriting their parents' money and property, we will, in a few generations, have a society in which people no longer work, based on the assumption that it is economic pressure that motivates people to work, and there is no economic pressure on a person who has inherited more money than he or she will ever need. And clearly this assumption is false.

7. Everyone must be allowed to speak his or her mind, because otherwise freedom of speech would be violated.

8. [A college debate team member arguing against legalization of marijuana.] The only possible justification its proponents can give for legalizing marijuana is that marijuana laws cannot be absolutely enforced. Obviously this is a very weak argument, since no one claims that any law can be absolutely enforced.

9. All people who like the novels of Emily Brontë are persons with excellent literary taste, since persons with excellent literary taste are persons who like Emily Brontë's novels.

10. He sent money to Somalia because the people there were starving, so he should send us money, too, because we are always starving by the time dinner is finally on the table.

11. Jogging is a better exercise than walking. The proof of this fact is that joggers are more energetic people than walkers. And the proof of *this* fact is that the joggers go jogging, while the walkers only walk.

12. The dance critic says Jones is very good. So Jones must be a very good person.

13. Gruber's argument begins with the premise, 'Cats are hairy animals.' But this statement does not take into account that a few cats have no hair at all. So Gruber's first premise is false and his argument is therefore unsound.

12.2 Valid but Fallacious Arguments

Arguments that are invalid can be determined to be so using one or more of the formal methods presented in Chapters 4, 6, and 8. As mentioned in Chapter 2 and demonstrated in some detail in Chapter 14, almost any argument (that is real, not disguised as real) can be treated as an enthymeme and reformulated as a valid (that is, deductive) argument. But in putting it into deductive form, we must often add premises that are highly questionable, if not blatantly false. The fallacies discussed in the remainder of this chapter are commonly found in a variety of everyday contexts.

A single basic method can be used in evaluating all fallacies involving real arguments (as opposed to disguised nonarguments). This method involves first determining that there is a real argument, which means that we must check to see that none of the fallacies discussed previously in this chapter are being committed. Once we have confirmed that we are dealing with a real argument, then we must add whatever premises are needed to make the argument valid. Then we must check the premises to determine whether any of them are highly questionable or blatantly false. Since fallacious arguments usually appear at first glance to be relatively good, the problematic premise is usually one that was not explicitly stated in the original presentation of the argument. Each of the fallacies to be discussed in the remainder of the chapter involves the use of particular suppressed premises.

12.2.1 Argument from Ignorance

Many people accept the argument that because no "hard" scientific proof has been given for the phenomenon of psychokinesis, or the ability to move physical objects with no devices or assistance other than one's mind, it does not exist. That is, they make their inability to verify the phenomenon a justification for labeling all claims of its occurrence as false. In doing so they are using a fallacious mode of argument called **argumentum ad ignorantiam,** or **argument from ignorance.**

The fact that a proposition has not been conclusively proved to be true or false establishes nothing but one's inability to prove or disprove it. In the case of our example, new methods are regularly being devised to test psychokinesis, and there may one day be sufficient data to formulate a sound argument for or against its existence. Until then, the reasonable way of arguing about it is to say that existing evidence has not conclusively proved anything one way or the other.

In its basic form, an *argumentum ad ignorantiam* requires use of a premise similar to the following statement:

> **If there is no evidence (or proof) that it is the case that X, then it is the case that not-X.**

By substituting 'cigarette smoking causes cancer' for 'X,' we produce the following argument:

> **There is no proof that cigarette smoking causes cancer.**
> **Therefore, cigarette smoking does not cause cancer.**

This argument is invalid as it stands, for the conclusion could be false even though the premise is true. In fact, the truth of the premise is itself somewhat open to debate, since some people (for example, the surgeon general) assert that it has been proved that smoking causes cancer, whereas others (for example, presidents of tobacco companies) deny this. For the purpose of this discussion, it is sufficient that the premise might be true. In any case, it is not unreasonable to treat the argument as an enthymeme and add a premise that makes it valid, as follows:

> **If there is no proof that something is the case, then that something is in fact not the case.**
> **There is no proof that cigarette smoking causes cancer.**
> **Therefore, cigarette smoking does not cause cancer.**

Although the argument is now clearly valid, the added premise is far from being obviously true. In fact, it is highly questionable, and might be downright false. Notice that the weakness of the argument now rests in this questionable premise rather than in the validity of the argument.

Some arguments can appear on the surface to commit the *ad ignorantiam* fallacy, but on closer inspection can be seen to be legitimate. In particular, certain inductive arguments are quite good, even though they appear to have the same form as an *ad ignorantiam* fallacy:

> **Every possible attempt has been made to prove that such-and-such is the case.**
> **Not one attempt to prove that such-and-such is the case has been successful.**
> **Therefore, it is probable that such-and-such is not the case.**

This is essentially the type of reasoning that some physicists used at the end of the nineteenth century in arriving at the conclusion that a gravitational aether does not exist. It is probably also the kind of reasoning that led to the demise of alchemy. The conclusion that a base metal, such as lead, probably cannot be turned into gold was not unreasonable in the seventeenth or eighteenth centuries, even though present-day theories indicate that such a transmutation might be at least theoretically possible. In any case, when confronted with an argument that appears to involve the *ad ignorantiam* fallacy, we should make sure that it cannot reasonably be interpreted as being a possibly good inductive argument.

12.2.2 False Dilemma

A fallacy that is often very convincing when used in public debates is the **false dilemma,** which consists of presenting an argument as if there were fewer possible solutions of the problem than is actually the case. Usually only two alternatives are offered, in an either/or fashion. For example:

> **If the new highway is built along the recommended route, the park will be destroyed.**
> **If it is built along the alternate route, a residential neighborhood will be destroyed.**
> **It must be built along either one route or the other.**
> **Therefore either the park or a residential neighborhood will be destroyed.**

This argument is formally valid. If the premises are true, the conclusion must also be true. But it is probable that the either/or premise is not true. Very likely, other possible routes for the highway exist that would destroy neither park nor homes. Or, possibly, the highway might not be built at all (which might be precisely what the speaker of the above argument is trying to accomplish). If there are in fact such other alternatives, the argument as given above commits the fallacy of false dilemma.

Let's consider one more example:

> **Either coal miners work, inhale coal dust, and develop black-lung disease, or they don't work and can't earn any money.**
> **They must earn money.**
> **Therefore, they must develop black-lung disease.**

Again, this argument is formally valid. But the 'Either . . . or . . .' statement is false, for, although miners can indeed develop black-lung disease as a consequence of inhaling coal dust, it is not necessary for them to inhale the dust. The use of proper safety equipment in the mines can prevent it. Thus, again, the two alternatives offered are not the only options, and the dilemma is a false one; other conditions exist under which miners can both earn money and avoid contracting an incurable disease.

© 1979 Jules Feiffer.

The executive in this cartoon commits the fallacy of false dilemma. Explain what is wrong with his formulation of the alternative courses of action.

Actually, true either/or situations are rare in the real world, and whenever a speaker, columnist, lobbyist, or advertiser confronts us with one we would do well to examine it carefully. Unless one alternative is a direct contradiction of the other ('either X or not-X'), there are probably other choices available—choices that the arguer does not want to make explicit.

Dilemmas—false or legitimate—do not always have to be simple either/or problems; they sometimes are quite complex, as in the item at the left. What makes a dilemma fallacious is the implicit suggestion that all of the options are listed, when in fact one or more are not given. This example is fallacious. Can you identify some of the omitted options?

12.2.3 Fallacy of False Cause

A person who lives in an apartment with damp walls and roaches might conclude that damp walls cause roaches or that roaches cause damp walls, but no proof has been offered for either contention. Republicans claim that the Democrats cause wars, and Democrats say that the Republicans cause depressions. All that is known for certain is that Democratic presidents were in office when two world wars broke out, and that Republican presidents were in office when two major depressions occurred. These are examples of one of another common fallacy, the fallacy of **false cause.**

Many difficulties surround the entire concept of causality, some of which are outlined in Chapter 10. Still, it is easy enough to recognize that the conjunction in space and time of two events or states of affairs is not sufficient to establish the existence of a causal relation between them. Coincidences do happen, and one must not draw the conclusion that, just because something occurs in time after something else, the earlier was the cause of the later.

This fallacy can be formulated as involving inductive arguments whose premises provide little support for their conclusions, although at first glance the argument might appear strong. However, it can be formulated as a valid argument—with an obviously false premise—as follows:

> **Any event that immediately precedes another event is the cause or part of the cause of that event.**
> **Event X immediately preceded event Y.**
> **Therefore, event X is the cause of event Y.**

Thus, as with arguments in general, this kind can be formulated as both an inductive and a deductive argument, and the addition of the premise(s) necessary to make it valid makes the weakness of this argument obvious.

12.2.4 Fallacy of Hasty Generalization

The fallacy of **hasty generalization** involves forming a generalization from a sample that is too small or poorly selected, thus allowing the possibility that all the cases might be exceptional rather than typical. The basic premise necessary to make valid an argument committing the fallacy of hasty generalization is the following statement, which is certainly less than plausible:

> **If something is true of a few things of a certain kind, then it is true of all things of that kind.**

This, at best, defines a very weak form of inductive argument as discussed in Chapter 2.

Formal criteria for constructing good generalizations are spelled out in some detail in Chapter 9, but there are several informal commonsense rules that we all recognize and use regularly in everyday situations. The most obvious is that, to make a reasonably safe generalization and avoid the fallacy of hasty generalization, it is necessary to collect enough data about the matter at hand to distinguish the typical from the accidental.

The Irish poet W. B. Yeats and many of his friends and colleagues were agnostics and admirers of the aristocracy, but their case cannot be used to generalize about all Irish people. Yeats and his circle were a small minority and were thus exceptions, not the rule. Most of the Irish were then, as now, Catholic and republican. To generalize about the Irish on the basis of what one knows about Yeats would be "jumping to a conclusion" on the basis of inadequate evidence. This type of fallacious thinking characterizes many forms of prejudice: Poles are stupid; Jews are avaricious; Latin lovers are sexy; women are catty; and so on.

Our tendency to make hasty generalizations is at least partially psychologically grounded. Researchers have compiled much evidence that people tend to seek out examples that reinforce their beliefs. The old woman who is mugged by a young Puerto Rican male—even if she is a liberal old woman—is likely afterward to be particularly alert to other examples of crimes committed by young Puerto Rican males, which then tend to support her conviction that all young Puerto Rican males are dangerous lawbreakers. But the fact—if it is a fact—that we tend to think in this way provides little if any justification for assuming that this is a good way to reason.

There is a certain similarity between the fallacies of false cause and hasty generalization, insofar as both involve going from an observation to a conclusion that simply has little support from that observation. The two fallacies can be easily distinguished if we are careful to determine which premise must be added to make the argument valid. Another way of keeping the two fallacies separate is to recognize that the conclusion of an argument involving the fallacy of false cause must explicitly assert that something is *the cause* of something else, while the conclusion of an argument committing the fallacy of hasty generalization must explicitly assert that *all* things of a certain kind have a specific characteristic (but it does not assert anything about a causal relation).

12.2.5 Fallacy of Composition

The fallacy of **composition** is sometimes confused with the fallacy of hasty generalization, although it is actually quite different. It does not involve generalizing from a few members of a group to all of the other members of the group. Rather, it involves an inference from something that is already known to be true of each of the members of the group to a conclusion concerning the group itself. The fallacy of composition has two distinct forms.

One form of the fallacy of composition looks like this:

> **Each part or component of object X has property A.**
> **If all the parts or components of an object have a property, then the object has that property.**
> **Therefore, object X has property A.**

The error in this form of the fallacy occurs when a person falsely argues that a whole (considered as a single entity) has a certain characteristic because each of its parts has that characteristic. Thus, a person would commit the fallacy of composition by concluding that, since each pane of glass in a geodesic dome is a two-dimensional triangle, the dome itself must be a two-dimensional triangle. The fact is that a geodesic dome is spherical (and thus also three-dimensional).

The second version of the fallacy of composition has the following form:

All members of group X have property A.
If all the members of a group have a property, then the group has that
**   property.**
Therefore, group X has property A.

For example, it would be fallacious to argue that if each individual member of an orchestra is an excellent musician, the orchestra will play excellently. The fallacy arises from taking an attribute common to all the members and assuming that it is a characteristic of the group, in a situation in which the group operates under some principle different from that of the members. Thus, the orchestra operates under a number of principles that do not reflect the skill of the individual members, such as the ability of the musicians to play together and the competence of the conductor.

We can understand this fallacy better if we make a distinction between the distributive and collective uses of general terms. A word is used in its distributive sense when it refers to properties possessed by the individual members of a collection. When it refers to a property possessed by the totality of members of a collection, it is being used in its collective sense. For example, every feather is light, but it is obviously erroneous to conclude that a ton of feathers is light. The fallacy here arises from applying a distributive concept to a collective entity. Each feather is distributively light, but a ton of feathers is not collectively light.

12.2.6 Fallacy of Division

The fallacy of **division** is the opposite of the fallacy of composition, in that it involves an inference from something that is known to be true of a group or entity to a conclusion concerning each member or component. Its valid form also includes a highly questionable, if not blatantly false, premise.

X has property A.
If some group (or entity) has a property, then all of its members (or
**   parts) have that property.**
Therefore, each and every member (or part) of X has property A.

Like the fallacy of composition, this fallacy also occurs in two forms. The first form occurs when it is falsely argued that because the whole has a certain attribute, each part also has that particular attribute. Sometimes the fallacy is obvious, as in the claim that because a joke is funny, every word in the joke is funny, or that because the jury is split over the decision, every juror must be split over the decision. Less obvious is the fallacy in the argument that Sue must be one of the best women basketball players in the world because she is on one of the teams in the world championship game. She might be the twelfth player on the team and might not be good enough to be on the first five of many other teams as well.

In the second form of the fallacy of division, one argues that what is true of a collection of items must be true of the items themselves. When the attribute being considered is a distributive attribute, the inference will be valid; but when it is a collective attribute, it will be invalid. Consider the following description of an entering class at Erehwon University:

> **The class of '99 comes to us from 13 countries and 48 states. Their varied interests include archeology, Chinese, stamp collecting, filmmaking, physics, and basket weaving. They are unmarried, 60 percent female, and range in age from 15 to 24.**

From this statement, it does not follow that a particular student in the class comes from 13 countries and 48 states, or is 60 percent female. To assume either of these would be to try to assign collective properties of the group distributively. The only one of these statements that is true of the group distributively as well as collectively is that any given student is single.

EXERCISE 12-2

Identify the informal fallacy, or fallacies—or at least one if there are several—involved in the following arguments. (All are from among those introduced in Section 12.2) You might also find it useful to reformulate each example as a valid deductive argument, adding premises as needed, and then identifying which of the added premises are questionable or blatantly false.

1. The Palace of Versailles gives us an idea of the elegance and luxury in which the people of France lived in the seventeenth and eighteenth centuries.

2. The counselor said I shouldn't have spanked Bennie for breaking the window; but isn't it better to do it right away rather than wait till my wife comes home in the evening and let her do it then?

3. The lab tests on the patient's blood and urine yielded negative results. The patient's illness is therefore psychological rather than physiological.

4. We in America today are more fortunate than our ancestors. While our present infant mortality rate is less than 1 percent, more than a third of my ancestors must have died during infancy, for the rate of infant mortality was 39 percent until 1910.

5. Faith healing is a fraud. There is no scientific evidence to suggest that any real medical healing takes place, although the power of suggestion may in some cases be great enough to make people think they are cured.

6. No one can prove that drivers who were drunk when they had accidents would not have the same accidents had they been sober. It is therefore unwarranted to claim that the driver's state of intoxication increases the likelihood of an accident.

7. The Controller's office reports that the city's revenues have fallen off considerably. I suggest that the City Council immediately approve a 25 percent

across-the-board budget cut for all departments. The people of the city will just have to learn to live with three-fourths of the services they have had up to this time.

8. With a laissez-faire policy, each member of society acts in a way that will best advance his or her own economic interest. Consequently, all individuals and ultimately society as a whole achieve the maximum economic advantages.

9. If we go to the club we'll pay the cover charge. If we go to the fraternity party we'll pay the admission fee. Either we're going to the club or to the fraternity party. So, we'll have to pay something.

10. Dr. Brown is brilliant, and he's bald; and Mr. Jinx is very smart, too, and he's bald. And Mrs. Echtleproctney is a genius, and she's going to lose her hair, too.

11. The choir sounds sounds terrible. So, each singer in the choir sounds terrible.

12. I'm always thirsty when I wake up in the morning. So waking up in the morning causes me to be thirsty.

13. It has never been proved that Johnson was the Quinstown pickpocket. So, Johnson wasn't the Quinstown pickpocket.

14. Each thread in my sweater is one color. So, my sweater is one color.

15. I recently toured several ocean-front mansions in Miami Beach. Floridians are obviously very wealthy.

16. Salesperson at an electronics store: "Sure you can afford this stereo system: you can afford the equalizer, you can afford the receiver, you can afford the CD changer, you can afford the cassette recorder, and you can afford the speakers."

17. We will never have good politicians. Ambitious politicians will sacrifice the good of the people for personal gain, and those who are not ambitious will be ineffective.

18. Over the last five years, the crime rate has risen proportionally to the increase in roller-blade sales. Clearly, roller-blades must be a cause of this increase.

12.2.7 Appeal to Force

Although it is one of the most obvious of the informal fallacies, the **appeal to force,** or **argumentum ad baculum,** is, nonetheless, one of the most effective. Literally translated, '*argumentum ad baculum*' means 'argument toward the stick.' Its power to persuade lies in its arousal of the listener's fear. Instead of obtaining agreement through cogent reasoning and the presentation of evidence, the appeal to force seeks to intimidate the listener into acquiescence.

The only possible premise that could be added to make an argument of this kind valid would be something like "might makes right." In complete form, it would have to look like the following:

> **Those who have the power to control other persons' health and welfare are always correct in their beliefs and opinions.**
> **X has the power to control other persons' health and welfare, and X believes that A is true.**
> **Therefore, A is true.**

The first premise might seem so obviously false that no one would ever commit this fallacy. Unfortunately, history books and newspapers provide all too many examples of its use.

The success of the Spanish Inquisition in "defending" the Roman Catholic faith was largely due to its free use of the appeal to force. Dissident Catholics were told that they would spend eternity in hell unless they recanted. And if their beliefs withstood this argument, there was the more immediate threat of torture or death. Although neither argument dealt directly with the religious doctrines under dispute, they both effected thousands of conversions. Such methods are by no means obsolete. In 1968, after the intelligence ship *USS Pueblo* was seized by North Korean gunboats, the commander admitted to spying activities when his adversaries told him, "You will sign this confession or we will begin to shoot your crew one at a time in your presence." The threat certainly gave the commander good grounds for signing the "confession," but it in no way proved that the statements therein were true.

The "force" appealed to need not be physical violence. Attempts to manipulate the views of a politician often include appeals to force, such as threats to withhold campaign financing unless the candidate reconsiders a position on some piece of proposed legislation. Here the appeal is to the politician's personal fear of financial embarrassment and loss of status, and it is used in place of arguments about the legislation itself. In the courtroom, jurors are sometimes the target of the appeal to force. The prosecutor might say to the jury, "Will you be safe in the streets at night if this man is not convicted and put behind

I long to hear that you have declared an independency. And in the new code of laws which I suppose it will be necessary for you to make, I desire you would remember the ladies and be more generous than your ancestors. . . . If particular care and attention is not paid to the ladies we are determined to foment a rebellion and will not hold ourselves bound by any laws in which we have no voice or representation.

ABIGAIL ADAMS, LETTER TO JOHN ADAMS, 1774

Was Abigail Adams committing the fallacy of appeal to force in her letter to her husband, or was she simply indicating that her position is a self-supported axiom and that she would not accept a shifting of the burden of proof, just as her husband and his colleagues were doing with the king of England?

"Sir, the logic of your argument is questionable, but your method of presentation is irrefutable."

Reprinted with permission of National Review.

bars?" Without offering any additional evidence of the defendant's guilt, the prosecutor has increased the chance of a "guilty" verdict by substituting the jurors' fears of being attacked for the proper criteria on which the guilt or innocence of the defendant should be determined. The defense, of course, will often respond in kind, "warning" the jury that "if you don't acquit this innocent person, you may some day be convicted of a crime you didn't commit."

The *ad baculum* argument is indeed so blatantly fallacious that it would not be a mistake simply to assert that it is not an argument at all. The premises that must be added to make it valid are certainly highly questionable. Thus, the response of the victim of the *ad baculum* in the cartoon is an accurate analysis of such an "argument."

12.2.8 Appeal to Authority

We regularly make appeals to authority by citing the opinion of experts to support our positions. Because what is taken as fact is often derived from statements by legitimate authorities on the topic under discussion, an argument that rests on such supporting opinion is not necessarily fallacious. An **appeal to authority** is fallacious, however, when the person appealed to is *not truly an authority on the subject under consideration.* It is such an *illicit* appeal to authority, or pseudo-authority, which constitutes this fallacy, the Latin name for which is the **ad verecundiam** fallacy. For instance, while it is legitimate to quote an internist's concurring opinion on the causes of appendicitis, it is hardly relevant to quote this medical doctor as an authority on the stock market (unless evidence is presented that the physician is *also* a legitimate authority on the stock market). Similarly, quoting a famous trial lawyer on the techniques of courtroom cross-examination might be appropriate, but using the attorney's opinions about a diet plan to persuade other people to buy it does commit the fallacy as long as there is no evidence that the lawyer has any more expertise about diet plans than the average person has.

The basic form of arguments that commit the fallacy of the appeal to authority is something like this:

Person A is an expert on subject X.
A says that such-and-such is the case about subject Z.
Therefore, such-an-such is the case about subject Z.

To make this argument valid, we would have to add a premise such as the following, which is clearly false.

Everything that an expert on subject X says about subject Z is true.

The only really plausible argument of this general form is the inductive one, which uses as its basic premise something like this:

Everything an expert on subject X says about subject X is probably true.

Who constitutes a genuine authority can be a matter of dispute, complicated by the fact that the evaluation of a particular authority might change with time. The arguments that Galileo's contemporaries marshaled against his contention that the sun stands still while the earth spins on its axis were based on the Bible, once accepted by Western society as the ultimate authority on everything. Today, many people would regard an attempt to refute empirical astronomical measurements and calculations with the words of the Old Testament as a fallacious appeal to authority.

Nor does appealing to one authority in the appropriate field always prove an argument conclusively, for authorities in the same field often subscribe to conflicting theories. It is reasonable to quote a renowned psychologist as saying that premarital sexual relations between men and women have doubled in the past twenty years. But another renowned psychologist holds that it is the freedom to discuss sex, not the incidence of premarital relations, that has grown. The opinions of the two authorities in this situation are contradictory, and it is important in such cases to acknowledge the controversial nature of the subject and the inconclusiveness of both arguments. It is even more important to recognize the need for going directly to the factual evidence whenever possible, rather than depending needlessly upon even legitimate authorities.

Advertisers frequently promote their products with the aid of pseudo-authorities. A favorite technique, until it was outlawed, was to dress an actor in a doctor's white coat and let him lecture the television audience on the benefits of some patent medicine. Advertisers also exploit the popularity of public figures whose only credentials as "authorities" are their fame as sports celebrities or television stars. They endorse products or services because they are paid to do so, not because they have made a study of all comparable products and found the ones they are endorsing to be superior.

12.2.9 Appeal to the People

Another common mode of argument that is often persuasive, in spite of its manifest error in reasoning, is the **argumentum ad populum,** or **appeal to the people.** Perhaps calling it an "error in reasoning" is itself somewhat erroneous, for the source of the argument's persuasiveness often lies in the fact that it bypasses reasoning altogether, to manipulate the passions, prejudices, and identity of an audience.

Put into valid form, most ad populum arguments look something like this:

> **If most people believe (or like, or want, etc.) something, then that something is true (or good, or valuable, etc.).**
> **Most people believe (or like, or want, etc.) X.**
> **Therefore, X is true (or good, or valuable, etc.).**

A common *ad populum* argument makes use of the "bandwagon effect:" "Everybody's doing it, so you should too." "Nineteen million people brush with Pearly Toothpaste." "It's all right to help yourself to a bit of the stuff in the stockroom now and then; all the employees do it."

An ironic version of the advertisers' favorite ad populum—the one that makes use of the desire "to be like everyone else"—is the appeal directed to the "individualist." One cigarette manufacturer, for example, challenges the consumer to identify which person in a group smokes its brand of cigarettes. The people in the photograph exhibit symptoms of everything from slavish conformity to mild insanity, except for the "right" woman who poses as an island of untroubled tranquility and independence. The appeal is direct: it's not "in" to be "out" and the right cigarette will help you get there.

Public health authorities expressed concern that surveys indicated in the early 1990s that the number of smokers under age 24 had increased, despite major efforts to provide the public with sound arguments and pertinent evidence about the risks of smoking. This suggests that the billions of dollars spent by cigarette companies on advertising—much of which involved *ad populum* elements—has been effective.

12.2.10 Argument against the Person

Some fallacies arise primarily in the context of responding to or criticizing someone else's argument or position. Such counterarguments are fallacious when they fail to identify any weakness in the other person's argument or conclusion. The fallacy of **argument against the person** consists of attacking a person's beliefs or assertions by attacking the person him- or herself in one way or another. It is often referred to by its Latin name, **argumentum ad hominem,** which, literally translated, means "argument toward the man." This fallacious

argument appears most often in one of three forms: the abusive, the circumstantial, and the **tu quoque** ("you, too").

12.2.10.1 Abusive Argument

A disputant is unlikely to change his opinion
because his opponent has dubbed him "an unrealistic fool." But it takes considerable independence of thought on the part of the listeners to support him
in spite of such a label. Thus, an **abusive argument** leveled against one's opponents can have the effect of discrediting any statements they make—something politicians seem to recognize. In the 1992 presidential campaign, one of
the main "arguments" used by the Republicans was that the Democrats were
"liberals"; they emphasized that this was a bad thing by referring to it as the
"l-word," which suggested that it was the same as an obscenity. Although the
Republicans lost the election, many observers felt that this particular strategy
was fairly effective in influencing some voters to vote against the Democrats.

To make an *ad hominem* argument valid, it is necessary to add a highly
questionable premise such as the following.

> **Anything that a person with characteristic A says (or believes or
>   advocates) is false.**
> **Person X has characteristic A and advocates P.**
> **Therefore, P is false.**

Unless characteristic A is something like "never tells the truth" or "has an IQ
of 10," and strong evidence is presented that X in fact has characteristic A, the
argument is fallacious.

Would it be fallacious for an attorney to challenge this witness' testimony on the grounds that she has a poor
sense of time? Why or why not?

Of course we say that we do not believe in god. We know perfectly well that the clergy, the landlords, and the bourgeoisie all claimed to speak in the name of god, in order to protect their own interests as exploiters.

V.I. LENIN

Lenin is committing the *ad hominem*-circumstantial fallacy in this statement. Why?

As well as using epithets, the abusive argument against the person can also operate with factual but irrelevant data about the opponent. It is, for instance, quite irrelevant to a debate about health care that the opponent is against capital punishment and in favor of legalizing marijuana use. Yet these facts might be so abhorrent to some hearers that they will not want to be associated with such a person on any issue, including health care. On the other hand, if in a trial the prosecution's key witness can be shown to be a habitual liar or mentally incompetent, this is quite relevant, since trustworthiness and competence are key factors in evaluating the reliability of testimony.

12.2.10.2 Circumstantial Argument   The **circumstantial argument** cites the opponent's personal circumstances as sufficient reason for dismissing a statement she has made. "Of course she favors highway construction: Her biggest campaign contributor was a manufacturer of road-building machinery." "Why shouldn't those welfare mothers support public day care? They're the ones who'll benefit from it, and they don't have to pay for it." These statements about individuals' personal circumstances might be perfectly true, but they do not by themselves constitute rational disproof of their positions on specific issues.

Other circumstantial *ad hominem* arguments might point out a contrast between the opponent's lifestyle and his or her expressed opinion, thereby suggesting that the opponent and his statements can be dismissed as insincere: for example, "If Mr. Jones really believed that the hospital is understaffed, he would work there as a volunteer." Such assumptions are, by themselves, quite clearly insufficient to support any conclusions as to the true staff situation at the hospital.

The premise that must be added to make an argument committing the circumstantial *ad hominem* fallacy into a valid argument is the following (or something similar to it):

If person A stands to benefit personally if the conclusion of an argument A is presenting is accepted, then the argument must be a bad one.

While this assertion might have a ring of truth to it, it should be clear upon reflection that it is not true that the fact that someone will benefit from the acceptance of the conclusion of an argument implies that the argument must be bad. Certainly we would not be foolish to look more closely at arguments being advocated by persons who stand to benefit from them, but we must still evaluate the argument by the same standards as any other argument and must be prepared to recognize it as a good argument if it in fact is good.

12.2.10.3 Tu Quoque Argument
In **tu quoque,** or "you too," arguments, people do not address themselves to the issues raised against them, but instead attempt to absolve themselves by proving the guilt of their opponents. In response to objections or accusations, the *tu quoque* has several tactical advantages: it allows one to avoid answering to the substance of the charges; it might throw the opponent off guard; and it directs the attention to the opponent's weakness and away from one's own.

A premise that can be added to make any *tu quoque* argument valid is

If someone else did X, then it is all right for me to do X.

For this reason, the fallacy is also sometimes called the "two wrongs make a right" fallacy. Another premise that might be supplied is one to the effect that 'similar cases should be treated similarly.' One could validly deduce from this the subprinciple that 'if your doing X was not considered wrong, then my doing X should not be considered wrong.' But this leaves open a second possibility, namely, 'If my doing X is considered wrong, then your doing X should also be considered wrong.' Thus, although this seems to be a reasonable premise, it is not sufficient to derive validly the conclusion, 'My doing X should be considered right.'

EXERCISE 12–3

Identify the informal fallacy, or fallacies—or at least one if there are several—involved in the following arguments. (All are from among those introduced in Section 12.3) You might also find it useful to reformulate each example as a valid deductive argument, adding premises as needed, and then identifying which of the added premises are questionable or blatantly false.

1. The theory of evolution cannot be true. The Bible says the world was created in seven days.

2. Take out a subscription to the *Investigator,* the nation's leading newsweekly, and be as well informed as your neighbors!

3. Insurance agents never tell you about the ways their company has to get out of paying insurance claims until you actually file a claim. So how can insurance companies blame people for padding their claims the next time they have an accident or burglary?

4. Two children playing a board game. Child A: I will throw the dice first. Child B: No, I'll throw first. Child A: No, it's only fair that I go first, because it's my game and I'll take it home if I can't go first.

MISTER PRESIDENT

We are a group of independent oil and gas men in Denver. Independent oil and gas men are a vital part of the oil and gas industry in America. We recognize the always difficult and sometimes awesome duties of the presidency. We share your concern over the many problems facing our nation, especially those concerning oil and gas.

We have looked to the White House for years in search of direction toward meeting the energy problem, some means of translating into understandable prose the sheaves of regulations, de-regulations, promises, threats and pure political expediency that make up government supervision of the economic metabolism of ALL the nations' industries, including the oil business. We are still looking.

In your address to the nation on April 5th, announcing your plan to de-control prices on crude oil, you promised the end of excessive government controls. You acknowledged that increased oil prices will insure more exploration, more refineries, more national petroleum production and less dependency on OPEC. That was all very good news.

However, the balance of your address of April 5th was a direct insult to the energy consuming public and to the oil industry in this country.

You made indelibly plain to the consumer that he can expect increased prices. Increases in the price of energy, Mr. President? This is hardly startling news.

Your White House statisticians spend endless hours tabulating surges in prices and in estimating future increases, not for oil products alone, but in other vital areas such as food, clothing, transportation housing, health and government. That, Mr. President is your own in-house evidence of inflation. It is all-consuming: and it goes on at a runaway pace.

You acknowledged the ineptitude of government control of the oil industry. To quote you: ..."the federal bureaucracy and red tape have become so complicated, it's almost unbelievable." **We** believe it, Mr. President.

You suggested that you will take away some of the pain of increased oil prices (gasoline prices) by the imposition of a windfall profits tax on the oil companies, and that this money will go to assist low income families, mass transportation and long range energy problems. Our Congress will determine this.

Some of the language in your address we find insulting, purely political and unnecessary. You called us cheats. You alleged that as the result of de-control the nation can expect the oil companies to reap "unearned" profits and "windfalls." You predicted price gouging of the public by oil companies. Your allegation was based on the valid premise that we must explore more, produce more and lessen our dependency on foreign oil imports.

You became prosecutor, judge and jury in your broad indictment of the oil industry. You then convicted us of terrible skulduggery even before your proposals are in effect. You plea bargained with the public in your distasteful announcement that our nation is in for price hikes. All before the fact.

Indeed, you emphasized your verdict against the oil and gas industry with this quote: "First, as surely as the sun will rise, the oil companies can be expected to fight to keep the profits which they have not earned."

You blamed part of the projected rise in consumer prices on the Congress. And you admonished the public to let the Congress know it favors the "windfall profit tax"... adding, "and that you do not want the need to produce more energy to be turned into an excuse to CHEAT the public and to damage our nation."

The oil industry in America is made up of millions of people from all avenues of commerce, including investors who receive yearly compensation from shares owned in oil companies and hundreds of thousands of farmers, ranchers and other individuals who receive a monthly royalty payment from oil and/or gas production. In fact, the largest single monthly oil and gas royalty payment recipient in America is the United States Government.

We resolutely and in the strongest terms object to you imprinting your presidential seal on broad-brush allegation that the oil industry is made up of "cheats," who rake in "unearned" profits on projected "windfalls" that might come from a not yet implemented White House proposal.

We know that other segments of American industry with which we are associated share our objection, our disbelief and resentment concerning your unrelenting and unjust public flogging of April 5.

Bill Callaway	Joe Bander	Tom Connelly	Al Hickerson
Paul Rothwell	Tom Jordan	Phil Anschutz	Bob Boekel
Ray Duncan	Bob Haynie	Vince Duncan	Ray Rader
Send inquiries to:	Fred Mayer		Dow and Marks

Bill Callaway, Denver Independant Oil Fund, 145 Security Life Bldg., Denver Colo., 80202

Courtesy William O. Callaway, 145 Security Life Bldg., Denver 80202.

How many informal fallacies do the oil producers accuse President Carter of committing? Do they appear to be committing any fallacies themselves in their ad?

CITIVIEWS

CITIVIEWS is distributed quarterly to Citicorp investors. It contains viewpoints on timely public issues. We believe the following may be of interest to you...

Is Capitalism Kaput?

Marx and Engels, writing at the inception of communism, gave capitalism great credit for its revolutionary role in history. One passage in their *Manifesto* is especially worth examining:

The bourgeoisie, wherever it has got the upper hand, has put an end to all feudal, patriarchal, idyllic relations. It has pitilessly torn asunder the motley feudal ties that bound man to his "natural superiors" and has left remaining no other nexus between man and man than naked self-interest, than callous "cash payment." It has drowned the most heavenly ecstasies of religious fervor, of chivalrous enthusiasm, of philistine sentimentalism, in the icy water of egotistical calculation. It has resolved personal worth into exchange value, and in place of the numberless indefeasible chartered freedoms, has set up that single, unconscionable freedom — Free Trade.

Since the authors of this statement clearly disapprove of the "motley feudal ties" that capitalism rent asunder, why does not capitalism emerge a hero? The clue is in that one word, *unconscionable*, which means "unrestrained by conscience." Why is Free Trade unconscionable? Because it is, by definition, free — and free means unrestrained. We are in the presence of a tautology, the absurdity of which can be shown by simply calling it Unrestrained Trade instead of Free Trade; thus capitalism is guilty of engaging in unrestrained Unrestrained Trade.

How many fallacies can you identify in the passage quoted from Marx and Engels? How many can you find in Citibank's counterargument? Which "argument" do you think is stronger? Explain why it is stronger.

5. The sixth commandment says "Thou shalt not kill." Yet you, Reverend Smith, claim that the United States was correct to send fighting men to Vietnam. Surely, you do not mean to contradict God's commandment!

6. This must be a good toy: it is advertised on TV.

7. People on welfare should not be allowed to vote, since they will obviously all vote to raise taxes on working people.

8. Republicans have no grounds for criticizing the Democratic administration's failure to balance the federal budget. Republicans failed to balance the budget for the twelve years they controlled the White House.

9. There is no real health care crisis. The doctors are just holding back their services to try to increase the demand, so they can raise their fees and increase their income.

10. If you really want to be in the swing of things, read our magazine every week.

11. Continuing to disagree with my interpretation of *Hamlet* could be risky when it comes to exam time. After all, I am the teacher and a Shakespearean scholar.

12. Eleven members of the jury have decided that Ms. Schlumph is guilty; only Bob hasn't made up his mind. There's obviously something wrong with him if he can't see the obvious verdict.

12.3 Other Informal Fallacies

The informal fallacies discussed above are only a small sampling of the almost unlimited number of kinds of bad argument that have been invented over a period of thousands of years of human civilization. They are sufficient to show the sublety and complexity of human communications and argumentation. Once again, it must be emphasized that there are often several different ways of interpreting particular sentences so that two people may even disagree as to what specific fallacy is committed by a specific case, or even as to whether it commits a fallacy at all. The subtlety and complexity of fallacious cases should be kept in mind when doing any of the exercises in this chapter, particularly those in the following set.

EXERCISE 12–4

Identify the informal fallacy, or fallacies—or at least one if there are several—involved in the following arguments. (All are from among those introduced in this chapter.) You might also find it useful to reformulate each example as a valid deductive argument, adding premises as needed, and then identifying which of the added premises are questionable or blatantly false.

1. Every time I think of Janey before the roulette wheel spins, it lands on black. So I'm going to bet on black and continue to think of Janey before the roulette wheel spins. Since my thinking of Janey makes the wheel land on black, I'm bound to win.

2. Socrates and Plato lived to be old men. So, the life span of ancient Greeks was generally very long.

3. I ate a delicious pomegranate when I was a child. So, all pomegranates are delicious.

4. All molecules of gas are small. So, all gas containers should be small as well.

5. Tim, Doug, Mary, Lou, and Tip—everybody in the club, in fact, owns a dog. So, the club must own a dog.

6. A pack of wildebeasts is always very large. So, wildebeasts themselves must be very large.

7. When the Fabulous Fabrizi Quartet stands on the freight balance, they are seen to weigh eight-hundred pounds. So Jim, Tad, Skip, and Jack—the four members of the quartet—must each weigh eight-hundred pounds.

8. You say that you're not a great singer anymore. But just look at that crowd! They've packed the auditorium, they're chanting your name; they love you! *They* know you're still a great singer. So buck up; all those fans couldn't be mistaken.

9. Dr. Blithe says that the test for the QXZ virus is not always reliable. But Dr. Blithe is a notorious womanizer. So you've got nothing to worry about; if the test says that you don't have the QXZ virus, you can be sure you don't have it.

10. Sure, he says the house is on fire, but he's a pessimist, and you can't trust a pessimist!

11. Of course Jones told you this was a great price; he makes a substantial commission if you buy the tickets from him. So don't believe a word he says, since he's the one who stands to benefit most if you take his advice.

12. Of course the defendant says he's innocent. But don't believe a word he says; he knows that if he doesn't convince you of his innocence, he's going to jail. That's why he's claiming he's innocent.

13. The Biblical account of creation cannot be true. Many intelligent scientists say that life as we know it evolved over billions of years.

14. After missing that open three-point shot, my teammate has no reason to criticize me for missing two free throws earlier.

15. If you wish to stay awake, you should drink lots of water. Whenever I need to study late at night, I drink coffee which is composed almost entirely of water.

16. Doctors are all incompetent; twenty had their licenses revoked just last year.

17. Of course UFOs are visitors from outer space. No one has ever been able to offer a shred of evidence to the contrary.

18. If you drop one page from the Manhattan telephone directory from the top of a ten-story building, it will float to earth very slowly. Therefore, if you drop that telephone directory from a ten-story building, it too will float to earth slowly.

19. None of my grandchildren likes science courses; it appears that the next generation will have no scientists.

20. Doctors who favor the extermination of rats and mosquitoes do so in violation of their Hippocratic oath, which binds them to do all they can to preserve life and nothing to destroy it.

21. If by the end of the class you are still convinced that I have not treated you fairly, you'll stay here in the classroom while the other students go out to the playground.

22. I'll bet that movie stinks. Of course Astella Boogie says it's great—she's the star. But you're not going to believe *her*, are you? I mean, she's the star!

23. Sodium is poisonous and chlorine is poisonous; therefore salt, which is composed of sodium and chlorine, must be poisonous.

24. The other executives find it helpful to do a few hours' work in the office on Saturday mornings. The person who was your predecessor never did; that's the reason we replaced him. We hope you'll agree to come in on weekends.

25. Good roast beef is rare these days, so you shouldn't order yours well done.

26. Since this committee began investigating abuses in nursing home care of the elderly, it has received one thousand letters from old people in nursing homes, complaining of poor conditions. Quite obviously, every nursing home is filled with abuses.

27. We may conclude that the gymnast is a nimble athlete. For we know that gymnasts are supple, and if they are supple then they are flexible. And all flexible athletes are nimble.

28. When Smith was in Rome it was ninety-five degrees (Fahrenheit) outside and there was hardly a cloud in the sky. Smith said it was average weather. Smith said it was average weather today, too, in Minneapolis. So if Smith was telling the truth in Rome and is telling the truth today, it must be ninety-five degrees (Fahrenheit) and cloudless in Minneapolis.

29. You said on the phone that you would be here in two seconds. Well, it's been nearly two minutes and you've just arrived. So you told a lie over the phone.

30. Your average liberal holds that in the name of justice we should radically redistribute the wealth held by the citizens of this country, so that beginning next year, every American adult will hold the same moderate sum in assets and earn the same modest salary. But it is obvious that it is not only unfeasible but wrong to take away from the successful what they have worked long and hard for. So the liberals are obviously wrong.

31. The only way to manage a company effectively is to instill fear in your workers. Either you treat employees kindly and they take advantage of you and goof off, or you are tough on them and they'll work hard for you.

32. Our cat died at the animal hospital, then on 65th Street in Manhattan. So our cat died twice.

33. Things that are difficult to find cost a lot, and secret hiding places are difficult to find, so secret hiding places cost a lot.

34. John says that he loves me and he must be telling the truth, because a person who says that he loves someone would never lie to the person he loves.

35. Nothing has ever been discovered that travels faster than the speed of light; therefore, it is impossible to travel faster than the speed of light.

36. President Kennedy died in office because, in this century, every president who was elected in a year with a number which ended in zero has died while he was in office.

37. Mr. Ball's argument is exactly what one can expect from a racist like him!

38. My opponent, who has so ably defended rent control, knows that there are more tenants who can give him their votes than there are landlords.

39. Kent can play each note contained in the score of Beethoven's Moonlight Sonata. Thus, he should be able to play the Moonlight Sonata.

40. That woman is a minister; of course she's going to support having prayers in our schools.

41. The All Stars should be the best college football team in the country, for it is composed of all the best college players in the country.

42. You really should vote for this bill, Senator; our fifty-thousand-member local union is in favor of it, and you are up for reelection this fall.

43. Uncle Homer says he has lived to celebrate his ninetieth birthday because all his life he ate a garlic clove and downed a shot of whiskey every day.

44. The peoples of the world necessarily face widespread and horrible death within the next century. If enough food is produced to feed the expanding world population, then water and air will be polluted beyond the tolerable limit by the amount of fertilizers and insecticides that are required. So people will die of water and air poisoning. If these fertilizers and insecticides are not used, not enough food will be able to be produced on the land available, and people will starve.

45. Why should we be so solicitous about protecting the legal rights of prisoners? They themselves chose to disregard the law when they committed the crimes that brought them to prison.

46. The Swedes are 90 percent Protestant. Uncle Gustav is a Swede. Therefore, he is 90 percent Protestant.

47. The world of science contains numerous examples of great men and women who believed in a god, so a god must exist.

48. Of course, you realize that if you fail to vote against the gun control bill, our organization will not support your next reelection drive with a donation as it has done in the past.

49. As sure as I am talking to you, Bob Davis is guilty of embezzlement. You know he has a criminal record; he was convicted of income tax evasion and stock fraud five years ago.

50. Either Frank is poor or he is rich, and by looking at the car he drives, you can see that he is rich.

51. If you study hard you'll graduate with honors; and if you don't study at all you won't graduate. Either you'll study hard or you won't study at all. So, either you'll graduate with honors or you won't graduate.

52. Night always follows day. Therefore, day causes night.

53. That you think it a failure of mine that I begin studying for exams only days before they are given reveals that you are a bit naive, Professor. If you looked a little more closely, you'd realize that Ms. Davies, one of your star pupils, begins studying the week of the exam, too.

Summary

1. Commonly used and often highly persuasive sets of statements that appear to present logical support for a conclusion sometimes do not provide any support at all or else involve an implicit premise that is blatantly false. Since some of these can be recognized with little or no reliance on the methods of formal logic, they are often referred to as informal fallacies.

2. Some fallacies do not involve real arguments at all, but are attempts to disguise the fact that a particular set of statements is a nonargument. The attempts to disguise nonarguments to make them look like arguments fall into several patterns.

3. Any argument that is such that, for its intended audience the conclusion is merely a restatement of something explicitly stated in the premises, commits the fallacy of **begging the question** (or **petitio principii**). Usually, the longer the circular argument, the more deceptive and persuasive it is likely to be.

4. The fallacy of **equivocation** involves the use of a word or phrase that can be interpreted in two or more different ways in the given context. The equivocal element might be used in one sense in the premise(s) and in another in the conclusion; or it might be used in different senses in different premises; or it might be used in such a way that it is impossible to determine the sense in which it is being used.

5. The fallacy of **amphiboly** occurs when a person tries to draw a conclusion from a faulty interpretation of a grammatically ambiguous statement. Amphiboly and equivocation are not a matter of erroneous reasoning so much as of erroneous interpretation.

6. When we interpret—or intentionally distort—an individual's statements on a given matter in such a way as to make them most vulnerable to attack and criticism, we are violating the principle of charity and committing the **straw person fallacy.** This fallacy often involves reducing a relatively complex argument to simple form, thereby leaving out some of its key elements.

7. Attempts to disprove an opponent's conclusion by presenting information that merely establishes another conclusion rather than refuting the one under criticism, involves committing the fallacy of **irrelevant conclusion.**

8. If a set of statements does in fact constitute a real argument but is still fallacious, the specific fallacy that it commits can often be identified by adding whatever premises are needed to make the argument valid. At least one of the added premises will be either blatantly false or highly improbable.

9. The fact that a proposition has not been conclusively proved to be true or false—especially when little or no real attempt has been made to verify or falsify it—often establishes nothing but one's inability to prove or disprove it. To treat this inability as establishing the truth or falsity of the proposition is to use a fallacious mode of argument known as the **argument from ignorance** (or **argumentum ad ignorantiam**). To make an argument that commits this fallacy into a valid argument, it is necessary to add a clearly false premise such as 'There is no evidence (proof) that it is the case that X; therefore, it is not the case that X.' When confronted with an argument that appears to have this form, we should make sure that it cannot be reasonably interpreted as a legitimate inductive argument before labeling it as fallacious.

10. The fallacy of **false dilemma** consists of presenting an argument as if there were fewer possible solutions to the problem than is actually the case. Usually two alternatives are offered in an either/or fashion, but other alternatives are available.

11. Underlying the fallacy of **false cause** is the mistaken notion that the conjunction in space and time of two events or states of affairs is sufficient to establish that one of them is the *cause* of the other.

12. Forming a generalization based on a small number of exceptional, or specially selected, cases constitutes the fallacy of **hasty generalization.** To avoid this fallacy, one should collect a sufficient number of typical, or randomly selected, cases so that there is enough data to distinguish the typical from the accidental.

13. The fallacy of **composition** has two forms. The first occurs when one argues that a single entity has a certain characteristic because each of its component parts has that characteristic. The second form occurs when one

concludes that a collective entity (such as a team or an orchestra) has a certain characteristic because each member of the collective group has this characteristic.

14. The fallacy of **division** also has two forms. The first form occurs when it is argued that each part of a single entity has a particular attribute because the entity has that attribute. The second form occurs when it is argued that what is true of a collective entity must also be true of each of the members of the collective.

15. The **appeal to force** (or **argumentum ad baculum**) attempts to get people to accept the conclusion by arousing their fears and intimidating them into acquiescence. The appeal to force might involve threats of immediate physical violence or threats against a person's status and general well-being.

16. Citing the opinion of a pseudo-expert as reinforcement for one's own opinion constitutes the fallacy known as the **appeal to authority** (or **argumentum ad verecundiam**). Identifying this fallacy can be difficult in cases where there is disagreement over who is a genuine authority in a given field. Appealing to a *legitimate* authority is not fallacious.

17. The **appeal to the people** (or **argumentum ad populum**) relies on the "bandwagon" effect and can be highly persuasive, since it manipulates the passions, prejudices, and identity of specific audiences and often bypasses reasoning altogether.

18. The fallacy of **argument against the person** (or **argumentum ad hominem**) consists of attacking a person's beliefs or assertions by attacking the person in one way or another. This fallacy usually appears in one of three forms: the abusive, the circumstantial, and the *tu quoque*. Using epithets, or factual but irrelevant data about one's opponents, the **abusive** argument is used in an attempt to discredit any statements they make. The **circumstantial** argument cites the opponents' personal circumstances (e.g., that they stand to gain financially if their argument is accepted) as sufficient reason for dismissing their arguments. **Tu quoque** ('you, too') arguments involve criticizing opponents as having acted contrary to the position for which they are arguing.

Chapter 13

Definitions

Definitions are significant to the study of the logic of propositions and arguments for several reasons. First, understanding the meaning of a particular word is often a critical part of analyzing and evaluating a statement or argument. Second, definitions often appear as premises, or need to be added as premises, in all types of arguments, so we need to be able to recognize them when they occur, to supply the proper ones when needed, and to determine whether they are good or bad. Also, many definitions are interesting and significant for their own sake, and it is important to recognize and appreciate them when we encounter them.

Definitions can have very significant economic and political ramifications. For example, in 1994 the U.S. Supreme Court ruled that certain emissions from incinerators qualify under statutory definitions as being hazardous waste. Some experts claimed that this single definition could increase waste disposal costs for some cities (and their taxpayers) by as much as 1000 percent.

Definitions also come into play in the areas of foreign policy and business competition. United States auto manufacturers lobbied to have special tariffs imposed on the portion of the cost of an automobile that is not "American." This legislation led to all sorts of debates, court suits and threats from foreign governments due in part to the problems associated with interpreting the definition of "American." Does it include products manufactured in the United States by a company that is entirely owned and managed by non-U.S. citizens? Or this such an interpretation too broad? One small example of the problem is shown in the box in the margin.

13.1 Kinds of Definitions

The technical term for *a word that is to be defined* is **definiendum**. The *symbols or words used to define it* are called the **definiens**. Thus, in the definition

square $=_{df}$ rectangle with four equal sides

'square' is the definiendum and 'rectangle with four equal sides' is the definiens.

It is always important to specify the context in which the definiendum is being used. For instance, the noun 'rest' can mean either 'repose,' or 'a measured period of silence in music,' or 'a written symbol that denotes this silence,' or 'a prop,' or 'a shelter,' according to the context in which it is used.

There are several different methods by which a given word may be satisfactorily defined. That is to say, one may use various types of definiens to define a given definiendum. Depending on the type of definiens provided, a definition may be classified as one of several kinds, four of which will be discussed here: synonymous, enumerative, connotative, and operational.

13.1.1 Synonymous Definitions

A **synonymous definition** is one in which *the definiens consists of only one word which, in appropriate contexts, can be used interchangeably with the definiendum.* The following are examples of synonymous definitions:

freedom $=_{df}$ liberty
conceal $=_{df}$ hide
quoted $=_{df}$ cited
intentionally $=_{df}$ purposely

As the term 'synonymous' is usually used in everyday discourse, any adequate definition is such that its definiens is synonymous with its definiendum. Thus, it is important to note that we are using the term with a special, technical meaning, such that only those definitions whose definiens consist of exactly one word qualify as synonymous definitions.

Synonymous definitions are the shortest of all definitions, but are not always the most precise and useful. Synonymous definitions are commonly used in teaching foreign languages even though it is likely that the meaning and usage of an English word and its foreign "synonym" will only overlap without being identical. That, however, is also the case with many English synonyms for English words. They usually share some, but not all, of their meanings. As long as there is a significant overlap in meaning between two such words, it is still all right to use one of them to define the other.

Give synonymous definitions for each of the following words. For words with multiple meanings, it is only necessary to give a synonym for one of the meanings. Don't hesitate to use a dictionary: this is not a vocabulary quiz!

1. canine
2. laudable
3. mistake (verb)
4. site (noun)
5. bandit
6. pot (slang)
7. rigid
8. viscous
9. idle
10. emend

13.1.2 Enumerative Definitions

In an **enumerative definition,** the definiens lists words referring to, or presents actual examples of, things, properties, relations, concepts, and so on to which the definiendum may be correctly applied. For instance, the enumerative definiens 'father, mother, son, daughter, uncle, aunt, grandparent, grandchild' may be given to clarify the sense in which the word 'relative' is being used in a particular context. Enumerative definitions are divided into two categories— ostensive definitions and denotative definitions.

13.1.2.1 Ostensive Definitions   In an ostensive definition, the meaning of the definiendum is presented by means of concrete examples. In teaching the meaning of 'nose' to a young child, you might point to your nose, to the child's nose, to the nose of anyone else present, while you repeat the word 'nose' until the child gets the idea of what a nose is. Similarly, the concept yellow might be defined by pointing to a daffodil, a lemon, and a grapefruit. Instead of using one's finger to point to a visible definiens, one can point out the definiens verbally. One could point one's finger and say, "That is a three-toed sloth," or one might merely say, "That rather dirty-looking animal that is hanging upside down in this tree is a three-toed sloth."

The definiens need not be perceivable solely by the eyes. One can provide ostensive definitions for terms such as 'hard,' 'fugue,' 'sweet,' and 'stink' by providing the appropriate nonvisual sensory experiences.

There are certain advantages to the use of ostensive definitions. They are easy to formulate. They can, as when noses are pointed out to babies, help to teach concepts that were previously unknown to the learner. They can also be understood in the absence of preexisting language, which makes them suitable for conveying meaning to small children or others whose vocabulary is limited.

Ostensive definitions also have disadvantages. They depend on the physical presence of the definiens, or at least a good picture of it. The most serious disadvantage of ostensive definitions is that they are more easily subject to misinterpretation than most other kinds of definition. The child, for instance, might conclude that 'nose' is the equivalent of 'face.' Or if one were trying to provide an ostensive definition of 'face' and happened to point to the middle of someone's face, the child might conclude that the word 'face' signifies the nose. In other words, a person might associate the definiendum with the whole of the ostensive definiens when it was intended for her to associate it with only a part, and vice versa. Furthermore, even a randomly chosen definiens can have more than one set of common characteristics, and so an unintended set might be presumed to be the intended set. For example, all the noses pointed to might be Roman noses. In this case, a child might conclude that a pug nose is not a nose.

13.1.2.2 Denotative Definitions
Unlike ostensive definitions, **denotative definitions** do not require the physical presence of the definiens; rather they list examples of things, or types or classes of things, to which the definiendum applies. The list constituting the definiens specifies what is known as the **denotation** or **extension** of the definiendum. If 'carnivore' is the definiendum, then the denotative definiens 'dogs and cats' would be correct; but it would not be adequate since the listener might well infer that the definiendum is synonymous with 'pets.' To rectify this, we might add 'tigers, wolves, foxes, and hyenas' to our list. The listener might now correctly understand 'carnivore' or might, on the other hand, think that it means 'mammal.' To prevent further misunderstanding, we might add 'dolphins, owls, and vultures' to the definiens. Had we left out 'dogs, cats, and hyenas,' the listener might well have inferred that our definiendum is synonymous with 'predator.'

Denotative definitions are easy to formulate, and they can be understood easily and correctly, at least when the listing in the definiens is exhaustive—that is, if it names *all* the things to which the definiendum refers. A definition of 'United States' as 'Alabama, Alaska, Arizona, Arkansas, California, etc.' would be a useful denotative definition only if the reader or listener is able to supply the meaning of 'etc.'

An extreme case arose in 1993 when the California legislature voted to tax snack foods. As the legislators worked to formulate a definition that would include all of the items that they wanted to tax without also including other items that they did not want taxed, they concluded that the only way that they could do so was to list each item in the new law. The law they passed thus includes an 87-page-long list of 4,000 items that are defined as being 'snack foods' and are subject to the tax. (Some of the items included on the list are gingerbread cake, gum, breath mints, Slime Slurp, and Goodman Matzo 5.

New Tax On Munchies Not So Sweet

SACRAMENTO, CA. Unable to find a definition that draws a sharp line between snack foods and "serious" foods, the California legislature has resorted to compiling a list of over 4000 specific products which will be subject to a 7% sales tax; all edibles not on the list are exempt from the tax.

Included on the 87-page list of snack foods are such items as Rain Blo Neon Gum Shipper and Pink Peeps, while former President George Bush's favorite snack fried pig skins is still exempt from the sales tax. The California Grocer's Association is considering challenging the new law in the courts.

Some items not included on the list—and thus not taxed—are cake icing, candied lemon drops, graham crackers, and fried pig skins.)

There are also some words for which it is not only difficult, but practically impossible to provide adequate denotative definitions. What kind of denotative definition could one give for words such as 'being,' 'understand,' 'infinity,' and 'infer'?

EXERCISE 13-2

Give denotative definitions for each of the following words and explain how an ostensive definition might be given for each. For words with multiple meanings, give a definition only for one of the meanings. Don't hesitate to use a dictionary; this is not a vocabulary quiz!

1. canine
2. champion
3. mistake (verb)
4. lake
5. bandit
6. grass
7. rigid
8. military
9. idle
10. letter (alphabet)

EXERCISE 13-3

Arrange the following terms in order of increasing extension (i.e., put the term with the smallest extension first and the term with the largest extension last).

1. beagle, mammal, dog, domestic pet
2. reading material, weekly newsmagazine, magazine, printed publication
3. symphony, music, classical music, sounds
4. flying object, eagle, bird, golden eagle
5. vehicle, Neon, automobile, Dodge

13.1.3 Connotative Definitions

In logic, the term **connotation** is used to refer only to the essential characteristic, or set of characteristics, of the thing(s) named or referred to by the definiendum. The definiens in a connotative definition pinpoints the meaning of the definiendum by listing the set of properties common to all and only the things to which the definiendum can be correctly applied. For example, 'hospital' might be defined connotatively as 'an institution staffed and equipped to provide the sick or the injured with diagnosis, medical or surgical treatment, temporary accommodation, and temporary custodial care.' Each property narrows down the possible meanings of the definiendum until, ideally, the sum total of the properties given applies not only entirely, but also exclusively, to the particular definiendum. *The sum total of a definiendum's essential properties* is called the **intension** or the **connotation** of the definiendum.

In the definiens above, the component 'institution' eliminates only some of the things that are *not* among the things referred to by the definiendum. For instance, it excludes the possibility that the term 'hospital' could apply to any living creature, natural occurrence, or manufactured article. The specification of the purpose of the things named by the definiendum (rendering services to the sick and the injured) eliminates all institutions that are primarily financial, political, punitive, or educational in their purpose. The requirement that anything called 'hospital' must provide accommodation eliminates clinics and doctors' offices; and the specification that the accommodation is temporary disqualifies homes for the terminally ill and homes for the chronically infirm from the class of things to which the word 'hospital' can be correctly applied. The references to sickness and medicine rule out 'hotel,' 'boarding house' and 'dormitory' as synonyms of 'hospital.' 'Custodial care' prevents the application of the term 'hospital' to some institutions in certain parts of the world, in which all other services are provided, but custodial care is not—members of the patient's families do their cooking, laundry, and so on. If we want to call such facilities hospitals, the reference to custodial care in the definiens must be removed.

An increase in the intension of a definition (the adding of properties) cannot result in an increase in the extension (or denotation) of the definiendum. Any properties added to the connotation will either diminish the denotation (extension) or leave it unchanged. Conversely, if there is a decrease in the connotation (intension)—that is, an elimination of some of the properties named by the definiens—the denotation of a term can only increase or remain unchanged; it cannot thereby be diminished. Thus, the word 'female' denotes slightly more than half the world's population. Expand this connotation to 'young female,' by adding the property of youth, and you have decreased the denotation by about two-thirds. If you now add the property 'intelligent' to the others, the extension shrinks again. By the time you have increased your intention to 'intelligent young female scientist,' the extension has undergone a drastic shrinkage, and this expression denotes a much smaller population than the original word 'female,' which had a lesser connotation.

There are some words for which it is possible to give a connotative definition, but quite impossible to give a denotative definition. 'Dragon,' 'werewolf,' 'unicorn,' and 'vampire' are cases in point. The fact that most people don't believe that these creatures do, or ever did, exist does not prevent us from explaining what it is that people have in mind when they use these words. One can, for example, define 'unicorn' as 'a horselike creature with a single, pointed conical horn in the middle of its forehead,' without implying that any such creature ever existed. One can even include 'mythical' as part of the definiens. (Remember, it is important to distinguish clearly between a picture or idea of a unicorn and a real unicorn. One can readily give an ostensive definition of 'picture of a unicorn.')

EXERCISE 13–4

Explain what happens to the extension of the following intensional definitions when they are changed as indicated.

1. a. mammal
   b. four-legged mammal
   c. brown four-legged mammal
   d. female brown four-legged mammal

2. a. vehicle
   b. four-wheeled vehicle
   c. self-propelled four-wheeled vehicle
   d. red self-propelled four-wheeled vehicle

3. a. book
   b. logic book
   c. hardcover logic book
   d. entertaining hardcover logic book

4. a. creature
   b. winged creature
   c. winged creature with a halo
   d. supernatural winged creature with a halo

5. a. painting
   b. watercolor painting
   c. miniature watercolor painting
   d. 100-year-old miniature watercolor painting

13.1.3.1 Definition by Genus and Difference

A **definition by genus and difference** is a type of connotative definition that *consists of specifying the general class of things to which the definiendum belongs and then further specifying the properties by which the definiendum can be distinguished from other things belonging to the same general class.* Traditionally, the general class is known as the genus and the distinguishing properties are called either the differentia or the difference.

Definitions by genus and difference are commonly used to define concepts pertaining to the natural sciences, though their use is not restricted to scientific contexts. In biology, a definition of 'gorilla' by genus and difference might begin by stating that the gorilla is an anthropoid ape. Then, because the genus 'anthropoid ape' includes not only gorillas, but also chimpanzees, orangutans, and gibbons, it is necessary to point out the characteristic or set of characteristics distinguishing the species 'gorilla' from the other species of the same genus. In this case, one might specify that the gorilla is the largest of the anthropoid apes.

The method of definition by genus and difference can also be used to define terms that are not part of such highly formalized systems as biology. In fact, it can be used for many words in our everyday vocabulary. 'Frying pan' might be defined as 'a cooking utensil, consisting of a shallow metallic bowl attached to a long handle.' 'Bed' might be defined as 'a common piece of furniture, constructed to support the human body lying horizontally.'

EXERCISE 13–5

Write a connotative definition (perhaps by genus and difference) for each of the following. Choose only one of the meanings of words with multiple meanings.

1. metropolis
2. movie
3. insect
4. cat
5. car
6. election
7. exploit
8. freedom
9. play
10. tyrant

13.1.4 Operational Definitions

An **operational definition** is one *in which the definiens provides a test or a formal procedure that is to be followed to determine whether or not the definiendum applies to a certain thing.* An operational definition of 'alkaline liquid' might read: 'If you immerse a piece of litmus paper in a liquid and the litmus paper turns blue, the liquid is alkaline.' Similarly, an operational definition of 'brain activity' might read: 'Brain activity produces visible oscillations on an electroencephalograph that has been properly attached to the head.'

The following example of an operational definition is taken from a physical science textbook: "If the substance fails to break down upon being heated to 1,000°, having an electric current passed through it, being treated with acid, etc., it is an 'element.'" The behavioral sciences also make frequent use of operational definitions, setting up testing procedures involving observable behavior patterns.

Household instructions routinely include operational definitions. A cake is 'done' when a toothpick inserted in it comes out dry and clean; an avocado is ripe if the pit inside rattles when you shake it.

"The Wizard of Id" by permission of Johnny Hart and Creators Syndicate, Inc.

Was the king entrapped by a definition? If so, what kind? How might he have avoided this predicament?

EXERCISE 13–6

Write an operational definition for each of the following.

1. magnet
2. buoyant
3. flammable
4. contagious
5. poison (noun)
6. even number
7. genius
8. acid
9. transparent
10. definition

EXERCISE 13–7

Decide whether each of the following definitions is synonymous, enumerative (ostensive or denotative), connotative (possibly by genus and difference), or operational.

1. 'Herbivorous' means 'feeding on plants.'
2. A copy is a reproduction.
3. Prime numbers: 1, 2, 3, 5, 7, 11, 13, 17, 19, 23, etc.
4. The piece of music we are listening to now is an example of a string quartet.
5. An icosahedron is a polyhedron having twenty faces.
6. Alcoholic beverage: If, as you drink more and more of a beverage, you become more and more drunk, the beverage is an alcoholic beverage.

7. Free trade: As applied to international trade, the absence of export and import duties and of regulations which are clearly designed to reduce or prevent such trade (Sloan and Zurcher, *Dictionary of Economics*).

8. Aleph is the first letter of the Hebrew alphabet.

9. Quercus alba is the scientific name for the American white oak.

10. A prevaricator is a liar.

11. The face cards in a deck of playing cards are all the jacks, queens, and kings.

12. Allergy: If a substance is placed on a person's skin and the person develops a rash, then that person has an allergy to that substance.

13. Stamina is the same thing as endurance.

14. An iguana is a large herbivorous tropical American lizard.

15. Noon (local time) is that time of day at which the sun is equidistant between the eastern and western horizons.

16. 'Wireless' means 'radio.'

17. Right triangle: Given any triangle, construct a circle around the triangle, using the longest side of the triangle as the diameter of the circle. If all three vertices of the triangle lie on the circle, the triangle is a right triangle.

18. The principal parts of a Latin verb: amo, amare, amavi, amatus.

19. The principal parts of a Latin verb are the first person singular present indicative active, the present infinitive active, the first person singular perfect active, and the perfect passive participle.

20. The principal parts of a Latin verb are those verb forms from which all other possible verb forms can be derived.

21. An object is fluorescent if, when you put it under an ultraviolet lamp, it gives off light, whereas it did not before.

22. The provinces of Canada are British Columbia, Alberta, Saskatchewan, Manitoba, Ontario, Quebec, Newfoundland, New Brunswick, Nova Scotia, Prince Edward Island, the Northwest Territories, and the Yukon Territories.

23. The gross national product is the total value at current market prices of all the goods and services produced by a nation in a given year, prior to the deduction of depreciation charges and other allowances.

24. The constellation Ursa Major is the Big Dipper.

25. A full house is a poker hand consisting of three of a kind and a pair.

26. [An experienced poker player to a beginner.] See, there you have a full house in your hand: three aces and two tens.

27. 'Myopia' means 'nearsightedness.'

28. Myopia is a condition of the eye in which images come to a focus in front of the retina because the eyeball is elongated or the lens is too convex, resulting in an inability to see distant objects well, if at all.

29. That's Nova Scotia off the bow, the only land visible on the horizon.

30. Marsupials are an order of mammals in which the females have an abdominal pouch for carrying their young.

31. Marsupials are animals such as kangaroos, wombats, and opossums.

32. Humans are rational animals.

33. A tango is a modern ballroom dance in 4/4 time that originated in Buenos Aires and is characterized by syncopated rhythm, long pauses, and stylized body positions.

34. The Pleiades is that cluster of seven stars over there in the eastern sky where I'm pointing.

35. Lambda is the eleventh letter of the Greek alphabet.

36. Alcoholic beverages are beer, wine, hard liquors (bourbon, scotch, gin, vodka, rum), and liqueurs.

37. A person has an addiction to a drug or an activity if he or she manifests high anxiety reactions when deprived of the drug or prevented from engaging in the activity.

38. Phytohormones are the same thing as plant hormones.

39. Grimm's law is a linguistic law, formulated by Jacob Grimm, describing a pattern of consonant changes in words as they passed from primitive Indo-European languages into early Germanic languages.

40. A series of numbers is a geometric progression in which the same answer results from dividing the second number by the first, the third by the second, the fourth by the third, and so on to the end of the series.

13.2 Uses of Definitions

Although our shorthand method of writing definitions (as 'definiendum $=_{df}$ definiens') can obscure the fact, all verbal definitions are sentences that can be used in many ways to perform a variety of tasks. Definitions can be used to express statements, but they are not always used in this manner, and the criteria for determining their truth or falsity can differ quite markedly from case to case. It is, therefore, important to briefly examine some of the more common uses of definitions.

13.2.1 To Report Meaning

Sometimes a definition is used to *report the meaning of a term as it is normally used and understood by most members of a specific group* (such as all U.S. citizens or all biologists). Such a definition is known as a **reportive** or **lexical definition.** It is the kind of definition one would expect to find in a dictionary ('lexicon' is a synonym for 'dictionary').

Lexical definitions can be enumerative, connotative, synonymous, or operational: 'dandelion,' for instance, can be defined as 'a yellow-flowered composite plant (genus Taraxacum): esp.: an herb (T. officinale) sometimes grown as a potherb and nearly cosmopolitan as a weed' (Webster), or as 'one of those plants growing out there in the lawn.' The first definition is connotative, the second enumerative (ostensive). 'Bachelor' can be defined as 'a member of the group that includes A, B, C, D, and E'—naming a number of bachelors known to the hearer—which is enumerative (denotative). Although each of these is a different kind of definition, they are all being used to do the same thing, namely, to report the generally accepted meaning of a word.

A lexical definition can be judged as being true or false according to whether it accurately reports the way the word is actually used by members of a specific group. Thus, " 'bachelor' means 'unmarried male' " is true, for 'unmarried male' is the meaning generally given to 'bachelor' in ordinary use by native English speakers.

A lexical definition is false only if the meaning it attributes to a word is one not normally associated with that word by the members of a specific group. But it can be true and yet flawed; that is, it might fail to give all the meanings normally associated with the word, or fail to indicate the context within which the word has a particular meaning. Thus, to define 'key' as 'a usually metal instrument by which the bolt of a lock is turned' is true as far as it goes; but it would be of little help to the student wanting to understand the use of the term 'key' in a music appreciation book, or in the answer key at the back of this text. To be complete, the lexical definition must deal also with these and other common uses of the term 'key' and must indicate the context within which each applies. In fact, *Webster's Ninth New Collegiate Dictionary* lists many separate categories of meaning for the term 'key,' some of them with several subdivisions, as shown below.

A lexical definition need not report the way an entire language group (such as all English speakers) uses a word; it may properly be limited to reporting

¹key \'kē\ *n* [ME, fr. OE *cæg;* akin to MLG *keige* spear] (bef. 12c) **1 a** : a usu. metal instrument by which the bolt of a lock is turned **b** : any of various devices having the form or function of such a key **2 a** : a means of gaining or preventing entrance, possession, or control **b** : an instrumental or deciding factor **3 a** : something that gives an explanation or identification or provides a solution ⟨the ∼ to a riddle⟩ **b** : a list of words or phrases giving an explanation of symbols or abbreviations **c** : an aid to interpretation or identification : CLUE **d** : an arrangement of the salient characters of a group of plants or animals or of taxa designed to facilitate identification **e** : a map legend **4 a** (1) : COTTER PIN (2) : ²COTTER **b** : a keystone in an arch **c** : a small piece of wood or metal used as a wedge or for preventing motion between parts **5 a** : one of the levers of a keyboard musical instrument that actuates the mechanism and produces the tones **b** : a lever that controls a vent in the side of a woodwind instrument or a valve in a brass instrument **c** : a digital that serves as one unit of a keyboard and that works usu. by lever action to set in motion a character or an escapement (as in some typesetting machines) **d** : KEYBUTTON **6** : SAMARA **7** : a system of seven tones based on their relationship to a tonic; *specif* : the tonality of a scale **8 a** : characteristic style or tone **b** : the tone or pitch of a voice **c** : the predominant tone of a photograph with respect to its lightness or darkness **9** : a decoration or charm resembling a key **10** : a small switch for opening or closing an electric circuit **11** : the set of instructions governing the encipherment and decipherment of messages **12** : KEYHOLE 2 — **keyed** \'kēd\ *adj* — **key·less** \'kē-ləs\ *adj*

color, colour. (1) The visual sensation caused by light. (2) Light of a definite wavelength or group of wavelengths which is emitted, reflected, refracted, or transmitted by an object. A c. is defined by three properties; *hue*, the wavelength of the monochromatic light, i.e., shade; *saturation*, the percentage of the light of the above wavelength present, i.e., strength; *brightness*, the amount of light reflected as compared with a standard under the same conditions, i.e., luminosity.

collision. Interaction between material systems (molecule, atom, or electron), or electromagnetic induction, resulting in a change in molecular energy.

Hackk's Chemical Dictionary, *4th ed., 1969.*

Is knowledge of chemical theory necessary for understanding these definitions?

"Obesity is a nonmental medical disorder with no psychopathological basis."

Artwork by Gerry Gersten, © 1978, Psychology Today *Magazine, (Sussex Publishers, Inc.).*

Can you translate this theoretical definition of 'obesity' into "ordinary" language? What is the theoretical content in this definition given in the basic psychology reference work, *Diagnostic and Statistical Manual of Mental Disorders,* 3rd ed.?

the way a term is used in a technical or otherwise limited context. For instance, a word may be *defined in terms of the meaning that it carries in the context of a particular theory,* in which case we have a **theoretical definition.**[1] Such definitions are useful when, as is often the case in scientific usage, the meaning of a term as used in a particular theory does not correspond in intension or extension to its ordinary lexical meaning. Thus, when used as a psychoanalytical term, 'ego' requires a theoretical definition, for its meaning in the context of Freudian theory is different from that which it has in common usage. In point of fact, 'ego' has several quite different meanings within different psychoanalytic theories, and has still other meanings in various philosophical systems.

Other words, such as 'proton' and 'mitochondria,' have *only* theoretical definitions, for they have been conceived in connection with particular theories, and whatever common usage they have has evolved out of their use in connection with those theories.

A theoretical definition, when contained in a textbook or presented in a classroom lecture, is either true or false, depending on whether or not it accurately gives the meaning of the word as used in the particular theory. However, *prior* to its incorporation into textbooks and other standard uses, the definition must go through an evolutionary evaluational process to determine its usefulness and appropriateness in the particular theory. During this process of introduction into the theory, the definition is being used stipulatively—a kind of use that we will discuss shortly.

Another case of a limited reportive definition is the **legal definition.** This is

---

[1]In a very real way, ordinary, everyday language can itself be said to embody, contain, or presuppose a "theory." In this sense, every lexical definition is a theoretical definition. The concept of a theory need not be restricted to scientific theories in the narrow sense of the term; there are theories of other kinds as well—such as ethical, religious, aesthetic, and metaphysical—that also give special meanings to certain words. We use the term 'theoretical' in a relatively broad sense which allows it to be applied to any "special" language group insofar as that group is also distinguished by any characteristics other than shared language. Thus, a definition reporting the way in which English speakers use a particular word would not be theoretical, but a definition regarding the way in which it is used by all (and only) Satanists, or by all (and only) abstract expressionists, would be theoretical.

VALID. Having legal strength or force, executed with proper formalities, incapable of being rightfully overthrown or set aside. Edwards v. O'Neal, Tex.Civ.App., 28 S.W.2d 569, 572. Of binding force; legally sufficient or efficacious; authorized by law. Anderson, L.Dict.; Morrison v. Farmers' & Traders' State Bank, 70 Mont. 146, 225 P. 123, 125. Good or sufficient in point of law; efficacious; executed with the proper formalities; incapable of being rightfully overthrown or set aside; sustainable and effective in law, as distinguished from that which exists or took place in fact or appearance, but has not the requisites to enable it to be recognized and enforced by law. Thompson v. Town of Frostproof, 89 Fla. 92, 103 So. 118; United States v. McCutchen, D.C.Cal., 234 F. 702, 709.

Black's Law Dictionary, *Rev. 4th ed., 1968.*

Compare this legal definition with the definition in logic given in Chapter 2 of this book, and with the definitions of 'valid' given in any standard dictionary.

a definition *specified in the laws as formulated by a legislative, judicial, or executive body.* If a motorist is stopped on the highway and given a summons for speeding, the verb 'to speed' is not being used in the same sense as in the proverbial injunction 'to speed the departing guest' or in that of the drug addict who 'speeds' on amphetamines. In the context of traffic law, as pertaining to any particular stretch of road, 'to speed' is defined as meaning 'to drive at a rate exceeding x miles per hour.' Similarly, the definition of 'valid' from a legal dictionary is very different from the theoretical definition in logic of 'valid.'

When used in court, or in some other situation with reference to a law that already exists and a definition that is generally accepted, a legal definition is being cited in a reportive way. However, when a proposed law is being debated by a legislative body, the use of definitions in it are most likely reportive.

EXERCISE 13–8

Give reportive definitions for each of the following words and explain how you obtained each of them. For words with multiple meanings, give a definition for only one of the meanings.

1. rap
2. jive
3. wipeout
4. cool
5. work
6. fun
7. fast
8. happiness
9. God
10. bird

13.2.2 To Introduce New Meaning

Occasionally, it is necessary to introduce new meanings. Sometimes this is done by "coining" words. For instance, in his book *Without Guilt and Justice,* philosopher Walter Kaufman analyzes the strategies people employ to avoid making fateful decisions, and suggests that the reason for this avoidance is the individual's fear of autonomy. "The fear of autonomy," he writes, "is a nameless dread, which leaves me free to coin a name for it: decidophobia."[2] In thus defining and then naming a new concept, Kaufman formulated what is known as a **stipulative definition.**

A word that is stipulatively defined need not be a newly coined word. It may be a word that has a generally accepted meaning, but which the speaker wants to use in a new sense and therefore stipulates that he or she will be using it in that sense. Legislatures sometimes stipulate new meanings in the writing of new laws; courts sometimes expand the meaning of terms in existing laws to cover new situations.

The sciences often provide even clearer examples of stipulative definitions, for they are likely to develop completely new concepts that need to be named. Psychoanalytical terminology was originally introduced through stipulative definitions by Freud and some of his followers. Some of these terms, such as 'neurosis' and 'sublimation,' were completely new words; others, such as 'transference' and 'repression,' were words already in the language to which new meanings were assigned.

Once a new word, or a new meaning for an old word, has been introduced, it might be absorbed into general usage or into the standard vocabulary of a particular discipline. What began as a stipulative definition then becomes a reportive definition, and can properly be cited as such.

EXERCISE 13–9

Give stipulative definitions for each of the following words.

1. passing grade
2. big
3. old
4. cool
5. work
6. fun
7. geek
8. humongous
9. sharp
10. fast

[2]Walter Kaufman, *Without Guilt and Justice.* New York: Wyden Press, 1973.

It's time
to hatch a better word.

When the world's top tennis professionals fought their way through the recent U.S. Open tennis tournament, the courts they played on caused almost as much comment as their drives and lobs. For the first time, the green grass of Forest Hills was gone, replaced by a clay-like composition that gave the ball a truer bounce.

Forest Hills' innovation is just one more example of a trend all of us now take for granted—toward synthetic products that are actually better than the real thing. Little ones, like synthetic vitamins. Big ones, like flood gates of rubber-coated nylon that may save Venice from a repetition of the 250 floods the medieval city has suffered in the past 15 years.

It occurs to us that the word "synthetic" no longer fits, because it somehow implies a pallid imitation, not something better. *Webster's New Collegiate Dictionary* defines "synthetic" as "devised, arranged, or fabricated for special situations to imitate or replace usual realities." But where's the "imitation" in an inflatable nylon body brace that allows paraplegics to walk on crutches? (It's a third as heavy as a regular metal brace.) And clothes made from synthetics mixed with cotton and wool go beyond the "usual." Wrinkle-free with no ironing, they represent a true revolution to the housewife.

Today's heat-resistant silicon carbides combine the best properties of ceramic and metal. Lush artificial furs, now being perfected, promise to save Africa's wild beasts from extinction. Plas-

tics do everything now from brightening lives with long-playing records to saving them with blood-storage bags. The list goes on and on, but the bottom line never changes: <u>developing products of the highest quality which improve on nature itself</u>.

At Mobil, we market a line of synthesized hydrocarbon fluids that industry uses as circulating and gear oils. Our scientists spent 10 years perfecting them. They last three to five times as long as conventional lubricants. And they perform over a much broader temperature range. They're oil we never drilled for, and in these days of energy conservation, that's a big plus.

The line includes an auto engine lubricant which Mobil introduced abroad two years ago and is now test marketing in eight areas around the U.S. Without going into a commercial, extensive tests show this new lubricant can increase gasoline mileage for the average car as much as 10 miles per tankful, by drastically reducing engine friction. Additionally, it reduces oil consumption dramatically and facilitates starting down to 40 degrees below zero.

The thousands of new products developed through science are certainly more than just "synthetic," as Americans have come to understand the word. They're not only better than nature's products, but they conserve nature's resources in the process.

And they deserve a better name.

Although it is possible to stipulate a new meaning for an existing word in a totally arbitrary way (e.g., 'logic' = $_{df}$ 'orange peel') or an arbitrary meaning for a new word, we almost always have some reason for offering a new definition. Sometimes we can and do offer quite elaborate and carefully reasoned justifications for introducing new words or changing meanings of existing words. This ad provides a good example of the kind of argument that can be given in support of a new definition. What additional reasons can you think of for inventing a new word for the kinds of objects mentioned for which 'synthetic' is inappropriate? What arguments might be given for continuing to refer to such objects as 'synthetic'? Since no new word is suggested in the ad, can you think of a new word that might be used to refer to these objects?

13.2.3 To Remove Ambiguity or Vagueness

Ambiguity is said to exist *when a word or phrase having two or more distinct meanings is used in such a way that it is not obvious from the context which meaning is intended.* When we are told that a person is 'funny,' we might not be immediately certain whether the speaker means 'funny-haha' or 'funny-peculiar.' 'There's a rook on the patio' might refer to a large black bird or to a chess piece.

Vagueness exists *when the meaning of a term is sufficiently imprecise that it is impossible to tell whether or not it applies to certain borderline cases.* For example, the term 'hill' might seem clear enough, but at what point does a rise in the surface of the earth become a hill? Suppose I add one grain of sand at a time to a small mound; eventually the mound will become a hill, but where is the dividing line? If 4,987,523,610 grains of sand do not make a hill, do 4,987,523,611 grains make a hill? How about 4,987,523,612? There is a range of sizes within which most people will agree that the mound does not fit the definition of 'hill'; there is another range of sizes within which most will agree that it does; but there is a third, in-between range within which it is impossible to obtain a consensus. Instances that fall in this last range are known as **borderline cases.** Thus, a word is vague if it has borderline cases.

Almost all words in ordinary language are somewhat vague. If they were not so, everyday communication would be almost unmanageably overburdened with precision. One could not say, "I had scrambled eggs for breakfast." One would need to use different words according to whether the eggs were large, small, or medium sized; fresh or less than fresh; brown or white; scrambled hard or soft. One would also have to specify which other foods the meal included, at what precise time it was eaten, and so on. As it is, we can add these details to the account if we wish, but the vagueness of the terms 'eggs,' 'scrambled,' and 'breakfast' enables us to leave more specific details out if they are not relevant to what we want to communicate at the moment. A certain degree of vagueness and imprecision, then, is valuable. But too much can be a handicap, and then definitions must be offered to make the meanings of key words more precise.

Definitions used to eliminate ambiguity or vagueness are called **precising definitions.** They may be synonymous, connotative, or any of the other kinds discussed previously. They can also simultaneously serve the purpose of reporting accepted general or theoretical meanings, or they can be stipulative. Frequently, but not always, they are explicitly limited to specific contexts:

> **Throughout this book the word 'sound' will be used to mean 'valid with true premises.' (Removes ambiguity of 'sound,' which has several distinct meanings.)**

> **For the purposes of this discussion, the word 'old' will be used to mean 'at least seventy-five years of age.' (Removes vagueness of 'old,' which otherwise has borderline cases.)**

If the universe were like this, there would be very few vague concepts.

Precising definitions are not evaluated strictly in terms of truth or falsity. They are to be judged by whether they adequately eliminate ambiguity or vagueness and whether they do it without distorting the generally accepted meaning of the word. A definition that significantly changes the accepted boundaries of the definiendum—that is, that allows the word to be applied in cases where it was clearly inapplicable before, or excludes it in cases where it was clearly allowed before—can be said to be false, if it is being offered as a precising definition. For this reason the following definition can be considered to be false:

> **The word 'old' in ordinary English usage means 'at least ten years of age.'**

While this definition certainly eliminates vagueness, it also distorts the generally accepted meaning of the word 'old' in our culture, for it allows it to be applied in cases to which it is clearly not applicable under the rules of general usage.

EXERCISE 13–10

Give precising definitions for each of the following words. Explain why your definition is reasonable. For words with more than one meaning, choose the one that is most appropriate for giving a precising definition.

1. genius
2. big
3. old
4. cool
5. successful
6. healthy
7. obscene
8. rich
9. violent
10. fast

13.2.4 To Persuade

Synonymous, enumerative, connotative, and operational definitions can also be used persuasively. **Persuasive definitions** are used to change the attitudes or feelings of people toward specific things. Thus, one may connotatively define 'chiropractor' as 'someone who claims to be able to treat illness by messing around with your spine, although not a licensed M.D.' or as 'a highly trained manipulative practitioner, who frequently succeeds in curing persons whom conventional medicine has been unable to help.' The first of these definitions is probably intended to persuade one not to consult a chiropractor; the second is quite possibly intended to persuade one to do so. 'The unemployed' may be defined enumeratively as 'bums, people too lazy to work, and people who got fired,' or as 'people between jobs, and people for whom the capitalist economy fails to provide job opportunities.' The first definition might be cited to persuade someone to oppose an increase in welfare benefits, the second to arouse support for a socialistic economic program. Thus, persuasive definitions are usually geared to implanting in someone else's mind one's own evaluation of the definiendum and to affecting other people's behavior in some significant way.

It is generally inappropriate to evaluate persuasive definitions in terms of truth or falsity. Rather, a persuasive definition can be said to be good if it succeeds in doing what it was intended to do, and bad if it fails.

13.2.5 To Serve Social or Political Purposes

It is not at all uncommon for words to be defined or redefined to serve certain social or political purposes. Definitions used for such purposes can be of any

DEPRESSIONS: Inflation fighter Alfred E. Kahn has taken to calling that unmentionable economic downturn a "kumquat" rather than a "banana." Reason: a letter from United Brands Co. asserting Chiquita Banana's patriotism and claiming that banana price rises are now within the anti-inflation guidelines.

Shortly after he was appointed to head the anti-inflation program established by President Carter in 1978, economist Alfred E. Kahn stated in a press conference that a serious economic depression was quite possible if the anti-inflation guidelines were not followed. After newspaper headlines reported that Kahn had said that a depression was possible, the president told Kahn not to use the word 'depression' again. Kahn complied, and told the press that he would only talk about 'bananas' from then on. Shortly thereafter, the item above appeared in *Business Week* (December 25, 1978).
What kind of a definition did Kahn give? What uses did this definition have?

Supreme Court Rules Against Alcoholic Vets

WASHINGTON, DC The Supreme Court ruled 4-3 that veterans who claim disabilities due to alcoholism can be denied benefits by the Veterans Administration. In its ruling, the court stated that "primary alcoholism" as defined by Congress in the pertinent statutes is caused by "willful misconduct" and that veterans with the condition are "at least to some extent responsible for their disabilities."

of the several kinds and can also serve other purposes as well. To take one relatively simple example, many people in our society are very much concerned with the problem of alcoholism, either because it affects them directly and personally or because of its impact on society as a whole. Two fundamental problems are related to the definition of 'alcoholism.'

One problem is that the definition is far from precise, and there is much disagreement as to who is an alcoholic. Many definitions have been offered. The Women's Christian Temperance Union, which wants to make the consumption of any and all alcoholic beverages illegal, defines an alcoholic as "anyone who drinks alcohol. As soon as they start to drink they're on that road downward." The Rutgers University Center for Alcohol Studies defines an alcoholic as "one who is unable consistently to choose whether he shall drink or not, and who, if he drinks, is unable consistently to choose whether or not he shall stop." The National Council on Alcoholism gives an operational definition. The council has constructed a checklist of twenty-six questions, and then defined a "potential alcoholic" as anyone who gives an affirmative answer to any one question. Their questions include "Do you drink heavily after a disappointment?" and "Are you secretly irritated when your family or friends discuss your drinking?" Other researchers don't believe it is possible to formulate a very precise definition. Which if any of these positions is correct?

The second difficult problem associated with the definition of 'alcoholism' is that of deciding whether it should be categorized as a mental illness, a physical illness, or a moral weakness. The way in which it is defined can have a very significant impact. For example, if alcoholism is defined as a physical illness, the costs of treatment for one's illness would have to be covered by regular medical insurance policies. If it is defined as a mental illness, its treatment costs would be covered only by policies that provide for the treatment of mental illnesses. And, if it is defined as a manifestation of moral weakness, its treatment would not be covered by any kind of health insurance policy. In addition, societal attitudes toward the alcoholic would be quite different depending on whether the alcoholic is assumed to be suffering from a physical disease or to be a weak-willed moral degenerate.

A third significant effect of the definition of 'alcoholism' is in the area of governmental support for research. If alcoholism is defined as a physical illness, most of the research funds would be channeled to physiologists and internists. If it is defined as a mental illness, most of the funds would go to psychologists and psychiatrists. If it is considered to be a moral weakness, research funds would not be justified at all. Thus, the debates over the definition of concepts such as 'alcoholism' ultimately can turn out to be about very real and significant social and political policy issues.

EXERCISE 13–11

Next to each word listed below is a use to which a definition for that word might be put. Write a definition for each word which functions according to the use indicated. Provide a context for each definition where necessary.

1. forecast (reportive)
2. pornographic (precising)
3. Z-ray (stipulative)
4. vase (reportive)
5. religion (persuasive)
6. good teacher (precising)
7. friend (reportive)
8. gimbit (stipulative)
9. lover (precising)
10. coup d'etat (reportive)
11. rich (precising)
12. socialism (persuasive)
13. closed shop (limited reportive-legal)
14. politician (persuasive)
15. force (limited reportive-theoretical)

16. recent (precising)
17. counsel (limited reportive-legal)
18. velocity (limited reportive-theoretical)
19. bail (limited reportive-legal)
20. transmission (limited reportive-theoretical)

EXERCISE 13–12

Each passage below is concerned with the definition of a word, and in some cases a particular context has been supplied. Read each passage carefully and then determine the use to which the definition has been put. Is it (a) reportive, (b) limited reportive (perhaps theoretical or legal), (c) precising, (d) stipulative, (e) persuasive, or (f) a combination of these?

1. A physics teacher defining 'gravity,' stating Newton's law of universal gravitation: Every body of matter in the universe attracts every other body with a force directly proportional to the product of their masses and inversely proportional to the square of the distance between them.

2. A professor to her graduate philosophy seminar: To eliminate confusion in this discussion, I propose that we define 'intuition' as 'unmediated knowledge' and find other words to express the other meanings that some of those involved in the discussion are attaching to the word 'intuition.'

3. A statement in 1974 by corporate executive Irving S. Shapiro, describing effective training programs for persons who will be working for industrial companies: Nearly 80 percent of the people who will be of working age in the year 2000 are already on the job or are now in school. These people are the direct bridge to the twenty-first century. They're what we might call our "people connection" with the future. (*The New York Times,* Dec. 15, 1974)

4. Walter Lippmann, on the duty of public officials: Those in high places are more than the administrators of government bureaus. They are more than the writers of laws. They are the custodians of a nation's ideals, of the beliefs it cherishes, of its permanent hopes, of the faith which makes a nation out of a mere aggregation of individuals.

5. A music teacher to the class: Quality is one of the attributes of a note. By their quality, notes of the same pitch and volume may be distinguished. Quality depends on the extent to which overtones are present with the fundamental.

6. In addition, the newly discovered subatomic particle may be the first to possess a combination of mathematical properties rather unscientifically known as "charm" (a term first coined by physicists Sheldon Glashow and James Bjorken), which involves such basic characteristics as the way in which the particle is produced and the means by which it breaks up into other particles. (*Newsweek,* Dec. 2, 1974)

7. A law school professor to his class: Escrow is defined as property placed by one person in the hands of a second person, usually a trust company, for the delivery to a third person upon the fulfillment by the latter of certain specific obligations.

8. A lobbyist who is against repealing marijuana laws: Marijuana is the devil's weed; it weakens the mind of the user and destroys the fabric of American society.

9. A social problems instructor to his class: There are many varying definitions of poverty. By 'poverty,' I mean any family unit of two or more persons which has a yearly income of $4,800 or less, or any individual living alone who has a yearly income of $2,000 or less.

10. A musician teaching his daughter to play the piano: A natural is a note which is neither a sharp nor a flat.

11. A judge to a lawyer defending a thirteen-year-old charged with burglary: In this district all charged persons under sixteen years of age are juveniles, and hence are subject not to the jurisdiction of this court, but rather to the jurisdiction of the juvenile court.

12. A sociologist in a paper about juvenile sexual attitudes: In my study, 120 juveniles, which we shall consider to mean persons between the ages of eleven and sixteen, were interviewed to determine their attitudes toward sex roles, premarital sexual activity, masturbation, and other sexual matters.

13. A teacher to her class of sixth-graders: The word 'juvenile' which you just came across in this book means 'a young person.'

14. A chemistry professor to his students: In chemistry, the term 'sublimation' refers to the process whereby a solid changes directly to the gaseous state without liquefaction.

15. A tour guide at the New York Stock Exchange to tourists: That area with the circular steps on which all those frantic people are standing is the pit, the place where traders buy and sell stocks.

16. From an article on the status of railroads in the United States: Railroads—as a system of transportation, not as companies—should begin to get equal treatment with the subsidized highway system. . . . If the railroads are dying, it is partly because our mental images equate 'railroad' with 'company,' and so see dangers of socialism in a mix of public and private finance and ownership. Yet we have long ago accepted that mix as a fact of life in our street and highway system.

17. One businessman to another: We work under a 'contract system' with the federal penitentiary in Smithsville. We sign a contract with the federal government for the use of convict labor. It's a way of keeping costs down and it's a socially valuable system as well, since we provide convicts with job training.

18. A science major to a friend: The steady state universe is really a theory which states that the universe is infinite and eternal and that new material is formed to fill the gaps that occur as the universe expands.

19. A certain lunatic is convinced that all dons [Oxford professors] want to murder him. His friends introduce him to all the mildest and most respectable dons that they can find and after each of them has retired, they say, "You see, he really doesn't want to murder you; he spoke to you in a most cordial manner; surely you are convinced now?" But the lunatic replies, "Yes, that was only his diabolical cunning; he's really plotting against me the whole time, like the rest of them." . . . Let us call that in which we differ from this lunatic, our respective bliks. He has an insane blik about dons; we have a sane one. (R. M. Hare, in Antony Flew and Alasdair MacIntyre, *New Essays in Philosophical Theology*).

20. A high school teacher to her students: The word 'revere,' which the poet uses, means 'to worship or adore someone.'

13.3 Criteria for Good Definitions

For any word you care to think of, no one definition is the best for all purposes and under all circumstances. Definitions are not made in a void. They are a part of the process of human communication and must, therefore, be formulated to suit the purpose for which they are given as well as the audience to which they are addressed.

It would be as inappropriate to list all the known properties of copper in answer to a small child's question, "What is copper?" as it would be to define 'copper' by its looks, tarnished and untarnished, when a chemistry major asks the same question in the classroom. Neither definition would be appropriate if the question were asked by a visiting professor of chemistry who had only a scant knowledge of English. Here, the detailed connotative definition would be needlessly cumbersome; the definition in terms of its appearance would be unnecessarily vague; and both might overtax the professor's knowledge of English. For the professor, the preferred definition would probably be 'Cuprum $=_{df}$ Cu'—the synonymous scientific word and the internationally recognized chemical abbreviation for the element copper.

While the type of definition appropriate in a given context is determined by that context itself, some general criteria for good definitions can be applied to any definiens, be it synonymous, enumerative, connotative, operational, or of any other kind.

13.3.1 Noncircularity

To be satisfactory, a definition must bridge the gap between the unfamiliar and the familiar, by relating the unfamiliar definiendum to something that is already known and understood. When a definiens contains the word that is to be defined, or contains a grammatical variation of this same word, this definition is said to be **circular**. One can compare it to a dog chasing its own tail instead of catching the rabbit.

Defining 'feoffer' as 'one who makes a feoffment,' is circular and unenlightening, for it can be presumed that people who do not know the term 'feoffer' are equally ignorant of the word 'feoffment.' The only thing this circular definition reveals about 'feoffer' is that the word refers to a person. This leaves us with an infinite number of choices as to what the word actually means. For reasons of space, this kind of definition appears in dictionaries. But in a good dictionary, this circular definition would be supplemented by the entry, 'feoffment: the granting of a fee.' The conjunction of the two definitions eliminates the circularity.

13.3.2 Affirmativeness

Assume a department store has one thousand sweaters, and you know which one you want to buy. You could either tell the salesperson that the sweater you want is medium-sized, green, made of orlon, and with a boatneck collar, or you could say: "The sweater I want is not extra small, small, large, etc.; not blue, pink, white, etc.; not wool, cotton, dacron; I don't want a turtleneck, V-neck, etc."

For almost any word you want to define, there are thousands of attributes or denotations that do not apply, and only a few that do apply. Consequently, an **affirmative** definiens, which states the applicable, is generally far more efficient at pinpointing a definition than a negative definiens, which states what is inapplicable.

DOONESBURY © G. B. Trudeau. Reprinted with permission of UNIVERSAL PRESS SYNDICATE. All rights reserved.

What, if anything, is wrong with the definition of 'crisis' being used in this scene? Is there some way that 'energy crisis' could be defined that would prevent the bureaucrat/politician from being justified in announcing the end of the energy crisis?

One exception to this rule is any definiens for words that in themselves signify an absence of something: baldness (no hair), broke (no money), spinster (no marriage), dead (no life).

You might at first think that a negative definition that consists of saying 'the word's antonym is not applicable' would point straight to the definiendum. But the result is usually ambiguous. By defining 'optimist' as 'someone who is not a pessimist' or (assuming that whoever does not know 'optimist' will also be unfamiliar with 'pessimist') as 'one who is not a despairing person and does not habitually perceive or expect the worst,' we have not precluded the inference that 'optimist' means 'someone who sees both good and bad in everything and expects that some things will go well and others will go badly.'

When there are only two mutually exclusive categories into which the definiendum can fall, as whole numbers must be either odd or even, a negative definition of 'odd' as 'not even' is a satisfactory definition if one has already given a positive definition of 'even.'

13.3.3 Accuracy

A definition should be neither too broad nor too narrow. If it is too broad, it applies not only to the things referred to by the definiendum, but to other things as well. If it is too narrow, some concepts or things normally referred to by the definiendum will not be referred to by the definiens.

Defining 'pianoforte' as 'a musical instrument that has a keyboard' is too broad, for it fails to eliminate organs, harpsichords, and accordions. The definition 'a three-legged musical instrument that produces sound by means of a keyboard connected to hammers that activate strings by striking them' does successfully eliminate organs, harpsichords, and accordions. Unfortunately, it also eliminates some upright pianos.

It is possible to fail on both counts simultaneously, especially with short definitions, such as 'eating implement' as a definition of 'knife.' This definition is too narrow, since it rules out woodcarving knives, penknives, and so forth; and it is also too broad, because it includes forks and spoons. Such errors result when a definition fails to mention the most telling characteristic of the thing named by the definiendum, which, in the case of the knife, is that it is an instrument used for cutting.

No man, not even a doctor, ever gives any other definition of what a nurse should be than this—'devoted and obedient.' This definition would do just as well for a porter. It might even do for a horse. It would not do for a policeman.

FLORENCE NIGHTINGALE

On what grounds is the definition of 'nurse' being criticized? What are the social and political implications of the definition and what is the political message of the criticism?

13.3.4 Clarity

The following definition of the concept of deception is taken from an excellent dictionary and observes all the criteria for good definitions we have mentioned so far:

Die arglistige Erregung oder Erhaltung eines Irrtums in einem anderen durch bewußte Angabe falscher oder Unterdrückung wahrer Tatsachen. *(Knaurs Konversationslexikon.)*

This example demonstrates that a definition, however good it is in all other respects, must also be understandable to those for whom it is intended. One must try to gauge the knowledge and the vocabulary of the intended audience and then frame the definition accordingly. A definiens couched in unknown or unfamiliar terms is as unenlightening as the definiens of a circular definition.

EXERCISE 13–13

Indicate which criterion (or criteria)—like noncircularity, affirmativeness, accuracy, and/or clarity—is (are) violated by each of the following definitions.

1. A teacher to fifth-grade students: A protester is a person who protests.

2. A student in a college physics course to another student in the course: Velocity is how fast something travels.

3. A science teacher to fifth-grade students: Velocity is equal to acceleration times time.

4. A logic student to another logic student: Valid means justifiable or well-founded.

5. A doctor to a patient: A depressant is not a stimulant.

6. A logic professor to students: Vagueness is the quality or state of being vague.

7. A prosecutor to a jury: A defendant is one who is on trial because he or she has committed a crime.

8. A biology student to another student: Genetics is the science that deals with inheritance.

9. A science teacher to sixth-grade students: A layman is someone who is not trained as a scientist.

10. An English major to another student: 'Vainglorious' refers to someone who has the character flaw of vainglory.

11. Father to his teenage son: A jury is a group of people at a criminal trial.

12. A member of a sailing club to a new member: A schooner is a large sailing ship.

13. A craft enthusiast talking to a friend who knows nothing about weaving: A warp is the opposite of woof.

14. A worker at an international currency exchange to a visiting German tourist: A penny is one-hundredth of a dollar.

15. A San Franciscan to a French visitor who speaks little English: A church is an edifice used as a place of worship by a religious group, usually Christian.

Summary

1. Definitions enable us to identify and deal with statements whose truth or falsity is determined by the meanings of the words of which they are comprised. They are also important in evaluating arguments in everyday contexts, in determining whether a given sentence expresses a proposition and is thus analyzable, and in determining whether two or more expressions have the same meaning. Meaning and the definition of words can also have a powerful effect on the practical course of people's lives.

2. In logic, all definitions are primarily used to define words, not concepts or ideas. The term that is to be defined is called the **definiendum.** The word or words used to define it are called the **definiens.** When formulating a definition, it is important to specify the context in which the definiendum is being used. A definition may be classified as one of several kinds, depending on the type of definiens being used.

3. A **synonymous definition** is one in which the definiens consists of only one word that in appropriate contexts can be used interchangeably with the definiendum. We are thus using a special meaning of the term 'synonymous,' since, as it is used in everyday discourse, any adequate definition is such that its definiens is synonymous with its definiendum.

4. **Enumerative definitions** are divided into two categories, according to the manner in which the definiens is presented: **ostensive definitions,** which present the meaning of the definiendum by providing concrete examples or appropriate sensory experiences; and **denotative definitions,** which name examples of things to which the definiendum applies, without requiring the physical presence of the definiens.

5. The definiens in a **connotative definition** pinpoints the meaning of the definiendum by listing a set of properties common to all the things to which the definiendum can be correctly applied, and common only to those things. The sum total of a definiendum's essential properties is variously called the **intension** or the **connotation** of the definiendum. An increase in the intension of a definition (the adding of properties) will either diminish the **denotation (extension)** or leave it unchanged; a decrease in the intension of a definition (the elimination of some of the properties named by the definiens) will either increase the denotation or leave it unchanged.

6. A **definition by genus and difference** is a type of connotative definition that consists of specifying the general class of things to which the definiendum

belongs (the genus), and then further specifying the properties (the differentia or difference) by which the definiendum can be distinguished from the other things that belong to the same class. This type of definition is especially useful in any field of study that has been exhaustively classified. Connotative definitions must list the **essential attributes** of a definiendum. 'Essential attributes' is a relative term that can be defined as 'those attributes which, when included in the definiens, are most informative, most characteristic of the definiendum, and least open to misinterpretation.'

7. In an **operational definition,** the definiens provides a test or a formal procedure that is to be followed in order to determine the applicability of the definiendum.

8. Definitions can serve a variety of functions. A **reportive or lexical definition** is used to report the meaning of a term as it is used and understood by a specific group. It can be enumerative, connotative, synonymous, or operational; it can be judged as being true or false according to whether it accurately reports the way the word is actually used and interpreted by the group in question. A limited reportive definition reports the way a term is used in a technical or otherwise limited context; for instance, a **theoretical definition** defines a word in terms of the meaning which it carries in a particular scientific theory. Some words have both lexical and theoretical definitions; others are used and understood only in terms of their theoretical definitions. A **legal definition** is one that is specified in laws as formulated by a legislative, judicial, or executive body. It serves a limited reportive function when it is used in reference to a law that already exists and to a definition that is generally accepted.

9. A **stipulative definition** introduces new meaning. It may define either a newly coined word or a word that has a generally accepted meaning, but which is now being used in a new sense. Since there is no precedent for the newly stipulated use of a word, a stipulative definition cannot be true or false. It can be judged good if it achieves the specific purpose for which it was introduced and bad if it does not.

10. **Ambiguity** is said to exist when a word or phrase having two or more distinct meanings is used in such a way that it is not obvious from the context which meaning is intended. **Vagueness** exists when the meaning of a term is sufficiently imprecise that it is impossible to tell whether or not it applies to certain **borderline cases.** Definitions that are used to eliminate ambiguity or vagueness are called **precising definitions** and can be of any of the kinds of definitions previously mentioned. They are evaluated according to how well they eliminate ambiguity or vagueness without distorting the generally accepted meaning of the word.

11. Synonymous, enumerative, connotative, and operational definitions may also be used persuasively. **Persuasive definitions** usually reflect the beliefs

or persuasive intent of the speaker; they are usually intended to influence someone else's evaluation of the definiendum and to affect other people's behavior in some significant way. They are thus often used to achieve various social and political goals.

12. Some general criteria for good definitions can be applied to any definiens. A good definition is not **circular,** that is, the definiens does not contain the word that is to be defined, nor does it contain a grammatical variation of the same word. An **affirmative** definiens (one that states those attributes applicable to the word being defined) is generally more efficient at pinpointing a definiendum than a negative definiens (one that states what is inapplicable to the word being defined). A definition should be **accurate**—neither too broad nor too narrow. The definiens must also be **clear**—free from any vagueness or ambiguities that can reasonably be removed; and, unless the definition is a persuasive one, the definiens should convey or describe any positive or negative overtones carried by the definiendum.

Chapter 14

Applied Logic

As indicated in Chapter 2, the logical analysis of arguments is an art as much as it is a science. Chapter 2 provides a sketch of some of the complexities and subtleties of argument analysis, as well as informal preliminary analyses of several sample arguments. But most of the succeeding chapters are devoted to the formal and more "scientific" aspects of logical analysis, although they also include discussions of some of the simpler problems involved in translating individual sentences into the form appropriate to a particular system of formal logic.

Doing complete logical analyses of arguments involves many complexities that exceed the time and space limits of this book. In this chapter we concentrate primarily on the problem of *choosing* from among the various systems of logic the one that is most appropriate for analyzing a particular argument. However, we first need to take a moment to recognize that arguments—either inductive or deductive—are not always required to support specific statements.

When confronted with a statement or set of statements, we should not immediately assume that an argument is being tacitly or explicitly asserted. We might instead be dealing with something else, such as the assertion of a definition or the presentation of what is called "exposition." Even when we encounter a statement or set of statements that might seem to involve a conclusion for which we must find premises, we need to recognize that not all statements require arguments to support them. In other words, some assertions are such that in appropriate contexts, any request for proof can be answered simply with the statement that no proof is necessary for this statement in this context. Whether such a claim is correct or not requires that we determine where the burden of proof lies in a specific situation.

14.1 Burden of Proof

We sometimes encounter situations in which we are asked to provide reasons in support of statements we make. Thus, if we assert that "George Washington wore wooden false teeth," someone might very well ask "How do you know that to be true?" We could answer this in a variety of ways. For example, we could respond that we were taught this in a history class in grade school. If pressed to give a reason for saying that what we were taught in a history course is true, we might give an answer to the effect that we have found over a period of time that most of what we were taught in that class (or even most of what we were taught in school in general) has proved to be true in subsequent experience. And we could then go on, if pressed further, to explain how the other things we were taught have been confirmed or to show how this general experience with things taught in school supports our belief that George Washington, in fact, wore wooden false teeth.

Of course, we must always keep an open mind and be ready to recognize and willing to admit that our reasons might not be good ones. But it is also important to recognize that our inability to give good reasons in support of some of our judgments is not always a bad thing. Indeed, it is generally recognized that it is not possible to give reasons for or proofs in support of every one of our beliefs, even though someone may demand such justifications.

By demanding proof (and tacitly questioning the truth of our assertion) that Washington wore wooden false teeth, the person who asked how we knew this was attempting to place on us what is known as the **burden of proof.** In giving our reasons above, we were accepting the burden of proof; but we could

TRUDY

Reprinted with special permission of King Features Syndicate.

I decline altogether to explain why I am not a vivisectionist. It is for the vivisectionists to explain their conduct, not to challenge mine. I am on the jury, not in the dock. We have not yet reached a pass at which normal sanity, kindliness, and regard for the honor of science can be waylaid and called to account by sadism, ethical imbecility, and invincible ignorance.

GEORGE BERNARD SHAW

have refused to do so. We could also stop with the reasons that we have given up to this point and refuse to accept the claim that it is up to us to further prove the truth of the reasons already offered. One of the most common strategies for shifting the burden of proof is that used by children as displayed in the Trudy cartoon—sheer stubborn persistence. However, there are other more reasonable strategies and rules that are part of various cultures for determining on whom the burden of proof should be placed.

It is possible to give various kinds of reasons in support of one's position concerning burden of proof, although the reasons are not necessarily going to be more effective than Trudy's effort in the cartoon. One good example of the utilization of the strategy of shifting the burden of proof is provided by George Bernard Shaw's response to persons who wanted him to prove why it is wrong to kill and dissect and otherwise use animals in biological research.

In many areas of our culture, informal conventions and sometimes even formal rules exist that specify on whom falls the burden of proof of a given statement. Thus, it would generally be agreed that it is the responsibility of the person who is asserting that Martians exist or that New York City is not in the United States to prove the truth of such assertions rather than to require

---

Judge Fisk left the bench.

Mason turned to where Paul Drake and Della Street were seated beside him.

"Well," he said, "this is a lawyer's nightmare. I'm going to listen to the evidence without having the faintest idea of what the prosecution is holding up its sleeve until they start throwing punches."

"You can't get a word out of the defendants?" Drake asked, looking over to where Morley Eden and Vivian Carson were seated between two officers.

"Not a word," Mason said.

"Well, the prosecution has got something all right," Drake said. "They're keeping it buttoned up, but Ormsby is as snug as a bug in a rug."

"I know," Mason said, "but he doesn't want to be *too*

sure. I'm going to use every psychological trick that I can. I'm going to keep within the letter of the law but I'm going to make him prove these defendants guilty beyond all reasonable doubt.

"This is a case that is going to depend almost entirely on circumstantial evidence. It is a rule of circumstantial evidence, a rule of law in this state, that if the circumstances can be explained by any reasonable hypothesis other than that of guilt, the jurors are bound on their oaths to accept that hypothesis, and acquit the defendants.

"That is of course merely another way of stating the rule of law that a defendant can't be convicted unless the evidence proves him guilty beyond all reasonable doubt. If there is a reasonable doubt in the minds of the jurors they must resolve that doubt in favor of the defendants, and acquit."

From Erle Stanley Gardner, The Case of the Fenced-In Woman, 1972.

others to prove that they are false. In a more formal way, as part of our legal system, we recognize that it is the responsibility of others to prove the truth of a charge that a person is guilty of a criminal offense. The principle "innocent until proven guilty" places the burden of proof on the accuser; the accused does not have to prove that the charges are false, a fact that is central to lawyer Perry Mason's strategy in the case described on the preceding page.

14.2 The Principle of Induction

Chapters 3 through 11 present a number of different systems of formal logical analysis, including syllogistic, propositional, quantificational, enumerative inductive (by analogy and generalization), probabilistic, and Mill's methods of causal analysis. You have presumably studied at least two or three of these systems by now, enough to get a feel for some of the differences among them as well as some understanding of the relative strengths and weaknesses of each. Before studying the problems of choosing the appropriate system for analyzing an argument, we need to examine a procedure for converting arguments that appear to be inductive into arguments that are explicitly deductive.

We have emphasized that it is usually difficult and often impossible to determine whether a particular set of statements is intended as an inductive or deductive argument. We have also pointed out that, in supplying missing premises in an enthymeme, we must exercise judgment in applying the principle of charity since it is possible to formulate almost any argument as a valid argument or as a strong inductive argument. This is illustrated clearly by the following example:

> **The Republicans have always controlled the council in this city in the past so they will do so again next year.**

It is reasonable to assume that this is being offered as an argument, with 'The Republicans will control the council next year' being the intended conclusion and 'The Republicans have always controlled the council in the past' being a premise. With only this one premise, we have what is a reasonably strong inductive argument with what we can only presume to be a well-established truth for the premise. If we add another premise such as 'The same candidates are running next year as ran last year,' the argument might even be stronger, although it is still inductive. However, if we add certain other new premises, we can make the argument valid, as in the following case.

> **The Republicans have always controlled the council in this city in the past.**
> **[All similar events occur similarly in similar circumstances.]**
> **[The circumstances surrounding the city council election next year will be similar in all relevant respects to last year's election.]**
> **Therefore, the Republicans will win control in the election next year.**

The first of the premises we supplied is a version of a basic principle known as the **principle of induction.** When used in arguments (as in this example), it can make most arguments valid, but often, if not always, at the cost of introducing a premise or premises of questionable truth.

From a strictly logical point of view, such arguments are valid, since the truth of their conclusions necessarily follows from the truth of their premises. Remember, too, that, from a strictly logical point of view, we are not concerned either with the factual truth of the premises of an argument or with any temporal relation between the premises and the conclusion. As logicians, we are concerned only with the relationship between the premises and the conclusion—that is, with the support the premises offer for the conclusion. Quite clearly, the argument above, with the suppressed premises added, is logically stronger than the original argument. Nevertheless, there are serious obstacles to carrying out this reduction of an inductive argument to deductive form.

The first such obstacle is the problem of establishing the truth of the principle of induction itself. Although from a strictly logical point of view we need not be concerned with the truth of the premises of an argument, from a practical point of view this matter is of great concern, since as human beings we are interested in determining the best possible arguments. The "obvious" justification for the principle of induction might seem to be that it does, in fact, work. For instance, from past observations of voter behavior, poll takers regularly predict the outcome of the next election. From past observations concerning the attraction of iron to a magnet, we correctly infer that in the next instance in which iron is placed near a magnet, it will be attracted to the magnet. But this seemingly well-founded pragmatic justification of the principle of induction has been criticized as being circular, since it can be formulated as follows:

> **In the past it was useful to assume that similar things behave similarly under similar circumstances.**
> **Therefore, it is always useful to assume that similar things behave similarly under similar circumstances.**

What has happened here is that an inductive argument has been used to justify the principle of induction. (Some philosophers have argued that in this case we are dealing with a special type of self-supporting argument, and that the circularity is legitimate. This claim is not universally accepted.)

Numerous other arguments have been offered in support of the principle of induction, but none has been generally accepted. This has led some philosophers to suggest that, in fact, there is no justification for the principle of induction. Proponents of this view sometimes support their position by means of an argument based on an analogy between logic and branches of mathematics. They assert that just as there is no way, without circularity, to justify the axiom in geometry that the whole must be equal to the sum of its parts, so too it is impossible, without circularity, to justify a fundamental principle of logic such as the principle of induction. This argument may seem sound on the surface, but it is itself inductive, since it is based on an analogy. Although certain principles of reasoning in mathematics might not be provable, the argument from this analogy does not itself prove that the principle of induction cannot be justified. Here, again, an inductive argument has been used to support a conclusion about the principle of induction—in this case, the conclusion that no justification for it can be given.

In summary, no one has yet been able to provide a satisfactory justification for the principle of induction, but it would be pessimistic to conclude, on this ground, that no such justification will ever be provided.

In addition to the problem of justifying the principle of induction, we find that the reduction of inductive arguments to deductive form faces another serious obstacle—that of resemblance. No two states of affairs resemble each other exactly; if they did they would be the same state of affairs. Such an objection might seem trivial, but it points out a significant flaw in the principle of induction—one with practical importance for many arguments that involve "less similar" things. For instance, the social sciences often make predictions about human behavior based on observed cases, yet no one would argue that two human beings resemble each other in every way. Quite obviously, since no two states of affairs (whether they be objects, human beings, plants, events, or whatever) are identical, a judgment must be made as to whether or not two cases resemble each other in relevant ways.

A deductive argument, it will be remembered, is such that no matter what premises we add to the original, the argument remains valid. But when the principle of induction is used as a premise, it usually remains possible to add other premises that will affect the strength of the inference from the premises to the conclusion. This is so because, as we have seen, it is difficult to determine absolutely that the observed and unobserved cases are similar in all relevant respects.

EXERCISE 14-1

Assuming ordinary context, evaluate each of the following as inductive arguments. (a) Identify the conclusion. (b) Identify the stated premise(s). (c) Add a premise that will make the argument stronger. (d) Add a premise that will make the argument weaker. (e) Discuss how adding the principle of induction as a premise might change the argument.

1. I liked the 1992 Beaujolais wine that I drank. I liked the 1993 Beaujolais wine that I drank. I liked the 1994 Beaujolais wine that I drank. Therefore, I will like the 1995 Beaujolais wine that I am going to drink.

2. The guests our family has to dinner always like my mother's pot roasts. The Karlans are coming to dinner and my mother is serving pot roast. Therefore, the Karlans will like her pot roast.

3. John has done very well on all of his algebra tests, so he will do well on his algebra final today.

4. All swans observed to date have been white. Therefore, any swan observed in the future will be white.

5. We will be able to see the partial eclipse of the sun, since the weatherman says we will have a clear day tomorrow, the same as today.

6. Sluggo Jones has hit more home runs this season than any other player on the team. Therefore, he is likely to hit a home run today.

7. I walked under a ladder and then a black cat crossed my path, so something terrible is going to happen to me.

8. No runoff will be necessary. The polls say 52 percent of the voters favor the mayor for reelection.

9. Most east coast newspaper editors are liberals. Mr. Harrison is an east coast newspaper editor. Therefore, Mr. Harrison is liberal.

10. You will live to be at least seventy years of age. The life expectancy of someone your age is seventy years and your health has been better than average.

11. Most members of the National Rifle Association (NRA) oppose all gun registration. Mr. Robinson is a member of the NRA. Therefore, he opposes all gun registration.

12. Since it's not supposed to rain, and enough people to make two teams have promised to come, and we reminded them to bring their gloves and bats and balls, we should have a good baseball game at the picnic.

13. I just know I'm going to win some money at the race track today, because five of the horses I've picked fit the system I've worked out for picking winners.

14. There has been an outbreak of the Asian flu in the United States this month. You are more likely to catch the flu than I am because I have had a flu vaccination but you have not.

15. The automobile as we know it will eventually have to be replaced with other means of transportation, since at the present rate of consumption the known world petroleum reserves will be exhausted by the year 2020.

14.3 Choosing the Appropriate System

Given that we have at least several different systems to choose from, one problem now is that of deciding which system is most appropriate for the evaluation of the quality of any particular argument. As suggested in Chapter 2, the answer to this question is not an easy one. In fact, as we have just demonstrated, arguments that are expressed in an apparently inductive form can also be analyzed as deductive arguments.

The "arguments" used in the exercises in the preceding chapters (with the exception of Chapter 2), for example, Exercises 4–1 and 6–1, clearly fit into

From Mother of Her Country *by Alan Green. Copyright © 1973 by Alan Green. Reprinted by permission of Random House, Inc.*

the specific system of logic being discussed in those contexts. But the arguments in those exercises were constructed specifically for the purpose of being analyzed in a particular logical system; we very seldom find an argument in an everyday context that fits a specific system of logic clearly and naturally.

The closest that one might come to such a "natural" fit is the argument implicit in Rex Stout's endorsement of the book *Mother of Her Country*, which appears quite clearly to fit the syllogistic system. The conclusion of this intended argument can be formulated as the standard-form sentence, 'Rex Stout is a person who loves this book.' The explicitly stated premise has as its standard-form wording, 'Rex Stout is a person who loves the First Amendment and who loves to laugh.' Since 'person who loves this book' is the predicate of the conclusion, it must also appear in what we can assume to be the suppressed major premise, which can be expressed in standard form as 'All persons who love the First Amendment and who love to laugh are persons who love this book.' (This is, of course, the message the publishers hoped would get across to readers.) The syllogism, a valid **AAA-1,** can be written out in complete standard form as follows:

All persons who love the First Amendment and who love to laugh are persons who love this book.
Rex Stout is a person who loves the First Amendment and who loves to laugh.
Therefore, Rex Stout is a person who loves this book.

However "naturally" Stout's argument fits the syllogistic system, it would not be inappropriate (although it might require a bit more work) to analyze his argument using quantificational logic. And it would not be farfetched for someone to say that the supplied premise is obviously too strong (and thus is false); such a person might prefer to use something like 'Most persons who love the First Amendment and who love to laugh are persons who love this book,' and then proceed to evaluate the argument as inductive.

Although any of the systems mentioned above are appropriate for analyzing the Stout argument, it would be inappropriate to analyze the argument using propositional logic. Because the strength of the argument comes from the internal structures of the simple propositions comprising it, propositional logic does not provide access to internal structures and it would give the result that the argument is truth-functionally invalid (which is true) without giving any indication that it can be proved valid using another system.

To understand better the problems of choosing the appropriate system, let us reconsider some of the sample arguments that are discussed only briefly at the end of Chapter 2, the first of which is:

Ed is going to study hard in his logic course because he is rational and he wants to go to a good law school.

We identified the given premises and conclusion, and added several other premises (using the principle of charity), as follows.

A. Ed is going to study hard in this logic course.

B. Ed is rational.

C. Ed wants to go to a good law school.

[D]. Ed believes that studying hard in logic will help him get into a good law school.

[E]. Every rational person who believes that doing a specific thing will get him or her something he or she wants will do that thing.

We judged intuitively that the basic structure of this argument is represented by the following diagram.

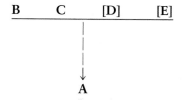

Remember that in Chapter 2, no method is available for proving that an argument is valid, and only the method of counterexamples is available for proving invalidity. Without a proof that the argument is valid we used the broken line in our diagram to indicate that the premises provide at most partial support for the conclusion, that is, that the argument is inductive. Now that we have several methods for proving validity and invalidity, we can see which if any of them might be appropriate for testing our sample argument.

Let us first try the system of syllogistic logic, since it is the simplest of those presented in this book. To use it, we must first translate the sentences expressing the premises and the conclusion into categorical standard form. For our sample argument, we get the following standard-form translation:

B. Ed is a rational person.

C. Ed is a person who wants to go to a good law school.

[D]. Ed is a person who believes that studying hard in logic will help him get into a good law school.

[E]. All rational persons who believe that doing a specific thing will get them something that they want are persons who will do that thing.

∴ A. Ed is person who is going to study hard in his logic course.

Since the argument has more than two premises, it is necessary to restructure it into a chain of syllogisms which are such that the conclusion of each becomes a premise of the next until the final conclusion is reached. But this cannot be done directly, since the premises in their present form do not fit together in such a pattern. 'Ed' is the subject of the ultimate conclusion and thus is the minor term and not the middle term. Is there any other possible middle term?

It might appear that the predicate term of [D] is the same as the subject term of [E], but a closer look reveals several small but significant differences, particularly that one term is singular and the other is plural and that the adjective 'rational' modifies 'person' in one but not in the other. Since no term other than 'Ed' appears more than once in the premises, we don't have any middle term. Thus, before proceeding we will either have to reformulate one or more of the premises that we already have, or else we will have to add some new premises that are reasonable and that will make the necessary connections between the premises. Further consideration indicates that this is not easily done for this particular argument. The most serious problem is the subject term of premise [E], which is a combination of the predicate terms of **B** and [D]. Since we have no procedure in syllogistic logic that allows us to combine two terms into one, the only other possibility would be to reconsider [E], which was not explicitly stated in the original version of the argument and which we added solely on the basis of intuition. But it is not at all clear that an alternative set of premises would do the job if they were added to the argument. Thus, instead of spending more time on this strategy (which might be nothing more than beating our heads against a brick wall), let us try another system to test the argument for validity.

Propositional logic is significantly simpler than quantificational logic. It also has the truth table procedure that gives us a definite answer, in a finite number of steps, as to whether an argument is valid or truth-functionally invalid. Thus, it is prudent to try it next. Premise **B** is a simple proposition since it contains no truth-functional operators, and **C**, [D], and [E], as well as the conclusion **A** are also truth-functionally simple. This means that each must be abbreviated by a different propositional constant. The schema of this argument is

1. p   Premise
2. q   Premise
3. r   Premise
4. s /∴ t   Premise/conclusion

Even if it seems intuitively obvious that this schema is truth-functionally invalid, we still need to *prove* that it is; we can easily prove its invalidity using the short truth table method and assigning the value **T** to each of the premises and **F** to the conclusion.

Since proving that an argument is truth-functionally invalid does not rule out the possibility that it can be proven to be valid in some other system, we still need to try quantificational logic to see if it might prove the argument valid.

The interior structure of the propositions constituting the argument about Ed can be made explicit using the more powerful symbolism of quantificational logic. First we must provide a dictionary indicating the meanings of specific individual and predicate constants. Many of these are relatively obvious, such as the following.

$$e = Ed$$
$$l = \text{the logic course Ed is taking}$$
$$Rx = x \text{ is rational}$$
$$Px = x \text{ is a person}$$
$$Gx = x \text{ goes to a good law school}$$
$$Sxy = x \text{ studies hard in } y$$
$$Wxy = x \text{ wants } y$$
$$Bxyz = x \text{ believes that doing } y \text{ will get them } z$$

Unfortunately, when we try to use this dictionary to symbolize the argument, we find that it is not sufficient. One premise, 'Ed is a rational person,' can be symbolized easily as '**Pe · Re.**' But the other three premises are at best problematic. The problems are caused primarily by the verbs 'wants' and 'believes,' which appear to be the same as verbs such as 'goes' or 'studies,' but which in fact operate quite differently in the contexts of these premises.

The term 'wants' often operates as an ordinary two-place predicate, as in 'Ed wants an apple,' which can be symbolized as '$(\exists x)(\mathbf{Ax} \cdot \mathbf{Wex})$' where '**Ax**' means 'x is an apple.' But 'to go to a good law school' is not a noun and it is not the main verb of the sentence; it is an infinitive phrase functioning as the direct object. We can easily symbolize 'Ed goes to a good law school' as '**Ge**,' but we cannot combine this with the main noun and verb 'Ed wants' in a grammatically correct way. Even if we were to use the ungrammatical formulation 'Ed wants Ed goes to a good law school,' we could not symbolize it because our system of quantificational logic does not allow us to symbolize the clause 'Ed goes to a good law school' as a predicate constant since it contains a proper name (which must be symbolized with an individual constant). Thus, the only way that we can symbolize premise **C** in quantificational logic is to lump everything together in the single predicate 'wants to go to a good law school.' Nothing is wrong with this in and of itself; the question is whether this symbolization is adequate for testing the argument for validity.

Similarly, the term 'believes' functions very differently from verbs such as 'goes' and 'studies.' The verb 'believes' is always followed by a complete clause, that is, an expression which if taken by itself is a grammatically complete sentence. As in our premises, 'believes' is often followed by a 'that.' We can easily symbolize 'Ed believes' as '**Be**,' but it is not at all clear what we can do with the 'that' or the clause following it in premise [**D**]. Even if we symbolize 'studying hard in logic' as '**Sx**,' it is hard to imagine which constant could be substituted for the '**x**' in a meaningful way. And even if we could figure something out here, there is simply no way that this could be connected to the basic clause 'Ed believes.'

The fact that we cannot adequately analyze this argument using any of the three systems of deductive logic presented in this book should not be interpreted to mean that these systems are not valuable. Syllogistic logic is quite useful for analyzing many arguments, such as the Rex Stout example. And propositional logic and quantificational logic are not only useful for a large number of arguments, as we shall see in the remainder of this chapter, but they are also very valuable insofar as they provide the foundations for a number of even more powerful (and complex) systems of deductive logic. Even though much material has been covered in this book, we have merely scratched the surface of the subject matter of logic. Methods for dealing with statements such as those in premises **C**, **[D]**, and **[E]** do exist, but they require systems of logic even more complex and sophisticated than the system of quantificational logic presented in this book. It is to be hoped that at the very least your appetite has been whetted and that you will go on to study more logic.

Although the more formal nature of systems of deductive logic restricts their utility for analyzing certain kinds of argument, the less formal systems of inductive logic can be used for the inductive interpretation of almost any argument. Thus, our example could be put in the following inductive form:

[1]. **Most people who are rational and who want something will do whatever is likely to help them get what they want.**

2. **Ed is rational and wants to go to a good law school.**

[3]. **All of the people whom Ed knows who studied hard in logic got into good law schools.**

4. **Therefore, Ed will study hard in his logic course.**

This interpretation actually involves one inductive argument inside of another. Premise [3] that we added provides inductive support for the conclusion that studying hard in logic helps one get into a good law school. Since Ed's range of personal acquaintances is presumably relatively limited, this inductive generalization has a weak negative analogy among the observed cases and is thus not a strong inductive argument. This inductively-arrived-at statement can then be used as a premise with [1] and 2 to provide inductive support for the conclusion that Ed will study hard. Since several of the premises are not themselves strongly supported, the argument is not very strong.

This example is evidence that arguments that appear intuitively to be relatively simple cannot always be easily analyzed, particularly in a system of formal deductive logic. Certainly, 'Ed is going to study hard in his logic course because he is rational and he wants to go to a good law school' appeared to be quite simple and straightforward when we first considered it in Chapter 2. But the attempts that we have just made to deal with it here, using the systems of deductive logic presented in this text, show that its analysis is not at all simple.

Finally, this example has also demonstrated that a knowledge of logic itself is not sufficient for analyzing arguments. It is equally important to develop the skill of being able to determine quickly and correctly which system of formal logic, if any, is appropriate for testing a particular argument for validity. And this skill can only be developed through patient and persistent practice. We can only help you begin this process here, by providing analyses of several more sample arguments and then giving a set of exercises on which you can practice.

Let us now consider the second example discussed in the final section of Chapter 2, an argument that looks a bit more complex on the surface but can in fact be analyzed adequately using one of the systems of logic presented in this book. The premises and conclusion of the argument are

B. At least one student in this logic course is lucky or works hard.

C. All students who work hard get As.

D. All students who are lucky get As.

∴ **A. Therefore, at least one student will get an A in this logic course.**

Seeing that each statement begins with either 'all' or 'at least one,' we should think immediately of the possibility of using syllogistic logic for testing the argument for validity. However, a closer look reveals that statement **B** contains an 'or'; we should remember that nothing in our discussion of syllogistic logic offers any way of dealing with a statement containing an 'or.' We know that propositional logic has the wedge, which can be used to symbolize the 'or' (which seems to be an inclusive 'or') in statement **B**. But propositional logic would require us to symbolize the component propositions as follows.

L = At least one student in this logic course is lucky.

W = At least one student in this logic course works hard.

H = All students who work hard get As.

S = All students who are lucky get As.

A = At least one student will get an A in this logic course.

Even though the statements abbreviated by 'L' and 'S' are similar to a certain degree, we cannot abbreviate both with the same propositional constant because they clearly do not say exactly the same thing. The same holds for the propositions abbreviated by '**W**' and '**H**.' The schema of this argument in propositional logic is

p ∨ q, r, s / ∴ t

The fact that it is possible to assign the value **F** to the conclusion and **T** to each of the premises is sufficient to prove that the schema is truth-functionally invalid. But this of course does not mean that the argument cannot be proved valid in another system, so let's try quantificational logic.

The following dictionary is one that appears to fit the original version sufficiently well to serve as the basis for abbreviating the argument.

S = is a student in this logic course

L = is lucky

W = works hard

A = will get an A in this logic course

Unfortunately, as soon as we start to symbolize the premises and conclusion using this dictionary, it becomes clear that things are not as simple as they first seemed. Part of the problem is a degree of vagueness in premises **C** and **D**. Does

C say that all students who work hard get As in all of their courses? If it does, then we cannot symbolize premise C using the predicate constant 'A' as defined above. Or does C make the more limited claim that all students who work hard in logic get As in logic? Or does it make the even more limited claim that all students who work hard in this logic course get As in this course? Since all that we need for this particular argument is the weakest claim about this logic course, we will interpret the premise in this sense, which means that we need to change the definition of one of the predicate constants to the following:

W = works hard in this logic course.

We probably don't need to be as specific about the predicate 'is lucky,' but we should interpret premise D as also asserting only that lucky students get As in this logic course.

Now the argument can be symbolized quite directly as

1. $(\exists x) (Sx \cdot (Lx \lor Wx))$ Premise
2. $(x)((Sx \cdot Wx) \supset Ax)$ Premise
3. $(x)((Sx \cdot Lx) \supset Ax) / \therefore (\exists x)(Sx \cdot Ax)$ Prem./concl.

The proof of the validity of this argument is relatively simple and straightforward, as long as the instantiation rules are applied in the proper sequence. To be specific, the rule of existential instantiation must be applied to premise **1** before universal instantiation is applied to either **2** or **3**. Our proof then goes as follows:

4. $Sa \cdot (La \lor Wa)$ EI, 1
5. $(Sa \cdot Wa) \supset Aa$ UI, 2
6. $(Sa \cdot La) \supset Aa$ UI, 3
7. $(Sa \cdot La) \lor (Sa \cdot Wa)$ Dist., 4
8. $Aa \lor Aa$ Dil., 5,6,7
9. Aa Taut., 8
10. Sa Simp., 4
11. $Sa \cdot Aa$ Conj., 9,10
12. $(\exists x)(Sx \cdot Ax)$ EG, 11

Thus our perseverance has paid off better with this argument than it did with the previous one, and we have found a formulation that we have proven to be valid. But there is still one other possibility that we need to consider.

When we considered the vagueness of premises C and D, we were concentrating on finding an interpretation of them that would be consistent with the original argument and would allow us to construct a proof in quantificational logic. But from a broader perspective, it is still possible to question whether the argument should be interpreted as deductive at all. Certainly the interpretations we have just used of premises C and D are as weak as possible to keep the argument valid, but they are still rather strong and their truth might be considered doubtful. Interpreting **C** as describing the past, for example, as 'All students who have worked hard in courses in the past have gotten As,' makes it more plausible that it is true. Likewise, changing the universal quantifier to 'most' or 'almost all' would also make premise **C** more plausible. The same changes could be made to premise **D.** But both of these interpretations make the argument inductive.

Examining this example as an inductive argument, we can see that its premises give relatively strong support for the conclusion, insofar as a strong positive analogy exists between the observed cases and the unobserved case. If we interpret **C** as referring to all students who have worked hard in all kinds of courses in the past, the negative analogy among the observed cases will be greater than if we interpret it as referring only to all students who have worked hard in logic courses. And if the negative analogy among the observed cases is greater, then the argument is inductively stronger.

In summary, this argument can be reasonably interpreted as a deductive argument that can be proven valid using quantificational logic and it can also be interpreted (at least as plausibly) as a relatively strong inductive argument.

The next example is the one from Chapter 2 about Susan and her logic course, which in its original form reads

> **Susan should do well in this logic course because she always does**
>   **well in science courses.**

We begin by considering how, if at all, this argument might be analyzed in syllogistic logic, proceeding from there to analyze it in terms of propositional, quantificational, and inductive logics.

In our preliminary analysis, we added a variety of possible suppressed premises and came up with three different formulations of the original argument. The formulation that appears to be most amenable to testing for validity using the methods of syllogistic logic is the following.

> **This logic course is a science course.**
> **Susan is taking this logic course.**
> **Susan always does well in science courses.**
> **Therefore, Susan will do well in this logic course.**

The first step in dealing with any argument in syllogistic logic is to express each proposition in standard form. This gives us:

> **This logic course is a science course.**
> **Susan is a person who is taking this logic course.**
> **Susan is a person who always does well in science courses.**
> **Therefore, Susan is a person who will do well in this logic course.**

We must now try to break the premises into a sequence of valid syllogisms that will ultimately lead to the desired conclusion. Unfortunately, the only term that appears twice in the three premises, and thus the only candidate for a middle term, is 'Susan,' and this is the minor term. Moreover, there is only one valid syllogism that can be constructed with two **A** premises in the third figure (that is, the middle term in the subject of each premise), namely the **AAI-3**. This would give us one of two intermediate conclusions: 'Some persons who are taking this logic course are persons who always do well in science courses' and its converse, neither of which could be used to support the **A** proposition in the principal conclusion. Thus we must write off the argument as invalid or find another plausible interpretation of the original argument that would test out favorably in syllogistic logic. The following reformulation would seem to satisfy this requirement.

> **All persons who always do well in science courses are persons who should do well in this logic course.**
> **Susan is a person who always does well in science courses.**
> **Therefore, Susan is a person who should do well in this logic course.**

This is an **AAA-1** syllogism that can be easily proven valid using the methods of syllogistic logic. Notice that this new version is still faithful to the original insofar as it includes everything that is explicitly stated in the original. As you gain experience, you will find that it gets easier to add premises that make the argument valid in a given system without running into dead ends as we did on our first try with this example.

Now let us try to analyze this argument using propositional logic. The premises and the conclusion contain no truth-functional operators, and thus each is a simple statement. We begin our analysis by underlining a letter in each sentence expressing a simple statement so that we can abbreviate the argument and give its schema.

> **This logic course is a science course.**
> **Susan is taking this logic course.**
> **Susan always does well in science courses.**
> **Therefore, Susan should do well in this logic course.**

If we symbolize this in the propositional calculus, we get the following abbreviation and schema:

$$
\begin{array}{ll}
\text{L} & \text{p} \\
\text{T} & \text{q} \\
\text{W} & \text{r} \\
\therefore \text{S} & \therefore \text{s}
\end{array}
$$

We can tell by inspection that the proposition in the conclusion is not contained in any of the premises, and we can also see that the premises are consistent and the conclusion is not a contradiction. We could, therefore, conclude immediately that this example is truth-functionally invalid. However, let us confirm this using the shorter truth table technique. If we assign the value **F** to the conclusion, it is still possible to assign the value **T** to each of the three premises as follows.

p, q, r ∴ s
T   T   T   F

Although this is sufficient to prove that the example is truth-functionally invalid, remember that it does not prove that it is not valid; this argument might still be proved to be valid using some other system of formal logic, and as we have already seen, it can be proven valid using syllogistic logic. Although we might try to come up with a creative reformulation of this argument that would be more suitable for analyzing in propositional logic, no point would be served by such an effort since it would be a less "natural" interpretation than the syllogistic one we have already used.

All arguments that can be proven valid in syllogistic logic can also be handled in quantificational logic, although because the two systems of logic have different assumptions about the existence of members in the classes of the various terms, some arguments that can be proven valid in syllogistic logic cannot be proven valid in quantificational logic. Let us symbolize in quantificational logic the syllogistic interpretation we have already formulated and then see if we can construct a proof for it.

s = Susan
S = is a person who always does well in science courses.
L = is a person who should do well in this logic course.

Using this dictionary, the argument can be symbolized and proved valid as follows:

1. $(x)(Sx \supset Lx)$ Premise
2. Ss / ∴ Ls Premise/conclusion
3. $Ss \supset Ls$ UI, 1
4. Ls M.P., 2,3

Finally, let us go back to the original formulation of the argument and see how it might be treated as an inductive argument. Its original form was

Susan should do well in this logic course, because she always does well in science courses.

In this form, these statements already constitute an inductive argument since the statement, 'She always does well in science courses,' provides some, but not absolute, support for the other statement. We saw in our preliminary analysis that there are many ways of interpreting these statements in conjunction with the addition of various possible (but relatively implausible) suppressed premises that can result in apparently valid arguments. We also saw that if the given premise is interpreted as applying only to science courses Susan has taken in the past—which makes it more plausible—several different inductive arguments can be formulated, one of which is the following:

> This logic course is a science course.
> Susan is taking this logic course.
> Susan has always done well in science courses in the past.
> Therefore, Susan will do well in this logic course.

You should now be able to recognize quickly that insufficient information is provided for this argument to have very much inductive strength. The premise asserting that Susan has always done well in science courses in the past does not really tell us much at all. For example, it does not specify how many science courses she has taken or what the nature of those courses was. It would certainly make some difference if she had taken three science courses or twenty of them. It is also important to know what kind of science courses Susan took so that we can assess the degree of positive and negative analogy among the past cases and between these cases and the present case (this logic course). The premise would be true even if Susan had taken only three science courses—all in geology—but, in such a case, it would provide much less support for the conclusion than if she had taken twenty very different courses, including topology, calculus, set theory, physical chemistry, and molecular biology, where the negative analogy among the observed cases is much greater. The argument would also be relatively strong if Susan had done well in only three courses, all of which are quite similar to logic (for example, Euclidean geometry, set theory, and computer programming) because this would create a strong positive analogy between the observed and unobserved cases.

Thus, as presented, the argument about Susan's grade is inductively weak because so little information is provided in the premise. As we have seen, if the facts underlying this premise were of a certain kind (for example, many courses similar in various ways to logic), and if they were made explicit, the argument could be made quite strong. But in its present form, we have no basis for assuming anything more than the weakest possible interpretation of this premise, namely that Susan has taken only a few science courses, none of which is very similar to logic.

Let us consider only briefly a deductive interpretation of the argument concerning the transmission of the smallpox virus. The preliminary formulation in Chapter 2 seems most amenable to analysis in propositional logic.

> Mrs. Parker was infected with the "Abid" strain of smallpox virus.
> A quantity of the "Abid" smallpox virus was being stored in the lab directly below Mrs. Parker's office.
> It is possible for smallpox virus to be transmitted through the air.
> There was no other possible source of the "Abid" virus than the downstairs lab.
> Mrs. Parker had not been in contact with any person or object from the downstairs lab.
> Therefore, Mrs. Parker must have been infected by a virus transmitted through the air from the downstairs lab.

A bit of thought reveals that since there are no recurring simple propositions in this formulation, it could not be truth-functionally valid. We must, therefore, try to add some compound statements that connect the other premises. The following appears to be a reasonable possibility:

> **If Mrs. Parker was infected with the "Abid" strain of smallpox virus, and there was no other possible source of the virus than the downstairs lab, then either she had been in direct contact with some person or object from the downstairs lab, or she was infected by a virus transmitted through the air from the downstairs lab.**

With the addition of this premise, the second and third premises become unnecessary. The argument can now be abbreviated and schematized as follows (eliminating unnecessary premises).

I	p
~S	~q
~C	~r
$(I \cdot {\sim}S) \supset (C \vee T)$	$(p \cdot {\sim}q) \supset (r \vee s)$
∴ T	∴ s

Since there are only four variables in the schema, the truth table would only have sixteen rows. However, a deductive proof would still probably be simpler, so we will try this method first:

1.	p	Premise
2.	~q	Premise
3.	~r	Premise
4.	$(p \cdot {\sim}q) \supset (r \vee s)$ / ∴ s	Premise/conclusion
5.	$p \cdot {\sim}q$	Conj., 1,2
6.	$r \vee s$	M.P., 4,5
7.	s	D.Syll., 6,3

Once again, proving validity for this truth-functional formulation is not that difficult. The significant question is whether the argument that we ultimately proved to be valid is essentially the same as the argument with which we began. In this case, it is not at all clear that it is the same.

Our preliminary analysis in Chapter 2 of this argument shows how it can be interpreted as an inductive argument. It is interesting to recognize now that this was not a "pure" form of enumerative induction. The argument qualified as an induction primarily because it was seen that the premises do not provide absolute support for the conclusion, that is, that it is possible to add certain premises that would make the conclusion false. Even though it is not an enumerative induction, the argument is worth taking another look at in this context. Our last formulation of it was as follows:

> The medical examiners reported that Mrs. Parker was infected with the "Abid" strain of smallpox virus.
>
> A quantity of the "Abid" strain of smallpox virus was being stored in the lab directly below Mrs. Parker's office.
>
> Of all the millions of cases of smallpox examined over the years, there was only one in which it appeared that the virus was transmitted through the air.
>
> Mrs. Parker was not known to have been in contact with any person or object from the downstairs lab.
>
> Therefore, Mrs. Parker must have been infected by a virus transmitted through the air from the downstairs lab.

To relate properly to the conclusion, the first premise needs to be interpreted as the premise of an enthymeme, because we are concerned with Mrs. Parker's illness, not with reports of medical examiners. The necessary argument is an enumerative induction something like the following:

> In the past, the medical examiners' reports have (usually) been correct.
>
> The medical examiners reported that Mrs. Parker was infected with the "Abid" strain of smallpox virus.
>
> Therefore, Mrs. Parker was infected with the "Abid" strain of smallpox virus.

The critical point in the general argument is not, however, whether Mrs. Parker had the "Abid" strain of smallpox but whether it was transmitted through the air. The support for this part of the argument is limited to two pieces of evidence—one to the affect that she was not known to have been in physical contact with any person or object from the downstairs lab, which was the only known source of the virus. It is doubtful that conclusive evidence could be given in support of either of these knowledge claims; it remains possible that she was in physical contact with someone or something that was carrying the virus, and it is also possible that there was some other source of the virus.

The other essential point concerning the transmission of the virus through the air is the claim that this is possible, based on the one documented case in which it was judged that such transmission had occurred. Given that only one such instance was ever documented out of the millions of cases of smallpox observed over the years, we would need a great deal of additional information about that one case before we could make a judgment as to how much weight it should be given in the evaluation of this argument. If the evidence was indeed strong in that case and if there is a strong similarity (that is, positive analogy) between that case and the present case, then this argument could be relatively strong even though the induction is based on only one observation. But this is only because the argument would then fit the model of Mill's methods for identifying causes (discussed in Chapter 10). For the moment, we can only judge that in its present form and with the information provided, it is not possible to evaluate this inductive argument as an enumerative induction.

Let us finally consider the argument concerning the motel operators. Our initial informal analysis in Chapter 2 is quite complex. Since no method of testing for validity is available there, we could only make an educated guess that the argument is probably not valid. The interpretation of this argument given in Chapter 2 in fact goes beyond the capabilities of any of the systems of logic presented in this text, insofar as premises **A** and **[J]** require a system that allows us to symbolize statements such as 'Somebody said that _____,' and this cannot be done even in quantificational logic as presented in Chapter 7. But insofar as we are now more familiar with the systems discussed in this book, we might be able to see another possible interpretation of the original argument that can be proved valid using one of these systems.

Since the argument seems to involve a number of 'if . . . then . . .' statements, let us see if we can formulate an interpretation of the argument that can be tested in propositional logic. Let us start with the following interpretation, which seems consistent with the original argument and which also seems to be analyzable in propositional logic.

> The resort motel operators in one Florida town all said that their business was fine.
> The parking lots of these motels were practically empty.
> The local bank reported that it had cashed many fewer travelers' checks than in the previous year.
> [If a resort motel's parking lot is almost empty, and its bank has not cashed many travelers' checks, then the resort motel's business is not good.]
> [If someone says business is good when it is not, then he is lying.]
> [If all of the resort motel operators interviewed in one Florida town lie about their business, then all resort motel operators lie about their business.]
> Therefore, all resort motel operators lie about their business.

The abbreviation and schema for this example are:

M	p
P	q
B	r
$(L \cdot {\sim}C) \supset {\sim}G$	$(s \cdot {\sim}t) \supset {\sim}u$
$S \supset H$	$v \supset w$
$I \supset O$	$x \supset y$
$\therefore O$	$\therefore y$

The symbolization of this example requires some explanation. At first glance, it might seem that the antecedent of the fourth premise should be abbreviated as '$P \cdot B$' rather than '$L \cdot {\sim}C$,' since it appears to be a conjunction of the second and third premises. This certainly would give the set of premises greater coherence, but unfortunately it does not represent the argument as we formulated it in our preliminary analysis. The second premise is about the specific set of resort motels in a particular town, whereas the first part of the fourth premise is about a randomly selected motel anywhere—and is thus about all motels everywhere. Likewise, the third premise is about a specific bank in the one town in Florida, while the fourth premise is about banks in general. Similarly, premise 5 is about anyone who misrepresents their business, which is quite different from the first premise that is about only the motel operators in one town. It is for this reason that different symbols had to be used in the abbreviation and schema of this argument. On this basis, the argument can be shown to be truth-functionally invalid using the shortened truth table method.

p,	q,	r,	(s	·	~	t)	⊃	~	u,	v	⊃	w,	x	⊃	y		∴ y
T	T	T	T	T	F	T	T	F	T	T	T	T	F	T	F		F

But let's not give up too quickly. Our educated guess was that the 'if . . . then . . .' structure of several premises indicates that the argument might be analyzable in propositional logic, so let's see if we can modify our interpretation of the premises not only so that they remain consistent with the original statement of the argument, but also so the argument will also test out as valid. Rather than formulate the added premises in a generalized form as we did originally, we can formulate them to refer to the same things as the explicit premises, so that the same symbols can be used in the abbreviations of two or more premises.

> The resort motel operators in one Florida town all said that their business was fine.
> The parking lots of these motels were practically empty.
> The local bank reported that it had cashed many fewer travelers' checks than in the previous year.
> If the parking lots of these motels were practically empty, and the local bank reported that it had cashed many fewer travelers' checks than in the previous year, then the business of these motels was not good.
> If the resort motel operators in one Florida town all said that their business was fine and the business of these motels was not good, then these motel operators lie about their business.
> If the resort motel operators in one Florida town lie about their business, then all resort motel operators lie about their business.
> Therefore, all resort motel operators lie about their business.

The abbreviation and schema for this formulation are as follows:

M	p
P	q
B	r
(P · B) ⊃ ~G	(q · r) ⊃ ~s
(M · ~G) ⊃ L	(p · ~s) ⊃ t
L ⊃ O	t ⊃ u
∴ O	∴ u

In this form, the argument schema has six variables, and thus its truth table would have 26, or 64, rows. It would, therefore, be most reasonable either to try to prove it to be invalid using the short truth table method, or to go with our intuitive hunch that the argument in this form is valid and try to prove that it is, using the method of deductive proof. Let us try the latter approach first. If after a while we can't complete the proof, then we can test it for invalidity using the short truth table method.

1. p		Premise
2. q		Premise
3. r		Premise
4. (q · r) ⊃ ~s		Premise
5. (p · ~s) ⊃ t		Premise
6. t ⊃ u / ∴ u		Premise/conclusion
7. q · r		Conj., 2,3
8. ~s		M.P., 4,7
9. p · ~s		Conj., 1,8
10. t		M.P., 5,9
11. u		M.P., 6,10

Thus, we have proven that in this formulation the argument is valid. The difficult judgments, of course, are whether this formulation is sufficiently close to the author's intent and whether the truth of the premises is reasonably well established, and these judgments are beyond the scope of the methods of formal logic.

EXERCISE 14–2

Reconsider the arguments for which you did a preliminary analysis in Exercises 2–12 and 2–13. Try to reformulate each argument in ways that are appropriate for analyzing it, using each of the systems of logic that you have studied thus far. Then carry out the analyses in each of the systems in which it seems possible. Compare your analyses here with those of the same arguments that you did in Exercise 2–12 and Exercise 2–13.

Summary

1. When we insist that someone give reasons in support of a particular statement, we are trying to place the **burden of proof** on that person. Informal conventions and sometimes even formal rules exist in every culture that help to determine where the burden of proof for various kinds of statements normally rests.

2. It is often asserted that all inductive arguments are grounded in the **principle of induction,** which can be formulated as the assertion that events in the future will resemble events in the past or that unobserved cases will resemble observed cases—i.e., that similar things behave similarly in similar circumstances.

3. It is sometimes argued that, if this principle is considered to be a suppressed premise, all inductive arguments can be reduced to deductive arguments. From a practical point of view, there are several obstacles to this reduction. One is in establishing the truth of the principle of induction itself.

4. Many arguments that we encounter in everyday contexts are such that it is not obvious at first glance whether they can be analyzed best using one particular system of logic or another. Depending on which set of statements one adds to those explicitly presented, one can convert an argument into one that is most appropriately analyzed using syllogistic logic, propositional logic, or even the concepts of the informal fallacies. This requires the development of skill through sustained practice.

Answers to Odd-Numbered Exercises

EXERCISE I–1

1. d	11. c
3. e	13. a
5. d	15. e
7. c	17. e
9. d	19. a

EXERCISE I–2

There are countless correct answers to each of these questions; the following are merely samples.

1. My torso, my head
   The Rosetta Stone, the Hope Diamond

3. Every intelligent person, 2 + 2 = 4
   Jackie Collins, she is a terrific writer

5. Alex has cleaned up her mess, she is lazy
   you like cartoons, you have no sense of humor

7. eat anchovies, eat goat cheese
   bet on horses, win

9. pyramids, spheres
   great artists, happy

EXERCISE I–3

1. _____ is happy.

3. Joe joined the _____.

5. Ben swam to _____ and Dave swam to
   ✱✱✱✱✱✱✱✱✱✱.

7. If Mt. Julio is taller than Everest, then if I
   climbed Mt. Julio, I'm ✱✱✱✱✱✱✱✱✱✱.

9. Either roses are _____ or violets are
   ✱✱✱✱✱✱✱✱✱✱.

11. Either I ate the _____ or I ate the
    ✱✱✱✱✱✱✱✱✱✱.

13. If _____ passed the ball then the Blankets
    ✱✱✱✱✱✱✱✱✱✱ the game.

15. _____ will _____ you if and only if
    you are ✱✱✱✱✱✱✱✱✱✱.

EXERCISE I–4

1. a	5. a
3. c	7. b

EXERCISE 1–1

A variety of correct answers are possible for this exercise.

EXERCISE 1–2

Sample answers for 1 only. A large variety of different correct answers are possible for each exercise. For example:

1. Groom's commitment to bride at a wedding ceremony

EXERCISE 1–3

A variety of correct answers are possible for this exercise.

EXERCISE 1–4

Sample answers for 1 only. A large variety of different correct answers are possible for each exercise. For example:

1. Cognitive context: A situation where a person uses this sentence to express the fact that he or she is cold. (I am feeling cold.)
Noncognitive context: A situation where one person orders another person to close the window of a chilly room.

EXERCISE 1–5

1. Cognitive: This sentence expresses a factual statement about which it is appropriate to say it is true or false.
3. Noncognitive: This sentence expresses a command not usually considered either true or false.
5. Cognitive
7. Noncognitive
9. Cognitive
11. Cognitive
13. Noncognitive
15. Noncognitive ('Leave my brother alone!')

EXERCISE 1–6

1. 1	9. 9
3. 2	11. 5
5. 10	13. 8
7. 11	15. 7

EXERCISE 1–7

1. Semantically analytic
3. Syntactically analytic
5. Semantically analytic
7. Semantically analytic
9. Syntactically analytic

EXERCISE 1–8

1. Synthetic
3. Semantically analytic
5. Synthetic
7. Synthetic
9. Syntactically analytic
11. Synthetic
13. Semantically analytic
15. Syntactically analytic

EXERCISE 1–9

1. Consistent
3. Consistent
5. Inconsistent
7. Inconsistent
9. Inconsistent

EXERCISE 1–10

1. Consistent
3. Consistent (if "neurotically fussy" means "careful, conscientious," otherwise probably inconsistent)

5. Consistent

7. Inconsistent

9. Inconsistent

EXERCISE 1–11

1. An apparent disagreement, since both statements may be true simultaneously.

3. An apparent disagreement/verbal; persons A and B are probably using different definitions for the term 'poor.'

5. Most likely an apparent/verbal disagreement with persons A and B having different ideas about what a long book is and what is exciting.

7. An apparent disagreement; statement A refers to a perception of the straw, while statement B refers to the way the straw really is.

9. A real disagreement

11. A real disagreement

13. An apparent disagreement; it may be true that the sun looks as though it revolves around the earth even though the earth may in fact revolve about the sun.

15. Most likely an apparent/verbal disagreement with persons A and B having different ideas about what indicates good academic performance.

EXERCISE 1–12

1. A implies B.

3. Independent

5. B implies A.

7. Independent

9. A implies B.

11. Logically equivalent

13. Logically equivalent (Both are syntactically analytically true.)

EXERCISE 1–13

1. (a) B must be true, (b) A must be true, (c) B must be false, (d) A must be false

3. (a) B must be true, (b) A must be true, (c) B must be false, (d) A must be false

5. (a) B must be false, (b) A must be false, (c) B must be true, (d) A must be true

7. (a) B is undetermined, (b) A must be true, (c) B must be false, (d) A is undetermined

9. (a) B must be false, (b) A must be false, (c) B is undetermined, (d) A is undetermined

EXERCISE 2–1

A variety of answers are possible.

EXERCISE 2–2

1. E	7. E
3. B	9. D
5. B	11. A

EXERCISE 2–3

A variety of answers are possible. For example:

1. If you chose (a) then you might argue as follows:
   The nation is great.
   All great nations were built by rugged individuals.
   Therefore, rugged individualism is one of the qualities that has contributed to the nation's greatness.

3. If you chose (b), you might argue as follows:
   Nuclear energy policies can either be determined by the public and legislators, an elitist team of experts, or big business interests.
   It would be a disaster if big business interests determined energy policies.
   Teams of experts are better at determining energy policies than the public and legislators.
   Therefore, nuclear energy policies will be best determined by an elitist team of experts.

EXERCISE 2–4

1. (a) Spiders are not insects. (b) Insects have only six legs.

3. (a) Frank could never become a policeman.
(b) He is only five feet two inches tall and
weighs only 120 pounds.

5. (a) Tom will never be able to climb the face of
that cliff. (b) He has no training in rock
climbing.

7. (a) Some mammals can fly. (b) Bats can fly.

9. (a) The sum of its (this figure's) interior angles
is 540°. (b) This figure is a pentagon.

11. (a) That is not a good French dictionary. (b) It
(that French dictionary) does not show how
each word should be pronounced.

13. (a) It (coffee) must contain a stimulant.
(b) Coffee keeps people awake.

15. (a) It will take two seconds for that rock to fall.
(b) It (that rock) is going to fall a distance of
sixty-four feet.

17. (a) This solution is an acid. (b) It (this solution)
turns litmus paper red.

19. (a) Starvation will inevitably occur somewhere
in the world. (b) The expanding world
population will eventually increase beyond the
capacity of the total world agricultural
resources to feed it.

21. (a) Our industrial system will eventually cease
to expand. (b) The functioning of an industrial
system depends on an abundance of raw
materials. Raw materials are running out.

23. (a) He (the defendant) did not commit the
crime. (b) The defendant was not present at the
scene of the crime.

25. (a) They (individuals) are responsible.
(b) Individuals are free.

27. (a) No one, including the defendant, could have
gotten off three shots in a span of five seconds.
(b) It takes three seconds to operate the bolt of
this rifle.

29. (a) The statement 'No statement can be proved
with absolute certitude' cannot be proved with
absolute certitude. (b) No statement can be
proved with absolute certitude.

EXERCISE 2–5

1. (a) No. (b) It is a conditional.

3. (a) No. (b) It is a conditional; also 'Give Joan a
call' expresses a command.

5. (a) No. (b) 'Since' is probably being used in a
temporal sense.

7. (a) No. (b) 'Please don't pick the flowers'
expresses a command, not a statement.

9. (a) Yes. (c) Conclusion: You are an idealist.
Premise: All Sagittarians are idealists.

11. (a) No. (b) 'Since' is being used in a temporal
sense.

13. (a) Yes. (c) Conclusion: Socrates is mortal.
Premises: All men are mortal. Socrates is a
man.

15. (a) No. (c) This is basically a compound 'either
. . . or . . .' statement. 'Either all citizens are
allowed to express their opinions freely or their
freedom of speech will be violated.'

17. (a) Yes. (c) Conclusion: It is stored in lead
containers. Premise: Hydrofluoric acid dissolves
glass.

19. (a) No. (b) 'Since' is being used in a temporal
sense.

21. (a) No. (b) This 'if . . . then' sentence is being
used to express a conditional statement.

23. (a) Yes. (c) Conclusion: French is called a
romance language. Premise: It (French) is
derived from Latin.

25. (a) No. (b) 'Since' is used in a temporal sense.

27. (a) No. (b) 'Don't use that book when you
write your paper' is a command.

29. (a) Yes. (c) Conclusion: It (this rock) is not
quartz. Premises: If a rock is quartz, it will
scratch glass, *and* This rock will not scratch
glass.

31. (a) Yes. (c) Conclusion: I don't think you will
agree with his conclusions in *Beyond Freedom
and Dignity*. Premise: Skinner is a determinist.

33. (a) No. (b) The passage is exposition; 'Since' is
used in the temporal sense.

EXERCISE 2–6

The following are the answers for Part I. A variety of answers are possible for Part II.

1. *****

   So, ***** and -----

3. All ***** are -----.
   All ----- are _____.
   So, all ***** are _____.

5. Some ***** are -----.
   Some ----- are _____.
   So, some ----- are _____ or some ----- are ++++.

7. Some +++++ are ***** and -----.
   No ***** and ----- thing is a _____.
   So, some +++++ are not _____.

9. No ***** are -----.
   Some ***** are _____.
   So, some _____ are not -----.

EXERCISE 2–7

1. c	7. c
3. c	9. c
5. b	

EXERCISE 2–8

Note that each of these is only one of many possible counterexamples for each argument.

1. If it rained, then the ground is wet. The ground is wet. Therefore, it rained. (The ground, of course, could be wet because someone hosed it down.)

3. All monkeys are mammals. No men are monkeys. Therefore, no men are mammals.

5. All whales are mammals. An ape is not a whale. Therefore, an ape is not a mammal.

7. Tomato juice is a delicious drink. Coffee is a delicious drink. Therefore, tomato juice-coffee is a delicious drink.

9. No Englishmen are Russians. No Englishmen are Americans. Therefore, all Russians are Americans.

11. If an animal is a mammal, then it bears its young live. A guppy is not a mammal. Therefore, a guppy does not bear its young live. (Guppies, a fish, do, in fact, bear their young live.)

13. All chimps are mammals. Some mammals are men. Therefore, some chimps are men.

15. Water extinguishes fires. Water is made of hydrogen and oxygen. Therefore, hydrogen extinguishes fires and oxygen extinguishes fires.

EXERCISE 2–9

Note for part (b) of the answers in this exercise: where the argument is deductive, it is so in all cases because the premise(s) provide(s) absolute support for the conclusion; where the argument is inductive, it is so because the premise(s) do(es) not provide absolute support for the conclusion. For inductive arguments, the answers given in (b) explain why the support is not absolute in each case.

1. (a) Inductive. (b) The fact that the person uttering the argument has not seen a bird that did not fly does not mean that such a bird could not exist. It is possible for the conclusion to be false while the premise is true.

3. (a) Deductive. (b) The conclusion can't possibly be false if both premises are true.

5. (a) Inductive. (b) It is possible for the premises to be true and the conclusion false.

7. (a) Inductive. (b) The truth of the premise does not necessitate the truth of the conclusion.

9. (a) Deductive

11. (a) Inductive. (b) The argument is weakened if a premise is added to the effect that Helen works as a waitress in a truck stop restaurant.

13. (a) Deductive

15. (a) Deductive

17. (a) Inductive. (b) The argument can be weakened if it is added that Bob's parents both have brown eyes.

19. (a) Inductive. (b) It is possible for the premises to be true and the conclusion false. (This is possibly even a nonargument, since the premises may provide no support whatsoever for the conclusion.)

21. (a) Inductive. (b) Even if the premises are true, it is still possible for the conclusion to be false. Someone who did not know how to shoot accurately may have made a lucky shot.

23. (a) Inductive. (b) The premise leaves open the possibility that some other species of animal may be observed in the future to be capable of rational thought.

25. (a) Deductive

EXERCISE 2–10

1. a. Yes   b. Yes
3. a. Yes   b. Yes
5. a. Yes   b. Yes
7. a. No   b. No
9. a. Yes   b. Yes

EXERCISE 2–11

Note that there are other possibilities for the supplied premises in each answer.

1. (a) That is not a rose bush. (b) It doesn't have thorns. (c) All rose bushes have thorns. (d) It has red flowers that look like roses.

3. (a) Death is the perfection of life. (b) The end of a thing is the perfection of life. (c) Death is the end of a thing. (d) The end of a thing is its goal or purpose.

5. (a) This wine is not Chablis. (b) This wine is red wine. (c) No red wine is Chablis. (d) Some Chablis wine is red.

7. (a) The baseball game was dull. (b) Both teams played poorly. (c) If both teams play poorly, a baseball game will be dull. (d) The score was 19–15, and there were three fights.

9. (a) Karl is eccentric. (b) All metaphysicians are eccentric. (c) Karl is a metaphysician. (d) Metaphysics is only Karl's hobby.

11. (a) He could not have stolen the money. (b) Mr. Poindexter did not work for the company. (c) If a person did not work for the company, he could not have stolen the money. (d) Mr. Poindexter's son was treasurer of the company.

13. (a) John makes mistakes. (b) All men make mistakes. (c) John is a man. (d) John was just born an hour ago.

15. (a) He must have lied. (b) He passed the examination. (c) If he passed the examination, he must have lied. (d) He almost never lies.

17. (a) He is a Democrat. (b) Senator Brandt is a major party candidate. He is not a Republican. (c) The Republican and Democratic parties are the only major parties. (d) Senator Brandt is head of the new Reform Party.

EXERCISE 3–1

1. A
3. O
5. I
7. A
9. O
11. E
13. E
15. E

EXERCISE 3–2

1. All typewriters are noisy things.

3. Some dodos are not extinct animals.

5. Some Toyotas are autos that get thirty miles to the gallon.

7. Cassius is a person with a lean and hungry look. *or* All persons who are members of the class of things that are Cassius are persons with a lean and hungry look.

9. Some cars are not vehicles that have pollution control devices.

11. [Already in standard form.]

13. No seals are animals with a smooth coat of fur.

15. No persons are persons who waved goodby.

EXERCISE 3–3

1. (a) All Italians are Europeans. (b) **A** (c) All I are E. (d) All S̲ are P̲.

3. (a) Some sailors are swarthy persons. (b) **I** (c) Some Sa are Sw. (d) Some S̲ are P̲.

5. (a) No ponderosas are shrubs. (b) **E** (c) No P are S. (d) No S̲ are P̲.

7. (a) All rappers are musicians. (b) **A** (c) All R are M. (d) All S̲ are P̲.

9. (a) Some dogs are not beagles. (b) **O** (c) Some D are not B. (d) Some S̲ are not P̲.

11. (a) *There are two possible interpretations:* Some politicians are not dishonest persons. *and* 'No politicians are dishonest persons. (The lack of context, however, indicates that the weaker **O** statement should be used.) (b) **O** (c) Some P are not D. (d) Some S̲ are not P̲.

13. (a) Some European families are not families that own an automobile. (b) **O** (c) Some E are not O. (d) Some S̲ are not P̲.

15. (a) Some paperbacks are inexpensive things *and* Some paperbacks are not inexpensive things. (b) **I** *and* **O** (c) Some P are I *and* Some P are not I. (d) Some S̲ are P̲ *and* Some S̲ are not P̲.

17. (a) All invited persons are members of the club. (b) **A** (c) All I are M. (d) All S̲ are P̲.

19. (a) Some college students are students who work part-time to pay for their education *and* Some college students are not students who work part-time to pay for their education. (b) **I** and **O** (c) Some C are W *and* Some C are not W. (d) Some S̲ are P̲ *and* Some S̲ are not P̲.

21. (a) Some professional basketball players are persons over six feet four inches tall *and* Some professional basketball players are not persons over six feet four inches tall. (b) **I** and **O** (c) Some B are T *and* some B are not T. (d) Some S̲ are P̲ *and* Some S̲ are not P̲.

23. (a) All persons who were invited to the party are his friends. (b) **A** (c) All I are F. (d) All S̲ are P̲.

25. (a) All persons who were able to get seats are persons who bought tickets in advance. (b) **A** (c) All S are B. (d) All S̲ are P̲.

EXERCISE 3–4

1. (a) Some wines are things made from dandelions. (b) Some W are D. (c) Some S̲ are P̲.

(d)
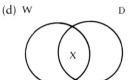

3. (a) All beetles are bugs. (b) All Be are Bu. (c) All S̲ are P̲.

(d)
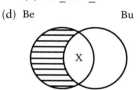

5. (a) No termites are ants. (b) No T are A (c) No S̲ are P̲.

(d)
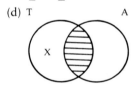

7. (a) Some Arabs are Moslems *and* some Arabs are not Moslems. (b) Some A are M *and* Some A are not M. (c) Some S̲ are P̲ *and* some S̲ are not P̲.

(d)
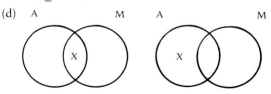

9. (a) Some <u>d</u>ancers are persons who can do the <u>C</u>harleston. (b) Some D are C. (c) Some <u>S</u> are <u>P</u>.

(d) D   C

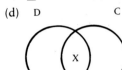

11. (a) All people who do well in <u>l</u>ogic are people with <u>g</u>ood study habits. (b) All L are G. (c) All <u>S</u> are <u>P</u>.

(d) L   G

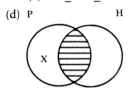

13. (a) No persons are people who scored <u>h</u>igher than 90 percent on the test. (b) No P are H. (c) No <u>S</u> are <u>P</u>.

(d) P   H

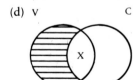

15. (a) All persons who can <u>v</u>ote are <u>c</u>itizens. (b) All V are C. (c) All <u>S</u> are <u>P</u>.

(d) V   C

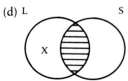

17. (a) No <u>l</u>ightning is a thing which <u>s</u>trikes twice in the same place. (b) No L are S. (c) No <u>S</u> are <u>P</u>.

(d) L   S

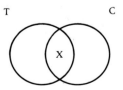

19. (a) Some <u>a</u>rt collectors are <u>r</u>ich persons *and* some <u>a</u>rt collectors are not <u>r</u>ich persons. (b) Some A are R *and* some A are not R. (c) Some <u>S</u> are <u>P</u> *and* Some <u>S</u> are not <u>P</u>.

(d) A   R   A   R

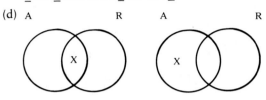

EXERCISE 3–5

Sentences from Exercise 3–1.

1. (a) All <u>t</u>ypewriters are <u>n</u>oisy things. (b) All T are N.

T   N

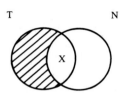

A: All T are N.

3. (a) Some <u>d</u>odos are not <u>e</u>xtinct things. (b) Some D are not E.

D   E

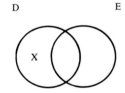

O: Some D are not E.

5. (a) Some <u>T</u>oyotas are <u>c</u>ars which get thirty miles to the gallon. (b) Some T are C.

T   C

I: Some T are C.

7. (a) All members of the class of which yon Cassius is the only member are people with a lean and hungry look. (b) All C are L.

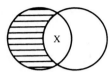

A: All C are L.

9. (a) Some cars are not things which have pollution control devices. (b) Some C are not P.

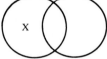

O: Some C are not P.

11. (a) No persons are islands. (b) No P are I.

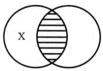

E: No P are I.

13. (a) No seals are animals having a smooth coat of fur. (b) No S are C.

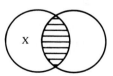

E: No S are C.

15. (a) No persons are persons who waved goodby. (b) No P̄ are W.

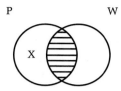

E: No P are W.

Sentences from Exercise 3–3

1. I   E

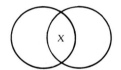

All I are E.

3. Sa   Sw

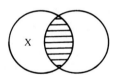

Some Sa are Sw.

5. P   S

No P are S.

7. R   M

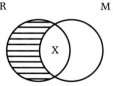

All R are M.

9.

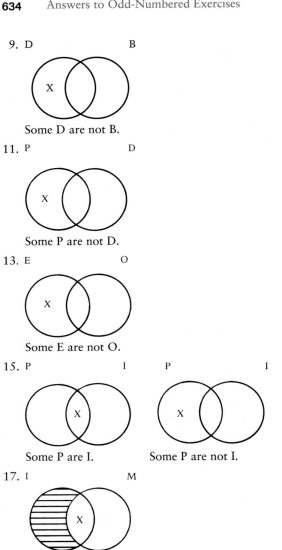

Some D are not B.

11. P   D

Some P are not D.

13. E   O

Some E are not O.

15. P   I   P   I

Some P are I.   Some P are not I.

17. I   M

All I are M.

EXERCISE 3–6

1. (a) Dependent (b) Consistent (c) Not logically equivalent

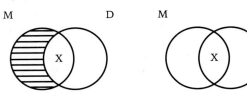

3. (a) Independent (b) Consistent (c) Not equivalent

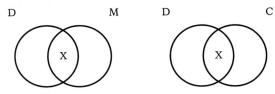

5. (a) Dependent (b) Inconsistent (c) Not equivalent

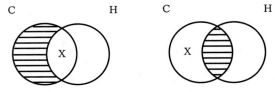

7. (a) Independent (b) Consistent (c) Not equivalent

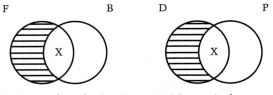

9. (a) Dependent (b) Consistent (c) Not equivalent

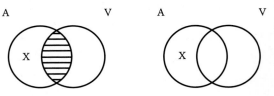

11. (a) Dependent (b) Consistent (c) Not equivalent

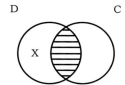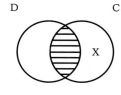

EXERCISE 3–7

1. (a) Contrariety (b) False (c) Undetermined

3. (a) Superimplication (b) Undetermined (c) False

5. (a) Superimplication (b) Undetermined (c) False

7. (a) Contrariety (b) False (c) Undetermined

9. (a) Contrariety (b) False (c) Undetermined

11. (a) Subimplication (b) True (c) Undetermined

13. (a) Contradiction (b) False (c) True

15. (a) Contrariety (b) False (c) Undetermined

EXERCISE 3–8

1. i. Relationship to original statement:
   (a) Contrary (b) Subimplicant (c) Contradictory
   ii. If original statement is true: (a) False (b) True
   (c) False
   iii. If original statement is false:
   (a) Undetermined (b) Undetermined (c) True

3. i. Relationship to original statement:
   (a) Subcontrary (b) Contradictory
   (c) Superimplicant
   ii. If original statement is true: (a) Undetermined
   (b) False (c) Undetermined
   iii. If original statement is false: (a) True (b) True
   (c) False

5. i. Relationship to original statement:
   (a) Contrary (b) Subimplicant (c) Contradictory
   ii. If original statement is true: (a) False (b) True
   (c) False
   iii. If original statement is false:
   (a) Undetermined (b) Undetermined (c) True

7. i. Relationship to original statement:
   (a) Subcontrary (b) Superimplicant
   (c) Contradictory

ii. If original statement is true: (a) Undetermined
(b) Undetermined (c) False
iii. If original statement is false: (a) True
(b) False (c) True

EXERCISE 3–9

1. (a) undetermined
   (b) undetermined

3. (a) undetermined
   (b) undetermined

5. (a) undetermined
   (b) undetermined

7. (a) undetermined
   (b) undetermined

9. (a) undetermined
   (b) undetermined

11. (a) undetermined
    (b) undetermined

13. (a) false
    (b) true

15. (a) undetermined
    (b) undetermined

EXERCISE 3–10

1. (a) All oaks are nonmaples. (b) Equivalent

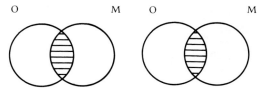

No O are M.   All O are nonM.

3. (a) No madrigal singers are nonmusicians.
   (b) Equivalent

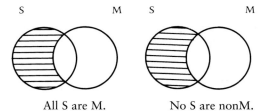

All S are M.   No S are nonM.

5. (a) Some g‌ifts are not nonex‌pensive things.
(b) Equivalent

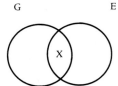

Some G are E.   Some G are not nonE.

7. (a) All bis‌cuits are nonmu‌ffins. (b) Equivalent

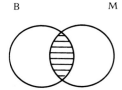

No B are M.   All B are nonM.

9. (a) Some mem‌bers are nonlaw‌yers.
(b) Equivalent

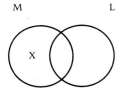

Some M are not L.   Some M are nonL.

EXERCISE 3–11

1. (a) All f‌ish are sal‌mon. (b) Not equivalent

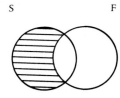

All S are F.   All F are S.

3. (a) Some Ca‌lifornians are Am‌ericans.
(b) Equivalent

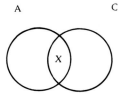

Some A are C.   Some C are A.

5. (a) All wr‌iting instruments are p‌ens. (b) Not equivalent

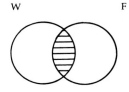

All P are W.   All W are P.

7. (a) No fo‌ols are wo‌men. (b) Equivalent

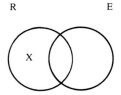

No W are F.   No F are W.

9. (a) Some el‌ected persons are not re‌presentatives.
(b) Not equivalent

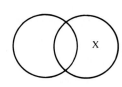

Some R are not E.   Some E are not R.

EXERCISE 3–12

1. (a) All nontools are nonhammers. (b) Equivalent

3. (a) Some nonbeverages are nondrinks. (b) Not equivalent

5. (a) No nonmen are nonmice. (b) Not equivalent

7. (a) No noncarnivores are nonelephants. (b) Not equivalent

9. (a)Some nonhammers are not nontools. (b) Equivalent

EXERCISE 3–13 (I)

1. (a) Obversion   (b) True

3. (a) Contradiction   (b) False

5. (a) Conversion   (b) Undetermined

EXERCISE 3–13 (II)

1. (a) Obversion   (b) True

3. (a) Contradiction   (b) False

5. (a) Conversion   (b) True

EXERCISE 3–13 (III)

1. (a) Obversion   (b) True

3. (a) Contradiction   (b) False

5. (a) Conversion   (b) True

EXERCISE 4–1

1. Categorical syllogism

3. Not a categorical syllogism

5. Categorical syllogism

7. Not a categorical syllogism

9. Not a categorical syllogism

11. Categorical syllogism

13. Categorical syllogism

15. Not a categorical syllogism

17. Not a categorical syllogism

19. Not a categorical syllogism

EXERCISE 4–2

1. Not in standard form: All bees are things that can sting. Some bees are insects. Therefore, some insects are things that can sting.

3. Not a categorical syllogism

5. Not in standard form: All drunkards are alcoholics. Some drinkers are drunkards. Therefore, some drinkers are alcoholics.

7. Not a categorical syllogism

9. Not a categorical syllogism

11. Not in standard form: All communists are Marxists. Some revolutionaries are not Marxists. Therefore, some revolutionaries are not communists.

13. Not in standard form: No kangaroos are soldiers. All generals are soldiers. Therefore, no generals are kangaroos.

15. Not a categorical syllogism

17. Not a categorical syllogism

19. Not a categorical syllogism

EXERCISE 4–3

1. (a)   All B are S.   (b)   All $\underline{M}$ are $\underline{P}$.
         Some B are I.   Some $\underline{M}$ are S.
         ∴Some I are S.   ∴Some $\underline{S}$ are $\underline{P}$.

3. Not a categorical syllogism.

5. (a)   All D are A.   (b)   All $\underline{M}$ are $\underline{P}$.
         Some Dr are D.   Some S are $\underline{M}$.
         ∴Some Dr are A.   ∴Some $\underline{S}$ are $\underline{P}$.

7. Not a categorical syllogism.

9. Not a categorical syllogism.

11. (a)   All C are M.   (b)   All $\underline{P}$ are $\underline{M}$.
          Some R are not M.   Some S are not $\underline{M}$.
          ∴Some R are not C.   ∴Some $\underline{S}$ are not $\underline{P}$.

13. (a)   No K are S.   (b)   No <u>P</u> are <u>M</u>.
       <u>All G are S.</u>   <u>All <u>S</u> are <u>M</u>.</u>
       ∴No G are K.   ∴No <u>S</u> are <u>P</u>.

15. Not a categorical syllogism.

17. Not a categorical syllogism.

19. Not a categorical syllogism.

EXERCISE 4–4

1. AII-3   11. A00-2

5. AII-l   13. EAE-2

EXERCISE 4–5

1. All <u>M</u> are <u>P</u>.   7. All <u>M</u> are <u>P</u>.
    <u>Some <u>M</u> are <u>S</u>.</u>   <u>All <u>M</u> are <u>S</u>.</u>
    ∴All <u>S</u> are <u>P</u>.   ∴All <u>S</u> are <u>P</u>.

3. Some <u>P</u> are not <u>M</u>.   9. Some <u>P</u> are <u>M</u>.
    <u>Some <u>M</u> are <u>S</u>.</u>   <u>Some <u>M</u> are <u>S</u>.</u>
    ∴No <u>S</u> are <u>P</u>.   ∴Some <u>S</u> are <u>P</u>.

5. No <u>P</u> are <u>M</u>.   11. All <u>M</u> are <u>P</u>.
    <u>All <u>M</u> are <u>S</u>.</u>   <u>Some <u>S</u> are <u>M</u>.</u>
    ∴Some <u>S</u> are not <u>P</u>.   ∴Some <u>S</u> are <u>P</u>.

EXERCISE 4–6

Note that each answer is only one of many possible answers.

1. All Buicks are autos. Some autos are Chevys. Therefore, some Chevys are Buicks.

3. No horses are flowers. No flowers are animals. Therefore, no animals are horses.

5. All Chicagoans are citizens. Some citizens are New Yorkers. Therefore, some New Yorkers are Chicagoans.

7. No pines are oaks. All pines are trees. Therefore, no trees are oaks.

9. All roses are plants. No roses are trees. Therefore, no trees are plants.

11. No beggars are rich. No millionaires are beggars. Therefore, no millionaires are rich.

13. Some animals are cats. All dogs are animals. Therefore, some dogs are cats.

EXERCISE 4–7

1. 1   5. 6
3. 7   7. 5

EXERCISE 4–8

1. Valid
   H = hippies
   L = law-abiding citizens
   P = pot smokers

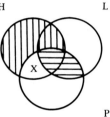

3. Valid
   Dr = drugs
   Da = dangerous things
   H = hallucinogens

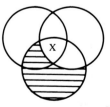

5. Valid
   Dr = drugs
   Da = dangerous things
   H = hallucinogens
   Standard form:
   All hallucinogens are dangerous things.
   All hallucinogens are drugs.
   Therefore, some drugs are dangerous things.

   Dr   Da

   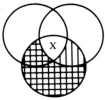

                    H

7. Valid
   P = powerful persons
   R = reactionaries
   D = dictators
   Standard form:
      Some dictators are reactionaries.
      All dictators are powerful people.
      Therefore, some powerful people are
         reactionaries.

   P   R

   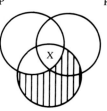

              D

9. Valid
   Standard form:
      All monks are ascetics.
      Some Buddhists are monks.
      ∴Some Buddhists are ascetics.

   B   A

   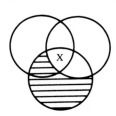

                        M

11. Invalid
    Standard form:
       No oak trees are pines.
       All pines are conifers.
       ∴No conifers are oak trees.

    C   O

    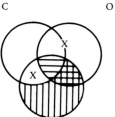

                         P

13. Invalid
    Standard form:
       No cats are canines.
       No cats are wolves.
       ∴Some wolves are canines.

    W   Ca

    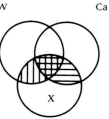

                    C

15. Valid
    Standard form:
       No edible things are toadstools.
       Some edible things are mushrooms.
    ∴Some mushrooms are not toadstools.

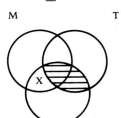

EXERCISE 4–9

1. Invalid
    All M are P.
    No M are S.
    ∴No S are P.

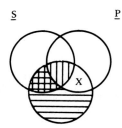

3. Invalid
    No M are P.
    All M are S.
    ∴No S are P.

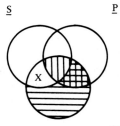

5. Invalid
    Some P are M.
    No M are S.
    ∴Some S are not P.

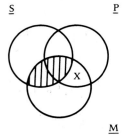

7. Invalid
    Some P are M.
    All S are M.
    ∴Some S are P.

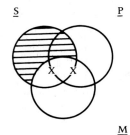

9. Valid
    All M are P.
    Some S are M.
    ∴Some S are P.

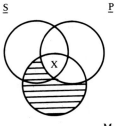

11. Valid
All <u>P</u> are <u>M</u>.
Some <u>S</u> are not <u>M</u>.
∴Some <u>S</u> are not <u>P</u>.

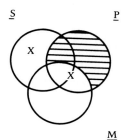

13. Invalid
Some <u>P</u> are <u>M</u>.
Some <u>S</u> are <u>M</u>.
∴Some <u>S</u> are <u>P</u>.

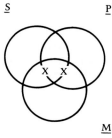

15. Invalid
Some <u>P</u> are not <u>M</u>.
Some <u>S</u> are not <u>M</u>.
∴No <u>S</u> are <u>P</u>.

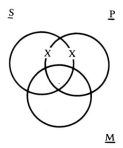

EXERCISE 4–10

Questions from 4-8

1. Valid

3. Valid

5. Valid

7. Valid

9. Valid

11. Violates rule 2. "Conifers" is distributed in the conclusion, but not in the minor premise.

13. Violates rule 3. There are two negative premises.

15. Valid

Questions from 4–9

1. Violates rule 2. Major term distributed in conclusion but not in premise.

3. Violates rule 2. Minor term distributed in conclusion but not in premise.

5. Violates rule 2. Major term distributed in conclusion but not in premise.

7. Violates rule 1. Undistributed middle term.

9. Valid

11. Valid

13. Violates rule 1. Undistributed middle term.

15. Violates rule 3. Both premises are negative.

EXERCISE 4–11

1. (b) Rule 2: Illicit major. (c) Invalid.

3. (b) Rule 3: Negative conclusion without a negative premise. (c) Invalid.

5. (b) Rule 1: Undistributed middle. (c) Invalid.

7. (b) Rule 1: Undistributed middle; *and* Rule 2: Illicit minor. (c) Invalid.

9. (b) Rule 2: Illicit major. (c) Invalid

11. (a) No trees are things having gangrenous limbs. All maples are trees. Therefore, no maples are things having gangrenous limbs. (b) No rules violated. (c) Valid.

13. (a) All sensitive people are people who suffer a lot in life. Some intelligent people are sensitive

people. Therefore, some intelligent people are people who suffer a lot in life. (b) No rules violated. (c) Valid.

EXERCISE 4–12

Questions from 4–8

1. Still valid

3. Still valid

5. Violates rule 4.

7. Still valid

9. Still valid

15. Still valid

Questions from 4–9

2. Still valid

4. Still valid

8. Still valid

14. Still valid

EXERCISE 4–13

1. All mushrooms are fungi. [All toadstools are mushrooms.] Therefore, all toadstools are fungi.

3. [No poisonous things are edible things.] Some mushrooms are poisonous things. Therefore, some mushrooms are not edible things *or* [No edible things are poisonous things.] Some mushrooms are poisonous things. Therefore, some mushrooms are not edible things.

5. [All foods that contain a lot of protein are nutritious foods.] All soybeans are foods that contain a lot of protein. Therefore, all soybeans are nutritious foods.

7. [No things written in foreign languages are understandable things.] All operas are things written in foreign languages. Therefore, no operas are understandable things. *or* [No understandable things are things written in foreign languages.] All operas are things written in foreign languages. Therefore, no operas are understandable things.

9. No reference books are books that can be taken out of the library. All foreign-language dictionaries are reference books. [Therefore, no foreign-language dictionaries are books that can be taken out of the library.] *or* All foreign-language dictionaries are reference books. No reference books are books that can be taken out of the library. [Therefore, no books that can be taken out of the library are foreign-language dictionaries.]

11. [All teachers of whom it can be said that all of the students in their class always get good grades are persons who must be terrific teachers.] All members of the class of which she is the only member are teachers of whom it can be said that all of the students in their class always get good grades. Therefore, all members of the class of which she is the only member are persons who must be terrific teachers.

13. [All movies that have plenty of violence and sex are movies that are sure to make a lot of money.] All members of the class of which that movie is the only member are movies that have plenty of violence and sex. Therefore, all members of the class of which that movie is the only member are movies that are sure to make a lot of money.

15. All lawyers are college graduates. [All members of the American Bar Association are lawyers.] Therefore, all members of the American Bar Association are college graduates.

17. [All persons who are members of Phi Beta Kappa are intelligent persons.] All members of the class of which Mary is the only member are members of Phi Beta Kappa. Therefore, all members of the class of which Mary is the only member are intelligent persons.

19. [All places where I smell smoke are places where there are fires.] All members of the class of which this place is the only member are places where I smell smoke. Therefore, all members of the class of which this place is the only member are places where there are fires.

21. [All places where grass is growing are places where water must be near.] All members of the class of which this place is the only member are places where grass is growing. Therefore, all members of the class of which this place is the only member are places where water must be near.

23. [All democratic countries are countries where all citizens can vote.] Some countries are not countries where all citizens can vote. Therefore, some countries are not democratic countries.

EXERCISE 4–14

Note that the reconstruction of complex and/or invalid sorites can often be facilitated by reconstructing syllogisms for individual stages of the argument starting from the conclusion and working backwards.

1. Valid
   (a) All <u>comets</u> are <u>wanderers in the zodiac</u>.
      No <u>terriers</u> are <u>wanderers in the zodiac</u>.
      [Therefore, no <u>terriers</u> are <u>comets</u>.]
   (b) All <u>curly-tailed creatures</u> are <u>terriers</u>.
      Therefore, no <u>curly-tailed creatures</u> are <u>comets</u>.

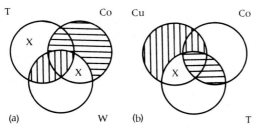

3. Valid
   (a) All <u>shade-grown fruit</u> is <u>unripe fruit</u>.
      No <u>wholesome fruit</u> is <u>unripe fruit</u>.
      [Therefore, no <u>wholesome fruit</u> is <u>shade-grown fruit</u>.]
   (b) All <u>apples in this basket</u> are <u>wholesome fruit</u>.
      Therefore, no <u>apples in this basket</u> are <u>shade-grown fruit</u>.

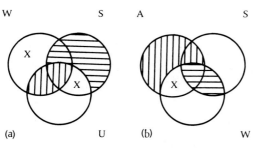

EXERCISE 5–1

1. (a) Yes. (b) 'Pines are evergreens'; 'Oaks are hardwoods.' (c) 'and' (d) Yes.

3. (a) Yes. (b) 'The earth is flat.' (c) 'It is not true that' (d) Yes.

5. (a) No.

7. (a) Yes. (b) 'The earth is not flat.' (c) 'You ought to know that.' (d) No.

9. (a) Yes. (b) 'Thomas Jefferson was the second president of the United States.' (c) 'I don't think that.' (d) No.

11. (a) Yes. (b) 'Joseph came out'; 'Joseph helped me shovel snow.' (c) 'and' (d) Yes.

13. (a)Yes. (b) 'Orrin Hatch is a liberal'; 'Edward Kennedy is a conservative.' (c) 'and' (d) Yes.

15. (a) Yes. (b) 'Orrin Hatch is a Republican'; 'Edward Kennedy is a Democrat.' (c) 'and' (d) Yes.

17. (a) No.

EXERCISE 5–2

1. A propositional constant is a symbol which represents a specific statement found in a compound proposition and which remains constant within a given context. A propositional variable is a symbol which serves as a *blank* in a compound proposition and into which a specific proposition may be substituted.

3. (a) '**A** and **B**' represents a particular compound proposition. (b) 'p and q' represents an infinite set of compound propositions.

5. The formula '**A** and **B**' has a specific truth value because it is an abbreviation of a sentence expressing a compound proposition containing propositions about which it is reasonable to say that they are true or false. The formula 'p and q' does not have a specific truth value because p and q do not represent specific propositions but merely represent blanks in a logical framework where statements may be placed.

EXERCISE 5-3

The particular letters used as constants here may differ from those chosen by the student, but the propositions symbolized remain the same.

 1. (a) Sense of temporal sequence lost. (b) R · G; R = The gunmen robbed the bank; G = The gunmen made their getaway.

 3. (a) Dot cannot properly be used; it does not convey the implication that the Oakland Athletics and Los Angeles Dodgers played *each other* in the World Series.

 5. (a) Dot cannot properly be used; it loses the essential meaning of 'rock and roll'.

 7. (a) Dot cannot properly be used; it loses the essential meaning of 'ball and chain'.

 9. (a) Dot cannot suitably be used; loss of essential meaning of 'hit-and-run accident'.

11. (a) Loss of time-sequence. (b) C · D; C = Jim climbed out of the water; D = Jim dried himself off.

13. (a) No significant meaning loss. (b) G · M; G = 'George is a character in Albee's *Who's Afraid of Virginia Woolf?*,' M = 'Martha is a character in Albee's *Who's Afraid of Virginia Woolf?*'

EXERCISE 5-4

 1. (a) T · O
    (b) T = Tom likes ice cream.
       O = Orrin Hatch was president in 1985.
    (c) No loss of meaning.

 3. (a) ~T · M
    (b) T = Tom can symbolize this problem.
       M = Mary can symbolize this problem.
    (c) The sense that this is a comparison between Tom and Mary is lost.

 5. (a) ~U · R
    (b) U = Sue understood the preceding section.
       R = Sue read the preceding section again more carefully.
    (c) The time sequence and possible causal relation are lost.

 7. (a) D · ~G
    (b) E = Bill found this to be difficult.
       G = Bill gave up.

    (c) The connection between the not giving up and the difficulty is lost.

 9. (a) ~W · C
    (b) W = The brakes worked.
       C = The car crashed.
    (c) The time sequence and the possibility of a causal connection are lost.

11. (a) S · B
    (b) S = Sue is engaged to be married.
       B = Bill is engaged to be married.
    (c) The fact that they are engaged to be married to each other is lost. It would be better to symbolize this proposition as 'E' where 'E' = 'Sue is engaged to be married to Bill.'

EXERCISE 5-5

 1. (a) T ∨ R
    (b) T = Tom likes ice cream.
       R = Orrin Hatch was president in 1985.
    (c) No loss of meaning.

 3. (a) T ∨ M
    (b) T = Tom can symbolize this problem.
       M = Mary can symbolize this problem.
    (c) No loss of meaning.

 5. (a) U ∨ R
    (b) U = Sue understood the preceding section.
       R = Sue read the preceding section very carefully.
    (c) The possibility of an exclusive disjunction is lost.

 7. (a) D ∨ E
    (b) D = Bill found this to be difficult.
       E = Mary found this to be easy.
    (c) No loss of meaning.

 9. (a) ~W ∨ C
    (b) W = The brakes worked.
       C = The car crashed.
    (c) No loss of meaning.

EXERCISE 5-6

 1. (a) L ⊃ R
    (b) L = You like ice cream.
       R = Ronald Reagan was president in 1985.
    (c) No loss of meaning.

3. (a) ~S ⊃ W
   (b) S = You can symbolize this problem.
      W = You will get this problem wrong.
   (c) Possible causal connection is lost.

5. (a) ~U ⊃ M
   (b) U = You understand the preceding section.
      R = You will probably miss this question.
   (c) Possibility of causal connection is lost.

7. (a) D ⊃ ~H
   (b) D = You find this to be difficult.
      H = It is helpful to get upset.
   (c) The possibility of a causal connection is lost.

9. (a) ~W ⊃ C
   (b) W = The brakes work.
      C = The car will crash.
   (c) The causal connection is lost.

EXERCISE 5–7

1. (a) R · B (b) R = Roses are red; B = Violets are
   blue. (c) No meaning loss.

3. (a) R · L (b) R = It rained today; L = The
   mailman was late. (c) Loss of a suggestion of
   possible causal connection.

5. (a) ~H (b) H = Hickory is a soft wood. (c) No
   loss of meaning.

7. (a) K · C (b) K = Joyce needs a kitchen table
   for her apartment; C = Joyce needs some chairs
   for her apartment. (c) None.

9. (a) Not adequately translatable.

11. (a) M ≡ E (b) M = Oil and water will mix;
    E = Oil and water are emulsified. (c) Loss of
    suggestion of causal relation.

13. (a) E ≡ P (b) E = A total eclipse of the sun
    occurs; P = The moon is positioned directly
    between the earth and the sun. (c) Suggestion of
    causal connection is lost.

15. (a) ~P (b) P = Sugar is a protein. (c) None.

17. (a) F ≡ G (b) F = This object will float; G =
    This object's specific gravity is less than .10
    (c) Loss of a suggestion of causal connection.

19. (a) E ≡ S (b) E = A geometrical figure is
    equilateral; S = All its (the geometrical figure's)
    sides have the same length.
    (c) Loss of meaning that the two components
    are synonomous.

21. (a) P ⊃ T (b) T = I will take the job; P = It
    (the job) pays well. (c) Loss of sense that I
    would take the job *because* it pays well.

23. (a) P ⊃ W (b) P = Pat is late; V = The world
    must be coming to an end. (c) Loss of meaning
    that it would be extremely unusual for Pat to
    be late.

25. (a) W · G (b) W = Most swans are white; G =
    Some swans are gray. (c) 'Although' connotes
    an exception to a rule.

27. (a) C ≡ P (b) C = A conjunction is true;
    P = Both its component propositions are true.
    (c) Loss of meaning that the two components
    are synonomous.

29. (a) P (b) P = People lose money. (c) Loss of the
    suggestion that the behavior of the stock
    market has no effect on whether people lose
    money or not.

31. (a) A ∨ ~C (b) A = He came after I left; C =
    He came. (c) Loss of suggestion that he didn't
    come while I was there.

33. (a) P ⊃ S (b) P = You will pass this exam; S =
    You study hard. (c) Loss of suggestion of
    causal connection.

35. (a) ~R · (D · O) (b) R = It rained; O = The
    clouds were ominous; D = The clouds were
    dark. (c) Loss of suggestion that dark, ominous
    clouds indicate that rain is likely to occur.

EXERCISE 5–8

1. (S · R) ⊻ D

3. S ⊻ (R · D)

5. S ⦂ (R · D)

7. ⁓(W ⊃ H)

9. W ⊇ ~H

11. ~W ⊇ H

13. C ⦂ ~M

15. ~C ⦂ ~M

17. ⁓(C · ~M)

19. (S · H) ⊇ ~C

21. S ⊇ (~H ∨ ~C)

23. S ⊇ (H ⊃ ~C)

25. Q ⊇ (H · C)

27. Q ⊇ (H ∨ C)

29. (K · M) ⊻ H

31. K ⊻ (M ∨ H) *or* (K ∨ M) ⊻ H

33. ⁓(K ∨ (M · H))

35. ⁓((K · M) ∨ H)

37. K ⊻ (M · ~H)

39. ~K ⦂ (M ∨ H)

EXERCISE 5–9

1.

p	q	p	·	~q
T	T		F	F
F	T		F	F
T	F		T	T
F	F		F	T
			(2)	(1)

3.

p	q	p	⊃	~q
T	T		F	F
F	T		T	F
T	F		T	T
F	F		T	T
			(2)	(1)

5.

p	q	~p	·	~q
T	T	F	F	F
F	T	T	F	F
T	F	F	F	T
F	F	T	T	T
		(1)	(2)	(1)

7.

p	q	~	(p ⊃ q)
T	T	F	T
F	T	F	T
T	F	T	F
F	F	F	T
		(2)	(1)

9.

p	q	p	∨	~q
T	T		T	F
F	T		F	F
T	F		T	T
F	F		T	T
			(2)	(1)

11.

p	q	~	(~p	∨	q)
T	T	F	F	T	
F	T	F	T	T	
T	F	T	F	F	
F	F	F	T	T	
		(3)	(1)	(2)	

13.

p	q	(p · q)	≡	p
T	T	T	T	
F	T	F	T	
T	F	F	F	
F	F	F	T	
		(1)	(2)	

15.

p	q	(p · q)	⊃	q
T	T	T	T	
F	T	F	T	
T	F	F	T	
F	F	F	T	
		(1)	(2)	

17.

p	q	r	(p ∨ q)	⊃	r
T	T	T	T	T	
F	T	T	T	T	
T	F	T	T	T	
F	F	T	F	T	
T	T	F	T	F	
F	T	F	T	F	
T	F	F	T	F	
F	F	F	F	T	
			(1)	(2)	

19.

p	q	r	~	(p · q)	⊃	~r
T	T	T	F	T	T	F
F	T	T	T	F	F	F
T	F	T	T	F	F	F
F	F	T	T	F	F	F
T	T	F	F	T	T	T
F	T	F	T	F	T	T
T	F	F	T	F	T	T
F	F	F	T	F	T	T
			(3)	(2)	(4)	(1)

21.

p	q	r	((p ∨ q)	·	p)	⊃	r
T	T	T	T	T	T		
F	T	T	T	F	T		
T	F	T	T	T	T		
F	F	T	F	F	T		
T	T	F	T	T	F		
F	T	F	T	F	T		
T	F	F	T	T	T		
F	F	F	F	F	T		
			(1)	(2)	(3)		

23.

p	q	r	(~ (p ∨ ~q) · p) ⊃ r
T	T	T	F T F F T
F	T	T	T F F F T
T	F	T	F T T F T
F	F	T	F T T F T
T	T	F	F T F F T
F	T	F	T F F F T
T	F	F	F T T F T
F	F	F	F T T F T
			(3) (2) (1) (4) (5)

25.

p	q	((p ⊃ q) · ~q) ⊃ ~p
T	T	T F F T F
F	T	T F F T T
T	F	F F T F F
F	F	T T T T T
		(2) (3) (1) (4) (1)

27.

p	q	~ (p · q) ≡ (~ p ∨ ~q)
T	T	F T T F F F
F	T	T F T T T F
T	F	T F T T F T
F	F	T F T T T T
		(3) (2) (4) (1) (2) (1)

29.

p	q	r	((p · q) ⊃ r) ≡ (p ⊃ (q ⊃ r))
T	T	T	T T T T T
F	T	T	F T T T T
T	F	T	F T T T T
F	F	T	F T T T T
T	T	F	T F T F F
F	T	F	F T T T F
T	F	F	F T T T T
F	F	F	F T T T T
			(1) (2) (3) (2) (1)

EXERCISE 5–10

1. (a) Equivalent

p	q	p · q	~ (~p ∨ ~q)
T	T	T	T F F F
F	T	F	F T T F
T	F	F	F F T T
F	F	F	F T T T
		(3)	(1) (2) (1)

3. (a) Equivalent

p	q	~p · q	~ (p ∨ ~q)
T	T	F F	F T F
F	T	T T	T F F
T	F	F F	F T T
F	F	T F	F T T
		(1) (2)	(3) (2) (1)

5. (a) Not equivalent

p	q	~ (p ∨ q)	~p ∨ q
T	T	F T	F T
F	T	F T	T T
T	F	F T	F F
F	F	T F	T T
		(2) (1)	(1) (2)

7. (a) Equivalent

p	q	p ⊃ q	~p ∨ q
T	T	T	F T
F	T	T	T T
T	F	F	F F
F	F	T	T T
		(1)	(2)

9. (a) Equivalent

p	q	~p ≡ q	p ≡ ~q
T	T	F F	F F
F	T	T T	T F
T	F	F T	T T
F	F	T F	F T
		(1) (2)	(2) (1)

11. (a) Equivalent

p	q	~ (p ⊃ q)	p · ~q
T	T	F T	F F
F	T	F T	F F
T	F	T F	T T
F	F	F T	F T
		(2) (1)	(2) (1)

13. (a) Not equivalent

p	q	~	(p ∨ q)	~p	∨	~q
T	T	F	T	F	F	F
F	T	F	T	T	T	F
T	F	F	T	F	T	T
F	F	T	F	T	T	T
		(2)	(1)	(1)	(2)	(1)

EXERCISE 5–11

1. (a) Contingent

p	q	p ⊃ q
T	T	T
F	T	T
T	F	F
F	F	T

3. (a) Contingent

p	p ⊃ ~p
T	F F
F	T T
	(2) (1)

5. (a) Tautology

p	q	p ⊃ (p ∨ q)
T	T	T T
F	T	T T
T	F	T T
F	F	T F
		(2) (1)

7. (a) Contradiction

p	q	((p ⊃ q)	·	~q)	· p
T	T	T	F	F	F
F	T	T	F	F	F
T	F	F	F	T	F
F	F	T	T	T	F
		(2)	(3)	(1)	(4)

9. (a) Tautology

p	q	(p ⊃ q)	≡	(~ p	∨ q)
T	T	T	T	F	T
F	T	T	T	T	T
T	F	F	T	F	F
F	F	T	T	T	T
		(2)	(3)	(1)	(2)

11. (a) Contradiction

p	q	(p ⊃ q)	≡	(p ·	~q)
T	T	T	F	F	F
F	T	T	F	F	F
T	F	F	F	T	T
F	F	T	F	F	T
		(2)	(3)	(2)	(1)

13. (a) Contradiction

p	q	((p ⊃ q)	·	p) ·	~q
T	T	T	T	F	F
F	T	T	F	F	F
T	F	F	F	F	T
F	F	T	F	F	T
		(2)	(3)	(4)	(1)

15. (a) Contingent

p	q	(p ∨ ~p)	⊃	(p ·	~q)
T	T	T F F	F	F	F
F	T	T T F	F	F	F
T	F	T F T	T	T	T
F	F	T T F	F	F	T
		(2) (1) (3)		(2)	(1)

17. (a) Contingent

p	q	~(p ⊃ q)	≡)	(~p ⊃	q)
T	T	F T	F	F	T
F	T	F T	F	T	T
T	F	T F	T	F	T
F	F	F T	T	T	F
		(3) (2)	(4)	(1)	(2)

EXERCISE 6–1

Note that the letters used in the following abbreviations are relatively arbitrary and need not match those letters you selected. In all cases, however, make certain that you have provided a dictionary indicating which letter stands for which proposition and that the *forms* of the abbreviations and schemas match those given here.

1. R = It is raining. W = The ground is getting wet.

    (a) R ⊃ W   (b) p ⊃ q
          R   p
         ∴W   ∴q

3. C = There are clouds in the sky. S = The sun is shining.

    (a) C ∨ S   (b) p ∨ q
          ~S   ~q
         ∴C   ∴p

5. S = That artifact is from the Stone Age. M = That artifact is made of metal.

    (a) S ⊃ ~M   (b) p ⊃ ~q
          M   q
         ∴~S   ∴~p

7. D = All dogs are carnivores. F = Fido is a carnivore.

    (a) D ⊃ F   (b) p ⊃ q
          ~F   ~q
         ∴~D   ∴~p

9. W = This chair is made of walnut. M = This chair is made of mahogany. T = This chair is made of teakwood.

    (a) (W ∨ M) ∨ T   (b) (p ∨ q) ∨ r
          ~W   ~p
         ∴M ∨ T   ∴q ∨ r

11. N = That glass you are holding contains nitroglycerin. D = You are dropping the glass. E = The nitroglycerin will explode.

    (a) (N · D) ⊃ E   (b) (p · q) ⊃ r
          N · D   p · q
         ∴E   ∴r

13. S = We are going to the state park for a picnic. J = We will take Johnny along. B = We will take Billy along.

    (a) S ⊃ (J ∨ B)   (b) p ⊃ (q ∨ r)
          S   p
         ∴J ∨ B   ∴q ∨ r

15. Using the same propositional constants as in 13:

    (a) (S · J) ⊃ B   (b) (p · q) ⊃ r
          S · J   p · q
         ∴B   ∴r

17. Using the same propositional constants as in 13:

    (a) (S ∨ J) ⊃ B   (b) (p ∨ q) ⊃ r
          J   q
         ∴B   ∴r

19. T = You put topspin on the cue ball. F = The cue ball will follow the six ball into the pocket. S = You will scratch.

    (a) T ⊃ (F · S)   (b) p ⊃ (q · r)
          T   p
         ∴F · S   ∴q · r

21. R = We are having a heavy rain. O = The sewers will be overloaded. F = The basement will flood.

    (a) R ⊃ O   (b) p ⊃ q
          O ⊃ F   q ⊃ r
          R   p
         ∴F   ∴r

23. S = It is snowing. F = Sleet is falling. G = We will go sledding.

    (a) S ⊃ G   (b) p ⊃ q
          S ∨ F   p ∨ r
          ~G   ~q
         ∴F   ∴r

25. R = It is raining. W = The wind is blowing. T = Water will get in the tent.

    (a) (R · W) ⊃ T   (b) (p · q) ⊃ r
          R   p
          W   q
         ∴T   ∴r

27. F = Snow is falling. C = It is getting cold. S = My car will start.

    (a) F ⊃ C   (b) p ⊃ q
          C ⊃ ~S   q ⊃ ~r
          F   p
         ∴~S   ∴~r

29. P = Peter is playing piano. B = Bob is playing base. D = Don is playing drums. C = Our regular combo is here.

    (a) ((P · B) · D) ⊃ C   (b) ((p · q) · r) ⊃ s
          ~C   ~s
         ∴~P ∨ (~B ∨ ~D)   ∴p ∨ (~q ∨ ~r)

31. E = The statement under discussion is an equivalence. I = The statement under discussion contains an implication. D = The statement under discussion is a disjunction.

(a)   E ⊃ I
      D ∨ E
      ~D
      ∴I

(b)   p ⊃ q
      r ∨ p
      ~r
      ∴q

33. C = The statement under discussion is a conjunction. D = The statement under discussion is a disjunction. I = The statement under discussion is an implication.

(a)   C ∨ D
      C ∨ I
      D ⊃ ~I
      ∴C

(b)   p ∨ q
      p ∨ r
      q ⊃ ~r
      ∴p

35. T = The statement is a truth-functional proposition. C = The statement is a command. P = The statement is a compound proposition. L = The statement contains a logical operator.

(a)   T ∨ C
      T ⊃ P
      P ⊃ L
      ~C
      ∴L

(b)   p ∨ q
      p ⊃ r
      r ⊃ s
      ~q
      ∴s

37. Y = The Cheshire cat is yellow. C = The Cheshire cat is colored. V = The Cheshire cat is visible. R = The Cheshire cat is real.

(a)   Y ⊃ C
      C ⊃ V
      V ⊃ R
      ~R
      ∴~Y

(b)   p ⊃ q
      q ⊃ r
      r ⊃ s
      ~s
      ∴~p

39. Using the same propositional constants as in 37:

(a)   R ∨ ~V
      V ∨ ~C
      C ∨ ~Y
      Y
      ∴R

(b)   p ∨ ~q
      q ∨ ~r
      r ∨ ~s
      s
      ∴p

41. H = Herb is a Hoosier. B = Herb is a Buckeye. I = Herb is from Indiana. O = Herb is from Ohio. C = Herb is a U.S. citizen.

(a)   H ⊃ I
      B ⊃ O
      (I ∨ O) ⊃ C
      H ∨ B
      ∴C

(b)   p ⊃ q
      r ⊃ s
      (q ∨ s) ⊃ t
      p ∨ r
      ∴t

43. R = We will have red wine for dinner. W = We will have white wine for dinner. B = We will have roast beef for dinner. S = We will have fillet of sole for dinner. F = We will have fruit salad for dessert.

(a)   R ∨ W
      B ⊃ R
      B ∨ S
      S ⊃ F
      ~R
      ∴S · (W · F)

(b)   p ∨ q
      r ⊃ p
      r ∨ s
      s ⊃ t
      ~p
      ∴s · (q · t)

45. P = Preston is a member of the Safari Club. Q = Quincy is a member of the Safari Club. R = Randolph is a member of the Safari Club. S = Stuart is a member of the Safari Club. T = Trumbull is a member of the Safari Club.

(a)   (P ⊃ Q) ∨ (R ⊃ S)
      (P ⊃ R) · (T ⊃ ~S)
      P
      ∴Q · (R · T)

(b)   (p ⊃ q) ∨ (r ⊃ s)
      (p ⊃ r) · (t ⊃ ~s)
      p
      ∴q · (r · t)

EXERCISE 6–2

1. Valid

p	q	p · q	p
T	T	T	T
F	T	F	F
T	F	F	T
F	F	F	F

3. Truth-functionally invalid

p	q	q ⊃ p	~q	⊃	~p
T	T	T	F	T	F
F	T	F	F	T	T
T	F	T	T	F	F
F	F	T	T	T	T

5. Valid

p	q	(p ⊃ q)	⊃	(p ∨ q)	(p ∨ q)	⊃	(q ∨ p)
T	T	T	T	T	T	T	T
F	T	T	T	T	T	T	T
T	F	F	T	T	T	T	T
F	F	T	F	F	F	T	F

7. Valid

p	q	p ∨ q	~p	q
T	T	T	F	T
F	T	T	T	T
T	F	T	F	F
F	F	F	T	F

9. Truth-functionally invalid

p	q	p ∨ q	q
T	T	T	T
F	T	T	T
T	F	T	F
F	F	F	F

11. Truth-functionally invalid

p	q	q	p · q
T	T	T	T
F	T	T	F
T	F	F	F
F	F	F	F

13. Truth-functionally invalid

p	q	r	p ⊃ q	p ⊃ r	q ∨ r
T	T	T	T	T	T
F	T	T	T	T	T
T	F	T	F	T	T
F	F	T	T	T	T
T	T	F	T	F	T
F	T	F	T	T	T
T	F	F	F	F	F
F	F	F	T	T	F

15. Valid

p	q	r	p ⊃ q	p ∨ r	~r	q
T	T	T	T	T	F	T
F	T	T	T	T	F	T
T	F	T	F	T	F	F
F	F	T	T	T	F	F
T	T	F	T	T	T	T
F	T	F	T	F	T	T
T	F	F	F	T	T	F
F	F	F	T	F	T	F

17. Valid

p	q	r	p ⊃ q	q ⊃ r	p ⊃ r
T	T	T	T	T	T
F	T	T	T	T	T
T	F	T	F	T	T
F	F	T	T	T	T
T	T	F	T	F	F
F	T	F	T	F	T
T	F	F	F	T	F
F	F	F	T	T	T

19. Valid

p	q	r	p	⊃	(q · r)	(q ∨ r)	⊃	~p	~p
T	T	T	T	T	T	T	F	F	F
F	T	T	F	T	T	T	T	T	F
T	F	T	T	F	F	T	F	F	F
F	F	T	F	T	F	T	T	T	F
T	T	F	T	F	F	T	F	F	F
F	T	F	F	T	F	T	T	T	T
T	F	F	T	F	F	F	T	F	F
F	F	F	F	T	F	F	T	T	T

21. Truth-functionally invalid

p	q	r	p ⊃ q	p ⊃ r	~r	~q
T	T	T	T	T	F	F
F	T	T	T	T	F	F
T	F	T	F	T	F	T
F	F	T	T	T	F	T
T	T	F	T	F	T	F
F	T	F	T	T	T	F
T	F	F	F	F	T	T
F	F	F	T	T	T	T

23. Valid

p	q	r	p ⊃ q	p ∨ r	~q	r
T	T	T	T	T	F	T
F	T	T	T	T	F	T
T	F	T	F	T	T	T
F	F	T	T	T	T	T
T	T	F	T	T	F	F
F	T	F	T	F	F	F
T	F	F	F	T	T	F
F	F	F	T	F	T	F

25. Truth-functionally invalid

q	r	~q	q ⊃ r	r
T	T	F	T	T
F	T	T	T	T
T	F	F	F	F
F	F	T	T	F

27. Truth-functionally invalid

p	q	p ⊃ q	~p	~q
T	T	T	F	F
F	T	T	T	F
T	F	F	F	T
F	F	T	T	T

29. Valid

p	q	r	p ⊃ q	r · p	q ∨ r
T	T	T	T	T	T
F	T	T	T	F	T
T	F	T	F	T	T
F	F	T	T	F	T
T	T	F	T	F	T
F	T	F	T	F	T
T	F	F	F	F	T
F	F	F	T	F	F

31. Valid

p	q	r	(p · q)	⊃	r	p	·	~r	~q
T	T	T	T	T			F	F	F
F	T	T	F	T			F	F	F
T	F	T	F	T			F	F	T
F	F	T	F	T			F	F	T
T	T	F	T	F			T	T	F
F	T	F	F	T			F	T	F
T	F	F	F	T			T	T	T
F	F	F	F	T			F	T	T

33. Truth-functionally invalid

p	q	r	p	⊃	(q ⊃ r)	p ⊃ q	q ⊃ r
T	T	T	T	T	T	T	T
F	T	T	F	T	T	T	T
T	F	T	T	T	T	F	T
F	F	T	F	T	T	T	T
T	T	F	T	F	F	T	F
F	T	F	F	T	F	T	F
T	F	F	T	T	T	F	T
F	F	F	F	T	T	T	T

35. Valid

p	q	r	~p	⊃	(q · r)	~r	p
T	T	T	F	T	T	F	T
F	T	T	T	T	T	F	F
T	F	T	F	T	F	F	T
F	F	T	T	F	F	F	F
T	T	F	F	T	F	T	T
F	T	F	T	F	F	T	F
T	F	F	F	T	F	T	T
F	F	F	T	F	F	T	F

39. Truth-functionally invalid

p	q	r	(~p ∨ q)	⊃	r	~r	~p
T	T	T	F T	T	T	F	F
F	T	T	T T	T	T	F	T
T	F	T	F F	T	T	F	F
F	F	T	T T	T	T	F	T
T	T	F	F T	F	F	T	F
F	T	F	T T	F	F	T	T
T	F	F	F F	T	F	T	F
F	F	F	T T	F	F	T	T

EXERCISE 6–3

1.

p	q	r	p	⊃	q	q	⊃	r	q	∨	r
F	F	F	F	T	F	F	T	F	F	F	F

3.

p	q	r	p	⊃	(q · r)	~p	~r
F	T	T	F	T	T T T	T	F
F	F	T	F	T	F F T	T	F

5.

p	q	r	p	·	q	p	∨	r	r
T	T	F	T	T	T	T	T	F	F

7.

p	q	r	p	⊃	q	p	∨	r	q	⊃	~r
T	T	T	T	T	T	T	T	T	T	F	FT
F	T	T	F	T	T	T	T	T	T	F	FT

9.

p	q	r	p	⊃	(q ∨ r)	~	q	r	⊃	p
F	F	T	F	T	F T T	T	F	T	F	F

11.

p	q	r	s	p	⊃	(q ∨ r)	q	⊃	s	p	r	⊃	s
T	F	T	F	T	T	F T T	F	T	F	T	T	F	F

13.

p	q	r	p	⊃	(q ⊃ r)	p	r
T	F	F	T	T	F T F	T	F

15.

p	r	s	t	(p ⊃ r)	·	(s ⊃ t)	r	∨	t	p	∨	s
F	T	F	T	F T T	T	F T T	T	T	T	F	F	F
F	T	F	F	F T T	T	F T F	T	T	F	F	F	F
F	F	F	T	F T F	T	F T T	F	T	T	F	F	F

17.

p	q	r	s	p	⊃	q	r	⊃	s	(p ∨ q)	⊃	(r · s)
T	T	F	T	T	T	T	F	T	T	T T T	F	F F T
F	T	F	T	F	T	T	F	T	T	F T T	F	F F T
T	T	F	F	T	T	T	F	T	F	T T F	F	F F F
F	T	F	F	F	T	T	F	T	F	F T F	F	F F F

EXERCISE 6–4

1. Tautology, ∴ valid

p	q	(p · q)	⊃	p
T	T	T	T	T
F	T	F	T	F
T	F	F	T	T
F	F	F	T	F

3. Contingent, ∴ truth-functionally invalid

p	q	(q ⊃ p)	⊃	(~q ⊃ ~p)
T	T	T	T	F T T F
F	T	F	T	F T T T
T	F	T	F	T F F F
F	F	T	T	T T T T

5. Tautology, ∴ valid

p	q	((p ⊃ q) ⊃ (p ∨ q))	⊃	((p ∨ q) ⊃ (q ∨ p))
T	T	T T T	T	T T T
F	T	T T T	T	T T T
T	F	F T T	T	T T T
F	F	T F F	T	F T F

7. Tautology, ∴ valid

p	q	((p ∨ q) · ~p)	⊃	q
T	T	T F F	T	T
F	T	T T T	T	T
T	F	T F F	T	F
F	F	F F T	T	F

9. Contingent, ∴ truth-functionally invalid

p	q	(p ∨ q)	⊃	q
T	T	T	T	T
F	T	T	T	T
T	F	T	F	F
F	F	F	T	F

11. Contingent, ∴ truth-functionally invalid

p	q	q	⊃	(p · q)
T	T	T	T	T
F	T	T	F	F
T	F	F	T	F
F	F	F	T	F

The same pattern as shown in these answers can be followed with answers 13–39.

EXERCISE 6–5

1. 3. Simp., 1
   4. Add., 3

3. 3. Simp., 2
   4. Add., 3

5. 3. Conj., 1,2
   4. Add., 2
   5. Conj., 3.4

7. 4. Simp., 3
   5. Simp., 3
   6. Conj., 2,5
   7. Conj., 4,6

9. 3. Simp., 2
   4. Simp., 1
   5. Simp., 2
   6. Add., 3
   7. Add., 6
   8. Conj., 4,7

EXERCISE 6–6

1. 1. p · r   Premise
   2. r   Simp., 1
   3. r ∨ s   Add., 2
   4. (r ∨ s) · (p · r)   Conj., 1,3

3. 1. t · r   Premise
   2. (q ∨ p) · s   Premise
   3. q ∨ p   Simp., 2
   4. t   Simp., 1
   5. (q ∨ p) · t   Conj., 3,4

5. 1. p   Premise
   2. t · p   Premise
   3. t   Simp., 2
   4. p · t   Conj., 1,3
   5. (p · t) · (t · p)   Conj., 2,4
   6. ((p · t) · (t · p)) · t Conj., 3,5

7. 1. p   Premise
   2. q · (r · s)   Premise
   3. t · (s ∨ (p ∨ t))   Premise
   4. s ∨ (p ∨ t)   Simp., 3
   5. r · s   Simp., 2
   6. r   Simp., 5
   7. r · (s ∨ (p ∨ t))   Conj., 4,6

9. 1. (((q · r) · s) · r)   Premise
   2. (t · u) · (p · t)   Premise
   3. t · u   Simp., 2
   4. u   Simp., 3
   5. ((q · r) · s)   Simp., 1
   6. p · t   Simp., 2

7. p	Simp., 6
8. p · u	Conj., 4,7
9. (p · u) ∨ t	Add., 8
10. ((p · u) ∨ t) · ((q · r) · s)	Conj., 5,9

EXERCISE 6–7

1. 4. M.T., 2,3
   5. M.T., 1,4

3. 4. M.T., 1,3
   5. M.P., 2,4

5. 5. M.T., 3,4
   6. M.T., 2,5
   7. M.P., 1,6

EXERCISE 6–8

1. 1. p ⊃ q   Premise
   2. q ⊃ r   Premise
   3. r ⊃ s   Premise
   4. p /∴ s   Premise/conclusion
   5. q   M.P., 1,4
   6. r   M.P., 2,5
   7. s   M.P., 3,6

3. 1. ~r ⊃ s   Premise
   2. r ⊃ ~t   Premise
   3. ~~t /∴ s   Premise/conclusion
   4. ~r   M.T., 2,3
   5. s   M.P., 1,4

5. 1. q ⊃ p   Premise
   2. p ⊃ t   Premise
   3. t ⊃ s   Premise
   4. ~s /∴ ~q   Premise/conclusion
   5. ~t   M.T., 3,4
   6. ~p   M.T., 2,5
   7. ~q   M.T., 1,6

EXERCISE 6–9

1. 4. Simp., 3
   5. M.T., 1,4
   6. Simp., 3
   7. M.T., 2,6

3. 3. Simp., 1
   4. M.P., 2,3
   5. Add., 4

EXERCISE 6–10

1. 1. p · q   Premise
   2. (p ∨ r) ⊃ s   Premise
   3. p   Simp., 1
   4. p ∨ r   Add., 3
   5. s   M.P., 2,4

3. 1. ~(p ∨ q) ⊃ (r · t)   Premise
   2. (p ∨ q) ⊃ s   Premise
   3. ~s   Premise
   4. ~(p ∨ q)   M.T., 2,3
   5. r · t   M.P., 1,4
   6. r   Simp., 5
   7. r · ~s   Conj., 3,6
   8. t   Simp., 5
   9. t ∨ p   Add., 8
   10. (r · ~s) · (t ∨ p)   Conj., 7,9

EXERCISE 6–11

1. 4. H.Syll., 1,2
   5. H.Syll., 3,4

3. 4. D.Syll., 1,2
   5. H.Syll., 3,4

5. 6. H.Syll., 2,3
   7. D.Syll., 1,4
   8. D.Syll., 5,7

EXERCISE 6–12

1. 1. p ⊃ r   Premise
   2. r ⊃ s   Premise
   3. s ⊃ t   Premise
   4. t ⊃ u   Premise
   5. p ⊃ s   H.Syll., 1,2
   6. p ⊃ t   H.Syll., 5,3
   7. p ⊃ u   H.Syll., 6,4

3. 1. (p ⊃ q) ∨ (t ⊃ u)   Premise
   2. (t ⊃ u) ∨ (q ⊃ s)   Premise
   3. ~(t ⊃ u)   Premise
   4. p ⊃ q   D.Syll., 1,3
   5. q ⊃ s   D.Syll., 2,3
   6. p ⊃ s   H.Syll., 4,5

5. 1. p ⊃ q   Premise
   2. q ⊃ r   Premise
   3. r ∨ (s ∨ t)   Premise
   4. ~r   Premise
   5. ~t   Premise

6. p ⊃ r	H.Syll., 1,2
7. s ∨ t	D.Syll., 3,4
8. s	D.Syll., 7,5

EXERCISE 6–13

1. 6. D.Syll., 3,4
   7. M.P., 2,6
   8. H.Syll., 1,7
   9. M.T., 1,5

3. 4. D.Syll., 1,3
   5. M.P., 2,4
   6. H.Syll., 4,5
   7. M.T., 6,3

EXERCISE 6–14

1. 1. p ∨ (q ⊃ r)	Premise
2. r ⊃ (s ⊃ p)	Premise
3. r	Premise
4. ~p	Premise
5. q ⊃ r	D.Syll., 1,4
6. q ⊃ (s ⊃ p)	H.Syll., 5,2
7. s ⊃ p	M.P., 2,3
8. ~s	M.T., 7,4

3. 1. (s · r) ∨ (t ⊃ (p ⊃ q))	Premise
2. t	Premise
3. q ⊃ (s · r)	Premise
4. ~(s · r)	Premise
5. ~q	M.T., 3,4
6. t ⊃ (p ⊃ q)	D.Syll., 1,4
7. p ⊃ q	M.P., 6,2
8. p ⊃ (s · r)	H.Syll., 7,3

EXERCISE 6–15

1. 5. ~r	M.T., 3,4
6. q ⊃ r	Simp., 1
7. ~q	M.T., 6,5
8. s	D.Syll., 2,7
9. p	Simp., 1
10. p · s	Conj., 9,8

3. 4. p	Simp., 3
5. s · r	M.P., 1,4
6. (s · r) ∨ p	Add., 5
7. ~t	M.P., 2,6

8. t ∨ ~~r	Simp., 3
9. ~~r	D.Syll., 9,7
10. ~~r · (s · r)	Conj., 5,9

5. 5. p ⊃ q	Simp., 4
6. p · (s ∨ r)	M.P., 1,5
7. p	Simp., 6
8. q	M.P., 5,7
9. s ∨ r	Simp., 6
10. ~s	Simp., 4
11. r	D.Syll., 9,10
12. (p ⊃ q) · ((t · r) ⊃ s)	Conj., 3,5
13. p ∨ (t · r)	Add., 7
14. q ∨ s	Dil., 12,13

7. 4. ~r	Simp., 2
5. (p ∨ s) ∨ t	D.Syll., 1,4
6. ~(p ∨ s)	Simp., 2
7. t	D.Syll., 5,6
8. t ∨ (r · p)	Add., 7
9. q	M.P., 3,8

9. 5. ~(s ∨ p)	Simp., 4
6. ~p	M.T., 3,5
7. ~(t · r)	M.T., 2,5
8. p ⊃ (s ∨ p)	H.Syll., 1,2
9. ~p · (p ⊃ (s ∨ p))	Conj., 6,8

EXERCISE 6–16

1. 1. ~p · (q ⊃ r)	Premise
2. r ⊃ ~t	Premise
3. s ⊃ t	Premise
4. s ∨ p	Premise
5. ~p	Simp., 1
6. s	D.Syll., 4,5
7. t	M.P., 3,6
8. r ∨ s	Add., 6
9. (r ⊃ ~t) · (s ⊃ t)	Conj., 2,3
10. ~t ∨ t	Dil., 9,8

3. 1. p · (q ⊃ (r ∨ t))	Premise
2. ~s ∨ ~r	Premise
3. ~~r · (s ∨ ~(r ∨ t))	Premise
4. p	Simp., 1
5. q ⊃ (r ∨ t)	Simp., 1
6. ~~r	Simp., 3
7. s ∨ ~(r ∨ t)	Simp., 3
8. ~s	D.Syll., 2,6
9. ~(r ∨ t)	D.Syll., 7,8
10. ~q	M.T., 5,9

5. 1. p ∨ (q ⊃ r)   Premise
   2. s ⊃ (p · (t ∨ q))   Premise
   3. ~p · (q ∨ s)   Premise
   4. ~p   Simp., 3
   5. q ⊃ r   D.Syll., 1,4
   6. (q ⊃ r) · (s ⊃ (p · (t ∨ q))) Conj., 2,5
   7. q ∨ s   Simp., 3
   8. r ∨ (p · (t ∨ q))   Dil., 6,7

7. 1. r ⊃ (s · ~t)   Premise
   2. r ∨ ~(s · ~t)   Premise
   3. ~~(s · ~t)   Premise
   4. r   D.Syll., 2,3
   5. s · ~t   M.P., 1,4
   6. s   Simp., 5
   7. r · s   Conj., 4,6
   8. (p ⊃ q) ∨ (r · s)   Add., 7

9. 1. ((p ∨ t) ∨ (s · r)) ⊃ q   Premise
   2. t   Premise
   3. (q ∨ (s · r)) ⊃ p   Premise
   4. p ∨ t   Add., 2
   5. (p ∨ t) ∨ (s · r)   Add., 4
   6. q   M.P., 1,5
   7. q ∨ (s · r)   Add., 6
   8. p   M.P., 3,7

EXERCISE 6–17

1. 3. (p · q) · r   Assoc., 1
   4. ~~s · t   Comm., 2
   5. s · t   D.N., 4

3. 2. (q ∨ p) · r   Comm., 1
   3. (q ∨ ~~p) · r   D.N., 2
   4. (q ∨ ~~p) · (r · r)   Taut., 3

5. 2. (p ∨ (p · q)) ∨ ~~r   Assoc., 1
   3. ~~r ∨ (p ∨ (p · q))   Comm., 2
   4. r ∨ (p ∨ (p · q))   D.N., 3
   5. r ∨ (p ∨ (q · p))   Comm., 4
   6. r ∨ (p ∨ ((q · p) · (q · p)))   Taut., 5
   7. r ∨ (p ∨ ((q · p) · (p · q)))   Comm., 6

7. 2. (s · (r · t)) · (p · q)   Comm., 1
   3. (s · (r · ~~t)) · (p · q) D.N., 2
   4. (s · (r · (~~t · ~~t)))
      · (p · q)   Taut., 3
   5. (s · (r · (~~ t · t)))
      · (p · q)   D.N., 4
   6. (s · (r · (~~ t · t)))
      · (q · p)   Comm., 5

EXERCISE 6–18

1. 1. (p · q) · (s · r)   Premise
   2. (s · r) · (p · q)   Comm., 1
   3. (r · s) · (p · q)   Comm., 2
   4. (r · s) · (q · p)   Comm., 3

3. 1. s · (r · ~t)   Premise
   2. (s · r) · ~t   Assoc., 1
   3. (s · r) · ~~~t   D.N., 2
   4. ~~~t · (s · r)   Comm., 3

5. 1. ((p · q) · s) · r   Premise
   2. (p · (q · s)) · r   Assoc., 1
   3. p · ((q · s) · r)   Assoc., 2
   4. ((q · s) · r) · p   Comm., 3
   5. ((q · ~~s) · r) · p   D.N., 4
   6. ((q · ~~s) · r) · (p ∨ p)   Taut., 5
   7. ((q · (~~s · ~~s)) · r)
      · (p ∨ p)   Taut., 6

7. 1. p ∨ q   Premise
   2. (p ∨ q) ∨ (p ∨ q)   Taut., 1
   3. (p ∨ q) ∨ ((p ∨ q)
      ∨ (p ∨ q))   Taut., 2
   4. ((p ∨ q) ∨ (p ∨ q))
      ∨ (p ∨ q)   Assoc., 3
   5. (~~(p ∨ q) ∨ (p ∨ q))
      ∨ (p ∨ q)   D.N., 4
   6. (p ∨ q) ∨ (~~(p ∨ q)
      ∨ (p ∨ q))   Comm., 5

9. 1. p   Premise
   2. p ∨ p   Taut., 1
   3. p ∨ (p · p)   Taut., 2
   4. (p ∨ p) ∨ (p · p)   Taut., 3
   5. (p ∨ (p ∨ p)) ∨ (p · p)   Taut., 4
   6. p ∨ ((p ∨ p) ∨ (p · p))   Assoc., 5
   7. ((p ∨ p) ∨ (p · p)) ∨ p   Comm., 6
   8. ((p ∨ p) ∨ (p · p)) ∨ (p · p)   Taut., 7

EXERCISE 6–19

1. 3. DeM., 1
   4. DeM., 2

3. 3. Dist., 1
   4. Dist., 2

5. 3. Dist., 1
   4. DeM., 3
   5. DeM., 4

6. Dist., 2
7. DeM., 6

EXERCISE 6–20

1. 1. ~(p ∨ q)   Premise
   2. ~p · ~q   DeM., 1

3. 1. (~(~p · ~q)
        · ~(~s ∨ ~r))   Premise
   2. ~((~p · ~q) ∨ (~s ∨ ~r))DeM., 1
   3. ~(~(p ∨ q) ∨ (~s ∨ ~r)) DeM., 2
   4. ~(~(p ∨ q) ∨ ~(s · r))   DeM., 3

5. 1. p · (q ∨ (r · (s ∨ t)))   Premise
   2. (p · q) ∨ (p · (r · (s ∨ t))) Dist., 1
   3. (p · q) ∨ (p · ((r · s)
        ∨ (r · t)))   Dist., 2
   4. ((p · q) ∨ p) · ((p · q)
        ∨ ((r · s) ∨ (r · t)))   Dist., 3

EXERCISE 6–21

1. 2. Comm., 1
   3. Dist., 2
   4. DeM., 3
   5. DeM., 4
   6. DeM., 5

3. 2. DeM., 1
   3. Taut., 2
   4. Assoc., 3
   5. DeM., 4
   6. DeM., 5
   7. Assoc., 6
   8. Taut., 7

EXERCISE 6–22

1. 1. (~~p · ~~q)
        ∨ (~~p · ~~r)   Premise
   2. ~~p · (~~q ∨ ~~r)   Dist., 1
   3. ~~p · ~(~q · ~r)   DeM., 2
   4. p · ~(~q · ~r)   D.N., 3
   5. ~(~q · ~r) · p   Comm., 4

3. 1. ~p ∨ (~q · ~r)   Premise
   2. (~p ∨ ~q) · (~p ∨ ~r)   Dist., 1
   3. ((~p ∨ ~q) · ~p)
        ∨ ((~p ∨ ~q) · ~r)   Dist., 2
   4. (~(p · q) · ~p)
        ∨ ((~p ∨ ~q) · ~r)   DeM., 3

5. ((~p ∨ ~q) · ~r)
      ∨ (~(p · q) · ~p)   Comm., 4
6. (~r · (~p ∨ ~q))
      ∨ (~(p · q) · ~p)   Comm., 5
7. ((~r · ~p) ∨ (~r · ~q))
      ∨ (~(p · q) · ~p)   Dist., 6
8. ((~r · ~p) ∨ (~r · ~q))
      ∨ (~p · ~(p · q))   Comm., 7

EXERCISE 6–23

1. 2. Exp., 1
   3. Trans., 2

3. 2. Exp., 1
   3. Exp., 2
   4. Trans., 3
   5. Exp., 4

5. 2. Exp., 1
   3. Exp., 2
   4. Trans., 3
   5. Trans., 4
   6. Trans., 5
   7. Exp., 6

EXERCISE 6–24

1. 1. (p · q) ⊃ (r ⊃ s)   Premise
   2. p ⊃ (q ⊃ (r ⊃ s))   Exp., 1
   3. p ⊃ ((q · r) ⊃ s)   Exp., 2
   4. p ⊃ (~s ⊃ ~(q · r))   Trans., 3
   5. ~(~s ⊃ ~(q · r)) ⊃ ~p   Trans., 4

3. 1. ((r ⊃ t) · (s ⊃ p))
        ⊃ (r ⊃ q)   Premise
   2. (r ⊃ t) ⊃ ((s ⊃ p)
        ⊃ (r ⊃ q))   Exp., 1
   3. (r ⊃ t)
        ⊃ (((s ⊃ p) · r) ⊃ q)   Exp., 2
   4. (r ⊃ t)
        ⊃ (~q ⊃ ~((s ⊃ p) · r)) Trans., 3
   5. (r ⊃ t) ⊃ (~q ⊃
        ~((~p ⊃ ~s) · r)   Trans., 4

5. 1. (((r · p) ⊃ s) · ~q)
        ⊃ ((r · s) ⊃ p)   Premise
   2. ((r · p) ⊃ s)
        ⊃ (~q ⊃ ((r · s) ⊃ p)) Exp., 1
   3. ((r · p) ⊃ s)
        ⊃ (~q ⊃ (r ⊃ (s ⊃ p))) Exp., 2
   4. ((r · p) ⊃ s) ⊃ (~q ⊃
        (r ⊃ (~p ⊃ ~s)))   Trans., 3

5. $(r \supset (p \supset s)) \supset (\sim q \supset$
   $(r \supset (\sim p \supset \sim s)))$ Exp., 4
6. $(\sim (p \supset s) \supset \sim r) \supset$
   $(\sim q \supset$
   $(r \supset (\sim p \supset \sim s)))$ Trans., 5
7. $(\sim (p \supset s) \supset \sim r) \supset$
   $(\sim q \supset ((r \cdot \sim p) \supset \sim s))$ Exp., 6

EXERCISE 6–25

1. 2. DeM., 1
   3. Trans., 2
   4. Trans., 3
   5. DeM., 4

3. 2. DeM., 1
   3. Exp., 2
   4. Trans., 3
   5. DeM., 4

EXERCISE 6–26

1. 1. $\sim ((p \cdot u) \supset r) \supset \sim (t \vee p)$ Premise
   2. $(t \vee p) \supset ((p \cdot u) \supset r)$ Trans., 1
   3. $(t \vee p) \supset (p \supset (u \supset r))$ Exp., 2
   4. $((t \vee p) \cdot p) \supset (u \supset r)$ Exp., 3
   5. $(((t \vee p) \cdot p) \cdot u) \supset r$ Exp., 4
   6. $\sim r \supset \sim (((t \vee p) \cdot p) \cdot u)$ Trans., 5

3. 1. $\sim ((t \vee (\sim s \supset \sim r)) \supset p)$
      $\supset (\sim t \cdot \sim q)$ Premise
   2. $\sim ((t \vee (r \supset s)) \supset p)$
      $\supset (\sim t \cdot \sim q)$ Trans., 1
   3. $\sim ((t \vee (r \supset s)) \supset p)$
      $\supset \sim (t \vee q)$ DeM., 2
   4. $(t \vee q) \supset ((t \vee (r \supset s))$
      $\supset p)$ Trans., 3
   5. $((t \vee q) \cdot (t \vee (r \supset s)))$
      $\supset p$ Exp., 4
   6. $(t \vee (q \cdot (r \supset s))) \supset p$ Dist., 5

EXERCISE 6–27

1. 2. Equiv., 1
   3. Impl., 2
   4. Impl., 3

3. 2. Equiv., 1
   3. Impl., 2
   4. Impl., 3
   5. Impl., 4
   6. Impl., 5

5. 2. Impl., 1
   3. Equiv., 2
   4. Impl., 3
   5. Impl., 4
   6. Impl., 5
   7. Impl., 6
   8. Impl., 7

EXERCISE 6–28

1. 1. $(\sim r \vee (p \cdot q)) \cdot$
      $\sim ((p \cdot q) \cdot \sim r)$ Premise
   2. $(\sim r \vee (p \cdot q)) \cdot$
      $((p \cdot q) \supset r)$ Impl., 1
   3. $(r \supset (p \cdot q)) \cdot ((p \cdot q) \supset r)$ Impl., 2
   4. $r \equiv (p \cdot q)$ Equiv., 3
   5. $(r \cdot (p \cdot q)) \vee$
      $(\sim r \cdot \sim (p \cdot q))$ Equiv., 4

3. 1. $(\sim q \vee \sim (t \vee p)) \cdot$
      $\sim (\sim (t \vee p) \cdot \sim q)$ Premise
   2. $(\sim q \vee \sim (t \vee p)) \cdot$
      $(\sim (t \vee p) \supset q)$ Impl., 1
   3. $(q \supset \sim (t \vee p)) \cdot$
      $(\sim (t \vee p) \supset q)$ Impl., 2
   4. $q \equiv \sim (t \vee p)$ Equiv., 3
   5. $(q \cdot \sim (t \vee p)) \vee$
      $(\sim q \cdot \sim \sim (t \vee p))$ Equiv., 4

5. 1. $((p \equiv q) \supset t) \equiv$
      $(\sim (s \cdot \sim t) \supset u)$ Premise
   2. $(((p \supset q) \cdot (q \supset p)) \supset t)$
      $\equiv (\sim (s \cdot \sim t) \supset u)$ Equiv., 1
   3. $(((\sim p \vee q) \cdot (q \supset p)) \supset t)$
      $\equiv (\sim (s \cdot \sim t) \supset u)$ Impl., 2
   4. $(((\sim p \vee q) \cdot \sim (q \cdot \sim p)) \supset$
      $t) \equiv (\sim (s \cdot \sim t) \supset u)$ Impl., 3
   5. $((((\sim p \vee q) \cdot \sim (q \cdot \sim p))$
      $\supset t) \supset (\sim (s \cdot \sim t) \supset u))$
      $\cdot (((\sim (s \cdot \sim t) \supset u) \supset$
      $(((\sim p \vee q) \cdot \sim (q \cdot \sim p))$
      $\supset t))$ Equiv., 4
   6. $((\sim \sim ((\sim p \vee q) \cdot \sim (q \cdot$
      $\sim p)) \supset t) \supset (\sim (s \cdot \sim t$
      $\supset u)) \cdot (((\sim (s \cdot \sim t) \supset$
      $u) \supset (((\sim p \vee q) \cdot \sim (q \cdot$
      $\sim p)) \supset t))$ DN, 5
   7. $((\sim ((\sim p \vee q) \supset (q \cdot \sim p))$
      $\supset t) \supset (\sim (s \cdot \sim t) \supset u))$
      $\cdot (((\sim (s \cdot \sim t) \supset u) \supset$
      $(((\sim p \vee q) \cdot \sim (q \cdot \sim p))$
      $\supset t))$ Impl., 5

EXERCISE 6–29

1. 2. Equiv., 1
   3. Impl., 2
   4. Trans., 3

3. 2. Equiv., 1
   3. Trans., 2
   4. Exp., 3
   5. Impl., 4
   6. Exp., 5
   7. Impl., 6

5. 2. Equiv., 1
   3. D.N., 2
   4. Impl., 3
   5. Exp., 4
   6. Trans., 5
   7. Impl., 6
   8. Impl., 7

EXERCISE 6–30

1. 1. $(\sim s \vee t) \cdot (\sim s \supset \sim t)$ Premise
   2. $(\sim s \vee t) \cdot (t \supset s)$ Trans., 1
   3. $(s \supset t) \cdot (t \supset s)$ Impl., 2
   4. $s \equiv t$ Equiv., 3
   5. $(s \cdot t) \vee (\sim s \cdot \sim t)$ Equiv., 4

3. 1. $((\sim q \vee \sim(\sim s \cdot \sim \sim t)) \supset p) \cdot (((p \cdot q) \cdot t) \supset s)$ Premise
   2. $((\sim q \vee (\sim s \supset \sim t)) \supset p) \cdot (((p \cdot q) \cdot t) \supset s)$ Impl., 1
   3. $((\sim q \vee (\sim s \supset \sim t)) \supset p) \cdot ((p \cdot q) \supset (t \supset s))$ Exp., 2
   4. $((q \supset (\sim s \supset \sim t)) \supset p) \cdot ((p \cdot q) \supset (t \supset s))$ Impl., 3
   5. $((q \supset (\sim s \supset \sim t)) \supset p) \cdot (p \supset (q \supset (t \supset s)))$ Exp., 4
   6. $((q \supset (t \supset s)) \supset p) \cdot (p \supset (q \supset (t \supset s)))$ Trans., 5
   7. $q \supset (t \supset s) \equiv p$ Equiv., 6

5. 1. $((p \supset s) \supset (\sim s \supset \sim(\sim s \vee p)))$ Premise
   2. $((p \supset s) \supset (\sim s \supset \sim(s \supset p)))$ Impl., 1
   3. $((p \supset s) \supset ((s \supset p) \supset s))$ Trans., 2
   4. $(((p \supset s) \cdot (s \supset p)) \supset s)$ Exp., 3
   5. $\sim(((p \supset s) \cdot (s \supset p)) \cdot \sim s)$ Impl., 4
   6. $\sim((p \equiv s) \cdot \sim s)$ Equiv., 5

EXERCISE 6–31

1. 2. Comm., 1
   3. Impl., 2
   4. Taut., 3
   5. D.N., 4

3. 2. Equiv., 1
   3. Trans., 2
   4. Trans., 3
   5. D.N., 4

5. 2. Assoc., 1
   3. Dist., 2
   4. Comm., 3
   5. D.N., 4
   6. D.N., 5
   7. Impl., 6

7. 2. Equiv., 1
   3. Exp., 2
   4. Comm., 3
   5. Trans., 4
   6. Impl., 5
   7. D.N., 6
   8. Trans., 7

9. 2. D.N., 1
   3. Impl., 2
   4. D.N., 3
   5. DeM., 4
   6. Impl., 5
   7. DeM., 6
   8. D.N., 7

EXERCISE 6–32

1. 1. $(p \cdot (s \cdot t)) \supset t$ Premise
   2. $p \supset ((s \cdot t) \supset t))$ Exp., 1
   3. $\sim((s \cdot t) \supset t) \supset \sim p$ Trans., 2
   4. $\sim(\sim t \supset \sim(s \cdot t)) \supset \sim p$ Trans., 3
   5. $\sim(\sim \sim t \vee \sim(s \cdot t)) \supset \sim p$ Impl., 4
   6. $\sim \sim(\sim \sim t \vee \sim(s \cdot t)) \vee \sim p$ Impl., 5
   7. $(\sim \sim t \vee \sim(s \cdot t)) \vee \sim p$ D.N., 6
   8. $(t \vee \sim(s \cdot t)) \vee \sim p$ D.N., 7

3. 1. $(s \vee t) \equiv (p \cdot q)$ Premise
   2. $((s \vee t) \supset (p \cdot q)) \cdot ((p \cdot q) \supset (s \vee t))$ Equiv., 1
   3. $(\sim(s \vee t) \vee (p \cdot q)) \cdot ((p \cdot q) \supset (s \vee t))$ Impl., 2

4. (~(s ∨ t) ∨ (p · q)) ·
   (~(s ∨ t) ⊃ ~(p · q))   Trans., 3
5. (~(s ∨ t) ⊃ ~(p · q)) ·
   (~(s ∨ t) ∨ (p · q))   Comm., 4

5. 1. t · ((s ⊃ p) ∨ (r ⊃ u))   Premise
  2. (t · (s ⊃ p)) ∨ (t · (r ⊃ u)) Dist., 1
  3. (t · (~p ⊃ ~s)) ∨
    (t · (r ⊃ u))   Trans., 2
  4. (t · (~~p ∨ ~s)) ∨
    (t · (r ⊃ u))   Impl., 3
  5. (t · (p ∨ ~s))
    ∨ (t · (r ⊃ u))   D.N., 4
  6. (t · (p ∨ ~s))
    ∨ (t · (~r ∨ u))   Impl., 5
  7. (t · (p ∨ ~s)) ∨ ((t · ~r)
    ∨ (t · u))   Dist., 6

7. 1. ~(t ⊃ s) · ~(~(p · q)
    ⊃ r)   Premise
  2. ~((t ⊃ s) ∨ (~(p · q)
    ⊃ r))   DeM., 1
  3. ~((t ⊃ s) ∨ ((~p ∨ ~q)
    ⊃ r))   DeM., 2
  4. ~((t ⊃ s) ∨ ((~p ∨ ~q)
    ⊃ (r · r))   Taut., 3
  5. ~((~t ∨ s) ∨ ((~p ∨ ~q)
    ⊃ (r · r))   Impl., 4
  6. ~((s ∨ ~t) ∨ ((~p ∨ ~q)
    ⊃ (r · r))   Comm., 5
  7. ~((~~s ∨ ~t) ∨
    ((~p ∨ ~q) ⊃ (r · r))   D.N., 6
  8. ~((~s ⊃ ~t) ∨
    ((~p ∨ ~q) ⊃ (r · r))   Impl., 7

9. 1. ((p · q) · (r · s)) ⊃ t   Premise
  2. (p · q) ⊃ ((r · s) ⊃ t)   Exp., 1
  3. (p · q) ⊃ (r ⊃ (s ⊃ t))   Exp., 2
  4. p ⊃ (q ⊃ (r ⊃ (s ⊃ t)))   Exp., 3
  5. p ⊃ (~(r ⊃
    (s ⊃ t)) ⊃ ~q)   Trans., 4
  6. p ⊃ (~(r ⊃
    (~t ⊃ ~s)) ⊃ ~q)   Trans., 5
  7. ~(~(r ⊃
    (~t ⊃ ~s)) ⊃ ~q) ⊃
    ~p   Trans., 6
  8. ~(~(r ⊃ (~~t ∨ ~s)) ⊃
    ~q) ⊃ ~p   Impl., 7

EXERCISE 6–33

1. Transportation

3. De Morgan's rules

5. Simplification

7. Error (Addition is being applied to a
   subcomponent.)

9. Exportation

11. De Morgan's rules

13. Error (not Distribution)

EXERCISE 6–34

1. 1. ~p / ∴ ~(p · q)   Premise/conclusion
  2. ~p ∨ ~q   Add., 1
  3. ~(p · q)   DeM., 2

3. 1. p   Premise
  2. ~q ⊃ ~p / ∴ q   Premise/conclusion
  3. p ⊃ q   Trans., 2
  4. q   M.P., 1,3

5. 1. p   Premise
  2. q ∨ (r · s)   Premise
  3. ~q ∨ ~p / ∴ s   Premise/conclusion
  4. ~~p   D.N.,1
  5. ~q   D.Syll., 3,4
  6. r · s   D.Syll., 2,5
  7. s   Simp., 6

7. 1. q ⊃ (p · r)   Premise
  2. ~ p / ∴ ~ q   Premise/conclusion
  3. ~p ∨ ~r   Add., 2
  4. ~(p · r)   DeM., 3
  5. ~q   M.T., 1,4

9. 1. ~r · ~s   Premise
  2. (p ∨ q) ⊃ (r ∨ s) /
    ∴ ~(p ∨ q)   Premise/conclusion
  3. ~(r ∨ s)   DeM., 1
  4. ~(p ∨ q)   M.T., 2,3

11. 1. p ⊃ (q ⊃ r)   Premise
  2. ~r / ∴ ~(p · q)   Premise/conclusion
  3. (p · q) ⊃ r   Exp., 1
  4. ~ (p · q)   M.T., 3,2

13. 1. ~p   Premise
  2. ~(p · q) ⊃ (~p ⊃ r) /
    ∴ r   Premise/conclusion

3. ~p ∨ ~q	Add., 1	9. ~s	M.T., 3,8
4. ~(p · q)	DeM., 3	10. r · ~s	Conj., 7,9
5. ~p ⊃ r	M.P., 2,4	11. ~~(r · ~s)	D.N., 10
6. r	M.P. 1,5	12. ~(r ⊃ s)	Impl., 11

15.
1. ~(p ∨ q)	Premise
2. r ⊃ p	Premise
3. s ⊃ q / ∴ ~(r ∨ s)	Premise/conclusion
4. ~p · ~q	DeM., 1
5. ~p	Simp., 4
6. ~r	M.T., 2,5
7. ~q	Simp., 4
8. ~s	M.T., 3,7
9. ~ r · ~s	Conj., 6,8
10. ~(r ∨ s)	DeM., 9

17.
1. ~r · ~s	Premise
2. (p ∨ q) ⊃ (r ∨ s) / ∴ ~q ∨ t	Premise/conclusion
3. ~(r ∨ s)	DeM., 1
4. ~(p ∨ q)	M.T., 2,3
5. ~ p · ~q	DeM., 4
6. ~ q	Simp., 5
7. ~q ∨ t	Add., 6

19.
1. ~r · ~s	Premise
2. (p ∨ q) ⊃ (r ∨ s) / ∴ ~ (p · q)	Premise/conclusion
3. ~(r ∨ s)	DeM.,1
4. ~ (p ∨ q)	M.T., 2,3
5. ~ p · ~ q	DeM., 4
6. ~ p	Simp., 5
7. ~p ∨ ~q	Add., 6
8. ~ (p · q)	DeM., 7

21.
1. ~(q ∨ ~p)	Premise
2. (p · ~q) ⊃ (p ⊃ r)	Premise
3. r ⊃ s / ∴ p⊃ s	Premise/conclusion
4. ~q · ~~p	DeM., 1
5. ~q · p	D.N., 4
6. p · ~q	Comm., 5
7. p ⊃ r	M.P., 2,6
8. p ⊃ s	H.Syll., 7,3

23.
1. ~(p ⊃ q)	Premise
2. p ⊃ r	Premise
3. s ⊃ q / ∴ ~(r ⊃ s)	Premise/conclusion
4. ~~(p · ~q)	Impl., 1
5. p · ~q	D.N., 4
6. p	Simp., 5
7. r	M.P., 2,6
8. ~q	Simp., 5

25.
1. p	Premise
2. q / ∴ p ≡ q	Premise/conclusion
3. q ∨ ~p	Add., 2
4. ~p ∨ q	Comm., 3
5. p ⊃ q	Impl., 4
6. p ∨ ~q	Add., 1
7. ~q ∨ p	Comm., 6
8. q ⊃ p	Impl., 7
9. (p ⊃ q) · (q ⊃ p)	Conj., 5,8
10. p ≡ q	Equiv., 9

27.
1. ~p ∨ q	Premise
2. (p ⊃ q) ⊃ (p ⊃ r)	Premise
3. p / ∴ r	Premise/conclusion
4. p ⊃ q	Impl., 1
5. p ⊃ r	M.P., 2,4
6. r	M.P., 5,3

29.
1. ~(p · ~q)	Premise
2. (p ⊃ q) ⊃ (p ⊃ r) / ∴ p ⊃ r	Premise/conclusion
3. p ⊃ q	Impl., 1
4. p ⊃ r	M.P., 3,2

31.
1. p · (q ∨ r)	Premise
2. ~(p · r) / ∴ q	Premise/conclusion
3. (p · q) ∨ (p · r)	Dist., 1
4. p · q	D.Syll., 2,3
5. q	Simp., 4

33.
1. (p · q) ⊃ r	Premise
2. (p · r) ⊃ q	Premise
3. p / ∴ r ≡ q	Premise/conclusion
4. p ⊃ (q ⊃ r)	Exp., 1
5. p ⊃ (r ⊃ q)	Exp., 2
6. q ⊃ r	M.P., 4,3
7. r ⊃ q	M.P., 5,3
8. (r ⊃ q) · (q ⊃ r)	Conj., 6,7
9. r ≡ q	Equiv., 8

35.
1. ~p ∨ (q · r)	Premise
2. r ⊃ p / ∴ p ≡ r	Premise/conclusion
3. (~ p ∨ q) · (~ p ∨ r)	Dist., 1
4. ~ p ∨ r	Simp., 3
5. p ⊃ r	Impl., 4
6. (p ⊃ r) · (r ⊃ p)	Conj., 2,5
7. p ≡ r	Equiv., 6

EXERCISE 6–35

1. 1. p ⊃ q / ∴ p ⊃ (p · q)　　Premise/conclusion
   2. p　　　　　　　　　　　Assumption
   3. q　　　　　　　　　　　M.P., 1,2
   4. p · q　　　　　　　　　Conj., 2,3
   5. p ⊃ (p · q)　　　　　　C.P., 2–4

3. 1. (p ∨ q) ⊃ (r · s) /
   　　∴ ~s ⊃ ~q　　　　　Premise/conclusion
   2. ~s　　　　　　　　　　Assumption
   3. ~s ∨ ~r　　　　　　　Add., 2
   4. ~r ∨ ~s　　　　　　　Comm., 3
   5. ~(r · s)　　　　　　　DeM., 4
   6. ~(p ∨ q)　　　　　　　M.T., 1,5
   7. ~p · ~q　　　　　　　　DeM., 6
   8. ~q　　　　　　　　　　Simp., 7
   9. ~s ⊃ ~q　　　　　　　C.P., 2–8

5. 1. p ⊃ (q ⊃ r) /
   　　∴ (~r · s) ⊃ (q ⊃ ~p)　Premise/conclusion
   2. ~r · s　　　　　　　　Assumption
   3. ~r　　　　　　　　　　Simp., 2
   4. (p · q) ⊃ r　　　　　　Exp., 1
   5. ~(p · q)　　　　　　　M.T., 3,4
   6. ~p ∨ ~q　　　　　　　DeM., 5
   7. ~q ∨ ~p　　　　　　　Comm., 6
   8. q ⊃ ~p　　　　　　　　Impl., 7
   9. (~r · s) ⊃ (q ⊃ ~p)　C.P., 2–8

7. 1. p ⊃ (q ⊃ r) /
   　　∴ (p · q) ⊃ r　　　　Premise/conclusion
   2. p · q　　　　　　　　Assumption
   3. p　　　　　　　　　　Simp., 2
   4. q ⊃ r　　　　　　　　M.P., 1,3
   5. q　　　　　　　　　　Simp., 2
   6. r　　　　　　　　　　M.P., 4,5
   7. (p · q) ⊃ r　　　　　C.P., 2–6

9. 1. q ⊃ r /
   　　∴ p ⊃ (q ⊃ (r ∨ s))　Premise/conclusion
   2. p　　　　　　　　　　Assumption
   3. q　　　　　　　　　　Assumption
   4. r　　　　　　　　　　M.P., 1,3
   5. r ∨ s　　　　　　　　Add., 4
   6. q ⊃ (r ∨ s)　　　　　C.P., 3–5
   7. p ⊃ (q ⊃ (r ∨ s))　　C.P., 2–6

11. 1. (p ∨ q) ⊃ (r ≡ s)　　Premise
    2. ~(~s · p)　　　　　　Premise
    3. ~t ⊃ ~r / ∴ p ⊃ (t · r)　Premise/conclusion
    4. p　　　　　　　　　　Assumption

5. p ∨ q　　　　　　　　Add., 4
6. r ≡ s　　　　　　　　M.P., 1,5
7. (r ⊃ s) · (s ⊃ r)　　Equiv., 6
8. ~ ~s ∨ ~p　　　　　　DeM., 2
9. s ∨ ~p　　　　　　　D.N., 8
10. ~~p　　　　　　　　　D.N., 4
11. s　　　　　　　　　　D.Syll., 9,10
12. s ⊃ r　　　　　　　　Simp., 7
13. r　　　　　　　　　　M.P., 12,11
14. ~~r　　　　　　　　　D.N., 13
15. ~~t　　　　　　　　　M.T., 3,14
16. t　　　　　　　　　　D.N., 15
17. t · r　　　　　　　　Conj., 16,13
18. p ⊃ (t · r)　　　　　C.P., 4–17

13. 1. ~p ⊃ (q ⊃ r)　　　　　Premise
    2. s ⊃ q / ∴ s ⊃ (~p ⊃ r)　Premise/conclusion
    3. s　　　　　　　　　　Assumption
    4. ~p　　　　　　　　　Assumption
    5. q　　　　　　　　　　M.P., 2,3
    6. q ⊃ r　　　　　　　　M.P., 1,4
    7. r　　　　　　　　　　M.P., 6,5
    8. ~p ⊃ r　　　　　　　C.P., 4–7
    9. s ⊃ (~p ⊃ r)　　　　C.P., 3–8

15. 1. (p · q) ⊃ r /
    　　∴ p ⊃ (q ⊃ r)　　　Premise/conclusion
    2. p　　　　　　　　　　Assumption
    3. q　　　　　　　　　　Assumption
    4. p · q　　　　　　　　Conj., 2,3
    5. r　　　　　　　　　　M.P., 1,4
    6. q ⊃ r　　　　　　　　C.P., 3–5
    7. p ⊃ (q ⊃ r)　　　　C.P., 2–6

17. 1. p · (q ∨ r)
    　　/ ∴ ~q ⊃ (p · r)　　Premise/conclusion
    2. ~q　　　　　　　　　Assumption
    3. q ∨ r　　　　　　　　Simp., 1
    4. r　　　　　　　　　　D. Syll., 3,2
    5. p　　　　　　　　　　Simp., 1
    6. p · r　　　　　　　　Conj., 5,4
    7. ~q ⊃ (p · r)　　　　C.P., 2–6

19. 1. s / ∴ p ⊃ (q ⊃ (r ⊃ s))　Premise/conclusion
    2. p　　　　　　　　　　Assumption
    3. q　　　　　　　　　　Assumption
    4. r　　　　　　　　　　Assumption
    5. s　　　　　　　　　　Premise 1
    6. r ⊃ s　　　　　　　　C.P., 4–5
    7. q ⊃ (r ⊃ s)　　　　C.P., 3–6
    8. p ⊃ (q ⊃ (r ⊃ s))　C.P., 2–7

EXERCISE 6–36

1.
1. ~q ⊃ (~p · r)　　Premise
2. ~r / ∴ q　　Premise/conclusion
3. ~q　　Assumption
4. ~p · r　　M.P., 1,3
5. r　　Simp., 4
6. r · ~r　　Conj., 5,2
7. q　　I.P., 3–6

3.
1. p ∨ (q · r)　　Premise
2. p ∨ t　　Premise
3. t ⊃ ~(q · r) / ∴ p　　Premise/conclusion
4. ~p　　Assumption
5. q · r　　D. Syll., 1,4
6. t　　D. Syll, 2,4
7. ~(q · r)　　M.P., 3,6
8. (q · r) · ~(q · r)　　Conj., 5,7
9. p　　I.P., 4–8

5.
1. (p ⊃ q) · (r ⊃ s)　　Premise
2. (q ∨ s) ⊃ t　　Premise
3. ~t / ∴ ~(p ∨ r)　　Premise/conclusion
4. ~~(p ∨ r)　　Assumption
5. p ∨ r　　D.N., 4
6. q ∨ s　　Dil., 1,5
7. t　　M.P., 2,6
8. t · ~t　　Conj., 7,3
9. ~(p ∨ r)　　I.P., 4–8

7.
1. p ⊃ (q ⊃ r)　　Premise
2. ~s ⊃ (p ∨ r)　　Premise
3. p ⊃ q / ∴ s ∨ r　　Premise/conclusion
4. ~(s ∨ r)　　Assumption
5. ~s · ~r　　DeM., 4
6. ~s　　Simp., 5
7. p ∨ r　　M.P., 2,6
8. ~r　　Simp., 5
9. p　　D.Syll., 7,8
10. q　　M.P., 3,9
11. q ⊃ r　　M.P., 1,9
12. r　　M.P., 11,10
13. r · ~r　　Conj., 8,12
14. s ∨ r　　I.P., 4–13

9.
1. (p · q) ⊃ r　　Premise
2. ~p ⊃ r　　Premise
3. q / ∴ r　　Premise/conclusion
4. ~r　　Assumption
5. ~ (p · q)　　M.T., 1,4
6. ~p ∨ ~q　　DeM., 5
7. ~~q　　D.N., 3

8. ~p　　D. Syll., 6,7
9. r　　M.P., 2,8
10. r · ~r　　Conj., 4,9
11. r　　I.P., 4–10

11.
1. p · q　　Premise
2. ~(p ⊃ q) / ∴ r ⊃ s　　Premise/conclusion
3. ~(r ⊃ s)　　Assumption
4. q　　Simp., 1
5. ~~(p · ~q)　　Impl., 2
6. p · ~q　　D.N., 5
7. ~q　　Simp., 6
8. q · ~q　　Conj., 4,7
9. r ⊃ s　　I.P., 3–8

13.
1. p ⊃ (q ∨ ~(r ∨ s))　　Premise
2. ~r ⊃ s / ∴ ~q ⊃ ~p　　Premise/conclusion
3. ~(~q ⊃ ~p)　　Assumption
4. ~p ∨ (q ∨ ~(r ∨ s))　　Impl., 1
5. (~p ∨ q) ∨ ~(r ∨ s)　　Assoc., 4
6. ~~r ∨ s　　Impl., 2
7. r ∨ s　　D.N., 6
8. ~(p ⊃ q)　　Trans., 3
9. ~(~p ∨ q)　　Impl., 8
10. ~(r ∨ s)　　D.Syll., 5,9
11. (r ∨ s) · ~(r ∨ s)　　Conj., 7,10
12. ~q ⊃ ~p　　I.P. 3–11

EXERCISE 6–37

1.
1. p ⊃ q　　Premise
2. p / ∴ q　　Premise/conclusion
3. q　　M.P., 1,2

3.
1. p ∨ q　　Premise
2. ~q / ∴ p　　Premise/conclusion
3. p　　D. Syll., 1,2

5.
1. p ⊃ ~q　　Premise
2. q / ∴ ~p　　Premise/conclusion
3. ~ ~q　　D.N., 2
4. ~p　　M.T., 1,3

7.
1. p ⊃ q　　Premise
2. ~q / ∴ ~p　　Premise/conclusion
3. ~p　　M.T., 1,2

9.
1. (p ∨ q) ∨ r　　Premise
2. ~p / ∴ q ∨ r　　Premise/conclusion
3. p ∨ (q ∨ r)　　Assoc., 1
4. q ∨ r　　D.Syll., 3,2

11.
1. (p · q) ⊃ r　　Premise

2. p · q / ∴ r   Premise/conclusion
3. r   M.P., 1,2

13. 1. p ⊃ (q ∨ r)   Premise
    2. p / ∴ q ∨ r   Premise/conclusion
    3. q ∨ r   M.P., 1,2

15. 1. (p · q) ⊃ r   Premise
    2. p · q / ∴ r   Premise/conclusion
    3. r   M.P., 1,2

17. 1. (p ∨ q) ⊃ r   Premise
    2. q / ∴ r   Premise/conclusion
    3. q ∨ p   Add., 2
    4. p ∨ q   Comm., 3
    5. r   M.P., 1,4

19. 1. p ⊃ (q · r)   Premise
    2. p / ∴ (q · r)   Premise/conclusion
    3. (q · r)   M.P., 1.2

21. 1. p ⊃ q   Premise
    2. q ⊃ r   Premise
    3. p / ∴ r   Premise/conclusion
    4. q   M.P., 1,3
    5. r   M.P., 2,4

23. 1. p ⊃ q   Premise
    2. p ∨ r   Premise
    3. ~q / ∴ r   Premise/conclusion
    4. ~p   M.T., 1,3
    5. r   D. Syll., 2,4

25. 1. (p · q) ⊃ r   Premise
    2. p   Premise
    3. q / ∴ r   Premise/conclusion
    4. p · q   Conj., 2,3
    5. r   M.P., 1,4

27. 1. p ⊃ q   Premise
    2. q ⊃ ~r   Premise
    3. p / ∴ ~r   Premise/conclusion
    4. q   M.P., 1,3
    5. ~r   M.P., 2,4

29. 1. ((p · q) · r) ⊃ s   Premise
    2. ~s / ∴ ~ p ∨ (~q ∨ ~r)   Premise/conclusion
    3. ~((p · q) · r)   M.T., 1,2
    4. ~ (p · q) ∨ ~r   DeM., 3
    5. (~p ∨ ~q) ∨ ~r   DeM., 4
    6. ~p ∨ (~q ∨ ~r)   Assoc., 5

31. 1. p ⊃ q   Premise
    2. r ∨ p   Premise
    3. ~r / ∴ q   Premise/conclusion

4. p   D.Syll., 2,3
5. q   M.P., 1,4

33. 1. p ∨ q   Premise
    2. p ∨ r   Premise
    3. q ⊃ ~r / ∴ p   Premise/conclusion
    4. (p ∨ q) · (p ∨ r)   Conj., 1,2
    5. p ∨ (q · r)   Dist., 4
    6. ~q ∨ ~r   Impl., 3
    7. ~(q · r)   DeM., 6
    8. p   D.Syll., 5,7

35. 1. p ∨ q   Premise
    2. p ⊃ r   Premise
    3. r ⊃ s   Premise
    4. ~ q / ∴ s   Premise/conclusion
    5. p   D.Syll., 1,4
    6. r   M.P., 2,5
    7. s   M.P., 3,6

37. 1. p ⊃ q   Premise
    2. q ⊃ r   Premise
    3. r ⊃ s   Premise
    4. ~s / ∴ ~p   Premise/conclusion
    5. ~r   M.T., 3,4
    6. ~q   M.T., 2,5
    7. ~ p   M.T., 1,6

39. 1. p ∨ ~q   Premise
    2. q ∨ ~r   Premise
    3. r ∨ ~s   Premise
    4. s / ∴ p   Premise/conclusion
    5. ~p   Assumption
    6. ~q   D. Syll., 1,5
    7. ~ r   D. Syll., 2,6
    8. ~ s   D. Syll., 3,7
    9. s · ~s   Conj., 4,8
    10. p   I.P., 5–9

41. 1. p ⊃ q   Premise
    2. r ⊃ s   Premise
    3. (q ∨ s) ⊃ t   Premise
    4. p ∨ r / ∴ t   Premise/conclusion
    5. (p ⊃ q) · (r ⊃ s)   Conj., 1,2
    6. q ∨ s   Dil., 4,5
    7. t   M.P., 3,6

43. 1. p ∨ q   Premise
    2. r ⊃ p   Premise
    3. r ∨ s   Premise
    4. s ⊃ t   Premise
    5. ~p / ∴ s · (q · t)   Premise/conclusion

6. q   D.Syll., 1,5
7. ~r   M.T., 2,5
8. s   D.Syll, 3,7
9. t   M.P., 4,8
10. (q · t)   Conj., 6,9
11. s · (q · t)   Conj., 8,10

45. Invalid. One (of several) short truth tables that proves this is the following.

(p ⊃ q) ∨ (r ⊃ s), (p ⊃ r) · (t ⊃ ~s), p/∴q · (r · t)

T T T T T T T   T T T T F T F T   T   T F T F F

EXERCISE 7–1

1. (a) Te
   (b) T = _____ is tall
       e = Ed
   (c) Tx

3. (a) Tso
   (b) T = _____ is the tallest building in _____
       s = the Sears Tower
       o = the world
   (c) Txy

5. (a) Tsp
   (b) T = _____ is taller than _____
       s = Sue
       p = Pat
   (c) Tuv

7. (a) Cds
   (b) C = _____ is the capital of _____
       d = Washington, D.C.
       s = the United States
   (c) Cxy

9. (a) Ltan
   (b) L = _____ likes _____ better than _____
       t = Ted
       a = Professor Allen
       n = Professor Nella
   (c) Lxyz

EXERCISE 7–2

1. (a) ~Te · ~Ts
   (b) T = _____ is tall

       e = Ed
       s = Sue
   (c) ~Tx · ~Ty

3. (a) Ts · Te
   (b) T = _____ is a tall building
       s = the Sears Tower
       e = the Empire State Building
   (c) Ty · Tz

5. (a) Tsp ∨ Ttp
   (b) T = _____ is taller than _____
       s = Sue
       t = Tony
       p = Pat
   (c) Txy ∨ Twy

7. (a) ~Cns · ~Cas *or* ~(Cns ∨ Cas)
   (b) C = _____ is the capital of _____
       n = New York
       a = Los Angeles
       s = the United States
   (c) ~Cwx · ~Czx *or* ~(Cwx ∨ Czx)

9. (a) Ltan · Ltal
   (b) L = _____ likes _____ better than _____
       t = Ted
       a = Professor Allen
       n = Professor Nella
       l = Professor Lean
   (c) Lxyz · Lxyw

EXERCISE 7–3

1. (a) (∃x)Tx
   (b) T = _____ is tall
   (c) At least one thing is tall. (No loss of meaning.)

3. (a) (∃x)(Tx · Bx)
   (b) T = _____ is tall
       B = is a building
   (c) At least one thing is tall and is a building. (No loss of meaning.)

5. (a) (∃x)Txp
   (b) T = _____ is taller than _____
       p = Pat
   (c) At least one thing is taller than Pat. (This loses the sense that there are *many* things taller than Pat.)

7. (a) (∃x)Bx

(b) B = _____ got broken
(c) At least one thing got broken. (This loses sense that more than one thing was broken.)

9. (a) (∃x)Lxmg
   (b) L = _____ likes _____ better than _____
      m = Mary
      g = George
   (c) There exists at least one thing that likes Mary better than George. (This loses the possible original sense that only one thing likes Mary better than George.)

EXERCISE 7–4

1. Tom is faster than something.

3. Something is a person.

5. Something borrowed Tom's logic book.

7. Somebody is happy.

9. Mary borrowed something.

11. Somebody borrowed Tom's logic book.

13. Somebody who passes the test is more logical than Mary.

15. Some nocturnal thing is more logical than Tom.

17. Mary borrowed Tom's logic book.

19. Somebody is happy.

EXERCISE 7–5

1. (a) (∃x)(Px · Tx)
   (b) P = _____ is a person
      T = _____ is tall
   (c) There is at least one thing which is a person and is tall. (No loss of meaning.)

3. (a) (∃x)(Px · (Tx · Hx))
   (b) P = _____ is a person
      T = _____ is tall
      H = _____ is heavy
   (c) There is at least one thing which is a person and is tall and heavy. (No loss of meaning.)

5. (a) (∃x)(Wx · Sxp)
   (b) W = _____ is a woman
      S = _____ is shorter than
      p = Pat

(c) There is at least one thing which is a woman and is shorter than Pat. (This loses the original sense that definitely more than one woman is shorter than Pat.)

7. (a) (∃x)(Dx · Fax) · (∃y)(Hy · Fay)
   (b) D = _____ is a dog
      H = _____ is a horse
      F = _____ is faster than _____
      a = Al's car
   (c) There is at least one thing which is a dog and Al's car is faster than it and there is at least one thing which is a horse and Al's car is faster than it. (This loses the meaning that Al's car is faster than more than one dog and more than one horse.)

9. (a) (∃x)(Vx · ~(~Cx ≡ Fx))
   (b) V = _____ is valuable
      C = _____ costs much
      F = _____ is free
   (c) There is at least one thing which is valuable, which is either free or does not cost much. (*Note:* This is the exclusive sense of 'or'. This loses the sense of most.)

11. (a) (∃x)((Px · Sx) · (Lx · Mx))
    (b) P = _____ is a person
       S = _____ is smart
       L = _____ studies logic
       M = _____ studies math
    (c) There is at least one person who is smart and who studies logic and math. Loses the sense that more than one smart person studies logic and math.

EXERCISE 7–6

1. (a) (x)Tx
   (b) T = _____ is tall
   (c) For any thing whatsoever, it is tall. *or* Everything is tall. (No loss of meaning.)

3. (a) (x)Rx
   (b) R = _____ is round
   (c) For any thing whatsoever, it is round. *or* Everything is round. (No loss of meaning.)

5. (a) (x)Mx
   (b) M = _____ has mass
   (c) For any thing whatsoever, it has mass. *or* Everything has mass. (No loss of meaning.)

7. (a) (x)Bx
   (b) B = _____ gets broken
   (c) For any thing whatsoever, it gets broken. *or* Everything gets broken. (No loss of meaning.)

1. (a) (x)(Px ⊃ Tx)
   (b) P = _____ is a person
   T = _____ is tall
   (c) For any thing whatsoever, if that thing is a person, then it is tall. *or* Everybody is tall. (No loss of meaning.)

3. (a) (x)(Px ⊃ (Tx · Hx))
   (b) P = _____ is a person
   T = _____ is tall
   H = _____ is heavy
   (c) For any thing whatsoever, if that thing is a person, then it is tall and heavy. *or* Everybody is tall and heavy. (No loss of meaning.)

5. (a) (x)((Px · Tx) ⊃ Hx)
   (b) P = _____ is a person
   T = _____ is tall
   H = _____ is heavy
   (c) For any thing whatsoever, if that thing is a tall person, then it is heavy. *or* Every tall person is heavy. (No loss of meaning.)

7. (a) (x)(Sx ⊃ Tx)
   (b) S = _____ is a student
   T = _____ studies
   (c) For any thing whatsoever, if that thing is a student, then it studies. *or* Every student studies. (No loss of meaning.)

9. (a) (x)(Fx ⊃ Bx)
   (b) F = _____ is fragile
   B = _____ is broken easily
   (c) For any thing whatsoever, if that thing is fragile, then it is broken easily. *or* Every fragile thing breaks easily. (No loss of meaning.)

1. ~(∃x)~Tx

3. ~(x)Dx

5. (∃x)~(Px ⊃ Jx)

7. (x)(Dx · Kx)

9. ~(x)(Px · Qx)

1. (a) ~(∃x)(Px · Tx)
   (b) P = _____ is a person
   T = _____ is tall
   (c) (x) ~(Px · Tx)   QE
   (x)(~Px ∨ ~Tx)   DeM
   (x)(Px ⊃ ~Tx)   Impl.
   (d) Nobody is tall. (No loss of meaning.)

3. (a) ~(x)(Px ⊃ (Tx · Hx))
   (b) P = _____ is a person
   T = _____ is tall
   H = _____ is heavy
   (c) (∃x)~(Px ⊃ (Tx · Hx))   QE
   (∃x)~~(Px · ~(Tx · Hx))   Impl.
   (∃x)(Px · ~(Tx · Hx))   DN
   (d) Someone is not both tall and heavy. (No loss of meaning.)

5. (a) ~(∃x)((Sx · Tx) · Hx)
   (b) S = _____ is a student
   T = _____ is tall
   H = _____ is heavy
   (c) (x)~((Sx · Tx) · Hx)   QE
   (x)~((Sx · Tx) · ~~Hx)   DN
   (x)((Sx · Tx) ⊃ ~Hx)   Impl.
   (d) For any thing whatsoever, if that thing is a tall student, then it is not the case that it is heavy. *or* No tall students are heavy. (No loss of meaning.)

7. (a) ~(x)((Ix · Cx) ⊃ Fx)
   (b) I = _____ is imported
   C = _____ is a car
   F = _____ is fast
   (c) (∃x)~((Ix · Cx) ⊃ Fx)   QE
   (∃x)~~((Ix · Cx) · ~Fx)   Impl.
   (∃x)((Ix · Cx) · ~Fx)   DN
   (d) There exists at least one imported car which is not fast. *or* Some imported cars are not fast. (No loss of meaning.)

9. (a) ~(x)(Vx ⊃ Ix)
   (b) V = _____ is valuable
   I = _____ is insured
   (c) (∃x)~(Vx ⊃ Ix)   QE
   (∃x)~~(Vx · ~Ix)   Impl.
   (∃x)(Vx · ~Ix)   DN

(d) Something is valuable and not insured. *or* Some valuable things are uninsured. (No loss of meaning.)

EXERCISE 7–10

1. (a) Tom is faster than everything.
   (b) ~(∃x)~Ftx
   (c) It is not the case that Tom is not faster than any thing. (No loss of meaning.)

3. (a) Everything is such that at least one thing is faster than it.
   (b) ~(∃x)~(∃y)Fyx   QE
       ~(∃x)(y)~Fyx   QE
   (c) There does not exist even one thing such that everything is not faster than it. (No loss of meaning.)

5. (a) Nothing is happier than everything.
   (b) (x)~(y)Hxy   QE
       (x)(∃y)~Hxy   QE
   (c) For any thing whatsoever, something exists such that the first thing is not happier than the second. (No loss of meaning.)

7. (a) Something is happier than everything, including itself.
   (b) ~(x)~(y)Hxy   QE
       ~(x)(∃y)~Hxy   QE
   (c) It is not the case that for any thing whatsoever, something exists such that the first thing is not happier than the second. (No loss of meaning.)

9. (a) All happy people are fast.
   (b) ~(∃x)~((Px · Hx) ⊃ Fx)   QE
       ~(∃x)~~((Px · Hx) · ~Fx)   Impl.
       ~(∃x)((Px · Hx) · ~Fx)   D.N.
   (c) There is not one happy person who is not fast. (No loss of meaning.)

11. (a) Everything is such that something other than itself is faster than it.
    (b) ~(∃x)~(∃y)(~Ixy ⊃ Fyx)   QE
        ~(∃x)(y)~(~Ixy ⊃ Fyx)   QE
        ~(∃x)(y)~~(~Ixy · ~Fyx)   Impl.
        ~(∃x)(y)(~Ixy · ~Fyx)   D.N.
    (c) It is not the case that something is such that everything else is not faster than it. (No loss of meaning.)

13. (a) It is not the case that everything that passes the test is happier than everything that does not pass the test.
    (b) (∃x)~(y)((Tx · ~Ty) ⊃ Hxy)   QE
        (∃x)(∃y)~((Tx · ~Ty) ⊃ Hxy)   QE
        (∃x)(∃y)~~((Tx · ~Ty) · ~Hxy)   Impl.
        (∃x)(∃y)((Tx · ~Ty) · ~Hxy)   D.N.
    (c) There exists at least one thing that passes the test that is not happier than something that does not pass the test. (No loss of meaning.)

15. (a) Tom likes every happy person better than any person who is not happy.
    (b) ~(∃x)~(y)(((Px · Hx) · (Py · ~Hy)) ⊃ Ltxy)   QE
        ~(∃x)(∃y)~(((Px · Hx) · (Py · ~Hy)) ⊃ Ltxy)   QE
        ~(∃x)(∃y)~~(((Px · Hx) · (Py · ~Hy)) · ~Ltxy)   Impl.
        ~(∃x)(∃y)(((Px · Hx) · (Py · ~Hy)) · ~Ltxy)   D.N.
    (c) Not even one happy person exists whom Tom does not like better than some person who is not happy. (No loss of meaning.)

EXERCISE 7–11

Many of the following statements are strange to say the least; the point is that the symbolizations must be translated precisely, not edited to sound better or less strange.

1. Something studies harder than everything (including itself).

3. Everything studies harder than something or other (possibly itself).

5. Everything is a person and a violinist.

7. Some specific nocturnal thing is more logical than everything (including itself).

9. Each person borrowed something.

11. Everything is more logical than some specific thing which is not a librarian.

13. Everything which is more logical than something will get an A in logic.

15. Each thing is a person who borrowed something or other.

17. Everybody is such that they are not more logical than somebody or other.

19. There exists some thing such that if it's a person, then it's a violinist.

21. Some (specific) person studies harder than everybody, including her/himself.

23. There exists some thing such that if it's a person, then it studies harder than everything.

25. Everybody is more logical than some specific thing (but that thing is not more logical than itself).

27. Each person is more logical than some person other than her- or himself.

EXERCISE 7–12

1. (a) Te · (∃x)(Tx · Bex)
   (b) T = _____ a tournament player
       B = _____ can beat _____
       e = Emil
   (c) Emil is in the tournament and there is some tournament player that Emil can beat. (No loss of meaning.)

3. (a) (x)(Fxg ⊃ Mxc)
   (b) F = _____ is a friend of _____
       M = _____ is a member of _____
       c = chess team
       g = George
   (c) Everyone who is a friend of George is a member of the chess team. (No loss of meaning.)

5. (a) (∃x)(Ax · Wx) ⊃ ~(x)(Ax ⊃ Mx)
   (b) A = _____ is a resident of Dorm A
       W = _____ is a woman
       M = _____ is a man
   (c) If at least one resident of Dorm A is a woman, then not every resident of Dorm A is a man. Loss of meaning that more than one resident of Dorm A is a woman.

7. (a) (x)(Lx ⊃ (y)((Py · Mxy) ⊃ Gxy))
   (b) L = _____ is a member of the L family
       P = _____ is a person
       M = _____ meets _____
       G = _____ greets _____
   (c) Every member of the L family greets everyone they meet. (No loss of meaning.)

9. (a) ~(∃x)(y)(Ixy)
   (b) I = _____ is identical to _____
   (c) It is not the case that something is identical to everything. (No loss of meaning.)

11. (a) (x)((Cx · Tgx) ⊃ Lgx)
    (b) C = _____ is a class
        T = _____ is taking _____
        L = _____ is late for _____
        g = George
    (c) George is late for every class that he takes. (No loss of meaning.)

13. (a) (∃x)(Cx · Mx)
    (b) C = _____ is a cigar smoker
        M = _____ prefers a mild tobacco
    (c) At least one cigar smoker prefers a mild tobacco. (This loses the sense that most cigar smokers like mild tobacco.)

15. (a) (x)(Dx ⊃ (Sx · Gx))
    (b) D = _____ is a member of the Dean's list
        S = _____ is a student
        G = _____ has good grades
    (c) All members of the Dean's list are students with good grades. (No loss of meaning.)

EXERCISE 8–1

1. It is not correct because universal instantiation can only be applied to a universal quantifier which is the main operator, and it is not here.

3. The main operator is the biconditional, not the universal quantifier.

5. The main operator is the horseshoe, not the quantifier.

7. The main operator here is the negation sign, not the universal quantifier.

9. Because there are two quantifiers, it takes two steps to go from the premise to the conclusion.

EXERCISE 8–2

1. Ta

3. Universal instantiation cannot be applied here because the biconditional (not the universal quantifier) is the main operator.

5. The main operator is the horseshoe, not the universal quantifier, so universal instantiation cannot be applied here.

7. The main operator is not the universal quantifier, but the negation sign, so application of universal instantiation is not correct.

9. (∃y)~((Pb · Py) ⊃ Gby)

EXERCISE 8–3

1. The main operator in the conclusion is the '·'; we cannot use EG when the new existential quantifier is not the main operator.

3. The new existential quantifier is not the main operator of the conclusion; the biconditional is.

5. The quantifier is being applied to more than one kind of constant (both the 'n' and the 'd').

7. The existential quantifier is not the main operator of the conclusion.

9. EG can only be applied once in a single step. We must do the '(∃x)' in a second step.

EXERCISE 8–4

1. (∃x)Tx

3. (∃y)(~Dy ≡ (x)Bx). EG cannot have its scope limited to only the '~Dm,' because the new existential quantifier would then not be the main operator of the step.

5. (∃y)((x)Px · Jy). If the '(∃y)' were added directly in front of 'Jy'; the new quantifier would not be the main operator of the step, so EG could not be applied in that way.

7. (∃x)(∃y)~(Dx · Ky). We cannot use a single variable to quantify more than one kind of individual constant. This must be done in two steps.

9. (∃y)(x)~((Px · Py) ⊃ Gxy)

EXERCISE 8–5

1. 1. (y)Dy / ∴ (∃y)Dy   Premise/conclusion
   2. Da   UI, 1
   3. (∃y)Dy   EG, 2

3. 1. ~(∃x)Bx / ∴ ~Bf   Premise/conclusion
   2. (x)~Bx   QE, 1
   3. ~Bf   UI, 2

5. 1. Pn ∨ (x)Jx   Premise
   2. ~ Pn / ∴ (∃y)Jy   Premise/conclusion
   3. (x)Jx   D.Syll., 1,2
   4. Ja   UI, 3
   5. (∃y)Jy   EG, 4

7. 1. ~(∃x)(Dx · ~Kx)   Premise
   2. ~K r / ∴ ~(x)(Dx · Kx)   Premise/conclusion
   3. (x)~(Dx · ~Kx)   QE, 1
   4. ~(Dr · ~Kr)   UI, 3
   5. Dr ⊃ Kr   Impl., 4
   6. ~Dr   M.T., 5,2
   7. ~Dr ∨ ~Kr   Add., 6
   8. ~(Dr · Kr)   DeM., 7
   9. (∃x)~(Dx · Kx)   EG, 8
   10. ~(x)(Dr · Kx)   QE, 9

9. 1. ~(Pf · Pq) ∨ ~(∃x)Qx   Premise
   2. (x)(Pf · Rx)   Premise
   3. ~Pq ⊃ ~Rj /
      ∴ (∃y)~Qy   Premise/conclusion
   4. Pf · Rj   UI, 2
   5. Rj   Simp., 4
   6. ~~Rj   D.N., 5
   7. ~~Pq   M.T., 3,6
   8. Pq   D.N., 7
   9. Pf   Simp., 4
   10. Pf · Pq   Conj., 8,9
   11. ~~(Pf · Pq)   D.N., 10
   12. ~(∃x)Qx   D.Syll., 1,11
   13. (x)~Qx   QE, 12
   14. ~Qb   UI, 13
   15. (∃y)~Qy   EG, 14

EXERCISE 8–6

1. EI cannot be applied here because '(∃x)' is not the main operator of the step.

3. EI cannot be used because the biconditional is the main operator of the step, not '(∃x)'.

5. '(∃x)' is not the main operator of the step.

7. '(∃x)' is not the main operator (the tilde is).

9. Only '(∃x)' can be operated on in this step by EI; '(∃y)' can only be operated on in another step after the '(∃x)' has been removed by EI.

11. The individual constant we use to replace the variable bound by the quantifier cannot be one already used in the premises or conclusion. Here we cannot use 'a' since it already appears in the premise.

EXERCISE 8–7

1. 1. (∃x)Tx / ∴ (∃y)(Ty ∨ Wy) Premise/conclusion
   2. Ta   EI, 1

3.   EI cannot be applied since '≡' is the main operator, not '(∃x)'.

5.   EI cannot be applied here since '(∃x)' is not the main operator.

7.   EI cannot be used here since '(∃x)' is not a main operator. It can be used if we use QE first to convert '~(x)' to '(∃x)~'.

9.   EI cannot be applied since the existential quantifier is not the main operator here.

EXERCISE 8–8

1. This is not correct because the new universal quantifier is not the main operator of the conclusion.

3. This is incorrect because '(y)' is not the main operator of the conclusion, and also because the 'm' was not introduced by UI.

5. UG is wrongly applied here because it was used on more than one constant in Step 4.

7. This is wrong because UG was not applied to all occurrences of constant 'd' in Step 3.

9. UG cannot be applied in Step 4 because Step 3 contains a constant introduced by EI.

EXERCISE 8–9

1. 1. (x)Tx / ∴ (y)Ty   Premise/conclusion
   2. Ta   UI, 1
   3. (y)Ty   UG, 2

3. 1. (x)Bx / ∴ (x)(Bx ∨ Kx)   Premise/conclusion
   2. Ba   UI, 1
   3. Ba ∨ Ka   Add., 2
   4. (x)(Bx ∨ Kx)   UG, 3

5. 1. (x)Px ∨ (y)Qy   Premise
   2. ~Pa · ~Qb /
         ∴ (x)(Px · Qx)   Premise/conclusion
   3. ~Pa   Simp., 2
   4. (∃x)~Px   EG, 3
   5. ~(x)Px   QE, 4

6. (y)Qy   D.Syll., 1,5
7. Qc   UI, 6
8. ~Qb   Simp., 2
9. (∃y)~Qy   EG, 8
10. ~(y)Qy   QE, 9
11. (x)Px   D.Syll., 1,10
12. Pc   UI, 11
13. Pc · Qc   Conj., 7,12
14. (x)(Px · Qx)   UG, 13

EXERCISE 8–10

1. 1. (x)Tx / ∴ (∃x)Tx   Premise/conclusion
   2. Ta   UI, 1
   3. (∃x)Tx   EG, 2

3. 1. (x)(Tx ⊃ (Nx ⊃ Cx)) /
        ∴ (x)((Tx · Nx) ⊃ Cx) Premise/conclusion
   2. Ta ⊃ (Na ⊃ Ca)   UI, 1
   3. (Ta · Na) ⊃ Ca   Exp., 2
   4. (x)((Tx · Nx) ⊃ Cx)   UG, 3

5. 1. (x)(Tx · Nx) /
        ∴ (x)Tx · (x)Nx   Premise/conclusion
   2. Ta · Na   UI, 1
   3. Ta   Simp., 2
   4. Na   Simp., 2
   5. (x)Tx   UG, 3
   6. (x)Nx   UG, 4
   7. (x)Tx · (x)Nx   Conj., 5,6

7. 1. (x)(y)Sxy / ∴ Sdd   Premise/conclusion
   2. (y)Sdy   UI, 1
   3. Sdd   UI, 2

9. 1. (x)(y)Sxy / ∴ (y)(x)Sxy   Premise/conclusion
   2. (y)Say   UI, 1
   3. Sab   UI, 2
   4. (x)Sxb   UG,3
   5. (y)(x)Sxy   UG, 4

11. 1. (∃x)Tx /
         ∴ ~(x)(~Tx · ~Nx)   Premise/conclusion
    2. Ta   EI, 1
    3. ~~Ta   D.N., 2
    4. ~~Ta ∨ ~~Na   Add., 3
    5. ~(~Ta · ~Na)   DeM., 4
    6. (∃x)~(~Tx · ~Nx)   EG, 5
    7. ~(x)(~Tx · ~Nx)   QE, 6

13. 1. (x)(Tx ⊃ Nx) /
　　∴(x)Tx ⊃ (x)Nx　　Premise/conclusion
　2. (x)Tx　　　　　　　Assumption
　3. Ta　　　　　　　　UI, 2
　4. Ta ⊃ Na　　　　　UI, 1
　5. Na　　　　　　　　M.P., 4,3
　6. (x)Nx　　　　　　　UG, 5
　7. (x)Tx ⊃ (x)Nx　　C.P., 2–6

15. 1. (∃x)(Tx ∨ Nx) /
　　∴(∃x)Tx ∨ (∃x)Nx　Premise/conclusion
　2. ~(∃x)Tx　　　　　Assumption
　3. (x)~Tx　　　　　　QE, 2
　4. Ta ∨ Na　　　　　EI, 1
　5. ~Ta　　　　　　　UI, 3
　6. Na　　　　　　　D.Syll., 4,5
　7. (∃x)Nx　　　　　　EG, 6
　8. ~(∃x)Tx ⊃ (∃x)Nx　C.P., 2–7
　9. ~~(∃x)Tx ∨ (∃x)Nx　Impl., 8
　10. (∃x)Tx ∨ (∃x)Nx　D.N., 9

17. 1. (∃x)(Cx · Hx) ⊃ (x)Ux　Premise
　2. (∃x)~Ux /
　　∴ (x)(Cx ⊃ ~Hx)　Premise/conclusion
　3. ~(x)Ux　　　　　QE, 2
　4. ~(∃x)(Cx · Hx)　M.T., 1,3
　5. (x)~(Cx · Hx)　QE, 4
　6. ~(Ca · Ha)　　　UI, 5
　7. ~(Ca · ~~Ha)　　D.N., 6
　8. Ca ⊃ ~Ha　　　Impl, 7
　9. (x)(Cx ⊃ ~Hx)　UG, 8

19. 1. (x)(y)(Mxy ⊃ ~Myx) /
　　∴ (x)~Mxx　　　Premise/conclusion
　2. (y)(May ⊃ ~Mya)　UI, 1
　3. Maa ⊃ ~Maa　UI, 2
　4. ~Maa ∨ ~Maa　Impl., 3
　5. ~Maa　　　　Taut. 4
　6. (x)~Mxx　　　UG, 5

1. Step 2; the 'Bg' was dropped illegitimately.

3. Step 6; UG is applied to a constant introduced by EI.

5. Step 3; UG is applied to a constant not introduced by UI (the 'g' in 'Bg').

7. No errors.

9. No errors.

Alternative correct symbolizations and proofs are possible for each of the exercises.

1. (a) 'Gx' = 'x grows on trees'; 'Tx' = 'x is a tomato'; 'Sx' = 'x is a squash'; 'Ax' = 'x is an acorn'.
　　1. (x)(Gx ⊃ ~Tx)　Premise
　　2. (x)(Gx ⊃ ~Sx)　Premise
　　3. (x)(Ax ⊃ Gx) /
　　　∴ (x)(Ax ⊃ ~(Tx ∨ Sx))　Premise/conclusion
　(b) 4. Ga ⊃ ~Ta　　UI, 1
　　5. Ga ⊃ ~Sa　　UI, 2
　　6. Aa ⊃ Ga　　　UI, 3
　　7. Aa　　　　　　Assumption
　　8. Ga　　　　　　M.P., 6,7
　　9. ~Ta　　　　　M.P., 4,8
　　10. ~Sa　　　　　M.P., 5,8
　　11. ~Ta · ~Sa　　Conj., 9,10
　　12. ~(Ta ∨ Sa)　DeM., 11
　　13. Aa ⊃ ~(Ta ∨ Sa)　C.P., 7–12
　　14. (x)(Ax ⊃ ~(Tx ∨ Sx))　UG, 12

But if symbolized as:
　　1. (x)(Gx ⊃ ~(Tx ∨ Sx))　Premise
　　2. (x)(Ax ⊃ Gx) /
　　　∴ (x)(Ax ⊃ ~(Tx ∨ Sx))　Premise/conclusion

then the deduction may be accomplished by UI (repeated), H. Syll., and UG.

3. (a) 'Jx' = 'x is injured on the job'; 'Zx' = is a member of group Z'; 'Ax' = 'x is alerted automatically'; 'f' = 'Felice'.
　　1. (∃x)Jx ⊃ (x)(Zx ⊃ Ax)　Premise
　　2. Zf · ~Af /
　　　∴ ~(∃x)Jx　　Premise/conclusion
　(b) 3. ~~(Zf · ~Af)　D.N., 2
　　4. ~(Zf ⊃ Af)　Impl., 3
　　5. (∃x)~(Zx ⊃ Ax)　EG, 4
　　6. ~(x)(Zx ⊃ Ax)　QE, 5
　　7. ~(∃x)Jx　　　M.T., 1,6

5. (a) 'Fx' = 'x finishes first'; 'Dx' = 'x is disqualified'; 'Sy' = 'y finishes second'; 'Py' = 'y is placed first'; 'b' = 'Lazy Bill'; 'm' = 'Maizy Dae'.

1. (∃x)(Fx · Dx)
   ⊃ (y)((Sy ·
   ~Dy) ⊃ Py)   Premise
2. Fb · Db   Premise
3. Sm · ~Pm /∴
   Dm   Premise/conclusion

(b) 4. (∃x)(Fx · Dx)   EG, 2
5. (y)((Sy ·
   ~Dy) ⊃ Py)   M.P., 1,4
6. (Sm · ~Dm)
   ⊃ Pm   UI, 5
7. ~Pm   Simp., 3
8. ~(Sm · ~Dm)   M.T., 6,7
9. Sm ⊃ Dm   Impl., 8
10. Sm   Simp., 3
11. Dm   M.P., 9,10

7. (a) 'Hx' = 'x is a human being'; 'Rxy' = 'x is
entitled to as much respect as y';
's' ='Sally';'j' = 'John'.
1. (x)(y)((Hx · Hy)
   ⊃ Rxy)   Premise
2. Hs · Hj /∴ Rsj   Premise/conclusion

(b) 3. (y)((Hs · Hy)
   ⊃ Rsy)   UI, 1
4. (Hs · Hj) ⊃ Rsj   UI, 2
5. Rsj   M.P., 2,4

9. (a) 'Qx' = 'x is a beauty queen'; 'Bx' = 'x is
beautiful'; 'Gx' = 'x is a college graduate'.
1. (x)(Qx ⊃ Bx)   Premise
2. (∃x)(Gx · Qx) /
   ∴ (∃x) (Gx · Bx)   Premise/conclusion

(b) 3. Ga · Qa   EI, 2
4. Qa ⊃ Ba   UI, 1
5. Ga   Simp., 3
6. Qa   Simp., 3
7. Ba   M.P., 4,6
8. Ga · Ba   Conj., 5,7
9. (∃x)(Gx · Bx)   EG, 8

11. (a) 'Tx' = 'x is a terrier'; 'Px' = 'x is a
poodle'; 'Dx' = 'x is a dog'; 'Cx' = 'x is a
Cairn'.
1. (x)((Tx ∨ Px)
   ⊃ Dx)   Premise
2. (x)(Cx ⊃ Tx) /
   ∴ (x)(Cx ⊃
   Dx)   Premise/conclusion

(b) 3. (Ta ∨ Pa) ⊃ Da   UI, 1
4. Ca ⊃ Ta   UI, 2

5. ~Ca ∨ Ta   Impl., 4
6. (~Ca ∨ Ta) ∨ Pa   Add., 5
7. ~Ca ∨ (Ta ∨ Pa)   Assoc., 6
8. Ca ⊃ (Ta ∨ Pa)   Impl., 7
9. Ca ⊃ Da   H.S., 8,3
10. (x)(Cx ⊃ Dx)   UG, 9

EXERCISE 8–13

1. Quantification can be avoided. 'If the pot's a
dollar short, somebody did not ante up. The
pot's a dollar short. Therefore, somebody did
not ante up.'

3. One reformulation would be: 'All experienced
gardeners who hear of a frost warning take
precautions. Jimmy is an experienced gardener.
If Jimmy hears of a frost warning he will take
precautions'. Abbreviating 'x is an experienced
gardener' by 'Gx', 'x hears of a frost warning' by
'Wx', 'x takes precautions' by 'Px', and 'Jimmy'
by 'j', we get: '(x)((Gx · Wx) ⊃ Px)', 'Gj';
therefore, 'Wj ⊃ Pj'. Proof takes just three steps:
instantiation to 'j', exportation, and *modus
ponens*.

EXERCISE 9–1

1. Explanation

3. Argument

5. Explanation

7. Explanation

9. Argument

EXERCISE 9–2

1. Inductive generalization

3. Inductive generalization

5. Induction by analogy

7. Inductive generalization

9. Inductive generalization

11. Inductive generalization

13. Inductive generalization

15. Induction by analogy.

17. Induction by analogy

EXERCISE 9–3

1. c, a, b, d, e
3. c, d, a, b, e
5. c, a, d, e, b
7. c, b, e, a, d

EXERCISE 9–4

1. (a)

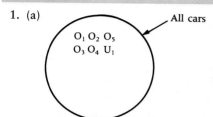

Slightly stronger than original statement.

(b)

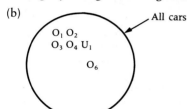

Stronger than a.

(c)

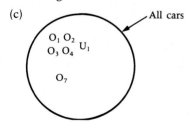

Stronger than b.

(d)

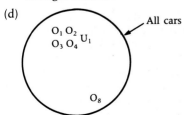

Stronger than c.

(e)

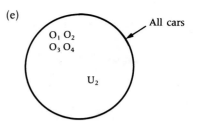

Weaker than original argument.

(f)

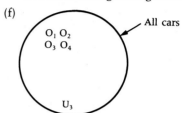

Weaker than e.

EXERCISE 9–5

1. (a)

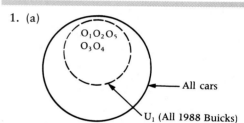

Slightly stronger than original.

(b)

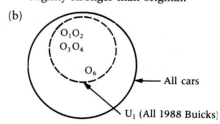

Stronger than a.

(c)

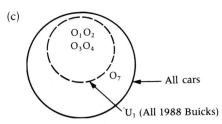

Stronger than b.

(d)

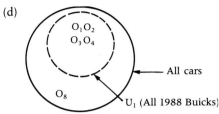

Stronger than c.

(e)

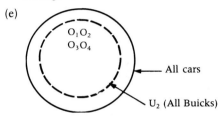

Weaker than original argument.

(f)

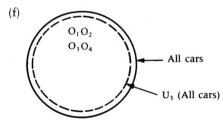

Weaker than e.

EXERCISE 9–6

1. (a) Strengthens by increasing the number of observed cases and increasing the negative analogy among them. (b) Strengthens by increasing the number of observed cases and increasing the negative analogy among them. (c) Destroys the argument by providing a

counterexample. (d) Destroys the argument by providing a counterexample. (e) Strengthens the argument by increasing the number of observed cases and increasing the negative analogy among them. (f) Destroys the argument by providing a counterexample.

3. (a) Strengthens by increasing the number of observed cases and increasing the negative analogy among them. (b) Weakens by increasing the positive analogy among the observed cases, if the location of the cats is considered to be relevant. (c) Weakens by presumably reducing the number of observed cases. (d) Strengthens by increasing the number of observed cases and increasing the negative analogy among them. (e) Strengthens by increasing the positive analogy among the observed cases and increasing the number of observed cases. (f) Weakens by both increasing the positive analogy among the observed cases and decreasing the number of observed cases.

5. (a) Weakens by increasing the negative analogy between the observed and unobserved cases. (b) Weakens by increasing the negative analogy between the observed and the unobserved cases, if one considers the type of soap powder used relevant. (c) Weakens by increasing the negative analogy between observed and unobserved cases, if one considers the type of bleach and fabric softener relevant. (d) Strengthens by increasing the number of observed cases. (e) Strengthens by increasing the positive analogy between observed and unobserved cases, if one considers the plant of manufacture, the inspector, and place of purchase relevant. (f) Weakens by increasing the negative analogy between observed and unobserved cases, if one considers the fact that the Corleones' washing machine was a floor model relevant.

7. (a) Increases the negative analogy among the observed cases; strengthens the argument that the Allens will get at least 25 miles to a gallon of gas (but would weaken an argument that they will get exactly 25 miles per gallon). (b) Weakens by decreasing the positive analogy between the observed and unobserved cases. (c) No effect, since color is presumably not relevant to mileage per gallon. (d) Strengthens by

increasing the positive analogy between the observed and unobserved cases, if the dealer and the date of purchase are considered relevant to mileage per gallon. (e) Weakens by increasing the negative analogy between the observed and unobserved cases. (f) Weakens by increasing the negative analogy between the observed and unobserved cases. (g) Weakens by increasing the negative analogy between observed and unobserved cases, if the octane level is considered relevant to mileage per gallon. (h) Weakens by increasing the negative analogy between observed and unobserved cases.

EXERCISE 9–7

1. (a) Frank has won at blackjack.
        Frank has won at seven-card stud.
        Frank has won at five-card draw.
        ∴ Frank will win at five-card stud.

   (b) Frank has won at blackjack.
        Frank has won at seven-card stud.
        Frank has won at five-card draw.
        ∴ Frank always wins at all kinds of poker.
        Five-card stud is a kind of poker.
        Frank will play five-card stud.
        ∴ Frank will win at five-card stud.

3. (a) It rained on Sunday.
        It rained on Monday.
        It rained on Tuesday.
        It rained on Wednesday.
        It rained on Thursday.
        It rained on Friday.
        ∴ It will rain on Saturday.

   (b) It rained on Sunday.
        It rained on Monday.
        It rained on Tuesday.
        It rained on Wednesday.
        It rained on Thursday.
        It rained on Friday.
        ∴ It rains every day.
        Saturday is a day.
        ∴ It will rain on Saturday.

5. (a) The flood crested in Pittsburgh this week.
        The flood crested in Cincinnati this week
        ∴ The flood will crest in Louisville this week.

   (b) The flood crested in Pittsburgh this week.
        The flood crested in Cincinnati this week.
        ∴ The flood is cresting in all cities on the Ohio River this week.
        Louisville is a city on the Ohio River.
        ∴ The flood will crest in Louisville this week.

7. (a) The Smiths own a Zowie Stereo and get excellent service.
        The Parkers own a Zowie Stereo and get excellent service.
        The Roberts own a Zowie Stereo and get excellent service.
        The Mitchells own a Zowie Stereo and get excellent service.
        The Conners own a Zowie Stereo and get excellent service.
        The Carters just bought a Zowie stereo.
        ∴ The Carters will get excellent service.

   (b) The Smiths own a Zowie Stereo and get excellent service.
        The Parkers own a Zowie Stereo and get excellent service.
        The Roberts own a Zowie Stereo and get excellent service.
        The Mitchells own a Zowie Stereo and get excellent service.
        The Conners own a Zowie Stereo and get excellent service.
        ∴ All persons who own Zowie Stereos always get excellent service.
        The Carters just bought a Zowie Stereo.
        ∴ The Carters will get excellent service.

9. (a) My grandfather went bald before he was thirty years old.
        My father went bald before he was thirty years old.
        My older brother went bald before he was thirty years old.
        ∴ I will go bald before I am thirty years old.

   (b) My grandfather went bald before he was thirty years old.
        My father went bald before he was thirty years old.
        My older brother went bald before he was thirty years old.
        ∴ All males in my family go bald before they are thirty years old.

I am a male in my family.
∴I will go bald before I am thirty years old.

11. (a)   Jan is Swiss and speaks German.
Hans is Swiss and speaks German.
Maria is Swiss and speaks German.
Karl is Swiss and speaks German.
Karin is Swiss and speaks German.
∴Antonio, who is Swiss, must speak German.

(b)   Jan is Swiss and speaks German.
Hans is Swiss and speaks German.
Maria is Swiss and speaks German.
Karl is Swiss and speaks German.
Karin is Swiss and speaks German.
∴All who are Swiss speak German.
Antonio is Swiss.
∴Antonio must speak German.

13. (a)   John got As in every course he took in his first semester in college.
John got As in every course he took in his second semester in college.
John got As in every course he took in his third semester in college.
John got As in every course he took in his fourth semester in college.
∴John will get As in every course he takes in this, his fifth semester in college.

(b)   John got As in every course he took in his first semester in college.
John got As in every course he took in his second semester in college.
John got As in every course he took in his third semester in college.
John got As in every course he took in his fourth semester in college.
∴John gets As in all his courses in every semester in college.
This is John's fifth semester in college.
∴John will get As in every course he takes in this, his fifth semester in college.

15. (a)   There were interesting people at Joe's last party.
There were interesting people at Joe's second to last party.
There were interesting people at Joe's third to last party.
Joe is having a party tonight.
∴There will be interesting people at Joe's party tonight.

(b)   There were interesting people at Joe's last party.
There were interesting people at Joe's second to last party.
There were interesting people at Joe's third to last party.
∴There are interesting people at all of Joe's parties.
Joe is having a party tonight.
∴There will be interesting people at Joe's party tonight.

EXERCISE 9–8

1. d, b, c, a

3. b, a, d, e, c

5. e, d, c, a, b

EXERCISE 9–9

1. (a) Weakens by decreasing the negative analogy among the observed cases. (b) Strengthens by increasing the number of observed cases. (c) Strengthens by increasing the negative analogy among the observed cases. (d) Strengthens by increasing the negative analogy among the observed cases. (e) Weakens by increasing the positive analogy among the observed cases, if the specified characteristics are considered relevant.

3. (a) Weakens by increasing the positive analogy among observed cases and increasing the negative analogy between observed and unobserved cases. (b) Strengthens by increasing the negative analogy among observed cases. (c) Weakens by increasing the positive analogy among observed cases and increasing negative analogy between observed and unobserved cases. (d) Weakens by increasing the positive analogy among observed cases, if one considers the sex of the students relevant.

EXERCISE 10–1

1. Ann is a student who took the logic exam.

3. *The Blithedale Romance* is an American novel.

5. Bill is a man.

7. K-2 is a mountain over twenty thousand feet in height.

9. Gabriela Sabatini is a professional tennis player.

EXERCISE 10–5

1. a, b, d, e, f

3. a, c, d

5. a, b

EXERCISE 10–6

Sample answer: Hypothesis: All planets in the solar system have satellites. *Supporting observation statements:* (a) The earth has one satellite, the moon. (b) Mars has two satellites. (c) Jupiter has twelve satellites. *Disconfirming observation statements:* (d) Mercury has no satellites. (e) Pluto has no satellites.

EXERCISE 10–7

1. *Inductive argument:*
   (a) Sergei, a Russian, can laugh.
   (b) Elena, a Spaniard, can laugh.
   (c) Muhammed, a Tunisian, can laugh.
   (d) Vani, a Bantu, can laugh.
   (e) Mikako, a Japanese, can laugh.
       ∴ All people can laugh.
   (b, c, d, e) These arguments take the same form as (a). *Order of decreasing inductive strength:* c, a, e, b, d.

3. *Inductive argument:*
   (a) Frenchie, a miniature poodle, is a carnivore.
   (b) Natasha, a Russian wolfhound, is a carnivore.
   (c) Pierre, a standard poodle, is a carnivore.
   (d) King, a German shepherd, is a carnivore.
   (e) Lassie, a collie, is a carnivore.
       ∴ All dogs are carnivores.
   Arguments b, c, d and e take the same form as argument a. *Order of decreasing inductive strength:* c, a, d, b, e.

EXERCISE 10–10

1. *Proximate:* l. *Remote:* a, b, c, e, g, i, j, k

EXERCISE 10–12

1. (a) Sufficient but not necessary. (b) Necessary but not sufficient. (c) Sufficient but not necessary. (d) Neither necessary nor sufficient. (e) Sufficient but not necessary. (f) Necessary but not sufficient. (g) Necessary but not sufficient. (h) Neither necessary nor sufficient. (i) Necessary and sufficient. (j) Necessary and sufficient. (k) Necessary but not sufficient. (l) Neither necessary nor sufficient.

3. *Necessary conditions:* age 23 or over, and the disjunction of previous communications experience and previous computer experience. However, this combination is not a sufficient condition as is shown by the fact that it was fulfilled by persons 4 and 8, who were not hired.

EXERCISE 10–13

Method of agreement. The proximate condition of cracking was probably the differential expansion, and the condition of this was the conjunction of sudden change in temperature, eastward exposure, and the presence of the varicolored paints on the glass. Since cracking occurred only where these conditions were present, the expansion and the conjunction which produced it were necessary conditions. They would not be shown to be sufficient conditions unless it could be demonstrated that cracking occurred in every case in which they were present.

EXERCISE 10–14

1. Method of difference. Since the only significant condition in which the contaminated broth differed from the uncontaminated was that of exposure to ordinary air (and to whatever microorganisms it contained), this exposure was established as probably a sufficient condition of the contamination.

EXERCISE 10–15

The necessary condition is probably the conjunction of crystal and zeroz—an answer arrived at by use of the method of agreement. (Of course, in real life it is highly unlikely that the different samples would vary as much as in this imaginary case.)

EXERCISE 10–16

1. Method of agreement: The only structural flaw common to all the malfunctioning sets was the improperly soldered wire. Therefore the presence of this improperly soldered wire was probably a necessary condition for this particular type of malfunction.

3. Method of concomitant variations: Expenditure in dollars varies positively with total income, and expenditure as a percentage of income varies inversely (though not perfectly so) with total income. It would not be unreasonable to conclude from this evidence that an increase in income is a necessary condition for an increase in expenditure on recreation and entertainment.

5. Method of difference: The various groups of chicks differed only in the substance with which they were inoculated (or not inoculated), and their subsequent death rates from the virus. Therefore, since the death rate of Group 3 was markedly lower than that of any other group, the vaccine given to this group was probably a sufficient condition of the lower death rate. Vaccines 1, 2, and 4 were also sufficient conditions for lowering the death rate, although they were less effective than Vaccine 3.

EXERCISE 10–17

1. This may have been either method of difference or joint method. If the random selection process resulted in two groups which, as groups, were alike in all relevant aspects save the one experimental difference, this represents use of the method of difference. If, as seems more likely with the fairly small groups of people involved, there were other possibly significant differences among them, it represents use of the joint method.

EXERCISE 10–18

1. Joint method. (a) Caffeine is the condition associated with Mr. Johnson's insomnia (it is present in coffee, tea, and coke, but not in the other foods or beverages consumed). (b) Caffeine is probably a necessary condition (insomnia occurred only when caffeine was present) and also a sufficient condition (insomnia occurred whenever caffeine was present).

EXERCISE 10–19

1. Method of agreement and method of difference. The successive findings that all the men were heavy drinkers, that they had all eaten at the same cafeteria, that they had all eaten oatmeal, and that they had all consumed a drug were important steps in leading investigators to the probable source of the poisoning and proved to be, in this particular case, necessary though not sufficient conditions. Working from these clues, and from the symptoms, the investigators eliminated one after another possible alternative explanations (gas poisoning, food poisoning) which failed to account for all the circumstances, until they arrived at one which could successfully explain all the known facts. The presence of the sodium nitrite in the oatmeal and in the salt-shaker, together with the other known conditions and the likelihood that the men had salted their oatmeal from that shaker, constituted what appeared to be sufficient conditions for the poisonings. That is, probably the only significant difference between the poisoning victims and others who had eaten at the cafeteria that morning was that the victims had all both eaten the contaminated oatmeal and salted it heavily from the contaminated shaker while the others had not fulfilled both these conditions. In effect, the investigators were assuming that use of the method of difference, had it been possible to check all the details, would have supported this conclusion.

EXERCISE 10–20

1. (1) Method of difference. Presumably the sudden-death victims, as a group, did not differ in other significant respects from the cardiac patients who did not die.

   (2) (a) The argument would be strengthened if studies of larger groups—say 1,000 or 10,000—of cardiac patients showed similar discrepancies between the smoking habits of those who did and those who did not suffer sudden cardiac death. (b) The argument would be weakened if it were shown that most of the current cigarette smokers among the sudden-death victims had been heavy smokers for ten years or more. (This might, however, provide strong evidence that prolonged heavy smoking is a cause of sudden cardiac death.) (c) It is doubtful that there is any single piece of evidence that would completely falsify the conclusion—or completely prove the truth of it.

   (3) 'Cause' is here being used to refer to a sufficient condition. The fact that some nonsmokers are also victims of sudden cardiac death is good evidence that there are other causes as well—that is, that smoking is not a necessary condition.

3. (1) Probably joint method. In the high-polio group, there was a general pattern, or condition, of drinking whiskey but not beer. In the lower ranks, this condition was reversed. Since other conditions (quality of living quarters, type of duty, and so on) were probably not always the same for the two groups, the method of difference cannot be used in this case.

   (2) (a) The argument would be strengthened if it were found that in every case of paralytic polio, the affected individual had drunk whiskey and had not drunk beer, or if studies among other population groups, in other parts of the world, showed a similar pattern. (b) The argument would be weakened if it were shown that certain other possibly relevant conditions were consistently different for the two groups: for instance, that all the officers, and only the officers, had eaten food from a particular source or had attended training sessions at a particular place. (c) The conclusion would be falsified if a high polio group were discovered in which beer rather than whiskey was the usual drink.

   (3) 'Cause' is here being used to refer to a sufficient condition. However, the evidence does not permit a conclusion as to whether the significant condition is the drinking of whiskey, or the nondrinking of beer, or both.

EXERCISE 11–2

1. Very close to 1.

3. This answer depends on the date and location of your answer. In Seattle during the summer the probability of this statement would be closer to 0. In Los Angeles in the summer, the probability would be closer to 1.

5. Close to 0.

7. Very close to 0.

9. Close to 1.

11. Very close to 1.

13. About .5.

15. 1

EXERCISE 11–3

1. No. Given the definitions of "hurricane" and "clear and calm," these statements are logically inconsistent.

3. Yes. These statements are consistent.

5. Yes. Sue Smith could have had twins.

7. No. Logically inconsistent.

9. Yes. Logically consistent.

11. No. Logically inconsistent.

EXERCISE 11–4

1. ½

3. ¹⁄₁₀₀

5. ²⁄₆ = ⅓

7. $\frac{1}{1000}$

9. $\frac{4}{5}$

EXERCISE 11–5

1. $\frac{5}{20} = \frac{1}{4}$

3. 0

5. $\frac{400}{1000} = \frac{2}{5}$

7. $\frac{55}{100} = \frac{11}{20}$

9. 1

11. $\frac{75}{100} = \frac{3}{4}$

13. $\frac{2}{12} = \frac{1}{6}$

15. 1

EXERCISE 11–6

1. Classical; $\frac{1}{100}$

3. (a) Classical; $\frac{1}{512}$
   (b) Classical; $\frac{8}{512} = \frac{1}{64}$

5. Relative frequency; $\frac{2,180,000}{4,258,000} = \frac{1090}{2129} =$ about .51

7. Classical; $\frac{14,000}{300,000} = \frac{7}{150}$

9. Relative frequency; $\frac{156}{342,576} = \frac{1}{2196}$ assuming that it is permissible to apply the relative frequency definition to single cases.

11. (a) $\frac{5}{6}$
    (b) $\frac{1}{6}$

13. $\frac{1}{15}$ for each, if we feel justified in applying the principle of indifference. If we feel that the probability for each driver is not the same, we cannot use the classical theory. The probabilities cannot be computed on the relative frequency theory, since we are not told how the three drivers have fared in races against each other, and against the rest of today's field of 15. We have only each driver's won-lost record to go on. The subjective theory is probably best.

15. (a) Relative frequency; $\frac{99,200}{100,000}$
    (b) Relative frequency; $\frac{800}{100,000}$

17. Classical; $\frac{20}{50} = \frac{2}{5}$

EXERCISE 11–7

1. (a) Initial probability of each outcome $= \frac{1}{6}$
   (b) Probability of conjuct outcome
   $$= \frac{1}{6} \times \frac{1}{6} \times \frac{1}{6} = \frac{1}{216}$$

3. (a) $\frac{1}{6}$
   (b) $\frac{1}{6} \times \frac{1}{6} \times \frac{1}{6} = \frac{1}{216}$

5. (a) $\frac{1}{2}$
   (b) $\frac{1}{2} \times \frac{1}{2} \times \frac{1}{2} = \frac{1}{8}$

7. (a) $\frac{1}{4}$
   (b) $\frac{1}{4} \times \frac{1}{4} \times \frac{1}{4} = \frac{1}{64}$

EXERCISE 11–8

1. (a) Independent
   (b) Restricted conjunction
   (c) The probability of each independent outcome $= \frac{1}{6}$
   (d) Probability of conjuct outcome
   $$= \frac{1}{6} \times \frac{1}{6} \times \frac{1}{6} = \frac{1}{216}$$

3. (a) Independent
   (b) Restricted conjunction
   (c) $\frac{1}{10}$
   (d) $\frac{1}{10} \times \frac{1}{10} = \frac{1}{100}$

5. (a) Independent
   (b) Restricted conjunction
   (c) $\frac{1}{365}$
   (d) $\frac{1}{365} \times \frac{1}{365}$

7. (a) Dependent
   (b) General conjunction
   (c) Initial probability of drawing a black ball $= \frac{10}{30} = \frac{1}{3}$; of drawing a second black ball given that the first was drawn $= \frac{9}{29}$; of drawing a third black ball given that the first two were drawn $= \frac{8}{28}$.
   (d) $\frac{1}{3} \times \frac{9}{29} \times \frac{8}{28}$

9. (a) Dependent
   (b) General conjunction

(c) Initial probability of drawing a red ball = ⅓, of drawing a white ball given that a red ball has been removed = ¹⁰⁄₂₉, and of drawing a black ball given that one red and one white ball have been removed = ¹⁰⁄₂₈.

(d) $\dfrac{10}{30} \times \dfrac{10}{29} \times \dfrac{10}{28}$

EXERCISE 11–9

1. (a) Initial probability of each outcome = ⅙; probability of disjunct outcome:

$$\frac{1}{6} + \frac{1}{6} = \frac{2}{6} = \frac{1}{3}$$

(b) Initial probability of each outcome = ⅙; probability of disjunct outcome:

$$\frac{1}{6} + \frac{1}{6} + \frac{1}{6} = \frac{3}{6} = \frac{1}{2}$$

3. Initial probabilities = ⁴⁰⁄₁₀₀ that an individual will have gray hair, ²⁵⁄₁₀₀ that an individual will have blond hair; probability of disjunct outcome:

$$\frac{25}{100} + \frac{40}{100} = \frac{65}{100}$$

5. Initial probability = ¹⁄₁₀; probability of disjunct outcome:

$$\frac{1}{10} + \frac{1}{10} + \frac{1}{10} = \frac{3}{10}$$

7. Initial probability = ¼. (For exactly one coin to come up heads when two are flipped, the other must come up tails. Thus, possible favorable outcomes are: coin A = H & coin B = T, or coin A = T & coin B = H. In either case, initial probabilities = ½ × ½ = ¼.); probability of disjunct outcome:

$$\frac{1}{4} + \frac{1}{4} = \frac{1}{2}$$

EXERCISE 11–10

1. (a) a. Specified outcomes are mutually exclusive
   b. Restricted disjunction
   c. Initial probability of each outcome = ⅙

d. Not relevant
e. Probability of disjunct outcome:

$$\frac{1}{6} + \frac{1}{6} = \frac{2}{6} = \frac{1}{3}$$

(b) a.–c. Same as above
d. Not relevant
e. Probability of disjunct outcome:

$$\frac{1}{6} + \frac{1}{6} + \frac{1}{6} = \frac{3}{6} = \frac{1}{2}$$

3. (a) Not mutually exclusive
   (b) General disjunction
   (c) Initial probabilities of having: gray hair = .4; blue eyes = .25; both gray hair and blue eyes = .15
   (d) P(x and y) = .15
   (e) .4 + .25 − .15 = .5

5. (a) Mutually exclusive outcomes
   (b) Restricted disjunction
   (c) Initial probability of drawing a white ball = ⁵⁄₃₀; of drawing a blue ball = ⁶⁄₃₀
   (d) Not relevant
   (e) $\dfrac{5}{30} + \dfrac{6}{30} = \dfrac{11}{30}$

7. (a) Not mutually exclusive
   (b) General disjunction
   (c) Initial probability of boy living to his twentieth birthday = .97; of girl living to her twentieth birthday = .96
   (d) P(x and y) = .97 × .96 = .9312
   (e) .97 + .96 − .9312 = .9988

11. (a) Not mutually exclusive
    (b) General disjunction
    (c) Initial probability = .7
    (d) P(x and y) = .7 × .7 = .49
    (e) .7 + .7 − .49 = .91

EXERCISE 11–11

1. (a) a. Outcomes are independent
   b Restricted conjunction
   c. Initial probability of each simple outcome = ⅙
   d. Not relevant
   e. Probability of conjunct event:

$$\frac{1}{6} \times \frac{1}{6} \times \frac{1}{6} = \frac{1}{216}$$

(b) a. Mutually exclusive
   b. Restricted disjunction
   c. Initial probability of each outcome = $\frac{1}{216}$ (from 1a.)
   d. Not relevant
   e. $$\frac{1}{216} + \frac{1}{216} = \frac{2}{216} = \frac{1}{108}$$

3. (a) a. Dependent simple outcomes
   b. General conjunction
   c. Initial probabilities of simple events: $\frac{2}{5}$ and $\frac{3}{5}$.
   d. Not relevant
   e. Probability of disjunct event: $\frac{3}{5}$, calculated as follows:
   Probability of first possible favorable event (drawing a dime and then a nickel).
   Equation: P(x & y) = P(dime & nickel) = P(dime) × P(nickel given dime on first draw)
   $$\frac{2}{5} \times \frac{3}{4} = \frac{6}{20} = \frac{3}{10}$$

   Probability of second possible favorable event (drawing a nickel and then a dime).
   Equation: P(x & y) = P(nickel and dime = P(nickel) × P(dime given nickel on first draw)
   $$= \frac{3}{5} \times \frac{2}{4} = \frac{6}{20} = \frac{3}{10}$$
   Probability of disjunction (either dime and nickel or nickel and dime). Equation: P(x or y) = P(dime and nickel or nickel and dime)
   $$= \frac{3}{10} + \frac{3}{10} = \frac{6}{10} = \frac{3}{5}$$

  (b) a. Dependent
   b. General conjunction rule
   c. Initial probability of each simple event: $\frac{3}{5}$
   d. Not relevant
   e. Probability of conjunct event:
   $$\frac{3}{5} \times \frac{2}{4} \times \frac{1}{3} = \frac{6}{60} = \frac{1}{10}$$

  (c) a Mutually exclusive
   b. Restricted disjunction rule
   c. Not relevant.
   d. Not relevant
   e. Probability of disjunct event:
   $$\frac{6}{10} + \frac{1}{10} = \frac{7}{10}$$

5. (a) Mutually exclusive (and so dependent)
   (b) Restricted disjunction
   (c) $$\frac{1}{10}, \frac{1}{10}, \frac{1}{10}, \frac{1}{10}, \frac{9}{10}, \frac{9}{10}, \frac{9}{10}, \frac{9}{10}$$
   (d) Not relevant
   (e) $(\frac{1}{10} \times \frac{1}{10} \times \frac{1}{10} \times \frac{1}{10})$
   $+ (\frac{9}{10} \times \frac{9}{10} \times \frac{9}{10} \times \frac{9}{10})$

EXERCISE 12–1

1. Equivocation (on 'well-done')
3. Begging the question
5. Amphiboly
7. Begging the question
9. Begging the question
11. Begging the question
13. Straw person

EXERCISE 12–2

1. Hasty generalization
3. Argument from ignorance
5. Argument from ignorance
7. Division
9. False dilemma
11. Division
13. Argument from ignorance
15. Hasty generalization
17. False dilemma

EXERCISE 12–3

1. Appeal to authority
3. *Ad hominem* (*tu quoque*)
5. *Ad hominem* (*tu quoque*)—this may also involve equivocation (on 'kill') *or* Straw Person.
7. *Ad hominem* (circumstantial)
9. *Ad hominem* (circumstantial)
11. *Ad baculum* (<u>not</u> appeal to authority)

EXERCISE 12–4

These sentences are rather complex and subtle, and it is possible to interpret many of them plausibly as involving fallacies other than the ones listed below.

1. False cause
3. Hasty generalization
5. Composition
7. Division
9. *Ad hominem* (abusive)
11. *Ad hominem* (circumstantial)
13. Hasty generalization or *ad populum*
15. Division
17. Argument from ignorance
19. Hasty generalization
21. *Ad baculum*
23. Composition
25. Equivocation (on 'rare')
27. Begging the question (assuming it is known that 'nimble,' 'supple,' and 'flexible' are synonyms)
29. Equivocation (on 'two seconds') or Straw Person
31. False dilemma
33. Amphiboly or Equivocation (on 'difficult to find')
35. Argument from ignorance
37. *Ad hominem* (abusive)
39. Composition
41. Composition
43. False cause
45. *Ad hominem* (tu quoque)
47. Appeal to authority
49. *Ad hominem* (abusive)
51. False dilemma

EXERCISE 13–3

1. Beagle, dog, domestic pet, mammal
3. Symphony, classical music, music, sounds
5. Neon, Dodge, automobile, vehicle

EXERCISE 13–4

Extension diminishes from (a) to (d) for all exercises.

EXERCISE 13–7

1. Connotative
3. Enumerative, denotative, unless one believes that numbers are nothing more than numerals, in which case it would be an ostensive definition.
5. Connotative, by genus and difference (genus = polyhedron)
7. Connotative
9. Connotative, by genus and difference (genus = oak).
11. Enumerative, denotative
13. Synonymous
15. Connotative
17. Operational
19. Enumerative, denotative
21. Operational
23. Connotative
25. Connotative (genus and difference)
27. Synonymous
29. Enumerative (ostensive)
31. Enumerative (denotative)
33. Connotative
35. Connotative
37. Operational
39. Connotative

EXERCISE 13–12

1. Limited reportive, theoretical
3. Stipulative
5. Limited reportive, theoretical
7. Reportive, legal. (This is not a limited reportive definition since the legal meaning of the word 'escrow' is its only meaning.)
9. Precising, possibly also stipulative

11. Limited reportive, legal

13. Reportive

15. Limited reportive

17. Limited reportive–legal, and persuasive

19. Stipulative

EXERCISE 13–13

1. Noncircularity

3. Clarity

5. Affirmativeness

7. Accuracy (too narrow) though it may be persuasively effective

9. Accuracy (too narrow) and affirmativeness

11. Accuracy (too narrow and too broad)

11. Clarity

15. Clarity

Index

Numbers in **boldface** indicate pages on which term or concept is defined.

Abbreviated sentences, **120**–21
Abbreviations
  constants and, 206–7
  letters in, 224n
  propositional, 205–8
  in quantificational logic, 335
  for syllogisms, 161–62
  for truth-functional arguments, 254–55
Abusive argument, **559**–61
Accuracy, of definitions, 596–97
Adams, Abigail, 555
Addition rule, **283**
Ad verecundiam fallacy, **557**
Advertising, ambiguous statements in, 542–43
Affirmative definiens, **595**–96
Affirmative quality statement, **115**
Affirmative statements, 117
Agreement
  and difference, 484–85
  method of, 475–80
Ambiguity, disagreement and, 50
Amphiboly fallacy, **541**–43
Analogy
  in advertising, 394
  elimination of inductions by, 425–28
  hypthetico-deductive method and, 441–42
  induction by, 392–99
  in inductive generalizations, 415–18
  positive and negative, 408–15
  statistical induction by, 428–38
Analysis of arguments. *See* Arguments
Analytically false statements, **245**
Analytic statement, **39**
  semantically analytic statement, 41–42

syntactically analytic statements and, 39–40, 41
Antecedent, **220**, 222
  fallacy of denying, 262–63
Apparent disagreement, 50
Appeal to authority, 556–558
Appeal to force (*argumentum ad baculum*), **554**–56
Appeal to the people fallacy (*argumentum ad populum*), **558**
Appearance, 70
Applied logic, 601–24
Argument abbreviations, truth tables and, 281n
Argument against the person (*argumentum ad hominem*), 558–59
Arguments, **64**
  analysis guidelines, 107
  analysis of informal, 62–112
  analyzing sample, 100–6
  Aristotelian logic and, 155–201
  categorical syllogism as, 156–58
  chain of, 96–97
  choosing system for, 607–23
  circular, 93
  circumstantial, 560–61
  complex structures in, 96–100
  criteria for, 92–94
  deductive, 80–86, 389–91
  defined, 64
  disguised nonarguments and, 537–46
  enthymemes and, 78–80
  equivalence rules and sample proofs of, 317–21
  from ignorance, **546**–48
  inductive, 80–81, 88–91, 94, 389–439
  inference and, 65–69

logical form and counterexamples, 86–88
logical sense of, **70**–71
logic in, 3
problems in recognizing intended, 75–78
propositional logic and, 251–332
quantificational logic and, 368–88
sample proof of schema, 293–94
subarguments in, 98–99
syllogistic, in ordinary language, 192–99
truth table validity testing for, 260–70
tu quoque, 561
valid, as deductive argument, 81–86
valid but fallacious, 546–64
validity of, 267, 368
See also Logical operators; Syllogisms; Truth-functional validity; Truth tables; Valid arguments; Validity
Argumentum ad baculum, **554**–56
Argumentum ad hominem, **259**, 558–61
Argumentum ad ignorantiam, **546**–48
Argumentum ad populum, **558**
Aristotelian logic
  arguments, 155–201
  statements and, 113–54
A sentences, **119**
Assertion, 70, 100
Association, 301, **303**
Assumptions, discharged, 322
A statements, **117**
Astrology, science and, 445
Astronomy, hypotheses about, 453–57
Asymmetrical relation, 55
Authority, appeal to, 556–58

Bakunin, Mikhail, 380
Begging the question (*petitio principii*), **538**–40
Biconditional statement, **240**
Biorhythms, impact of, 457–59
Blanks, and symbols in schemas, 121–22
Boolean interpretation, 142–52, **143**, **191**
  complementarity and, 144–45
  contraposition and, 149–52
  conversion and, 147–49
  obversion and, 145–47
  summary of equivalences on, 151
Bound variable, **343**
Breuer, Marcel, 147
Burden of proof, 39, **602**–4

Calculus, propositional, 276–77
Calculus of probability, 524–34
  combining rules for, 533–34
  general conjunction rule, 526–28
  general disjunction rule, 530–33
  restricted disjunction rule, 529–30
Carter, Jimmy
  inductive argument about, 432
  informal fallacies in accusations against, 462
Categorical propositions, **114**–20
  logical relations between, 133–36
  quality of, 114–15
  quantity of, 115–17
  standard-form sentences as, 118–20
Categorical statements, 113–20
  immediate inferences and, 136–40
  schema of, 121–29
  standard-form sentences and, 118–20
  Venn diagrams and, 129–33
Categorical syllogism, **156**–57
  Boolean inerpretation of, 191–92
  diagramming, 171–82
  mood and figure in, 164–66
  standard-form, 158–64
  testing by rules, 182–91
  validity of, 166–67
Causal explanations, 462–63
Causal relations, 221–22
  counterfactuals and, 223n
Cause(s)
  kinds of, 463–74
  as necessary and sufficient conditions, 469–74

Chain of interlocking syllogisms, sorites as, 197
Charity, principle of. *See* Principle of charity
Circular argument, 93
Circular definition, **594**–95
Circumstantial argument, 560–61
Clarity, of definitions, 597
Classical theory, of probability, **515**–17
Cognitive uses of sentences, 32–33
Commands, logic of, 35
Commutation, 301, **303**
Complement of a class, **144**–45
Composition fallacy, **551**–52
Compound propositions, 337–39
  existentially quantified, 343
  and logical operators, 202–3
  universally quantified, 348–52
Conclusion
  in arguments, 70–71, 96–97
  indicators, 73
  induction and, 433–34
  inference and, 65
  standard-form syllogism and, 158
  support for, 100
Concomitant variations, method of, 485–89
Conditional proof, **321**–25
Conditionals, **220**
  corresponding, 274
  truth-functional arguments and, 273–76
Conditional words, 76
Conditions, cause as necessary and sufficient, 469–74
Conflict, 4
Conjunction, 209–14, **210**
  of conditions, **471**
  truth tables and, 210–11, 214–15
Conjunction rule, **282**–83
Conjuncts, **210**
Connotation, **575**–76
Connotative definitions, 575–77
Consequent, **220**
Consistent statements, 45–48, **134**–35
Constants
  abbreviations and, 206–7, 335
  variables and, 335–37
Construction, of truth tables, 233–37
Constructive dilemma, **275**, 290–93
Context, of sentences, 36–37, 192
Contingent proposition, **42**–43
Contingent statement, **245**–46
Contradictions, 244–45

Contradictory premises, and tautological conclusions, 253–54
Contradictory propositions, **136**–37, 143–44
Contraposition, 149–52
Contraries, **137**–38
Controls, and Mill's methods, 489–90
Converse, **147**
Conversion, **147**–49
Convertend, **147**
Coolidge, Calvin, 41
Copernicus, 454
Corresponding conditional, **274**
Counterexample
  in argument, 86–88
  of syllogism, 167–70
Counterfactual conditional, **223n**
Crucial experiments, and hypothetico-deductive method variation, 452–59

DeBakey, Michael, 486
Decision making, 4
Decision procedure, for syllogisms, **169**
Declaration of Independence, self-evident statements in, 39
Declarative sentences, 35–36
Deduction, of observation statements, 442–44. *See also* Induction
Deductive arguments, 80–86, 389–91
  criteria for, 92–94
  as valid argument, 81–86
Deductive completeness, **327**–29
Deductive proof, method of, 276–77
Deductive strength, 402–7, **405**
Definiendum, **572**
Definiens, **572**
Definitions, 571–600
  criteria for, 594–98
  to introduce new meaning, 585, 586
  kinds of, 572–81
  to report meaning, 581–84
  for social or political purposes, 589–92
DeMorgan's rules, **239**, 301, **305**–08
Denotation, of definiendum, **574**
Denotative definitions, **574**
Dependent outcomes, **523**
Descriptive statement, **16**
Diagrams
  for analogy in inductive generalizations, 415–17
  of categorical syllogisms, 171–82

of positive and negative analogy, 408–15
of syllogistic schemas, 170–71
See also Venn diagrams
Dictionary. *See* Abbreviations
Difference
agreement and, 484–85
method of, 480–83
Dilemma, constructive, 275, 290–93
Disagreements
arguments and, 64
real vs. apparent, 49–52
verbal, 52–54
Discharged assumption, **322**
Disguised nonarguments, 538–46
begging the question, 538–40
fallacy of amphiboly, 541–43
fallacy of irrelevant conclusion, 544–45
straw person fallacy, 543–44
Disjunction, 217–19, **471**
Disjunctive syllogism, **274**–75, 288–93
Distributed term, 183–84
Distribution, 301
DeMorgan's rules and, 305–8
Division fallacy, **552**–53
Dot operator, 209–10, 282–83
translation from English to, 212–13
Double negation, 238–39, 301, **302**
Double parenthesis unit, 234
Dyadic relational predicate, 336

Eddy, Mary Baker, 196
Efficient cause, **465**
EG. *See* Existential generalization
Eliot, George (Mary Ann Evans), 246
Engels, Friedrich, informal fallacies and, 563
English, translation to dot operator, 212–13. *See also* Ordinary language
Enthymemes, 78–80, 94–96, 193–97
Enumerative arguments
number of observed cases and, 420–21
relevance and, 422–25
Enumerative definitions, **573**–75
Enumerative generalization, 400–1
Enumerative induction, **391**–402
observed and unobserved cases of, 407
positive and negative analogy, 408–15

relative strength of, 402–25
rules about, 434
Equivalence(s), 301
on Boolean interpretation, 151
logical, 55–56, 238–40
material, 225–27, 239–42, 311
Equivalence rules, for arguments, 317–21
Equivocation fallacy, **540**–41
E sentences, **119**
E statements, **118**
Evans, Mary Ann. *See* Eliot, George
Events, cause of, 463–64
Examinations, graduate and professional school, 68–69
Exceptive statements, 127–28
Excluded middle, law of, 243
Exclusive disjunction, 218–19
Exclusive sense, **217**
Exclusive statement, **128**
Existential fallacy, 191–92
Existential generalization (EG), **372**–75
Existential instantiation, 375–78
Existential quantifiers, 339–46, **340**
Experiments
on biorhythms, 457–59
crucial, 452–59
locating center of universe and, 453–57
Exportation, 301, **308**–11
Exposition, statements as, 75

Fallacies
appeal to authority (*ad verecundiam*), 556–58
appeal to the people (*argumentum ad populum*), 558
argument against the person (*argumentum ad hominem*), 558–61
composition, 551–52
of denying the antecedent, **262**–63
division, 552–53
existential, 191–92
false cause, 549–50
false dilemma, 548–49
hasty generalization, 550–51
of illicit major, **186**
of illicit minor, **186**
informal, 537–70
for syllogisms, 184–88

of undistributed middle, **185**
See also Informal fallacies
Fallacious arguments, valid but fallacious, 546–64
Fallacious syllogisms, **185**
False cause fallacy, **549**–50
False dilemma, **548**–49
Figure, of standard-form syllogism, **165**
Final (purposive) cause, **466**
Form
logical, 10–11
of standard-form syllogism, **165**
Formal cause, **465**
Formal deductive proof, for argument schema, 324
Formal logic, 12–13
Formal proof, 277–**81**
Free variable, **343**–44

Galileo, 454
General conjunction rule, 526–28, **527**
General disjunction rule, **530**–32
Generalization
existential (EG), 372–75
formulation, 442
inductive, 392, 399–402
statistical, 428–29
universal, 378–87
General noun, **335**
Genus and difference, definition by, 579
Grouping, **228**–33

Hasty generalization fallacy, **550**–51
Homelessness, debate about, 23
Horseshoe operator, 219–22, 286, 288
Hypotheses, about universe, 453–57
Hypothetical syllogism, 290–93
as argument schema, **264**–65
for proving argument schema validity, 278–81
Hypothetico-deductive method, **441**–47
crucial experiments and, 452–59
and inductive generalization, 447–52

Identity, symbol for, 226n
Ignorance, argument from, 546–48
Immediate inferences, 136–40
Implication, **54**–55, 311
Inclusive disjunction, **217**–19

Inclusive sense, **217**
Inconsistent premises, **253**
Inconsistent statements, 45–48
Independent outcomes, **522**
Independent statements, **56–60, 133–34**
Indicator words, **73**
Indifference principle, 515
Indirect proof, **325–27**
Individuals, predicates and, 333–35
Individual variables, **336**
Induction
    by analogy, **392–99**
    elimination by analogy, 425–28
    principle of, 604–6
Inductive argument, 80–81, **88–91,** 389–439
    analogy and, 425–28
    criteria for, 92–94
    enumerative inductions, 391–425
    statistical inductions, 428–38
Inductive generalization, **392,** 399–402
    analogy in, 415–18
    hypothetico-deductive method and, 447–52
Inductive strength, 402–7
Inference(s), **65–69**
    analogy and, 392–93
    immediate, 136–40
    mediated, 156
    rules of, 281–94
    valid forms of, 301
Informal analysis
    of arguments, 62–112
    of statements, 30–61
Informal fallacies, **537–70**
    disguised nonarguments, 538–46
    examples of, 564–68
Informal logic, **12–13**
Instantiation
    existential, 375–78
    universal (UI), 369–72
Intended argument, recognizing, 75–78
Intension of definiendum, **576**
Intention, 70
Interrogative sentences, 35
Intuition, 20
    in inductive arguments, 418–21
    logical relationships between propositions and, 45
    See also Arguments
Invalidity
    logic system and, 267

shortened truth table method and, 271
    See also Valid argument; Validity
Irrelevant conclusion fallacy, **544–45**
I sentences, **119**
I statements, **117**

Jacobson, Lenore F., 480
Jefferson, Thomas, self-evident statements and, 39
Joint method of agreement and difference, **484–85**
Judgments, analogy and, 393, 395

Kahn, Alfred E., 589
Kissinger, Henry, 395

Language(s), differences among, 36. *See also* Ordinary language
Laws
    descriptive and prescriptive, 16–17
    of double negation, **238–39**
    of excluded middle, **243**
    of noncontradiction, **243**
Legal definition, **583–84**
Lenin, V.I., 560
Lexical definition, **581–85**
Liars, Roberts' article on, 104, 105–106
Lieber, Arnold L., 487–88
Linguistic entity, sentence as, 34
Logic
    applied, 601–24
    Aristotelian, 113
    concerns of, 18–19
    formal and informal, 12–13
    inductive, 389–439
    learning about, 9–16
    and psychology, 16–19
    and science, 501–5
    syllogistic, 133
    symbolic, 205–6
    value and uses of, 2–4
    See also Aristotelian logic; Propositional logic; Quantificational logic; Syllogistic logic
Logical consistency. *See* Consistent statements
Logical effort, **446**

Logical equivalence and material equivalence, 239–42
Logical form, **10**
    in argument, 86–88
    schema of categorical statement and, 121
    and structure of statements, 10–11
Logically equivalent categorical propositions, **135,** 136
Logically equivalent statements, **55–56,** 238–39
    DeMorgan's rules and, 239
    law of double negation, 238–39
Logical operators, **203**
    grouping and, 228–33
    for material equivalence, 225–26
    for material implication, 219–20
    negation and, 215–17
    propositions with more than one, 228–33
    truth-functional, 203–5
Logical relations
    arguments and, 71
    between categorical propositions, 133–36
    traditional square of opposition and, 140–41
Logical structure, Venn diagrams and, 131–32
Loomis, W.F., 477n

Main operator, **229–31,** 237
Major premise, **158.** *See also* Categorical syllogism, diagramming
Major term, **158**
Marx, Karl, informal fallacies and, 563
Material cause, **465**
Material equivalence, **225–27, 301, 311–17**
    logical equivalence and, 239–42
Material implication, **219–25, 301, 311–17**
    horseshoe operator and, 286
Mediated inferences, **156**
Merely verbal disagreement, **53**
Method of agreement, **475–80**
Method of concomitant variations, **485–89**
Method of crucial experiments, 452–59
Method of deductive proof, **276–77**
Method of difference, **480–83**

Methods, of Mill. *See* Mill's methods
Middle term, **158**
Mill, John Stuart, 475
Mill's methods, 475–89
 agreement, 475–80
 difference, 480–83
 joint method of agreement and
  difference, 484–85
 method of concomitant variations,
  485–89
 replicability, controls, and, 489–501
Minor premise, **158**. *See also*
 Categorical syllogism,
 diagramming
Minor term, **158**, 159
Modus ponens, **263**, 286–88
Modus tollens, **262**, 287–88
Moral laws, 17
Multiple-choice question, argument,
 inference, and, 66–67
Multiple predicates, negation and, 354–
 57
Multiple quantifiers, 357–66
Murphy, Raymond E., 539n
Mutually exclusive outcomes, 523

Natural languages, sentences and, 33
Necessary conditions, 469–74
Negation, **215–17**
 law of double, 238–39, 301, 302
 and multiple predicates, 354–57
 and quantifier exchange, 352–54
 truth table for, 233
Negative analogy, **408–15**
Negative quality statement, **115**
Negatives, in complex subject or
 predicate term, 120, 123
Negative statements, 118
Nightingale, Florence, 596
Nixon, Richard, 395
Noncircularity, of definitions, 594–95
Noncognitive uses of sentences, 32–33
Noncontradiction, law of, 243
Nonreflexive predicates, 358
Noun
 general, 335
 proper, 334–35
Noun phrases, sentences and, 120

Observation statements
 deduction of, 442–44
 testing, 444–47

Obversion, **145–47**
Obvertend, **145**
Ochsner, Alton, 486
Omniscience principle, 515
Operational definitions, 578–81
Operators, main, 237. *See also* Logical
 operators
Opposition, traditional square of, 140–
 41
Ordinary language
 arguments in, 256n
 conditionals in, 222–24
 as contexts, 222–24
 syllogistic arguments in, 192–99
 translation to dot operator, 212–13
O sentences, **119**
O statements, **118**
Ostensive definition, 573–74
Outcomes, independent and mutually
 exclusive, 523

P (specified outcome), **511**
P (y given x), **522–23**
Parenthesis unit, **233–34**
Particular affirmative statements (I
 statements), **117**, 124–25
Particular categorical statements, **115**
Particular negative statements (O
 statements), **118** 125–27
Perception, and reality, 51
Persuasive definitions, **589**
Petitio principii, **538–40**
Physical entity, sentence as, 34
Political laws, 17
Positive analogy, **408–15**
Precising definitions, **587–88**
Predicate constants, 337
Predicate logic, **333**
Predicates
 and individuals, 333–35
 negation and multiple, 354–57
 two-place relational, 336
 See also Statements
Predicate terms, 113–14
Premise indicators, 73
Premises
 in arguments, 65, 70–71, 95–99
 and conclusions, 72–75
 See also Arguments; Categorical
  syllogism; Deductive arguments;
  Inductive arguments
Prescriptive statement, **16**

Principle of charity, 79, **194**
Principle of indifference, **515**
Principle of omniscience, **515**
Probability, 509–36
 classical theory of, 515–17
 general principles of, 513–14
 independent and mutually exclusive
  outcomes of, 522–23
 indifference principle of, 515
 omniscience principle of, 515
 relative frequency theory of, 517–
  19
 subjectivist theory of, 519–22
 terminology in, 510–12
Probability calculus, 524–34
Professional schools, admission exams
 for, 2
Proof(s), 1, 39
 burden of, 602–4
 conditional, 321–25
 and equivalence rules for
  arguments, 317–21
 formal, 277–81
 indirect, 325–27
 reductio ad absurdum, **325–27**
 of validity in quantificational logic,
  383–87
Proof construction, rules of thumb for,
 294–96
Proper noun, **334–35**
Proposition(s), **34**, 202
 Boolean interpretation of, 142–52
 categorical, 114–20
 compound, 337–39
 contingent, 42–43
 contradictory, 136–37
 contraries, 137–38
 definitions of, 571–600
 existentially quantified compound,
  343
 relationships between two or more,
  44–45
 sentences and, 34n
 subcontraries, 138
 synthetic, 42–43
 truth-functional, 202–3
 universally quantified compound,
  348–52
 See also Arguments
Propositional abbreviations, and
 schemas, 205–8
Propositional calculus, 276–77
Propositional constant, **206**

Propositional logic
arguments, 251–332
formal proof for, 277–81
statements, 202–50
Propositional schema, 207–8
Propositional variable, **207–8**
Proximate causes, **466–67**
Pseudodisagreement, 50, 53
Psychology, 16–19
Ptolemy, 453–54
Purposive cause, **466**

Qualifiers, existential, 339–46
Quality, **114**–15
Quantificational logic, **333**
arguments, 368–88
proofs of validity in, 384–87
statements, 333–67
Quantifier exchange, **353**
negation and, 352–54
rule for, 353
Quantifiers, **115**, **340**
exceptive statements and, 127
multiple, 357–66
scope of, 343–46
universal, 346–52
Quantity, of categorical propositions, **115**
Questions, logic of, 35

Random sampling, 411
Real disagreement, 49–52
Reality, perception and, 51
Reasoning, **16**
Reasons, in argument analysis, 62–64
Reductio ad absurdum proof, **325–27**
Reflexive relation, 358
Relational predicate, dyadic, 336
Relations, symmetrical, 55
Relationships, between two (or more) propositions, 44–45
Relative frequency theory, **517**–19
Relative strengths, of inductive arguments, 402–25
Remote causes, **467**
Replacement rule, 300–2
Replicability, of Mill's methods, **489–91**
Reportive definition, **581–84**
Restricted conjunction rule, 524–26, **525**

Restricted disjunction rule, **529–30**
Rigor, rules of, 296–300
Rivers, Howard, 539n
Roberts, Edwin A., Jr., "List of the 10 Greatest Liars" by, 104, 105–6
Roland, Joseph, 539n
Rosenthal, Robert, 480
Rule(s)
addition, 283
association, **303**
combining conjunction and disjunction, 533–34
commutation, 303
conjunction, 282
DeMorgan's, 305–8
double negation, 302
exportation, 301, 308–11
general conjunction, 526–28
general disjunction, 530–31
of inference, **281–94**, **283**
for proof construction, 294–96
for quantifier exchange, 353
of replacement, 300–302
restricted conjunction, 524–26
restricted disjunction, 529–30
of rigor, 296–300
simplification, 282–83
for symbolizing English statements in quantificational logic, 364
tautology, 303
testing categorical syllogisms by, 182–91
transportation, 301, 308–11
Russell, Bertrand, 4

Sample proof, of argument schema, 293–94
Schema, **121–29**
hypothetical syllogism, 264–65
modus ponens, 263
modus tollens, 262
for syllogisms, 162–64
for truth-functional arguments, 255–60
valid argument, 257
See also Truth tables
variables and, 207–208
Science
consistency or inconsistency of competing statements in, 502n
role of logic in, 501–5
Scientific method, 459–63, 441–508

causal explanations and, 462–63
hypothetico-deductive method, 441–47
Self-evident statements, 38
Semantically analytic statements, **41–42**
Sentences, **31–38**, **34**
abbreviated, 120–21
causal relations in, 221
cognitive and noncognitive uses of, 32–33
ordinary language vs. standard-form, 192
propositions expressed by, 256n
standard-form, 118–20
syllogism and, 158
used to express statements, 35–38
See also Abbreviations; Statements
Shaw, George Bernard, 603
Sherin, Carolyn R., 487–88
Short truth table method, 270–72
Simple propositions, 334
Simplification rule, **282–83**
Single parenthesis unit, 234
Singular affirmative statements, 122–23
Singular statement, **116–17**
Sorites, 197–99, **198**
Specified outcome, **511**
Standard form, **158**
Standard-form sentences, 118–20
for particular affirmative statements, 124–25
for particular negative statements, 125–27
for universal affirmative statements, 122–23
for universal negative statements, 123–24
Standard form syllogism, 158–64
abbreviating, 161–62
schema of, 162–63
Venn diagrams and, 170–82
See also Syllogism
Statements, **30**, **34–35**
analytic, 39
analytically false, 245
argument and, 70–71, 75–77
Aristotelian logic and, 113–54
asserted, 100
biconditional as, 240
categorical, 113–20
categorical propositions as, 114–20
consistent, 45–48, 134–35
contradictions, 244–45

exceptive, 127–28
exclusive, 128
inconsistent, 45–48
independent, 56–60, 133–34
informal analysis of, 30–61
logical form and structure of, 10–11
logically equivalent, 238–39
logical substitution and, 301
missing, in arguments, 78–80
particular affirmative (I statements), 117, 124–25
particular negative (O statements), 118, 125–26
as premise or conclusion, 404n
propositional logic, 202–50
quantificational logic, 333–67
self-evident, 38
semantically analytic, 41–42
sentence used to express, 34–38
singular, 116–17
standard-form sentences for universal affirmative, 122–23
supported, 38
universal affirmative (A statements), 117
universal negative (E statements), 118
See also Sentences
Statistical generalization, **428–29**
Statistical induction by analogy, **428–38**
Stein, Gertrude, 356
Stevens, Francis B., 539n
Stipulative definition, **585**, 586
Straw person fallacy, **543–44**
Subarguments, in complex argument, 98–99
Subcontraries, **138**
Subimplicants, **139**, 140
Subimplication, 138–**39**
Subject. *See* Statements
Subjectivist theory, **519–22**
Subject terms, 113–14
Sufficient conditions, 469–74
Superimplicants, **139**, 140
Superimplication, 138–**39**, 140
Supported statements, **38**
Syllogism, 156
  abbreviating, 161–62
  categorical, 156–57
  counterexamples for testing, 167–70
  decision procedure for, **169**

disjunctive, 274–75, 290–93
hypothetical, 264–65, 290–93
mood and figure of, 164–66
schema for, 162–64
testing using rules, 188–91
valid forms for, 190
validity of, 166–67, 183
Venn diagrams for testing, 170–82
Syllogistic arguments
  enthymemes and, 193–97
  in ordinary language, 192–99
  sorites and, 197–99
Syllogistic logic, 333
Symbolic logic, **205–6**
Symbolization
  of English statements in quantificational logic, 364
  in quantifiers, 343–45
  and universally quantified compound propositions, 348–51
Symbols
  for blanks in schemas, 121–22
  for identity, 226n
  for material equivalence, 225–26
  See also Abbreviations; Definitions
Symmetrical relation, **55**
Synonymous definition, **572–73**
Syntactically analytic proposition, 39–40
Synthetic proposition, **42–43**

Tautology, 242–45, **243**, 253, 301, 303
  conditional and, 275–76
  contradictory premises and, 253–54
Terminology, in probability, 510–12
Terms, distribution of, 183–84
Testing, of observation statements, 444–47
Testing of syllogisms
  Boolean interpretation of, 191–92
  counterexamples for, 167–70
  rules for, 182–91
  validity of, 166–67
Theoretical definition, **583**
Theories
  concept of, 452n
  about theories, 459–60
Traditional square of opposition, 140–41
Transportation, 301, **308–11**
Truth-functional arguments
  abbreviating, 254–55

and corresponding conditionals, 273–76
  schematizing, 255–60
Truth-functional logic, 221
Truth-functionally invalid argument, 269
Truth-functional operators, **203–5**, 209
Truth-functional proposition, **202–3**, 209–10, 251
Truth-functional validity, 252–53
Truth tables, 214–15
  for arguments of argument abbreviations, 281n
  construction of, 233–37
  horseshoe symbol and, 221
  hypothetical syllogism and, 278
  limitations on, 266–69
  short method of, 270–72
  testing validity by, 260–70
Truth value, **202**
Tubman, Harriet, 242
Tu quoque argument, **561**
Twain, Mark, 20, 46
Two-place (dyadic) relational predicate, **336**
Two-step argument, in inductions by analogy and inductive generalizations, 425–27

UI. *See* Universal instantiation
Universal affirmative statements (A statements), **117**
Universal generalization, 378–87, **379**
Universal instantiation (UI), 369–72
Universal negative statements (E statements), **118**, 123–24
Universal quantifiers, 346–52
Universal quantity statements, **115**
Universe, locating center of, 453–57

Vagueness, **587**
Valid arguments, **81–83**, 251–52
Valid argument schema, **167**
Valid but fallacious arguments, 546–64
Valid inference forms, 301
Validity
  testing by truth tables, 260–70
  truth-functional, 252–53
  types of logic and, 368
Valid syllogisms, 166–67, 183
  rules for, 184–88

Values
    truth and, 202
    truth tables and, 214–15
Variables
    bound and free, 343–44
    and constants, 335–37
    eliminating, 295
    propositional, 207
    and schemata, 207–8
Variants, **283**
Variations, concomitant, 485–89

Venn, John, 129
Venn diagrams, 170–82
    Boolean interpretation and, 143
    categorical statements and, 129–33
    for contrapositive, 150
    for conversion, 147–48
    logical equivalence of two
       categorical propositions and, 135
    for obversions, 145–46
Verbal disagreements, 52–54
Vos Savant, Marilyn, 10

Will, George, 32
Wollstonecraft, Mary, 384

"You-too" argument. *See Tu quoque*
    argument

Zuckerman, Ed, 323

Propositional Logic

The **rules of inference** are valid argument schemas, and therefore *cannot be applied to sub-components of compound propositional schemas within a single step of an argument.* In other words, these eight rules *can be applied only to the main operators of entire lines of a deductive proof.*

Conjunction (Conj.)

p
q
∴ p · q

Addition (Add.)

p
∴ p ∨ q

Simplification (Simp.)

p · q   p · q
∴ p   ∴ q

Modus Ponens (M.P.)

p ⊃ q
p
∴ q

Modus Tollens (M.T.)

p ⊃ q
~q
∴ ~p

Hypothetical Syllogism (H.Syll.)

p ⊃ q
q ⊃ r
∴ p ⊃ r

Disjunctive Syllogism (D.Syll.)

p ∨ q   p ∨ q
~p   ~q
∴ q   ∴ p

Constructive Dilemma (Dil.)

(p ⊃ q) · (r ⊃ s)
p ∨ r
∴ q ∨ s

Equivalence Rules

The rule of **Replacement** allows that *a statement can be substituted for a logically equivalent statement anywhere in a proof, even in the middle of a line. It is not necessary to replace only whole lines with equivalent statements.* In symbolic language, it states:

The two following schemas are valid inference forms:

... Φ ...   ... Ψ ...
Φ ≡ Ψ   *or*   Φ ≡ Ψ
... Ψ ...   ... Φ ...

where 'Φ ≡ Ψ' is one of the equivalences listed below:

De Morgan's rules (De M.):   ~(p · q) ≡ (~p ∨ ~q)
                                                           ~(p ∨ q) ≡ (~p · ~q)

Commutation (Com.):   (p ∨ q) ≡ (q ∨ p)
                                                (p · q) ≡ (q · p)

Association (Assoc.):   (p ∨ (q ∨ r)) ≡ ((p ∨ q) ∨ r)
                                            (p · (q · r)) ≡ ((p · q) · r)

Distribution (Dist.):   (p · (q ∨ r)) ≡ ((p · q) ∨ (p · r))
                                         (p ∨ (q · r)) ≡ ((p ∨ q) · (p ∨ r))

Double Negation (D.N.):   p ≡ ~~p